Natural Resource Management and Policy

Volume 63

There is a growing awareness to the role that natural resources, such as water, land, forests and environmental amenities, play in our lives. There are many competing uses for natural resources, and society is challenged to manage them for improving social well-being. Furthermore, there may be dire consequences to natural resources mismanagement. Renewable resources, such as water, land and the environment are linked, and decisions made with regard to one may affect the others. Policy and management of natural resources now require interdisciplinary approaches including natural and social sciences to correctly address our society preferences. This series provides a collection of works containing most recent findings on economics, management and policy of renewable biological resources, such as water, land, crop protection, sustainable agriculture, technology, and environmental health. It incorporates modern thinking and techniques of economics and management. Books in this series will incorporate knowledge and models of natural phenomena with economics and managerial decision frameworks to assess alternative options for managing natural resources and environment.

Nicoletta Batini
Editor

The Economics of Non-Human Animals

Revaluing Life for a Liveable Planet

Springer

Editor
Nicoletta Batini
Independent Evaluation Office
International Monetary Fund
Washington D. C., USA

ISSN 0929-127X ISSN 2511-8560 (electronic)
Natural Resource Management and Policy
ISBN 978-3-032-17579-3 ISBN 978-3-032-17580-9 (eBook)
https://doi.org/10.1007/978-3-032-17580-9

This Springer imprint is published by the registered company Springer Nature Switzerland AG
The registered company address is: Gewerbestrasse 11, 6330 Cham, Switzerland

To Gnomo and Yang—who walked with me for so many years, and to Baby—who still does. We are one soul, always.

Foreword

In a now-classic publication of 1987, known as the Brundtland Report, the World Commission on Environment and Development defined "sustainable development" as development that meets the needs of the present without compromising the ability of future generations to meet their own needs. I don't know of another idea in growth and development economics and the economics of poverty that caught the imagination of the public as quickly as the notion of sustainable development did, but it deserved its immediate acceptance as a tool for thinking about economic possibilities for the future.

The Brundtland criterion asks us to compare economic opportunities at different points in time and defines sustainable development to be paths along which those opportunities expand continually (more accurately, where they don't ever contract). Macroeconomists have interpreted Brundtland to be advocating GDP growth. Their presumption has been that GDP growth creates economic opportunities, so national governments should pursue it. In this they have been utterly wrong.

By opportunities facing an economy we should mean the economic futures available to the economy. As capital stocks are an economy's productive base, the available set of options at any date depends on the portfolio of assets the economy holds at that date. Just as the acquisition of human capital (health, education, skills, aptitude, character) is a means for people to expand their life opportunities, enlargement of an economy's portfolio of capital stocks creates greater opportunities for the economy. The Brundtland criterion for sustainable development can thus be interpreted as development along which an economy's portfolio of assets expands over time (more accurately, don't ever contract).

Although it is near-universal practice to use GDP as a measure of sustainable development, it is unsuitable and for two reasons. First, GDP is a flow (so many billions of dollars per year), and flows can tell us nothing about what lies ahead, only stocks of capital can. Second, the "G" in the acronym GDP is "gross," meaning that GDP does not deduct the depreciation of capital that accompanies production and consumption. If you want to know whether someone is wealthy, you should not ask how much he spends on goods and services, because the person could be spending a lot of money by simply liquidating his assets, but by doing that he would become poor, even bankrupt, in time. You should instead ask what the market value of his assets is.

For national economies the matter is more complicated by the fact that market prices of goods and services don't necessarily reflect their social values. So, we need to make two adjustments to the way we measure economic opportunities. First, instead of GDP, offices of national statistics should be estimating the value of an economy's stocks of capital assets, which includes the value of produced capital (roads, buildings, ports, machines), human capital (education, health, aptitude), and natural capital (ecosystems, sub-soil resources, sand, and gravel). Second, the assets should be valued at "shadow prices," reflecting the assets' social worth, which are not necessarily reflected in market prices (many natural resources are not traded in markets). We call the sum of the social values of an economy's entire stock of capital assets its "wealth." Offices of national statistics should be estimating the wealth of nations.

Of the three major classes of assets that add up to make for wealth, the one almost invariably ignored in mainstream economics is natural capital. Barring the atmosphere as a sink for carbon emissions, you will be hard pressed to find an item of natural capital being the object of study in any leading economics journal. What does not exist is most often not missed, so you will not hear mainstream economists complaining of the big hole in the conception of capital assets used by them for understanding the dynamics of contemporary economies. Fortunately, there is now a growing literature that embeds the human economy in Nature, meaning that natural capital is increasingly recognized as being the bedrock of economies. The term "bedrock" is all important here. The common practice of national accounting is to track the output of economic activity (GDP), whereas the bedrock peers at an economy's underbelly, and that is where natural capital lodges itself.

Natural capital comes in various shapes and sizes—from microbes, via fungal networks, to tropical rainforests, and, of course non-human animals such as bees, elephants, and fish, which play critical roles in pollination, seed dispersal, and nutrient cycling across ecosystems. When we speak of ecosystems, we have in mind a complex of living organisms (plans, animals, fungi, and microorganisms) and their non-living environment in a particular location that together combine to control such natural processes as energy flows, and material recycling. Ecosystems therefore range from a drop of water to the Amazon rainforest. Individual animals and plants are ecosystems, as are the larger ecosystems that are home to them. But it is only in the post-War period (starting around 1950) that ecosystems as communities of organisms in their non-living environment have come to find a central place in the biological sciences. Previously, the study of animal and plant behavior dominated zoology and what used to be called "botany." The present collection of essays returns to that practice and is especially valuable for that. Animals, from oxen to sperm whales have been essential to economic activity since immemorial times—providing labor, transport, food, clothing, and companionship, and playing a vital role in agriculture, trade, and cultural development. This work adds indispensable analysis to this often-overlooked dimension of natural capital, studying animals, not only from an anthropocentric viewpoint, but also for their intrinsic worth. It reminds us that protecting animals and ensuring they thrive is essential to sustain life and prosperity for all. Indeed, I know of no other book that studies animals as a normative category from as wide a range of angles as to be found here. It is a tremendous achievement.

August 2025

Partha Dasgupta
St John's College
Cambridge, UK

Preface

When we think of the global economy, we often picture bustling stock exchanges, multinational corporations, and the invisible hand of market forces. We might invoke bull and bear markets, and economies destabilized by unpredictable "animal spirits." We might reach for pork belly futures when we try to explain commodity markets or refer to pork barrel politics when it comes to the political allocation of resources. But there our consideration of animal kingdom ends. Rarely, if ever, do we think of a sled dog braving the Arctic, a pigeon soaring through enemy fire, or a monkey in a laboratory. Yet, these animals—and countless others—have shaped the very foundations of our economic systems. Without their labor—for they are workers too—our economies, societies, and political systems would not exist. This book is a tribute to them: to the animals who have carried us, fed us, clothed us, healed us, entertained us, and, above all, died for us. We do not usually think of them, and we should at least acknowledge them. But it is also a call to reimagine economics itself—to make it both more just and more faithful to the realities of the living world.

From the earliest days of human civilization, animals have been indispensable economic agents. Two million years ago, our ancestors began hunting wild species for food, setting in motion a relationship that would evolve, far more recently, into domestication, agriculture, and to intensive animal farming systems that are no more than a few decades old. Animals thousands of years ago became our laborers, our transport, our raw materials, and our companions. They pulled our plows, turned our mills, and carried our goods. They continue to provide us milk, meat, wool, leather, and even the enzymes for our medicines, though now on a vast and unprecedented scale. Oxen and draft horses may have disappeared from daily life in many modern economies, but they continue to serve as silent engines of economic growth in communities around the world.

And yet, despite their centrality, animals remain largely invisible in economic theory. They are absent from production functions, ignored in national accounts, and undervalued in policy decisions. When they are assigned a value, it is often only the price of their flesh, their fur, or the functions they perform—never the full value of their contributions, let alone the measure of their suffering. Such erasure is not the result of animals' weakness or lesser intelligence, but of "economic speciesism" and the systematic manipulation of value to serve human interests. In conventional economic logic, which is anthropocentric to the core, animals have no intrinsic value. This book seeks to confront that neglect and reframe how we understand animals' place in our economies.

The misvaluation of animals is a root cause of both ecological and economic imbalance. Today, the combined biomass of humans and their domesticated animals vastly outweighs that of all wild mammals. As most commonly eaten animal, the broiler chicken outweighs wild birds three times over, and layers of discarded chicken bones may end up as the fossil record of our late industrial age. This disproportionate reliance on domesticated animals reflects an economic system that relentlessly commodifies life, treating sentient beings as mere inputs while ignoring the broader costs of their exploitation. The consequences are far-reaching: biodiversity loss, degraded ecosystems, and deepening social inequalities. In many cases, the burdens of animal-based industries—such as pollution, disease exposure, and food insecurity—fall disproportionately on low-income communities around the world, reinforcing cycles of poverty and marginalization and centuries of human as well as animal exploitation. These are not just environmental or ethical concerns—they are also structural economic failures, and because of them, the long-term sustainability of the global economy is parlous. Restoring some kind of balance is not only a moral imperative—it is in our collective interest too.

Beyond many of the animals whose stories have had profound social, technological, and economic consequences—Laika, the first living being to orbit Earth; Togo, the Siberian Husky who led the 1925 serum run to Nome; Snowman, the horse rescued from a slaughterhouse who became a champion show jumper; Lulu, the pot-bellied pig who saved her guardian's life by seeking help during a medical emergency; or Axel, the therapy dog who brought comfort and healing to children and families after the 2022 school shooting in Uvalde, Texas, USA—are the trillions of unnamed animals who have built our world. The oxen who plowed our fields. The silkworms who clothed our emperors. The horses who pulled wagons and won wars. The bees who pollinate our crops. The fish who feed our nations. The mice sacrificed in the search for cures. The dogs who help raise more kind-hearted children, assist people who need support, and offer comfort across all stages of life. Even the earthworm, quietly turning the soil to help plants grow. Each of these animals, willingly or unwittingly, plays a role in the complex web of economic activity that sustains human life.

This book shows that by honoring animals' lives and contributions, we can unlock not only moral clarity but also economic benefits for all. It offers a framework for reassessing the full worth of animals—economically, ecologically, and ethically—across the many dimensions of human–animal interaction. It presents examples of how more humane, animal-free systems can reduce inefficiencies, spark innovation, and enhance both ecological and economic resilience. It explains the worth of a world in which animals are no longer reduced merely to commodities but instead acknowledged as co-creators of value. This would be a world of lower costs, greater stability, and richer possibilities. By recognizing animal agency and ecological interdependence, we can build more inclusive models of production and consumption, more efficient and sustainable economies, and fairer futures too.

To help bring about this transformation, the book proposes a set of policy reforms designed to align economic incentives with animal welfare, biodiversity conservation, and ecosystem health. These include smarter economic policies, targeted market mechanisms, and institutional changes that internalize the hidden costs of animal exploitation and reward practices that foster coexistence.

Ultimately, this book is a call to action. A call to economists to expand their models. A call to policymakers to rethink their priorities. A call to consumers to reconsider their choices. And above all, a call to humanity to recognize the animals who brought us here—not just on their backs, but in their hearts.

To Laika, Togo, Snowman, Lulu, and Axel, and the trillions of others who have shaped our world: this book is for you.

Independent Evaluation Office,
International Monetary Fund,
Washington D. C., USA
June 2, 2025

Nicoletta Batini

Acknowledgements

In 2021, I completed *The Economics of Sustainable Food*, a book that explored how the way we produce and consume food harm people and planet, touching on conservation, megafauna, insects, and nature-positive practices. But something felt unfinished. There was no space to examine one of the most profound and urgent topics of our time: the economics of other sentient beings. So, I followed that thread. The more I thought about it, the more I saw the vast, unspoken gap in economic theory—an absence in how we economists account for the lives, experiences, and contributions of animals. What began as a conceptual challenge quickly became a personal journey.

To get a better handle on the topic, I reached out to all kinds of experts—from ethologists, to ecological and agricultural economists, animal law scholars, historians, and, conservation biologists—each bringing their own perspective on the tangled ways animals are caught up in our economic systems. These conversations were enriched by insights from thinkers like Peter Singer, whose ethical frameworks provided a foundational lens; Carl Safina and Jared Kukura, who offered ecological and conservationist perspectives; and Brian Kateman, whose work on reducetarianism challenged conventional dietary paradigms. I also drew inspiration from Andrew Linzey, whose pioneering work in animal theology offered a powerful moral and spiritual dimension to the conversation. I benefited from the economic insights of Luigi Durand and colleagues at Sveriges Riksbank, as well as the thoughtful contributions of Clair Smith on the financial dimensions of moving toward an animal-positive economic model. Beyond academia, I spoke with seasoned hunters and fishers, and individuals from diverse food cultures and traditions—dialogues that were often challenging, but always illuminating.

What I heard confirmed my hunch: this was a path few had walked, but one that mattered and was worth exploring. So, I set out to find the right authors to bring this vision to life—and I did. Each one brought not just expertise, but conviction, creativity, and a deep sense of purpose. Their chapters are not just examinations, they are proposals. They offer concrete, original, and often bold solutions to the challenges of reimagining our economies with animals in mind. Many of these contributions were shaped through rich, collaborative discussions—including the final chapter, which benefitted from a dedicated workshop and collective reflection among the book's authors. I am deeply grateful to each of them—for their insight, their generosity, and their belief in this project. Their work gives this volume its depth, its reach, and its hope.

To Niko Chtouris at Springer, thank you for believing in this project and supporting it with care and commitment. To my family, thank you for your love, your questions, and your unwavering support. To my colleagues and friends, thank you for your insights, your encouragement, and your time.

All in all, I have learned so much from the people involved in this project—from the conversations, the collaborations, and their thought-provoking and deeply inspiring insights.

But perhaps the most profound lessons came from the animals themselves. Not through arguments or analysis, but through their presence. Through the quiet ways they connect, communicate, and simply are. In their gestures, their resilience, and their joy, they have shown me new ways of seeing the world—and myself. They remind us that another kind of economy is possible—one rooted in attentiveness, respect, and the shared moments that make life meaningful, if we are willing to truly listen.

Just like sister wolves in a pack, Gnomo—my rescue Jack Russell from Peru—helped me raise my kids, always by my side with calm, emotional support, and a steady sense of safety. My cat Yang taught me what unconditional love really looks like—and showed me how to grow old with grace and let go with peace. And Baby, my forever pup, so in love with the world, reminds me every day how to roll with people's moods and just get along (postmen excluded, of course). From the right whale off the coast of the Dominican Republic, who surfaced to show us her calf, I learned the meaning of trust. From the new born turtles in Todos Santos, scrambling toward the sea guided only by an ancient instinct, I discovered the strength it takes to take the first step. From the swallows who nest at the highway gas station, I appreciated the art of thriving in unlikely places. From the seabreams in Elba, who swim in a shimmering shoal beside me, I came to understand the power of unity. From the blue-footed booby in Galapagos, who sometimes lets one chick go so the other may thrive, I learned that love sometimes means making impossible choices. I could add countless more lessons I have received from animals—the serenity of a black bear in West Virginia, the mysticism of a red deer in Killarney, the primal strength of a buffalo in Yellowstone, the majesty of a whale shark in the Sea of Cortez, the courage of an elephant calf in Chobe, and the quiet diligence of an orb-weaver spider outside my garden door—each encounter left its mark.

Some animals taught me through fear: the chained ink-black German shepherd at the end of the alley, the massive bull with the ringed nose in Maremma, my friend's Doberman who lunged, the asp viper under my dad's bench in the Alps, the scorpionfish I brushed against while swimming in Corfu. These moments, too, shaped my understanding of our complex, often fraught relationships with other species. And yet, even in these encounters, I came to see that life is not only beauty and grace, but also struggle, instinct, and survival and that within this tension lies the possibility of coexistence, if we choose awareness over fear, and compassion over control.

And I have learned, painfully, through the captivity of others. Like the orca circling endlessly in a tank at a safari park near London, the bear pacing in its stone jail in Bern—a living “emblem” of the city’s flag. The black panther caged in Manaus’ zoo, the crocodile confined to a barred pit in a home in Aswan—beings whose suffering from the loss of their wildness I once grasped only faintly, if at all. As a child, zoos and wildlife parks were places of wonder—because there, I could meet the animals—so magical, so beautiful, so near to my heart. But over time, those same places became sites of reckoning. Their confinement became a mirror to our own limitations, and their endurance a call to do better. I began to see not just the animals, but the systems that hold them—and us—captive.

I cannot ever fully repay the animals for what they have given me. I continue to learn from them—intellectually, emotionally, and spiritually. This book is a small gesture of gratitude, and a step in my lifelong journey with them. May all who read these pages feel what I have felt—your presence, your wisdom, and your beauty. And may we come to recognize, in each of you, your true and immense value.

Praise for *The Economics of Non-Human Animals: Revaluing Life for a Liveable Planet*

"**This pioneering collection of essays** raises an issue that economists have ignored for far too long: How are we to include non-human animals in economic evaluations of policies and practices? Fortunately, interest in this important question is now growing rapidly. The essays brought together in this volume sketch the outlines of a rich and extensive new field of thought."

—Peter Singer, *Emeritus Professor of Bioethics, Princeton University; Visiting Professor, National University of Singapore; author of* Animal Liberation *and* Animal Liberation Now.

"**A brilliant and ground breaking book** that demonstrates how sentient animals have become a forgotten consideration in economic theory. It provides a whole new way of thinking about economics and the status of animals."

—Andrew Linzey, *Director, Oxford Centre for Animal Ethics; member, Faculty of Theology, University of Oxford; author of* Animal Theology.

"**The field of economics has helped us solve some of the most important problems** in the society of humans. This book shows it can lead the way when this society is expanded to include animals."

—F. Bailey Norwood, *Professor of Agribusiness, Department of Agricultural Economics, Oklahoma State University; author of* Compassion by the Pound: The Economics of Farm Animal Welfare.

"Trillions of animals—tame, wild, domesticated—have clothed us, fed us, comforted us, and suffered for us. In dozens of ways explained in this astonishing book, humanity and culture depend heavily on animals for our existence as we know it. And in a surprising twist, the authors show us that there would be no human economy without animals. But a rethink and a moral reckoning are now due. A towering, singular achievement of information merging insight and empathy, this is one of those rare works that changes our view of everything. And I don't say that lightly."

—Carl Safina, *author of* Beyond Words, *and*, Alfie and Me.

Disclaimer

The views expressed in this book are those of the authors/editor and do not necessarily represent the views of the International Monetary Fund (IMF), its Executive Board, or IMF Management, nor of the IMF's Independent Evaluation Office (IEO), nor of Sveriges Riksbank.

This book was edited while Nicoletta Batini was affiliated with Sveriges Riksbank.

Contents

Part I
Our Economic Symbiosis with Other Animal Species

Chapter 1
Human and Non-Human Animals: A Complex Relationship

Harriet Ritvo and Rebecca J. H. Woods

> "Animals are not brethren, they are not underlings; they are other nations, caught with ourselves in the net of life and time."
> —Henry Beston

Abstract This chapter traces the complex and evolving relationship between human and nonhuman animals across history, exploring the ways these interactions have shaped, and been shaped by, cultural, economic, and ethical frameworks. From hunting and domestication to spectacle, labor, and pet-keeping, it maps a long historical arc of entanglement in which animals have been alternately valued as companions, commodities, symbols, and subjects of affection. Yet these relationships, however intimate or cooperative, are never innocent. They are inflected by structures of power, shaped by human interests, and limited by cultural specificity. Even apparent recognitions of sentience or agency—seen in practices like training or co-working—remain bounded within anthropocentric systems. Emotional bonds, while significant, are not immune from complicity. As the chapter concludes, an ethical reckoning with human–animal relations must move beyond isolated moments of care to confront the broader asymmetries that define our shared yet unequal worlds.

Defining the Human–Animal Connection

Human interactions with other species are at the very root of economic thought, theory, and action, and core components of economic thought and action—exchange, valuation, transmutation, accumulation—lurk in relations between humans and other animals. This is true even for those forms of engagement that seem most distant from

H. Ritvo (✉)
Massachusetts Institute of Technology, Cambridge, MA, USA
e-mail: hnritvo@mit.edu

R. J. H. Woods
Institute for the History and Philosophy of Science, University of Toronto, Toronto, ON, Canada
e-mail: rebecca.woods@utoronto.ca

N. Batini (ed.), *The Economics of Non-Human Animals*, Natural Resource Management and Policy 63, https://doi.org/10.1007/978-3-032-17580-9_1

capital economies. It is no accident that *species* and *specie* share a Latin root. For at least ten thousand years, domestic animals have been a regenerative source of wealth for many human communities. In the longue durée of history, human engagements with wild and domesticated creatures—those hunted and herded, on whom we rely for companionship, labor, and/or sustenance—have been and remain largely economic.

Species of Prey

Undoubtedly among the earliest forms of human–animal interaction, for much of human history hunting constituted the primary way in which humans encountered other animals. Prior to the domestication of other animals, hunting (along with scavenging) was the primary method by which animal protein entered human diets. Indeed, long before the evolution of *Homo sapiens* 300,000 years ago, hominids were hunters. Archeological evidence, in the form of stone tools and butchered bones, demonstrates that our ancestors, *Homo erectus*, hunted as early as 1.8 million years ago.[1] Over the course of human evolution, many creatures large and small, winged, aquatic, and terrestrial, have been targets of the chase. While smaller animals could be trapped or snared, often single-handedly or by the young, bringing down larger prey required complex group cooperation, and was thus a spur to social organization. In many ways, then, hunting is part of what has made us human. Notably, for the last approximately 40,000 years, humans have relied—and continue to rely—on our longstanding co-evolutionary companions, *Canis familiaris*, to succeed in predating other species.

Just how important hunting and the species of prey were to early human cultures can be seen in cave art, in archeological evidence of animal rituals, and in the very early history of technology. Ritual and taboos surrounding hunters, and prominent symbolism accorded to both prey animals and other predators, speak to the significance of hunting in early human cultures. Hunting developed, persisted, evolved, and diversified over the last approximately two million years. It became embedded in taboo and ritual, and imbued with social and spiritual significance. Fundamentally, hunting is about feeding and sustaining human bodies and societies.

In more recent history, the economics of hunting have shifted, taking on new trappings, meanings, symbolisms, and economics.[2] The late medieval and early modern periods saw hunting become the privilege of ruling classes from Western Europe to South Asia, with wild animals increasingly classed as either game or vermin. "Game" animals were those properly the subject of elaborate elite hunting cultures, whose death at the hands of an English lord or Mughal prince could confer qualities of strength, prowess, and masculinity. Which species in particular constituted prized

[1] José Ferraro et al. (2013). See also Jayne Wilkins et al. (2012).

[2] Chapters 7 and 10 in this book delve on today's economics of hunting.

game depended on local ecologies; aurochs (extinct by 1627),[3] stags, and wild boar were among those most prized in Western Europe; tigers, lions, and boar in South Asia; and tigers in East Asia.[4]

Often, whether a species fell into one category or the other reflected the extent to which it competed with, or preyed upon, domesticates, especially sheep and cattle. For example, quaggas, a now-extinct subspecies of zebra, competed for fodder with imported settler livestock in nineteenth-century Southern Africa, and were therefore considered vermin,[5] while in the western United States, wolves, coyotes, and cougars—all of whom preyed on ranchers' sheep and cattle, similarly suffered the very real consequences of the label "vermin," with state-sanctioned bounties contributing to their dramatically reduced numbers.[6] As hunting became the preserve of elite classes, hunting for subsistence, often called "pot hunting," was reclassed as poaching—the unauthorized appropriation of game species for personal consumption—and subject more often than not to the full weight of the penal code.[7] The value systems of elite hunting cultures were primarily symbolic and emblematic of political power and social worth, while reliance on hunting for subsistence was often a marker of marginal economic status.[8]

The expansion of European imperialism in the seventeenth and eighteenth centuries profoundly altered the literal and symbolic values of wild animals and hunting practices. European encounters with Indigenous hunting cultures transformed practices in the colonies and Europe. As Marcy Norton argues, pre-Columbian Amazonian practices of trapping and taming small mammals and wild birds profoundly influenced the rise of pet-keeping in early modern Europe.[9] More broadly, colonists selectively adopted and incorporated local hunting practices, learning from natives and then claiming their skills along with their lands as rightfully their own. In colonial New England, where Indigenous modes of hunting and warfare closely overlapped, English colonists relied on Indigenous hunters and their techniques from forest-clearing to game-stalking. Colonists embraced Indigenous hunting practices and transformed them into methods of total war that they ultimately used against their native foes and allies alike in wars of colonial domination.[10] In Africa and South Asia, Europeans embraced existing princely hunting cultures, producing syncretic modes such as the modern safari, heavily reliant upon the skills and labor of Indigenous guides and porters, who were invariably denigrated

---

[3] https://www.rewildingbritain.org.uk/why-rewild/reintroductions-key-species/key-species/aurochs-cow.

[4] For hunting in European history, see Eric Joseph Goldberg (2020), Richard Almond (2003), Marcy Norton (2024). For hunting in South Asia, see Julie E. Hughes (2013).

[5] Harriet Ritvo (2020).

[6] Michael D. Wise (2016), Alison Laurence (2025), Jon T. Coleman (2004).

[7] Roger B. Manning (1993), Charles Pocklington Chenevix Trench (1967). See also Karl Jacoby (2001).

[8] Umberto Albarella and Veronica Aniceti (2024).

[9] Marcy Norton (2015); also Mackenzie Cooley (2022).

[10] Patrick M. Malone (1991).

as mere "boys" or "coolies."[11] At the same time, colonial expansion also democratized hunting for lower-class European colonists, who for the first time had relatively unrestricted access to game in places like Australia and New Zealand, where pot hunting literally sustained nascent colonies.[12]

Perhaps most significantly, hunting was industrialized under the expansion of imperial economies.[13] From elephant ivory to beaver pelts, from whale oil to sealskins, parts of wild animals—but usually not their flesh—became commodities for globalizing markets.[14] The local and aggregate ecological impacts of industrialized hunting from the eighteenth century on have been enormous, pushing species to or beyond the brink of extinction.[15] Not only have whole ecosystems been transformed in the absence of bison, beavers, tigers, and elephants. As recent ethological research demonstrates again and again that mammals have culture,[16] we must surmise that for both victims and survivors, the demographic collapses wrought by industrialized hunting were profound. And they are ongoing, as the so-called sixth extinction continues apace all around us.

The Domestication Imperative

In the past as at present, hunting was a hazardous activity, and its results were unpredictable. With regard to species that were expected to provide substantial nourishment, it was obviously safer and more convenient to keep them close by and under control. Humans have developed a variety of methods to accomplish this, and consequently consensus around a single definition of domestication has been elusive. There is, however, significant convergence. For example, one group of zoologists specifies "four main characteristics" of domesticated animals that allow plenty of room for individual judgment or for argument: breeding controlled by humans; provision of a useful product or service; tameness; selection away from the wild type.[17] However, all four contribute to the productivity of the desired commodity (meat) and the efficiency and ease of obtaining it. As a side benefit, the domestication of some species also gave access to secondary commodities, such as milk and fiber.

The first animal to be domesticated, however, offered none of these commodities. Dogs were domesticated more than 30,000 years ago in Eurasia.[18] Uncertainty

---

[11] John M. MacKenzie (1997); Vijaya Ramadas Mandala (2019).

[12] Kathryn Hunter (2015).

[13] Bathsheba Demuth (2019).

[14] Helen Cowie (2022) and John Soluri (2024).

[15] Ryan Tucker Jones (2014).

[16] Andrew Whiten (2021).

[17] Anthea Gentry et al. (2004). For an overview of domestication, see Juliet Clutton-Brock (1987).

[18] https://www.scientificamerican.com/article/how-wolf-became-dog/ "Out of Southeastern Asia: the natural history of domestic dogs across the world," *Scientific American*, December 2015. https://www.nature.com/articles/cr2015147.

remains about exactly where the original domestication took place or whether it occurred more than once, especially since it is possible that some ancient domesticated lineages died out and left no contemporary descendants. It was formerly theorized that, since humans and wolves were attracted to the same game animals, domestication resulted from both species' recognition that collaboration led to more effective predation, but it now seems more likely that dogs were attracted to the garbage that inevitably accompanies human settlements. Thus, scavenging was the basis of a relationship that came to include cooperative hunting, guarding, and, ultimately, herding. The much later domestication of the cat, approximately 10,000 years ago at the eastern end of the Mediterranean, seems to have followed a similar pattern. Members of the wildcat species *Felis silvestris* were attracted by anthropogenic waste, and were tolerated (or admired) because they also hunted mice and other pests.[19]

The domestication of various livestock species happened during the same general period. It is notable that although humans seem to have had the same intellectual capacities for more than a hundred thousand years, and hunting has been difficult and dangerous for much longer, domestication of food animals occurred so recently. (Plant domestication follows a similar chronology; gathering wild plants is less dangerous than killing wild animals, but it is nevertheless much more convenient to have them close at hand.) The likeliest explanation is that, in many places around the world, the climate became more predictable and moderate as the glaciers receded at the end of the Pleistocene. Thus, sheep, goats, pigs, and cattle were domesticated in Southwest Asia around 10,000 years ago, and pigs were domesticated in China a little later, as were llamas and alpacas in the Andean region of South America.[20] Chickens were domesticated in Southeast Asia by 8,000 years ago, and turkeys were domesticated in North America approximately 2,000 years ago.[21] Domesticated horses (like dogs, they were primarily valued as labor, not as food) spread across Eurasia from the lower Volga region around 4,000 years ago.[22] As is the case with dogs (but unlike cats), the wild ancestors of most domesticated species live in social groups with a leader, and so the process of domestication involves both increasing tolerance of human contact and willingness to recognize a human replacement for the conspecific leader.

The value of most domesticates has most obviously been expressed in money, paid either for their products or for the animals themselves. But it has also conventionally been expressed more abstractly by placing the domesticated animals in distinct species, even though all of them will produce fertile offspring (the traditional, though unsatisfactory, definition of species) when mated with their close wild relatives. Most versions of modern systematic taxonomy have enshrined these categories in the form

[19] https://www.scientificamerican.com/article/the-taming-of-the-cat/

[20] https://pmc.ncbi.nlm.nih.gov/articles/PMC8214435/

[21] https://www.science.org/content/article/turkeys-so-good-people-tamed-them-twice https://www.nature.com/articles/s41598-021-81589-7.

[22] https://www.nature.com/articles/s41586-021-04018-9.

of nomenclature, emphasizing the value added by domestication with latinate binomials: so that *Bos taurus* is the offspring of the extinct ancestral *Bos primigenius* and *Canis familiaris* is the offspring of the still extant ancestral *Canis lupus*. Two hundred years ago, in the freewheeling early days of systematic zoology, domesticated animal kinds were frequently elevated to the level of genus, with breeds of dogs or cattle consequently allotted their own species or subspecies.[23] The guidance offered on this point by the International Commission on Zoological Nomenclature, which, by its own declaration, "acts as adviser and arbiter for the zoological community by generating and disseminating information on the correct use of the scientific names of animals,"[24] is not particularly firm.[25] And many taxonomists continue to stress the importance of maintaining separate binomials, not only for reasons of intellectual clarity, but also because in many cases both the lived experience and the legal status of the two forms are very different.[26]

Breeding Wealth

Wealth and domestication have been deeply entwined, possibly since the advent of pastoralism. A cursory glance at English etymology makes plain the shared roots of capital accumulation and animal agriculture. Terms such as "breed wealth" and "livestock," the latter of which came into usage in the sixteenth century, indicate the tight coupling of domesticated animals and the accumulation of wealth. Chattel and cattle share even closer roots. In medieval English, the two were used interchangeably to refer to capital, moveable property, and domesticated animals, differentiating into distinct forms of property only in the fifteenth century.[27]

In point of fact, animal economies function by capitalizing on the reproductive capacity of domesticated organisms.[28] This is why control over reproduction has been so central to understandings of domestication. Feeding, tending, and caring for an animal or group of animals enhances not only the wellbeing of individuals, but the health and number of their offspring as well. In this way, care compounds. Several animals become more, become many, and profits flow in the form of both "renewable"

---

23 See Harriet Ritvo (1997).

24 ICZN website, accessed 28 February 2016. http://iczn.org/

25 "Wild vs. domestic animal names. The majority of domestic animals and their wild ancestors share the same name but in a few cases the two forms were named separately, which has created confusion. It was proposed that the first available specific name based on a wild population be adopted. Therefore, despite the fact that these names post-dated or were contemporary with those based on domestic derivatives, the Commission recently conserved, as valid, the usage of 17 species names based on wild species." "Biodiversity Studies," ICZN website, accessed 28 February 2016. http://iczn.org/content/biodiversity-studies.

26 Anthea Gentry et al. (2004).

27 *Oxford English Dictionary*, "chattel (n.)," June 2024, https://doi.org/10.1093/OED/4008666338; *Oxford English Dictionary*, "cattle (n.)," June 2025, https://doi.org/10.1093/OED/5036159615.

28 Sarah Franklin (2007).

products (milk and other dairy, wool, blood, labor) and "terminal" products, those dependent upon the death of a creature, such as hide, flesh, fat, and horns. By the eighteenth-century, earlier associations between cattle, chattel, stock, and livestock, had morphed into new expressions of breed wealth, in which the genetic potentiality embodied in particular animals constituted a primary source of value, giving rise to modern breeds of sheep, cattle, horses, pigs, and eventually, cats, dogs, poultry, and so on.[29]

In the modern era, as with so many other forms of engagement with other animals and facets of animal economies, these basic premises were scaled up and intensified. Many animals became multitudes, particularly with the imperial expansion of Europe, which offered unprecedented opportunities for the biotic explosions of European domesticates in novel ecologies. In the wake of imperial expansion, populations of colonial livestock exploded, to the detriment of indigenous ecologies. Historians have demonstrated how livestock were central to European "conquests" of "new" worlds, literally facilitating Europe's demographic takeover of much of the world. Sometimes, their role was unwitting. As Alfred Crosby has shown, "crowd" diseases produced from livestock husbandry and its accumulations, including urban living, gave colonists both an edge and a weapon in their encounter with Indigenous Americans.[30] In other instances, livestock animals were deliberate tools of colonization. A pair of goats deposited on an oceanic island became a living larder for passing voyagers, thus keeping sailors and soldiers alive, and extending the potential of European imperial ambitions across oceanic environments. On mainlands, domesticates occupied Indigenous lands, often in advance or outside of the scope of direct colonial oversight, disrupting Indigenous practices of land management, cultivation, and ecological relations, almost invariably to the advantage of colonists.[31] Their biological and reproductive flourishing supported the demographic explosion of settler societies in North and South America, Australia, New Zealand, and Southern Africa—places where, by the mid-nineteenth century, cattle, and especially sheep, dramatically outnumbered human settlers, who enjoyed animal protein as part of their diets at levels undreamt of in Europe.[32]

This was an era of globalizing food systems, occasioned and furthered by Empire itself.[33] As alimentary networks extended across oceans and continents, regimes of livestock husbandry intensified, stratified, and specialized. Livestock breeders increasingly specialized in the production of studs, animals capable of imparting their preferred genetic traits to their offspring, and distinct breeds of sheep, cattle, pigs, and chickens proliferated. The introduction of artificial feed unyoked grazing animals from their fodder, increasing the density of animals per acre of land and permitting more concentrated modes of cattle raising in particular that gave rise, eventually,

---

[29] Harriet Ritvo (1995), Ritvo (1987a, b), Rebecca J. H. Woods (2017a, 2017b), Margaret C. Derry (2003), and Nicholas Russell (1986).

[30] Alfred W. Crosby (1986).

[31] Virginia DeJohn Anderson (2006), Elinor G. K. Melville (1994).

[32] Rebecca J. H. Woods (2015).

[33] Chris Otter (2020).

to twentieth-century confined animal feeding operations (CAFOs).[34] Geographies of slaughter, too, evolved, concentrating first in major conurbations before being banished from cities as technologies of preservation, notably artificial refrigeration, made it possible to produce meat (that is, to slaughter and butcher animals) at vast distances from their sites of consumption.[35]

All these transformations had profound impacts on how animal lives were lived. A sheep or a cow might change hands several times, as it passed from breeder to grazier to drover to slaughterhouse. Animals lived in increasingly concentrated herds and flocks, with commercial flocks of merino sheep regularly numbering in the tens of thousands in nineteenth-century Australia. Dairy production requires pregnant cows; male offspring, as is well known, are surplus to the industry, unless diverted into markets for veal. As the dairy industry transformed along a pattern similar to that of meat, in which pasteurization provided the key technological component permitting scaled up dairy production, the fate of bobby cows became a rallying cry for animal rights and slow food activists in the twentieth century.[36]

From Menagerie to Marketplace

The deployment of animals as entertainers in public and private menageries, staged combats, and as performers in other contexts is not as obviously economic as their role in producing agricultural commodities. Nevertheless, at least occasionally, there has been greater overlap between them than may appear at first glance. For example, when the London Zoo opened to the public in 1828, the exotic animals on display were not its only occupants. Two years earlier, the founders of the Zoological Society of London had outlined sweeping and ambitious goals for the new institution, including "the introduction of new and curious subjects of the Animal Kingdom" to enhance and diversify existing British livestock. Thus, at first, a small area was reserved for what were termed breeding experiments, although its inhabitants were soon moved to more commodious quarters in a farm outside the city.[37] The farm animals were not different in kind (or kinds) from the animals in the menagerie, but the range of species was significantly smaller and there was room for more individuals of each. They included various species of deer, sheep, goats, zebras, kangaroos, zebu cattle, rabbits, ostriches, emus, gallinaceous fowls (wild relatives of chickens and turkeys), ducks, and geese.[38] That is, allowing for a few imaginative flights of fantasy, they were close allies of the domesticated animals that occupied most British barns and fields.

---

[34] Chapter 6 explores modern animal agriculture practices in greater depth globally.

[35] Chris Otter (2006), Thomas Almeroth-Williams (2019), Woods (2017a, 2017b).

[36] Ruth Harrison (1964).

[37] P. Chalmers Mitchell (1929).

[38] Henry Scherren (1905).

They had also been selected to accommodate a much narrower human constituency than the one that was drawn to Regent's Park. Many of the fellows of the Zoological Society were also elite agriculturalists who shared more practical concerns with regard to animal breeding and husbandry. Indeed the original governing Council of the Society was fairly evenly split between anatomists and naturalists based in the capital and gentlemanly nonspecialists of much grander social position.[39] It was to accommodate them that the core aim of the farm was "effecting improvements in the quality or properties of [domesticated Quadrupeds and Birds] used for the table; and likewise in domesticating subjects from our own or foreign countries, which have not hitherto been inmates of our poultry or farm yards."[40] This was the reason why the zoo farm circulated a questionnaire to poultry breeders, asking them to rate types of domesticated fowls and game birds with regard to such qualities as beauty, productivity, and courage; why it mated zebras with donkeys to see if the resulting hybrids were better in some way; and why it responded positively to requests like the following: "the Duke of Bedford presents his compliments [to the ZSL secretary], and begs to know whether he can spare him a Cereopsis male goose…"[41]

The zoo farm only lasted a few years, after which the landowners interested in the introductions and enhancements it had offered had to transfer their activities to their own estates. For example, the Earl of Derby's menagerie included Asian species of pheasants, all four species of South American camelids, and a breeding herd of elands, the largest and meatiest of the antelopes.[42] In addition, they founded what were called acclimatization societies to support their efforts. In Europe and North America, such societies had little impact—the Society for the Acclimatization of Animals, Birds, Fishes, Insects, and Vegetables within the United Kingdom lasted only a few years, and the more robust French Société d'Acclimatation, which lasted longer and possessed a zoo in Paris, had a similarly minimal influence on French livestock. The most influential acclimatization societies, for better or for worse, were on the other side of the world.

The faunas of both Australia and New Zealand have been radically altered over the last two centuries. This was not completely the fault of acclimatization societies—much of this transformation resulted from the operation of forces that Alfred Crosby has labeled as "ecological imperialism"—that is, the effect of transplanting an integrated European system of agriculture. But the deer and stoats of New Zealand, and the rabbits and foxes of Australia, among many other kinds, constitute a continuing memorial to the aspirations and inclinations of their nineteenth-century introducers.[43]

The purely spectatorial aspect of live animal collections is not, of course, completely divorced from economic concerns. Acquiring and maintaining large exotic animals has always been expensive. To give an extreme example, the National Zoo in Washington pays China $1,000,000 per year to rent the recently arrived pair

---

39 Mitchell, 26.

40 Scherren, 43.

41 Scherren, 66–69.

42 Clemency Fisher (2002).

43 On acclimatization, see Harriet Ritvo (2018).

of pandas, in addition to $2,800,000 in annual maintenance costs.[44] Menageries were supported by wealthy and powerful individuals in ancient Egypt, China, India, and Rome, and this continued through the medieval period.[45] Modern zoos, open to the public and relying on admission fees for significant support, evolved from private forebears, sometimes literally. The Schönbrunn Zoo in Vienna, which calls itself the oldest zoo in the world, was founded as an imperial menagerie in 1752, but opened to the public soon afterward.[46] The zoo at in the Jardin des Plantes in Paris opened in 1794 to accommodate animals who had lived in the royal menagerie at Versailles before the French Revolution.[47] Similarly, if less disruptively, the London Zoo absorbed some of the animals from the royal menagerie at the Tower of London when it was disbanded in 1835.[48]

Like zoos, a range of other animal performances supported human employment as well as ancillary products and services. Individual exotic animals or small collections in traveling menageries, could be exhibited at taverns or fairs.[49] Animal combats have always attracted audiences, whether or not they were legal—and whether the animals were fighting each other, as in cockfights and badger baits, or people, as in bullfights. Observation of exotic animals in situ, as on safari, has been available to affluent consumers since the steamship made travel relatively efficient in the nineteenth century; the less prosperous could enjoy their observations vicariously, in the form of written accounts and (later) documentary films.

Valuing Pets

The value of animal companions is not usually expressed in financial terms.[50] The importance of such connections is obvious from their owners' responses to their loss, and, often, the time, effort, and money they devote to maintaining them, but, like other emotional values, it is difficult to quantify. That is particularly true of the close relationships that must always have existed between at least some working animals and their owners, especially since, before the nineteenth century, pet ownership—that is, the support of animals whose only purpose was friendship—was considered an unjustifiable luxury for people of modest means. Women who seemed too close to their nonhuman companions could be burned as witches, and it is not a coincidence that a still popular toy spaniel breed was named after King Charles. Well into the

[44] https://nationalzoo.si.edu/animals/giant-panda-faqs.

[45] Eric Baratay and Elisabeth Hardouin-Fugier (2002).

[46] Cara Parks (2015).

[47] https://www.jardindesplantesdeparis.fr/en/history-of-the-menagerie-the-zoo-of-the-jardin-des-plantes.

[48] https://www.hrp.org.uk/tower-of-london/history-and-stories/the-tower-of-london-menagerie/#gs.mrgw15.

[49] Harriet Ritvo (1987a, b).

[50] Chapter 20 delves deeply into the pet industry, tracing its history and transformation over time.

eighteenth century, Humphrey Morice, a gentleman of some distinction who had served as a member of the Privy Council, wished to provide for the maintenance of his aged dogs and horses after he died. Because he feared posthumous public ridicule (and possibly a challenge to the will), he chose not to include this bequest in the main body of his will, hiding it instead in a secret codicil included in a letter to a friend.[51] When pet-keeping did become widely acceptable, a market for goods such as toys and canned food and for veterinary and other services emerged to accommodate the increasing numbers of dog and cat owners.

Formalized first in Britain, the modern infrastructure of domesticated animal breeding emerged in the eighteenth and nineteenth centuries, based on earlier, less formalized practices of evaluation and selection. It includes the breed societies that record and validate pedigrees and establish standards, as well as the competitive shows that illustrate and reinforce them. Racehorses and then economically valuable livestock species were the first to benefit from such attention. Later in the nineteenth century, the proprietors of small carnivores adopted the practices that had been developed to establish, validate, and maintain the breeds of large ungulates. The first formal dog show was held in Newcastle in 1859, followed by increasingly large and numerous shows in other cities and around the world. The Kennel Club was founded in 1873 and published its first *Stud Book* the next year. Applying practices that had been developed for livestock was not, however, always straightforward. Livestock standards ultimately reflected economic value based on utility—at least, this was routinely asserted, although the definition of utility could vary; for example, the selection of some breeds of cattle and sheep for extreme fatness provoked intense debate and criticism about both the healthiness and the palatability of the resulting meat. In contrast, analogous claims could not be made about pet poodles or toy spaniels, whose value was primarily sentimental. Moreover, the increasing popularity of pet-keeping meant that some owners of dogs like setters or collies or bulldogs, whose original purposes had been utilitarian, might wish to apply modified standards when they were kept as companions.

Nevertheless, lack of utility did not mean lack of value. One reason for the proliferation of institutionalized and accredited breeds in the course of the nineteenth century (and subsequently), is that the value of pedigreed animals can be expressed in cash, both purchase price and the cost of what are genteelly referred to as "services." Dogs are among the most malleable of mammals, both physically and temperamentally, which was as observable at Victorian dog shows as it is at present. This gave breeders a lot to work with. The same, however, could not be said of cats. Cat breeds exhibit far less variation than dog breeds; in fact, even distinct feline species tend to resemble one another closely, apart from differences in size. Nevertheless, the first public cat show—held in 1871 at the Crystal Palace in London—drew more than 20,000 visitors.[52] As with other domesticated animals, pedigrees and breed books conferred legitimacy that could enhance the perceived value of individual cats. Indeed, in some cases, the mere identification of a breed (that is, the assertion that the breed existed)

51 Dix Harwood (1928).

52 Harrison Weir (1889).

could increase the value of individual animals who belonged to it. That is, documentation could actually create value, not just recognize it and report on it. In this way, word might actually be turned into flesh—or at least into money.

Conclusions

As this brief tour through the *longue durée* of human–animal relations reveals, there is no pure, innocent, or uncomplicated form of engagement between humans and other animals. Our interactions are always shaped by context, culture, and power—never entirely free from the imprint of human interests. Yet, within this entangled history, we find many ways in which humans have recognized and responded to the capacities of other creatures. Sentience, for instance, is often acknowledged—sometimes tacitly, sometimes overtly—when working animals are given commands, or when companion animals like dogs participate in hunting, herding, or sport.[53] These moments suggest a kind of interspecies communication, a recognition of agency, even if bounded by human frameworks.

Emotional bonds also form a significant part of this landscape. People admire, care for, and even grieve nonhuman animals. From the affection shown to pets, to the awe inspired by wild animals, these attachments are often held up as evidence of a more ethical or empathetic mode of engagement—one that stands in contrast to the more brutal realities of exploitation, particularly in industrialized systems like factory farming.

However, such relationships—rooted in care, admiration, or collaboration—have their limits. Not only are they historically recent and culturally specific, but they also tend to benefit only a small subset of animals, often those closest to human domestic life. While the lives of some individual animals may be enriched through these bonds, they do little to alter the broader structures that govern human–animal relations. In the aggregate, animals remain subject to systems that prioritize human needs, desires, and economies. The ethics of our engagement, then, cannot be measured solely by isolated acts of kindness or recognition. They must also confront the persistent asymmetries that define our collective relationship with the animal world—where even care can coexist with control, and affection with appropriation.[54]

References

Albarella U, Aniceti V (2024) 'Unmaking' the deer in Medieval Europe: historical and archaeological evidence. Eur J Archaeol 27(3):353–371

Almeroth-Williams T (2019) City of beasts: how animals shaped Georgian London. Manchester University Press, Manchester

---

[53] Donna J. Haraway (2003, 2008).

[54] Even this may be overstating the benefits. See Laurel Braitman (2014).

Anderson VDJ (2006) Creatures of empire: how domestic animals transformed early America. Oxford University Press, New York
Baratay E, Hardouin-Fugier E (2002) Zoo: a history of zoological gardens in the west (trans: Welsh O). Reaktion, London
Braitman L (2014) Animal madness: how anxious dogs, compulsive parrots, and elephants in recovery help us understand ourselves. Simon & Schuster, New York
Clutton-Brock J (1987) A natural history of domesticated mammals. Cambridge University Press, Cambridge
Coleman JT (2004) Vicious: Wolves and Men in America. Yale University Press, New Haven
Cooley M (2022) The perfection of nature: animals, breeding, and race in the Renaissance. The University of Chicago Press, Chicago
Cowie H (2022) Victims of fashion: animal commodities in Victorian Britain. Cambridge University Press, Cambridge
Crosby AW (1986) Ecological imperialism: the biological expansion of Europe, 900–1900. Cambridge University Press, Cambridge
Demuth B (2019) Floating coast: an environmental history of the Bering Strait. W.W. Norton & Company, New York
Derry MC (2003) Bred for perfection: shorthorn cattle, collies, and Arabian horses since 1800. Johns Hopkins University Press
Ferraro J et al (2013) Earliest archaeological evidence of persistent hominin Carnivory. PLoS One 8(4):e62174. https://doi.org/10.1371/journal.pone.0062174
Fisher C (ed) (2002) A passion for natural history: the life and legacy of the 13th Earl of Derby. National Museums and Galleries on Merseyside, Liverpool, pp 87, 102, 114, 116
Franklin S (2007) Dolly mixtures: the remaking of genealogy. Duke University Press, Durham
Gentry A, Clutton-Brock J, Groves CP (2004) The naming of wild animal species and their domestic derivatives. J Archaeol Sci 31:645–651
Goldberg EJ (2020) In the manner of the Franks: hunting, kingship, and masculinity in early medieval Europe. University of Pennsylvania Press, Philadelphia
Haraway DJ (2003) The companion species manifesto: dogs, people, and significant otherness. Prickly Paradigm Press, Chicago
Haraway DJ (2008) When species meet. University of Minnesota Press, Minneapolis
Harrison R (1964) Animal machines: the new factory farming industry. Vincent Stuart, London
Harwood D (1928) Love for animals and how it developed in great Britain. Columbia University Press, New York, p 216
Hughes JE (2013) Animal kingdoms: hunting, the environment, and power in the Indian princely states. Harvard University Press, Cambridge, Mass
Hunter K (2015) Colonial Hunting Cultures. In: Beattie J, Melillo E, O'Gorman E (eds) Eco-cultural networks and the British empire: new views on environmental history. Bloomsbury, New York, pp 180–201
Jacoby K (2001) Crimes against nature: squatters, poachers, thieves, and the hidden history of American conservation. University of California Press, Berkeley
Jones RT (2014) Empire of extinction: Russians and the North Pacific's strange beasts of the sea, 1741–1867. Oxford University Press, Oxford
Laurence A (2025) Coyotes, Cougars, Californians: views on changing animal relations at the natural history museum of Los Angeles County. Animal History 1(3):1–27
MacKenzie JM (1997) The empire of nature. Manchester University Press, Manchester
Malone PM (1991) The Skulking way of war: technology and tactics among the New England Indians. Madison Books, Lanham, MD
Mandala VR (2019) Shooting a Tiger: big-game hunting and conservation in Colonial India. Oxford University Press, New Delhi, India
Manning RB (1993) Hunters and Poachers: a social and cultural history of unlawful hunting in England, 1485–1640. Clarendon Press, Oxford, UK

Melville EGK (1994) A plague of sheep : environmental consequences of the conquest of Mexico. Cambridge University Press, Cambridge
Mitchell PC (1929) Centenary history of the zoological society of London. Zoological Society of London, London, p 93
Norton M (2015) The Chicken or the Iegue: human-animal relationships and the Columbian exchange. Am Hist Rev 120(1):28–60
Norton M (2024) The tame and the wild: people and animals after 1492. Harvard University Press, Cambridge, Mass
Otter C (2006) The vital city: public analysis, dairies and slaughterhouses in nineteenth-century Britain. Cult Geogr 13(4): 517–537
Otter C (2020) Diet for a large planet : industrial Britain, food systems, and world ecology. The University of Chicago Press, Chicago
Parks C (2015) The world's oldest zoo is a modern attraction with a storied past. Smithsonian Magazine. https://www.smithsonianmag.com/travel/zoo-endured-inside-worlds-oldest-zoo-180957191/
Richard A (2003) Medieval hunting. Sutton, Stroud, UK
Ritvo (1987a) The animal estate: the English and other creatures in the victorian age. Harvard University Press, Cambridge, Mass
Ritvo H (1987b) The animal estate: the English and other creatures in the victorian age. Harvard University Press, Cambridge, MA, pp 206–209
Ritvo H (1995) Possessing mother nature: genetic capital in eighteenth-century Britain. In: Staves S, Brewer J (eds) Early modern conceptions of property. Routledge, pp 413–426
Ritvo H (1997) The Platypus and the Mermaid. Harvard University Press, Cambridge
Ritvo H (2018) The world as zoo. In: Minteer B et al (ed) The ark and beyond: the evolution of zoo and aquarium conservation. University of Chicago Press, Chicago
Ritvo H (2020) Q is for Quagga. In: Mawani R, Burton A (eds) Animalia: an anti-imperial bestiary. Duke University Press, Durham, NC
Russell N (1986) Like Engend'ring like: heredity and animal breeding in early modern England. Cambridge University Press, Cambridge
Scherren H (1905) The zoological society of London: a sketch of its foundation and development, and the story of its farm, museum, gardens, menagerie and library. Cassell, London, pp 66–73
Soluri J (2024) Creatures of fashion: animals, global markets, and the transformation of Patagonia. The University of North Carolina Press, Chapel Hill
Trench CC (1967) The Poacher and the Squire: a history of poaching and game preservation in England. Longmans, London
Weir H (1889) Our cats and all about them. Their varieties, habits, and management; and for show. The standard or excellence and beauty described and pictured. Houghtob Mifflin, Boston, pp 123–124
Whiten A (2021) The burgeoning reach of animal culture. Science 372:6537
Wilkins J et al (2012) Evidence for early hafted hunting technology. Science 338:942–946. https://doi.org/10.1126/science.1227608
Wise MD (2016) Producing predators: wolves, work, and conquest in the Northern Rockies. University of Nebraska Press, Lincoln
Woods RJH (2015) From colonial animal to imperial edible: building an empire of sheep in New Zealand, ca. 1880–1900. Comp Stud South Asia Afr Middle East 35(1):117–136
Woods RJH (2017a) Nature and the refrigerating machine: the politics and production of cold in the nineteenth century. In Kowal E, Radin J (eds) Cryopolitics. The MIT Press, pp 89–115
Woods RJH (2017b) The herds shot round the world: native breeds and the British empire, 1800–1900. The University of North Carolina Press, Chapel Hill

Chapter 2
Economic Speciesism

Brian A. Swartz and Brent D. Mishler

> "The most important scientific revolutions all include … the dethronement of human arrogance from … our centrality in the cosmos."
> —Stephen Jay Gould

Abstract *Speciesism*, as diagnosed by Swartz and Mishler (2022), is the belief that species are uniquely real biological entities and that the human species is superior to nonhuman life. This view reflects human exceptionalism rooted in cultural institutions and is reinforced by scientific practices that impose arbitrary species-level boundaries across the Tree of Life. This perceived separation has long been used to justify prioritizing human interests, including the systematic use of nonhuman organisms for human purposes. Building on this, *economic speciesism* can be understood as the normalization of extracting value from nonhuman life through market logic that favors utility and disregards agency, sentience, and ecological functions. We introduce a dual-layered valuation model that distinguishes *instrumental value*—based on the utility life provides—from *intrinsic value*, which reflects both the structural, energetic, and evolutionary roles of organisms within complex systems, as well as ethical considerations of other lineages. Using carbon as a biospheric currency, we quantify contributions across trophic levels and explore tools like trophic network modeling and dependency mapping to make systemic interdependence visible for policy development. Although economic considerations alone cannot fully capture the ethical value of nonhuman life, they serve as a strategic entry point to foster broader scientific and ethical appreciation of life's complexity and interdependence.

B. A. Swartz (✉) · B. D. Mishler
Department of Integrative Biology, University of California, Berkeley, CA, USA
e-mail: brian.darwin@berkeley.edu

B. D. Mishler
e-mail: bmishler@berkeley.edu

B. A. Swartz
Millennium Alliance for Humanity and the Biosphere, Department of Biology, Center for Conservation Biology, Stanford University, Stanford, CA, USA

N. Batini (ed.), *The Economics of Non-Human Animals*, Natural Resource Management and Policy 63, https://doi.org/10.1007/978-3-032-17580-9_2

From Crown to Soil: Tracing Value from Humans to Whales to Worms[1]

If a single blue whale is valued at $2 million for its role in carbon sequestration, ecotourism appeal, and ecological contributions, then how much are ants, nematodes, or soil microbes worth? And what impact does the disappearance of these unseen "ecosystem workers" have on the human economy?

This is not a rhetorical question. Economists have proposed monetary valuations for whales, mangroves, and honeybees (Costanza et al. 1997; Chami et al. 2019), aiming to influence policy and market behavior. While these figures sometimes guide environmental planning or pilot projects, they are rarely formalized into enforceable systems. Their role is best seen as part of the conceptual groundwork of biodiversity economics, rather than as a strict regulatory standard (OECD 2020). Of course, even these high-profile valuations—though incomplete and rarely enforceable—are more than most organisms ever receive. Smaller and less visible organisms are often overlooked, not because their contributions are insignificant, but because their activities happen out of sight, underground, or at scales too small to draw public attention or influence policy. This illustrates that economic speciesism isn't a simple yes-or-no issue—it varies in degree. Some lineages are completely ignored, others are partially recognized, and a few are narrowly valued for the small parts of their labor that we can measure. The result is a deeply uneven economy of attention.

But if a whale is valued for its ecosystem services, does that value disappear when human-made technologies—like direct air carbon capture systems—can replicate those services (Meckling and Biber 2021; Küng et al. 2023)? What happens to the whale's worth once it has been replaced?

These questions expose a deeper issue: the logic of natural capital depends on instrumental value—life only matters when it serves human interests. This goes beyond a narrow economic perspective; it reveals a core speciesism rooted in human exceptionalism and justified by arbitrary distinctions at the species level (Swartz and Mishler 2022). It is not only a moral oversight but a cognitive pattern: humans tend to apply status-based reasoning to a biosphere governed by interdependence, not social hierarchy.

Instrumental reasoning can help translate ecosystems into economic terms, but it also hides the structural and intrinsic conditions that allow Earth's ecosystems to exist. Instrumental value draws attention; intrinsic value sustains life. A valuation model that ignores this distinction doesn't just miss part of the picture—it misreads the foundation of what it aims to protect.

---

[1] This chapter examines the scientific and ethical foundations of such valuation systems, while Chapter 5 discusses valuation methods.

Instrumental Value and the Cognitive Architecture of Speciesism

If whales have a "market value," then so do other organisms. If we are willing to assign a price to whales, why are we opposed to pricing humans? This question lies at the core of biodiversity economics. Many people feel moral disgust at the idea of placing a financial value on human beings, yet they often have no hesitation in doing so for nonhuman organisms. Why is that? The answer is speciesism—a cognitive bias that views *Homo sapiens* as fundamentally different from and superior to all other life. As Swartz and Mishler (2022) argue, speciesism is conceptually parallel to racism, operating at a higher phylogenetic level.

This double standard has evolutionary roots. Humans evolved to care deeply for kin—those who share our genes—and to extend that concern to ingroup members (Hamilton 1964a, b; Tomasello 2016). As societies grew and ethical reasoning expanded, this kinship logic was abstracted to include broader communities, sometimes even humanity as a whole (Singer 1981; Greene 2013). Yet nonhuman organisms, lineages that share our deep evolutionary ancestry, are often excluded from that moral boundary. They are treated as "other," and their value is justified not in terms of inherent worth but in terms of the services they provide.

There is something deeper at play as well. Speciesism isn't just rooted in tribal loyalty; it also reflects how our minds evolved to navigate social hierarchies and status games (Boehm 1999; Sapolsky 2017). We don't only care more about those who are "like us"—we also rank everything, placing ourselves at the top (Cheng et al. 2013; Henrich 2020). From a geocentric cosmos to the *scala naturae*—with humans at the pinnacle—we project our social logic onto the structure of nature (Lovejoy 1936; Crosby 1996). See Fig. 2.1. This is a predictable bias rooted in the cognitive patterns of highly social primates. Human cognition evolved to monitor rank and dominance. Culture reinforced this by depicting nonhuman life as inferior, turning animality into an insult rather than a kinship. So deeply are we attuned to status that we instinctively elevate ourselves, even when no hierarchy exists to climb.

Stephen Jay Gould captured this recurring tendency with characteristic clarity. "The most important scientific revolutions," he wrote, "all include, as their only common feature, the dethronement of human arrogance from one pedestal after another" (Gould 1989). Thus, Copernicus displaced us from the center of the cosmos, while Darwin shifted our status from divine image to naked, upright ape (Copernicus 1543; Darwin 1859). What remains might be the last illusion to dispel: that human life has inherent superiority over other life, not only in moral or metaphysical terms but on any objective or empirical basis. The idea of human exceptionalism may soothe cultural sensibilities, but evidence from evolution, ecology, and thermodynamics all show such distinctions to be artificial.

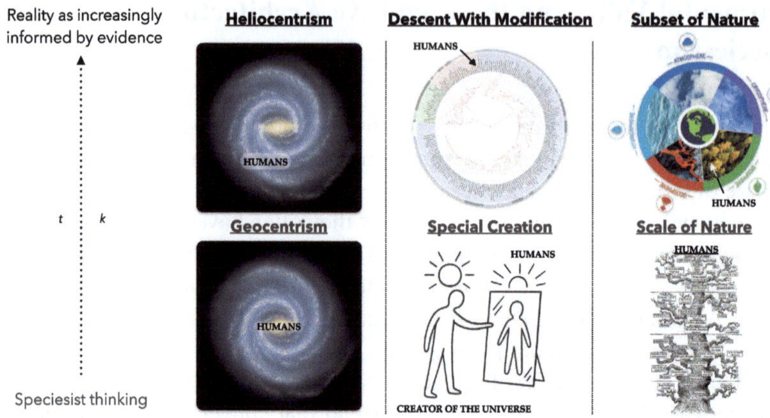

Fig. 2.1 A visual genealogy of speciesist worldviews and their scientific undoing. Across three domains—cosmology, biology, and ontology—humans have repeatedly positioned themselves as central, superior, or distinct from other entities. Each vertical pair contrasts a traditional, speciesist frame with its evidence-based alternative. Together, the panels illustrate what Stephen Jay Gould called "the dethronement of human arrogance" from one pedestal after another (Gould 1989). $t =$ time; $k =$ knowledge. *Source* Authors' own work

The Valuation Trap: Measuring Life by What It Does, Not What It Is

This chapter is not a critique of anthropocentrism itself. We recognize its evolutionary and cognitive roots. The human tendency to prioritize our group was beneficial during early evolution (Hamilton 1964a, b; Silk 2007). However, past adaptive value does not justify current actions. Rather than outright rejecting anthropocentrism, we propose that instrumental value, although limited, can serve as a practical entry point for engaging people because it uses language they already understand. Framing biodiversity in economic terms doesn't fully capture its worth, but it provides a reason for people to care. That alone might be enough to trigger behavior change. Yet instrumental reasoning reveals an ethical inconsistency. If we recoil at the idea of assigning a price to humans, why are we comfortable putting dollar values on other lineages? This inconsistency—what we call *economic speciesism*—highlights the different valuation systems applied to human and nonhuman life. Some lineages, like our own, are assumed to have intrinsic worth, while others are valued only for their utility to humans (e.g., fungi, ants, whales).

Yet even this boundary is more permeable than it seems. Human life is often described as "priceless," but it is frequently assigned a monetary value in practice. During the COVID-19 pandemic, governments weighed the economic costs of lockdowns against the expected number of deaths (Cutler and Summers 2020). In regulatory systems, actuarial models assign a dollar value to human life, guiding decisions in healthcare, transportation, and environmental safety (Aldy and Viscusi

2003). The claim that human life cannot be priced is more often a moral stance than a policy fact, which clearly shows the difference between intrinsic and instrumental valuation.

So, what determines which lineages are considered inherently valuable and which are not? The answer does not lie in empirical differences but in how we categorize them. Once we draw a boundary between "us" and "them," we justify that boundary using social and cognitive shortcuts. Ingroup members are given intrinsic value; outgroups—whether human or nonhuman—are judged based on their function relative to the ingroup (Brewer 1999; Brown 2004). This illustrates the application of a deeply rooted bias, discussed earlier, that prioritizes kin and familiar allies. That same heuristic continues to influence how we value life today. Rejecting speciesism involves recognizing that species are not uniquely real and that the perceived superiority of the human species is culturally and cognitively reinforced rather than empirically grounded. Choosing to extend ethical consideration beyond the human ingroup is a normative decision—but one that may be informed by empirical insights into our evolutionary continuity with other organisms, our ecological entanglement with them, and the cognitive biases that shape how we assign value.

The intrinsic value of biodiversity depends not only on ethical arguments but also on scientific facts. Biological lineages are not interchangeable. Each one results from enormous thermodynamic costs (Schrödinger 1944)—millions of years of energy, mutation, selection, and other evolutionary processes that have built complex, self-sustaining systems (Szathmáry and Smith 1995). Each is uniquely historical and unreproducible, following a singular journey through evolutionary space that cannot be repeated or recreated, even if de-extinction technologies can produce functionally similar descendants from different ancestral origins (Gedman et al. 2025). A "restored" lineage is not the same lineage, just perhaps a similar one. These organisms are also part of ecological networks that support the biosphere and create conditions necessary for life. These are not subjective statements; they are empirical facts showing that life, in its structure and history, has immense value that is independent of human use or attitudes.

Our goal in this chapter is not to dismiss the usefulness of instrumental reasoning but to use it as a bridge to intrinsic valuation. By engaging with people within the frameworks they already use, we can guide those frameworks to be more evidence-based and ethically consistent. Intrinsic value, in this context, is not just a moral idea; it's an acknowledgment of the physical, historical, and biological factors that enable life and the planet to exist.

This chapter unfolds in three parts. It starts by examining how natural capital frameworks assign economic value to nonhuman life, mainly focusing on animals—such as whales, livestock, and pollinators—whose instrumental value is increasingly shaping environmental policy. Next, the discussion shifts to the ethical tensions this perspective creates, exploring how speciesism influences which lives are valued and which are ignored. Finally, the chapter questions whether valuation can go beyond utility, recognizing life not only for its economic roles but also for the complex ecological systems it helps maintain.

If you've ever wondered why whales are valued while beetles, nematodes, springtails, and other decomposers are overlooked—along with the immense microbial world beneath them—this chapter offers answers and a framework to fix that imbalance.

Pricing Life: Economic Speciesism and the Market Logic of Nature

Animals as Capital: How Economic Systems Enfold the Living World

Ecosystems are more than just scenic landscapes or wildlife refuges. They are dynamic, productive systems that provide essential services for the human economy (Daily et al., 2000). Rainforests absorb atmospheric carbon, wetlands filter water, and coral reefs protect coastlines from storms (Pan et al. 2011; Ferrario et al. 2014; Barbier 2019). These processes are active and energy-intensive forms of work. Fundamentally, life regulates food webs, cycles, and nutrients and maintains conditions that enable ecosystems to function. Among these life forms, animals contribute in particularly dynamic ways—cycling nutrients, shaping food webs, and affecting energy flows. From the largest mammals to the tiniest detritivores, they help stabilize the climate and support the living infrastructure of ecosystems (Costanza et al. 1997).

For centuries, this work has been regarded as "free labor"—an endless supply of benefits from unseen forces of nature. However, that idea was an illusion. The costs of nature's work have always been real, but they were never officially recorded in the world's balance sheets, profit statements, or national GDPs (Dasgupta 2021). Businesses, governments, and investors used these services without paying for them, believing that the mechanisms of open natural systems represented an endless, inexhaustible resource (Guerry et al. 2015).

However, this approach is changing. Over the past twenty years, economists have started valuing ecosystem services as natural capital. This concept treats ecosystems, biodiversity, and natural processes as economic assets (Bateman and Mace 2020). Just like machines, factories, and infrastructure are viewed as "capital" in the traditional economy, forests, rivers, and organisms are now recognized as productive assets that deliver benefits such as carbon offsets, flood protection, and pollination services (Daily et al. 2000; Folke et al. 2021). These benefits are practical, measurable, tradable, and increasingly priced in markets for ecosystem services (Salzman et al. 2018).

What Counts as Natural Capital?

To understand natural capital, think of it like a financial economy. When a company builds a new factory, it is viewed as an asset—a form of capital—because it produces valuable goods. Likewise, nonhuman animals, forests, wetlands, and coral reefs are increasingly recognized as productive assets because they perform services that support the human economy (Daily et al. 2000). Whales help regulate carbon cycles, pollinators support agriculture, and bats and birds control pests. These organisms are not just background elements of ecosystems—they are active contributors to global productivity. But unlike human-owned machines or workers, they operate independently and without being compensated.

Lineages are not paid when wetlands clean water, forests store carbon, or bees assist with fruit harvesting. This lack of ownership and legal recognition means no stakeholder has both the authority and incentive to claim their value. As a result, the work of animals and other vital contributors remains economically invisible—a common market failure that occurs when essential work isn't included in the accounting system (Costanza et al. 1997). This shift in thinking of life as capital is no longer just an idea; it has become a reality. It supports natural capital accounting systems (Bateman et al. 2011), which measure ecosystem services in monetary terms. For example:

- *Carbon sequestration*: Whales, forests, and mangroves absorb carbon. Markets currently value this service at $10 to over $100 per ton of CO_2 (Agnolucci et al. 2023; Döbbeling-Hildebrandt et al. 2024).
- *Water filtration*: Wetlands naturally clean water, but much of this work is carried out by filter-feeding animals, such as freshwater mussels, which can collectively filter tens of thousands of liters of water each day. When mussel populations decline due to pollution or habitat loss, governments often face high costs in building artificial treatment facilities to mimic their service (Postel and Thompson 2005; Vaughn 2018).
- *Pollination*: Bees, bats, butterflies, and other animal pollinators contribute over $200 billion annually to agriculture (Gallai et al. 2009)—yet this work remains unpaid.

Each of these examples demonstrates animal labor embedded in natural capital. Although it appears "free," the costs are simply deferred. When pollinators fail, humanity bears the burden (Lautenbach et al. 2012). When wildfires destroy habitats, humanity pays the price (NOAA 2025). When natural carbon sinks decline, we pay in atmospheric instability (Kikstra et al. 2022).

We are not separate from these systems. Animals, large and small, are woven into the thermodynamic flows that sustain life. When their work is devalued or disrupted, ecosystems reorganize toward new equilibria—often less favorable to us (Kleidon 2010). These shifts cause economic volatility, ecological risk, and increasing pressure to replace nature's labor with costly human-made infrastructure (Rockström et al. 2009; Barnosky et al. 2012).

In short, when we overspend ecological capital, we still pay the bill. Nature bats last and always balances its books, whether or not we choose to track the ledgers.

Seeing the Unseen: Why Valuing Nature Still Favors the Visible

Two main forces have driven the shift toward natural capital: first, ecological breakdown has made invisible labor visible. When pollinators decline, pest regulators vanish, or keystone lineages are lost to wildfire, the once "free" services provided by nature suddenly carry billion-dollar price tags (Herweijer et al. 2020). Second, carbon sequestration is uniquely measurable, enabling economists to assign market value to whales, mangroves, or forests based on their ability to capture carbon (Rogelj et al. 2015; Agnolucci et al. 2023).

One well-known example is the "$2M blue whale." By diving and fertilizing phytoplankton, each whale helps draw down carbon levels, which equates to millions of dollars in climate mitigation (Chami et al. 2019). This valuation is now used in marine finance and conservation.

But what happens when this logic is applied more broadly? How much is a mussel worth? A beetle? A nematode? These tiny decomposers filter water, build soil, and recycle nutrients, yet they remain economically invisible. The issue isn't their ecological contribution but their absence from the accounting system.

This is where economic speciesism shows itself. Even when we manage to value some forms of life, it's usually only those we perceive as large, visible, or charismatic that we value. The rest—despite their crucial systemic importance—remain overlooked. Valuation reflects our perception, not nature's actual functional networks. To address this, we need a framework that recognizes the structural contributions of all life, including animals, not just the visible ones.

While natural capital offers a way to recognize the worth of "lineage labor," its perspective remains limited, favoring what can be seen, measured, and marketed. Even when we assign value, it often supports human-centered hierarchies, emphasizing whales or pollinators while ignoring less prominent contributors like beetles, mussels, or soil microbes. However, new tools—such as remote sensing, soil diagnostics, and AI-driven biodiversity models—are beginning to close this gap. By expanding what we can observe, we can also broaden what and who we are willing to value.

Carbon: The Currency of Life

Carbon is the currency of the biosphere—a unit of exchange, store of value, and measure of ecological impact. Just as dollars or euros power financial systems, carbon fuels ecosystems. It moves through food webs like money through markets: captured, exchanged, stored, and recycled. Recognizing carbon as a biospheric currency allows the integration of ecosystem functions into market logic, making them legible, investable, and tradable (Guerry et al. 2015).

Like currency, carbon is divisible, portable, and interchangeable. It accumulates in plants, moves through consumers, and is recycled by decomposers. This analogy links ecological flow (carbon moving through an ecosystem) to financial flow (money circulating through human markets).

- Producers (plants) capture carbon from the atmosphere, much like central banks print money.
- Consumers (animals) circulate it through feeding, echoing market exchange.
- Decomposers return it to the system, much like reinvested capital.

Carbon throughput measures the amount of work an ecosystem performs. The more carbon flows, the higher its biological productivity. By monitoring this flow, we can start to value the ecological contributions of individual lineages and trophic groups.

Valuing Trophic Contributions

To understand the economic roles of nonhuman life, we trace carbon through the food web.

1. Producers as carbon engines

Primary producers—trees, plants, and photosynthetic microbes—convert CO_2 into biomass, forming the foundation of all animal food webs (Field et al. 1998). In tropical secondary forests, fast-growing trees can sequester 10–30 tons of CO_2 per hectare each year (Chazdon et al. 2016). With carbon priced at $50/ton, this results in hundreds of dollars of carbon value per hectare each year.

But forests aren't just carbon factories—they're interconnected systems where carbon flows among trees, fungi, microbes, and animals. Productivity doesn't come from a few key lineages but from ecological cooperation across many. Trying to identify "the most valuable species," whatever that means, since they are arbitrary constructs anyway, will miss the bigger picture. True value lies in relationships: how carbon is captured, transferred, broken down, and reused over time.

This prepares us to examine the next link in the chain: animals as consumers, whose ecological work keeps carbon moving and sets up decomposers to keep productivity alive.

2. Consumers are carbon transfer agents

Primary producers capture carbon, but animals—herbivores, carnivores, and top consumers—keep it moving. Insects, rodents, and ungulates transfer carbon into biomass; predators sustain the flow. Although they don't create new carbon inputs, animal consumers are essential for mobilizing and cycling carbon through ecosystems (Schmitz et al. 2010).

Blue whales, for example, promote phytoplankton growth by fertilizing surface waters with nutrient-rich waste, similar to how grazing herbivores stimulate vegetation (Roman and McCarthy 2010). Their contributions also include nutrient redistribution and long-term carbon storage through sinking biomass after death (Lavery et al. 2010). One estimate values a whale's lifetime contribution at \$2 million, reflecting not only carbon services but also tourism and cultural effects (Chami et al. 2019).

However, Table 2.1 shows conservative, carbon-only estimates priced at \$50 per ton—excluding non-carbon services—to demonstrate how broader valuations can distort visibility. A biologically accurate perspective also recognizes diversity among whale lineages: baleen whales fertilize oceans through nutrient cycling, while toothed whales influence food webs through predation (Roman and McCarthy 2010; Lavery et al. 2010; Estes et al. 2011; Roman et al. 2014). Whales are, therefore, not a single economic asset but a group of evolutionary roles within the marine carbon cycle. Accurate valuations must consider that complexity.

The estimates above represent the lifetime carbon value of living whales, calculated by multiplying each group's average contribution by its global population and pricing that output at around \$50 per ton of CO_2. This provides a "stock-based" valuation: a projection of whales' total carbon offset potential over their natural lifespans

Table 2.1 Carbon-based economic estimates of conspicuous and less conspicuous whales

Group	Est. Global Pop. (indiv.)	Avg. Lifetime CO_2 (tons)	Carbon Price (\$/ton)	Lifetime Value/Whale (\$, carbon-only)	Total Lineage Value (\$B, lifetime stock)	Avg. Lifespan (years)	Annualized Flow Value (\$M/year)
Blue whales	10,000	2000	\$50	\$100,000	\$1B	80	\$12 M
Other baleen whales	750,000	1200	\$50	\$60,000	\$45B	65	\$692 M
Sperm whales	736,000	3500	\$50	\$175,000	\$128.8B	70	\$1840 M
Other toothed whales	1,500,000	800	\$50	\$40,000	\$60B	45	\$1333 M

(based on population data and calculations after Thomas et al. (2016), Cooke (2018), Whitehead and Shin (2022), and Braulik et al. (2023)).

But we can also consider annual ecological income. By dividing total lifetime value by the average lifespan (see Table 2.1), we obtain a flow-based measure—how much carbon value whales produce each year through fertilization, trophic regulation, and carbon storage via whale falls (Roman and McCarthy 2010; Lavery et al. 2010). From this perspective, whales are not just long-term carbon reservoirs but active contributors, performing measurable ecological work.

For example, the global sperm whale population has a stock value surpassing $128.8 billion, but an estimated annual carbon flow of about $1.84 billion, comparable to the yearly output of major economic sectors (Chami et al. 2019). All whales combined—including blue, other baleen, sperm, and other toothed whales—contribute over $3.8 billion annually in carbon services, underscoring their cumulative ecological and economic importance.

This shift in framing moves us from symbolic stories to quantifiable, function-based valuation. Whales are no exceptions; they are essential ecosystem workers embedded in a planetary carbon cycle.

Importantly, this logic is scalable. The same approach applies to marine mammals, terrestrial herbivores, and decomposers. By translating biological activity into carbon-based value, we establish a common accounting system—one that captures ecological complexity while communicating in the language of finance, policy, and return on life.

3. Decomposers: the currency recyclers

Decomposers are the last link in the biosphere's carbon economy. They don't capture or move carbon through typical food webs—they return it from the dead. This process isn't just decay for its own sake but a crucial step in restoring ecological function. Decomposers include fungi, bacteria, and animal detritivores like earthworms, termites, and millipedes. Their roles—breaking down, digesting, and transforming organic material—make carbon available again (Bradford et al. 2016; Fierer 2017; Yang et al. 2012). Although invisible to most accounting systems, they are essential for nutrient cycling and maintaining long-term soil health (Gleixner 2013).

In tropical forests, decomposition occurs rapidly and has been widely studied. These ecosystems cover about 1.8 billion hectares (FAO 2020). Heterotrophic respiration—mainly driven by decomposers—ranges from 7.5 to 15 tons of CO_2 per hectare per year (Wei et al. 2015; Riutta et al. 2021), valued at $375–$750 per hectare annually at $50 per ton (Agnolucci et al. 2023). This results in a global annual carbon value of $675–$1350 billion in tropical forests alone. To put this into perspective: the total annual carbon value of all whales worldwide is around $3.8 billion. Decomposers in tropical forests thus contribute 174–348 times more than whales, even though they are mostly absent from policy and economic models.

Their labor is distributed, self-organized, and often invisible without scientific tools (Loreau 2010). However, invisibility does not mean worthlessness. When the most functionally essential organisms are priced lower than the most charismatic, it reveals not ecological insight but aesthetic and perceptual bias. We don't value ecosystems based on what sustains them but on what we recognize.

Transitioning to an Intrinsic Valuation of Biodiversity

In the previous section, we pushed the limits of instrumental valuation. We measured carbon flow through producers, consumers, and decomposers, assigning dollar values to the ecological work performed by different lineages. We showed that this method allows policymakers to make decisions with immediate, tangible effects.

However, in this process, a deeper problem has emerged. The organisms that perform the most vital ecological roles are often undervalued (Gleixner 2013). Decomposers, for instance, sequester more carbon and support greater productivity than whales, yet they are usually left out of most pricing models and conservation efforts (Brussaard et al. 2007; Dominati et al. 2010). This issue isn't due to a lack of data—it exposes a structural bias in how we perceive value. We tend to value what we can see, name, or emotionally connect with. However, ecosystems do not operate based on visibility; they operate based on function.

This is where instrumental thinking begins to break down. If our methods of assigning value consistently overlook what matters most, then those methods are no longer sufficient. They are incomplete. They measure parts but not systems. They favor charisma over necessity. And if we develop policies and markets based on such partial logic, we risk misallocating attention, protection, and resources—ultimately weakening the very systems we are trying to conserve.

The path forward isn't to abandon instrumental value but to understand its limits. We need a broader framework—one that allows us to see value not only through services provided but also in lineages maintained as vital parts of complex systems, relationships nurtured, and evolutionary histories carried forward. That is the role of intrinsic valuation. And that's where we now focus.

What Makes Life Intrinsically Valuable?

We often view intrinsic value as an ethical intuition—something we feel rather than calculate. This naturally extends from our ethical intuitions about other humans, whom we see as relatives. Science has now clearly demonstrated that all living organisms are genealogically connected, forming a vast Tree of Life. Our family is much larger than we previously believed throughout most of human history. Part of overcoming speciesism involves broadening ethical principles to include these newly discovered relatives.

And yet, recognizing intrinsic value does not have to be based only on moral or sentimental grounds. It can also be understood as an acknowledgment of what life is and what it does. This involves grounding intrinsic value in biophysical, structural, and measurable qualities—features that make living systems not just functional but fundamentally different from nonliving things. While ethical reflections offer important insights, the value itself can be informed by empirical realities separate from them.

At its core, life operates in a state of thermodynamic disequilibrium. Living systems sustain order by resisting entropy, expending energy to create and maintain structure (Kleidon 2010). This is not a metaphor—it is physics. Organisms, ecosystems, and the biosphere exist only by continuously cycling energy and materials through structured networks. This organization is sustained through metabolic work, trophic exchange, and feedback regulation, none of which occur spontaneously (Jørgensen and Svirezhev 2004). As an open system, life is an ongoing act of persistence against the universal drift toward disorder.

Intrinsic value is not solely about structure; it also encompasses history. Every organism is the product of an unbroken evolutionary lineage that stretches back billions of years (Knoll 2015). While some functions may converge across distant lineages, no two lineages are identical in their evolutionary past, physiological traits, or ecological relationships (Stayton 2015). Even organisms that seem functionally redundant can vary in their interactions, adaptability, or roles within feedback systems (Raup and Sepkoski 1982; Bambach 2006). This shows that biodiversity loss isn't just about losing function; it's about losing our evolutionary heritage and ecological solutions that cannot simply be recreated.

Finally, life has relational value through its involvement in complex systems. Organisms are part of self-organizing, adaptive networks, where their value arises not from their individual existence but from how they contribute to system-level properties like resilience, stability, feedback, and adaptation (Levin 1998). These emergent traits can't be predicted solely from the characteristics of individual parts; they depend on the presence of specific relationships (Bascompte 2009). Thus, intrinsic value encompasses not just the organism itself but also its integration within systems that cannot operate without it.

What follows from this? If life is thermodynamically exceptional, evolutionarily unique, and relationally embedded, it holds value not only in its outputs but also in its existence and structure. Recognizing this type of value does not replace instrumental logic; it complements it. It helps us see organisms not just as services but as our relatives and partners in a continuous, co-constructed Earth system, whose full value becomes clear when we stop trying to reduce it to its parts.

Complexity, Contingency, and Irreplaceability

Living systems are complex in a precise, physical sense. They are open systems that maintain thermodynamic disequilibrium by continuously cycling energy and materials through structured networks (Schramski et al. 2015). In a universe where net entropy always increases, life is the rare exception: a persistent pocket of order maintained by the work of living matter (England 2013). Complexity arises when interacting components give rise to emergent behaviors—properties that cannot be predicted from the parts alone. Their structure emerges from local interactions, feedback loops, and energy flows—not from top-down control (Levin 2005). Ecosystems exemplify this architecture, as they regulate the climate, recycle nutrients, and sustain productivity through self-organization (Loreau 2010).

In such systems, the role of any component is not diagnosed solely by its traits but by how it participates in the network (Bascompte 2009). A forest is not just a sum of its trees—it is an integrated system of trees, fungi, microbes, herbivores, decomposers, and climate. Remove one lineage, and the whole may appear intact; yet its function or stability may shift in unpredictable, nonlinear ways (Hastings and Wysham 2010). The components are not interchangeable because their value lies in their relationships.

This is the foundation of irreplaceability. Lineages that appear functionally similar—such as two nitrogen-fixing plants or two decomposers—often differ in metabolic rate, climate tolerance, seasonal timing, or symbiotic dependencies (Hooper et al. 2005). These differences matter because they shape the system's tempo, feedback sensitivity, and resilience (Bardgett and Wardle 2010). A slow decomposer in wet soil regulates nutrients differently than a fast one in dry soil. The effects ripple throughout the system. Similarity does not guarantee substitutability.

Evolution reinforces this point. Lineages result from unique evolutionary histories shaped by constraints and contingencies. Even traits that evolved multiple times, like the various forms of flight or photosynthesis, arose through separate pathways with unique outcomes (Rosenblum et al. 2014). A lost lineage cannot simply be recreated from its analogs. Consequently, what disappears involves more than just function; it includes a set of interactions and a structural thread in the fabric of complexity.

This is why intrinsic value is not just about ethical values. It also pertains to the structure and function of the earth and its inhabitants. In complex systems, value emerges from participation in a larger framework, not from isolated actions (Barabási 2009). To value life intrinsically means to take seriously the architecture of complexity itself.

Leaving Speciesism Behind: A Smarter Valuation Future

The logic of instrumental value converts ecological value into economic value by assigning a price to the benefits ecosystems provide. It enables policymakers to quantify services like carbon sequestration, pollination, water filtration, and flood protection, making ecological processes easier to grasp in terms of markets, budgets, and cost-benefit analysis. In this way, it makes conservation financially justifiable within the framework of economic planning (TEEB 2010).

However, as we have shown, this logic consistently underestimates the most crucial parts of living systems. Animal decomposers, microbial guilds, and feedback-regulating lineages remain economically invisible despite their essential roles in planetary function. This is more than a theoretical mistake; it distorts budgets, incentives, and risk assessments. When valuation tools ignore complexity, decision-makers are misled about the sources of stability and where failures occur. The result is a conservation economy that values visibility more than importance. In complex systems, that's a dangerous mismatch.

The solution is not to fully abandon instrumental logic but to complement it. What's missing is a *two-layered framework*—one that differentiates between what ecosystems produce and what they need to remain functional. To show how these two layers of value work in practice, Table 2.2 highlights key differences relevant to environmental planning, budgeting, and system resilience.

These two forms of valuation operate at different levels. Instrumental value pertains to measurable outputs, such as carbon capture, pollination, and water purification—services with clear utility (TEEB 2010). In contrast, intrinsic value includes both ethical considerations and system-critical ecological roles—those that are less visible but essential for the system's functioning. These can be mapped using tools like dependency analysis (Thébault and Fontaine 2010; Saavedra et al. 2017), trophic modeling (Berlow et al. 2009; Allesina and Tang 2012), and ecosystem stress tests (Dakos et al. 2011; Scheffer et al. 2012).

Understanding this difference is crucial because not all losses are equal. Some impact visible services, while others destabilize the systems that generate them. For

Table 2.2 Complementary dimensions of ecological valuation: A comparative framework for ecological assessment

Dimension	Instrumental value	Intrinsic value
What it captures	Tangible benefits ecosystems provide	Systemic roles ecosystems need to remain functional; ethical status extended to the broader Tree of Life
Examples	Carbon sequestration, water filtration, pollination, erosion control	Nutrient cycling by decomposers, symbioses, predator-prey regulation, microbial community structure
Measurement methods	Market-based valuation, cost-benefit analysis, ecosystem service pricing	Dependency mapping, trophic network modeling, ecosystem stress tests
Visibility	High: Services are often visible, symbolic, or monetizable	Low: Roles are often invisible, slow-moving, or underappreciated
Valuation risk	Overprioritizes charismatic or visible organisms	May be ignored due to lack of market data or visibility
Policy blind spots	Underrepresents foundational lineages and processes	Lacks integration into funding models, assessments, and conservation incentives
What failure looks like	A service stops delivering—e.g., crop failure, flooding, loss of carbon sink	The system loses resilience—e.g., collapses after stress, can't adapt, slow erosion of function
Policy implication	Guides where to act, top-down	Reveals what to protect, bottom-up

instance, the extinction of a microbial group vital for nutrient cycling may cause more long-term damage than losing a top animal predator—yet it is far less likely to be recognized or funded (Estes et al. 2011; Ripple et al. 2014; Delgado-Baquerizo et al. 2016; Maron et al. 2018; Wagg et al. 2021).

To operationalize intrinsic value, we need to reevaluate how we measure return, cost, and risk. Return should reflect future ecological performance under stress. Cost must include the delayed impacts of lost complexity. Risk needs to account for systemic vulnerabilities that increase the chances of breakdowns over time. From this logic, several policy directions emerge. See Fig. 2.2.

(1) Track functional and stabilizing organisms, not just those that are abundant or charismatic.
(2) Design incentives for ecosystem-supporting lineages, including microbial and decomposer communities.
(3) Expand carbon accounting to include below-ground ecological labor. Invest in long-term system resilience rather than short-term gains.

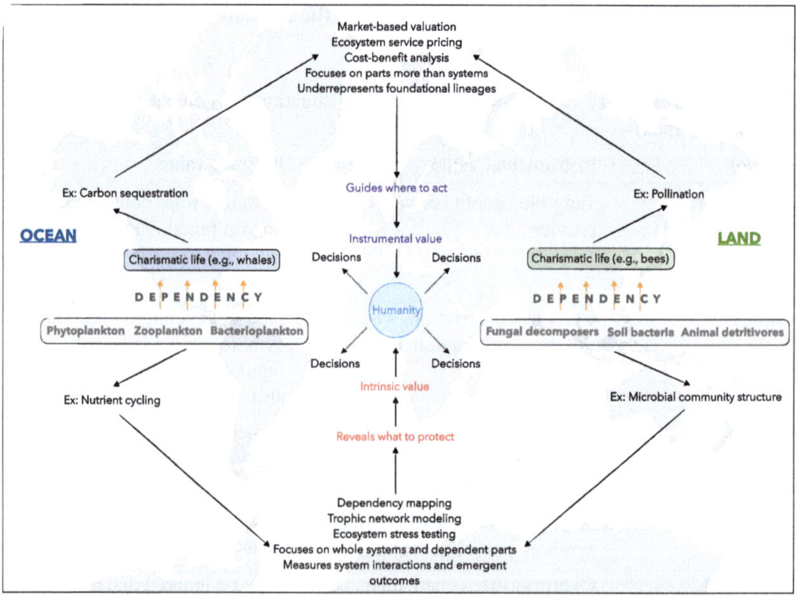

Fig. 2.2 A conceptual map comparing two different frameworks for valuing life and ecological systems—instrumental value (purple) and intrinsic value (red). Instrumental valuation focuses on the tangible services ecosystems offer—such as carbon sequestration or pollination—highlighting parts, visibility, and market-based decision tools. In contrast, intrinsic valuation encompasses systemic roles and interdependencies: the entire web of life, including evolutionarily contingent, complex adaptive systems that exist in thermodynamic disequilibrium. The perspective we choose influences how we interpret the Earth system, shaping what we measure, what we overlook, and what we ultimately protect

Policymakers already value infrastructure for its reliability. Considering the interconnectedness and dependencies involved, it is wise to treat ecosystems with the same importance. A more innovative valuation system doesn't force us to choose between instrumental and intrinsic worth—it recognizes that one shows what ecosystems do, and the other reveals what they need to survive.

Conclusions

What we have traced in this chapter is not just a new way to value life—it is a deeper understanding of what life is and what value means. We began with what is measurable: carbon captured, services provided, and returns modeled. These serve as the entry points through which biodiversity becomes clear to policy and markets. However, beneath that measurement lies a more fundamental insight: ecosystems are not machines that produce outputs on demand. They are living systems composed of our relatives, shaped by contingent relationships, feedback loops, and distributed labor. Thus, the rest of the Tree of Life is also connected to us in genealogical, ecological, and economic terms.

Animals are not just parts of ecosystems; they are active participants within them. From carbon cycling to nutrient redistribution, their roles are vital and ongoing. However, most valuation systems reward visibility and economic convenience, often excluding even iconic groups like whales from recognition for much of history. When they are valued, it's usually belated, linked to specific services like carbon sequestration or tourism, and fails to fully capture their broader ecological contributions. Many organisms remain undervalued not because they do less, but because their contributions don't fit neatly into existing models. This reflects the structure of economic speciesism: a system that favors what is familiar, measurable, or marketable, while ignoring the structural labor of both small and large creatures. Even well-meaning tools reinforce these biases, misallocating attention and resources in ways that quietly weaken the very systems we aim to sustain.

This is not a technical glitch but rather a cultural blind spot. If we only monitor outputs, we risk undermining the conditions that generate them. Valuation, then, isn't a neutral tool. It's a systems-level decision about what and who we choose to make visible.

But there is another way forward. We can develop valuation frameworks that accurately reflect the structure of ecosystems as interconnected, nonlinear, and dependent on all participating members. Instrumental logic guides us on where to intervene. However, intrinsic logic explains why life matters, even when no transaction occurs. To live wisely within the biosphere, we need to value not just what ecosystems provide, but also what sustains their ability to provide anything at all.

In this context, resilience is not just an accessory—it is the currency of the future. Safeguarding it requires moving beyond speciesism and spectacle to adopt a valuation framework rooted in evolutionary kinship, ecological interdependence, and the thermodynamic principles that govern all complex adaptive systems. Life persists not because it is static, but because it operates far from equilibrium, fueled by constant energy flow and structured by both constraint and opportunity. That's the invitation—and the obligation—of this chapter.

References

Agnolucci P, Fischer C, Heine D et al (2023) Measuring total carbon pricing. World Bank Res Obs 39:227–258. https://doi.org/10.1093/wbro/lkad009

Aldy JE, Viscusi WK (2003) The value of a statistical life: a critical review of market estimates throughout the world. J Risk Uncertain 27:5–76. https://doi.org/10.1023/a:1025598106257

Allesina S, Tang S (2012) Stability criteria for complex ecosystems. Nature 483:205–208. https://doi.org/10.1038/nature10832

Bambach RK (2006) Phanerozoic biodiversity mass extinctions. Annu Rev Earth Planet Sci 34:127–155. https://doi.org/10.1146/annurev.earth.33.092203.122654

Barabási A-L (2009) Scale-free networks: a decade and beyond. Science 325:412–413. https://doi.org/10.1126/science.1173299

Barbier EB (2019) The value of coastal wetland ecosystem services. In: Perillo GME, Wolanski E, Cahoon DR, Hopkinson CS (eds) Coastal Wetlands. Elsevier, pp 947–964

Bardgett RD, Wardle DA (2010) Aboveground-belowground linkages: biotic interactions, ecosystem processes, and global change. Oxford University Press

Barnosky AD, Hadly EA, Bascompte J et al (2012) Approaching a state shift in Earth's biosphere. Nature 486:52–58. https://doi.org/10.1038/nature11018

Bascompte J (2009) Disentangling the web of life. Science 325:416–419. https://doi.org/10.1126/science.1170749

Bateman IJ, Mace GM (2020) The natural capital framework for sustainably efficient and equitable decision making. Nat Sustain 3:776–783. https://doi.org/10.1038/s41893-020-0552-3

Bateman IJ, Mace GM, Fezzi C et al (2011) Economic analysis for ecosystem service assessments. Environ Resour Econ 48:177–218. https://doi.org/10.1007/s10640-010-9418-x

Berlow EL, Dunne JA, Martinez ND et al (2009) Simple prediction of interaction strengths in complex food webs. Proc Natl Acad Sci 106:187–191. https://doi.org/10.1073/pnas.0806823106

Boehm C (1999) Hierarchy in the forest. Harvard University Press

Bradford MA, Berg B, Maynard DS et al (2016) Understanding the dominant controls on litter decomposition. J Ecol 104:229–238. https://doi.org/10.1111/1365-2745.12507

Braulik GT, Taylor BL, Minton G, Notarbartolo di Sciara G, Collins T, Rojas-Bracho L, Crespo EA, Ponnampalam LS, Double MC, Reeves RR (2023) Red-list status and extinction risk of the world's whales, dolphins, and porpoises. Conservation Biology 37(5):e14090. https://doi.org/10.1111/cobi.14090

Brewer MB (1999) The psychology of prejudice: ingroup love and outgroup hate? J Soc Issues 55:429–444. https://doi.org/10.1111/0022-4537.00126

Brown DE (2004) Human universals, human nature & human culture. Dædalus 133:47–54. https://doi.org/10.1162/0011526042365645

Brussaard L, de Ruiter PC, Brown GG (2007) Soil biodiversity for agricultural sustainability. Agric Ecosyst Environ 121:233–244. https://doi.org/10.1016/j.agee.2006.12.013

Chami R, Cosimano T, Fullenkamp C, Oztosun S (2019) Nature's solution to Cliamte Change. A Strategy to protect whales can limit greenhouse gases and global warming. IMF Finance & Development 56:34–38

Chazdon RL, Broadbent EN, Rozendaal DMA et al (2016) Carbon sequestration potential of second-growth forest regeneration in the Latin American tropics. Sci Adv 2:e1501639. https://doi.org/10.1126/sciadv.1501639

Cheng JT, Tracy JL, Foulsham T et al (2013) Two ways to the top: evidence that dominance and prestige are distinct yet viable avenues to social rank and influence. J Pers Soc Psychol 104:103–125. https://doi.org/10.1037/a0030398
Cooke JG (2018) *Balaenoptera musculus* (errata version published in 2019). The IUCN Red List of Threatened Species 2018:e.T2477A156923585. https://doi.org/10.2305/IUCN.UK.2018-2.RLTS.T2477A156923585.en
Copernicus N (1543) De revolutionibus orbium coelestium [On the revolutions of the heavenly spheres]. Johannes Petreius, Nuremberg
Costanza R, d'Arge R, de Groot R et al (1997) The value of the world's ecosystem services and natural capital. Nature 387:253–260. https://doi.org/10.1038/387253a0
Crosby AW (1996) The measure of reality. Cambridge University Press, Cambridge
Cutler DM, Summers LH (2020) The COVID-19 pandemic and the $16 trillion virus. JAMA 324:1495–1496. https://doi.org/10.1001/jama.2020.19759
Daily GC, Söderqvist T, Aniyar S et al (2000) The value of nature and the nature of value. Science 289:395–396. https://doi.org/10.1126/science.289.5478.395
Dakos V, Kéfi S, Rietkerk M et al (2011) Slowing down in spatially patterned ecosystems at the brink of collapse. Am Nat 177:E153–E166. https://doi.org/10.1086/659945
Darwin C (1859) On the origin of species. John Murray, London
Dasgupta P (2021) The economics of biodiversity: the Dasgupta review. Abridged version
Delgado-Baquerizo M, Maestre FT, Reich PB et al (2016) Microbial diversity drives multi-functionality in terrestrial ecosystems. Nat Commun 7:10541. https://doi.org/10.1038/ncomms10541
Döbbeling-Hildebrandt N, Miersch K, Khanna TM et al (2024) Systematic review and meta-analysis of ex-post evaluations on the effectiveness of carbon pricing. Nat Commun 15:4147. https://doi.org/10.1038/s41467-024-48512-w
Dominati E, Patterson M, Mackay A (2010) A framework for classifying and quantifying the natural capital and ecosystem services of soils. Ecol Econ 69:1858–1868. https://doi.org/10.1016/j.ecolecon.2010.05.002
England JL (2013) Statistical physics of self-replication. J Chem Phys 139:121923. https://doi.org/10.1063/1.4818538
Estes JA, Terborgh J, Brashares JS et al (2011) Trophic downgrading of Planet Earth. Science 333:301–306. https://doi.org/10.1126/science.1205106
FAO (2020) Global forest resources assessment 2020: main report. Food and Agriculture Organization of the United Nations. https://doi.org/10.4060/ca9825en
Ferrario F, Beck MW, Storlazzi CD et al (2014) The effectiveness of coral reefs for coastal hazard risk reduction and adaptation. Nat Commun 5:3794. https://doi.org/10.1038/ncomms4794
Field CB, Behrenfeld MJ, Randerson JT, Falkowski P (1998) Primary production of the biosphere: integrating terrestrial and oceanic components. Science 281:237–240. https://doi.org/10.1126/science.281.5374.237
Fierer N (2017) Embracing the unknown: disentangling the complexities of the soil microbiome. Nat Rev Microbiol 15:579–590. https://doi.org/10.1038/nrmicro.2017.87
Folke C, Polasky S, Rockström J et al (2021) Our future in the Anthropocene biosphere. Ambio 50:834–869. https://doi.org/10.1007/s13280-021-01544-8
Gallai N, Salles J-M, Settele J, Vaissière BE (2009) Economic valuation of the vulnerability of world agriculture confronted with pollinator decline. Ecol Econ 68:810–821. https://doi.org/10.1016/j.ecolecon.2008.06.014
Gedman GL, Pirovich KM, Oppenheimer J et al (2025) On the ancestry and evolution of the extinct dire wolf. bioRxiv 2025.04.09.647074. https://doi.org/10.1101/2025.04.09.647074
Gleixner G (2013) Soil organic matter dynamics: a biological perspective derived from the use of compound-specific isotopes studies. Ecol Res 28:683–695. https://doi.org/10.1007/s11284-012-1022-9
Gould SJ (1989) Wonderful life: the Burgess Shale and the nature of history. WW Norton & Company

Greene JD (2013) Moral tribes: emotion, reason, and the gap between us and them. Penguin Press

Guerry AD, Polasky S, Lubchenco J et al (2015) Natural capital and ecosystem services informing decisions: From promise to practice. Proc Natl Acad Sci 112:7348–7355. https://doi.org/10.1073/pnas.1503751112

Hamilton WD (1964a) The genetical evolution of social behaviour. I. J Theor Biol 7:1–16. https://doi.org/10.1016/0022-5193(64)90038-4

Hamilton WD (1964b) The genetical evolution of social behaviour. II. J Theor Biol 7:17–52. https://doi.org/10.1016/0022-5193(64)90039-6

Hastings A, Wysham DB (2010) Regime shifts in ecological systems can occur with no warning. Ecol Lett 13:464–472. https://doi.org/10.1111/j.1461-0248.2010.01439.x

Henrich J (2020) The WEIRDest people in the world: how the west became psychologically peculiar and particularly prosperous. Farrar, Straus and Giroux

Herweijer C, Evison W, Mariam S et al (2020) Nature risk rising: why the crisis engulfing nature matters for business and the economy. In: World Economic Forum and PwC. World Economic Forum, pp 1–34

Hooper DU, III FSC, Ewel JJ et al (2005) Effects of biodiversity on ecosystem function: a consensus of current knowledge. Ecological Monographs 75:3–35. https://doi.org/10.1890/04-0922

Jørgensen SE, Svirezhev YM (2004) Chapter 3 - Second and Third Law of Thermodynamics in open systems. In: Jørgensen SE, Svirezhev YM (eds) Towards a Thermodynamic Theory for Ecological Systems. Pergamon, Oxford, pp 41–67

Kikstra JS, Nicholls ZRJ, Smith CJ et al (2022) The IPCC Sixth Assessment Report WGIII climate assessment of mitigation pathways: From emissions to global temperatures. Geosci Model Dev 15:9075–9109. https://doi.org/10.5194/gmd-15-9075-2022

Kleidon A (2010) Life, hierarchy, and the thermodynamic machinery of planet Earth. Phys Life Rev 7:424–460. https://doi.org/10.1016/j.plrev.2010.10.002

Knoll AH (2015) The first three billion years of evolution on earth - updated edition, Revised. Princeton University Press

Küng L, Aeschlimann S, Charalambous C et al (2023) A roadmap for achieving scalable, safe, and low-cost direct air carbon capture and storage. Energy Environ Sci 16:4280–4304. https://doi.org/10.1039/d3ee01008b

Lautenbach S, Seppelt R, Liebscher J, Dormann CF (2012) Spatial and temporal trends of global pollination benefit. PLoS One 7:e35954. https://doi.org/10.1371/journal.pone.0035954

Lavery TJ, Roudnew B, Gill P et al (2010) Iron defecation by sperm whales stimulates carbon export in the Southern Ocean. Proc R Soc B Biol Sci 277:3527–3531. https://doi.org/10.1098/rspb.2010.0863

Levin SA (1998) Ecosystems and the biosphere as complex adaptive systems. Ecosystems 1:431–436. https://doi.org/10.1007/s100219900037

Levin SA (2005) Self-organization and the emergence of complexity in ecological systems. Bioscience 55:1075–1079. https://doi.org/10.1641/0006-3568(2005)055[1075:sateoc]2.0.co;2

Loreau M (2010) From populations to ecosystems. Princeton University Press

Lovejoy AO (1936) The great chain of being. Harvard University Press

Ma H, Zeng J, Chen N et al (2019) Satellite surface soil moisture from SMAP, SMOS, AMSR2 and ESA CCI: a comprehensive assessment using global ground-based observations. Remote Sens Environ 231:111215. https://doi.org/10.1016/j.rse.2019.111215

Maron P-A, Sarr A, Kaisermann A et al (2018) High microbial diversity promotes soil ecosystem functioning. Appl Environ Microbiol 84:e02738-e2817. https://doi.org/10.1128/aem.02738-17

Meckling J, Biber E (2021) A policy roadmap for negative emissions using direct air capture. Nat Commun 12:2051. https://doi.org/10.1038/s41467-021-22347-1

NOAA NC for EI (NCEI) (2025) U.S. billion-dollar weather and climate disasters

Odum HT (1983) Systems ecology: an introduction. Wiley

OECD (2020) Biodiversity and the economic response to COVID-19: ensuring a green and resilient recovery. OECD Polic Responses Coronavirus (COVID-19). https://doi.org/10.1787/d98b5a09-en

Pan Y, Birdsey RA, Fang J et al (2011) A large and persistent carbon sink in the world's forests. Science 333:988–993. https://doi.org/10.1126/science.1201609
Postel SL, Thompson BH Jr (2005) Watershed protection: capturing the benefits of nature's water supply services. Natural Resources Forum 29:98–108
Raup DM, Sepkoski JJ (1982) Mass extinctions in the marine fossil record. Science 215:1501–1503. https://doi.org/10.1126/science.215.4539.1501
Ripple WJ, Estes JA, Beschta RL et al (2014) Status and ecological effects of the world's largest carnivores. Science 343:1241484. https://doi.org/10.1126/science.1241484
Riutta T, Kho LK, Teh YA et al (2021) Major and persistent shifts in below-ground carbon dynamics and soil respiration following logging in tropical forests. Glob Chang Biol 27:2225–2240. https://doi.org/10.1111/gcb.15522
Rockström J, Steffen W, Noone K et al (2009) A safe operating space for humanity. Nature 461:472–475. https://doi.org/10.1038/461472a
Rogelj J, Luderer G, Pietzcker RC et al (2015) Energy system transformations for limiting end-of-century warming to below 1.5 °C. Nat Clim Chang 5:519–527. https://doi.org/10.1038/nclimate2572
Roman J, Estes JA, Morissette L et al (2014) Whales as marine ecosystem engineers. Front Ecol Environ 12:377–385. https://doi.org/10.1890/130220
Roman J, McCarthy JJ (2010) The whale pump: Marine mammals enhance primary productivity in a coastal basin. PLoS One 5:e13255. https://doi.org/10.1371/journal.pone.0013255
Rosenblum EB, Parent CE, Brandt EE (2014) The molecular basis of phenotypic convergence. Annu Rev Ecol Evol Syst 45:1–24. https://doi.org/10.1146/annurev-ecolsys-120213-091851
Saavedra S, Rohr RP, Bascompte J et al (2017) A structural approach for understanding multispecies coexistence. Ecol Monogr 87:470–486. https://doi.org/10.1002/ecm.1263
Salzman J, Bennett G, Carroll N et al (2018) The global status and trends of payments for ecosystem services. Nat Sustain 1:136–144. https://doi.org/10.1038/s41893-018-0033-0
Sapolsky RM (2017) Behave: the biology of humans at our best and worst. Penguin
Scheffer M, Carpenter SR, Lenton TM et al (2012) Anticipating critical transitions. Science 338:344–348. https://doi.org/10.1126/science.1225244
Schmitz OJ, Hawlena D, Trussell GC (2010) Predator control of ecosystem nutrient dynamics. Ecol Lett 13:1199–1209. https://doi.org/10.1111/j.1461-0248.2010.01511.x
Schramski JR, Gattie DK, Brown JH (2015) Human domination of the biosphere: Rapid discharge of the earth-space battery foretells the future of humankind. Proc Natl Acad Sci 112:9511–9517. https://doi.org/10.1073/pnas.1508353112
Schrödinger E (1944) What is life?
Silk JB (2007) The adaptive value of sociality in mammalian groups. Philos Trans R Soc B Biol Sci 362:539–559. https://doi.org/10.1098/rstb.2006.1994
Singer P (1981, 2011) The Expanding Circle: Ethics, evolution, and moral progress. Princeton University Press
Stayton CT (2015) The definition, recognition, and interpretation of convergent evolution, and two new measures for quantifying and assessing the significance of convergence. Evolution 69:2140–2153. https://doi.org/10.1111/evo.12729
Swartz B, Mishler BD (2022) Speciesism, science, and society. In: Swartz B, Mishler BD (eds) Speciesism in biology and culture. Springer-Nature International Publishing, Cham, pp 3–31. https://doi.org/10.1007/978-3-030-99031-2_1
Szathmáry E, Smith JM (1995) The major evolutionary transitions. Nature 374:227–232. https://doi.org/10.1038/374227a0
TEEB (2010) The economics of ecosystems and biodiversity: mainstreaming the economics of nature. A synthesis of the approach, conclusions and recommendations of TEEB.
Thébault E, Fontaine C (2010) Stability of ecological communities and the architecture of mutualistic and trophic networks. Science 329:853–856. https://doi.org/10.1126/science.1188321

Thomas PO, Weller DW, Burdin AM (2016) Status of the world's baleen whales. Mar Mamm Sci 32(4):682–734. https://doi.org/10.1111/mms.12380
Tomasello M (2016) A natural history of human morality. Harvard University Press
Vaughn CC (2018) Ecosystem services provided by freshwater mussels. Hydrobiologia 810:15–27. https://doi.org/10.1007/s10750-017-3139-x
Wagg C, Hautier Y, Pellkofer S et al (2021) Diversity and asynchrony in soil microbial communities stabilizes ecosystem functioning. eLife 10:e62813. https://doi.org/10.7554/elife.62813
Wei H, Chen X, Xiao G et al (2015) Are variations in heterotrophic soil respiration related to changes in substrate availability and microbial biomass carbon in the subtropical forests? Sci Rep 5:18370. https://doi.org/10.1038/srep18370
Whitehead H, Shin M (2022) Current global population size, post-whaling trend and historical trajectory of sperm whales. Sci Rep 12(1):19468. https://doi.org/10.1038/s41598-022-24107-7
Yang X, Yang Z, Warren MW, Chen J (2012) Mechanical fragmentation enhances the contribution of Collembola to leaf litter decomposition. Eur J Soil Biol 53:23–31. https://doi.org/10.1016/j.ejsobi.2012.07.006

Chapter 3
The Impact of Thriving Animal Populations on Today's Economies

Benedetta Falsetti, Giacomo Novelli, and Stefano Tripodi

"The wildness is the preservation of the world"
—Henry David Thoreau

Abstract Thriving animal populations could be more than an ecological asset—they might also bolster economies. This chapter examines the economic impact of faunal diversity, with Brazil as a case study. Using indices like the Biodiversity Intactness Index, the Ecosystem Condition Index, and the IUCN Vertebrates Red List, the findings reveal a strong correlation between rich animal populations and higher GDP per capita, although causation remains unclear. Brazil, a biodiversity hotspot, showcases how ecological wealth can drive economic growth and enhance social inclusion. Protecting such natural assets is not merely a responsibility—it is a strategic opportunity. By linking the spatial distribution of species to economic outcomes, this analysis underscores the dual importance of faunal biodiversity for economic resilience and environmental sustainability, particularly in nations abundant in renewable natural resources. Designing policies that balance economic ambitions with wildlife protection is critical for long-term prosperity.

B. Falsetti · G. Novelli (✉) · S. Tripodi
Macroeconomic and Finance Research Area, Prometeia, Bologna, Italy
e-mail: giacomo.novelli@prometeia.com

B. Falsetti
e-mail: benedetta.falsetti@gmail.com

S. Tripodi
e-mail: trp.stefano@gmail.com

G. Novelli
ClimaTRACES Lab, Cambridge, UK

N. Batini (ed.), *The Economics of Non-Human Animals*, Natural Resource Management and Policy 63, https://doi.org/10.1007/978-3-032-17580-9_3

The Importance of Faunal Diversity

Faunal biodiversity, or the variety of animal species within ecosystems, is crucial for sustaining ecosystem health and productivity. In turn, healthy ecosystems provide essential services such as pollination, carbon storage, flood control, and food production, and in turn, these services underpin human economic prosperity. Thriving animal populations, as a key component of natural capital, contribute to the stability of ecosystems and enable the regeneration of natural resources, which are fundamental to economic production (Dasgupta 2021).

Natural capital encompasses the stock of renewable and non-renewable natural assets, such as soil, water, plants, and animals that provide goods and services essential to human well-being and economic activity. Animals play an indispensable role, performing functions like seed dispersal, pest control, and the regulation of food chains (see Chapter 18 in this book). These processes are intertwined with plant and microbial activity, forming a complex web of life that ensures ecosystem resilience and supports sustainable resource use. Disruptions in faunal biodiversity, whether through over-abundance or scarcity of species, weaken these systems, reducing their capacity to deliver services that societies and economies rely on.

Ecosystems rely on a balance of species performing complementary roles to thrive. Vertebrates, for instance, regulate prey populations and shape vegetation patterns, which are critical for maintaining ecosystem productivity. Evidence suggests that faunal diversity enhances productivity through these complementary functions. For example, keystone species, such as sea otters or vultures, have disproportionate impacts on ecosystem balance. Their role in controlling sea urchin populations helps sustain kelp forests, which are primary producers vital for carbon storage and nutrient cycling. When keystone species populations decline, the resulting disruptions ripple through ecosystems, diminishing their capacity to support human needs (Gregr et al., 2020; Frank and Sudarshan 2024).

Giglio et al. (2024) highlight that ecosystem productivity increases with biodiversity, though the returns diminish as biodiversity reaches higher levels. This relationship underscores the importance of maintaining sufficient levels of faunal diversity for optimal ecosystem performance. Thriving animal populations are not only vital for ecological health but also directly contribute to human prosperity by sustaining the natural processes that drive agricultural productivity, forestry, and fisheries, among other industries.

However, faunal biodiversity is on a decreasing path worldwide, with animal populations suffering particularly severe declines. In the last century, the rate of vertebrate species extinction has been 50 to 100 times higher than the mean extinction rate in the Cenozoic fossil records (Pereira et al. 2020). The root causes for this loss are anthropogenic, as a growing population exerts increasing pressures on the natural world, extracting resources at a faster rate than nature's regenerative capacity. The main drivers of biodiversity loss are land-use change, resource exploitation, climate change, and pollution.

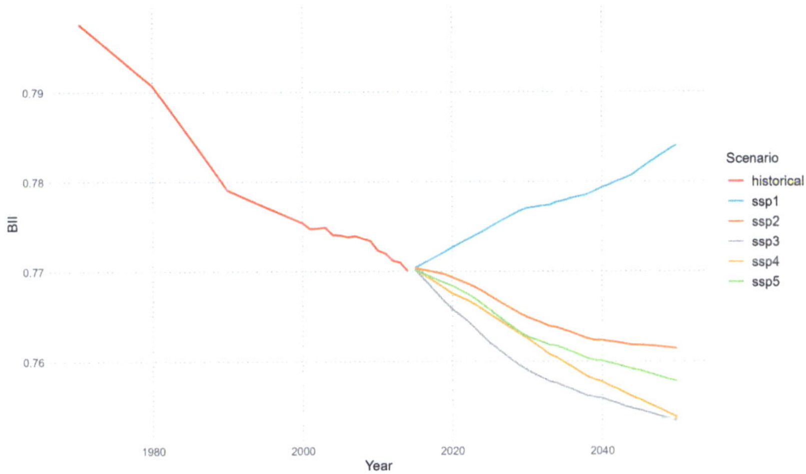

Fig. 3.1 BII worldwide. *Notes* This figure shows historical and projected trends in the Biodiversity Intactness Index. Historical data until 2015. From 2016 onwards, the data represent simulations under five SSP scenarios

Figure 3.1 shows worldwide historical and projected trends for the Biodiversity Intactness Index (BII, Philips et al. 2021), an index measuring how total abundance of organisms and compositional similarity responded to land use and related pressures. Worldwide, the BII has relentlessly decreased from 1975 to 2015, and this decreasing trend will continue further in the future, unless strong and sound policies aimed at changing the global economy productive structure are taken.

Across all Shared Socioeconomic Pathways (SSPs),[1] the only scenario which projects global biodiversity to eventually increase is SSP1, where the world transitions gradually toward a more inclusive and sustainable development path. In the remaining SSPs, where mitigation and adaptation to climate change face medium to high challenges, the level of biodiversity maintains its decreasing trend.

Faunal biodiversity provides both direct and indirect economic benefits. Its direct value arises from people's valuation of species and habitats—through wildlife tourism, recreational activities, or simply the willingness to pay for preserving a species' existence. These nonmarket values often focus on iconic and/or threatened animal populations, generating significant public support for conservation across diverse socioecological contexts (Hanley and Perrings 2019).

At the same time, faunal diversity is essential for maintaining healthy ecosystems providing goods and services "for free". From crop pollination to natural pest management and flood control via soil retention, these processes rely on a wide range of species working together (Di Falco and Perrings 2005; IPBES 2018; and Chapter 18 in this book). For instance, maintaining habitat heterogeneity and functional group diversity can stabilize essential services when facing climatic or

[1] Shared Socioeconomic Pathways are climate change scenarios of projected socioeconomic changes up to 2100 as defined by the United Nations Intergovernmental Panel on Climate Change.

economic shocks (Millennium Ecosystem Assessment 2005), ultimately lowering production risks for land managers. In this sense, faunal biodiversity not only contributes cultural and esthetic value but also acts as a form of "natural insurance" by preserving ecosystem functionality and productivity.

This chapter introduces a novel spatial framework to measure faunal biodiversity and explore the relationship between different levels of biodiversity and the performance of economies. Traditional faunal and floral biodiversity indicators often lack a spatial dimension, limiting their ability to capture complex patterns. Widely used measures, such as protected area coverage and biodiversity hotspots, provide valuable insights but offer only a partial perspective. To address these limitations, this chapter utilizes three spatial indicators of faunal biodiversity, and applies them to the case of Brazil—a faunal biodiversity hotspot. By integrating spatial data on animal diversity with economic metrics, the framework sheds light on how thriving animal populations contribute to both ecological balance and economic development in Brazil. The findings show that the link between biodiversity and economic performance varies across income levels and biomes, highlighting the importance of creating tailored policies. There seems to be significant value in leveraging faunal biodiversity to promote sustainable growth.

Measuring Faunal Biodiversity

Measuring faunal biodiversity, as measuring biodiversity more generally, is complex because it goes beyond the diversity of a single attribute. Here, we focus on the composition of animal communities using measures of species richness. We adopt a spatial approach, using fine-grained gridded data to build three indicators of faunal biodiversity. In this chapter, we concentrate on Brazil, given its significant share of global biodiversity across multiple biomes and ecosystems, including the Amazon, the world's largest rainforest.

First, we calculate the animal component of the Ecosystem Condition Index (henceforth Animal ECI) proposed in Falsetti et al. (2025). Formally, it is defined as $AnimalMSA_i^{(1+T_i)^{-1}}$, where *AnimalMSA* is animal Mean Species Abundance (MSA) taken from GLOBIO Integrated Assessment Model (Schipper et al. 2020) and T is the number of threatened animal species according to the IUCN Red List (IUCN 2024). We compute the index for each grid cell i, which has a 1 km resolution, and then aggregate at the Municipio level (i.e., the lowest administrative unit in Brazil) by taking the index average.

Mean Species Abundance (MSA) is a biodiversity indicator that provides information on relative species richness by comparing the number of species present in a given area under perturbed conditions with those under undisturbed conditions.[2] We augment the MSA metric with data on threatened animal species in the same

[2] Perturbed conditions reflect the main human pressures acting on the level of biodiversity: climate change, nitrogen deposition, land use and land use change, road and hunting.

grid cell i (from the IUCN Red List), thereby giving greater weight to at-risk species and accounting for animal species' fragility. Preserving the actual animal species is crucial since some considered species may be simultaneously endangered and acting as keystone species in the ecosystem.

Although the GLOBIO data are spatially comprehensive, they are available only for the reference year 2015. Consequently, we construct two additional indicators of ecosystem composition using information on vertebrate species richness and threatened vertebrate species from IUCN Red List for the year 2017 and 2021. Vertebrate species richness is defined as the number of vertebrate species (assessed by the IUCN Red List) found in grid cell i, while threatened vertebrate species refers to those classified as critically endangered, endangered, or vulnerable. Because the IUCN's assessed species pool grows annually, we calculate, for both 2017 and 2021, the proportion of "world" vertebrate species in each cell i as the ratio between the number of species present in cell i and the total number of species assessed by IUCN worldwide. Again, we aggregate at the Municipio level by taking the average.

The correlation between these measures is high and positive, as shown in Table 3.1.

Table 3.1 Correlation across biodiversity measures

	ECI animal (2015)	Vertebrate proportion (2017)	Vertebrate proportion (2021)	Threatened vertebrate proportion (2017)	Threatened vertebrate proportion (2021)
ECI Animal (2015)	1				
Vertebrate Proportion (2017)	0.71	1			
Vertebrate Proportion (2021)	0.76	0.75	1		
Threatened Vertebrate Proportion (2017)	0.75	0.97	0.75	1	
Threatened Vertebrate Proportion (2021)	0.49	0.33	0.44	0.45	1

Notes This Table shows the statistical correlation among several biodiversity measures

The Case of Brazil

Brazil ranks first among the 18 megadiverse countries.[3] It hosts between 15 and 20% of the world's biological diversity, with more than 120,000 species of invertebrates, about 9000 vertebrates and more than 4000 plant species.[4] Brazil plays a pivotal role in global climate regulation and biodiversity conservation. Protecting Brazil's landscapes, therefore, has a far-reaching impact: it stabilizes the global climate, safeguards irreplaceable genetic resources, and preserves the ecological processes upon which local and international communities depend. However, many areas in Brazil with high biodiversity and healthy ecosystems are under threat from human activities. Among these, the mining industry is especially damaging, with mines often located in near-pristine areas. We find that in such mining sites, the Animal ECI is high (around 0.95 on a scale up to 1), indicating that some of the country's most valuable natural areas face a significant risk of degradation in the coming years.

The overall distribution of Animal ECI is shown in Fig. 3.2. Based on the Ecosystem Condition Index (Falsetti et al. 2025), the animal condition index applied here shows the ecological integrity of the animal species, considering both abundance and risk of species. While this indicator provides valuable insights into ecosystem health, our understanding of ecological networks remains incomplete, particularly when it comes to identifying which species play keystone roles. Since the loss of even a seemingly minor species can trigger cascading effects across an ecosystem, conserving ecosystems in their natural complexity offers an optimal best strategy for maintaining long-term ecological balance.

To prioritize the conservation of areas rich in biodiversity but under severe threat from human activity, scholars rely on the concept of biodiversity hotspots (Myers et al. 2000, and Mittermeier et al. 2004). According to this concept, vast portions of Brazil, most notably the Cerrado and Mata Atlântica biomes (Fig. 3.3, Panel A.), qualify as biodiversity hotspots (Fig. 3.3, Panel B.) hosting high levels of endemic species while facing intense human pressure from agricultural expansion, urban development, infrastructure growth, and deforestation. These pressures include the deliberate use of fire to clear native vegetation, causing severe ecosystem destruction and major losses in animal wildlife, to convert it into cropland or pastureland. Despite its global reputation for biodiversity, the Amazon is not classified as a hotspot because much of it remains relatively undisturbed by human activity, albeit this situation is rapidly changing. In contrast, Cerrado and Mata Atlântica are home to some of Brazil's most densely populated and economically developed regions, including São Paulo, Rio de Janeiro, and Brasília, where the recent growth has dramatically reduced wildlife habitats.[5]

---

[3] https://www.unep.org/news-and-stories/story/megadiverse-brazil-giving-biodiversity-online-boost.

[4] Ibidem.

[5] 2024 has seen a record in wildfires for Brazil. The number of wildfires has increased by 120% from 2023 to 2024 (194% in Amazonia, 27% in Caatinga, 85% in Cerrado, 47% in Mata Atlântica, −65% in Pampa, 1628% in Pantanal). The total burned area has increased by 7% from 2023 to 2024

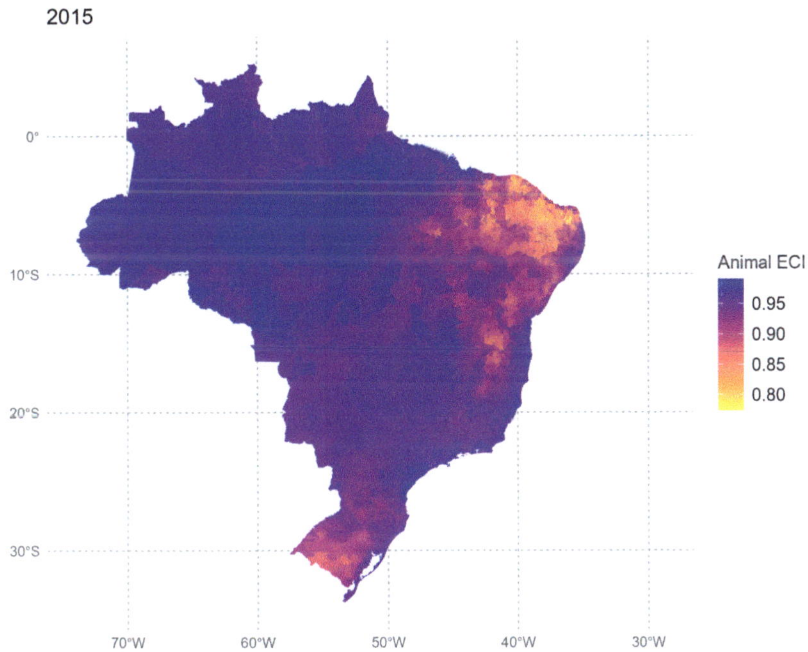

Fig. 3.2 Spatial distribution of Animal ECI

Unfortunately, the creation or the expansion of protected areas alone is not sufficient to address this challenge. Brazil's vast territory contrasts sharply with the relatively limited extent of land currently under protection (Fig. 3.3, Panel B.). Moreover, law enforcement across such large and often remote landscapes is a significant constraint. Strengthening economic incentives for conservation, in tandem with more effective governance and enforcement, could prove crucial for preserving Brazil's unique plant and animal life. Indigenous communities, which are widely recognized for their role in conserving biodiversity, should be part of this strategy as they inhabit some key regions. However, their number is relatively small, and legal and material protections intended to support them are poorly implemented.

The current fragmented approach to conservation overlooks a crucial issue: Brazil's biomes are deeply interconnected, and wildlife moves freely across the landscape, not respecting the artificial boundaries of protected areas. Many species depend on large, continuous habitats and migrate across regions in search of food, water, or breeding grounds. Yet, Brazil's protected areas are disconnected and frequently embedded within manage land. Nevertheless, healthy ecosystems where wildlife can thrive must be preserved, not only for their intrinsic value, but also because they serve as insurance against various risks, particularly climate-related

(4% in Amazonia, 13% in Caatinga, 12% in Cerrado, 5% in Mata Atlântica, 0% in Pampa, 18% in Pantanal). Data Source: Queimadas Program of the National Institute for Space Research (INPE).

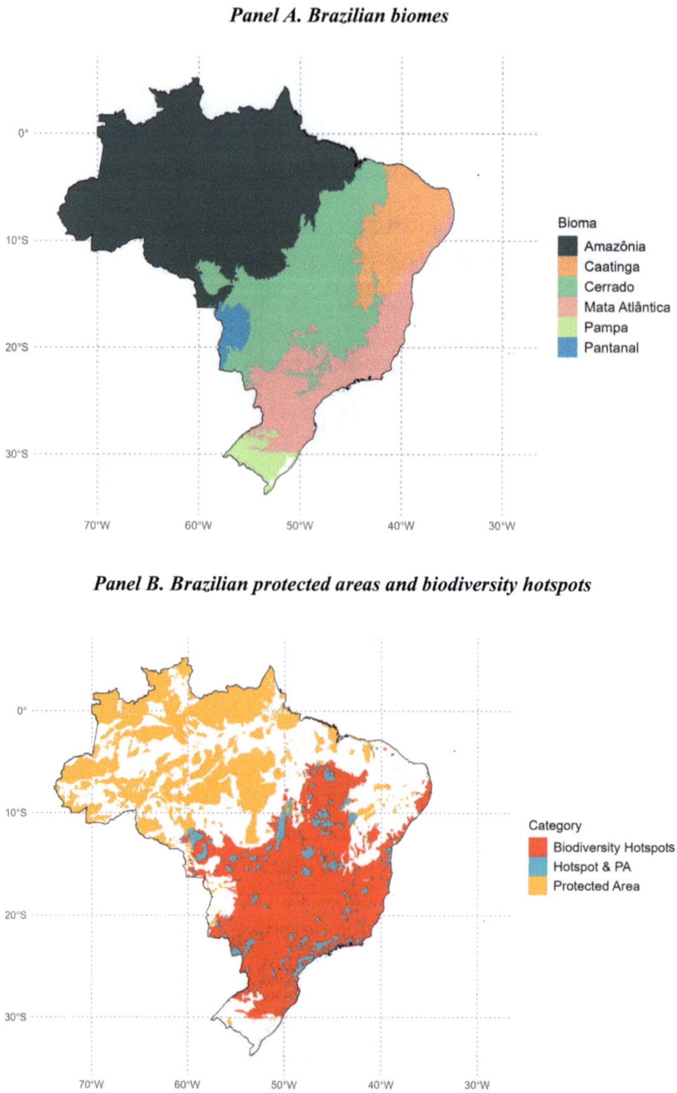

Fig. 3.3 Brazilian biomes (Panel A.) and biodiversity hotspots and protected areas (Panel B.)

ones, which are becoming increasingly intimidating in the face of a rapid climate change.

For instance, land-use change in the Cerrado undermines its biodiversity while also affecting ecological balance in neighboring biomes, including the Amazon and the Pantanal. These disruptions contribute to water scarcity and boost the frequency and intensity of extreme whether events such as droughts, wildfires, and heatwaves, threatening the stability of the economic system and of the ecosystems across the country. Therefore, preserving a single biome is not enough. Brazil needs coordinated, integrated conservation policies that recognize the ecological interdependence of its natural wildlife. Although limiting deforestation is necessary, it is not sufficient; broader transformation of the country's productive structure is also essential. Such measures could deliver substantial global benefits since Brazil is indispensable in the global strategy to manage climate change.

The Link Between Faunal Biodiversity and Economic Activity

I. Data and Sample

To explore quantitatively the link between faunal biodiversity and economic activity in Brazil, we use data from the following sources:

(1) *IUCN.* The number of species (species richness) and the number of threatened species are taken from IUCN (IUCN 2024). The data are provided as a spatial grid with resolution 30 km. Species richness is a count of the number of species belonging to any red list category potentially occurring in each grid cell, while the number of threatened species is a count of the number of species belonging to the critically endangered, endangered, or vulnerable categories. We calculate the number of species in each Municipio by averaging the grid cell specific number of species across all grid cells within a given Municipio.
(2) *GLOBIO.* Mean Species Abundance values for both plants and animals come from the GLOBIO model. The model is characterized by a set of quantitative relationships that assess the impacts of anthropogenic pressures on biodiversity intactness (Schipper et al. 2020). Pressures included are climate change, land use, roads, atmospheric nitrogen deposition, and hunting. Impacts are quantified based on Mean Species Abundance (from now onward MSA) metric. We use the baseline scenario that represents the degree of biodiversity intactness in 2015, based on historical pressures. MSA values are provided as regular spatial grid, with resolution 300 m.
(3) *Biodiversity Intactness Index.* The Biodiversity Intactness Index (Philips et al. 2021), measures how total abundance of organisms and compositional similarity responded to land use and related pressures. It consists of country-level time series data, historical and in projection, from which we also extract data relative to Brazil.
(4) *IBGE.* We take GDP per capita data at the Municipio level from the Instituto Brasileiro de Geografia e Estatística for the years 2017 and 2021.
(5) *Climate Data Store.* The dataset provides satellite global gridded data that categorize land surface into 22 classes, plus additional regional classes (CDS 2019) in a regular spatial grid, with resolution 300 m. Classes have been defined using UN FAO Land Cover Classification System (LCCS). We extract data for 2017

and 2021, aggregate them into seven macro classes, and calculate the extent of each land cover category in square kilometers for each Municipio.

(6) *World Database on Protected Areas.* The World Database on Protected Areas (WDPA) is a global dataset of marine and terrestrial protected areas (UNEP-WCMC and IUCN 2024). The location and the extent of each protected area are provided as polygons part of a shapefile. For the purpose of this chapter, we only consider terrestrial protected areas. We calculate the extent of a Municipio area under protected status in square kilometers by overlying the location of protected areas to Municipio shapes.

(7) *Climatic Research Unit gridded Time Series (CRU TS).* CRU TS provides high-resolution (0.5° regular grid), monthly time series of precipitation and temperature at a global scale from 1900 to 2022 (Harris et al. 2020). We take monthly precipitation, measured in mm, and temperature, measured in °C. For each Municipio, we calculate climate anomalies as the difference between yearly-specific and historical averages.

Our sample is made of 5570 Municipios, observed over two years (2017 and 2021), for a total of 11,140 observations. Summary statistics are shown in Table 3.2.

The proportion of "world" vertebrates present in a Municipio decreased from 1.18% to 1.03%, on average, from 2017 to 2021, while a relatively larger number of species became either endangered, critically endangered or vulnerable. This suggests a decline in the extent of animal biological diversity over time. We do not observe huge changes in land use, most likely because of the relatively short time span covered by our sample. While precipitation patterns are different, with 2021 presenting a much larger deviation from the long-term historical average, temperatures anomalies have been smaller in 2021 compared to 2017.

The spatial distribution of the biodiversity measures we use in our analysis is shown in Fig. 3.4. Over time, Brazil lost a considerable number of vertebrate species included in the IUCN Red List, and species richness considerably decreased (Panel A. of Fig. 3.4). The areas which experienced a sizeable decline correspond to the Amazonia, Cerrado, Mata Atlântica, and Pantanal biomes. The decline primarily affected central areas of Brazil, i.e., those where biodiversity was higher in 2017. Panel B. of Fig. 3.4 shows the proportion of threatened world vertebrate species, which generally increased from 2017 to 2021, especially in coastal areas.

II. Empirical Strategy

To assess the link between faunal biodiversity and economic activity, we focus on the relationship between our measures of biodiversity and GDP per capita at the Municipio level. We do so by running an Ordinary Least Squares (OLS) regression with the (logarithm) of GDP per capita on the left-hand side and the (logarithm) of one biodiversity measure on the right-hand side, controlling for observable covariates determining both economic activity and biodiversity levels. Since our preferred biodiversity indicator is observed over two different periods, we can add year fixed effects to the regression, controlling in this way for time-varying shocks occurring at

Table 3.2 Summary statistics of selected variables

Variable	Mean	S.D	Median	N.Obs
Panel A. 2017				
PIB per capita (ths BRL)	21.991	20.946	16.599	5570
Animal species proportion (%)	1.186	0.224	1.189	5570
Threatened animal species proportion (%)	0.026	0.012	0.026	5570
Protected Area size (ths km^2)	0.453	3.915	0.000	5570
Cropland (ths km^2)	0.375	0.711	0.137	5570
Grassland/Shrubland (ths km^2)	0.308	0.742	0.080	5570
Tree and shrub (flooded) (ths km^2)	0.045	0.570	0.000	5570
Tree cover (ths km^2)	0.768	5.013	0.065	5570
Urban areas (ths km^2)	0.005	0.021	0.001	5570
Water bodies (ths km^2)	0.026	0.153	0.000	5570
Sparse vegetation (ths km^2)	0.000	0.003	0.000	5570
Precipitation anomaly (mm)	−131.988	192.286	−139.358	5570
Temperature anomaly (°C)	0.607	0.252	0.610	5570
Panel B. 2021				
PIB per capita (ths BRL)	33.871	41.909	23.401	5570
Animal species proportion (%)	1.031	0.195	1.034	5570
Threatened animal species proportion (%)	0.032	0.025	0.028	5570
Protected Area size (ths km^2)	0.459	3.952	0.000	5570
Cropland (ths km^2)	0.374	0.713	0.136	5570
Grassland/Shrubland (ths km^2)	0.305	0.738	0.079	5570
Tree and shrub (flooded) (ths km^2)	0.045	0.570	0.000	5570
Tree cover (ths km^2)	0.772	5.008	0.070	5570
Urban areas (ths km^2)	0.005	0.021	0.001	5570
Water bodies (ths km^2)	0.026	0.153	0.000	5570
Sparse vegetation (ths km^2)	0.000	0.003	0.000	5570
Precipitation anomaly (mm)	−167.280	255.801	−142.053	5570
Temperature anomaly (°C)	0.352	0.215	0.386	5570

the national level. In addition, we include state fixed effects, which allow to control for time-constant state-level unobservables.

Formally, the main model is

$$\log(GDP)_{it} = \alpha + \beta \log(BIO)_{it} + \lambda' \boldsymbol{X}_{it} + \delta_t + \gamma_i + \varepsilon_{it} \tag{3.1}$$

where BIO_{it} is either the proportion of world vertebrates or the proportion of threatened world vertebrates in Municipio i and year t, $\boldsymbol{X}_{it}$ is a matrix of covariates for Municipio i and year t which include land use and climate anomalies, δ_t and γ_i are

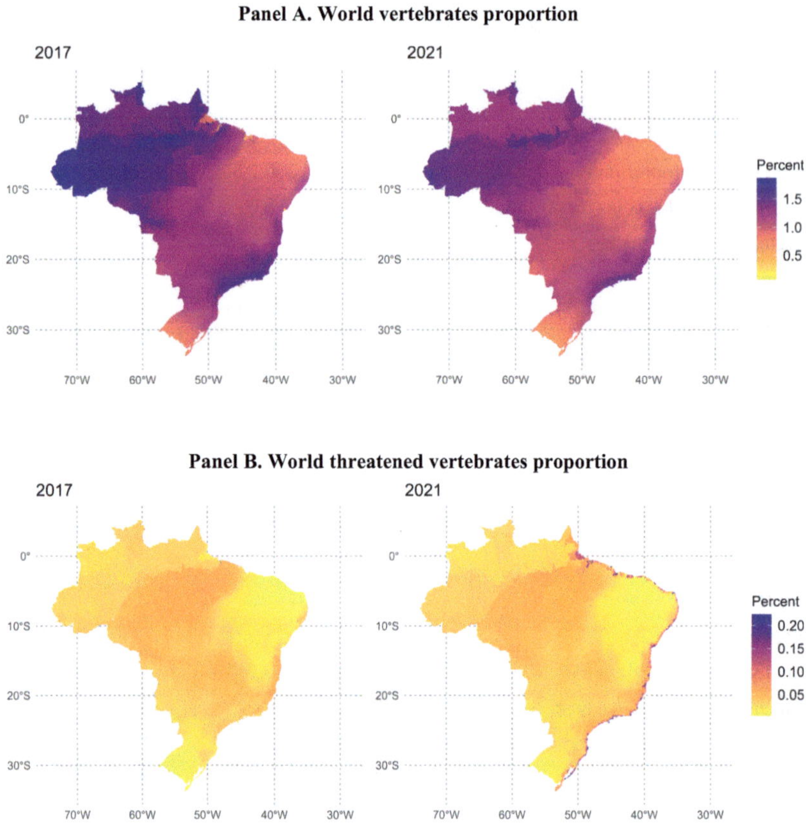

Fig. 3.4 Spatial distribution of world vertebrates (Panel A.) and threatened vertebrates (Panel B.) proportion in Brazil

year and Municipio fixed effects, and ε_{it} are standard errors clustered at the Municipio level. The parameter β tells us the elasticity of GDP per capita with respect to the level of biodiversity.

We also explore how the relationship between biodiversity and the level of economic activity changes across the distribution of the GDP per capita. To do so, we run Equation (3.1) at different quantiles of the distribution of GDP per capita and calculate the β parameter at each quantile.

III. Results

We explore the relationship between a more general measure of biodiversity, the BII, and economic conditions in Brazil by exploiting the relatively lengthy time series of BII. Figure 3.5 plots the relationship between the level of BII and the growth rate of (national) GDP per capita over the years from 1975 to 2015.

We find a positive correlation between these two variables over time: when BII is higher, national Brazilian GDP grows faster. However, this relationship is likely

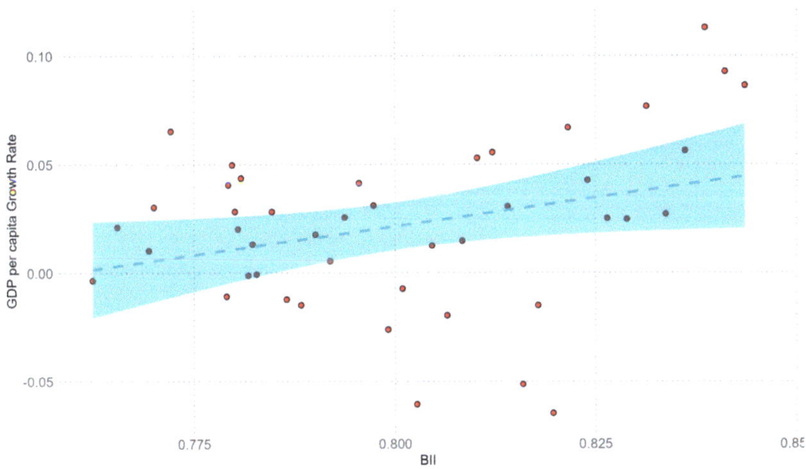

Fig. 3.5 Relationship between BII and GDP per capita growth rate in Brazil. *Notes* shaded area represents 95% confidence bands

underlying the effect of unobservables determining both the growth rate of national GDP and the level of BII, rather than a pure positive boosting effect of biodiversity on economic growth. One likely alternative explanation is the fact that, at low levels of income, nature is pristine, and the economy grows fast to "catch up" with its optimal level. Once the economy approaches its potential, growth slows down and nature has been exploited to foster economic development. Hence, the positive correlation observed in the data. In addition, BII measures overall biodiversity, rather than focusing solely on faunal biodiversity.

A. Nationwide

We explore the relationship between faunal biodiversity and economic activity using Municipio-level information. Figure 3.6 shows that ECI Animal, calculated using 2015 data, is overall positively correlated with the level of economic activity in Brazilian Municipios. In addition, the positive relationship is strong in the right side of the ECI Animals support, suggesting that relatively higher levels of biodiversity are associated with relatively higher levels of economic activity. However, this relationship might be confounded by unobservables.

To control for state- and time-varying confounding factors, as well as to control for observable Municipio characteristics, we analyze the relationship between economic activity and biodiversity using the specification described in Equation (3.1). Results are shown in Table 3.3.

The proportion of vertebrates hosted in a given Municipio is overall positively and significantly correlated with the level of economic activity (columns (i) and (ii)). The elasticities are around 0.43, implying that a one percent increase in the proportion of vertebrates increases GDP per capita by around 0.43%. Similarly, the proportion

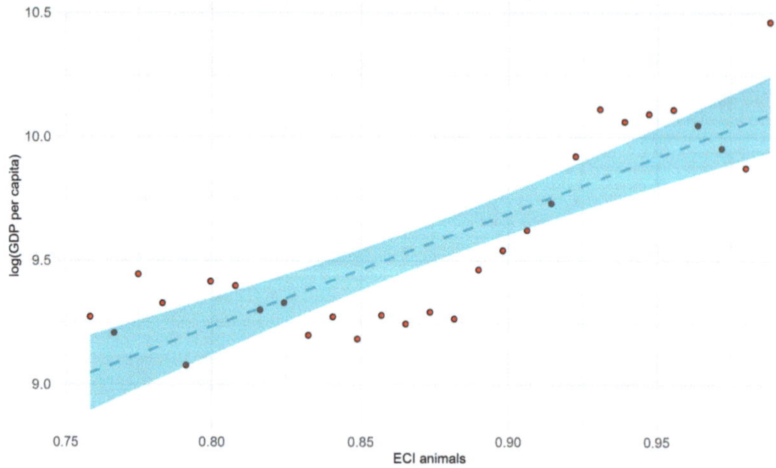

Fig. 3.6 Relationship between ECI animals and the logarithm of GDP per capita. *Notes* shaded area represents 95% confidence bands. Each dot represents the average level of log (GDP per capita) in a given ECI Animals bin, where we defined 30 bins. Data are pooled across years

of threatened vertebrates shows a positive and significant correlation with GDP per capita, with an estimated elasticity of about 0.15 (columns (iii) and (iv)).

The contribution of animal wildlife to economic activity is larger when we consider diversity across all vertebrate species, rather than focusing on species that are threatened or endangered. A larger overall proportion of vertebrates in a Municipio is likely to be associated with a greater ecosystems' functional diversity, therefore to a provision of ecosystem services which is higher in both quantity and quality. These results suggest that overall animal biological diversity matters more for economic activity, than the diversity of threatened species. However, it would be misleading to conclude that preservation efforts should be focused only on preserving biodiversity as a whole, rather than directing resources toward endangered species. The disappearance of few animal species, in fact, might disrupt the overall functioning of a given ecosystem if they are keystone species, completely halting the provision of ecosystem services and their contribution to the economic system.

We explore how the relationship uncovered in Table 3.3 varies at different levels of GDP per capita. We do so by running a quantile regression, where the main coefficient of interest is estimated at each specified quantile of the dependent variable. The results of this exercise are shown in Fig. 3.7, separately for the proportion of world vertebrates and the proportion of world threatened vertebrate species (estimated coefficients and standard errors are reported in Appendix Table A1 and Table A2 for the proportion of world vertebrates and the proportion of world threatened vertebrates, respectively).

The magnitude of the elasticity of GDP to vertebrate species decreases as GDP per capita increases, reaching zero from the 8th decile and onwards. On the other

Table 3.3 The effect of faunal biodiversity on GDP per capita

	log (GDP per capita)			
	(i)	(ii)	(iii)	(iv)
Log vertebrates prop	0.4284 ***	0.4389 ***		
	[0.1161]	[0.1208]		
Log threatened vertebrates prop			0.1587 ***	0.1549 ***
			[0.0137]	[0.0143]
Precipitation anomaly		−0.0002 ***		−0.0002 ***
		[0.0000]		[0.0000]
Temperature anomaly		0.2432 ***		0.2537 ***
		[0.0407]		[0.0386]
Protected Area size [km^2]	0.0008	0.0006	0.0008	0.0007
	[0.0011]	[0.0011]	[0.0010]	[0.0010]
Cropland [km^2]	0.0437 ***	0.0413 ***	0.0461 ***	0.0427 ***
	[0.0054]	[0.0053]	[0.0053]	[0.0052]
Grassland/Shrubland [km^2]	−0.0090 *	−0.0076	−0.0086 *	−0.0072
	[0.0050]	[0.0050]	[0.0045]	[0.0045]
Tree and shrub (flooded) [km^2]	0.0080 ***	0.0074 ***	0.0055 ***	0.0049 ***
	[0.0017]	[0.0016]	[0.0016]	[0.0016]
Tree cover [km^2]	−0.0078 **	−0.0077 **	−0.0058 **	−0.0056 *
	[0.0030]	[0.0030]	[0.0029]	[0.0029]
Urban areas [km^2]	0.0319 ***	0.0316 ***	0.0311 ***	0.0311 ***
	[0.0022]	[0.0022]	[0.0022]	[0.0022]
Water bodies [km^2]	0.0024 *	0.0026 *	0.0017	0.0018
	[0.0014]	[0.0014]	[0.0014]	[0.0014]
Sparse vegetation [km^2]	0.0128 ***	0.0124 ***	0.0117 ***	0.0113 ***
	[0.0023]	[0.0023]	[0.0023]	[0.0023]
State FE	Yes	Yes	Yes	Yes
Year FE	Yes	Yes	Yes	Yes
Adj. R2	0.588	0.592	0.592	0.595
Num. obs	11,028	11,026	11,028	11,026

Notes Standard errors clustered at the Municipio level in brackets. *, ** and *** indicates 10, 5 and 1% significance levels, respectively

hand, the elasticity of GDP to threatened vertebrate species monotonically increases across GDP per capita distribution.

The divergent behavior between all species and threatened species that can be appreciated in Fig. 3.7 is quite peculiar since the lines cross in the highest income decile, which includes highly urbanized areas such as Rio de Janeiro, São Paulo, Brasilia, and other major cities. The regression highlights the complexity of the

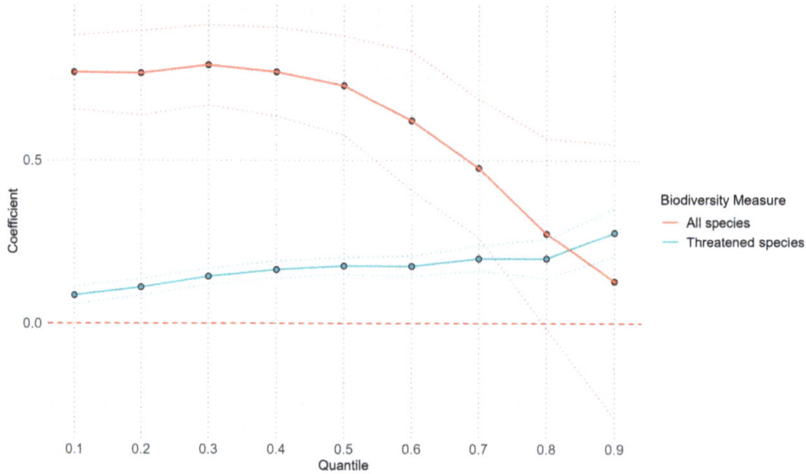

Fig. 3.7 Quantile regression coefficients. *Notes* dotted lines represent 95% confidence bands

GDP per capita—faunal biodiversity relationship, which varies substantially across the income distribution if we consider a specific indicator (i.e., faunal biodiversity as a whole or "all species"), while remains relatively stable using another indicator (i.e., threatened species only). This difference may arise from the dominant economic activity in the area, being primary, secondary, or tertiary sector. For instance, wealthier regions may leverage threatened species for ecotourism or conservation-related services, while simultaneously trying to reduce the presence of species—many species—from which they cannot directly extract economic value. In contrast, less developed areas, where primary sector activities are prevalent, may rely on goods and services provided by animal-rich ecosystems. In this latter case, certain threatened species may even be considered harmful to their livelihoods. On the other hand, the specific nature of the biome may be relevant to determine how the productive structure and faunal biodiversity interact.

B. By Bioma

Building on previous results and noting that 7 of the 10 richest metropolitan areas in Brazil are located within the Cerrado or Mata Atlântica, we continue our analysis focusing on these two biomes, whose territory, as previously underlined, is mostly considered as a biodiversity hotspot.[6] We then re-estimate Equation (3.1) for each of these two biomes. Results are shown in Table 3.4.

Our analysis shows a statistically significant and positive correlation between income per capita and biodiversity in both biomes, with the effect being particularly pronounced in the Cerrado. Analogously to Table 3.3, this holds whether we consider

6 98% of Mata Atlântica area and 90% of Cerrado area is a biodiversity hotspot, whereas only 10% of Mata Atlântica and 12% of Cerrado is a protected area.

Table 3.4 The effect of faunal biodiversity on GDP per capita by biome

	log (GDP per capita)			
	Cerrado	Mata Atlântica	Cerrado	Mata Atlântica
Log vertebrates prop	2.6284 ***	0.3106 **		
	[0.2778]	[0.1304]		
Log threatened vertebrates prop			0.3610 ***	0.0729 ***
			[0.0482]	[0.0179]
Precipitation anomaly	0.0001	−0.0002 ***	−0.0001	−0.0002 ***
	[0.0001]	[0.0000]	[0.0001]	[0.0000]
Temperature anomaly	0.7260 ***	0.0666	0.4133 ***	0.0905 *
	[0.1107]	[0.0465]	[0.1005]	[0.0465]
Protected Area size [km^2]	−0.0050 **	0.0018	0.003	0.0022 **
	[0.0024]	[0.0015]	[0.0018]	[0.0011]
Cropland [km^2]	0.1429 ***	0.0569 ***	0.1556 ***	0.0539 ***
	[0.0174]	[0.0073]	[0.0125]	[0.0048]
Grassland/Shrubland [km^2]	0.0347 **	−0.0547 ***	0.008	−0.0499 ***
	[0.0168]	[0.0084]	[0.0126]	[0.0052]
Tree and shrub (flooded) [km^2]	0.0057	0.0029	0.005	0.0022
	[0.0040]	[0.0021]	[0.0031]	[0.0017]
Tree cover [km^2]	−0.0400 ***	−0.0008	−0.0496 ***	−0.0001
	[0.0142]	[0.0049]	[0.0101]	[0.0035]
Urban areas [km^2]	0.0196 ***	0.0405 ***	0.0250 ***	0.0406 ***
	[0.0053]	[0.0032]	[0.0041]	[0.0024]
Water bodies [km^2]	0.0015	0.0053 ***	0.0022	0.0044 ***
	[0.0035]	[0.0019]	[0.0026]	[0.0015]
Sparse vegetation [km^2]	0.0097 **	0.0229 ***	0.0098 ***	0.0222 ***
	[0.0047]	[0.0046]	[0.0035]	[0.0028]
State FE	Yes	Yes	Yes	Yes
Year FE	Yes	Yes	Yes	Yes
Adj. R2	0.56	0.514	0.537	0.513
Num. obs	2102	5425	2102	5425

Notes Standard errors clustered at the Municipio level in brackets. *, ** and *** indicates 10, 5 and 1% significance levels, respectively

all vertebrates species or threatened species only, but the coefficient is higher in the first case rather than in the latter.

Therefore, our findings support the case for comprehensive protection of faunal biodiversity even across diverse biomes. Being the two biomes rich in biodiversity and characterized by a strongly present and expected to grow human activity, further reinforces the importance of our findings.

The Monetary Value of Faunal Biodiversity

We can calculate the monetary loss in GDP per capita following a loss of faunal biodiversity. We do so by applying the elasticity formula and defining a hypothetical negative shock to the number of species. In this hypothetical scenario, we define the loss in the proportion of world (threatened) vertebrates equal to the year-specific standard deviation. The decline in GDP per capita is then defined as the average GDP per capita in each year multiplied by the estimated elasticity, and by the shock size. Results of this exercise are shown in Table 3.5.

We estimate a decline in GDP of about 8.3% (8.6%) in 2017 and 8.6% (14.6%) in 2021, following a one standard deviation decline in the proportion of world (threatened) vertebrate species, respectively. Although this is a sizeable loss in GDP, the shock is large, and the monetary loss is within the range of that estimated by Falsetti et al. (2025).

In a hypothetical scenario where it is conservatively assumed that a biodiversity shock of magnitude equal to 0.195 (that is, a loss equal to one standard deviation of faunal biodiversity in 2017) occurs every ten years, and considering Brazil's actual GDP growth rate of approximately 2.2% and its population trends during the period 2000–2023, such shocks could result in a cumulative GDP per capita loss of 27% by 2050 relative to 2023. This projected decline underscores the economic risks associated with biodiversity loss, which could exacerbate inequality, particularly in regions and sectors highly dependent on natural resources for livelihoods and economic stability. Addressing these challenges would require prioritizing biodiversity conservation to ensure long-term economic resilience and equity.

Given these conservative estimates, investing even a fraction of this potential loss in the form of government spending in conserving animal wildlife offers a win-win-win strategy for human welfare, animal welfare, and economic stability. Protecting faunal biodiversity supports critical ecosystem services like pollination and carbon storage, sustains productivity in key sectors such as agriculture, and reduces risks to GDP from biodiversity shocks. It also ensures continued resources for livelihoods, enhances resilience to climate change, and fosters ecological balance by safeguarding wildlife habitats. Strategic conservation spending now can prevent far greater ecological and economic losses in the future.

Table 3.5 Monetary impacts of biodiversity loss

Year	Vertebrates prop. (avg.)	Threatened vertebrates prop. (avg.)	Vertebrates prop. (s.d.)	Threatened vertebrates prop. (s.d.)	GDP per capita	GDP change	
						Shock to vert. prop	Shock to threatened vert. prop
2017	1.186	0.026	0.224	0.012	21990.76	−1837.54	−1889.24
2021	1.031	0.032	0.195	0.025	33871.28	−2808.95	−4934.23

Conclusions

Faunal biodiversity is essential for ecosystem function, as animals are a foundational pillar of ecosystems and a critical component of the intricate web of life. Through their roles and contributions, animals do not merely sustain ecosystems—they fundamentally determine their health, balance, and regenerative capacity. This is especially important as faunal biodiversity represents a form of natural capital that directly contributes to human economic production and prosperity by supporting vital ecosystem services.

In our analysis of Brazil, using a novel spatial framework, we identified key complementarities between the health of wild animal populations and the performance of economic activity. The relationship between faunal biodiversity and economic outcomes is influenced by numerous factors, including income levels, biomes, and the types of vertebrate species considered. While all income groups benefit from thriving animal populations, those engaged in the primary sector are particularly vulnerable to losses in faunal biodiversity due to their direct reliance on natural ecosystems. Furthermore, it is the collective richness of vertebrate species, rather than the health of iconic vertebrates alone, that proves most consequential for fostering favorable economic outcomes.

Our experiment estimating per capita GDP loss due to biodiversity shocks demonstrates the tangible economic risks of faunal biodiversity depletion. Importantly, this analysis underscores the value of employing spatial frameworks in policy design, as they capture the nuanced, context-dependent relationships between biodiversity and economic activity. Such approaches enable more effective and targeted interventions, tailored to specific biomes, income levels, and species compositions.

Strategic conservation spending, informed by spatial analyses, promises substantial returns by reducing economic vulnerabilities, ensuring ecological stability, and advancing human welfare. Allocating resources to protect wildlife populations and biodiversity represents a holistic win-win-win strategy—bolstering the prosperity of human economies, safeguarding animal populations, and strengthening ecosystem resilience for future generations. Conservation is not just an ecological necessity; it is a smart economic imperative.

Appendix Tables

Table A1 Quantile regression coefficients

	Quantile								
	$\tau = 0.1$	$\tau = 0.2$	$\tau = 0.3$	$\tau = 0.4$	$\tau = 0.5$	$\tau = 0.6$	$\tau = 0.7$	$\tau = 0.8$	$\tau = 0.9$
β	0.7709	0.7684	0.7930	0.7718	0.7300	0.6215	0.4768	0.2758	0.1285
SE	0.0596	0.0625	0.0641	0.0703	0.0796	0.0888	0.1385	0.1298	0.2118

Coefficients are calculated using the log of the proportion of world vertebrates as independent variable

Table A2 Quantile regression coefficients

	Quantile								
	$\tau = 0.1$	$\tau = 0.2$	$\tau = 0.3$	$\tau = 0.4$	$\tau = 0.5$	$\tau = 0.6$	$\tau = 0.7$	$\tau = 0.8$	$\tau = 0.9$
β	0.0856	0.1105	0.1434	0.1641	0.1753	0.1741	0.1977	0.1981	0.2792
SE	0.0134	0.0132	0.0135	0.0143	0.0117	0.0152	0.0166	0.0316	0.0438

Coefficients are calculated using the log of the proportion of world threatened vertebrates as independent variable

References

Climate Data Store (2019) Land cover classification gridded maps from 1992 to present derived from satellite observation. Copernicus Climate Change Service (C3S)

Chaplin-Kramer R et al (2022) Mapping the planet's critical natural assets. Nat Ecol Evol 7(1):56–61

Dasgupta P (2021) The economics of biodiversity: the Dasgupta review. HM Treasury, London

Di Falco S, Perrings C (2005) Crop biodiversity, risk management and the implications of agricultural assistance. Ecol Econ 55(4):459–466

Falsetti B et al (2025) Quantifying nature-related risks and opportunities: a novel metric for assessing ecosystem integrity and its economic impact. SSRN Working Paper 4948659

Frank E, Sudarshan A (2024) The social costs of keystone species collapse: Evidence from the decline of vultures in India. Am Econ Rev 114(10):3007–3040

Giglio S et al (2024) The economics of biodiversity loss. NBER Working Paper Series 32678

Gregr EJ et al (2020) Cascading social-ecological costs and benefits triggered by a recovering keystone predator. Science 368(6496):1243–1247

Hanley N, Perrings C (2019) The economic value of biodiversity. Annual Review of Resource Economics 11:355–375

Harris I et al (2020) Version 4 of the CRU TS monthly high-resolution gridded multivariate climate dataset. Scientific Data 7(1):109

IBGE (2017, 2021) Produto Interno Bruto dos Municípios. Diretoria de Pesquisas, Coordenação de Contas Nacionais e Diretoria de Geociências, Coordenação de Geografia e Coordenação de Recursos Naturais e Estudos Ambientais

Instituto Nacional de Pesquisas Espaciais (INPE) (2025) Programa Queimadas. https://queimadas.dgi.inpe.br/queimadas/. Accessed on 24 March 2024
IPBES (2018) The IPBES assessment reports on biodiversity and ecosystem services. IPBES, Bonn, Germany
IUCN (2024) The IUCN red list of threatened species. Version 2024-2. https://www.iucnredlist.org. Accessed 12 Dec 2024
Millennium Ecosystem Assessment (2005) Ecosystems and human well-being: biodiversity synthesis. World Resources Institute, Washington, DC
Mittermeier RA et al (2004) Hotspots revisited: earth's biologically richest and most endangered terrestrial ecoregions, Preface by Peter A. Seligmann, Foreword by Harrison Ford, Cemex/Conservation International. Sierra Madre/Monterrey/Mexico 392
Myers N et al (2000) Biodiversity hotspots for conservation priorities. Nature 403(6772):853–858
Pereira HM et al (2020) Global trends in biodiversity and ecosystem services from 1900 to 2050. Science 384(6694):458–465
Philips H et al (2021) The Biodiversity Intactness Index - country, region and global-level summaries for the year 1970 to 2050 under various scenarios. Natural History Museum
Schipper AM et al (2020) Projecting terrestrial biodiversity intactness with GLOBIO 4. Glob Change Biol 26(2):760–771
TEEB (2010) Mainstreaming the economics of nature: a synthesis of the approach, conclusions and recommendations of TEEB. UNEP, Geneva
Tilman D et al (1997) The influence of functional diversity and composition on ecosystem processes. Science 277(5330):1300–1302
UNEP-WCMC and IUCN (2024) Protected planet: the world database on protected areas

Chapter 4
Animal Welfare Is Human Economic Welfare

Linda J Keeling

> 'What we do to the animals, we do to ourselves.'
> —*Marc Bekoff*

Abstract In the scientific literature, animal welfare is usually defined in terms of the quality of an animal's life—how well it is coping with and experiencing its environment. While this concept centers on the animal itself, it also has important implications for human economic welfare. There are two primary reasons for this connection. First, because animals are sentient and capable of feelings, how we treat them matters ethically. Second, the majority of non-human animals are domesticated, and this has significant economic implications. Despite this, there has been limited research into the true costs and benefits of current animal management practices. A deeper understanding of these interconnections would highlight the critical role animal welfare plays in promoting economic, environmental, and social sustainability. Ultimately, the well-being of humans and animals is deeply interconnected, and it is essential to reexamine how this relationship is managed. This chapter explores how animal welfare can be meaningfully measured, the limitations of existing approaches, and their potential to inform policies that benefit both animals and the economy. Even imperfect metrics can bring animal welfare into the conversation alongside economic, environmental, and social indicators—supporting a more holistic and integrated approach to sustainability.

What Does Animal Welfare Really Mean?

The term 'animal welfare' is widely used, and often loosely, in media and society generally. In scientific contexts, however, the term refers to the state of an individual animal, rather than to human responsibilities or ethical obligations. According to the

L. J. Keeling (✉)
Department of Applied Animal Science and Welfare, Swedish University of Agricultural Sciences, Uppsala, Sweden
e-mail: Linda.Keeling@slu.se

N. Batini (ed.), *The Economics of Non-Human Animals*, Natural Resource Management and Policy 63, https://doi.org/10.1007/978-3-032-17580-9_4

World Organisation for Animal Health (WOAH 2024), animal welfare means 'the physical and mental state of an animal in relation to the conditions in which it lives and dies.' Other definitions emphasize the animal's quality of life as perceived by the animal itself (Bracke et al. 1999) highlighting that welfare is about the animal's subjective experience, including its feelings (Duncan 1996).

Welfare can range from very poor to very good, depending on how well the animal is coping with its environment (Broom 1996). Scientists assess animal welfare using an increasing number of behavioral, physiological, and cognitive indicators. What individuals or society ought to do to ensure animals have a good life—or at least a life worth living—is an ethical question. Much of the apparent disagreement between people about animal welfare stems from mixing scientific questions about animal welfare with ethical questions about how animals ought to be treated.

Historically, humans have always been concerned about animals, in part due to our dependence on them. Over time, sections of society became distanced from animals. This did not mean that people were no longer concerned about the pain and suffering of animals. They were concerned and this led to the formation of animal protection and antivivisection societies. The modern animal welfare debate started following the publication of Ruth Harrison's book 'Animal Machines,' which criticized industrial farming and coined the term 'factory farm' (Harrison 1964). In response to public outcry, the UK government established the Brambell Committee, which proposed that scientific evidence was needed 'concerning the feelings of animals that can be derived from their structure, functions and also from their behavior' (HMSO 1965).

This was visionary, especially considering that at the time it was not widely accepted that animals felt pain, and most behavioral studies focused on wild animals. There was even debate about whether domesticated animals could show 'natural' behaviors. While centuries of domestication has led to animals being easier to handle, stronger, more productive, or more beautiful to look at, it has not eliminated their species—specific behavior patterns.

One enduring societal concern is whether animals suffer when they cannot perform their natural behavior. The key question for welfare science is not whether the environment is 'natural,' but the extent to which an animal is motivated to perform and has the possibility to express specific behavior patterns. For example, populations of gulls are successful in Europe though foraging in very artificial environments like garbage dumps and nesting on buildings. For those behaviors that have been essential to perform in order to survive and reproduce, it seems there is a behavioral need. Young mammals have a need to suckle to get milk from their mother. On most modern dairy farms, however, calves are separated from their mothers at birth and fed milk from buckets. Research shows that the act of sucking plays an important role in satisfying feeding motivation, independent of milk intake. Likewise, chickens peck and scratch, pigs root, and horses graze. Providing food that is consumed quickly, and without opportunities to express the natural behavior that over evolutionary time has become so intimately connected with it, can lead to abnormal behavior, such as stereotypies. The emergence of abnormal behavior indicates that the animal is unable to adapt to its housing conditions, suggesting unmet behavioral needs and compromised welfare. Recognizing which behaviors matter to animals and designing environments that support them has led to significant improvements in animal welfare. In many regions—particularly across the European Union, in New Zealand, and in a limited number of jurisdictions in North America—such provisions are now mandated by legislation. These laws often require that animals be given opportunities to express key natural behaviors, such as nesting in hens or rooting in pigs. However, this is not yet a global standard. In many countries, especially where animal welfare regulations are less developed or poorly enforced, such behavioral needs may still be overlooked. Even within the EU, and despite a commitment to propose legislation phasing out cage systems, restrictive housing systems remain in use. For example, gestation crates are still permitted for the first four weeks of pregnancy, and farrowing crates, which similarly confine sows during birth and nursing, are widely used. And while New Zealand has long banned gestation crates and is phasing out farrowing crates, Australia continues to allow both, with some variation between states.

While there are welfare concerns about systems that severely limit movement and natural behaviors, not all natural behaviors are desirable in managed settings. Flight responses and aggression are natural, but they may pose risks to animals or humans in confined environments. Social species may also experience welfare issues due to dominance hierarchies, where low-ranking individuals struggle to compete for food, resting places, or other resources.

These complexities highlight the need to better understand what animals themselves consider important—bringing us back to the Brambell Committee's emphasis on feelings. Even Charles Darwin addressed this in 'The Expression of the Emotions in Man and Animals' (Darwin 1872). Emotions in animals are thought to have evolved to help guide prioritizing behavior. Negative states occur in need situations and drive goal—directed action, while positive states are rewarding and motivate the animal to perform the behavior again, if the opportunity arises. For example, hunger and thirst motivate the animal to find food and water, while the benefits of play behavior can include improved coordination, and play fighting can help improve skills that will be beneficial later in life.

Moving from behavior to health, it seems self-evident that good health is important for good welfare. For a long time, if an animal appeared healthy, it was assumed to have good welfare. Failing to treat disease or injury is broadly recognized as neglect and a violation of basic tenets of animal care. Nearly all welfare assessment programs include checks for disease and injury. Pain is a particularly important negative state, but animals can also suffer from frustration, fear, anxiety, and other negative emotional states. There may even be states that we, as humans, find hard to imagine. What does it feel like for a wild bird in captivity not to be able to migrate?

Efforts to improve animal welfare focus primarily on reducing negative states. However, there is growing interest in promoting positive emotional states in animals, such as comfort, pleasure, and excitement. Good animal welfare is more than just the absence of suffering. Including positive emotions in welfare considerations brings the field of animal welfare in line with the increasing emphasis within human health on quality of life as a balance between negative and positive experiences. Yet while we can ask humans how they feel, it is more difficult to ask animals.

One method is to observe their preferences. Preference tests provide a simple way of asking animals what they like. Animals approach things they want and avoid things they do not. We can also quantify these preferences by training animals to press a lever or push through a weighted barrier to make a choice. Animals will work harder to obtain things they value, such as a favorite food, in the same way as humans are willing to pay more for something they desire. This approach, rooted in consumer demand theory, was proposed to estimate how much animals value specific resources (Dawkins 1983).

Research in this area has helped identify which natural behaviors are most important to animals, that is, their behavioral needs. For example, pigs will work hard to access straw for rooting, and chickens for litter in which to peck and dust-bathe. Chickens also work hard to access perches in the evening, even in the absence of nighttime predators. Behavior is also influenced by underlying emotional states. Like humans, non-human animals are more likely to make optimistic judgments when they are in a positive emotional state and more pessimistic ones when they are in negative emotional states (Mendl et al. 2010). These cognitive judgement bias tests are another way to ask animals how they feel and have been adapted from studies on young children.

Today, animal welfare is recognized as multidimensional. Physical health includes not only disease and injury but also subclinical conditions, such as immunosuppression which can be caused by prolonged stress. Stress hormone levels are also used as welfare indicators. Mental health includes the absence of fear and distress, the ability to perform motivated behaviors, and the experience of positive emotional states.

A continuing challenge is how to integrate these various indicators into a single measure of overall welfare. A basic principle is that all relevant dimensions must be assessed. One common framework identifies four key principles: good feeding, good housing, good health, and appropriate behavior. These are further divided into 11 more specific criteria. This structure forms the basis of the widely used Welfare Quality® protocols for farm animals (Blokhuis et al. 2013). More recently, the Five Domains model has gained popularity (Mellor et al. 2020). It consists of four functional domains; nutrition, physical environment, health, and behavior—and a fifth domain that reflects the animal's mental state. This model has also been applied to wildlife. For example, Nicol et al. (2020) used it to evaluate anthropogenic threats to cetaceans, such as whale watching, ship strikes, entanglement, and marine contaminants, offering a science—based tool to inform policy.

Another challenge in welfare assessment is that people have differing views on what constitutes a good life for animals, which leads them to prioritize different aspects of welfare (Fraser et al. 1997). Some emphasize natural living—believing animals should express species-specific behaviors in environments that resemble their natural habitats. Others focus on biological functioning, prioritizing health, growth, and the absence of disease. A third view centers on affective states, highlighting the importance of animals' emotional experiences, such as comfort or fear. While these perspectives often overlap, they can lead to different conclusions in practice. For instance, a pig may be physically healthy in a controlled indoor system but unable to root or explore, raising concerns from a natural living or emotional well-being standpoint. These differing views are still debated, although modern frameworks aim to integrate them.

Beyond Ethics: The Economic Case for Animal Welfare

Traditionally, economic calculations associated with animal welfare have focused on the costs of housing, feeding, and caring for the animals, weighed against revenues from their use. In farming, this means income from milk, eggs, or meat. In other contexts, income may be derived from ticket sales at zoos, fees for horseback riding, or guided tours in nature reserves etc. Across these sectors, a common argument has been that improving animal welfare increases costs, typically because it involves changes to buildings, management or some aspect of infrastructure.

However, even early studies in farm animal welfare economics showed this view was overly simplistic. For example, McInerney's framework from the 1990s proposed that modest investments in welfare can lead to gains in productivity, through improved animal health and reduced stress (See McInerney 2004). These gains benefit humans through cheaper products. Yet, there is a tipping point: as productivity is pushed further, animal welfare begins to decline. Beyond a certain threshold, welfare compromises can become so severe that productivity actually drops. In such cases, animals are no longer efficient producers because they are operating beyond their biological limits (Fig. 4.1).

In this sense, society places an implicit monetary value on animal welfare. The market price of products like eggs or milk reflects, in part, the welfare of the animals that produced them. If we had a clearer understanding of public preferences, society might choose to accept lower outputs in exchange for higher animal welfare. Indeed,

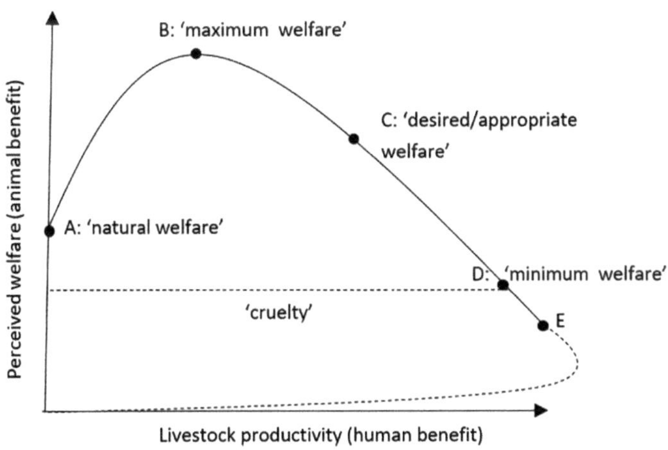

Fig. 4.1 Trade—offs between human and farm animal welfare. *Source* Adapted from McInerney (2004)

research suggests some consumers are willing to pay more for products perceived as coming from well—treated animals. However, this 'willingness to pay' is often limited. People may express concern as citizens but act differently as consumers. Niche markets for higher—welfare products, such as those from organic or extensive systems, do exist, but most consumers remain price sensitive.

As a result, farmers often operate in a narrow economic margin, caught between keeping production costs low and meeting consumer expectations. Retailers, also under pressure, are reluctant to pay more for higher—welfare products. This restricts farmers' options for improving housing conditions. Nevertheless, there are other ways to improve welfare that do not cost money and which, in the long term, can be economically beneficial. One example is that slightly lower productivity in the short term can lead to better animal health and longer productive life spans. High-producing dairy cows are more prone to mastitis (udder infections), lameness due to joint stress, and metabolic disorders like ketosis, and often have shorter productive lives now than in the past. Producing slightly less milk for more lactations per cow can be cost—effective, in part due to reduced veterinary costs but mainly because of the reduced need for rearing replacement cows. Thus, even if poor housing is always a risk factor for poor welfare, focusing on the welfare of the animal itself makes good economic sense.

The shift toward using animal-based measures in welfare assessment has helped support this transition. These measures, which reflect animals' health, physiology, and behavior, are more reliable indicators of welfare than resource—based measures, which only describe the environment (e.g., space per animal or number of feeders). Animal—based measures also allow for earlier detection of problems. Improved monitoring enables timely interventions that can prevent costly disease outbreaks, injuries, or reproductive failures. For instance, stress can reduce fertility in livestock, and lameness in horses can affect their usability and market value.

Good husbandry—being skilled at interpreting and responding to animals—is already a core competence of experienced farmers. But it is not necessarily very transparent compared to benchmarking of animal-based measures. Emerging technologies can now help support this. Automated sensors, accelerometers, and camera systems can detect subtle changes in animal behavior before even trained staff would notice. This allows for proactive management that benefits both welfare and productivity. Although less developed than in farming, similar principles apply in other sectors. In riding schools and private stables, reputation and customer trust depend partly on how horses are perceived to be treated. In laboratory settings, animal welfare is directly linked to the validity of scientific research. Stressed animals may yield unreliable data, contributing to the broader reproducibility crisis in biomedical science. As the saying goes, 'Good welfare is good science' (Neville et al. 2022).

Toward a Unified Measure of Animal Welfare

As discussed earlier, animal welfare is a multidimensional concept and while it is important to assess each component separately to identify specific problems, there are situations where a single, integrated welfare metric is useful. A single unit or simple series of categories is much easier to communicate. Systems similar to the one-to-five-star categories used for hotels, or a range of different smiley faces, are already used for labeling products or to indicate compliance with animal welfare quality assurance schemes. A more precise welfare metric, however, can be needed for policy comparisons or economic modeling.

In human health, Disability—Adjusted Life Years (DALYs) are used to quantify disease burden by combining years of life lost with years lived with disability. Similarly, Welfare—Adjusted Life Years (WALYs) have been proposed to estimate the impact of poor welfare in animals. WALYs are most applicable for assessing physical health impacts like disease, but less so for mental health or behavioral restriction. Budolfson and colleagues (2024) suggest translating traditional animal welfare indicators into a Quality—Adjusted Life Years (QALYs) framework to generate 'Animal QALYs', which could then be monetized or compared to human impacts within a cost–benefit analysis. While this remains theoretical and faces challenges, it could offer a framework for evaluating cross-species impacts on a common scale.

The Welfare Footprint Framework is a different and relatively new approach that came originally from assessment of pain in humans and clearly shifts the focus to animals' subjective experiences. It estimates the intensity and duration of both negative and positive affective states (such as pain, fear, or joy), to get an estimate of 'cumulative pain' and 'cumulative pleasure' over time. This approach reflects the growing emphasis on animals' emotional experiences and aligns with the idea that welfare is not only about preventing negative states, but also about promoting positive ones. Although assigning probabilities to mental states is complex, the framework is gaining traction. One study using the Welfare Footprint Framework compared conventional fast—growing broiler chickens with slower—growing strains (Schuck-Paim and colleagues 2025). Although the slower birds take longer to reach slaughter weight, raising costs, their welfare outcomes are usually better. For every additional US dollar per kilogram of meat, it was estimated that by adopting these slower-growing breeds (as part of complying with the European Chicken Commitment), between 5 and 100 h of intense pain could be prevented. This kind of analysis highlights that improving welfare may be economically feasible, especially when societal costs are taken into account.

It is also worth noting that increases in farm—level production costs do not translate linearly to consumer prices. The farm gate price typically accounts for only about a quarter of the retail cost. Slaughter, processing, distribution, and marketing contribute significantly to the final price. Moreover, animal—based food products usually represent a small proportion of household expenditure. This means substantial improvements in animal welfare might only lead to modest price increases for consumers.

Integrating Animal Welfare Within Sustainability and Human Economic Welfare

In 2015, the United Nations launched the 2030 Agenda for Sustainable Development, outlining 17 Sustainable Development Goals (SDGs) and 169 associated targets (UN 2015). The vision was a world free from poverty, hunger, and environmental degradation. Notably, however, animal welfare was not mentioned. This omission has since been acknowledged and in 2022, the UN Environment Assembly adopted a resolution recognizing the interconnectedness of animal welfare, the environment, and sustainable development (UNEP 2022).

While it is increasingly accepted that improving animal welfare contributes to sustainability, identifying exactly how to integrate it into global frameworks remains a challenge. (Buller et al. 2018)). Like the SDGs, that are interlinked and interdependent, animal welfare is connected to multiple goals—sometimes synergistically, sometimes in conflict (Keeling et al. 2022). For example, the goal of reducing greenhouse gas (GHG) emissions can conflict with efforts to improve animal welfare. The global scale of livestock production—particularly the vast number of ruminants—poses significant environmental challenges, not because of the animals themselves, but due to the cumulative impact of maintaining such large herds on land use, resource consumption, and ecological balance (Batini 2021). Numerous strategies have been proposed to reduce methane emissions from ruminants, including dietary additives, gene-editing to change cows microbiomes and experimental technologies like methane-capturing masks. Yet the animal welfare implications of these mitigation strategies have not received much attention and there is a risk that some climate actions will inadvertently harm animal health and welfare (See Verkuijl et al. 2024). At the same time, well-managed grazing systems can enhance biodiversity and support ecosystem services. Thus, the environmental impact of animal production systems must be balanced with their welfare outcomes.

The concept of One Health emphasizes the interconnected health of humans, animals, and ecosystems (OHHLEP et al. 2022). One Welfare builds on this, recognizing that mental health and social well-being also depend on the treatment of animals (Pinillos et al. 2016). Animal welfare thus plays a role in public health, food security, biodiversity, and resource efficiency. A key example is antimicrobial resistance. According to the World Health Organization, the overuse of antibiotics in intensive animal production contributes significantly to antimicrobial resistance. Approximately 70% of antibiotics sold globally are used in food—producing animals. Often, antimicrobials are administered preventively to compensate for stressful housing conditions and compromised immunity, whereas improving animal welfare reduces disease risk, thus lowering the need for antibiotics (lbernaz-Gonçalves et al. 2022). Sweden provides an illustrative case of this with its strong focus on animal welfare and restrictive antibiotic-use policies. Furthermore, it is common sense that poor health and welfare also leads to inefficient use of resources, such as feed and energy by animals, adding both environmental and economic costs to production costs.

Not only animal farming, but activities like poaching, overhunting, and the trade in wild animals similarly carry public health risks. The capture and sale of wild animals is linked to biodiversity loss and the emergence of infectious diseases that affect humans as well as farmed and wild animals (Verkuijl et al. 2024). An estimated 60–75% of new infectious diseases have animal origins, and zoonoses account for billions of illnesses and millions of deaths each year. Improving animal welfare—both in domestic and wild populations—can reduce these risks.

Beyond health and sustainability, welfare improvements can have direct social benefits. In many parts of the world, working equids are crucial for livelihoods. Better treatment improves productivity and helps alleviate poverty (Kubasiewicz et al. 2022). There are also links between positive human–animal relationships and improved mental health. Animal-assisted interventions are increasingly used in therapy and rehabilitation (see Chapter 16 in this book). Conversely, human mental health issues can negatively affect animals, highlighting the need for coordinated welfare services. In disaster response, recognizing emotional bonds between humans and animals can improve outcomes for both. These examples fall under the umbrella of One Welfare, and are studied often within the interdisciplinary field of anthrozoology—the science of human–animal interactions (Tarazona et al. 2020).

Taken together, the evidence supports the view that animal welfare is a crucial aspect of sustainable development. Given this, one wonders why we still focus only on the conflicts and costs of improving animal welfare when there are also many synergies that will save money in the long term (Keeling 2025).

Conclusions and Implications for Future Policy

This chapter has presented the scientific foundations of animal welfare and demonstrated how animal welfare is intimately connected to human economic welfare, sustainability, and global health. As understanding of animal sentience and emotional complexity advances, it becomes increasingly evident that safeguarding animal welfare is not just an ethical imperative but a strategic policy goal.

Policymakers need tools to account for animal welfare in ways that are compatible with economic modeling and sustainability assessments. Science-based welfare indicators, especially animal-based measures, should be integrated into policy evaluations across agriculture, trade, health, and environmental domains. Quantitative frameworks, such as Welfare Footprints and QALYs-adapted metrics, can help translate animal experiences into comparable terms that inform cost–benefit analyses.

Furthermore, aligning animal welfare policy with initiatives such as the UN Sustainable Development Goals, One Health, and One Welfare provides a route to address interconnected challenges—from antimicrobial resistance to zoonotic risk, from food system resilience to mental health. Evidence shows that improved animal welfare can support human well-being, social equity, and environmental sustainability.

For future policy, animal welfare should be regarded not as a constraint, but as a multiplier of long-term value. Embedding animal welfare science into legislation, incentives, and sustainability governance will help create a future that is not only more humane but also more economically and ecologically resilient.

References

Batini N (2021) The economics of sustainable food: smart policies for health and the planet. Island Press and International Monetary Fund, p 320. ISBN-10 (1642831611)

Blokhuis HJ, Miele M, Veissier I, Jones B (eds) (2013) Improving farm animal welfare: science and society working together: the welfare quality approach. Wageningen Academic Publishers, p 232. ISBN 9789086867707

Bracke MBM, Spruijt BM, Metz JHM (1999) Overall animal welfare assessment reviewed. Part 1: is it possible? Neth J Agric Sci 47:279–291. https://library.wur.nl/ojs/index.php/njas/article/view/466/182

Broom DM (1996) Animal welfare defined in terms of attempts to cope with the environment. Acta Agric Scand Sec A Anim Sci Suppl 27:22–28

Budolfson M, Espinosa R, Fischer B, Treich N (2024) Monetizing animal welfare impacts for benefit–cost analysis. J Benefit-Cost Anal 15(S1):206–23. https://doi.org/10.1017/bca.2024.19

Buller H, Blokhuis H, Jensen P, Keeling L (2018) Towards farm animal welfare and sustainability. Animals 8(81). https://doi.org/10.3390/ani8060081

Darwin C (1872) The expression of the emotions in man and animals. John Murray. https://doi.org/10.1037/10001-000

Dawkins MS (1983) Battery hens name their price: Consumer demand theory and the measurement of ethological 'needs.' Anim Behav 31(4):1195–1205. https://doi.org/10.1016/S0003-3472(83)80026-8

Duncan IJH (1996) Animal welfare defined in terms of feelings. Acta Agric Scand Sec A Anim Sci Suppl 27:29–35

Fraser D, Weary DM, Pajor EA, Milligan BN (1997) A scientific conception of animal welfare that reflects ethical concerns. Anim Welf 6:187–205

Harrison R (1964) Animal machines. Vincent Stuart Ltd., London

Her Majesty's Stationery Office HMSO (1965) Report of the technical committee to enquire into the welfare of animal kept under intensive livestock husbandry systems. Command Paper 2836 Her Majesty's Stationery Office, London

lbernaz-Gonçalves R, Olmos Antillón G, Hötzel MJ (2022) Linking Animal Welfare and Antibiotic Use in Pig Farming-A Review. Animals 12(2):216. https://doi.org/10.3390/ani12020216. PMID: 35049838; PMCID: PMC8773261

Keeling LJ (2025) Animal welfare: part of the solution, not part of the problem in the move toward achieving sustainable development in animal agriculture. Anim Front 15(2):8–11. https://doi.org/10.1093/af/vfaf009

Keeling LJ, Marier EA, Olmos Antillón G, Blokhuis HJ, Staaf Larsson B, Stuardo L (2022) A global study to identify a potential basis for policy options when integrating animal welfare into the UN Sustainable Development Goals. Front Anim Sci 3:974687. https://doi.org/10.3389/fanim.2022.974687

Kubasiewicz LM, Watson T, Norris SL, Chamberlain N, Nye C, Perumal RK, Saroja R, Raw Z, Burden FA (2022) One welfare: linking poverty, equid ownership and equid welfare in the brick kilns of India. Anim Welf 31(4):517–528. https://doi.org/10.1017/S0962728600032504

McInerney J (2004) Animal welfare, economics and policy. Report on a study undertaken for the Farm & Animal Health Economics Division of Defra. https://citeseerx.ist.psu.edu/document?repid=rep1&type=pdf&doi=3ee106ec1b5c7e58e0ff2144a11057ab23347486

Mellor DJ, Beausoleil NJ, Littlewood KE, McLean AN, McGreevy PD, Jones B, Wilkins C (2020) The 2020 five domains model: including human—animal interactions in assessments of animal welfare. Animals 10(10):1870. https://doi.org/10.3390/ani10101870

Mendl M, Burman OHP, Paul E (2010) An integrative and functional framework for the study of animal emotion and mood. Proc Roy Soc B 277: 2895–2904. https://doi.org/10.1098/rspb.2010.0303

Neville V, Lecorps B, Mendl M (2022) Good science requires better animal welfare. Science 376(6595):809–809. https://doi.org/10.1126/science.abq7198

Nicol C, Bejder L, Green L, Johnson C, Keeling L, Noren D, Van der Hoop J, Simmonds M (2020) Anthropogenic threats to wild cetacean welfare and a tool to inform policy in this area. Front Vet Sci 7(57). https://doi.org/10.3389/fvets.2020.00057

One Health High-Level Expert Panel OHHLEP, Adisasmito WB, Almuhairi S, Behravesh CB, Bilivogui P, Bukachi SA, et al (2022) One health: a new definition for a sustainable and healthy future. PloS Pathog 18(6):e1010537. https://doi.org/10.1371/journal.ppat.1010537

Pinillos RG, Appleby MC, Manteca X, Scott-Park F, Smith C, Velarde A (2016) One welfare—a platform for improving human and animal welfare. Vet Rec 179(16):412–413. https://doi.org/10.1136/vr.i5470

Schuck-Paim C, Alonso WJ, Verkuijl C, Hegwood M, Hartcher K (2025) The welfare footprint framework can help balance animal welfare with other food system priorities. Nat Food 6(8):737–739. https://doi.org/10.1038/s43016-025-01213-z

Tarazona AM, Ceballos MC, Broom DM (2020) Human relationships with domestic and other animals: one health, one welfare, one biology. Anim 10(1):43. https://doi.org/10.3390/ani10010043

United Nations Environment Programme UNEP (2022) Animal welfare–environment–sustainable development nexus. Resolution adopted by the United Nations Environment Assembly on 2 March 2022. UK. https://wedocs.unep.org/20.500.11822/39791

United Nations (2015) Transforming our World: the 2030 agenda for sustainable development. https://sdgs.un.org/2030agenda

Verkuijl C, Smit J, Green JMH, Nordquist RE, Sebo J, Hayek MN, Hötzel MJ (2024) Climate change, public health, and animal welfare: towards a one health approach to reducing animal agriculture's climate footprint. Front Anim Sci 5:1281450. https://doi.org/10.3389/fanim.2024.1281450

World Organisation for Animal Health (WOAH) (2024) Terrestrial animal health code. 32nd ed. Paris (France): WOAH; 2024. Chapter 7.1. Introduction to the recommendations for animal welfare, p 3. https://www.woah.org/fileadmin/Home/eng/Health_standards/tahc/2023/chapitre_aw_introduction.pdf

Chapter 5
The Value of Non-Human Animals' Life

Simone Martino and Jasper O. Kenter

> The worth of a life, human or otherwise, cannot be reduced to income or consumption.
> —*Amartya Sen*

Abstract This paper explores how we can understand and measure the value of non-human animals' lives in economic terms. It explains why this kind of valuation matters—for shaping conservation policies, recognising different kinds of value (like usefulness, emotional connection, and inherent worth), and supporting better decision-making. We start by outlining the basic ideas behind economic valuation, including how it views markets, values, and human behaviour. Then, we look at some of the main criticisms, especially around fairness, power dynamics, and the role of institutions. Finally, we suggest that including public discussion and participation in the valuation process can help capture a broader range of values and lead to more inclusive and effective policies.

Economics for Animals: A Pluralistic Approach to Valuation and Conservation

Economics has widely supported animal conservation strategies by recognising their material and nonmaterial contributions to human wellbeing (Díaz et al. 2018). Since the original recognition of intrinsic values supported the designation of protected

S. Martino (✉)
The James Hutton Institute, Aberdeen, UK
e-mail: simone.martino@hutton.ac.uk

J. O. Kenter
Aberystwyth Business School, University of Aberystwyth, Aberystwyth, UK

Environment and Geography, University of York, York, UK

Ecologos Research, Aberystwyth, UK

J. O. Kenter
e-mail: mail@jasperkenter.com

N. Batini (ed.), *The Economics of Non-Human Animals*, Natural Resource Management and Policy 63, https://doi.org/10.1007/978-3-032-17580-9_5

species and areas (Dixon and Sherman 1991), the acknowledgement of animals as part of natural capital generating instrumental, anthropocentric values (Subroy et al. 2019) has been an increasingly important lever to reduce market and wider institutional failures (Hanley and Perrings 2019), through the introduction of penalties and economic incentives to regulate hunting, human-animal conflicts (Hanley et al. 2010), poaching (Johannesen and Skonhoft 2005) and illegal trade (van Uhm 2016). More recently, private finance has started promoting innovative tools to tackle the reduction of biodiversity by the introduction of tradable credits (Antonelli et al. 2024).

The implementation of such tools to protect animals is supported by economic valuation, a collection of methods that can recognise the importance of animals to human wellbeing (Methorst et al. 2020), medicine (Jobstvogt et al. 2014a, b), and food security (García-Díez et al. 2021), but also considering animal welfare (Schrobback et al. 2023), the functioning of natural processes (Holtmeier 2015), and the constraints of planetary boundaries (Bowles et al. 2019). Valuation, as an approach to human preferences elicitation, building on conventional economics principles, reflects instrumental (anthropocentric) values of nature as rooted in Judeo-Christian traditions (Parks and Gowdy 2013) and rea-affirmed in Bentham's utilitarianism (Bentham and Mill 2004). However, emphasis on a plurality of values proposed by the Intergovernmental Science Policy Platform on Biodiversity and Ecosystem Services (Christie et al. 2019; IPBES 2019; Raymond et al. 2023) advocates for a closer synergy between 'nature and people' (Mace 2014), as an approach to conservation. This new pluralistic paradigm also attends to problems of environmental justice (Figueroa 2022) and how to circumvent concerns arising from individualistic and utilitarian value assumptions of neoclassical economics (Kenter et al. 2015).

Based on these premises, the aim of this paper is to: (1) provide an overview of economic valuation to those engaged in animal management and conservation; (2) describe the diverse valuation approaches that may facilitate livestock and wildlife protection; and (3) highlight novel deliberative approaches in valuation that could help incorporate a plurality of values in decision-making instead of relying on a single dominant value perspective.

Valuing Animals Through the Neoclassical Lens

Neoclassical economics suggests that goods and services in themselves have no value (Parks and Gowdy 2013). Conversely, values emerge as expression of the subjective 'utility' of the good at stake. Utility here reflects the strength of someone's preference for a good, such as the conservation of an animal species, over other goods, such as consumer items. The relative value to society of different goods and services is then defined by the aggregation of individual preferences (Hockley 2014). An economic measure of utility is the willingness to pay (WTP), a concept that reflects the benefit for the individual of one additional unit of a good, keeping the amount of all other goods constant. A less-used counterpart, the willingness to accept (WTA), is adopted as a compensation needed in lieu of relinquishing something of value to us. The two measures may diverge substantially for the same good, because people typically attach more value to avoiding losses than gains (Hanemann 1991).

The framework adopted in economics to categorise utilitarian values for nature is called Total Economic Value (TEV) (Turner et al. 2003). It recognises two categories of value: use and non-use values. The first includes non-consumptive use, for instance generated by recreational experience (Getzner 2015) and consumptive use of resources such as livestock production, hunting, and fishing (Berman and Kofinas 2004). Non-use values, also called passive use values, include value for the sake of knowing that others (altruistic value), future generations (bequest value) or non-human nature (existence value) may benefit (Morse-Jones et al. 2012).

The TEV monetizes values under the assumptions that preferences are considered as individual, self-regarding, pre-formed, and rational. Examples of valuation operating under these assumptions are proposed in the next section, while relaxations of these principles and implication for values are considered in section on the limitations and critiques of standard valuation approaches below.

Standard Approaches to Animal Valuation

Conventionally, values of animals are assessed through market prices and non-market valuation. Market prices are commonly used to assess the benefits (use value) of domestic animals (Schrobback et al. 2023), their role within the economy of the farm (Herrero et al. 2013) and the added value to the economy of a nation (Tyohen and Mbakpenev 2023), providing insights on the effects of environmental conditions, market dynamics, and political stability to market prices. Conversely, passive, recreational, and cultural values are marginally considered, although preferences for some farmed animals can be reconnected to the local cultural context (Smith et al. 2013).

As for livestock, markets may reveal direct benefits of wildlife, including commercial and recreational hunting, and viewing. However, markets are incapable of capturing most components of TEV such as passive values or indirect uses of wildlife like pollination services (Lewis et al. 2024; Martino and Kenter 2023). Therefore, methods for assessing non-market values have been designed.

Non-market valuations adopt stated preference to elicit unobservable values and revealed preferences to infer values from observed expenditures. Stated preferences, including the contingent valuation method (CVM) (Hanemann 1994) and choice experiments (CE) (Hanley et al. 1998), elicit respondents' preferences in hypothetical policy scenarios by questionnaire survey. In CVM, WTP or WTA become a monetary measure of a clearly stated policy change as for the conservation of charismatic species such as rhino (Saayman and Saayman 2014) or sea turtle (Cazabon-Mannette et al. 2017). In CE, WTP reflects the rate of substitution of preferred choice between attributes of the environmental good, with cost being one of the attributes, as in

(Bach and Burton 2017) who used a CE to explore trade-offs between conservative and recreational measures for dolphins' management.

Hedonic pricing (HPM) and the travel cost method (TCM), conversely, are used to infer revealed preferences for environmental properties associated with an ordinary commodity (house, land, or other marketed goods) (Bockstael and McConnell 1993). HPM is used to infer the marginal value of animals through the analysis of hunting licences, and is adopted to adjust wildlife hunting policy (Mensah and Elofsson 2017), while TCM to reveal preferences from money spent in travelling to measure recreational experiences such as wildlife watching (Lewis et al. 2024; Martino and Kenter 2023).

Indirect benefits of animals can be assessed exploring their productivity on marketed products through dose–response relationships capturing the impact on crop production of pollination services (Breeze et al. 2016).

Approaches based on costs can be also adopted. In the avoided damage-cost approach, the benefit is assumed equal to the cost of preventing damage. For instance, natural pest control can be assumed at least equal to the value of the damage to food production incurred in case of absence of this ecosystem service (Naranjo et al. 2015) or to the increased value of human health because of the reduced use of insecticides (Frank 2024). In the replacement cost approach, the minimum value of environmental goods is equated with the cost of replacing them by manufactured capitals. For instance, the cost of renting honey beehives can be seen as a proxy for the value of wild pollinators (Sandhu et al. 2015).

Limitations and Critiques of Standard Valuation Approaches

The conventional economic assumptions underpinning TEV have been critiqued because of their individualism (whereas many values for nature are shared), the focus on instrumentalism (whereas many values of nature are intrinsic or relational and do not 'trade-off' in the ways assumed by conventional economics), and because of the narrow resource-focussed environmental worldview that considers nature as separate from people and merely as a stock of natural capital that provides anthropocentric benefits. To address these critiques, expand the scope of valuation, and help navigate more diverse worldviews and knowledge systems (Vatn et al. 2024), IPBES has adopted the *Life Framework* (O'Connor and Kenter 2019; Kenter and O'Connor 2022) of values, where nature is considered in terms of not just *living from nature* (nature as a resource), but also *living with nature* (nature as an important other), *living in nature* (nature as place), and *living as nature* (nature as self) (Pascual et al. 2023; Vatn et al. 2024). Aligned with this perspective, non-traditional approaches question whether values are a merely product of utilitarian preferences (Isacs et al. 2023). People might be willing to pay for animal conservation because they feel it is the right thing to do, rather than because it satisfies their preferences. Moreover, they often do not have clearly pre-formed individual values (Kenter et al. 2016a) and may prefer eliciting them through group deliberation to shape decisions under societal perspectives (Kenter et al. 2016b; Orchard-Webb et al. 2016). These shared values operate at the level of communities and cultures rather than individuals (Irvine et al. 2016).

These new critiques also emphasise the role that power and justice play in value formation (Kenter et al. 2019). When aggregating values, agreement is needed on how much each individual counts. Conventionally, cost–benefit analysis (CBA) is a key approach to assess trade-offs between benefits and costs to different stakeholders. However, in identifying economically optimal decisions via CBA, it is typically assumed that different groups in society have the same weight, although it is demonstrated that unweighted CBA can exacerbate social disparities with the poorest gaining less than the richest (Pearce et al. 2006). CBA also assumes that different dimensions of value (e.g. ecological, social, and cultural) can be fully monetised, therefore reduced to economic or financial benefits. If the benefits outweigh the costs after compensation of losers, the project would be 'efficient' and deliver a net value to society (regardless of whether these compensations take place). However, CBA does not deal with a fully and just compensation (Atkinson and Mourato 2015). Unless all parties agree on how different dimensions should be traded off against each other, it is not possible to come to any single legitimate conclusion. For this reason, conventional economic valuation and appraisal have only limited use in complex and contested situations (Hockley 2014). The use of these approaches can increase conflicts when people feel that their other values are not taken into consideration (Martino et al. 2019; O'brien 2003). However, to address the issues described above, it is possible to adopt valuation frameworks that move beyond individualism and utilitarianism to deliberative, non-monetary, and integrated valuation approaches.

Deliberative Valuation Methods

We advocate a set of methodologies termed d*eliberative monetary valuation* (DMV) that are used to integrate participation and social learning into monetary valuation (Bartkowski and Lienhoop 2018; Bunse et al. 2015; Kenter 2017; Lo and Spash 2013; Orchard-Webb et al. 2016). These approaches provide participants time to discuss and help them become familiar with the environmental goods they are being asked to (Christie et al. 2006), but can also consider broader sets of values and what policy options are deemed socially optimal based on these multiple underlying types of values. In DMV, values may be expressed distinguishing between the value provider (individual vs. group) and scale (individual vs. societal), providing four main types of monetary value indicator (Spash 2007):

1. a deliberated individual WTP for individuals (Voelker and Lienhoop 2016),
2. a deliberated group 'fair price' for individuals (Kenter et al. 2011),
3. a deliberated social WTP value determined by individuals (no studies),

4. a deliberated social WTP value determined by groups (Ainscough et al. 2024).

Most of these studies focussed on individual values expressed by individuals, and 'fair price', the equitable value deliberated by group bringing in the valuation process a moral context. However, only a few studies apply DMV to animal valuation using individual WTP for wildlife conservation (Table 5.1). The majority considers the broader implications of wildlife within the context of ecosystems conservation (Martino and Kenter 2023) but also introduces the analysis of social WTP and fair prices (Table 5.2).

The advantage of adopting deliberative forum in valuation gives the opportunity to link monetary methods to a broad range of values expressed by non-monetary approaches to consider experiences, identities, capabilities, and relational values to places (Bryce et al. 2016). In addition, DMV studies show that deliberated preferences are promising in relation to unknown ecosystems, such as underwater wildlife and habitats, where absence of preformed preferences is frequently observed (Hanley et al. 2015; Jobstvogt et al. 2014a, 2014b; Kenter et al. 2016a).

A further departure from the assumption of neoclassical economics is provided by deliberative democratic monetary valuation (DDMV), where goal is to get group consensus directly on the common good (Kenter 2017). Participants consider benefits and costs of different policy options alongside non-instrumental concerns, including social norms, rights and duties, virtues such as fairness or responsibility, and narratives—stories that can implicitly and explicitly express values (Kenter 2017). There have been at least two DDMV studies referring to animals, where participants in a deliberation on hypothetical policy options for strategic local development around fisheries and the broader coastal environment established a social WTP (Orchard-Webb et al. 2016), and where fisheries management was considered within the broader context of regional marine planning (Ainscough et al. 2024).

Animal Valuation for Decision-Making

Valuation has been often used to assess recreational and non-use values of mammals in temperate habitats (bears, wolves, lynx, deer, etc.) (Johansson et al. 2012) and charismatic species in tropical countries (Rathnayake 2016; Wang et al. 2018). Common is the assessment of conservation values using CVM [e.g. griffon vulture (Becker et al. 2009); dolphin (Wang et al. 2016); catfish (Hutt et al. 2013); red grouse (Hanley et al. 2010)], while CE is used to explore animals' relationships with ecosystems (e.g. forest and wetland) for better habitat management (Dias and Belcher 2015). Conversely, few papers have addressed the value of single individual animals (Lewis et al. 2024), whose estimate can be relevant for compensation in case of poaching or wildlife-human conflicts.

Decades of research have evidenced the contribution of animals to people (Methorst et al. 2020) showing how underestimating a range of values has led to poor

Table 5.1 Studies applying DMV with relevance to animal conservation applying to the category of deliberated individual WTP/WTA

Authors/ year	Object of values	Aim of the study	Type of value	Geographic area	Payment term
Kenter et al. (2016a)	Sea birds	The study proposes a deliberative choice experiment considering the value of sea birds (abundance and diversity) vs other environmental amenities in context of coastal realignment and habitat restoration	Use and non-use values	UK	Three-stage process comparing individual WTP, deliberated individual WTP, and deliberated group fair price
Lienhoop and Fischer (2009)	Large Blue butterfly	A market stall provides information on Large Blue butterfly and elicit WTP for conservation. Motivations from the respondents to protect Large Blue are captured by video recordings. Indicators of motivation correlate significantly with WTP statements	Non-use value	Germany	Deliberated individual WTP, recorded twice: during group meeting and later during telephonic interview
MacMillan et al. (2006)	Red Kite	DVM shows that conservation values of red kite require time to be elicited, compared to the introduction of green power energy by wind farm, a subject where interviewees showed to have higher preformed knowledge and preformed preferences	Non-use value	UK	Deliberated individual WTP, recorded twice: during group meeting and later during telephonic interview
MacMillan et al. (2002)	Wild goose	CVM and DMV are used to estimate the benefits of wild goose conservation and compare them with compensation provided by government to farmers	Use and non-use value	UK	Deliberated individual WTP, recorded twice: during group meeting and later during telephonic interview

(continued)

Table 5.1 (continued)

Authors/year	Object of values	Aim of the study	Type of value	Geographic area	Payment term
Philip and MacMillan (2005)	American mink, hedgehog, capercaillie, European beaver	Market stall is used to elicit preferences for different conservation policies in Scotland such as population culls, translocation, protection of species facing extinction, and the issue of species reintroduction for several mammals	Non-use value	UK	Deliberated individual WTP, recorded twice: during group meeting and later during telephonic interview
Wätzold et al. (2008)	Large Blue butterfly	The research estimates the optimal level of conservation of Large Blue by estimating benefits (WTP) and costs (WTA) of conservation measures such as agri-environmental schemes for agriculturists. Valuation of benefits (demand for conservation) is achieved by market stall	Non-use value	Germany	Individual WTP, recorded twice: during group meeting and later during telephonic interview

Modified from Martino and Kenter (2023)

biodiversity outcomes with negative consequence for people livelihoods (Chaplin-Kramer et al. 2025; Christie et al. 2012). For instance, research in dryland ecosystems has suggested how wildlife conservation in private ranches may be more remunerative than livestock production (Cloete and Spies 2013) under the right to 'exploit' animals for recreational purposes (Child et al. 2012). In addition, studies showing that wildlife viewing provides recreational benefits to consumers were used to set economic instruments on tourism activities, reflecting the consumer surplus of the recreational experience (Kaffashi et al. 2015). Since 2000s, research has focussed on setting entrance fees (Fix et al. 2005; Kaffashi et al. 2015; Rathnayake 2016); property or user rights (Harihar et al. 2015); taxes or charges to induce behavioural changes in the use and exploitation of marine (Batel et al. 2014) and terrestrial habitats and species (Dalrymple et al. 2012).

Notwithstanding the widely recognised economic benefits of protection, conservation of animals can be resisted and considered a costly option because of strong interference with human activities such as livestock predation, destruction of crops, traffic collisions, and transmission of diseases (Gren et al. 2018). Agricultural users, mainly in developing countries, have frequently raised these conflicts (Ninan and Sathyapalan 2005). Attempts to elicit the marginal values of actions supporting strategies for the coexistence between elephant, wolves, bears, livestock, and humans are still at an early stage, although physical barriers, training in animal husbandry, and

Table 5.2 Studies applying DMV with relevance to animal conservation within their ecosystems applying to the category of social WTP and fair prices

Authors/ year	Object of values	Aim of the study	Type of value	Geographic area	Payment term
Kenter et al. (2011)	Rainforest areas	CV and DMV are used to determine the value people placed on ecosystem services and whether participatory interventions influenced their preferences. Under CV, ecosystem services were valued at 30% of household income, but after deliberation, ecosystem services became priceless	Use and non-use value	Solomon Islands (Oceania)	Deliberated group fair price, elicited twice interspersed with several deliberative exercises
Orchard-Webb et al. (2016)	Marine fisheries	Study investigating the importance of fisheries and marine ecosystems more broadly in cultural and economic terms; set within stakeholder deliberation on sustainable development policies; values reflect allocations of public funds to different priorities	No assumptions made	UK (Europe)	Deliberated social willingness to pay (group consensus of social values)

(continued)

Table 5.2 (continued)

Authors/ year	Object of values	Aim of the study	Type of value	Geographic area	Payment term
Kenter et al. (2016b)	Marine wildlife and habitats	Study investigating value of different charismatic and non-charismatic species and marine habitats in context of marine p rotected area designation; differences between individual non-deliberated and deliberated WTP, and group-deliberated fair prices, and impacts of two interventions (information-based vs values-based discussion and storytelling), and relation between monetary and non-monetary wellbeing values	Use and non-use values	UK (Europe)	Five stage process comparing individual WTP, deliberated individual WTP (twice) and deliberated group fair price (also twice), interspersed with information and values-based interventions
Kenter (2016)	Sea birds and intertidal habitats	Deliberative choice experiment considering the value of sea birds in terms of abundance and diversity vs other environmental amenities in context of coastal realignment and habitat restoration. Multi-stage DMV looking at differences between individual, individual deliberated, and group-deliberated values	Use and non-use values	UK (Europe)	Three-stage process comparing individual WTP, deliberated individual WTP, and deliberated group fair price

Modified from Martino and Kenter (2023)

other non-lethal activities are expected to reduce human-wildlife conflicts (van Eeden et al. 2021).

The disconnect between non-human and human animals complicates the proper recognition of the role of non-human animal communities in supporting ecosystem functions, reducing traction for correct management (Dee et al. 2019) and conservation policies. For instance, the Global Biodiversity Framework and the EU Biodiversity Strategy 2030 consider targets for reversing the degradation of ecosystems but barely recognise the role of animals in supporting and regulating ecosystem services (Chaplin-Kramer et al. 2025). This prevents from fully protecting ecosystems from overexploitation, pollution, and substitution of natural capital with built infrastructures.

Economists have also valued some cultural and regulating services provided by animals to ecosystems and societies. A comparison between these benefits and conservation costs is considered for vulture (Johansson et al. 2012), elephant (Sutton et al. 2008), deer (Bowker et al. 2003), and duck (Bennett and Whitten 2003) as a step in CBA of conservation policies. However, CBAs do not necessarily reduce conflicts between different parties even under scenarios depicting positive economic return. An attempt to reintroduce the Eurasian lynx in the UK, while supported by a positive CBA (White et al. 2015) failed because of the negative inclination of key stakeholders (farmers) and an absence of positive attitudes from the public to co-exist with it (Hawkins et al. 2020). Deliberating on the stances at stake to help bridge economic, scientific, and local knowledge was considered the most transparent approach for converging towards a common position.

While environmental cost–benefit analyses (CBAs) include a range of instrumental values (Duffield and Neher 2021; Richardson and Lewis 2022), cases like the UK lynx reintroduction (Hawkins et al. 2020), and others as proposed by (Kenter et al. 2014), highlight how certain values—those incommensurable with conventional valuation methods—and the conflicts they generate on the ground, may require alternative approaches to assessment and decision-making. Involving people more directly in how we value animals through deliberative approaches can help make clearer how animals benefit humans, shape our relationships with wildlife—both good and bad—and allow space to express deeper, intrinsic values (O'Connor and Kenter, 2019). These more participatory and less traditional approaches to valuation can support planning that balances multiple goals, such as conservation, livelihoods, and community needs (Chaplin-Kramer et al. 2025). By relaxing some of the strict assumptions of conventional economics (i.e. people expected to think or behave purely following criteria of rationality)—we can explore more collaborative, community-based ways to manage natural resources (Roe et al. 2009). This shift could also help reduce conflict and inequality in decisions about animals, which have often been reinforced by neoclassical economic models (Methorst et al. 2020).

Conclusions

Valuing animal life is not just a technical exercise—it is a deeply ethical and political act that shapes how societies relate to the natural world. While economic valuation has helped highlight the many ways animals contribute to human wellbeing—through recreation, ecosystem services, and cultural significance—it has also revealed the limitations of viewing animals solely through a market-based lens.

Conventional approaches have often focussed on species-level or aggregate values, overlooking the importance of individual animals and the complex relationships people have with them. These methods tend to prioritise instrumental values—what animals can do for us—while sidelining intrinsic and relational values that reflect care, respect, and coexistence. As a result, policies based on narrow economic metrics can fail to resonate with local communities, especially when conservation is perceived as a threat to livelihoods or autonomy.

At the same time, the growing recognition of animals as part of natural capital has opened new opportunities for integrating them into decision-making frameworks. Economic tools like compensation schemes, tourism pricing, and habitat management incentives have shown promise in aligning conservation goals with human interests. Yet, these tools are not neutral—they reflect assumptions about human behaviour, rationality, and value that may not hold across cultures or contexts.

To move forward, there is a need to embrace a more pluralistic and participatory approach to valuation. This means creating spaces where different voices—scientific, local, indigenous, and experiential—can come together to articulate what animals mean to them. It also means acknowledging that some values cannot be easily measured or compared, and that decision-making must sometimes accommodate incommensurable perspectives.

Deliberative and knowledge co-creation approaches offer a way to bridge these gaps. By involving people directly in the process of defining and expressing values, we can build more inclusive, transparent, and context-sensitive policies. These approaches can help reduce conflict, foster trust, and support more just outcomes—especially in situations where human and animal interests intersect or collide.

Ultimately, valuing animal life is about more than assigning numbers. It is about recognising animals as part of our shared world, with roles, rights, and relationships that matter. A more reflective, inclusive, relational, and ethical approach to valuation can help us make decisions that are not only economically sound, but also socially and ecologically responsible.

References

Ainscough J, Kenter OJ, Azzopardi E, Meriwether A, Wilson M (2024) Participant perceptions of different forms of deliberative monetary valuation: Comparing democratic monetary valuation

and deliberative democratic monetary valuation in the context of regional marine planning. Environ Values 33. https://doi.org/10.1177/0963271924123151
Antonelli A, Rueda X, Calcagno R, Nantongo Kalunda P (2024) How biodiversity credits could help to conserve and restore nature. Nature 634:1045–1049. https://doi.org/10.1038/d41586-024-03475-2
Atkinson G, Mourato S (2015) Cost-benefit analysis and the environment (No. 97). OECD, Paris, France.
Bach L, Burton M (2017) Proximity and animal welfare in the context of tourist interactions with habituated dolphins. J Sustain Tour 25:181–197. https://doi.org/10.1080/09669582.2016.1195835
Bartkowski B, Lienhoop N (2018) Beyond rationality, towards reasonableness: enriching the theoretical foundation of deliberative monetary valuation. Ecol Econ 143:97–104. https://doi.org/10.1016/j.ecolecon.2017.07.015
Batel A, Basta J, Mackelworth P (2014) Valuing visitor willingness to pay for marine conservation—the case of the proposed Cres-Lošinj marine protected area, Croatia. Ocean Coast Manag 95:72–80. https://doi.org/10.1016/j.ocecoaman.2014.03.025
Becker N, Choresh Y, Bahat O, Inbar M (2009) Economic analysis of feeding stations as a means to preserve an endangered species: the case of Griffon Vulture (*Gyps fulvus*) in Israel. J Nat Conserv 17:199–211. https://doi.org/10.1016/j.jnc.2009.04.004
Bennett J, Whitten S (2003) Duck hunting and wetland conservation: compromise or synergy? Canadian Journal of Agricultural Economics/revue Canadienne D'agroeconomie 51:161–173. https://doi.org/10.1111/j.1744-7976.2003.tb00171.x
Bentham J, Mill JS (2004) Utilitarianism and other essays. Penguin UK.
Berman M, Kofinas G (2004) Hunting for models: grounded and rational choice approaches to analyzing climate effects on subsistence hunting in an Arctic community. Ecol Econ 49:31–46. https://doi.org/10.1016/j.ecolecon.2003.12.005
Bockstael NE, McConnell KE (1993) Public goods as characteristics of non-market commodities. Econ J 103:1244–1257. https://doi.org/10.2307/2234250
Bowker JM, Newman DH, Warren RJ, Henderson DW (2003) Estimating the economic value of lethal versus nonlethal deer control in suburban communities. Soc Nat Res 16:143–158. https://doi.org/10.1080/08941920309197
Bowles N, Alexander S, Hadjikakou M (2019) The livestock sector and planetary boundaries: a 'limits to growth' perspective with dietary implications. Ecol Econ 160:128–136. https://doi.org/10.1016/j.ecolecon.2019.01.033
Breeze TD, Gallai N, Garibaldi LA, Li XS (2016) Economic measures of pollination services: shortcomings and future directions. Trends Ecol Evol 31:927–939. https://doi.org/10.1016/j.tree.2016.09.002
Bryce R, Irvine KN, Church A, Fish R, Ranger S, Kenter JO (2016) Subjective well-being indicators for large-scale assessment of cultural ecosystem services. Ecosystem Services, Shared, Plural and Cultural Values 21:258–269. https://doi.org/10.1016/j.ecoser.2016.07.015
Bunse L, Rendon O, Luque S (2015) What can deliberative approaches bring to the monetary valuation of ecosystem services? A literature review. Ecosyst Serv 14:88–97. https://doi.org/10.1016/j.ecoser.2015.05.004
Cazabon-Mannette M, Schuhmann PW, Hailey A, Horrocks J (2017) Estimates of the non-market value of sea turtles in Tobago using stated preference techniques. J Environ Manage 192:281–291. https://doi.org/10.1016/j.jenvman.2017.01.072
Chaplin-Kramer R, Miller CR, Dee LE, Bennett NJ, Echeverri A, Gould RK, Gregr EJ, Kinnaird MF, Leidner AK, Naidoo R, Nicholas KA, Zhao J (2025) Wildlife's contributions to people. Nat Rev Biodivers 1:68–81. https://doi.org/10.1038/s44358-024-00006-9
Child BA, Musengezi J, Parent GD, Child GFT (2012) The economics and institutional economics of wildlife on private land in Africa. Pastoralism 2:18. https://doi.org/10.1186/2041-7136-2-18
Christie M, Fazey I, Cooper R, Hyde T, Kenter JO (2012) An evaluation of monetary and non-monetary techniques for assessing the importance of biodiversity and ecosystem services to

people in countries with developing economies. Ecological Economics, Sustainability in Global Product Chains 83:67–78. https://doi.org/10.1016/j.ecolecon.2012.08.012
Christie M, Hanley N, Warren J, Murphy K, Wright R, Hyde T (2006) Valuing the diversity of biodiversity. Ecol Econ 58:304–317. https://doi.org/10.1016/j.ecolecon.2005.07.034
Christie M, Martín-López B, Church A, Siwicka E, Szymonczyk P, Mena Sauterel J (2019) Understanding the diversity of values of "Nature's contributions to people": insights from the IPBES Assessment of Europe and Central Asia. Sustain Sci 14:1267–1282. https://doi.org/10.1007/s11625-019-00716-6
Cloete PC, Spies DC (eds) (2013) PR—farm level financial analysis of the wildlife sector in South Africa, IFMA19. https://doi.org/10.22004/ag.econ.345663
Dalrymple CJ, Peterson MN, Cobb DT, Sills EO, Bondell HD, Dalrymple DJ (2012) Estimating public willingness to fund nongame conservation through state tax initiatives. Wildl Soc Bull 36:483–491. https://doi.org/10.1002/wsb.164
Dee LE, Cowles J, Isbell F, Pau S, Gaines SD, Reich PB (2019) When do ecosystem services depend on rare species? Trends Ecol Evol 34:746–758. https://doi.org/10.1016/j.tree.2019.03.010
Dias V, Belcher K (2015) Value and provision of ecosystem services from prairie wetlands: a choice experiment approach. Ecosyst Serv 15:35–44. https://doi.org/10.1016/j.ecoser.2015.07.004
Díaz S, Pascual U, Stenseke M, Martín-López B, Watson RT, Molnár Z, Hill R, Chan KMA, Baste IA, Brauman KA, Polasky S, Church A, Lonsdale M, Larigauderie A, Leadley PW, van Oudenhoven APE, van der Plaat F, Schröter M, Lavorel S, Aumeeruddy-Thomas Y, Bukvareva E, Davies K, Demissew S, Erpul G, Failler P, Guerra CA, Hewitt CL, Keune H, Lindley S, Shirayama Y (2018) Assessing nature's contributions to people. Science 359:270–272. https://doi.org/10.1126/science.aap8826
Dixon JA, Sherman PB (1991) Economics of protected areas. Ambio 20:68–74
Duffield J, Neher C (2021) Incorporating deer and turtle total value in collision mitigation benefit-cost calculations. Nevada Department of Transportation.
Figueroa RM (2022) Environmental justice. In: The Routledge companion to environmental ethics. Routledge.
Fix PJ, Manfredo MJ, Loomis JB (2005) Assessing validity of elk and deer license sales estimated by contingent valuation. Wildl Soc Bull 33:633–642. https://doi.org/10.2193/0091-7648(2005)33[633:AVOEAD]2.0.CO;2
Frank EG (2024) The economic impacts of ecosystem disruptions: Costs from substituting biological pest control. Science 385:eadg0344. https://doi.org/10.1126/science.adg0344
García-Díez J, Gonçalves C, Grispoldi L, Cenci-Goga B, Saraiva C (2021) Determining food stability to achieve food security. Sustainability 13:7222. https://doi.org/10.3390/su13137222
Getzner M (2015) Importance of free-flowing rivers for recreation: case study of the River Mur in Styria, Austria. J Water Resour Plan Manag 141:04014050. https://doi.org/10.1061/(ASCE)WR.1943-5452.0000442
Gren I-M, Häggmark-Svensson T, Elofsson K, Engelmann M (2018) Economics of wildlife management—an overview. Eur J Wildl Res 64:22. https://doi.org/10.1007/s10344-018-1180-3
Hanemann WM (1994) Valuing the environment through contingent valuation. J Econ Perspect 8:19–43. https://doi.org/10.1257/jep.8.4.19
Hanemann WM (1991) Willingness to pay and willingness to accept: how much can they differ? Am Econ Rev 81:635–647
Hanley N, Czajkowski M, Hanley-Nickolls R, Redpath S (2010) Economic values of species management options in human–wildlife conflicts: Hen Harriers in Scotland. Ecol Econ 70:107–113. https://doi.org/10.1016/j.ecolecon.2010.08.009
Hanley N, Hynes S, Patterson D, Jobstvogt N (2015) Economic valuation of marine and coastal ecosystems : is it currently fit for purpose? J Ocean Coast Econ 2. https://doi.org/10.15351/2373-8456.1014
Hanley N, Perrings C (2019) The economic value of biodiversity. Ann Rev Res Econ 11:355–375. https://doi.org/10.1146/annurev-resource-100518-093946

Hanley N, Wright RE, Adamowicz V (1998) Using choice experiments to value the environment. Environ Res Econ 11:413–428. https://doi.org/10.1023/A:1008287310583
Harihar A, Veríssimo D, MacMillan DC (2015) Beyond compensation: integrating local communities' livelihood choices in large carnivore conservation. Glob Environ Chang 33:122–130. https://doi.org/10.1016/j.gloenvcha.2015.05.004
Hawkins SA, Brady D, Mayhew M, Smith D, Iversen SV, Lipscombe S, White C, Eagle A, Convery I (2020) Community perspectives on the reintroduction of Eurasian lynx () to the UK. Restor Ecol 28:1408–1418. https://doi.org/10.1111/rec.13243
Herrero M, Grace D, Njuki J, Johnson N, Enahoro D, Silvestri S, Rufino MC (2013) The roles of livestock in developing countries. Animal 7:3–18. https://doi.org/10.1017/S1751731112001954
Hockley N (2014) Cost-benefit analysis: a decision-support tool or a venue for contesting ecosystem knowledge? Environ Plann C Gov Policy 32:283–300. https://doi.org/10.1068/c1384j
Holtmeier F-K (2015) Animals' influence on the landscape and ecological importance: natives, newcomers, homecomers. Springer Netherlands, Dordrecht. https://doi.org/10.1007/978-94-017-9294-3
Hutt CP, Hunt KM, Schlechte JW, Buckmeier DL (2013) Effects of catfish angler catch related attitudes on fishing trip preferences. North Am J Fish Manag 33:965–976. https://doi.org/10.1080/02755947.2013.822443
IPBES (2019) Summary for policymakers of the global assessment report on biodiversity and ecosystem services of the intergovernmental science-policy platform on biodiversity and ecosystem services. IPBES Secretariat, Bonn. https://doi.org/10.5281/zenodo.3553579
Irvine KN, O'Brien L, Ravenscroft N, Cooper N, Everard M, Fazey I, Reed MS, Kenter JO (2016) Ecosystem services and the idea of shared values. Ecosystem Services, Shared, Plural and Cultural Values 21:184–193. https://doi.org/10.1016/j.ecoser.2016.07.001
Isacs L, Kenter JO, Wetterstrand H, Katzeff C (2023) What does value pluralism mean in practice? An empirical demonstration from a deliberative valuation. People and Nature 5:384–402. https://doi.org/10.1002/pan3.10324
Jobstvogt N, Hanley N, Hynes S, Kenter J, Witte U (2014a) Twenty thousand sterling under the sea: estimating the value of protecting deep-sea biodiversity. Ecol Econ 97:10–19. https://doi.org/10.1016/j.ecolecon.2013.10.019
Jobstvogt N, Watson V, Kenter JO (2014b) Looking below the surface: the cultural ecosystem service values of UK marine protected areas (MPAs). Ecosyst Serv 10:97–110. https://doi.org/10.1016/j.ecoser.2014.09.006
Johannesen AB, Skonhoft A (2005) Tourism, poaching and wildlife conservation: what can integrated conservation and development projects accomplish? Resour Energy Econ 27:208–226. https://doi.org/10.1016/j.reseneeco.2004.10.001
Johansson M, Sjöström M, Karlsson J, Brännlund R (2012) Is human fear affecting public willingness to pay for the management and conservation of large carnivores? Soc Nat Resour 25:610–620. https://doi.org/10.1080/08941920.2011.622734
Kaffashi S, Yacob MR, Clark MS, Radam A, Mamat MF (2015) Exploring visitors' willingness to pay to generate revenues for managing the National Elephant Conservation Center in Malaysia. Forest Policy Econ 56:9–19. https://doi.org/10.1016/j.forpol.2015.03.004
Kenter JO (2016) Integrating deliberative monetary valuation, systems modelling and participatory mapping to assess shared values of ecosystem services. Ecosyst Serv 21:291–307.
Kenter, J.O., 2017. Deliberative Monetary Valuation, in: Routledge Handbook of Ecological Economics. Routledge.
Kenter JO, Hyde T, Christie M, Fazey I (2011) The importance of deliberation in valuing ecosystem services in developing countries—evidence from the Solomon Islands. Global Environ Change, Special Issue on the Politics and Policy of Carbon Capture and Storage 21:505–521. https://doi.org/10.1016/j.gloenvcha.2011.01.001
Kenter JO, Jobstvogt N, Watson V, Irvine KN, Christie M, Bryce R (2016a) The impact of information, value-deliberation and group-based decision-making on values for ecosystem services:

Integrating deliberative monetary valuation and storytelling. Ecosyst Serv Shared, Plural and Cultural Values 21:270–290. https://doi.org/10.1016/j.ecoser.2016.06.006
Kenter JO, O'Brien L, Hockley N, Ravenscroft N, Fazey I, Irvine KN, Reed MS, Christie M, Brady E, Bryce R, Church A, Cooper N, Davies A, Evely A, Everard M, Fish R, Fisher JA, Jobstvogt N, Molloy C, Orchard-Webb J, Ranger S, Ryan M, Watson V, Williams S (2015) What are shared and social values of ecosystems? Ecol Econ 111:86–99. https://doi.org/10.1016/j.ecolecon.2015.01.006
Kenter JO, O'Connor S (2022) The Life Framework of values and living as nature; towards a full recognition of holistic and relational ontologies. Sustain Sci. https://doi.org/10.1007/s11625-022-01159-2
Kenter JO, Raymond CM, van Riper CJ, Azzopardi E, Brear MR, Calcagni F, Christie I, Christie M, Fordham A, Gould RK, Ives CD, Hejnowicz AP, Gunton R, Horcea-Milcu A-I, Kendal D, Kronenberg J, Massenberg JR, O'Connor S, Ravenscroft N, Rawluk A, Raymond IJ, Rodríguez-Morales J, Thankappan S (2019) Loving the mess: navigating diversity and conflict in social values for sustainability. Sustain Sci 14:1439–1461. https://doi.org/10.1007/s11625-019-00726-4
Kenter JO, Reed MS, Fazey I (2016b) The Deliberative value formation model. Ecosyst Serv Shared, Plural and Cultural Values 21:194–207. https://doi.org/10.1016/j.ecoser.2016.09.015
Kenter JO, Reed MS, Irvine KN, O'Brien L, et al (2014) UK national ecosystem assessment follow-on. Work Package Report 6: Shared, plural and cultural values of ecosystems, UNEP-WCMC, LWEC, UK. ed. Cambridge
Lewis L, Raynor J, Richardson L (2024) The nature of the beast: wildlife valuation from the iconic to the ordinary. Ann Rev Res Econ 16:167–186. https://doi.org/10.1146/annurev-resource-101623-093149
Lienhoop N, Fischer A (2009) Can you be bothered? The role of participant motivation in the valuation of species conservation measures. J Environ Planning Manage 52:519–534. https://doi.org/10.1080/09640560902868405
Lo AY, Spash CL (2013) Deliberative monetary valuation. in search of a democratic and value plural approach to environmental policy. J Econ Surv 27:768–789. https://doi.org/10.1111/j.1467-6419.2011.00718.x
Mace GM (2014) Whose conservation? Science 345:1558–1560. https://doi.org/10.1126/science.1254704
MacMillan D, Hanley N, Lienhoop N (2006) Contingent valuation: environmental polling or preference engine? Ecol Econ 60:299–307. https://doi.org/10.1016/j.ecolecon.2005.11.031
MacMillan DC, Philip L, Hanley N, Alvarez-Farizo B (2002) Valuing the non-market benefits of wild goose conservation: a comparison of interview and group based approaches. Ecol Econ 43:49–59. https://doi.org/10.1016/S0921-8009(02)00182-9
Martino S, Kenter JO (2023) Economic valuation of wildlife conservation. Eur J Wildl Res 69:32. https://doi.org/10.1007/s10344-023-01658-2
Martino S, Tett P, Kenter J (2019) The interplay between economics, legislative power and social influence examined through a social-ecological framework for marine ecosystems services. Sci Total Environ 651:1388–1404. https://doi.org/10.1016/j.scitotenv.2018.09.181
Mensah JT, Elofsson K (2017) An empirical analysis of hunting lease pricing and value of game in Sweden. Land Econ 93:292–308. https://doi.org/10.3368/le.93.2.292
Methorst J, Arbieu U, Bonn A, Böhning-Gaese K, Müller T (2020) Non-material contributions of wildlife to human well-being: a systematic review. Environ Res Lett 15:093005. https://doi.org/10.1088/1748-9326/ab9927
Morse-Jones S, Bateman IJ, Kontoleon A, Ferrini S, Burgess ND, Turner RK (2012) Stated preferences for tropical wildlife conservation amongst distant beneficiaries: Charisma, endemism, scope and substitution effects. Ecol Econ 78:9–18. https://doi.org/10.1016/j.ecolecon.2011.11.002

Naranjo SE, Ellsworth PC, Frisvold GB (2015) Economic value of biological control in integrated pest management of managed plant systems. Annu Rev Entomol 60:621–645. https://doi.org/10.1146/annurev-ento-010814-021005
Ninan KN, Sathyapalan J (2005) The economics of biodiversity conservation: a study of a coffee growing region in the Western Ghats of India. Ecol Econ 55:61–72. https://doi.org/10.1016/j.ecolecon.2004.10.005
O'Connor S, Kenter JO (2019) Making intrinsic values work, integrating intrinsic values of the more-than-human world through the Life Framework of Values. Sustain Sci 14(5):1247–1265.
O'brien EA (2003) Human values and their importance to the development of forestry policy in Britain: a literature review. Forestry: Int J For Res 76, 3–17. https://doi.org/10.1093/forestry/76.1.3
Orchard-Webb J, Kenter JO, Bryce R, Church A (2016) Deliberative democratic monetary valuation to implement the ecosystem approach. Ecosyst Serv Shared, Plural and Cultural Values 21:308–318. https://doi.org/10.1016/j.ecoser.2016.09.005
Parks S, Gowdy J (2013) What have economists learned about valuing nature? A review essay. Ecosyst Serv 3:e1–e10. https://doi.org/10.1016/j.ecoser.2012.12.002
Pascual U, Balvanera P, Anderson CB, Chaplin-Kramer R, Christie M, González-Jiménez D, Martin A, Raymond CM, Termansen M, Vatn A, Athayde S, Baptiste B, Barton DN, Jacobs S, Kelemen E, Kumar R, Lazos E, Mwampamba TH, Nakangu B, O'Farrell P, Subramanian SM, van Noordwijk M, Ahn S, Amaruzaman S, Amin AM, Arias-Arévalo P, Arroyo-Robles G, Cantú-Fernández M, Castro AJ, Contreras V, De Vos A, Dendoncker N, Engel S, Eser U, Faith DP, Filyushkina A, Ghazi H, Gómez-Baggethun E, Gould RK, Guibrunet L, Gundimeda H, Hahn T, Harmáčková ZV, Hernández-Blanco M, Horcea-Milcu A-I, Huambachano M, Wicher NLH, Aydın Cİ, Islar M, Koessler A-K, Kenter JO, Kosmus M, Lee H, Leimona B, Lele S, Lenzi D, Lliso B, Mannetti LM, Merçon J, Monroy-Sais AS, Mukherjee N, Muraca B, Muradian R, Murali R, Nelson SH, Nemogá-Soto GR, Ngouhouo-Poufoun J, Niamir A, Nuesiri E, Nyumba TO, Özkaynak B, Palomo I, Pandit R, Pawłowska-Mainville A, Porter-Bolland L, Quaas M, Rode J, Rozzi R, Sachdeva S, Samakov A, Schaafsma M, Sitas N, Ungar P, Yiu E, Yoshida Y, Zent E (2023) Diverse values of nature for sustainability. Nature 620:813–823. https://doi.org/10.1038/s41586-023-06406-9
Pearce D, Atkinson G, Mourato S (2006) Cost-benefit analysis and the environment: recent developments. OECD, Paris, France
Philip LJ, MacMillan DC (2005) Exploring values, context and perceptions in contingent valuation studies: the CV market stall technique and willingness to pay for wildlife conservation. J Environ Planning Manage 48:257–274. https://doi.org/10.1080/0964056042000338172
Rathnayake RMW (2016) Pricing the enjoyment of 'elephant watching' at the Minneriya National Park in Sri Lanka: an analysis using CVM. Tour Manag Perspect 18:26–33. https://doi.org/10.1016/j.tmp.2016.01.002
Raymond CM, Anderson CB, Athayde S, Vatn A, Amin AM, Arias-Arévalo P, Christie M, Cantú-Fernández M, Gould RK, Himes A, Kenter JO, Lenzi D, Muraca B, Murali R, O'Connor S, Pascual U, Sachdeva S, Samakov A, Zent E (2023) An inclusive typology of values for navigating transformations towards a just and sustainable future. Curr Opin Environ Sustain 64:101301. https://doi.org/10.1016/j.cosust.2023.101301
Richardson L, Lewis L (2022) Getting to know you: individual animals, wildlife webcams, and willingness to pay for brown bear preservation. Am J Agr Econ 104:673–692. https://doi.org/10.1111/ajae.12249
Roe D, Nelson F, Sandbrook C (2009) Community management of natural resources in Africa. IIED.
Saayman M, Saayman A (2014) Who is willing to pay to see the big 7? Tour Econ 20:1181–1198. https://doi.org/10.5367/te.2013.0347
Sandhu H, Wratten S, Costanza R, Pretty J, Porter JR, Reganold J (2015) Significance and value of non-traded ecosystem services on farmland. PeerJ 3:e762. https://doi.org/10.7717/peerj.762

Schrobback P, Dennis G, Li Y, Mayberry D, Shaw A, Knight-Jones T, Marsh TL, Pendell DL, Torgerson PR, Gilbert W, Huntington B, Raymond K, Stacey DA, Bernardo T, Bruce M, McIntyre KM, Rushton J, Herrero M (2023) Approximating the global economic (market) value of farmed animals. Glob Food Sec 39:100722. https://doi.org/10.1016/j.gfs.2023.100722
Smith J, Sones K, Grace D, MacMillan S, Tarawali S, Herrero M (2013) Beyond milk, meat, and eggs: role of livestock in food and nutrition security. Anim Front 3:6–13. https://doi.org/10.2527/af.2013-0002
Spash CL (2007) Deliberative monetary valuation (DMV): Issues in combining economic and political processes to value environmental change. Ecological Econ Sustainability and Cost-Benefit Analysis 63:690–699. https://doi.org/10.1016/j.ecolecon.2007.02.014
Subroy V, Gunawardena A, Polyakov M, Pandit R, Pannell DJ (2019) The worth of wildlife: A meta-analysis of global non-market values of threatened species. Ecol Econ 164:106374. https://doi.org/10.1016/j.ecolecon.2019.106374
Sutton WR, Larson DM, Jarvis LS (2008) Assessing the costs of living with wildlife in developing countries using willingness to pay. Environ Dev Econ 13:475–495. https://doi.org/10.1017/S1355770X08004397
Turner RK, Paavola J, Cooper P, Farber S, Jessamy V, Georgiou S (2003) Valuing nature: lessons learned and future research directions. Ecol Econ 46:493–510. https://doi.org/10.1016/S0921-8009(03)00189-7
Tyohen BI, Mbakpenev TJ (2023) Impact of livestock farming on economci growth in Nigeria. UMM J Account Financ Manag 3:124–150
van Eeden LM, Bogezi C, Leng D, Marzluff JM, Wirsing AJ, Rabotyagov S (2021) Public willingness to pay for gray wolf conservation that could support a rancher-led wolf-livestock coexistence program. Biol Cons 260:109226. https://doi.org/10.1016/j.biocon.2021.109226
van Uhm DP (2016) The illegal wildlife trade: Inside the world of poachers. Springer, Smugglers and Traders
Vatn A, Pascual U, Chaplin-Kramer R, Termansen M, Arias-Arévalo P, Balvanera P, Athayde S, Hahn T, Lazos E (2024) Incorporating diverse values of nature in decision-making—theory and practice. Philos Trans R Soc B. https://doi.org/10.1098/rstb.2022.0315
Voelker M, Lienhoop N (2016) Exploring group dynamics in deliberative choice experiments. Ecol Econ 123:57–67. https://doi.org/10.1016/j.ecolecon.2016.01.006
Wang K, Liu H, Hu W, Cox L (2016) Using online self-assessment tool to improve conjoint analysis: application in choices of wildlife excursions. Internet Res 26:644–660. https://doi.org/10.1108/IntR-04-2014-0105
Wang Z, Gong Y, Mao X (2018) Exploring the value of overseas biodiversity to Chinese netizens based on willingness to pay for the African elephants' protection. Sci Total Environ 637–638:600–608. https://doi.org/10.1016/j.scitotenv.2018.04.417
Wätzold F, Lienhoop N, Drechsler M, Settele J (2008) Estimating optimal conservation in the context of agri-environmental schemes. Ecol Econ 68:295–305. https://doi.org/10.1016/j.ecolecon.2008.03.007
White C, Convery I, Eagle A, O'Donoghue P, Piper S, Rowcroft P, Smith D, van Maanen E (2015) Cost-benefit analysis for the reintroduction of lynx to the UK: main report (Report). AECOM

Part II
Predatory Interactions

Chapter 6
Animals as Food

Kelly McNamara

> "Barbarism is not outside civilization but built into its very structures."
> —*Timothy Pachirat*

Abstract Animal-sourced foods have long been central to human diets and economies, but their production today is dominated by industrial systems that externalize vast environmental, social, and ethical costs. This chapter reviews the limitations of neoclassical economic models in capturing these impacts and explores alternative valuation frameworks such as True Cost Accounting and Doughnut Economics. It then outlines a suite of policy reforms—including subsidy shifts, environmental regulation, financial disclosure standards, and animal welfare protections—that could realign food systems with ecological and ethical imperatives. By rethinking how we value and govern animal agriculture, we can move toward a more sustainable and humane future.

Industrial Appetite: The Global Economy of Animal-Based Foods

Throughout human history, animal-source foods (ASFs)—meat, dairy, eggs, and seafood—have been central to human sustenance and have profoundly shaped the evolution of societies, economies, and cultures. From early hunting and gathering to the domestication of livestock, these foods have long been associated with prosperity, health, and rising socioeconomic status across individuals, communities, and nations.

While hundreds of millions of smallholders, pastoralists, and Indigenous and traditional farmers raise livestock and rely on them for subsistence and income generation, modern animal agriculture is dominated by large-scale feed and animal production systems, including commercial fishing and aquaculture. In North America, an estimated 99% of animals used for food are bred and reared slaughtered in concentrated

K. McNamara (✉)
Food System Innovations, Climate & Nature Program, San Francisco, CA, USA
e-mail: kelly.mcnamara@fsi.org

N. Batini (ed.), *The Economics of Non-Human Animals*, Natural Resource Management and Policy 63, https://doi.org/10.1007/978-3-032-17580-9_6

animal feeding operations (CAFOs), or factory farms; globally, this figure is ~74%, including farmed fish (Ritchie 2023).

Since the mid-twentieth century, a combination of agricultural technologies, government subsidies, corporate consolidation, and international trade has transformed animal agriculture into a global industrial complex. Each year, 100 billion animals are used and/or killed for food that is then ill-distributed, leading to obesity and various co-morbidities in half the world's population and hunger among nearly 10% of it (Schlottmann and Sebo 2019; FAO, IFAD, UNICEF et al. 2024). In addition, an estimated 1–2.7 trillion wild fish and over 100 billion farmed fish are killed annually for human consumption, along with tens of thousands of marine mammals. Industrial mono-cropping of soy, corn, and other crops for livestock feed has additional negative impacts on human and ecological health. The rise of modern animal agriculture has also resulted in the displacement of smallholder farmers capable of rearing livestock in ways that promote animal health and welfare and derive utility from the sustainable integration of animals into organic, agroecological, and/or genuinely regenerative mixed crop systems that can preserve, rather than destroy, Earth's land, air, and water.

Adding to these negative impacts on human health, intensive systems of breeding, rearing, and slaughtering animals inflict extreme—and avoidable—physical and psychological suffering of tens of billions of land animals and hundreds of billions of sea creatures each year. Extreme confinement routine mutilations, the stress-inducing separation of mothers from their young, and pain and terror during transport and slaughter are ubiquitous across farmed animal species. Such cruelty is inflicted not only on cows, pigs, chickens, and other terrestrial animals on factory farms and feedlots but also on fish, shrimp, and other sea creatures in commercial fishing and aquaculture operations, which subject marine animals to overcrowding, injury, stress, and inhumane slaughter while contributing to ocean degradation, biodiversity loss, and the depletion of wild fish stocks.

The various cruelties inflicted on farmed and/or fished animals are designed to minimize costs, which generally rules out the extra expense of alleviating animals' suffering (Table 6.1). For example, chickens are "debeaked" with hot blades to minimize the injuries that hyper-confined birds may inflict on each other. Globally, egg producers cull billions of male chicks each year, primarily by dropping them alive into high-speed grinders, or "macerators". Piglets are subjected to surgical castration, generally without pain relief, to avoid naturally occurring "boar taint", which diminishes the palatability of pork. Piglets also have their ears "notched" in a painful process for purposes of identification and their teeth "clipped" or ground down to improve their general manageability in high-density industrial settings. Cow calves are separated from their mothers shortly after birth in a process that is highly distressing to mothers and their young to preserve all mothers' milk for dairy processing, and calves are also "disbudded" to prevent natural horn growth, generally with hot irons in a procedure generally regarded as among the cruelest in animal agriculture.

Fish and crustaceans are not spared. Marine caught and farmed fish are generally slaughtered while fully conscious, including by prolonged methods, farmed fish

Table 6.1 Sample harms suffered by factory-farmed animals

Species	Confinement	Mutilation/physical harm	Other cruelties
Pigs	Gestation crates (sows); farrowing crates	Manual castration of piglets; teeth clipping; tail docking; ear notching	Early weaning; inability to root or express natural behavior
Cows (beef/dairy)	Tie-stalls (dairy); veal crates (calves); feedlots (beef cattle)	Castration; branding (hot-iron or freeze); disbudding/dehorning	Separation of calves from mothers shortly after birth (dairy)
Chickens (broilers and layers)	Battery cages (layers); overcrowded barns (broilers)	Beak trimming (generally by hot blades)	Live maceration of male chicks (layers); rapid growth leads to leg deformities and other painful and/or death-inducing conditions (broilers)
Turkeys	Overcrowded barns	Beak and toe trimming (hot blades)	Selective breeding leads to crippling weight gain
Sheep	Feedlots; intensive wool farming	Mulesing; tail docking	Rough handling; shearing injuries; exposure to elements
Goats	Cramped dairy stalls	Disbudding; castration	Kid removal (dairy); poor flooring causes joint injuries
Fish (farmed)	High-density pens or cages	Fin and scale damage from crowding; forced starvation prior to slaughter	Asphyxiation or slow death via ice baths; parasite infestations (e.g., sea lice in salmon)
Shrimp (farmed)	High-density ponds; poor water quality	Eyestalk ablation (performed manually with scissors or hot blade to disrupt hormone cycles and accelerate reproduction in female shrimp)	Long-distance live transport; often boiled alive
Marine fish/shrimp (wild-caught)	Long trawl net confinement; crushing in nets	Fin damage; suffocation on decks	Massive bycatch; slow deaths; stress and injury from capture methods

suffer in conditions of extreme confinement and overcrowding, and female shrimp are subjected to "eyestalk ablation", the controversial and painful practice of slicing off their eyes to accelerate reproduction.

While some practices are restricted or banned in some regions, global trade combines with slim margins to make such bans politically unpopular and the practices persist. And animals are not the only ones who suffer. Several studies have examined the negative psychological impacts on the humans pressed into inflicting severe pain and suffering on completely defenseless and harmless creatures (Dillard 2007). Such impacts compound the various physical risks laborers in industrialized ASF production operations face. On a global basis, jobs in slaughterhouses and factory farms are characterized by physically demanding, repetitive, and hazardous work, long hours, low wages, and limited legal protections.

For all its negative impacts, the value of modern animal agriculture (inclusive of terrestrial and aquatic animal-based foods) is vast, with annual market values estimated between $1.6 trillion and $3.3 trillion (OECD-FAO 2022; Schrobback et al. 2023). Across regions and complementary industries, meat, dairy, egg, and seafood production employs hundreds of millions of workers, contributes significantly to global GDP, and is widely viewed as essential to nutrition and food security for much of the world's population. Yet these apparent benefits are measured almost entirely in transactional terms (i.e., outputs, revenue, trade) without accounting for the full costs of production.

Traditional economic valuation models fall short in three critical ways. First, they ignore externalities—the unpriced costs borne by ecosystems, animals, and future generations. Second, they treat animals as inert capital inputs rather than sentient creatures, thereby failing to capture the value of non-human animal suffering despite the fact that such suffering involves negative economic impacts. Third, traditional models equate price with value, excluding ethical, environmental, public health, and other costs associated with industrial animal agriculture.

This chapter challenges that paradigm. As we navigate an era of ecological crisis and food system transformation, we argue that securing a livable planet requires accounting for the true economic costs of producing and consuming animal-sourced foods. These include vast environmental damages—from deforestation and greenhouse gas emissions to water depletion and biodiversity collapse—as well as social costs such as chronic illness, antimicrobial resistance, zoonotic pandemic risk, labor exploitation, and the systematic suffering of non-human animals.

In what follows, we take a closer look at the global production and consumption of ASFs, examine the environmental and social externalities this creates, explore why current economic models misrepresent animal agriculture's negative environmental and social impacts, and propose an alternative valuation framework grounded in ecological, ethical, and economic integrity. Understanding and rethinking our economic approach to animal agriculture may hold the key to ensuring food security, environmental resilience, and ethical progress in the decades to come.

From Smallholders to Giants: The Economic Scale of ASF Production

Estimates of the total value of ASF production converge around US$ 1.6 T annually (OECD-FAO 2022; Schrobback et al. 2023), representing roughly 35% of global crop and livestock output (FAO 2024). (An estimate of farmed animals' total economic value (TEV) is higher, falling between the lower boundary of farmed animals' output value of $1.6 T and the higher boundary of their combined asset and output value of US$ 3.3 T. (See Schrobback et al. 2023). According to the UN Food and Agriculture Organization (FAO), the livestock sector accounts for approximately 35% of the global agricultural gross domestic product and supports the livelihoods of at least 1.3 billion people (FAO 2018).

Here, it is important to note that livestock/ASF production is far from monolithic. The sector spans a variety of species and systems that vary among and within global regions. However, production is highly concentrated among seven species (cattle [beef and dairy], chickens, cattle [beef and dairy], ducks, pigs, sheep, goats, and farmed fish) and two types of systems: (1) small-scale, traditional and/or agroecological and (2) industrial, or "factory farming".[1] While these systems intersect and sometimes overlap, a closer look at each is instructive.

On one end of the spectrum are hundreds of millions of subsistence and smallholder farmers, pastoralists, and fisherfolk for whom livestock are sources of labor, food, and wealth. According to the FAO, livestock-related activities account for roughly 15% of pastoralist and smallholder incomes, though in some regions, this figure is much higher (FAO 2018). Importantly, the majority of smallholder livestock farmers raise animals in mixed crop and livestock systems, with livestock serving as a buffer against losses during periods of low rainfall or crop failures and potentially providing resiliency against climatic shocks (Thornton and Herrero 2015).

On the other end of the spectrum are large-scale industrialized production systems. These extend from multi-thousand-hectare plantations dedicated to mono-cropping soy, corn, and other agri-commodities used for animal feed to CAFOs housing between thousands and hundreds of thousands of animals in cages and sheds, their manure stored in pits, lagoons, or tanks, and/or sprayed across sprawling fields of feed crops. Large-scale slaughtering plants can kill 5,000 cattle, 25,000 pigs, or 550,000 chickens per day (Saitone et al. 2024). A steady stream of inputs combines with modern logistics to facilitate distribution to retail, hospitality, and restaurant outlets, providing various types of ASFs via a range of outlets to billions of people. Dominated by multinational corporations headquartered across the Global North and

---

[1] Hunting (wild meat) remains an important source of food for several African nations that are also among the world's most food insecure, including Botswana, Côte d'Ivoire, Madagascar, Republic of Congo, Guinea, Rwanda, Central African Republic, and Zimbabwe, and whaling remains a source of meat and other products for indigenous and other populations in countries including Greenland, Iceland, Japan, Norway, and Russia (Booth et al. 2021; National Resources Defense Council [NRDC] 2020). Hunting and whaling both involve risks relating to biodiversity loss, zoonotic disease risk, and animal cruelty, all of which are relevant to this chapter. On a volume basis, however, neither yields a statistically relevant amount of ASFs.

South, industrial systems are establishing footholds in frontier markets, most notably Africa, where expanding urban populations and rising incomes are expected to fuel demand for industrially produced ASFs (Latino et al. 2020).[2]

This transformation is mirrored in the fisheries sector, where small-scale, community-based fishing—once the dominant mode of aquatic food production—has been increasingly displaced by large-scale industrial operations. Traditional fisherfolk, who historically relied on low-impact, seasonal, and regionally adapted practices, are now competing with multinational fleets employing massive trawlers, longlines, and purse seines capable of harvesting thousands of tons of fish in a single voyage. Industrial aquaculture has also expanded rapidly, often replacing coastal ecosystems such as mangroves and estuaries with high-density fish farms. These shifts have not only altered the economic geography of aquatic food systems but have also intensified ecological degradation, reduced marine biodiversity, and marginalized small-scale fishing communities.

The Road to Industrial Animal Agriculture

Since the mid-twentieth century, global ASF production has experienced unprecedented expansion, surpassing population growth rates and fundamentally transforming agricultural systems, dietary patterns, and environmental dynamics. In 1961, global terrestrial animal meat production totaled approximately 70 million tons. By 2022, the world's population had doubled while meat production had increased more than fourfold, exceeding 360 million tons (Roser 2023; Fig. 6.1). Seafood production followed a similar trend, more than quadrupling between 1970 and 2020. As marine fishing depleted natural stocks, aquaculture (farmed fishing) scaled to meet rising global demand and now accounts for roughly 60% of seafood production worldwide (Ritchie 2019; Fig. 6.1).

The expansion of ASF production is attributable to a series of factors: the convergence of population growth, rising per capita incomes, accelerating urbanization, and the proliferation of industrial agricultural systems spurred by the so-called Green Revolution, which involved technological innovations such as synthetic fertilizers, high-yield crop varieties, and advanced animal feed formulations that facilitated substantial increases in feed crop productivity.

However, the distribution of these gains has been highly unequal. High-income countries (HICs) have experienced elevated availability—and overconsumption—of animal-sourced foods, while some low and middle-income countries (LMICs) have continued to suffer food and nutrition insecurity that, in some cases, is attributable to a lack of access to meat and/or dairy products. Per capita meat consumption in the United States now exceeds 120 kg per person annually, representing an increase

[2] While each of these types of systems can stand in opposition to each other, they can also combine. Particularly in low and middle-income countries, smallholder and even pastoralist systems can be integrated into broader enterprises that provide farmers with access to urban and other retail markets.

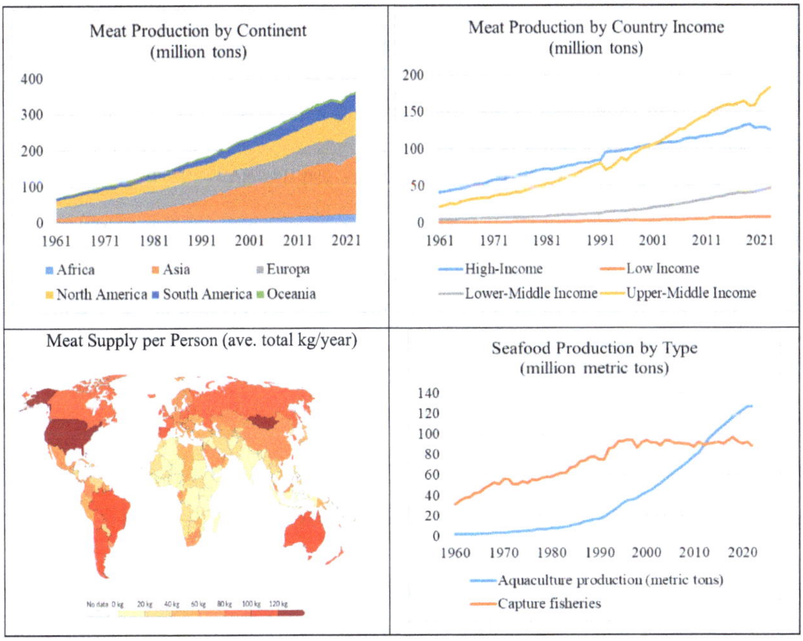

Fig. 6.1 Meat and seafood production, and meat consumption per person—1961–2023. 2024, 2025*Note* Total meat production includes both commercial and farm slaughter. Data are given in terms of dressed carcass weight, excluding offal and slaughter fats. Data excludes fish and other seafood sources. Figures do not correct for waste at the household/consumption level so may not directly reflect the quantity of food finally consumed by a given individual *Source* Meat data: Food and Agriculture Organization of the United Nations ()—with major processing by Our World in Data. OurWorldinData.org/meat-production (CC BY). Seafood data: Food and Agriculture Organization of the United Nations (via World Bank) (2025)—processed by Our World in Data (CC BY).

of 30% since 1960. This contrasts sharply with consumption rates of less than 10 kg observed in some LMICs (Our World in Data 2022).

Compounding the negative impacts of misdistribution is the high degree of waste involved in ASF production and distribution. Global estimates of food loss and waste (FLW) converge around 30% (UNEP 2024). While estimates of ASF FLW are generally lower than the total global average, an estimated 18B slaughtered animals are wasted each year, whether during the production or consumption phase (Klaura et al. 2023). Here, lower and higher levels of industrialization have conflicting impacts. Lower levels of industrialization (e.g., lack of access to markets, cold storage chain infrastructure) can mean higher levels of waste during production. Higher levels of industrialization associated with low prices can involve increased consumer-based losses, particularly in HICs.

Whatever the costs and benefits, ~74% of the world's ASF production now occurs in industrialized or "factory farm" settings, and the figure is increasing. Arguments in favor of industrializing ASF production include enhanced economic opportunities for farmers as well as modern infrastructure and technology reducing spoilage, improving animal health, and raising yields, helping countries meet rising protein demand while addressing micronutrient deficiencies (Adesogan et al. 2020). Arguments against the spread of factory farming into regions where it does not yet dominate it include the marginalization of smallholder farmers, loss of traditional agricultural knowledge and practices, environmental degradation, diminished market opportunities for farmers, and increased poverty among rural communities (Howard 2016).

Missing from all these arguments are broader questions about the costs of keeping animals at the center of our plates and assuming that increasing production, consumption, and industrialization of ASFs is both inevitable and sustainable when, in fact, it is neither.

These broader questions comprise the basis of inquiry for the remainder of this chapter.

The Hidden Bill: Environmental and Social Externalities

Contemporary animal agriculture systems impose far-reaching environmental and social externalities from ecological destruction to public health risks that remain unaccounted for in traditional economic assessments.

Clearing land for cattle grazing and feed production is the leading cause of deforestation worldwide, and livestock production is a major contributor to biodiversity loss, soil degradation, desertification, and eutrophication (pollution of estuaries and coastal waters), all of which negative impacts threaten to constrain global food production (Harwatt et al. 2022; Li et al. 2022; WRI 2024). Industrial fishing and aquaculture contribute to the degradation of marine ecosystems through overfishing, habitat destruction, nutrient pollution, and the spread of disease, further threatening aquatic biodiversity and the sustainability of global food systems (FAO 2020).

The livestock sector also involves negative social impacts with significant economic—and moral—consequences. In developed and emerging economies, the overconsumption of animal-based foods is a leading cause of chronic diseases including obesity, cancer, diabetes, and heart disease, the public costs of which are significant across low, middle, and high-income countries (Salter 2013; Bouvard et al. 2015; Barnard and Leroy 2020). Modern livestock operations are also notorious sources of animal diseases, including zoonoses with global pandemic potential like COVID-19, and the sector's persistent dependence on antibiotics means that by 2050, antimicrobial resistance (AMR) is on track to kill 10 M people per year (WHO 2019).

In every global region, industrial breeding, rearing, and slaughtering operations pollute the air, land, and water of the communities where they are located, putting residents at significant risk of related negative health impacts including cancer, heart disease, and respiratory illness (Walter et al. 2025; Hribar 2010; Miller and Murren 2019). Adding to these negative impacts, slaughterhouse workers rank among the world's most vulnerable to injury, illness, and lack of legal protections, and consolidation continues to threaten the livelihoods of smallholder and contract farmers across all global regions (Pew Charitable Trusts 2012; Eurofound 2018). Commercial fishing crews, particularly those working aboard distant-water fleets, also face exploitative and hazardous conditions. Many endure long hours, physical abuse, and in some cases, forced labor—conditions so severe that the International Labour Organization has identified fishing as one of the most dangerous professions globally, with labor abuses that often meet the threshold of trafficking and modern slavery (ILO 2013).

Paradoxically, livestock production also exacerbates the problem of human malnutrition and hunger by diverting resources to feed animals instead of humans. The European Commission's Joint Research Centre has called the use of highly productive croplands to produce animal feedstuffs a "net drain on the world's potential food supply", and the FAO has warned that further use of cereals as animal feed could threaten food security by diminishing supplies available for human consumption (European Commission 2019; Gerber et al. 2013).

In the remainder of this section, we take a closer look at how modern animal agriculture poses existential threats to other animals and their ecosystems in addition to jeopardizing the health of the human population, and we consider arguments for incorporating relevant costs into assessments of the sector's value.

Environmental Externalities of Industrial Animal Agriculture

The economic consequences of biodiversity loss are rapidly accelerating (WHO 2025). Modern animal agriculture is a primary driver and vulnerable to relevant impacts.

The World Economic Forum (WEF) estimates that over half of global GDP—approximately $44 trillion—is moderately or highly dependent on natural services, including pollination, water purification, and climate regulation (WEF 2024). Industrial animal agriculture systematically undermines these ecosystem services. Loss of pollinators alone could reduce global agricultural output value by $577 billion annually (IPBES 2016). Biodiversity loss also involves significant public health threats involving severe economic consequences. The World Health Organization has identified biodiversity loss as having significant implications for nutrition and health, including elevated risks of novel pandemic emergence.

Land-based livestock production constitutes a primary driver of global biodiversity loss through three interconnected mechanisms: (1) deforestation and land-use conversion; (2) industrial monoculture feed cropping (including widespread synthetic pesticide application and genetic modification); and (3) genetic engineering of livestock and aquatic species. These processes fundamentally alter ecosystems, diminish genetic diversity, and accelerate species extinction, generating substantial economic consequences via diminished agricultural productivity, negative public health impacts, and the degradation of natural resources on which various elements of the global economy depend. In addition, terrestrial livestock operations are significant sources of air pollution, emitting ammonia, methane, and particulate matter that contribute to respiratory illness, climate change, and environmental degradation.

In parallel, commercial fishing and aquaculture are major contributors to biodiversity loss in marine ecosystems. Overfishing has led to the collapse of numerous fish populations, disrupting food webs and reducing ocean resilience. Bycatch—the unintentional capture of non-target species such as dolphins, turtles, and seabirds—further accelerates species decline. Bottom trawling destroys seafloor habitats, while aquaculture operations contribute to genetic pollution, disease transmission, and nutrient loading in coastal waters. These impacts threaten the long-term viability of marine biodiversity and the ecosystem services it provides, including carbon sequestration, fisheries productivity, and coastal protection—services that are vital to both environmental stability and economic security.

1. Deforestation and Land-Use Conversion

The clearing of forests and entire ecosystems for industrial cattle grazing and feed production represents the leading global driver of tropical deforestation (WRI 2024). Despite numerous corporate zero-deforestation commitments and anticipated enforcement of the EU Deforestation Regulation (EUDR), 2024 witnessed record levels of tropical deforestation driven by illegal clearing and fires (Goldman et al. 2025).

Land conversion systematically replaces complex ecosystems with simplified landscapes that support merely a fraction of previous biodiversity levels. Such losses affect not only wildlife populations but also microbial communities vital for soil health, water filtration, and carbon sequestration. This transformation of land use has also drastically altered the global distribution of biomass among mammals and birds. Today, the vast majority of terrestrial mammalian biomass is composed of humans and their domesticated livestock, with wild mammals representing only a small fraction. Similarly, poultry now vastly outnumber wild birds (Fig. 6.2).

2. Industrial Monoculture Feed Cropping

An estimated 35–40% of the global cropland is dedicated to animal feed crops, primarily monocultures such as soy and corn (Cassidy et al. 2013; Ritchie and Roser 2019). Large-scale industrial mono-cropping operations rely heavily on synthetic fertilizers and pesticides to maintain yields and enable the consolidation of farmland into large, homogeneous blocks. This structural transformation has systematically devastated plant and insect diversity (Benton et al. 2021).

Industrial mono-cropping supports substantially fewer species than diversified cropping systems and inflict considerable harm on critical pollinators, including bees and butterflies (van der Sluijs and Vaage 2016). Widespread pesticide application has been definitively linked to declines in insect biomass and diversity, which subsequently affects avian populations and other wildlife dependent on insects for sustenance (Forister et al. 2019).

The pollution generated by industrial livestock operations extends beyond terrestrial systems. In addition to nitrogen and phosphorus from synthetic fertilizers,

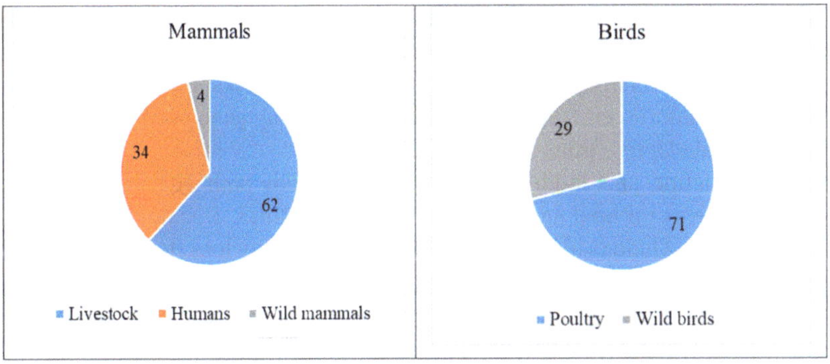

Fig. 6.2 Global share of wildlife versus humans and domesticated animals. *Source* Bar-On et al. (2018). The biomass distribution on Earth. Proceedings of the National Academy of Sciences. OurWorldinData.org.—Research and data to make progress against the world largest problems. Licensed under CC-BY by the authors Hannah Ritchie and Klara Auerbach. https://ourworldindata.org/wild-mammals-birds-biomass

contaminants include heavy metals from feed additives, ammonia from concentrated animal waste, nitrates, antibiotics, and disease-causing pathogens. These pollutants have contaminated and continue to contaminate air, land, and water resources with global consequences, contributing to the current exceedance of safe planetary boundaries for biodiversity loss and oceanic pollution (Richardson et al. 2023).

3. Genetic Engineering of Livestock and Aquatic Species

Contemporary breeding practices in industrial livestock production prioritize traits such as rapid growth, high feed conversion efficiency, and phenotypic uniformity. This approach has generated an alarming reduction in genetic diversity, with a limited number of highly selected breeds now dominating not only global livestock populations but also global human and non-human animal populations more generally.

Such genetic homogeneity increases vulnerability to disease outbreaks, as single pathogens can rapidly spread through genetically similar populations with minimal resistance (Springbett et al. 2003; Hayek 2022). Such vulnerability creates substantial risks for CAFOs and similar intensive systems. Beginning in the mid-late 2010s, outbreaks of African Swine Fever (ASF) and Highly Pathogenic Avian Influenza (HPAI) resulted in the destruction of billions of animals, raising pollution and animal welfare concerns with respect to the methods used (Bolotnikova 2022; Khanna 2022).

Genetic engineering of farmed animals raises additional concerns around animal welfare. Genetically manipulated farmed animals frequently exhibit compromised immune systems and chronic health disorders. Broiler chickens bred for accelerated growth, for example, commonly experience skeletal disorders and organ failure (Nuffield Council on Bioethics 2021; CiWF 2023). These welfare issues represent not only ethical concerns but also economic risks, resulting in elevated mortality rates and increased dependence on antibiotic interventions.

Aquaculture systems increasingly utilize genetically modified or selectively bred fish, particularly salmon and tilapia. These practices mirror terrestrial systems in reducing genetic diversity while also creating ecological risks. For example, escaped farmed fish can interbreed with wild populations, diluting gene pools and potentially introducing maladaptive traits (Muir 2004).

Food production and biodiversity preservation will both become increasingly important as stress on land and other resources intensifies. Because any shift from natural to managed land is likely to result in net biodiversity loss (Benton et al. 2021), it is imperative to prioritize the use of agricultural land in ways that preserve ecological balance and diversity and demonstrate enhanced resiliency to environmental shocks. It is also imperative that we use agricultural land to feed humans instead of farmed animals.

4. Air Pollution from Animal Agriculture

Modern animal agriculture is a major source of air pollution, emitting a range of harmful substances that affect both environmental and human health. Livestock operations release large quantities of ammonia, which reacts with other pollutants in the atmosphere to form fine particulate matter (PM2.5), a leading cause of respiratory and cardiovascular disease (Batini 2021). Methane, produced during enteric fermentation in ruminants and from manure storage, is released in vast quantities, contributing to atmospheric instability and the degradation of air quality. In addition, hydrogen sulfide, volatile organic compounds (VOCs), and bioaerosols are emitted from concentrated animal feeding operations (CAFOs), often affecting nearby communities and ecosystems.

These emissions are frequently unregulated or under-monitored, despite their well-documented health risks and environmental impacts (Heinzen 2015). These combined impacts—air, water, and odor pollution—not only create serious public health risks but also reduce the economic value of nearby assets, particularly residential property. Studies have shown that proximity to large-scale livestock operations can significantly lower housing prices, deter investment, and erode local tax bases (Herriges et al. 2003).

Social Externalities of Industrial Animal Agriculture

Modern animal agriculture generates a range of social externalities—costs borne not by producers or consumers, but by the broader public. Among the most pressing are the rise of non-communicable diseases (NCDs), the global threat of antimicrobial resistance (AMR), the displacement of smallholder farmers, labor exploitation, and the exacerbation of global food insecurity. These impacts are deeply intertwined with the structure and scale of industrial animal production systems.

1. Chronic Disease and Overconsumption of Animal-Sourced Foods

Animal-sourced foods (ASFs) are rich in essential nutrients such as protein, vitamin B12, iron, calcium, and omega-3 fatty acids. However, in high-income and increasingly in middle-income countries, excessive consumption of industrially produced meat, eggs, and dairy has been linked to a surge in diet-related NCDs, including heart disease, obesity, and certain cancers. The Harvard T.H. Chan School of Public Health estimates that the United States alone spends over $50 billion annually on health care costs related to diet-driven illnesses associated with high ASF consumption (Jardim et al. 2019).

These health burdens are not evenly distributed. While some populations suffer from overconsumption, others face undernutrition and hunger—both outcomes of a global food system that prioritizes industrial animal agriculture over equitable food access. The EAT-Lancet Commission (Willett et al. 2019) has shown that many of the nutrients provided by ASFs can be obtained from plant-based sources with significantly lower environmental and health costs.

2. Public Health Risks from Proximity to Industrial Operations

Beyond dietary impacts, communities living near concentrated animal feeding operations (CAFOs), slaughterhouses, and monoculture feed plantations face direct health threats. These include exposure to airborne pollutants, contaminated water, and hazardous chemicals. Studies have linked proximity to industrial livestock operations with increased risks of cancer, respiratory illness, and cardiovascular disease (Hribar 2010; May et al. 2012). In the United States, industrial animal agriculture is estimated to cause approximately 13,000 premature deaths annually due to air pollution alone (Animal Legal Defense Fund 2021). These impacts disproportionately affect low-income and marginalized communities, raising serious environmental justice concerns.

3. Antimicrobial Resistance (AMR)

Industrial livestock systems routinely administer antibiotics to animals—not only to treat illness but also to promote growth and prevent disease in overcrowded, unsanitary conditions. In the United States, approximately 80% of all antibiotics sold are used in animal agriculture (Martin et al. 2015), with the global figure estimated at around 70% (Ritchie and Spooner 2024). This widespread use of antimicrobials has accelerated the emergence of AMR, rendering many antibiotics less effective or even obsolete. According to Naghavy et al. (2024), drug-resistant infections are projected to cause over 39 million deaths between 2025 and 2050. The World Bank (2017) warns that AMR could reduce global GDP by 3.8% by 2050, with losses reaching $3.4 trillion as early as 2030.

4. Zoonotic Disease Emergence

A century after the 1918 H1N1 avian influenza killed 50 million people, deadly infectious diseases continue to emerge from intensive agriculture operations. Since the mid-1980s alone, several have caused outbreaks among animals and humans and remain persistent threats to each. Creutzfeldt-Jakob ("mad cow") disease (1986), H5N1 avian flu (1997), severe acute respiratory syndrome (SARS, 2003), H1N1 swine flu (2009), and H7N9 avian flu (2013) all spread among animals in livestock operations before spreading among and sickening and/or killing humans.

Terrestrial and aquatic livestock production systems involving close confinement of animals in unsanitary conditions, poor air quality, and untreated animal illness, injury, and stress combine to increase the likelihood and spread of infectious disease among farmed animals (Sebo 2022). At least some of these diseases are "zoonotic", or transmissible to humans. The abysmal conditions in which most farmed animals live operate synergistically with biodiversity loss resulting from deforestation and habitat conversion as well as genetic engineering to drive pathogen adaptation and emergence (Wallace 2016; Sebo 2022).

Changes in land use, including deforestation, involve human interaction with wildlife that contributes to the emergence of zoonotic diseases, while the lack of genetic diversity among animals in high-density systems facilitates pathogen spread. Industrial agriculture's reliance on genetic monocultures of domesticated birds eliminates natural immunity barriers and facilitates rapid pathogen transmission through susceptible populations (Wallace 2016). Waste management and live animal transport, including international trade, also facilitate pathogen spread, while biosecurity measures may eliminate less virulent pathogen strains that might provide natural inoculation effects, creating ecological niches for more dangerous variants (Wallace 2016). Prophylactic antibiotic use drives the origination of antibiotic-resistant pathogens, presenting threats to livestock populations and humans (Pew Charitable Trusts 2017).

Zoonotic diseases represent 60% of total human pathogens and roughly 75% of novel pathogens that have emerged since the mid-1980s (WHO 2014; UNEP and ILRI 2020).

5. Food Insecurity and Resource Inefficiency

Industrial animal agriculture also contributes to global hunger by diverting vast quantities of food and land toward livestock feed. While nearly 9 million people die from hunger-related causes each year, factory-farmed animals consume over 75% of the world's soy and 36–40% of all cereals (Cassidy et al. 2013; Ritchie and Spooner 2024). Yet these systems return only 37% of the world's protein and 18% of its calories (Poore & Nemecek 2018).

The European Commission's Joint Research Centre has described the use of prime cropland for animal feed as a "net drain on the world's potential food supply" (European Commission 2019). The FAO has similarly warned that continued diversion of cereals to livestock could undermine global food security (Gerber et al. 2013). If land and crops currently used for animal feed were redirected to human consumption, an additional 3.5 to 4 billion people could be fed each year (Cassidy et al. 2013). Table 6.2 below illustrates the inefficiency of converting plant-based calories and protein into animal products, reinforcing the argument that current livestock feeding practices squander valuable food resources that could otherwise nourish billions of people directly.

Table 6.2 Livestock conversion efficiencies in calories and protein

	Dairy	Eggs	Chicken	Pork	Beef
Calorie conversion efficiency (%)	40	22	12	10	3
Protein conversion efficiency (%)	43	35	40	10	5

Source This table is adapted (formatting only) from Cassidy et al. (2013). *Redefining agricultural yields: from tons to people nourished per hectare, Environmental Research* Letters 8, no. 3, 034015, Table 6.1. https://doi.org/10.1088/1748-9326/8/3/034015.

Note Feed-to-food calorie conversions for milk, eggs, chicken, pork, and beef are shown from left to right

6. Labor Exploitation and Displacement

The industrialization of animal agriculture has also reshaped rural economies and labor markets. Decades of corporate consolidation have displaced smallholder farmers—whom the World Economic Forum (2022) identifies as "central" to global food security. In their place, industrial operations rely on a labor force that is often underpaid, undocumented, and exposed to hazardous working conditions, including children in some regions.

The Corporate Grip on Animal Farming

The rise of modern agricultural technologies, globalization, and market liberalization has enabled large agribusiness corporations to deliver standardized animal-sourced products to global consumers with remarkable efficiency. These corporations benefit from economies of scale, vertically integrated supply chains, and concentrated market power. However, this consolidation has also produced significant negative externalities, particularly for smallholder farmers and rural communities.

During the past several decades, corporate control over livestock supply chains has intensified, displacing small-scale producers and reducing their bargaining power. This has led to widespread economic instability and the erosion of rural livelihoods. The imperative to "get big or get out" has proven financially devastating for many farmers and communities in both developed and emerging markets (Pew Charitable Trusts 2012; Meemken and Bellemare 2020; Gliessman 2022). Even hybrid systems, such as peri-urban landless dairies, often result in economic hardship due to high input costs and environmental degradation from improper waste disposal (FAO 2025).

In developed markets, particularly the United States, the livestock sector is dominated by a handful of powerful corporations. For example, just four companies—JBS, Tyson, Cargill, and National Beef (owned by Marfrig)—control over 80% of US beef processing. These firms wield significant political influence, spending over $500 million between 2019 and 2023 to shape legislation such as the US Farm Bill (Tarrant 2024). This lobbying has often delayed or weakened environmental and social regulations intended to protect ecosystems and communities.

Moreover, labor conditions in industrial animal agriculture are often exploitative. As discussed earlier in this chapter, jobs in slaughterhouses and factory farms are characterized by physically demanding, repetitive, and hazardous work, long hours, low wages, and limited legal protections. In addition to the psychological trauma associated with inflicting painful injuries and death on defenseless animals, laborers also face elevated risks of injury, chronic illness, and exposure to zoonotic pathogens.

Behind the Barn Doors and Inside the Nets

The Scale and Nature of Animal Suffering

Industrial animal agriculture is built on a foundation of systemic animal suffering. Large-scale breeding, rearing, and slaughter operations prioritize productivity and efficiency over welfare, subjecting animals to overcrowded conditions, routine mutilations without anesthesia, and unnatural environments that deprive them of the ability to express basic behaviors.

Beef cattle may be confined in feedlots where they are fattened rapidly on grain-based diets that can cause digestive disorders. Pigs are often kept in gestation crates so small they cannot turn around, and piglets routinely have their tails docked and teeth clipped without pain relief. Chickens raised for meat (broilers) are bred to grow so quickly that many suffer from leg deformities and organ failure, while egg-laying hens are confined in battery cages with less space than a sheet of paper per bird. Ducks and geese, especially in foie gras production, are force-fed multiple times a day through metal tubes inserted into their throats, leading to liver disease and severe discomfort.

Animals raised for food are not only killed for meat but also suffer even when used for products like milk and eggs. Dairy cows are repeatedly impregnated to maintain milk production and are routinely separated from their calves within hours of birth, causing distress to both mother and offspring. Goats and sheep used for milk endure similar reproductive exploitation, with kids and lambs often removed shortly after birth. Egg-laying hens are confined in battery cages or crowded cage-free barns, where they may suffer from feather loss, bone fractures, and stress-induced behaviors like pecking. Chicks deemed male and therefore unproductive in the egg industry are typically culled shortly after hatching, often by maceration or gassing. Quail, used increasingly for eggs and meat, are also kept in cramped, barren cages with little to no enrichment.

These practices are standard, not exceptional, and they cause immense suffering from birth to death. The physical toll is compounded by psychological distress, as animals are denied the ability to engage in natural behaviors such as nesting, rooting, grazing, or social bonding. In industrial systems, animals are treated as units of production rather than sentient beings, with suffering embedded into the very structure of vertically integrated supply chains.

Fish, too, suffer immensely in food production systems, though their suffering is often overlooked. Commercial fishing and aquaculture subject trillions of fish annually to prolonged and painful deaths (Van de vis 1996). Many fish are asphyxiated over the course of 25–250 min, sometimes while being gutted alive or chilled in ice water—methods that prolong distress. Capture methods such as trawling, gillnetting, and long-lining often cause severe exhaustion, injury, and stress, with some fish trapped for hours or even days. The scale of this suffering is staggering: estimates suggest that over 1 trillion fish are killed each year, making commercial fishing one of the largest and most severe animal welfare issues globally.

The Human Cost of Animal Suffering

The consequences of poor animal welfare extend beyond the animals themselves. Overcrowded and stressed animals are more susceptible to disease, increasing the risk of foodborne illnesses and zoonotic disease outbreaks. The 2008 Hallmark/Westland Meatpacking Company case in the United States revealed how animal cruelty can lead to massive food safety violations. Weeks after an exposé of animal cruelty at the Chino, California-based facility, Hallmark/Westland recalled a record 143 million pounds of beef. Following a protracted legal battle, the company declared bankruptcy in 2012.

Poor welfare conditions also contribute to non-zoonotic disease spread, pollution, and economic losses associated with food recalls, public health crises, and environmental degradation from concentrated animal feeding operations (CAFOs). These costs are rarely accounted for in economic models but are borne by taxpayers, consumers, and ecosystems.

Psychological and Social Impacts

The normalization of animal suffering in industrial systems contributes to a broader dissociation from the realities of food production. This dissociation limits empathy and desensitizes society to the suffering of the most vulnerable—both human and non-human. It also reflects a deeper moral and democratic crisis, as laws like the US Animal Enterprise Terrorism Act (AETA) and other countries' similar "ag-gag" laws restrict public access to information about how animals are treated, undermining transparency and the public's right to know.

This erosion of empathy and accountability comes at a time when the planet is facing unprecedented ecological and ethical challenges. The refusal to confront the suffering embedded in our food systems represents a profound opportunity cost—a missed chance to build more just, sustainable, and compassionate systems.

Shifting Norms and Legal Reforms

Despite industry resistance, consumer awareness and concern are growing. Public pressure has led to significant reforms in animal welfare laws and corporate practices.

Since the late 1990s, the European Union has banned several confinement systems, including veal crates, the continuous use of gestation crates for sows, and unenriched battery cages for laying hens. While the United States has failed to implement any such bans at the federal level, twelve states have imposed restrictions on the in-state sale of products from pigs raised in systems that use gestation crates. To date, legal challenges to these restrictions have failed, including a 2019 attempt to overturn California's Proposition 12.

What's Missing from the Price Tag? Rethinking Valuation in Animal Agriculture

Neoclassical economic models, which dominate food system analysis, are fundamentally ill-equipped to assess the true costs of animal agriculture. By focusing narrowly on human preferences and utility maximization, these models treat animals as non-sentient capital inputs and ignore the ethical and ecological dimensions of food production. As Peter Singer has long argued, the failure to account for animal suffering in economic systems reflects a profound moral blind spot—one that enables the continued exploitation of sentient beings on an industrial scale. These models also externalize major environmental and social costs such as biodiversity loss, public health risks, and greenhouse gas emissions, creating the illusion that cheap animal products are economically efficient. Market prices reflect only short-term exchange value, while long-term planetary and moral costs remain invisible. Discount rates further obscure the consequences of today's agricultural practices for future generations.

Emerging frameworks offer more comprehensive approaches. True Cost Accounting seeks to quantify externalities and assess agriculture's net social and environmental value. The TEEBAgriFood Framework (2018) is one such model already in use, aiming to integrate these hidden costs into decision-making. Doughnut Economics, proposed by Kate Raworth (2017), goes further by embedding economic activity within ecological ceilings and social foundations. This model reveals how industrial animal agriculture overshoots planetary boundaries while failing to meet basic standards of justice and welfare.

Policy and Market Reforms for a Smart and Just Food Future

Transforming the global food system requires more than consumer awareness or technological innovation—it demands bold, systemic policy change. Industrial animal agriculture is sustained by a web of subsidies, weak regulations, and market distortions that obscure its true costs. To build a food system that is equitable, sustainable, and humane, governments and institutions must adopt policies that internalize externalities, protect public goods, and reflect the intrinsic value of non-human animals.

1. Redirecting Public Funds

Globally, approximately $470 billion of the $540 billion in annual agricultural subsidies support environmentally harmful practices (FAO, UNDP, UNEP 2021). Redirecting these funds toward plant-based, agroecological, traditional husbandry, and polycultural systems could accelerate the transition to sustainable food production.

2. Promoting Healthy, Plant-Forward Diets

National dietary guidelines, public education, and institutional procurement policies can promote plant-based diets that meet nutritional needs while reducing environmental and ethical harms. The EAT-Lancet Commission (Willett et al. 2019) confirms that well-planned plant-based diets can provide all essential nutrients.

3. Environmental and Fiscal Policies

Proponents of the "polluter pays" principle have advocated for regulations that impose the costs associated with damage to the environmental and/or human health on the entities that have caused it. However, unlike other major polluting industries, livestock producers have historically been subjected to minimal environmental regulation despite generating significant air, water, and soil contamination. So-called agricultural exceptionalism has enabled animal agriculture to remain largely exempt from the pollution control standards applied to manufacturing, energy, and transportation sectors while also keeping government subsidies intact (Trebilcock and Pue 2015; Levandowski 2020).

Taxes on ASFs have emerged as a potential alternative or complement to environmental regulations. Modeled after excise taxes on products such as tobacco and carbon-intensive fuels, proposals have sought to adjust market prices to reflect the true societal costs of meat production, which are typically excluded from current pricing structures. Proponents argue that taxes offer a range of potential benefits, including reducing polluting emissions from large-scale operations, minimizing land and water degradation, lowering public healthcare expenditures associated with high meat consumption, and generating public revenue that could be reinvested in health or environmental initiatives. However, critics warn of taxes' regressive nature, noting that lower-income households—who spend a larger proportion of their income on food—may be disproportionately affected.

While no country has yet adopted a comprehensive national meat tax, several have contemplated such measures, in some cases in conjunction with subsidy reforms (Kmeťková et al. 2025).

In addition to such environmental and/or fiscal measures, regulations such as the EU Corporate Sustainability Reporting Directive (CSRD) and global disclosure frameworks such as those published by the International Sustainability Standards Board (ISSB), the Taskforce on Climate-Related Financial Disclosures (TCFD), and the Taskforce on Nature-Related Financial Disclosures (TNFD), can help expose and hold industrial ASF producers accountable for the negative environmental and social impacts of their operations and redirect capital away from high-impact industries toward regenerative, nature-positive systems. These include agroforestry and circular livestock systems that integrate animals into ecosystems rather than isolate them from them.

4. Transparency, Accountability, and Consumer Protection

Mandatory labeling on animal welfare and environmental impact can empower consumers to make informed choices. Repealing ag-gag laws would increase transparency and industry accountability.

5. Strengthening Animal Welfare Laws

Regulations should ban confinement systems and routine mutilations in addition to requiring higher-welfare practices such as in-ovo sexing (to avoid the mass killing of billions of male chicks each year), medical castration of pigs and other animals, and controlled atmospheric stunning (CAS) of chickens and pigs prior to/at the time of slaughter. Adherence to the most recent Office of Economic Development (OECD) Guidelines for Multinational Enterprises on Responsible Business Conduct (2023) would require that farmed animals do not suffer from pain, fear, or distress and are able to express behaviors that are essential for their physical and mental well-being. By requiring sufficient space and freedom from physical and psychological suffering, such adherence would effectively eliminate conventional factory farming.

6. Investing in Innovation

Public and private investment in plant-based meat alternatives and cellular agriculture can reduce reliance on traditional animal farming while creating new economic opportunities.

These policy reforms are not only feasible but also essential. By aligning economic incentives with ecological and ethical imperatives, governments can help transition the food system toward one that nourishes people, protects the planet, and respects the lives of animals. The path forward requires courage, coordination, and a willingness to rethink the rules that have long governed what—and whom—we value in our economies.

Conclusions

This chapter has examined the economic structures, valuation gaps, and policy failures that underpin the global animal agriculture system. From the invisibilized suffering of animals to the externalized costs borne by ecosystems and communities, the current model is neither sustainable nor just.

Yet alternatives exist. By adopting more holistic valuation frameworks and implementing bold policy reforms, we can build a food system that respects animals, protects the planet, and promotes human well-being. The future of food must be measured not only in profits and calories, but also in sound economics, social equity, ecological resilience, and compassion for animals. A food system that prioritizes justice and well-being across species is not just ethically necessary. It is economically smarter, more sustainable, and more resilient in the face of global challenges.

References

Adesogan AT, Havelaar AH, McKune SL, et al (2020) Animal source foods: Sustainability problem or malnutrition and sustainability solution? Perspective Matters. Glob Food Secur 25.

Animal Legal Defense Fund (2021) Urging the EPA to regulate factory farms' air pollution. https://aldf.org/case/urging-the-environmental-protection-agency-to-stop-giving-factory-farms-a-free-pass-on-air-pollution/#:~:text=A%20recent%20study%20on%20the,are%20raised%20for%20food%20production

Barnard ND, Leroy F (2020) Children and adults should avoid consuming animal products to reduce risk for chronic disease: YES. Am J Clin Nutr 112(4):926–930. https://doi.org/10.1093/ajcn/nqaa235. PMID: 32889521

Bar-On YM, Phillips R, Milo R (2018) The biomass distribution on Earth. Proc Natl Acad Sci 115(25):6506–6511. https://doi.org/10.1073/pnas.1711842115

Batini N (ed) (2021) The economics of sustainable food: smart policies for health and the planet. Island Press, Washington, D.C.

Benton TG, Bieg C, Harwatt H et al (2021) Food system impacts on biodiversity loss three levers for food system transformation in support of nature. Chatham House, London

Bolotnikova M (2022) 'They're cooking them alive': calls to ban 'cruel' killing methods on US farms. Guardian. https://www.theguardian.com/environment/2022/mar/08/theyre-cooking-them-alive-calls-to-ban-cruel-killing-methods-on-us-farms

Booth H, Clark M, Milner-Gulland EJ, et al (2021) Investigating the risks of removing wild meat from global food systems. Curr Biol 31(8)

Bouvard V, Loomis D, Guyto KZ et al (2015) Carcinogenicity of consumption of red and processed meat. Lancet Oncol 16(16):1599–1600

Cassidy ES, West PC, Gerber JS, et al (2013) Redefining agricultural yields: from tonnes to people nourished per hectare. Environ Res Lett 8(3). https://doi.org/10.1088/1748-9326/8/3/034015

Compassion in World Farming (CiWF) (2023) Factory farming: who benefits? how a ruinous system is kept afloat. https://www.ciwf.org.uk/news/who-benefits-big-ag-myths-shot-down/

Dillard J (2007) A slaughterhouse nightmare: psychological harm suffered by slaughterhouse employees and the possibility of redress through legal reform. Georgetown J Poverty Law Policy

European Commission (2019) Global impact of livestock. https://wad.jrc.ec.europa.eu/impactlivestock

European Foundation for the Improvement of Living and Working Conditions (Eurofound) (2018) Meat processing workers: occupational report. https://euagenda.eu/upload/publications/untitled-178347-ea.pdf
FAO (2018) World livestock: transforming the livestock sector through the sustainable development goals. Rome. https://doi.org/10.4060/ca1201en
FAO (2020) The state of world fisheries and aquaculture 2020: sustainability in action. Rome. https://doi.org/10.4060/ca9229en
FAO (2024) The state of food and agriculture 2024—value-driven transformation of agrifood systems. Rome. https://doi.org/10.4060/cd2616en
FAO (2025) Gateway to dairy production and products. https://www.fao.org/dairy-production-products/production/production-systems/en/
FAO, IFAD, UNICEF, et al (2024) The state of food security and nutrition in the world 2024: financing to end hunger, food insecurity and malnutrition in all its forms. Rome. https://doi.org/10.4060/cd1254en
FAO, UNDP, UNEP (2021) A multi-billion-dollar opportunity—Repurposing agricultural support to transform food systems. Rome, FAO. https://doi.org/10.4060/cb6562en
Forister ML, Pelton EM, Black SH (2019) Declines in insect abundance and diversity: We know enough to act now. Conservation Science and Practice 1:e80. https://doi.org/10.1111/csp2.80
Gerber PJ, Steinfeld H, Henderson B, et al (2013) Tackling climate change through livestock—a global assessment of emissions and mitigation opportunities. Rome
Gliessman S (2022) Smaller farms or factory farms?: an agroecological perspective. Agroecol Sustain Food Syst 46(10):1443–1444. https://doi.org/10.1080/21683565.2022.2124661
Goldman E, Carter S, Sims M (2025) Fires drove record-breaking tropical forest loss in 2024. World Resources Institute (WRI) Global Forest Watch. https://gfr.wri.org/latest-analysis-deforestation-trends
Hansen ME, Rosini S (2018) Meat processing workers: Future of manufacturing in Europe. European Foundation for the Improvement of Living and Working Conditions (Eurofound), Dublin.
Harwatt H, Wetterberg K, Giritharan A, Benton TG (2022) Aligning food systems with climate and biodiversity targets: Assessing the suitability of policy action over the next decade. R Inst Int Affairs, London. https://doi.org/10.55317/9781784135416
Hayek MN (2022) The infectious disease trap of animal agriculture. Sci Adv 8(44)
Heinzen T (2015) Recent developments in the quantification and regulation of air emissions from animal feeding operations. Curr Environ Health Rep 2(1):25–32. https://doi.org/10.1007/s40572-014-0038-4. PMID: 26231239
Herriges JA, Secchi S, Babcock BA (2003) Living with Hogs in Iowa: The Impact of Livestock Facilities on Rural Residential Property Values. Working Paper 03-WP 342, Center for Agricultural and Rural Development, Iowa State University. https://www.card.iastate.edu/products/publications/pdf/03wp342.pdf
Hribar C (2010) Understanding concentrated animal feeding operations and their impact on communities. National Association of Local Boards of Health; National Center for Environmental Health (U.S.) Environmental Health Services Branch. https://stacks.cdc.gov/view/cdc/59792
Howard P (2016) Concentration and power in the food system: who controls what we eat? Bloomsbury, London
International Labour Organization (ILO) (2013) Caught at sea: forced labour and trafficking in fisheries. https://www.ilo.org/publications/caught-sea-forced-labour-and-trafficking-fisheries
Jardim TV, Mozaffarian D, Abrahams-Gessel S, et al (2019) Cardiometabolic disease costs associated with suboptimal diet in the United States: A cost analysis based on a microsimulation model. PLoS Med 16(12):e1002981. https://doi.org/10.1371/journal.pmed.1002981
Khanna K (2022) African swine fever virus: a global concern. Am Soc Microbiol. https://asm.org/articles/2022/march/african-swine-fever-virus-is-a-global-concern
Klaura J, Breeman G, Scherer L (2023) Animal lives embodied in food loss and waste. Sustainable Production and Consumption 43:308–318. https://doi.org/10.1016/j.spc.2023.11.004

Kmeťková D, Zvěřinová I, Ščasný M, et al (2025) Acceptability of meat tax and subsidy removal by meat eaters: insights from five European countries. Agri Food Econ 13. https://doi.org/10.1186/s40100-025-00359-5
Latino LR, Pica-Ciamarra U, Wisser D (2020) Africa: the livestock revolution urbanizes. Glob Food Sec. https://doi.org/10.1016/j.gfs.2020.100399
Levandowski R (2020) Polluting 'til the cows come home: how agricultural exceptionalism allows CAFOs free range for climate harm. Georgetown Environmental Law Review 33:151–171
Li Y, Wang M, Chen X, et al (2022) Multi-pollutant assessment of river pollution from livestock production worldwide. Water Res 209. https://doi.org/10.1016/j.watres.2021.117906
Martin MJ, Thottathil SE, Newman TB (2015) Antibiotics overuse in animal agriculture: a call to action for health care providers. Am J Public Health 105(12):2409–2410. https://doi.org/10.2105/AJPH.2015.302870
May S, Romberger DJ, Poole JA (2012) Respiratory health effects of large animal farming environments. J Toxicol Environ Health B 15(8):524–541. https://doi.org/10.1080/10937404.2012.744288
Meemken E-M, Bellemare MF (2020) Smallholder farmers and contract farming in developing countries. Proc Natl Acad Sci 117(1):259–264. https://doi.org/10.1073/pnas.1909501116
Miller DL, Murren G (2019) CAFOs: what we don't know is hurting us. National Resources Defense Council (NRDC). https://www.nrdc.org/sites/default/files/cafos-dont-know-hurting-us-report.pdf
Muir WM (2004) The threats and benefits of GM fish. EMBO (Eur Mol Biol) Reports 5(7):654–659. https://doi.org/10.1038/sj.embor.7400197
Naghavy M et al (2024) Global burden of bacterial antimicrobial resistance 1990–2021: a systematic analysis with forecasts to 2050. The Lancet 404(10459):1199–1226
Nuffield Council on Bioethics (2021) Genome editing and farmed animal breeding: social and ethical issues. https://cdn.nuffieldbioethics.org/wp-content/uploads/Genome-editing-and-farmed-animal-breeding-FINAL-WEB-PDF.pdf
OECD, FAO. 2022. OECD-FAO agricultural outlook 2022–2031. Paris, OECD Publishing. https://doi.org/10.1787/f1b0b29c-en
Our World in Data (OWID) (2022) Per capita meat consumption by type, 1961 to 2022. https://ourworldindata.org/grapher/per-capita-meat-consumption-by-type-kilograms-per-year?country=USA~AUS
Pew Charitable Trusts (2012) How corporate control squeezes out small farms. https://www.pewtrusts.org/en/research-and-analysis/fact-sheets/2012/07/18/how-corporate-control-squeezes-out-small-farms
Pew Charitable Trusts (2017) Antibiotic use in food animals poses risk to public health. https://www.pew.org/en/research-and-analysis/issue-briefs/2017/11/antibiotic-use-in-food-animals-poses-risk-to-public-health
Poore J, Nemecek T (2018) Reducing food's environmental impacts through producers and consumers. Science 360:987–992. https://doi.org/10.1126/science.aaq0216
Raworth K (2017) Doughnut economics. Random House, London
Richardson K, Steffen W, Lucht W, et al (2023) Earth beyond six of nine planetary boundaries. Sci Adv9. https://doi.org/10.1126/sciadv.adh2458
Ritchie H (2019) The world now produces more seafood from fish farms than wild catch. OurWorldinData.org. https://ourworldindata.org/rise-of-aquaculture
Ritchie H (2023) How many animals are factory-farmed? OurWorldinData.org. https://ourworldindata.org/how-many-animals-are-factory-farmed
Ritchie H, Roser M (2019) Half of the world's habitable land is used for agriculture. OurWorldinData.org. https://ourworldindata.org/global-land-for-agriculture
Ritchie H, Spooner F (2024) Large amounts of antibiotics are used in livestock, but several countries have shown this doesn't have to be the case. OurWorldinData.org. https://ourworldindata.org/antibiotics-livestock#article-citation

Roser M (2023) How many animals get slaughtered every day. OurWorldinData.org. https://ourworldindata.org/how-many-animals-get-slaughtered-every-day
Saitone TL, Schaefer KA, Scheitrum D et al (2024) Consolidation and concentration in U.S. meat processing: updated measures using plant-level data. Rev Ind Organ 64(1):35–56. https://doi.org/10.1007/s11151-023-09923-z
Salter AM (2013) Impact of consumption of animal products on cardiovascular disease, diabetes, and cancer in developed countries. Anim Front 3(1):20–27. https://doi.org/10.2527/af.2013-0004
Schrobback P, Dennis G, Li Y, et al (2023) Approximating the global economic (market) value of farmed animals. Global Food Secur 39:100722. https://doi.org/10.1016/j.gfs.2023.100722
Walter S, Elaine ZC, Tierney R et al (2025) Foodborne illness acquired in the United States—major pathogens, 2019. Emerg Infect Dis 31(4):669–677. https://doi.org/10.3201/eid3104.240913
Schlottmann C, Sebo J (2019) Food, animals, and the environment: an ethical approach. Routledge, London
Sebo J (2022) Saving animals, saving ourselves: Why animals matter for pandemics, climate change and other catastrophes. Oxford University Press, London
Springbett AJ, MacKenzie K, Woolliams JA et al (2003) The contribution of genetic diversity to the spread of infectious diseases in livestock populations. Genetics 165(3):1465–1474. https://doi.org/10.1093/genetics/165.3.1465
Tarrant G (2024) Examining corporate influence over food and farm bill. Foodtank. https://foodtank.com/news/2024/07/examining-corporate-influence-over-food-and-farm-bill/
The economics of ecosystems and biodiversity, agrifood (TEEBAgriFood) (2018) https://teebweb.org/our-work/agrifood/understanding-teebagrifood/evaluation-framework/
Thornton P, Herrero M (2015) Adapting to climate change in the mixed crop and livestock farming systems in sub-Saharan Africa. Nat Clim Chang 5:830–836. https://doi.org/10.1038/nclimate2754
Trebilcock M, Kristen P (2015) The puzzle of agricultural exceptionalism in international trade policy. J Int Econ Law 18:233–260. https://doi.org/10.1093/jiel/jgv022
United Nations Environment Programme (UNEP) (2024) Food Waste Index Report. Nairobi, Kenya
UNEP and International Livestock Research Institute (ILRI) (2020) Preventing the next pandemic: zoonotic diseases and how to break the chain of transmission. Nairobi, Kenya.
Van de Vis K. (1996) Killing of fishes: literature study and practice-observations (field research). Report number: C 037/96 1996 RIVO DLO
van der Sluijs JP, Vaage NS (2016) Pollinators and global food security: the need for holistic global stewardship. Food Ethics 1:75–91. https://doi.org/10.1007/s41055-016-0003-z
Wallace R (2016) Big farms make big flu. Monthly Review Press, New York
World Bank (2017) Drug resistant infections: a threat to our economic future. https://documents1.worldbank.org/curated/en/323311493396993758/pdf/final-report.pdf
World Economic Forum (WEF) (2022) Why smallholder farmers are central to new food security interventions. https://www.weforum.org/stories/2022/09/smallholder-farmers-key-achieving-food-security/
WEF (2024) Investing in natural capital: innovations supporting much-needed financing for nature. Geneva
Willett W et al (2019) Food in the anthropocene: the EAT–*Lancet* Commission on healthy diets from sustainable food systems. Lancet 393(10170):447–492
World Health Organization (WHO) (2014) Zoonotic disease: emerging public health threats in the Region. https://www.emro.who.int/fr/about-who/rc61/zoonotic-diseases.html
WHO (2019) New report calls for urgent action to avert antimicrobial resistance crisis. https://www.who.int/news/item/29-04-2019-new-report-calls-for-urgent-action-to-avert-antimicrobial-resistance-crisis
WHO (2025) Biodiversity. https://www.who.int/news-room/fact-sheets/detail/biodiversity#:~:text=Biodiversity%20loss%20can%20have%20significant,cause%20or%20exacerbate%20political%20conflict

World Resources Institute (WRI) (2024) Deforestation linked to agriculture. Global Forest Review. Washington, DC, World Resources Institute. https://gfr.wri.org/forest-extent-indicators/deforestation-agriculture

Chapter 7
Animals for Recreational Hunting

Erica von Essen and Erika Andersson Cederholm

"There are some who can live without wild things and some who cannot."
—*Aldo Leopold*

Abstract Wildlife in recreational hunting exists within a complex intersection of economic, ethical, and ecological concerns. Hunting offers personal fulfillment and supports conservation, while also driving a broader market of hunting-related goods and services. Yet, wildlife is often treated as unowned (*res nullius*) until harvested, leaving its value largely unregulated before capture or death. Yet we show that value imbues wildlife at *all* points of its life as a game species, from commodity value, to encounter value, non-encounter value, aesthetic value, biopolitical value, and relational value. Through unpacking these categories of wildlife value, this chapter explores wildlife's role in hunting—from its intrinsic and instrumental value to hunters and the industry to its function in conservation. It examines how hunting technologies, tourism, and economic systems shape the regulation of game animals and how internalizing costs where possible—such as adaptive population monitoring and peer enforcement of hunting ethics—can create more sustainable frameworks.

The Price of the Wild: Understanding the Value of Hunting

Where does the value of wildlife come into hunting? Some scholars argue that it is in their potential and anticipatory forms; it is the mere *chance* of seeing a wild animal that confers value (Forssman & Root-Bernstein 2018; Marvin 2003). Others point to

E. von Essen (✉)
Stockholm Resilience Center, Stockholm, Sweden
e-mail: Erica.von.essen@su.se

Faculty of Applied Ecology, Agricultural Sciences and Biotechnology, Inland Norway University of Applied Sciences, Evenstad, Norway

E. A. Cederholm
Department of Service Studies, Lund University, Lund, Sweden
e-mail: erika.andersson_cederholm@ses.lu.se

N. Batini (ed.), *The Economics of Non-Human Animals*, Natural Resource Management and Policy 63, https://doi.org/10.1007/978-3-032-17580-9_7

the value for hunters being in *actual* sighting and using their skills in bringing about the presences of wild animals (Makoto Su and Cheon 2017). Still another group points to the value of hunting animals deriving from a successful harvest (Ebeling-Schuld and Darimont 2017). In the latter case, it is relatively straightforward to speak of wildlife commodity or use value in hunting. This much is often supported in legislation: it is at the *point of death* where the ownership of the animal is conferred to the hunter, becoming circulatable value in an economy (Snijders 2012). Before then, wildlife is commonly *res communis* or *res nullius*—belonging to no one individual. This lack of ownership is perhaps both optimistic—in terms of not imposing human structures on wild populations—and problematic, in terms of circumscribing responsibility and ability to regulate at this stage.

But even in its most hypothetical forms prior to harvest, wildlife has value for the recreational hunter throughout multiple phases in the animal's life. Some of these values are of a direct sort: wildlife provides an aesthetic asset, a cultural symbol, and experiential commodity. Some values are indirect. Wildlife do not provide the value *per se*, but become anchors around which other forms of value and goods can proliferate. These include, for example, the social value of hunting and its reproduction of community and cultural continuity (Giacomelli and Gibbert 2018). Wildlife also often becomes a focal point for commoditized technologies, equipment, and other miscellaneous goods, to be generated (Fischer et al. 2012).

In addition to an analytical separation between direct and indirect values, one can also consider a potential separation of intrinsic and instrumental values of wildlife. In the former category, so-called relational values derive from the connection between predator (hunter) and prey. In the latter category of instrumental values, by contrast, wildlife is valued in terms of *the services and goods it provides the hunter*: meat, recreation, or trophy. In practice, however, the boundaries between both direct and indirect, and intrinsic and instrumental, collapse somewhat in regard to the complex ways in which hunters relate to and make use of their game animals. Indeed, intrinsic values, such as aesthetic and relational experiences, are commodified products today. In the recreational hunting tourism industry, it is the whole package that is being sold: atmosphere, setting, anticipation (Cederholm and Sjöholm 2023; Lundhede et al. 2015).

Whether the product of wildlife is experiential or product-based, direct or indirect, there is an increasing moral sensitivity around commodifying nature, and wildlife in particular. What is striking about these reservations to commodification is that they do not only originate among e.g., animal rights activists and the non-hunting public. Today, hunters *themselves* are among the most vocal critics against commodification of hunting and wildlife (Øian and Skogen 2016; von Essen 2017). On hunters' critique, commodification is said to reduce wildlife to their object lives, outprice local hunters, and even promote harmful practices that eschew ethics and animal welfare. Our premise in this chapter is that because of the difficulty of valuing wildlife based solely on conventional economic parameters (Boman and Mattsson 2012), because of its status as *res nullius* prior to death, and following vocal reservations from hunters about commodifying it (while nevertheless contributing to it), wildlife in recreational hunting may hence be said to constitute a commodity that partly *resists* commodification. The result is an uncertainty in the sort of market that is to regulate this good; wildlife value is divided and contested between moral, economic, and socio-cultural spheres in most modern hunting cultures.

With this complexity in mind, we focus this chapter on, first, highlighting the diversity of values attributed to wildlife in recreational hunting. Second, we consider how we can conceptualize the complexities of valuation and the resistance of wildlife to commodification more generally. Hence in the first part, we synthesize values along both instrumental and intrinsic dimensions by drawing from posthuman conceptualisations of animal value that build on Marxist ecology (Barua 2017; Collard and Dempsey 2017; Lorimer et al. 2017) which we adapt to the case of contemporary recreational hunting. This conceptual approach involves new ways of thinking about how animals can inhabit e.g., encounter value, commodity value, biopolitical value, aesthetic, and relational value. In the second part of the chapter, we suggest that these values point to the nature of wildlife value in hunting as being *elusive or resistant*. Here we discuss how the seemingly intrinsic values of hunting overlap with instrumental values, creating a tension that is actively experienced for hunters as well as for society at large. Indeed, we highlight how the complex economics of hunting is both part of, and beyond, a market. We conclude our chapter by showing and explaining how hunting, as well as wildlife, can be seen as a 'peculiar good' (Fourcade 2011a, b) and why this is a more instructive approach than extant economic evaluations.

Commodity Value

Although wildlife officially becomes property at the point of death, their commodity value is not actually limited to their terminal object life, or dead forms. Their numbers and presences in life can boost the value of land, and they promise—without necessarily needing to deliver on—eventual products. Animal body parts such as antlers, horns, and hides are most often thought of as material trophies. In these instances, the animal enters their 'object life' (Collard 2014). Their meat is sometimes sold locally and informally, or exchanged as gifts, but at other times may be consumed directly by the hunter and their family. Ecofeminist scholars Adams (1991) and Kheel (1995) famously critique the object life being reflected in terms we use for the meat from the dead animal. Such terms, they argue, are invariably predicated upon absent referent: deer becomes venison, boar becomes pork, birds become fowl. This is said to facilitate their consumption by severing links to the living beings.

Depending on the setting, permits, tags, or tenancy of hunting grounds may be purchased transactionally—or exchanged for other goods. Rare wildlife species or particularly rich hunting grounds sell at a premium (Mensah and Elofsson 2017), sometimes outpricing local hunters (Cohen 2014; Øian and Skogen 2016). In this way, both hunting lands and the animals in them may become "difficult-to-attain positional goods", whose desirability is predicated at least in part on short supplies, limited access, higher prices, and consequent privilege in attaining them (Eliason

2008). Owning or having access to game-rich land is a major social currency for hunters, as it is increasingly difficult to attain (Tickle et al. 2024).

Buttressing the hunting commodity economy is also a steadily growing industry of gear, weapons, and paraphernalia. A rising class of 'gearhead' hunters can now purchase tracking and weapons equipment modeled on military technology (Littlefield and Ozanne 2011). Fashions for hunting, partly based on utility—such as thermal wear—and partly based on trends, is an industry valued around \$2.3 billion in 2022 with a projection to rise to \$3.7 billion by 2032. On social media, so-called hunting influencers are now sponsored by clothing manufacturing companies and sell brands in a way that has greatly boosted this dimension of the hunting industry. Game features are here not as purchasable in themselves but facilitate, or even necessitate, expenditure in this commodified industry of paraphernalia. This is sometimes termed an auxiliary industry to recreational hunting (Bauer and Alexander 2004).

Encounter Value

Whereas commodity value focuses on material aspects and is thus easier to attribute a monetary value to, the encounter value of wildlife comprises both intrinsic and instrumental values. Nevertheless, encounter value is created through relations that are primarily experiential rather than market-ready. While it is difficult to claim that any wildlife values in recreational hunting are purely 'non-use values' (Aylward 2019) given the consumptive nature of the activity, a maxim among recreational hunters that one can have a good day of hunting without felling game (Cahoone 2009). This reflects the value of wildlife as sightings, hypothetical harvests, and as providing an atmosphere. LeCain (2019) discusses how for some hunters in North America, the potential for large carnivore sightings in the area can be a boon to their deer hunt. As an 'experiential commodity' (p. 681)—the off-chance to be attacked by a wild animal—the hypothetical encounter with a grizzly bear adds flavor to their trip. Although this may be a rare example, the fact is that a majority of hunting stories of memorable encounters often center on unexpected background species they encounter, and not always the primary target.

Encountering wildlife in its natural habitat, pursuing it, and having it evade the hunter, provides the basis for thrill, sport, and leisure (Makoto Su and Cheon 2017). These are at once relational values that speak about an interplay between hunter and prey, and recreational value in providing entertainment and enjoyment for the hunter. Unlike wildlife in its object life, which becomes an exclusive and private value, encounter values can be collective and non-exclusive—one live animal may provide joy to multiple hunters. While some species promise high encounter values by for example being associated with good fighting spirit, an elusive nature (thus making the encounter rare in the first place) or impressive physique, individual encounters can also become memorable given the circumstances and the individual animal agency (von Essen et al. 2020): a boar outsmarting the hunter, a rabbit fooling the hunting dog by doubling back on its tracks, deer exhibiting playful behavior, or game fowl appearing at an unexpected time or place. Both private, introspective encounters between the hunter and an animal, and between several hunters to mutually experience an animal, carry their different values. In the latter, cumulative excitement may be generated among the hunters.

Wildlife encounters are drawn out in anticipatory, stalking, confronting, and retelling modalities. In the first stage, encounter value is indirect: most hunters encounter wildlife in the form of their traces: scat left, a branch felled, a deer path, or otherwise (Gregory 2005). Some of the indirect encounters as traces are perceptible to an attuned hunter but other traces may be sensed through the hunter's dog (Keil 2021). In these cases, the dog becomes a relay agent of encounter value. In a related form of co-witnessing, hunters report great enjoyment seeing their dog pick up a scent, partly for its encounter with the wildlife trace, and partly for the potential for an upcoming physical encounter (Chitwood et al. 2011).

While encounter value may seem to culminate in the physical meeting stage, value may be extended in the afterlives of the hunt by sharing stories, pictures, or clips or the encounter to peers afterward (von Essen 2020). In these cases, the encounter value also produces social currency and relational value in terms of bonding with other hunters. The value of wildlife encounter hence transcends the initial encounter and goes on to provide spiritual fulfillment, health effects, or social capital (Ebeling-Schuld and Darimont 2017).

Non-Encounter Value

In a less acknowledged case, we feel it important to mention, the *absence* of wildlife can also constitute a source of value. We include this, first, because it can paradoxically increase the value of some species. In the first case, the rarity or removal of wildlife species from the wild increases their symbolic and economic value. 'Guaranteed bags' or 'guaranteed sightings' both denigrate the value of a species by making it common, but can also be a clever marketing technique for a species that is so rare its presence needs to be lured and baited. In these instances, anticipation and failure to see them on the first or second day of hunting trips boost their value to later dates.

In the second case of non-encounter value of wildlife, there are some species whose values come explicitly through their elimination at the hands of hunters. Saha (2021) talks about unwanted species as having 'dead value', where bounties and subsidies encourage its removal from the wild. This is often to maximize the value of another, protected species or good whose value exceeds that of the killed species. Bounty business has historically been lucrative for hunters, turning in body parts of proof of the animal's death, even fraudulently. Today, a substantial portion of recreational hunting has also become a matter of necessary culling to remove surplus populations that would otherwise cause damage. Wild boar, for example, has both value as a good sport species and as having non-encounter value (Pereyra-Ceretta et al., 2025): a kind of elimination.

In the third and final case, the absence of some wildlife species in a hunting area can increase the attraction of the place and thus price of the grounds for tenants. In hunting grounds teeming with large carnivores and meso-predators, the value of the land is usually low. Oppositely, lands that can show an absence of e.g., wolves provide the promise of both safety for the hunter (whose dogs may be at risk) and more ample prey populations.

Ecological Value

Hunting has undergone an ecologicalization in the past decades (Gieser 2020). This means that even recreational hunting is increasingly framed and understood as an ecological service, wildlife management, and as hunters exercising trophic responsibility in the environment (Holsman 2000). Wildlife forms both a natural resource to manage in this perspective, and as a fellow trophic actor. Hunters have been criticized on account of maintaining artificially high game populations (Hummel and Goedeke 2005), which they often defend on accounts of ecological balance. In addition to this, recreational hunting is in a troubled relationship with carnivores (Nelson 1986): these ostensibly 'do the job' of hunters, maintaining prey guilds and shaping the ecosystem top-down (Komi and Kröger 2024). Hence, much of hunting involves wrestling with acknowledging the ecosystem value provided by wildlife, and how hunters can figure into this equation.

In several more recent studies, hunters seem to recognize the ecological utility of diversity more broadly and emphasize that each species has a role to play and hence must be maintained to some degree (Donfrancesco and Sandbrook 2025). That hunters should be the arbiters of such valuation, and experts on what constitutes a healthy ecosystem, remains a controversial point.

Biopolitical Value

In most democratic countries, multiple societal actors vie for control over various aspects of wildlife species, such as its monitoring, reproduction, and harvest quotas. To be charged with the mandate of managing a wildlife species comes with both responsibilities and obligations (Bellalba and Marin 2025). Actors leverage state funding for managing or monitoring several game species. Some 'hot potato' species, like wild boar, do not willingly become the mandate of anyone, but may nonetheless end up the responsibility of hunters to cull, or they may get fined for boar-caused damages on agricultural crops (Vajas et al. 2023). In Sweden, the moose has profound biopolitical value. Whoever controls moose, by way of knowledge, monitoring, access, and decision-making, exhibits much power (von Essen and Peterson 2024).

In the biopolitical apparatus of wildlife management, wildlife also holds scientific and education value. In most places, there is increasing infrastructure for an adaptive management of valued wildlife species that tracks migration patterns or population dynamics (ENETWILD-consortium et al. 2022). Although this is rarely big business, perhaps beyond competitive funding schemes for ecologists and biologists, there may be subsidies, grants, compensation, or easements involved for hunters as citizen scientists who record observations about wildlife. In the Nordic countries, there is a strong tradition of citizen science (Singh et al. 2014). In some instances, this has helped hunters consolidate their positioning as a mentor of sorts to society at large over wildlife. All of this indicates that wildlife has biopolitical value on the level of governance and society: it can empower, exclude or selectively call upon the expertise of particular actors.

Aesthetic Value

Some species have high encounterability—in terms of providing good sport or memorable interactions—but others may have eye-pleasing appeal through physical and behavioral characteristics alone. Majestic appearances have long been valued by hunters: large antlers are emblems of strength, big male specimens as indicative of population health. In Victorian era big-game hunting, size glorified the hunter who felled it (Donald 2006). Size is not the only factor in determining aesthetic value, however. Rarity in coloring, patterns, or features increases both the trophy value of an animal (in case one shoots it) or its encounter value (if the hunter decides to leave it). This can make the animal more attractive to shoot, but also more likely to be spared. Lorimer (2007) writes about non-human charisma, a key constituent of aesthetic value and vice versa, and suggests this may be unpredictable. At the very least, aesthetic charisma is more diverse than previously conceded: although universal characteristics of beauty exist, species appeal by being both 'awesome and awful'. Others may be aesthetically prized for exhibiting characteristics similar to humans, so that we may project ideas onto them. In other cases, the monstrosity of certain specimens may increase their aesthetic value for hunters.

Aesthetic appeal is sometimes tied to health, like a particularly fluffy, well-fed-looking deer or lynx. But aesthetics can also wholly disconnect from practical utility. In game ranches, bucks may be selectively bred for desirable traits to the point where they have trouble holding up their large antlers (Simon 2019). Just as often as they are singled out as aesthetically appealing specimens, moreover, wildlife also exhibit aesthetic value in situ—that is, in relation to their natural surroundings. On this perspective, wildlife are inseparable from the beautiful, pristine landscapes in which they are encountered. Historically, many game species—like pheasants—were introduced in large part for providing a picturesque appeal in enriching the landscape tableau, particularly in noble estates (van Heijgen et al. 2025).

Today an increasing part of hunting culture revolves around picture-taking of wildlife in their natural environment, as well as of felled specimens. von Essen (2020) showed that the aesthetic value of living wildlife among hunters is heavily tied to their surroundings, insofar as these provide the most popular and marketable photos and magazine covers. Photos are the *new trophies,* mobile and shareable across social media. Composition and framing, particularly of wildlife-in-landscape shots, appear just as important as the wildlife subject. Finally, as Keil (2021) notes, it needs to be remembered that aesthetics do not comprise solely the visual. It includes scentscapes, weatherworlds, and sounds. The rutting of elk, calls of birds, and grunts of deer contributes to immersion and atmosphere for hunters.

Relational Value

Hunting creates connection with wildlife through activities beyond killing, including supplementary feeding, habitat maintenance, monitoring populations, and photographing them (Oldfield et al. 2003). Hunters have both connections to individual animals, such as a known local buck or fox, and toward populations they have been stewarding over generations. Hunters approximate a (albeit dubious) care ethic in some regards, imbued with paternalistic stewardship value, coming to refer to e.g., moose populations as 'our moose' (Bell 2015). The implication is that their labour over time has created a relationship of that of a steward to their flock.

Research shows that relational value to wildlife most commonly accrues in familiar areas where there is already a sense of place for the hunters, i.e., a connection to the local landscape (Knight 2012; Svensson 2016). Oppositely, tourist hunts and trophy hunts have been criticized for not imbuing wildlife with any meaningful relational value, but seeing them as transactions and objects to whom no lasting relationship is formed beyond the kill (Franklin 2007). On Gunnarsdotter (2005)'s analysis, the hunter-forest-game-place history is impossible to recreate in day hunts or trips that are clearly purchased. By contrast, relational value is maximized when hunters have enduring relationships that go beyond the killing to include wildlife management more broadly, before and after the kill, and beyond the shot individual. Shephard et al. (2024) suggested that engaging in all of these parts is what fosters stewardship and relationship.

Finally, wildlife can also act as the anchor by which relations are (re)produced between people. Much research points toward the social value, camaraderie, and community maintenance function of hunting (Daigle et al. 2002; Franklin 2007). There is no space here to review all of these values. In times where the relations in hunting go on to strengthen traditions and reproduce customs, we can also talk about wildlife as having cultural value. The annual moose hunt in Sweden is a strong example of this, serving as connector of diverse people and as continuity of the countryside (Gunnarsdotter 2005). Equally, seasonal deer hunts elsewhere are much celebrated as ritual social gatherings.

Values Within and Beyond a Market

What distinguishes recreational hunting from subsistence, commercial, or management hunting (normally ‘culling’) is that experiential values typically top the value hierarchy. Hence, more importance is placed on relational, aesthetic, and social values of wildlife than its commodity or object life. Yet this is exactly the reason why recreational or sport hunting has been subject to outside criticism in recent years: the ‘goods’ provided by hunting e.g., companionship, nature experience, aesthetic appreciation, physical exercise, can be attained by non-lethal means: there is no need to *kill* the animals to attain these goods (List 2004).

However, as we have shown above, recreational hunting is also multifaceted and relies on animal deaths at its core. First, research shows that different recreational hunters place differential importance on experiential vs. commodity/achievement values at different points in their hunting lives, with different crowds, and depending on the game species (Gigliotti and Metcalf 2016). Second, we see a tight entanglement between these domains of value in the first place. Recreational hunting invariably has experiential values that can be linked to the object status of the game—meat, trophies, or the story of the killed or nearly killed game. Even values that may seem more instrumental, such as ecological and biopolitical values, are for many hunters linked to a sense of obligation to nature, the land, and wildlife. This is sometimes called a stewardship value (Aylward 2019).

Furthermore, even those values that appear to be intrinsic, such as encounter, aesthetic, and relational value, are to some extent commoditized—or at least possible to commoditize. In many countries, there is an established hunting tourism, which may be more or less packaged and marketed (Bauer and Alexander 2004; Cederholm and Sjöholm 2023). Here, the encounter, aesthetic, and relational value are often explicitly emphasized. Some companies offer complete packages with travel, guides, meals, and accommodation, while others are more low-key. Sometimes, only accommodation is offered if the customer is a hunting party where they already know each other and they take care of other services themselves. In these cases, commercial hunting tourism is similar to the kind of exchange hunting that is common among everyday local hunters, i.e., an informal exchange of friendship (Lundhede et al. 2015). Someone gets a hunt in exchange for helping out on another hunt, or as a way of returning the favor if they have previously been invited on a hunt (Andersson Cederholm and Sjöholm 2022, 2023).

A large part of hunting seems to operate according to this principle of informal exchange, that is, a socio-economic exchange according to a gift economy logic, rather than a market logic. However, one condition for this to work is that there are established social networks of hunters. Not all hunters are part of such a network and there is a growing market for those hunters who do not have contacts with local hunting teams, or who want to hunt on attractive hunting grounds, perhaps in countries other than their own (Tickle et al. 2022). Online sites and apps like Infinite Outdoors, Landtrust.com and Outdoor Access in the US, form part of a growing digital landscape of hunting access platforms that provide such a good, for a fee (Venker et al., 2026).

Who Attributes Value to Wildlife in Hunting?

How does the valuation—attribution of values—to wildlife look like and take place in recreational hunting? The attributers of value are mainly hunters themselves, following principles of supply and demand. But the valuation is neither wholly rational nor constant over time and place. Hunting trophies provides an instructive example of this. Trophies sometimes have high monetary value, which the hunter pays when he or she fells the game. The supply of huntable game with high trophy value thus has a high market value. The value is far from standardized, however, rather belonging to a (shifting) status market where the object has a singular and strong symbolic value, like an art market (Aspers 2009). Hence, this type of good is difficult to quantify and prices may seem arbitrary, despite a strong commitment to measuring and weighing trophies among hunters. Boone and Crocket Club have different criteria, for example, than does Safari Club International or the International Council for Game and Wildlife Conservation with the former penalizing asymmetry and the latter taking into account ecological values.

Experiential values are particularly subjective. Personal preferences and idiosyncrasies among hunters can make them value certain animal individuals—like ones that got away, or species that lead them to 'tick off' a box of achievement they have aspired to—more highly than an abstract market valuation would (Tickle and von Essen 2020). An outstanding question from scholars on animal value is whether the animals themselves have agency in influencing their relative value in recreational hunting. Collard (2014) suggests that there are ways in which animals can 'opt out' of their commodity/object lives, such as by being taken out of the wildlife trade or hunt to sanctuaries. As yet, however, more research is needed on how game animals specifically can influence their worth and resist commodification. But in a time of even ecologists coming to acknowledge the role of animal personality, it has been observed that the wiles, tricks, and bravery of certain individuals or even species can grant them a 'free pass' out of respect from hunters (von Essen et al. 2020).

Resisting Commodification of Recreational Hunting

If animals sometimes resist their capture and commodification by exercising agency, hunters, too, exhibit some resistance toward market forces taking over hunting. Hunters condemn a type of hunting that they feel has become too commercialized—or commercialized in the 'wrong' way, so that it appears as if it is only economic values that govern (Andersson Cederholm and Sjöholm 2023; Øian and Skogen 2016). In these contexts, to compensate, hunters often highlight the intrinsic values:

that hunting is a cultural heritage that should be managed, and that wildlife has intrinsic value.

For some hunting entrepreneurs, the marketing of non-quantifiable values, such as holistic and contemplative nature experiences, togetherness, and exclusive meals with game meat, also becomes a way of steering away from excessive focus on the quantifiable values, such as the number of game killed or the size of the trophy (Andersson Cederholm and Sjöholm 2023; Kola et al. 2017). The marketing of hunting experiences with an emphasis on holistic nature experiences and sustainable meat consumption thus represents new expressions of how intrinsic and instrumental values are combined in hunting.

In some cases, hunters' personal resistance to commodification of wildlife and hunting goes even further. This has manifested in trying to distance themselves from what they see as lavish, gadgeteer, and all-frills hunts in order to get back to a closer relation with the wildlife. This may be seen, in part, as a way of decentering the instrumental values of wildlife and its auxiliary industries—fancy parties, expensive gear, high-tech weapons—in favor of the relational value at the heart of the hunt. Indeed, such recreational hunters, while a diverse group, pride themselves on being bare-bones, no-frills, back-to-basics, and close-to-nature (Littlefield and Ozanne 2011; Skogen and Thrane 2007; Stinson 2017).

The logic of such hunts is that they seek to eliminate the mediating technologies between the hunter and the prey by creating an embodied encounter with the animal (Keil 2021). While this may be taken partly as a rejection of the market structuring hunting in favor of the primeval and the value of the human-animal connection, it does not always achieve this. Indeed, in recent years even tourist hunts seeking to cash in on this atavistic trend can now sell bare-bones hunting and the aesthetic of rusticity and simplicity as added values at a premium. In addition to this, both comfort goods and technological aids are used to make the hunt safer and more humane. Hence, eliminating these may paradoxically have animal welfare consequences.

Toward a Fair Game: Social, Economic, and Ecological Strategies for Regulation

Guarding against some of the dangers of excessive commodification on wildlife requires a nuanced approach. One key aspect of hunting regulation is closely monitoring animal populations to prevent overhunting and to ensure hunting quotas align with ecological stability. Governments should prioritize the development of rigorous monitoring schemes on wildlife, both in their *res nullius* state—before deaths—and as harvest data submitted by hunters. At present, European networks are seeking to harmonize and systematize such monitoring for European countries, but encounter wildly disparate systems, of often poor transparency (Åhl et al. 2020). Some hunters have themselves criticized bag reporting systems in their countries for not being sufficiently adaptive, or for processing their data too late in the season to make a difference in informing the sustainability of next year's hunt (ibid). Such bottlenecks need to be remedied in improved systems, perhaps with increased automation where possible. Sweden's annual moose population surveys provide an example of effective monitoring, allowing authorities to set hunting limits that support long-term population health. With more robust monitoring of recreational hunting, it will be easier to see how some species may require extended periods of uninterrupted recovery and hunting moratoriums. If hunters can appreciate that such decisions not only emanate from their own submitted data, but also promote the long-term viability of populations to which they ascribe relational value, they are more likely to get onboard with such restrictions.

Beyond regulating direct hunting practices, it is critical for hunters to find new ways of relating to predators in many hunting systems—beyond seeing these in terms of non-encounter or dead value, competing over prey animals. A vexing topic, the role of natural predators in ecosystems which is also used and shaped by hunters, needs to be acknowledged beyond seeing them as obstacles. Experts are suggesting that we are entering into a new era of predator coexistence that is characterized by uncharted territory: predators have had remarkable recoveries under the EU Habitats Directive, and now need to be brought into a new relationship that avoids the dichotomies of total protection—alienating local communities and causing human-wildlife conflict—and persecution, as has characterized much of human-predator socioecological history (von Essen and Pettersson 2024; Linnell and Boitani 2025). At present, measures like compensation for predator-induced losses represent regulatory opportunities, but remain end-of-line mechanisms.

Effective enforcement of hunting conduct can be a way forward to safeguard ethical conduct in communities and hunting teams While hunter enforcement is sometimes enacted by governments, such as in the form of anti-poaching units that patrol protected areas and police hunters, the majority of research on this topic demonstrates that the most effective and durable way for hunters to behave ethically is a type of social control or peer pressure (Brymer 1991; Gezelius 2004). Specifically, this refers to hunters experiencing that they are part of a hunting collective in which there are shared norms for proper conduct, as pertains to animal welfare and sustainability (von Essen and Hansen 2018). The success of such norm systems lies in penalties for hunters who violate norms, which are usually social in nature, like exclusion from hunting teams, or not being invited back to a hunt. Outside penalties have been shown to engender the opposite effect, leading hunters to turn away from the law more broadly and to potentially position themselves toward outside interference (Enticott 2011). One of the primary ways in which successful internal regulation may proceed is to ensure robust hunting exam requirements, minimizing the risk of irresponsible hunters already at the level of legal entry into the hunting community. To this end, all sources which socialize and enculturate hunters into hunting, particularly at early stages of their hunting lives but also continuously, need to uphold standards of respectful representation of wildlife, acknowledging their multiple and intrinsic values. This is done on the level of images presented, language used to refer to them, and directives to other hunters.

Finally, the role of economic incentives needs to be considered and carefully tailored to specific hunting contexts to foster sustainable practices. The *Common Agricultural Policy* has successfully compensated EU landowners like farmers and hunters for leaving land to nature, maintaining wetlands and hedgerows. Going forward, it will be important to subsidize non-lead ammunition to protect the environment and animal health and, where possible, encourage the supply chain of game meat by facilitating regulation. By firmly coupling recreational hunting to both environmental improvement and to locally sourced game meat consumption, hunting for the sake of sport alone, where surplus animal bodies may have to be discarded, may be counteracted.

By integrating clearer regulation of species populations, the enforcement of ethical practices, and economic incentives, hunting can evolve into an economically sustainable and ecologically responsible activity or secure its place as such in cultures where this is already established. The future of hunting regulation must not only secure the interests of hunters but also guarantee the longevity and health of the wildlife populations they rely on. Through economic incentives, monitoring programs, peer enforcement strategies, and occasional moratoriums that correspond to adaptive management, it is both necessary and possible to establish a hunting framework that respects both the traditions of hunters and the integrity of nature.

Conclusions

Wildlife occupies a unique space in economic and ethical discourse, simultaneously commodified yet resistant to conventional economic valuation. Wildlife can be transformed into tangible assets—trophies, meat, or fur—while also serving as the foundation for the hunting experience itself, which is marketed as an adventure or cultural tradition. However, wildlife's pre-harvest status as an unowned resource complicates its integration into standard market structures. As discussed in this chapter, this 'no-owner' condition leads to economic uncertainty, the potential for exploitation, and ethical dilemmas over whether wildlife should be freely accessible or strictly regulated.

Economic sociology describes such entities as 'peculiar goods' (Fourcade 2011a, b)—commodities that carry multifaceted and sometimes conflicting values, making them difficult to price. Wildlife fit this definition, much like human organs or surrogate motherhood, where attempts to assign market value provoke ethical debates. The resistance to pricing these goods often stems from their intrinsic worth, which many argue is immeasurable or even sacred. In recreational hunting, this resistance manifests in multiple ways—through shifting, subjective values, through moral debates among hunters themselves, and through the complex regulatory frameworks that attempt to balance market forces with conservation imperatives.

As seen in our discussion of structured hunting policies, wildlife cannot be effectively managed using conventional economic parameters alone. Much of hunting conduct, including ways of relating to wildlife, is shaped by norms, traditions, and values rather than regulation or economic deterrents. Hence, the latter need to be cautiously applied so as to not be automatically rejected as outside interference. Indeed, the ongoing debates over how—or even whether—wildlife should be priced underscore how economic valuation is never static but instead shaped by cultural, social, and moral contexts. Hunting provides economic value not just through direct commodities but through experiential, aesthetic, and relational value—creating an industry surrounding equipment, conservation funding, and tourism. Yet, as demonstrated, wildlife and hunting resist full market integration due to their evolving moral significance. The contradictions within hunting—where hunters both contribute to commodification while simultaneously rejecting excessive commercialization—illustrate why wildlife remains difficult to regulate within standard economic frameworks.

References

Andersson Cederholm E, Sjöholm C (2022) Jaktturism – ett delikat balansarbete i en komplex ekonomi. RIG Kulturhistorisk tidskrift (3):129–146

Andersson Cederholm E, Sjöholm C (2023) The tourism business operator as a moral gatekeeper—the relational work of recreational hunting in Sweden. J Sustain Tour 31(5):1126–1141. https://doi.org/10.1080/09669582.2021.1922425

Adams CJ (1991) The sexual politics of meat: a feminist-vegetarian critical theory. Continuum

Åhl M, Elmhagen B, Bergqvist G (2020) Survey of methods for harvest reporting of game species in Europe (Viltforum, Issue). https://jagareforbundet.se/vilt/viltforum/

Aspers P (2009) Knowledge and valuation in markets. Theory Soc 38(2):111–131. https://doi.org/10.1007/s11186-008-9078-9

Aylward B (2019) Appropriating the value of wildlife and wildlands. In: Economics for the wilds. Routledge, pp 34–64

Barua M (2017) Nonhuman labour, encounter value, spectacular accumulation: the geographies of a lively commodity. Trans Inst Br Geogr 42(2):274–288. https://doi.org/10.1111/tran.12170

Bauer J, Alexander H (2004) Hunting and fishing tourism. In: Bauer J, Alexander H (eds) Wildlife tourism: impacts, management and planning. Common Ground Publishing in Association with Cooperative Research Centre for Sustainable Tourism, pp 57–77

Bell J (2015) Hierarchy, intrusion, and the anthropomorphism of nature: hunter and rancher discourse on North American wolves. In: Masius P, Sprenger J (eds) A fairytale in question: historical interactions between humans and wolves. White Horse Press, pp 282–303

Bellalba P, Marin C (2025) À la recherche de données: Nature et flux des informations au fondement des politiques de gestion du sanglier urbain. L'exemple bordelais. Cybergeo: Eur J Geogr

Boman M, Mattsson L (2012) The hunting value of game in Sweden: have changes occurred over recent decades? Scand J for Res 27(7):669–674. https://doi.org/10.1080/02827581.2012.683533

Brymer RA (1991) The emergence and maintenance of a deviant sub-culture: the case of hunting/poaching sub-culture. Anthropologica 33(1/2):177–194. https://doi.org/10.2307/25605608

Cahoone L (2009) Hunting as a moral good. Environ Values 18(1):67–89. https://doi.org/10.3197/096327109X404771

Cederholm EA, Sjöholm C (2023) Jaktturism-avvägningar, utmaningar och möjligheter.

Chitwood MC, Peterson MN, Deperno CS (2011) Assessing dog hunter identity in coastal North Carolina. Hum Dimens Wildl 16(2):128–141. https://doi.org/10.1080/10871209.2011.551448

Cohen E (2014) Recreational hunting: ethics, experiences and commoditization. Tour Recreat Res 39(1):3–17. https://doi.org/10.1080/02508281.2014.11081323

Collard R-C (2014) Putting animals back together, taking commodities apart. Ann Assoc Am Geogr 104(1):151–165. https://doi.org/10.1080/00045608.2013.847750
Collard R-C, Dempsey J (2017) Capitalist natures in five orientations. Capital Nat Social 28(1):78–97
Daigle JJ, Hrubes D, Ajzen I (2002) A comparative study of beliefs, attitudes, and values among hunters, wildlife viewers, and other outdoor recreationists. Hum Dimens Wildl 7(1):1–19. https://doi.org/10.1080/108712002753574756
Donald D (2006) Pangs watched in perpetuity: Sir Edwin Landseer's pictures of dying deer and the ethos of Victorian sportsmanship. In: Group TAS (ed) Killing Animals. University Press of Illnois, pp 50–68
Donfrancesco V, Sandbrook C (2025) From biopower to affirmative biopolitics: a (bio)political ecology of becoming with wolves. Trans Inst Br Geogr n/a(n/a):e12744. https://doi.org/10.1111/tran.12744
Ebeling-Schuld AM, Darimont CT (2017) Online hunting forums identify achievement as prominent among multiple satisfactions. Wildl Soc Bull 41(3):523–529. https://doi.org/10.1002/wsb.796
Eliason SL (2008) A statewide examination of hunting and trophy nonhuman animals: perspectives of Montana hunters. Soc Anim 16(3):256–278
ENETWILD-consortium, Acevedo P, Aleksovski V, Apollonio M, Berdión O, Blanco-Aguiar J, del Rio L, Ertürk A, Fajdiga L, Escribano F, Ferroglio E, Gruychev G, Gutiérrez I, Häberlein V, Hoxha B, Kavčić K, Keuling O, Martínez-Carrasco C, Palencia P, Vicente J (2022) Wild boar density data generated by camera trapping in nineteen European areas. EFSA Support Publ 19(3):7214E. https://doi.org/10.2903/sp.efsa.2022.EN-7214
Enticott G (2011) Techniques of neutralising wildlife crime in rural England and Wales. J Rural Stud 27(2):200–208. https://doi.org/10.1016/j.jrurstud.2011.01.005
Fischer A, Sandström C, Delibes-Mateos M, Arroyo B, Tadie D, Randall D, Hailu F, Lowassa A, Msuha M, Kereži V, Reljić S, Linnell J, Majić A (2012) On the multifunctionality of hunting—an institutional analysis of eight cases from Europe and Africa. J Environ Planning Manage 56(4):531–552. https://doi.org/10.1080/09640568.2012.689615
Fourcade M (2011a) Cents and sensibility: economic valuation and the nature of "nature." Am J Sociol 116(6):1721–1777
Fourcade M (2011b) Price and prejudice: on economics and the enchantment (and disenchantment) of nature. In: Beckert J, Aspers P (eds) The worth of goods: valuation and pricing in the economy. Oxford University Press
Forssman N, Root-Bernstein M (2018) Landscapes of anticipation of the other: ethno-ethology in a deer hunting landscape. J Ethnobiol 38:71–87. https://doi.org/10.2993/0278-0771-38.1.071
Franklin A (2007) The 'Animal Question' and the 'consumption' of wildlife. https://doi.org/10.4324/9780203934326-11
Gezelius S (2004) Food, money, and morals: compliance among natural resource harvesters. Hum Ecol 32(5):615–634. https://doi.org/10.1007/s10745-004-6099-5
Giacomelli S, Gibbert M (2018) He likes playing the hero—I let her have fun shooting. Gender games in the Italian forest during the hunting season. J Rural Stud 62:164–173. https://doi.org/10.1016/j.jrurstud.2018.08.005
Gieser T (2020) Hunting wild animals in Germany: conflicts between wildlife management and 'traditional' practices of Hege. In: Fenske M, Tschofen B (eds) Managing the return of the wild: human encounters with wolves in Europe. Routledge, pp 164–179
Gigliotti LM, Metcalf EC (2016) Motivations of female black hills deer hunters. Hum Dimens Wildl 21(4):371–378. https://doi.org/10.1080/10871209.2016.1157714
Gregory NG (2005) Bowhunting deer. Anim Welf 14(2):111–116. https://www.ingentaconnect.com/content/ufaw/aw/2005/00000014/00000002/art00003
Gunnarsdotter Y (2005) Från arbetsgemenskap till fritidsgemenskap. Den svenska Landsbygdens omvandling ur Locknevis perspektiv. Doctoral, Swedish University of Agricultural Sciences, Uppsala.

Holsman RH (2000) Goodwill hunting? exploring the role of hunters as ecosystem stewards. Wildl Soc Bull 28(4):808–816

Hummel R, Goedeke TL (2005) The hunters and the hunted: Context and evolution of game management in Germanic countries versus the United States. In: Mad about Wildlife. Brill, pp 171–191

Keil PG (2021) Rank atmospheres: the more-than-human scentspace and aesthetic of a pigdogging hunt. Aust J Anthropol 32(S1):96–113. https://doi.org/10.1111/taja.12382

Kheel M (1995) License to kill: an ecofeminist critique of hunters' discourse. In: Adams, CJ, Donovan J (eds) Animals and women: feminist theoretical explorations. Duke University Press

Knight J (2012) The Anonymity of the Hunt: a Critique of Hunting as Sharing 53(3):334–355. https://doi.org/10.1086/665535

Kola A, Ratna A, Dashper K (2017) 'On the hunt for belonging': culture, hunting and indo-Muslim men in South Africa. Ann Leis Res 1–17. https://doi.org/10.1080/11745398.2017.1415153

Komi S, Kröger M (2024) Predators in the web of life: World ecology of historical human–wolf relations in Finland. J Agrarian Change n/a(n/a). https://doi.org/10.1111/joac.12533

LeCain TJ (2019) The consumption of humans: how the danger of Grizzly Bear attacks in American National Parks became a commodity. Environ Hist 24(4):680–687

Linnell JD, Boitani L (2025) Developing methodology for setting Favourable Reference Values for large carnivores in Europe. Report to the European Comission under contract N° 09.0201/2023/907799/SER/ENV. D. 3 "Support for Coexistence with Large Carnivores. Task B. 3–Assessment of large carnivores' conservation status"

List C (2004) On the moral distinctiveness of sport hunting. Environ Ethics 26(2):155–169

Littlefield J, Ozanne J (2011) Socialization into consumer culture: hunters learning to be men. Consum Mark Cult 14(4):333–360. https://doi.org/10.1080/10253866.2011.604494

Lorimer J (2007) Nonhuman Charisma. Environ Plann D Soc Space 25(5):911–932. https://doi.org/10.1068/d71j

Lorimer J, Hodgetts T, Barua M (2017) Animals' atmospheres. Prog Hum Geogr 43(1):26–45. https://doi.org/10.1177/0309132517731254

Lundhede TH, Jacobsen JB, Thorsen BJ (2015) A hedonic analysis of the complex hunting experience. J For Econ 21(2):51–66. https://doi.org/10.1016/j.jfe.2015.01.001

Makoto Su N, Cheon E (2017) Reconsidering nature: the dialectics of fair chase in the practices of American midwest hunters. In: Proceedings of the 2017 CHI conference on human factors in computing systems. Denver, Colorado, USA

Marvin G (2003) A passionate pursuit: foxhunting as performance. Sociol Rev 51:46–60. https://doi.org/10.1111/j.1467-954X.2004.00450.x

Mensah JT, Elofsson K (2017) An empirical analysis of hunting lease pricing and value of game in Sweden. Land Econ 93(2):292–308. https://doi.org/10.3368/le.93.2.292

Nelson RK (1986) Make prayers to the Raven: a Koyukon view of the Northern forest. University of Chicago Press

Øian H, Skogen K (2016) Property and possession: hunting tourism and the morality of landownership in rural Norway. Soc Nat Resour 29(1):104–118. https://doi.org/10.1080/08941920.2015.1041658

Oldfield TE, Smith RJ, Harrop SR, Leader-Williams N (2003) Field sports and conservation in the United Kingdom. Nature 423(6939):531–533

Pereyra-Ceretta V, Dabezies J-M, Ruiz-Ballesteros E (2025) Ambivalent animalities: wild boars in Uruguay. Ethnos 1–15. https://doi.org/10.1080/00141844.2025.2500314

Saha J (2021) Regulating death. In: Colonizing animals. Cambridge University Press, pp 83–106. https://doi.org/10.1017/9781108990240.004

Shephard S, von Essen E, Gieser T, List CJ, Arlinghaus R (2024) Recreational killing of wild animals can foster environmental stewardship. Nature Sustainability 7(8):956–963. https://doi.org/10.1038/s41893-024-01379-7

Simon A (2019) The competitive consumption and fetishism of wildlife trophies. J Consum Cult 19(2):151–168. https://doi.org/10.1177/1469540517690571

Singh NJ, Danell K, Edenius L, Ericsson G (2014) Tackling the motivation to monitor: success and sustainability of a participatory monitoring program. Ecol Soc 19(4):Article 7. https://doi.org/10.5751/ES-06665-190407
Skogen K, Thrane C (2007) Wolves in context: using survey data to situate attitudes within a wider cultural framework. Soc Nat Resour 21(1):17–33. https://doi.org/10.1080/08941920701460408
Snijders D (2012) Wild property and its boundaries—on wildlife policy and rural consequences in South Africa. J Peasant Stud 39(2):503–520. https://doi.org/10.1080/03066150.2012.667406
Stinson J (2017) Re-creating Wilderness 2.0: Or getting back to work in a virtual nature. Geoforum 79:174–187. https://doi.org/10.1016/j.geoforum.2016.09.002
Svensson G (2016) Do you have any particular favorite place? Hunters' and Anglers' secrets meet tourism in Northern Norway. Arctic Anthropol 53(1):58–68. http://www.jstor.org/stable/26449437
Tickle L, von Essen E (2020) The seven sins of hunting tourism. Ann Tour Res 84:102996. https://doi.org/10.1016/j.annals.2020.102996
Tickle L, von Essen E, Fischer A (2022) Expanding arenas for learning hunting ethics, their grammars and dilemmas: an examination of young hunters' enculturation into modern hunting. Sociol Rural *n/a*(n/a). https://doi.org/10.1111/soru.12371
Tickle L, von Essen E, Fischer A (2024) Fresh meat: women's motivations to hunt and how they challenge hunting structures. Environ Plan E-Nat. https://doi.org/10.1177/25148486241239822
Vajas P, Von Essen E, Tickle L, Gamelon M (2023) Meeting the challenges of wild boar hunting in a modern society: the case of France. Ambio. https://doi.org/10.1007/s13280-023-01852-1
van Heijgen E, Turnhout E, Driessen C (2025) Haunted by hunting: a landscape geneology of the biopolitics, necropolitics, and sovereign power of red deer and wild boar management at the Veluwe. Environ Plan E-Nat Space. https://doi.org/10.1177/25148486241301251
Venker NT, Epstein K, Venker M (2026) PropTech goes wild: hunting access platforms and the neo liberalization of rural land relations. Digit Geogr Soc 100159. https://doi.org/10.1016/j.diggeo.2026.100159
von Essen E (2017) The impact of modernization on hunting ethics: emerging taboos among contemporary Swedish hunters. Hum Dimens Wildl 23(1):21–38. https://doi.org/10.1080/10871209.2018.1385111
von Essen E (2020) The changing wildlife tableau of hunting magazine covers. Soc Anim 1–23. https://doi.org/10.1163/15685306-BJA10002
von Essen E, Allen M, Tickle L (2020) Game of Drones: on the moral significance of deception in modern sport hunting. Philosophical Journal of Conflict and Violence 4(2):137–157
von Essen E, Hansen HP (2018) Policing peers between law and morality: a socio-legal perspective on managing misconduct in hunting. Int J Rural Criminol 1(4)
von Essen E, Peterson J (2024) Digital wildlife expeditions and their impact on human-wildlife relations: Inside the phenomenon of livestreaming an annual moose migration. Digit Geogr Soc 7:100097. https://doi.org/10.1016/j.diggeo.2024.100097

Chapter 8
Animals for Recreational Fishing

Christopher Bova and Warren Potts

> "If I fished only to capture fish, my fishing trips would have ended long ago."
> —*Zane Grey*

Abstract Recreational fishing is a widespread activity shaped by diverse human motivations, from food provision to sport and cultural expression. This chapter explores how these motivations influence the economic, ecological, and social value of recreational fisheries. By challenging the traditional divide between subsistence and recreation, it proposes a more inclusive framework for assessing value, one that accounts for both visible economic contributions and less tangible benefits like nutrition and well-being. The chapter sets the stage for deeper discussions on specialised and trophy fisheries, highlighting the need for balanced, context-sensitive management.

Recreational Fishing and Its Global Significance

The relationship between fish and humans predates historical record, with evidence of human exploitation of fish using tools dating back to the Middle Palaeolithic Era, circa. 75,000 years (Henshilwood et al. 2002). Early forms of fishing rods can be seen as far back as 7000 years ago through ancient Egyptian depictions (Sahrhage 2008). However, the use of rod, reel, line, and hook, which is commonplace in recreational fisheries today, was depicted in artwork by Ma Yuan circa 1160–1225 AD (Needham 1974). While it is unclear when fishing was motivated by anything other than food and sale, it is possible that there were always some motivations that aligned with recreation.

C. Bova (✉) · W. Potts
Department of Ichthyology and Fisheries Science, Rhodes University, Grahamstown, South Africa
e-mail: c.bova@ru.ac.za

W. Potts
e-mail: w.potts@ru.ac.za

N. Batini (ed.), *The Economics of Non-Human Animals*, Natural Resource Management and Policy 63, https://doi.org/10.1007/978-3-032-17580-9_8

In modern times, recreational fishing is generally defined as the capture of fish and other aquatic organisms for personal enjoyment, sport, or cultural expression rather than subsistence or commercial economic gain (Arlinghaus et al. 2013). However, the definition has been expanded to acknowledge the various provisions of recreational fisheries (Cooke et al. 2018). Recreational fishing takes place in virtually every water body that has fish, from deep canyons in the largest oceans to the smallest freshwater streams. Recreational fishing is extremely popular, with an estimated 10% of the world's population participating in some form (Arlinghaus et al. 2021). It is particularly prevalent in High Income Countries (HICs) (Hyder et al. 2018), although there is evidence to suggest that participation rates in Lower Middle-Income Countries (LMICs) are growing rapidly (Bower et al. 2020). This scale makes recreational fishing a significant social phenomenon and an essential contributor to economies, food systems, and human well-being.

Despite its popularity and growth, people's motivations for recreational fishing are far from homogeneous and may vary from essential food provision to spending casual time with family and friends, to competitive sport, or elite trophy-seeking behaviour (Nguyen et al. 2025). This diversity leads to the conceptualisation of recreational fishing as a motivational spectrum or continuum. The position of a recreational angler on this spectrum has profound implications for the economic, ecological, and social dimensions of recreational fisheries.

Cooke et al. (2018) provide a key perspective on the food provision component of recreational fishing, referring to it as the "nexus of fun and nutrition". This work emphasised that recreational fishing is not solely a leisure activity but is often connected to food provisioning and nutritional needs. It also confronted the traditional divide between subsistence and recreation, arguing that fishing frequently exists at the intersection of necessity and enjoyment, particularly in marginalised or resource-limited communities. This viewpoint highlights both the complexity and the necessity for reassessing the value of recreational fisheries. For instance, fishers who are driven by food have different constraints and priorities compared to those seeking to fulfil personal challenges or aesthetic experiences. Furthermore, an individual may not be constrained to a single point in this continuum as their primary motivation may change based on various factors, such as target species, current economic status, customary practices, season, fishing from boat or from shore, freshwater or marine, whether they are on vacation or fishing in their own backyard, the availability of fish at local markets, or countless other contexts. Acknowledging this continuum is vital for fair management; policies focused solely on one type of angler may neglect others fishing for entirely different reasons or limiting the ability to shift motivation along the spectrum.

Recreational fishing is a multifaceted activity that attracts diverse individuals, each driven by their distinct motivations. These motivations can range from the desire to catch fish for food to the pursuit of larger, more impressive trophies that symbolise achievement (Birdsong et al. 2021). The reasons behind people's engagement in recreational fishing can influence various outcomes, including significant impacts on natural resources, the economic landscape, and even considerations regarding food security. When applying the motivation spectrum, from those focused on catching fish primarily for sustenance to those who fish predominantly for sport and leisure, it is evident that each type of fishing carries its own set of consequences. For example, the management of food-oriented fishing often emphasises resource sustainability, ensuring that fish populations remain viable for future generations (Galligan 2021). Conversely, trophy fishing might promote fish populations that are dominated by large individuals, instead of promoting high productivity. Fisheries managed as food fisheries will also have different economic benefits from trophy fisheries, which will tend to stimulate local tourism and possibly increase recreational licence sales (Arostegui et al. 2021).

The different economic benefits from the different types of recreational fisheries reflect a broader and more layered understanding of value. They demonstrate the need for recognising that not all benefits are captured through direct expenditure or conventional market metrics. While some anglers contribute through high per-trip spending, others offer support to local economies and food systems in less apparent but equally meaningful ways. To fully grasp the values associated with recreational fishing, it is necessary to adopt a more inclusive valuation approach that accounts for both direct economic or financial flows and the less visible, yet socially, economically, and culturally significant outcomes. Approaching value in this fishery from a broader perspective can also allow for more balanced management strategies that reflect the diverse motivations and behaviours of anglers and the population groups they affect.

Shared Waters, Diverging Values

Recreational fisheries frequently coexist with commercial and small-scale operations in the same aquatic ecosystems, vying for the same fish stocks despite contrasting objectives. While small-scale and commercial fisheries generally aim to maximise economic returns through the harvesting and selling of fish, recreational anglers typically fish for enjoyment, be it the pleasure of the activity, the excitement of the catch, or the eventual consumption of the fish, which can be an essential source of food and nutritional benefits. However, policy decisions frequently prioritise commercial harvest values, largely because these values reflect their direct contributions to GDP, employment, and trade. This emphasis often results in the social, cultural, and nutritional benefits provided by recreational fisheries being undervalued or outright excluded from management frameworks (Scheufele and Pascoe 2022). Despite their significant importance in shaping equitable and sustainable access to fishery resources, the economic contributions associated with recreational fishing as a leisure activity are similarly overlooked (Potts et al. 2022). Such neglect can create imbalances in policy frameworks that should ideally support both commercial and recreational interests.

Resource Competition and Equity

Resource conflicts between recreational and commercial fisheries are extensively documented in both marine and freshwater ecosystems. In certain instances, particularly where charismatic or high-value species (i.e. sea bass, salmon, tuna) are pursued by both sectors, tensions may escalate into highly politicised debates regarding access, allocation, and equity. Recreational fisheries are frequently characterised as "low-impact", yet this characterisation can be misleading when participation levels reach significant numbers. The combined impact of thousands or millions of anglers, particularly in nearshore ecosystems, can exceed levels of commercial exploitation, even if the individual catch is small (Lewin et al. 2019). The principal distinction is that recreational fishers seldom encounter direct market constraints; their activities are self-subsidised, relying on leisure time and disposable income rather than the imperative for profitability.

This distinction may yield significant ecological repercussions. Within commercial fisheries, a decrease in catch-per-unit-effort (CPUE) generally prompts an economic withdrawal, thereby hindering the total extinction of species solely by the commercial sector. Conversely, recreational anglers may continue fishing activities despite reduced catches, often motivated by non-harvest-related reasons such as enjoyment, tradition, or relaxation. Therefore, effort levels and corresponding resource impacts in recreational fisheries do not necessarily align with declines in fish stocks, raising concerns about sustainability, particularly for vulnerable species or those with slow growth rates.

Benefit Sharing and Sectoral Imbalances

Another significant issue is how benefits are distributed across different sectors. Recreational fisheries often contribute significantly to indirect economic activity, particularly in tourism-centric environments; however, these contributions are not always fairly recognised in national accounting or policy-making. Additionally, commercial fisheries usually take precedence in allocation discussions because of their importance in employment and food supply; even though recreational fisheries can occasionally produce greater economic returns per unit of fish harvested (Scheufele and Pascoe 2022).

However, this comparison may lead to misunderstandings. Recreational and commercial fisheries create distinct types of value, often measured through incompatible methods. While the value of commercial fisheries is evaluated by landed value or Gross Value Added (GVA) (Cai et al. 2019), recreational fisheries are generally assessed using tourism expenditure, contingent valuation, or Travel Cost Methods (TCM) (Loomis and Brown 1984; Potts et al. 2022). These differing approaches reflect various economic aspects, complicating direct comparisons and potentially leading to misconceptions. Consequently, recreational fisheries are often undervalued in management decisions, particularly regarding non-market or social benefits, such as well-being, food access, or community involvement, are omitted.

Ecological Externalities and the "Invisible Impact"

Recreational fishing is often seen as having a relatively low impact on the environment, especially when compared to the impacts of large-scale commercial fishing. One of the reasons for this is the difficulty in measuring catch rates in recreational fisheries, where the highly mobile and often well-resourced fishers move from areas with low to areas with high catch rates (Post 2013). Consequently, catch rates may remain largely stable despite considerable declines in fish populations. Aside from the impacts being ecological, the targeting of fish species that may hold ecological or cultural importance may also render even minor removals as socially controversial (Lewin et al. 2019). Ultimately, the perception that recreational fishing is an innocuous activity may mask any of its ecological effects, such as localised depletion near access points, unintended post-release mortality, and alterations in fish behaviour or reproductive patterns (Radford et al. 2018) as well as the complex social conflicts related to the "asymmetric antipathy" of users and stakeholders (Arlinghaus et al. 2015).

On the other hand, recreational fisheries can also act as significant platforms for conservation. Often, anglers are some of the most vocal supporters for habitat protection, water quality enhancement, and biodiversity preservation. When effectively engaged, communities involved in recreational fishing can assist in monitoring, enforcement, and stewardship efforts that benefit the wider ecosystem (Shephard et al. 2023). This potential for shared benefits highlights the necessity for policy frameworks that go beyond simple trade-offs, acknowledging the intricate interaction of ecological, economic, and social values in common water systems.

Typical Recreational Fishing Value Assessments

Historically, efforts to quantify the value of recreational fisheries have primarily focused on their economic contributions, which include the monetary spending related to fishing trips, gear purchases, licences, travel, accommodation, and related services (Cauvin 1980; Whitehead et al. 2025). Such estimates, commonly produced using TCM or input–output models, have identified recreational fisheries as important elements within regional economies. In areas reliant on tourism, recreational fishing is often portrayed as an economic engine driving local employment, service sectors, and infrastructure growth. However, while expenditure-based valuation highlights one dimension of the importance of recreational fisheries, it only captures part of the overall picture and presents several methodological and interpretive challenges.

Comparisons to Commercial Fisheries: Apples and Pears

A constant challenge that arises in discussions about fisheries policy is the comparison of economic contributions from recreational and non-recreational (including commercial and small-scale) sectors. Commercial fisheries, generally evaluated by GVA, reflect economic output derived from landed value and supply chain activity. On the other hand, recreational fishing valuations frequently rely on gross expenditure, which can encompass spending that does not remain within the local economy or expenditures that could happen even without fishing, such as general tourism. These outputs are not comparable as they assess different forms of economic value.

The GVA provides an indicator of net production (Cai et al. 2019), while the TCM or input–output models reflect consumer behaviour (Southwick et al. 2016). Direct comparisons may over- or underestimate the contribution of recreational fisheries to society without proper adjustments, potentially leading to flawed policy decisions yielding various externalities. Additionally, neither method considers non-market values, such as social cohesion, mental health benefits, cultural practices, or household nutrition; themes that can be especially important for marginalised or coastal communities (Bennett et al. 2021). As many of these non-market values are particularly relevant for recreational fisheries, the reliance on estimates based on expenditure alone may result in the undervaluing of these fisheries when compared with commercial enterprises.

Expenditure Footprints Along the Recreational Fishing Spectrum

Spending patterns of recreational fisheries participants can vary greatly depending on the angler's motivation and resources. For example, fishers motivated by food usually spend less per trip, particularly when fishing takes place locally with basic gear. However, their dependence on what they catch can be substantial, making their contribution to food provisioning disproportionately significant. In contrast, trophy or tourism-focused anglers tend to invest much more in travel, guides, and premium equipment, leading to notable economic impacts despite often harvesting few or no fish at all. Box 8.1 provides some details on this phenomenon. These differences are illustrated in Fig. 8.1: Expenditure Nexus, which plots angler primary motivation categories (Food, Fun, Competition, Trophy) against typical expenditures and economic contributions. It suggests that as you move further along the spectrum from purely food motivations to catching trophy specimens, economic contributions from expenditures increase. This heterogeneity complicates management and investment decisions. Should priority be given to low-expenditure but food-reliant fishers in coastal towns? Alternatively, to high-spending tourists who contribute to the service

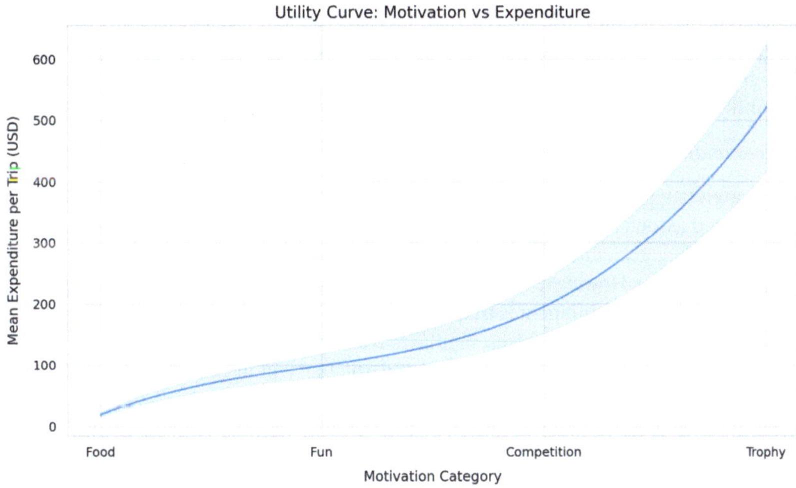

Fig. 8.1 Recreational fishery expenditure nexus linking primary motivation to expenditure-related economic contributions. *Source* Authors' own work

economy but rely heavily on carbon-intensive travel and target ecologically sensitive species? The answer depends on which values are recognised and prioritised in decision-making frameworks.

Context-Dependent Valuation

A growing body of literature calls for a context-sensitive approach to recreational fisheries valuation, one that recognises that economic metrics alone are insufficient, and that values vary across place, culture, and ecosystems (Bennett et al. 2021). In small island states, for example, recreational fishing may play a vital role in access to food and cultural identity. In urban centres, it may contribute more to mental health and social cohesion. A "one-size-fits-all" valuation approach is therefore inadequate. This recognition paves the way for multi-dimensional valuation frameworks, which incorporate not just monetary metrics but also social, nutritional, and ecological considerations. The conceptual utility figure suite developed for this chapter offers a foundation for this broader perspective, and we now turn to some key case studies and emerging evidence that demonstrate how these values materialise in real-world contexts.

Box 8.1 Two Anglers, Two Economies—A Comparative Look at Recreational Fishing Value in the Seychelles

Recreational fisheries contribute to local and national economies in diverse ways, depending heavily on the profile of participating anglers. This case study contrasts two archetypes—the local angler and the tourist angler—to highlight how different user groups generate distinct economic, social, and environmental impacts, using the Republic of Seychelles as a focal example.

Understanding Angler Profiles

Local anglers typically fish close to home, often using modest, self-owned equipment with limited associated travel costs. Their expenditures may include fuel, bait, maintenance of fishing gear, and small-scale retail purchases, many of which circulate within the local economy. However, in contexts such as small island developing states (SIDS), even modest fishing equipment is frequently imported, resulting in considerable expenditure leakage. In ecological terms, regular and extractive fishing by local residents can also exert sustained pressure on fish stocks, particularly in inshore areas.

In contrast, tourist anglers spend significantly more per trip, especially when engaging in guided fishing excursions, charter trips, or destination tournaments. Their spending supports a broader array of economic activities, including accommodation, transport, professional guiding services, and hospitality. Unlike local expenditures, this is often considered new money entering the economy; essentially an export of recreational services that generates a measurable economic impact. In some settings, such as the remote atolls of the Seychelles, tourist anglers engage in non-extractive or low-impact fishing practices (e.g., catch-and-release fly-fishing), resulting in high economic value with relatively low ecological cost.

However, this model is not without caveats. Tourist anglers may preferentially target charismatic or vulnerable species, potentially creating ecological hotspots of pressure, especially where marketing outpaces regulation. Additionally, unlike resident anglers, tourists may not have a long-term connection to local ecosystems, which underscores the need for effective regulatory frameworks and benefit-sharing mechanisms to safeguard sustainability.

Local vs. Tourist: Comparing Value and Impact in the Seychelles

In the Seychelles, a remote island state in the Western Indian Ocean, recreational fisheries span both high-end tourist operations and domestic, often subsistence- or consumption-driven, angling. A notable example is the exclusive catch-and-release fly-fishery located in the nation's outer atolls. Access is limited not only by participatory quotas but also by the high costs involved. Participants must first travel to the main island of Mahé, then charter additional flights to access remote fishing resorts. Packages typically include guides, flights, and accommodation, with additional spending on food, beverages, fishing gear, and additional tourism experiences. With an estimated 555 participants per year, each spending a roughly of USD $17,500, this fishery contributes over USD $4.6 million annually in retained income to the Seychellois economy.

By comparison, local recreational anglers, while spending far less per trip, collectively generate substantial economic activity due to high participation rates. Total spending by resident anglers in the Seychelles is estimated at approximately USD $95 million per year, reflecting not just routine expenditures but also the capital costs of boats, vehicles, and equipment. However, because this spending originates within the domestic economy, it does not constitute net economic inflow. Additionally, local fishing tends to be more extractive, raising ecological concerns, particularly when aggregate effort is high and regulation is limited.

Management Questions and Policy Implications

This comparison presents complex policy trade-offs. Should recreational fisheries management prioritise high-revenue, low-impact tourist anglers, or frequent, place-based local users whose cultural ties are stronger but whose cumulative impacts may be greater? How can regulations ensure that economic value supports local livelihoods without degrading marine ecosystems?

These questions cannot be answered through expenditure data alone. Instead, decision-makers should incorporate additional metrics such as:

- Value retention (how much expenditure stays in the local economy),
- Ecological footprint (per-unit and cumulative impacts),
- Nutritional contribution (especially in food-insecure areas), and
- Social connection and stewardship (the likelihood that users will support conservation outcomes).

Sustainable management of recreational fisheries, particularly in island economies, requires a nuanced understanding of angler heterogeneity and a willingness to balance economic development with ecological responsibility and social equity.

Beyond Leisure: Fishing as Food Provisioning

Although recreational fishing is frequently perceived as a leisure pursuit, it also plays a critical role in food provisioning, particularly in coastal, rural, and economically marginalised communities (Nguyen et al. 2025). In these contexts, fish caught recreationally are not incidental or symbolic; they form a meaningful part of household nutrition, contributing to dietary diversity, protein intake, and cultural food practices. This realisation challenges the artificial binary between "subsistence" and "recreational" fishing. In many countries, especially where formal rights or reporting systems are limited, the line between subsistence and recreation is blurred. Fishers may not sell their catch, but they do rely on it for sustenance (Sunde and Erwin 2020). In such cases, recreational fishing provides an informal safety net, helping buffer against food insecurity and fluctuating access to markets. Indeed, there is a relationship on the motivational context and the dependency on the activity for food (Fig. 8.2).

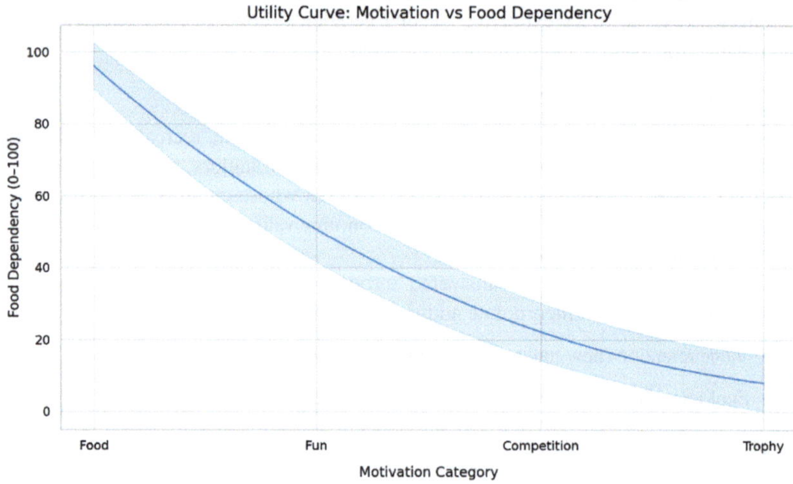

Fig. 8.2 Recreational fishery food dependency nexus linking primary motivation to reliance on food obtained from the activity. *Source* Authors' own work

The Overlooked Nutritional Value of Catch

The *nutritional value of* recreationally caught fish is often underestimated in national food security statistics, despite emerging evidence that it may be substantial in certain regions (Lynch et al. 2024). Many species targeted by recreational fishers, such as mackerel, seabass, mullet, or *tunas* offer high-value nutrition, including essential fatty acids, micronutrients, and digestible protein (Hicks et al. 2019). In areas where access to affordable animal protein is limited, recreational fishing may fill *nutritional demands* not easily met through market systems—as highlighted in Box 8.2. Furthermore, *the practice of catch sharing*, where fishers distribute surplus catch to family, friends, or neighbours, can further diffuse these nutritional benefits across communities (Cooke et al. 2018; Nguyen et al. 2025). These informal food flows rarely show up in economic or health impact studies, yet they form a crucial part of how recreational fisheries function socially and nutritionally.

Inequities in Recognition and Access

Despite this important role, food-provisioning recreational fishers are often marginalised in management regimes. Regulations that assume all recreational fishers are affluent leisure-seekers may disproportionately burden those who fish out of necessity. Bag limits, seasonal closures, license costs, or gear restrictions may unintentionally exclude or criminalise low-income fishers whose primary interest is food, not sport. This disconnect raises questions of equity in access to natural resources, especially where public waters and wild fish stocks are governed in ways that may favour tourism or elite recreational practices. In these contexts, valuing recreational fishing solely through the lens of tourist expenditures risks erasing the food security functions that some segments of the population derive from fishing.

Box 8.2: Case Study: Recreational Fishing and Food Security in Coastal and Urban Communities

Recreational fisheries are often characterised by their contributions to leisure, tourism, and economic value. However, in many regions, particularly in the Global South and within marginalised communities globally, recreational fishing also plays a critical, yet under-recognised, role in food security and household nutrition.

Regional Insights from Southern Africa

In countries such as South Africa and Namibia, informal surveys and ethnographic studies have revealed that shore-based recreational fishers, especially those living in peri-urban areas or informal settlements, frequently rely on their catch as a consistent source of protein and micronutrients. These fishers may not operate within formally recognised small-scale or subsistence frameworks but nonetheless often comply with recreational size and species regulations. Despite their informal status, they contribute meaningfully to local food systems.

Emerging research (e.g., Freire et al. 2020) indicates that in some coastal areas, the volume of fish harvested by recreational or "non-commercial" fishers may equal or even exceed that of formally designated small-scale sectors. However, these contributions are typically absent from national fisheries statistics and food system assessments, leading to policy blind spots regarding their social and nutritional value.

Parallel Dynamics in the Global North

Similar dynamics are observed in North America and parts of Europe, though often less visibly. Research by Joosse et al. (2021) highlights how, in low-income urban neighbourhoods, some individuals engage in nearshore or urban freshwater fishing as a means of supplementing household diets with affordable protein. These practices are often embedded in cultural traditions and passed through generations, particularly within immigrant and Indigenous communities, linking fishing to both food sovereignty and cultural identity (Nguyen 2025).

Implications for Valuation and Governance

Recognising the food provisioning role of recreational fisheries requires a conceptual shift in how these sectors are valued and managed. Traditionally assessed through metrics such as participation rates, expenditure, or economic multipliers, recreational fisheries are seldom evaluated for their contributions to nutrition, food access, or poverty alleviation. To address this gap, policymakers and researchers should consider the following:

- Revising data collection frameworks to include indicators of household reliance on recreationally caught fish;

- Legitimising informal provisioning fisheries as legitimate users of aquatic resources, particularly where their practices are sustainable and community-embedded;

- Designing access and conservation policies that account for both leisure-oriented and needs-based fishers, ensuring that vulnerable groups are not excluded by blanket restrictions.

By integrating food security into the governance and valuation of recreational fisheries, a more holistic and equitable understanding of their societal role can emerge, one that reflects not only economic and recreational dimensions but also the essential connections between fisheries, nutrition, rights, and resilience. Such an approach aligns with the broader imperatives of sustainable development, biodiversity conservation, and social inclusion. However, an increased focus on this type of consumptive value must also heavily consider the costs of the associated ecosystem impacts and find a sustainable solution.

Fishing for More Than Fish

Recreational fishing delivers more than economic or nutritional value; it also contributes meaningfully to mental health, physical activity, social cohesion, and personal well-being (Pita et al. 2022). These benefits are increasingly recognised in public health and environmental psychology research, yet they are often excluded from conventional fisheries management or economic valuation frameworks. Various examples from contemporary literature point to recreational fishing as a unique form of "blue space" interaction, a category of nature-based activity that offers cognitive restoration, stress relief, and emotional regulation (White et al. 2020). Time spent in natural aquatic environments, whether it be a riverbank, beach, or offshore reef, can foster mindfulness, connection to nature, and reduced physiological markers of stress (Djernis et al. 2019).

Psychological and Social Value

Anglers often highlight relaxation, solitude, escapism from everyday stress, and a bond with nature as primary motivations for fishing, regardless of their catch. These reasons become even more pronounced in urban areas, where access to nature is often limited (Arlinghaus et al. 2017; Joosse et al. 2021). For older adults, those with mental health challenges, and individuals who feel socially isolated, recreational fishing provides a structured and accessible way to engage with nature, promoting psychological resilience (Wilson et al. 2023).

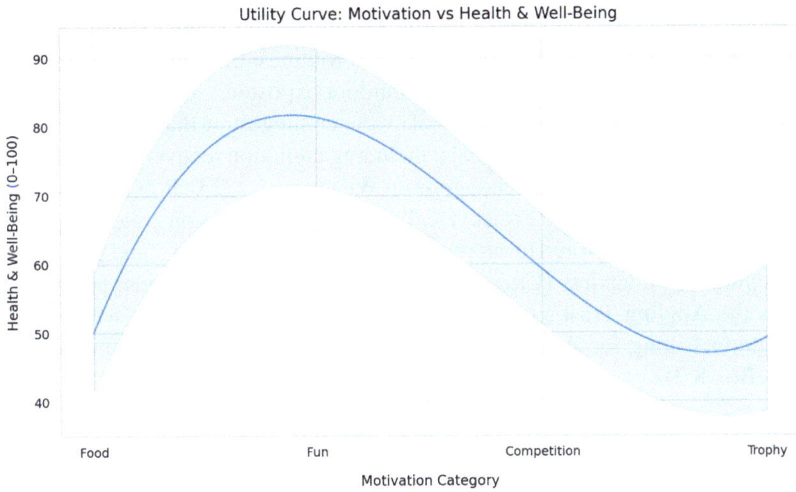

Fig. 8.3 Recreational fishery health and well-being nexus linking primary motivation to experienced health and well-being benefits. *Source* Authors' own work

At a broader level, recreational fishing can enhance social networks and strengthen intergenerational connections. Shared fishing experiences among parents and their children, friends, or community groups can foster trust, facilitate knowledge sharing, and create a sense of belonging (Gustavsson and Riley 2018). In many cultures, fishing extends beyond a mere hobby; it is a cultural practice that conveys values, narratives, and identity, especially in Indigenous and coastal communities (Liu et al. 2019). While these benefits are challenging to quantify from a traditional monetary standpoint, they remain significant. Their intangible qualities make them particularly at risk of being overlooked in policy decisions that focus on market-driven evaluations. Unlike the previous metrics, the contributions of health and well-being benefits are generally experienced at higher levels across the motivation continuum (Fig. 8.3).

Physical and Behavioural Health Benefits

From a public health perspective, recreational fishing provides an accessible form of low-impact physical activity, particularly valuable for individuals with limited access to conventional exercise infrastructure. The physical demands of fishing, such as walking to remote sites, casting, wading, or paddling, offer moderate movement that supports cardiovascular and musculoskeletal health (Griffiths et al. 2017). In addition, the goal-oriented or socially and culturally meaningful nature of fishing may enhance motivation and encourage prolonged engagement compared to more abstract or repetitive forms of physical exercise (Pita et al. 2022). This structured and purposeful activity may thus hold particular value for populations less inclined to participate in organised sport or gym-based routines, offering both physical and psychological benefits through sustained outdoor exposure.

This is supported by a growing body of evidence suggesting that angling participation supports behavioural health goals, including addiction recovery, post-traumatic stress management, and social reintegration (Wilson et al. 2023). Programmes such as Fishing for Heroes (UK) and Project Healing Waters (US) demonstrate how angling-based therapy can be tailored to support veterans, trauma survivors, and people living with depression or anxiety (Craig et al. 2020). Additionally, wellness programmes, such as the Angling Trust's *Get Fishing for Wellbeing* programme, which enables prescription fishing for those with qualifying conditions, aim to promote mental health (Box 8.3).

Lines in the Water, Scars in the Ecosystem: The Hidden Costs of Recreational Fishing

So far the chapter has focused on the economic value of recreational fishing, particularly the benefits it brings to fishers, tourism, and local economies. However, there is another side to this story, one that is often overlooked, which is ethical considerations in recreational fishing.

Many organisations and advocacy-based reviews in the scientific literature have raised concerns around recreational fishing, suggesting that fish caught in recreational contexts are frequently subjected to significant suffering. Probably the most contentious subject on the ethics around recreational fishing is whether fish feel pain? Scholars such as Lynne Sneddon and Victoria Braithwaite have argued that fish are sentient beings capable of experiencing pain, fear, and stress, and that these capacities should be taken seriously in ethical and regulatory discussions (Sneddon 2015; Braithwaite 2010). Their work draws on both behavioural and neurophysiological evidence, showing that fish respond to noxious stimuli in ways that suggest more than mere reflex, responses that are modulated by analgesics and involve learning and avoidance behaviours.

At the same time, Rose et al. (2014) and Diggles et al. (2024) have expressed scepticism about the idea that fish experience pain in a way analogous to humans. They argue that fish lack the neurological structures (such as a neocortex) required for conscious experience and that their responses to injury are better explained as unconscious, reflexive reactions. This perspective is summarised in Box 1 of Browman et al. (2019), which outlines the neurobiological basis for doubting fish sentience.

A clearer understanding of how fish respond to potentially harmful human interactions remains an important area of scientific inquiry. The ongoing debates within the literature, between those who argue that fish experience pain and those who remain unconvinced, reflects a genuine uncertainty rather than disagreement over the importance of the question itself. Much of this uncertainty stems from differing definitions of pain and from the challenges in interpreting behavioural and physiological responses in fishes. Given these contrasting perspectives, progress is most likely to emerge from collaborative research efforts that establish shared conceptual foundations, apply clearly defined and falsifiable hypotheses, and use methods that can be independently replicated. Advancing knowledge in this way would help move the field beyond entrenched positions and towards a more coherent and evidence-based understanding of fish responses to human activities.

Box 8.3: Case Study: Promoting Public Health Through Angling in the United Kingdom

Recreational fishing is increasingly recognised not only for its economic and ecological dimensions, but also for its contributions to public health and social well-being. In the United Kingdom, these benefits have been formalised through the integration of angling into social prescribing models, a health care approach in which clinicians refer patients to non-clinical, nature-based activities as part of broader therapeutic interventions.

Angling as a Nature-Based Health Intervention

One leading example is the Angling Trust's *Get Fishing for Wellbeing* programme, which partners with health care providers, community organisations, and mental health services to offer "prescribed" angling experiences for individuals experiencing psychological distress, social isolation, or physical inactivity. These interventions aim to reconnect individuals with outdoor environments, foster social engagement, and provide a sense of purpose through regular and meaningful activity.

Initial evaluations of the programme have revealed positive mental health outcomes, including improved mood, reduced symptoms of anxiety and depression, increased motivation to spend time outdoors, and enhanced feelings of self-worth. In some cases, participants report that angling served as a gateway to re-engagement with nature and community life after long periods of social withdrawal or clinical treatment. These benefits are particularly relevant in underserved communities where access to nature and structured recreation is limited.

Rethinking Value: Well-Being as a Policy Outcome

Despite its demonstrated benefits, the role of recreational fishing in improving human health and well-being remains largely invisible in traditional fisheries governance. Conventional management frameworks tend to prioritise metrics such as biomass, catch rates, and economic impacts, leaving out the qualitative, cumulative, and often intangible dimensions of personal and community health.

Integrating well-being into the valuation of recreational fisheries demands a fundamental shift in how benefits are conceptualised and measured. This includes:

- Moving beyond outcomes quantified in kilograms or dollars, toward outcomes measured in lives improved, mental health gains, or community cohesion;
- Shifting from resource allocation based purely on economic efficiency to resource sharing grounded in collective social benefit.

As environmental and health planning increasingly intersect, particularly in the face of rising mental health challenges and growing interest in nature-based solutions, recreational fishing stands out as a relatively low-cost, high-impact intervention.

Recognising and supporting this role can help align blue economy strategies with public health objectives, ensuring that fisheries policy reflects not only ecological and economic sustainability, but also the broader well-being of the communities it serves.

Recognising recreational fishing as a practice that enhances health and well-being is essential for integrating biodiversity and nature into economic and social decisions. Nature is not just a setting for recreation; it actively contributes to human flourishing. It is clear that recreational fisheries serve as a significant platform for this interaction.

While this process may take some time, several organisations and scholars have called for the precautionary approach in this matter. In other words, assume that fish do feel pain in the same way as birds or mammals, and that they are sentient beings, until proven wrong. This will require changes in the approach to fishes in many countries. For example, many countries in the EU and North America view fish primarily as natural resources rather than sentient individuals. Thus, their fisheries policies (for example, the EU's Common Fisheries Policy) focus on sustainable exploitation, not welfare. This is unlike most terrestrial animals, which benefit from more robust protections under animal welfare legislation. However, some countries (e.g. the United Kingdom) are already adopting a precautionary approach and are beginning to implement welfare legislation that recognises fish as sentient beings. These changes are likely to have implications beyond recreational fisheries and include all capture fisheries and the aquaculture industries. It is likely that these changes may lead to profound economic, social, and environmental consequences.

In the context of recreational fisheries, it is unlikely that welfare legislation will support the notion of catch-and-release. This welfare approach has already led to a ban of catch-and-release in some countries, such as Germany. Many may feel that this approach is sensible, particularly since a meta-analysis by Bartholomew and Bohnsack (2005), which reviewed 274 studies, found that post-release mortality in recreational fisheries ranges from 0 to 95%, with a median of 11% and a mean of 18%. Indeed, for some species, under certain conditions, such as deep hooking, warm water, or prolonged handling, mortality rates can be alarmingly high. However, for most species, catch-and-release is vital to maintain sustainable fish populations. In fact, fisheries regulations require catch-and-release for fish that are immature or larger individuals that contribute disproportionately more to the reproductive output of the population. Failure to control fisheries using catch-and-release regulations can have profoundly negative consequences for some species, ecosystems, and communities that are reliant on these resources.

In other cases, coastal economies are often driven by the tourism associated with catch-and-release fisheries. For example, The Bahamas has a tourist-based catch-and-release flats fishery that brings significant economic benefit to its citizens and the country. The fishery resources of this fishery would be rapidly depleted, and the local benefits would be undermined if catch-and-release were banned. This will lead to job losses (for example, the guides), economic hardship, and further pressure on aquatic resources as actors in this non-consumptive fishery shift to consumptive resource utilisation.

Although wholescale changes to the way we perceive fisheries resources are not recommended, unless there is unequivocal evidence for the sentience of fishes, we do need to incorporate fish welfare considerations into fisheries management systems. In a recreational fisheries context, there are many practices, including retaining fish in live wells for hours or the use of inhumane techniques to dispatch fish, and poor catch-and-release practices that need urgent attention. These fish welfare concerns should be solved by working with recreational angling communities to determine the most appropriate interventions to improve fish welfare, be they awareness drives, knowledge dissemination, or legislative amendments with appropriate enforcement. Ultimately, a more balanced and ethical approach to fisheries management must recognise the hidden costs associated with fish welfare and work towards practices that respect both ecological integrity and social justice.

Recognising the Full Spectrum of Value

Recreational fisheries generate a diverse array of benefits, from local economic activity and tourism revenue to food provisioning, mental health, and community cohesion. However, these values are rarely assessed together and even less frequently integrated into management decisions. Most fisheries governance systems still rely on narrow metrics, such as economic output, biomass harvested, or compliance rates, which fail to reflect the multi-dimensional societal contributions that recreational fishing provides as a Social-Ecological System (SES) (Hunt et al. 2013). To better align policy with reality, there is an urgent need to move beyond traditional, market-based valuation frameworks and towards holistic, inclusive approaches that reflect the entire spectrum of benefits and trade-offs pertaining to recreational fishing activities.

Addressing Allocation Challenges: Apples, Pears, and Blind Spots

One of the central problems in managing recreational fisheries is the tendency to treat different sectors, commercial, recreational, and small-scale, as comparable based on singular metrics like GVA or catch volume. This often can lead to false equivalences that obscure underlying differences in motivation, impact, and societal function. For example, consider the contrasting contributions of different angler groups within a coastal community. A small number of affluent tourist anglers might spend heavily on guided trips, accommodation, and gear, resulting in a relatively high economic return per person. However, their impact on local food systems or social networks tends to be limited, often confined to the tourism sector. In contrast, a much larger group of local, low-spending resident anglers may not generate the same level of gross value added, but they play a critical role in other dimensions of value. These community-based fishers often rely on their catch for nutrition, share traditional ecological knowledge across generations, and strengthen local resilience by embedding fishing practices into everyday life. While their direct economic footprint may appear modest, their broader contributions to social and food systems are substantial. Neither group in this example is necessarily more "valuable" than the other. Instead, each contributes to different types of value, requiring tailored strategies to assess and manage them. This insight challenges policymakers to reconsider how resource access is allocated, and how value is defined in the first place.

Integrating Food, Fun, and Function into Valuation

The example utility figures given earlier in this chapter, depicting how angler motivations span spending patterns, food reliance, and well-being, are not merely illustrative concepts. They also provide a starting point for rethinking how we assess the value of recreational fisheries and some potential trade-offs to consider when prioritising values. These figures invite us to move beyond traditional economic metrics and towards a more inclusive framework that recognises the diverse forms of value anglers bring to the table, whether they be purely economic, nutritional, social, or cultural. They also highlight the need to account for different types of anglers, each with unique relationships to fishery resources. Importantly, this approach encourages us to view value cumulatively, acknowledging the broader significance of widespread participation rather than reducing impact to singular, isolated indicators. Such frameworks would allow for better-informed trade-offs, especially in contexts where management actions may unintentionally marginalise food-reliant or culturally connected or wellness-focussed fishers in favour of high-expenditure anglers.

The trade-offs for management prioritising expenditure over food dependency or health and well-being are apparent in Fig. 8.4.

Policy Focus: Sustainability and Equity Together

The future of recreational fisheries management depends on a holistic balance between conservation of ecosystems and ensuring that benefits are accrued by participants from all walks of life; between promoting economic well-being and opportunities while safeguarding biodiversity; and between recognising fishing as a source of food, enjoyment, well-being, and cultural identity. Achieving this balance calls for a paradigm shift in governance strategies. Rather than relying only on instrumental approaches to management (i.e. regulations, economic outputs), more adaptive, inclusive frameworks that are attuned to the contextual needs, motivations, and outcomes of different user groups are needed. Also required is a change of mindset; moving beyond the outdated notion that recreational fishing is simply a low-impact leisure

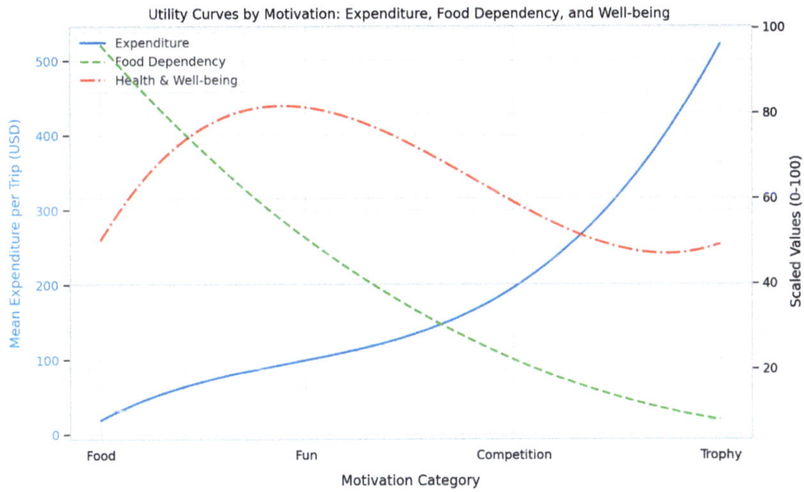

Fig. 8.4 Overlaid utility curves of expenditure, food dependency, and health and well-being benefits derived from various recreational fishery participation motivations. *Source* Authors' own work

activity and beginning to view it as part of a wider entanglement of well-being, food systems, and ecosystem service contributions.

Bridging to the Next Conversation: Specialised and Trophy Fisheries

While considering the need for more inclusive valuation frameworks, we must recognise that recreational fishing varies in sustainability risk and societal return. Highly specialised fisheries like those focusing on rare or vulnerable species or designed for elite tourism present unique challenges and opportunities. These fisheries tend to produce significant economic gains and attract intense ecological examination, particularly when associated with international travel, carbon emissions, or practices that hinder conservation efforts. In the next section, we explore the world of trophy fishing, examining how highly specialised recreational practices intersect with questions of sustainability, ethical treatment of animals, and benefit-sharing. This final piece adds nuance to our understanding of value by showing how intensity and exclusivity can shape both outcomes and perceptions.

Conclusions

The future of recreational fisheries management hinges on achieving a delicate balance between conserving ecosystems and ensuring equitable access to benefits; between fostering economic opportunities, protecting biodiversity, and enhancing fish welfare; and between recognising fishing as a source of food, cultural identity, and personal well-being. This balance cannot be achieved through traditional, one-size-fits-all approaches. Instead, it demands a paradigm shift towards governance strategies that are adaptive, inclusive, and responsive to the diverse motivations and needs of recreational fishers.

Such a shift involves moving beyond instrumental management tools focused solely on regulation and economic output. It requires embracing frameworks that account for the full spectrum of values (nutritional, social, cultural, and ecological) that recreational fishing provides. Equally important is a change in mindset: recreational fishing must no longer be viewed as a low-impact leisure activity, but as a complex and influential component of global food systems, well-being, and ecosystem services. The assumption that practices like catch-and-release are inherently harmless must be re-evaluated, and efforts to improve fish welfare in recreational fisheries should be pursued.

As we move forward, it is also essential to recognise that not all recreational fisheries are created equal. Specialised and trophy fisheries, often associated with high economic returns and elite tourism, present unique sustainability challenges. These include increased ecological scrutiny, ethical concerns over fish welfare, and questions around equitable benefit-sharing—particularly in regions where recreational use may compete with local subsistence or Indigenous fishing traditions. Chapter 9 delves into these specialised fisheries to explore how exclusivity and intensity shape both the impacts and the perceived value of recreational fishing.

References

Arlinghaus Retal (2017) Understanding and Managing Fresh water Recreational Fisheries as Complex Adaptive Social-Ecological Systems. Reviews in Fisheries Science & Aquaculture 25: 1–41.

Arlinghaus R, Cooke SJ, Potts W (2013) Towards resilient recreational fisheries on a global scale through improved understanding of fish and fisher behaviour. Fish Manage Ecol 20:91–98. https://doi.org/10.1111/fme.12027

Arlinghaus R, Tillner R, Bork M (2015) Explaining participation rates in recreational fishing across industrialised countries. Fish Manage Ecol 22:45–55. https://doi.org/10.1111/fme.12075

Arlinghaus R, Aas Ø, Alós J et al (2021) Global participation in and public attitudes toward recreational fishing: International perspectives and developments. Reviews in Fisheries Science & Aquaculture 29:58–95. https://doi.org/10.1080/23308249.2020.1782340

Arostegui MC, Anderson CM, Benedict RF et al (2021) Approaches to regulating recreational fisheries: balancing biology with angler satisfaction. Rev Fish Biol Fisheries 31:573–598. https://doi.org/10.1007/s11160-021-09662-y

Bartholomew A & Bohnsack J A (2005) A Review of Catch-and-Release Angling Mortality with Implications for No-take Reserves. Rev Fish Biol Fisheries 15: 129–154.
Bennett NJ, Schuhbauer A, Skerritt D, Ebrahim N (2021) Socio-economic monitoring and evaluation in fisheries. Fish Res 239:105934. https://doi.org/10.1016/j.fishres.2021.105934
Birdsong M, Hunt LM, Arlinghaus R (2021) Recreational angler satisfaction: what drives it? Fish Fish 22:682–706. https://doi.org/10.1111/faf.12545
Bower SD, Aas Ø, Arlinghaus R et al (2020) Knowledge gaps and management priorities for recreational fisheries in the developing world. Rev Fish Sci Aqua 28:518–535. https://doi.org/10.1080/23308249.2020.1770689
Braithwaite V (2010) Do Fish Feel Pain? (Oxford Univ. Press, Oxford).
Browman H I etal (2019) Welfare of aquaticanimals: where things are, where they are going, and what it means for research, aquaculture, recreationalangling, and commercialfishing. ICESJ Mar Sci 76: 82–92.
Cai J, Huang H, Leung P (2019) Understanding and measuring the contribution of aquaculture and fisheries to gross domestic product (GDP). FAO, Rome
Cauvin D (1980) The valuation of recreational fisheries. Can J Fish Aquat Sci 37:1321 1327. https://doi.org/10.1139/f80-169
Cooke SJ, Twardek WM, Lennox RJ et al (2018) The nexus of fun and nutrition: recreational fishing is also about food. Fish Fish 19:201–224. https://doi.org/10.1111/faf.12246
Craig P, Alger D, Bennett J, Martin T (2020) The transformative nature of fly-fishing for veterans and military personnel with posttraumatic stress disorder. TRJ 54. https://doi.org/10.18666/TRJ-2020-V54-I2-9965
Diggles BK et al (2024) Reasons to Be Skepticalabout Sentience and Painin Fishes and AquaticInvertebrates.Reviews in Fisheries Science & Aquaculture 32: 127–150.
Djernis D, Lerstrup I, Poulsen D et al (2019) A systematic review and meta-analysis of nature-based mindfulness: effects of moving mindfulness training into an outdoor natural setting. Int J Environ Res Public Health 16:3202. https://doi.org/10.3390/ijerph16173202
Freire KMF etal. (2020) Estimating Global Catches of Marine Recreational Fisheries. Front. Mar. Sci. 7.
Galligan BP (2021) Fisheries extractivism and the right to subsistence: conflicting governance models and the legal structures that enact them. Mar Policy 133:104729. https://doi.org/10.1016/j.marpol.2021.104729
Griffiths SP, Bryant J, Raymond HF, Newcombe PA (2017) Quantifying subjective human dimensions of recreational fishing: does good health come to those who bait? Fish Fish 18:171–184. https://doi.org/10.1111/faf.12149
Gustavsson M, Riley M (2018) The fishing lifecourse: exploring the importance of social contexts, capitals and (more than) fishing identities. Sociol Rural 58:562–582. https://doi.org/10.1111/soru.12181
Henshilwood CS, d'Errico F, Yates R et al (2002) Emergence of modern human behavior: middle stone age engravings from South Africa. Science 295:1278–1280. https://doi.org/10.1126/science.1067575
Hicks CC et al (2019) Harnessing global fisheries to tacklemicronutrient deficiencies. Nature 574: 95–98.
Hunt LM, Sutton SG, Arlinghaus R (2013) Illustrating the critical role of human dimensions research for understanding and managing recreational fisheries within a social-ecological system framework. Fish Manage Ecol 20:111–124. https://doi.org/10.1111/j.1365-2400.2012.00870.x
Hyder K, Weltersbach MS, Armstrong M et al (2018) Recreational sea fishing in Europe in a global context—participation rates, fishing effort, expenditure, and implications for monitoring and assessment. Fish Fish 19:225–243. https://doi.org/10.1111/faf.12251
Joosse S, Hensle L, Boonstra WJ, et al (2021) Fishing in the city for food—a paradigmatic case of sustainability in urban blue space. NPJ Urban Sustain 1:1–8. https://doi.org/10.1038/s42949-021-00043-9

Lewin W-C, Weltersbach MS, Ferter K et al (2019) Potential environmental impacts of recreational fishing on marine fish stocks and ecosystems. Rev Fish Sci Aquacult 27:287–330. https://doi.org/10.1080/23308249.2019.1586829

Liu Y, Bailey JL & Davidsen JG (2019) Social-Cultural Ecosystem Services of Sea Trout Recreational Fishing in Norway. Front. Mar. Sci. 6.

Loomis J, Brown W (1984) The use of travel cost models to estimate the net economic value of recreational fishing at new and existing sites. In: Making economic information more useful for Salmon and Steelhead production decisions. National Marine Fisheries Service, Seattle

Lynch AJ et al (2024) In land recreational fisheries contribute nutritional benefits and economic value but are vulnerable to climate change. Nat Food 5: 433–443.

Needham J (1974) Science and civilisation in China. Cambridge University Press

Nguyen VM-A, Fiorella KJ, Castello L, et al (2025) Provisioning fisheries: A framework for recognizing the fuzzy boundary around commercial, subsistence, and recreational fisheries. Fisheries, vuae31. https://doi.org/10.1093/fshmag/vuae031

Pita P, Gribble MO, Antelo M et al (2022) Recreational fishing, health and well-being: findings from a cross-sectional survey. Ecosyst People 18:530–546. https://doi.org/10.1080/26395916.2022.2112291

Post JR (2013) Resilient recreational fisheries or prone to collapse? A decade of research on the science and management of recreational fisheries. Fisheries Management and Ecology 20: 99–110.

Potts WM, Saayman M, Saayman A et al (2022) Understanding the economic activity generated by recreational fishing in South Africa provides insights on the role of recreational fisheries for social development. Fish Manage Ecol 29:29–43. https://doi.org/10.1111/fme.12515

Radford Z, Hyder K, Zarauz L et al (2018) The impact of marine recreational fishing on key fish stocks in European waters. PLoS ONE 13:e0201666. https://doi.org/10.1371/journal.pone.0201666

Rose JD et al (2014) Can fish really feel pain? Fish and Fisheries 15: 97–133.

Sahrhage D (2008) Fishing in Ancient Egypt. Encyclopaedia of the history of science, technology, and medicine in non-Western cultures. Springer, Dordrecht, pp 922–927

Scheufele G, Pascoe S (2022) Estimation and use of recreational fishing values in management decisions. Ambio 51:1275–1286. https://doi.org/10.1007/s13280-021-01634-7

Shephard S, List CJ, Arlinghaus R (2023) Reviving the unique potential of recreational fishers as environmental stewards of aquatic ecosystems. Fish Fish 24:339–351. https://doi.org/10.1111/faf.12723

Sneddon LU (2015) Pain in aquaticanimals. J Exp Biol 218: 967–976.

Southwick R, Maycock D, Bouaziz M (2016) Recreational fisheries economic impact assessment manual and its application in two study cases in the Caribbean: Martinique and The Bahamas. Food and Agriculture Organization of the United Nations, Rome

Sunde J, Erwin K (2020) Cast out: The systematic exclusion of the KwaZulu Natal Subsistence Fishers from the fishing rights regime in South Africa. KZN Subsistence Fisher's Forum and South Durban Community Environmental Alliance (SDCEA), Durban

White MP, Elliott LR, Gascon M et al (2020) Blue space, health and well-being: a narrative overview and synthesis of potential benefits. Environ Res 191:110169. https://doi.org/10.1016/j.envres.2020.110169

Whitehead JC, Cornicelli L, Bragg L, Southwick R (2025) The aggregate economic value of Great Lakes recreational fishing trips. J Great Lakes Res 51:102529. https://doi.org/10.1016/j.jglr.2025.102529

Wilson JJ, Trott M, Tully MA et al (2023) Mental health and recreational angling in UK adult males: a cross-sectional study. Epidemiologia 4:298–308. https://doi.org/10.3390/epidemiologia4030030

Chapter 9
Animals for Trophy Angling

Samuel Blyth

> "A gamefish is too valuable to only be caught once."
> —*Lee Wulff*

Abstract This chapter examines the complex role of trophy fishing at the intersection of ecology, economy, and ethics. It explores how the pursuit of large or unique fish shapes angler behavior, influences fisheries management, and contributes to local and global economies. Drawing on global case studies, it highlights the potential for well-managed trophy fisheries to support conservation goals through catch-and-release practices, citizen science, and incentive-based regulation. At the same time, the chapter critically considers the experience of the fish, emphasizing the need to reduce suffering, sublethal impacts, and mortality through best practices and ethical frameworks. It argues for policy reforms that internalize the ecological and welfare costs of fishing, expand the definition of a "trophy" to include species diversity and local significance, and promote stewardship that respects both human and non-human interests. The chapter proposes an integrated governance approach that includes differentiated licensing and conservation fees, species-specific bag and slot limits, mandatory reporting and citizen science platforms, recognition programs for ethical and diverse catches, precautionary risk assessments for vulnerable species, and enforceable rules for catch-and-release practices. Together, these tools aim to align biological sustainability, economic value, and ethical responsibility in recreational fisheries.

Beyond the Catch: The Trophy Economy of Recreational Fishing

As indicated in this chapter, trophy fishing occupies a unique position at the end of the spectrum of recreational fishing activities. Here trophy fishing deserves further exploration and explanation as it represents certain extremes of recreational fishing

S. Blyth (✉)
Earth Sciences, Uppsala University, Visby, Sweden
e-mail: samuel.blyth@geo.uu.se

N. Batini (ed.), *The Economics of Non-Human Animals*, Natural Resource Management and Policy 63, https://doi.org/10.1007/978-3-032-17580-9_9

activity that have unique impacts on human-nature relations and have spillover effects on ecosystems, economies, and other forms of recreational fishing.

Big fish stories and the pursuit of trophy fish have shaped human-nature interactions throughout history and continue to play this important role in art and media today (White and McLaren 2024). Ernest Hemingway's (1952) masterpiece "The Old Man and the Sea" is perhaps the most famous piece of literature about fishing, which uses the struggle of fishing for the largest of fish as a metaphor for life, although the protagonist is an artisanal rather than recreational fisher. In decades before this, the prolific author Zane Grey wrote several books introducing readers and the general public to trophy fishing for large game fish around the world during the early twentieth century (ZGWS 2025). Modern media continues to use trophy fish as a key component in story telling with television programs such as Extreme Fishing with Robson Green (2008–2011), River Monsters (2009–2017), and Wicked Tuna (2012–2024); as well as countless YouTube channels and videos on other platforms.

At one end of the trophy spectrum is pursuit of the absolute largest individuals of a species with the aim of having a record-sized specimen certified by a central authority (Shiffman et al. 2014). This has historically been associated with particularly large and charismatic species such as billfish, tuna, and sharks (Boon et al. 2024). The certification of trophy-sized specimens extends to species that do not grow so large, with micro-fishing being an extreme example of the pursuit of smaller species of fish (Cooke et al. 2020b). The trophy concept also extends to awards for angling skill (and associated prestige within some segments of the angling community) are also granted in tournaments for the largest individual or combined group of individual fish from a given body of water during a given time period (e.g., bass tournaments), largest number of fish caught without regard for size (e.g., fly-fishing tournaments), or the number of species captured. In some cases, anglers are recognized not only for individual feats but also for lifetime achievements, such as awards for the total number of species caught across different regions or ecosystems—highlighting both dedication and breadth of experience in the sport.

Of course, the competitive spirit at the heart of trophy fishing is not limited to tournaments or record books—it also applies to individual anglers. Many fishers set personal goals, celebrate memorable catches, and recognize what constitutes an exceptional fish for a specific body of water, even if that species grows larger elsewhere. In this context, a "trophy" is not just about size or rarity—it represents added symbolic value. It elevates a fish beyond its market price, its utility as food, its ecological role, or even the challenge of catching it. A trophy fish becomes a marker of personal achievement, connection to place, and the meaning anglers assign to the experience. Yet from the fish's perspective, this symbolic value is irrelevant—what matters is survival. The same qualities that make a fish a trophy to humans often make it the most vulnerable to capture, raising important ethical and ecological questions about how we define and pursue value in nature.

Measuring Success: Trophy Fishing and Conservation Challenges

Trophy fishing is far from a modern phenomenon—it has deep roots in how humans have long measured fishing success. The size or number of fish caught has been measures of fishing success throughout history. In subsistence contexts, this would advertise skill and convey status, where a good catch and surplus harvest ensured both short-term survival and the ability to save food for future consumption. In recreational fisheries, this emphasis remains evident in the common angler motivation to catch the longest or heaviest fish possible (Arlinghaus 2006). This focus on catching the biggest fish is exemplified by the International Game Fish Association (IGFA), which certifies and maintains records of the largest fish caught by anglers around the world. National and regional organizations, as well as a host of angling competitions, mirror this competitive record-keeping structure.

Formal recognition of a trophy-sized catch typically requires a verified and credible measurement of the fish. Following the IGFA as an example, most record systems have historically been based on weight. Often, this requires fish to be transported to accredited scales at a land-based weighing station, effectively eliminating the option of catch-and-release for large traditional trophy species (e.g., tuna, billfish, sharks) and dramatically complicating it for smaller species (Brownscombe et al. 2017; Shiffman et al. 2014). Harvested trophies are also consumed, which adds value and reduces waste. However, transporting the fish whole and intact to maintain weight can result in poorer food quality relative to immediately processing the fish (Tuna Champions 2025).

Record-setting is increasingly open to length-based measures, reflecting the fact that many anglers' desire to catch a trophy-sized fish is not associated with a desire to harvest it. Fish of that size are often released (Blyth et al. 2025; García-Asorey et al. 2011). The IGFA's All-Tackle Length records are based on length measurements, which make it easier to maintain best practices for catch-and-release, as catches do not need to be lifted from the water—let alone taken to shore or killed (IGFA 2025).

Yet even when catch-and-release focused, record-seeking trophy fishing can have large impacts on fish populations and ecosystems, particularly for freshwater fish where commercial and other fishing is not present (Arlinghaus et al. 2007; Joubert et al. 2020). Pressure is focused on the biggest and best fish through harvest and direct mortality, and in the form of indirect mortality and sublethal effects during catch-and-release (Brownscombe et al. 2017; Sutter et al. 2012). Additionally, it can contribute to a hierarchy of values where anglers and managers focus attention on a limited number of species or the largest individuals in a population (Rypel et al. 2021; Sutter et al. 2012).

Targeting threatened and endangered species—as listed by the International Union for the Conservation of Nature (IUCN) Red List—is a well-documented problem for trophy and non-trophy recreational fisheries, as well as artisanal and commercial fisheries (Boon et al. 2024; Cooke et al. 2016; Shiffman et al. 2014, 2015). Depletion of stocks by all forms of fishing is a serious issue that—even if it does not result in extinction—can take decades to rectify (Nøttestad et al. 2020). There are many jurisdictions where threatened species are protected from commercial harvest, yet regulations (or a lack of regulations) allow them to be targeted or caught as bycatch by recreational anglers (Cooke et al. 2016). Further, it is argued that awarding records (including records for released fish) causes anglers to target the most fecund individuals in populations of threatened and endangered species (Shiffman et al. 2014), with the removal of even a small number of individuals resulting in disproportionately large negative impacts on population dynamics (Sutter et al. 2012).

For several of these threatened species, it has also been argued that the potential to certify a record has not resulted in higher catch rates and submission to the IGFA, particularly when compared to commercial catches. Examples include a single critically endangered southern bluefin tuna (*Thunnus maccoyii*) being submitted for an IGFA All-Tackle record between 1991 and 2011, while total landings for the period were 293,695 metric tons, and a single mako shark (*Isurus spp.*) being submitted in contrast to total landings of 1264 metric tons for the same period (Schratwieser 2015).

All-Tackle record counts and applications for records for threatened and endangered species have declined substantially over recent decades, with no records for threatened species being awarded in 2018 (Boon et al. 2024; Shiffman et al. 2015). However, this trend should also be considered in the context that many anglers land large fish with the goal of obtaining a world record, but then do not report it when realizing the fish is short of record size (Shiffman et al. 2015; Wilde and Pope 2004).

In summary, trophy fishing continues to be a central and culturally significant aspect of recreational angling, deeply rooted in historical measures of success and personal achievement. While evolving practices such as length-based records and increased conservation awareness offer more sustainable alternatives, the ecological and ethical challenges remain substantial. These include the impacts of targeting large individuals, the unintended consequences of catch-and-release, and the risks posed to threatened species. As the sport progresses, aligning recognition systems and angler incentives with conservation goals will be critical to ensuring that trophy fishing contributes positively to both human experience and ecological sustainability.

More Than a Catch: The Power and Impact of Trophy Photos

The idea of a trophy in fishing has always been about more than just size—it is about preserving a moment of success. Historically, this meant food security or a physical memento like jaws, skin, or taxidermy. Today, it often means a photograph or video. Whether it is a replica, a gyotaku print, or a digital image, the trophy has evolved into something symbolic—proof of skill, connection to nature, and personal achievement.

Photographs have long been used to display fishing success. From black-and-white images of abundant harvests to dockside displays of big game species, these visuals have shaped public perceptions of fishing. Literary figures like Hemingway and Zane Grey helped popularize this imagery, turning the act of catching a fish into a cultural moment. Today, photographs allow anglers to preserve the memory while releasing the fish, and many record-keeping bodies now accept length-based photographic evidence. This shift supports catch-and-release practices that reduce environmental impact—when done correctly (Cooke et al. 2020a).

Trophy photos also serve science and management. Historical images help establish baselines for fish populations (McClenachan 2009), while modern digital platforms offer real-time data on catch rates, fish size, and angler behavior (Lennox et al. 2022). These insights would be costly to gather through traditional surveys (Venturelli et al. 2017).

Social media has amplified the role of trophy photos. Guides and gear brands use them for marketing, while everyday anglers seek recognition—even without financial reward. This visibility can promote conservation behaviors, such as proper catch-and-release techniques, and help fill gaps in enforcement through peer influence (Allison et al. 2023; Cooke et al. 2013; Guckian et al. 2018).

However, there are trade-offs. Handling fish for photos can increase stress and mortality, especially if best practices are not followed (Cook et al. 2015; Joubert et al. 2020). Shared images can also attract crowds to sensitive areas, increasing pressure on fish stocks, damaging habitat, and altering the social experience of fishing. In some cases, the pursuit of the "biggest and best" elsewhere can diminish appreciation for local species and waters.

Importantly, a trophy does not have to be the largest fish caught. It can be a child's first fish, a rare micro-fishing catch, or a personal milestone. These moments carry meaning and value, often with less ecological cost. As such, the trophy is not just the fish—it's the story, the memory, and the connection to nature that it represents.

Big Fish, Big Money

> Advertisers believed then – and still believe now – that if you just showed a picture of a guy holding a big enough fish, you could claim he caught it because of the brand of underwear he had on and people would run out and buy it.
>
> —*John Gierach* (2014)

While humorous, Gierach's quote captures a persistent truth: the image of a trophy fish remains a powerful marketing tool. Phrases like "catch of a lifetime" and "chance at a trophy" are used to sell everything from hooks to high-end travel packages. Trophy fishing is not just a pastime—it's a global economic engine. As outlined in this chapter, recreational fisheries generate a host of benefits to society and hundreds of billions of dollars in economic activity annually (Arlinghaus 2020), and in many cases this activity is driven by the allure of catching something big.

This economic potential has led to trophy fisheries being positioned not only as recreational opportunities but also as tools for conservation and rural development. The high spending per fish caught, and the geographic distribution of that spending, are often used to justify allocating marine and freshwater resources to recreational rather than commercial use (Borch et al. 2008; Golden et al. 2019; Joshi et al. 2021; Zwirn et al. 2005). In many cases, the monetary and social value of trophy fisheries drive investments in habitat restoration and species protection (Lennox et al. 2022).

Competitive angling further amplifies the economic and cultural visibility of trophy fisheries. Fishing tournaments—some with multimillion-dollar prize pools—serve as high-profile platforms that project the value of large fish. In 2023, the White Marlin Open awarded $6.2 million to a team that landed a 274.2 kg Atlantic blue marlin (*Makaira nigricans*) (White Marlin Open 2025). Professional leagues such as Major League Fishing and the Bassmaster Elite Series extend this visibility through televised events, sponsorships, and media coverage, reinforcing the prestige and profitability of catching big fish.

In Costa Rica, for example, recreational fishing was the fourth most common reason for visiting the country in 2009, accounting for over 21% of tourists and generating 63,000 jobs (Chacon et al. 2010). Target species such as billfish, tuna, and mahi (*Coryphaena hippurus*) have shown stable or increasing populations in areas where recreational fishing dominates (Chacon et al. 2010; Chaves-Campos et al. 2025). However, these gains remain vulnerable to commercial longline fisheries, which continue to impact key stocks despite regulatory efforts.

Elsewhere, trophy fisheries have become catalysts for conservation innovation. In India, endangered mahseer (*Tor spp.*) have benefited from angler-driven conservation. Former poachers have been retrained as fishing guides, and stretches of river managed for catch-and-release angling now offer better protection than unmanaged areas (Bower et al. 2017; Pinder and Raghavan 2013). Similarly, in Mongolia, the taimen (*Hucho taimen*) fishery has become a model for community-based conservation (Cooke et al. 2016; DeNies 2020; Golden et al. 2019). Anglers pay up to $7000 per week for the experience (Golden et al. 2019), and during the COVID-19 pandemic, many donated thousands of dollars to support local guides and maintain protections (Cooke et al. 2016; DeNies 2020).

Organizations such as Indifly and the Taimen Fund have played a key role in these efforts, empowering Indigenous and local stakeholders, funding scientific research, and providing economic compensation for conservation (Galland et al. 2021; Indifly 2024; Lennox et al. 2018). When managed responsibly, these initiatives help maintain community connections to aquatic resources while reducing harvest pressure—especially where catch-and-release is feasible and ethical.

The economic footprint of trophy fisheries is not limited to developing countries. In Canada, white sturgeon (*Acipenser transmontanus*) were targeted on just 1% of fishing days in British Columbia in 2022, yet accounted for over 5% of freshwater fishing expenditures—totaling $34 million CAD (DFO 2024). In Sweden, anglers on the Mörrum River spent approximately $5.1 million during the 2019 Atlantic salmon (*Salmo salar*) season, averaging $5900 per fish caught, with only 17.3% of those fish harvested (author's calculation). In Florida, bonefish (*Albula spp.*) have been valued at $3500 per fish in a catch-and-release fishery (Ault 2008), underscoring the high economic value of non-consumptive use.

However, the benefits of trophy fishing are not always equitably distributed. In Angola, a trophy fishery for Giant African Threadfin (*Polydactylus quadrifilis*) generated $236,826 in just four months, yet 86.1% of that revenue leaked out of the local economy due to limited community integration and involvement (Butler et al. 2020). In Kenya, similar disparities exist. While billfish tourism generates substantial income, few local fishers own sportfishing boats, limiting their share of the benefits (Kadagi et al. 2020). Artisanal fishers earn between $9 and $40 per day (Kimani et al. 2020), while charter rates in the same region range from $250 to $1500 per trip (Fishing Booker 2025, Hemingways 2025).

The structure of Kenya's billfish fishery reflects these inequalities. Approximately three-quarters of Kenyan recreational fishers targeting billfish operate professionally, relying on charter income from sportfishing tourists (Kadagi et al. 2020). In contrast, only a small fraction of artisanal fishers target billfish full-time and about one-fourth offer occasional recreational charters during peak tourist seasons. Artisanal landings are mostly for sale, while recreational catches are largely catch-and-release. Yet effort in the artisanal sector has been estimated to exceed sustainable levels by 20% (Tuda and Wolff 2015). A shift toward more inclusive recreational trophy fishing could help reduce pressure on fish stocks while maintaining livelihoods and direct human-nature connections. Income differences between sectors are substantial, suggesting that even modest redistribution could have meaningful impacts (Potts et al. 2021; Teh et al. 2020).

Tagging and releasing trophy fish has also become a key part of conservation branding. In Kenya, charter operators use billfish tagging to demonstrate both angling success and commitment to sustainability (Fish Your Dream 2021, Hemingways 2025). These efforts support research, monitoring, and public engagement—sometimes even funded by anglers themselves. However, the exclusivity of some trophy fisheries raises important questions: if only a privileged few can access these resources, why should the broader public invest in their conservation?

In conclusion, trophy fishing sits at the intersection of recreation, conservation, and global economic flows. When managed inclusively and responsibly, it can generate substantial revenue, incentivize habitat protection, and support rural livelihoods. But without equitable access and local integration, much of this potential is lost to economic leakage and social exclusion. As global interest in trophy fisheries grows, ensuring that benefits are shared and ecosystems are protected will be essential to their long-term sustainability and legitimacy.

The Experience of the Fish: Welfare and Sublethal Impacts

While recreational fishing is often framed as a low-impact or even conservation-positive activity, it can have significant consequences for the fish involved—especially in trophy fisheries where larger individuals are targeted and frequently handled.

For an individual fish being caught has two potential outcomes: harvest-guaranteed death or release-possible survival, but release is not without its costs. Scientific evidence increasingly supports the view that fish are sentient animals capable of experiencing pain, stress, and fear (Brown 2015; Sneddon et al. 2014). These experiences are not only ethically relevant but also biologically consequential.

Physiological stress responses in fish include elevated cortisol levels, increased ventilation rates, and metabolic disturbances, which can impair immune function and recovery (Cooke and Suski 2005). Physical injuries from hooks, handling, and air exposure can lead to infections, impaired swimming, and reduced feeding success, or even delayed mortality (Cook et al. 2015). Once released, these sublethal effects can cause reduced growth, or altered behavior—possibly compromising their survival and ecological function (Arlinghaus et al. 2007; Brownscombe et al. 2017). In some cases, these stresses may impair spawning or ability to defend territory, undermining population-level benefits of catch-and-release. Larger fish, often considered trophies, may be particularly vulnerable due to their size, age, and reproductive importance. Trophy fish may be subject to multiple capture events over their lifetime, a situation that is being compounded by advances in fishing technology and pressure from social media that have made it easier to find and target specific individuals. Furthermore, prolonged air exposure during photo-taking has been shown to significantly increase mortality in species like bull trout (*Salvelinus confluentus*) and bonefish (Joubert et al. 2020; Lennox et al. 2017).

These impacts are especially concerning for threatened or endangered species, where the loss of even a few individuals can have disproportionate effects on population viability (Cooke et al. 2016; Sutter et al. 2012). As such, ethical and scientifically informed handling practices are essential—not only to reduce suffering but to ensure that recreational fisheries contribute positively to conservation.

Aligning Ecology, Economy, and Angler Behavior

Managing fisheries to support more and larger trophy fish offers a rare alignment of biological, economic, and social goals. Larger individuals often have the highest reproductive potential and pass on traits for size and growth (Matsumura et al. 2011). They also play key roles in ecosystem stability, particularly as top predators (Eklöf et al. 2020). Economically, anglers are often willing to pay more for the chance to catch fewer but larger fish. In Oklahoma, for example, recreational fishing generated $68.51 million in net benefits, and a 25% increase in trophy catch rates was projected to add $28.58 million more (Joshi et al. 2021). Similarly, in high-threshold fisheries like fly-fishing for taimen in Mongolia, anglers express a clear preference for size over quantity (Golden et al. 2019).

Trophy fisheries also contribute to science and management. Improving knowledge of fish population and associated ecosystems, long-term monitoring, and data collection are essential for sustainability (Gusha et al. 2024; Holder 2020). The detailed reporting protocols used by the IGFA, tournament organizers, and others are valuable sources of reliable data (Boon et al. 2024). Catch-and-release trophy fisheries for white sturgeon (*Acipenser transmontanus*) in Canada's Lower Fraser River (Challenger et al. 2021; DFO 2024; Robichaud et al. 2017), and Atlantic bluefin tuna (*Thunnus thynnus*) in Canada and Europe (Ferter et al. 2024; Nielsen et al. 2024; Stokesbury et al. 2011) have supported both conservation and economic goals.

The behavioral dimension is equally important. The added status and recognition associated with trophy catches can shape angler expectations and norms. In high-value fisheries, anglers often hire guides to increase their chances of success. In British Columbia, 46% of white sturgeon trips involve guides—compared to just 9% for all freshwater trips (DFO 2024). Guides not only support local economies but also serve as behavioral models, promoting best practices and conservation ethics (Farthing et al. 2022a). However, this influence can be challenged when client satisfaction conflicts with ecological integrity (Farthing et al. 2022b). Angling competitions and record systems also shape behavior. Their rules and visibility often exceed those of formal management institutions. The IGFA's global catch-and-release guidelines, translated into nine languages, are a prime example (IGFA 2022, 2025). Nationally televised tournaments and social media amplify these norms, with high-profile anglers influencing gear choices, techniques, and attitudes across the broader community (Allison et al. 2023; Mannheim et al. 2018).

Associating trophy or special status with individual catches can also deepen anglers' emotional connection to species and locations. According to value-belief-norm theory, personally valuing a fishery broadens pro-environmental beliefs activating personal norms and pro-environmental behavior (Han et al. 2024; Stern et al. 1995). When catch registration is framed as citizen science, it enhances anglers' sense of ownership and agency—especially when the data informs management (Phillips et al. 2019; Thiel et al. 2014). Participation in catch reporting has been linked to a desire to catch large fish, a sense of conservation responsibility, and access to useful information like regulations and catch statistics (Gundelund et al. 2020; van den Heuvel et al. 2020). These factors, in turn, can motivate stewardship and increase support for management interventions (Adams et al. 2024; Gallagher et al. 2015; Gervasi et al. 2022; van den Heuvel et al. 2025).

The traditional concept of trophy fish has focused on only the largest and hardest-fighting species of fish, and tournaments often target single or select groups of species. In some cases species that would be considered valuable catches, food, or even trophies in their own right are only valued as bait for bigger fish (Cooke et al. 2020b; Viana et al. 2025) or labeled as trash (Rypel et al. 2021). This narrow species focus can diminish ecosystem-level attention with potential negative impacts on biodiversity, and the behavior and growth of other species (Detmer et al. 2025; Kirk et al. 2022; Long and Seguy 2024).

Fishery managers and record keepers can redefine what success looks like through broader trophy categories, and tools like size and bag limits that can help shape angler expectations. Programs such as Vermont's Master Angler Program and Sweden's Storfiskregistret recognize a wide range of species and sizes, rewarding diversity and local excellence rather than just record-breaking size (Sportfiskarna 2025;

Vermont 2023). Similarly, Minnesota's Native Fish Bill (Minnesota Session Law 2024, Chapter 90, Article 2) aims to elevate the value of all native species, not just traditional gamefish (Winter 2024). These initiatives broaden the definition of a trophy and encourage appreciation for biodiversity. This shift is also reflected in the IGFA's expanding record categories, which now include many smaller-bodied species (Boon et al. 2024). The rise of micro-fishing—akin to birdwatching in its focus on diversity and detail—further supports this trend (Cooke et al. 2020b). By celebrating a wider range of species and catch types, these programs help align angler motivations with ecological sustainability.

Best Practices and Policy Reforms for Ethical and Sustainable Trophy Fishing

Sustaining the ecological, economic, and cultural value of trophy fisheries requires more than just managing fish populations—it demands thoughtful regulation, ethical angling practices, and policies that internalize the true costs of fishing on biodiversity and animal welfare.

One of the most direct ways anglers can contribute to sustainability is through responsible catch-and-release. When done properly, this practice increases the likelihood that small fish survive to reach trophy size and that large fish can reproduce and pass on their genetics (Brownscombe et al. 2017; Cooke and Suski 2005). However, what constitutes "best practice" varies by species, environment, and gear type. For threatened or endangered species, getting it right is especially critical—whether they are targeted directly or caught as bycatch (Cooke et al. 2016).

Across the globe, engaged anglers, guides, and researchers have collaborated to reduce post-release mortality and sublethal impacts in high-value fisheries. These include mahseer in India (Bower et al. 2022), sturgeon in Canada (McLean et al. 2020), arapaima in Guyana (Lennox et al. 2018), tuna in the Pacific (Sepulveda et al. 2020), and billfish in Australia (Tracey et al. 2023). These partnerships demonstrate the potential of community-driven science and stewardship.

Regulatory frameworks can reinforce these practices. Many record-keeping bodies and fishing tournaments now require adherence to specific rules for catch-and-release, including gear restrictions, handling protocols, and photographic verification. When these systems are aligned with best practices, they create powerful incentives for ethical behavior.

To further institutionalize these norms, mandatory or incentivized training in best practices for guides and anglers could be implemented. Such training has been shown to improve knowledge, attitudes, and behavior in trophy fisheries (Farthing et al. 2022a, b). Certification programs could be tied to licensing, tournament eligibility, or access to high-value fisheries.

From a policy perspective, risk assessments should be conducted for all species targeted in recreational fisheries, with special attention to those pursued as trophies, used in competitive events, or listed as threatened or endangered (Cooke et al. 2016). These assessments should adopt a precautionary, qualitative approach that considers not only population status but also vulnerability to handling, gear type, and angler behavior.

Importantly, economic policy must reflect the unique value of trophy fisheries. This includes recognizing the ecological role of large individuals, the food webs that support them, and the non-market values they provide—such as cultural identity, recreational satisfaction, and conservation awareness. Management decisions should account for the disproportionate economic contributions of trophy fisheries and the human-nature relationships they foster.

To internalize the ecological and ethical costs of trophy fishing, several policy tools could be considered:

- Differentiated license fees or conservation stamps for access to trophy fisheries, with revenues earmarked for habitat protection, monitoring, and education.
- Mandatory reporting and citizen science platforms that treat catch registration as a form of stewardship, increasing angler engagement and data quality.
- Recognition programs that reward not only size but also species diversity, ethical practices, and conservation contributions.
- Bag limits and slot limits that shape expectations and redefine success—not just to limit harvest, but to promote ecological integrity and long-term value.

Ultimately, reducing suffering and mortality in trophy fisheries requires a shift in how we define success. Ethical angling must go hand-in-hand with ecological sustainability. By embedding best practices into policy, regulation, and angler culture, we can ensure that trophy fishing continues to deliver value—without compromising the well-being of the fish or the ecosystems they inhabit.

Conclusions

Trophy fishing, rooted in ancient subsistence practices and immortalized in literature by figures like Hemingway, has evolved into a modern pursuit shaped by social media, status signaling, and economic opportunity. Today, the image of an angler posing with a prized catch circulates globally within seconds, reinforcing cultural narratives of conquest and achievement. Yet behind these images lie complex realities: the physical distress of individual fish, declining stocks, the ecological consequences of selective pressure, and the commodification of wildlife for cash and prestige.

This chapter has argued that while trophy fishing can contribute to conservation and local economies, it must be reimagined through a more ethical and ecologically grounded lens. The costs of regulation—such as monitoring, enforcement, and education—are real, but so too are the long-term costs of inaction: degraded ecosystems, lost biodiversity, and diminished public trust.

Proposals for reform include redefining what constitutes a "trophy" to emphasize species diversity and local significance, implementing differentiated licensing and conservation fees, and promoting citizen science and ethical recognition programs. These tools, combined with enforceable catch-and-release standards and precautionary protections for vulnerable species, offer a path forward. By aligning biological sustainability, economic value, and ethical responsibility, we can transform trophy fishing from a symbol of dominance into a model of stewardship.

References

Adams AJ, Boucek RE, Lewis JP, Lombardo SM, Perez AU, Wilson JK, Brownscombe JW, Griffin LP (2024) Stakeholder engagement as a core component of recreational marine fisheries research, education, and conservation. Fisheries 49:565–576

Allison C, Winkler AC, Childs AR, Muller C, Potts WM (2023) Can social media platforms be used to foster improved environmental behaviour in recreational fisheries? Fish Res 258:106544

Arlinghaus R (2006) On the apparently striking disconnect between motivation and satisfaction in recreational fishing: the case of catch orientation of German anglers. North Am J Fish Manag 26:592–605

Arlinghaus R, Cooke SJ, Lyman J, Policansky D, Schwab A, Suski C, Sutton SG, Thorstad EB (2007) Understanding the complexity of catch-and-release in recreational fishing: an integrative synthesis of global knowledge from historical, ethical, social, and biological perspectives. Rev Fish Sci 15:75–167

Arlinghaus R et al (2020) Global participation in and public attitudes toward recreational fishing: international perspectives and developments. Rev Fish Sci & Aquacult, 1–38

Ault JS (2008) Biology and management of the world Tarpon and Bonefish fisheries. Taylor & Francis Group CRC Press.

Blyth S, Stensland S, Rönnbäck P (2025) Imagination, reality, and reproduction: comparing perceptions of coastal sea trout anglers, real catches, and sea trout spawning activity. Fish Manage Ecol 32:e12745

Boon JS, Vaudin G, Millward-Hopkins H, O'Leary BC, McClean CJ, Stewart BD (2024) Shifts in the size and distribution of marine trophy fishing world records. Aquat Conserv Mar Freshwat Ecosyst 34:e4051

Borch T, Aas Ø, Policansky D (2008) International fishing tourism: past, present and future. In: Aas Ø (ed) Global challenges in recreational fisheries. Blackwell Publishing Ltd., Oxford, UK, pp 268–291

Bower SD, Danylchuk AJ, Raghavan R, Danylchuk SC, Pinder AC, Alter AM, Cooke SJ (2017) Involving recreational fisheries stakeholders in development of research and conservation priorities for mahseer (Tor spp.) of India through collaborative workshops. Fish Res 186:665–671

Bower SD, Szekeres P, Raghavan R, Danylchuk AJ, Cooke SJ (2022) Consequences of simulated multiple catch-and-release events and different handling procedures on reflex impairment, ventilation rate, and body condition in Tor khudree. Fish Res 246:106175

Brown C (2015) Fish intelligence, sentience and ethics. Anim Cogn 18:1–17

Brownscombe JW, Danylchuk AJ, Chapman JM, Gutowsky LFG, Cooke SJ (2017) Best practices for catch-and-release recreational fisheries—angling tools and tactics. Fish Res 186:693–705

Butler EC, Childs A-R, Saayman A, Potts WM (2020) Can fishing tourism contribute to conservation and sustainability via ecotourism? a case study of the fishery for Giant African Threadfin Polydactylus quadrifilis on the Kwanza Estuary, Angola. Sustainability 12:4221

Chacon MY, Li AG, García CF, Bolaños RL, Rojas F, González G (2010) Final report analysis of the economic contribution of recreational and commercial fisheries to The Costa Rican Economy. Instituto de Investigaciones en Ciencias Economicas of Universidad de Costa Rica

Challenger W, Nelson TC, Robichaud D, English KK, Mochizuki T, Thibault T (2021) Status of White Sturgeon in the Lower Fraser River in 2020: Report for Fraser River Sturgeon Conservation Society, Vancouver, BC, and BC Ministry of Forest, Lands, Natural Resource Operations and Rural Development, Victoria, BC
Chaves-Campos J, Marrari M, Mug Villanueva M (2025) Temporal trends in relative abundance of Billfish and other large Pelagic Fish in recreational fisheries of Costa Rica. Fisheries Management and Ecology n/a:e12821
Cooke SJ, Suski CD (2005) Do we need species-specific guidelines for catch-and-release recreational angling to effectively conserve diverse fishery resources? Biodivers Conserv 14:1195–1209
Cooke SJ, Suski CD, Arlinghaus R, Danylchuk AJ (2013) Voluntary institutions and behaviours as alternatives to formal regulations in recreational fisheries management. Fish Fish 14:439–457
Cook KV, Lennox RJ, Hinch SG, Cooke SJ (2015) Fish out of water: how much air is too much? Fisheries 40:452–461
Cooke SJ, Hogan ZS, Butcher PA, Stokesbury MJW, Raghavan R, Gallagher AJ, Hammerschlag N, Danylchuk AJ (2016) Angling for endangered fish: conservation problem or conservation action? Fish Fish 17:249–265
Cooke SJ, Abrams AEI, Zolderdo A, Suski CD (2020a) On improved care of black bass during live-release competitive angling events—recent innovations and associated research needs. Fisheries 45:178–183
Cooke SJ, Lennox RJ, Cantrell B, Danylchuk AJ (2020b) Micro-fishing as an emerging form of recreational angling: research gaps and policy considerations. Fisheries 45:517–521
DeNies R (2020) Mongolia's Taimen Rivers Have answers, April 6. https://wildsalmoncenter.org/2020/01/17/in-landlocked-mongolia-taimen-rivers-have-answers/
Detmer TM, Airey ME, Jirka KJ, Randall EA, Zarri L, McIntyre PB, Kraft CE (2025) Community-wide transient dynamics of lake fish populations in response to two decades of suppressing an introduced predator. J Appl Ecol
DFO (2024) Results of the British Columbia freshwater recreational fishing survey, 2022 in Canada FaO, ed
Eklöf JS, Sundblad G, Erlandsson M, Donadi S, Hansen JP, Eriksson BK, Bergström U (2020) A spatial regime shift from predator to prey dominance in a large coastal ecosystem. Comm Biol 3:459
Farthing MW, Childs AR, Mann-Lang JB, Bova CS, Potts WM (2022a) Are recreational fishing guides role models for their clients? Fish Res 254:106408
Farthing MW et al (2022b) Assessment of fishing guide knowledge, attitudes, and behaviours in global recreational fisheries. Fish Res 255:106453
Ferter K et al (2024) Atlantic bluefin tuna tagged off Norway show extensive annual migrations, high site-fidelity and dynamic behaviour in the Atlantic Ocean and Mediterranean Sea. Proceed Royal Society B: Biol Sci 291:20241501
Fish Your Dream (2021) We tagged and released trout for 1.5 years. C&R study on sea trout. Pages https://youtu.be/MWwjl_Q9pmU?si=uhYW7YsAzqo4Yvtl in Hansson R, ed
Fishing Booker (2025) Kenya fishing charters, May 22. https://fishingbooker.com/destinations/country/ke
Gallagher AJ, Cooke SJ, Hammerschlag N (2015) Risk perceptions and conservation ethics among recreational anglers targeting threatened sharks in the subtropical Atlantic. Endangered Species Research 29:81–93
Galland LM, Simmons JB, Jahner JP, Luzuriaga-Neira AR, Sloat MR, Chandra S, Hogan Z, Jensen OP, Parchman TL (2021) Hierarchical genetic structure and implications for conservation of the world's largest salmonid, Hucho taimen. Scientific Reports 11:20508
García-Asorey MI, Escati-Peñaloza G, Parma AM, Pascual MA (2011) Conflicting objectives in trophy trout recreational fisheries: evaluating trade-offs using an individual-based model. Can J Fish Aquat Sci 68:1892–1904

Gervasi CL, Massie JA, Rodemann J, Trabelsi S, Santos RO, Rehage JS (2022) Recreational angler contributions to fisheries management are varied and valuable: case studies from South Florida. Fisheries 47:469–477

Gierach J (2014) Fishing bamboo: an Angler's passion for the traditional fly rod. Rowman & Littlefield

Golden AS, Free CM, Jensen OP (2019) Angler preferences and satisfaction in a high-threshold bucket-list recreational fishery. Fish Res 220:105364

Guckian ML, Danylchuk AJ, Cooke SJ, Markowitz EM (2018) Peer pressure on the riverbank: assessing catch-and-release anglers' willingness to sanction others' (bad) behavior. J Environ Manage 219:252–259

Gundelund C, Arlinghaus R, Baktoft H, Hyder K, Venturelli P, Skov C (2020) Insights into the users of a citizen science platform for collecting recreational fisheries data. Fish Res 229:105597

Gusha NMC, Wilhelm MR, Bova CS, Engelhard GH, Hyder K, Potts WM (2024) Horizon scan survey to identify key research questions to promote sustainability of the marine recreational fishery in Namibia. Fish Manage Ecol 32:e12709

Han H, Kim S, Chiriko AY, Quan L (2024) Fishing tourism and the environment: examining fishing tourists' resource consumption reduction and recycling behaviors at fishing destinations. J Vacation Market, 22

Hemingway E (1952) The old man and the sea. Scribner

Hemingways W (2025) Hemingways Watamu—fishing—the unrivalled thrill of a big catch, May 22. https://www.hemingways-collection.com/watamu/fishing/

Holder PE et al (2020) Preparing for a changing future in recreational fisheries: 100 research questions for global consideration emerging from a horizon scan. Rev Fish Biol Fish

IGFA (2022) IGFA codifies new release rules and recommendations, Schratwieser J, ed. International Game Fish Association, Dania Beach, Florida

IGFA (2025) IGFA international angling rules and world record requirements in association TIGF, ed. The International Game Fish Association, Dania Beach, Florida

Indifly (2024) All about indifly, May 11. https://www.indifly.org/about

Joshi O, Chapagain BP, Long JM, York B, Taylor AT (2021) Estimating the effects of fish quality and size on the economic value of fishing in Oklahoma streams and rivers: a revealed preference and contingent behavior approach. Fish Res 244:106116

Joubert BA, Sullivan MG, Kissinger BC, Meinke AT (2020) Can smartphones kill Trout? mortality of memorable-sized Bull Trout (Salvelinus confluentus) after photo-releases. Fish Res 223:105458

Kadagi NI, Wambiji N, Swisher ME (2020) Potential for conflicts in recreational and artisanal billfish fisheries on the coast of Kenya. Mar Policy 117:103960

Kimani P, Wamukota A, Manyala JO, Mlewa CM (2020) Factors influencing financial performance in marine small-scale fisheries value chain in Kenya. Mar Policy 122:104218

Kirk MA, Maitland BM, Hickerson BT, Walters AW, Rahel FJ (2022) Climatic drivers and ecological impacts of a rapid range expansion by non-native smallmouth bass. Biol Invasions 24:1311–1326

Lennox RJ, Filous A, Clark Danylchuk S, Cooke SJ, Brownscombe JW, Friedlander AM, Danylchuk AJ (2017) Factors influencing postrelease predation for a catch-and-release tropical flats fishery with a high predator burden. North Am J Fish Manag 37:1045–1053

Lennox RJ, Brownscombe JW, Cooke SJ, Danylchuk AJ (2018) Post-release behaviour and survival of recreationally-angled arapaima (Arapaima cf. arapaima) assessed with accelerometer biologgers. Fisheries Research

Lennox RJ et al (2022) Digital fisheries data in the internet age: emerging tools for research and monitoring using online data in recreational fisheries. Fish Fish 23:926–940

Long JM, Seguy L (2024) Global status of non-native largemouth bass (Micropterus Salmoides, Centrachidae) and smallmouth bass (Micropterus Dolomieu, Centrarchidae): disparate views as beloved sportfish and feared invader. Rev Fish Sci Aquacult 32:81–98

Mannheim SL, Childs A-R, Butler EC, Winkler AC, Parkinson MC, Farthing MW, Zweig T, McCord M, Drobniewska N, Potts WM (2018) Working with, not against recreational anglers: evaluating

a pro-environmental behavioural strategy for improving catch-and-release behaviour. Fish Res 206:44–56
Matsumura S, Arlinghaus R, Dieckmann U (2011) Assessing evolutionary consequences of size-selective recreational fishing on multiple life-history traits, with an application to northern pike (Esox lucius). Evol Ecol 25:711–735
McClenachan L (2009) Documenting loss of large trophy fish from the Florida keys with historical photographs. Conserv Biol 23:636–643
McLean MF, Litvak MK, Stoddard EM, Cooke SJ, Patterson DA, Hinch SG, Welch DW, Crossin GT (2020) Linking environmental factors with reflex action mortality predictors, physiological stress, and post-release movement behaviour to evaluate the response of white sturgeon (Acipenser transmontanus Richardson, 1836) to catch-and-release angling. Comp Biochem Physiol A: Mol Integr Physiol 240:110618
Nielsen Einar E et al (2024) Genetic sex and origin identification suggests differential migration of male and female Atlantic Bluefin Tuna (Thunnus thynnus) in the Northeast Atlantic. Evol Appl 17:e70009
Nøttestad L, Boge E, Ferter K (2020) The comeback of Atlantic bluefin tuna (Thunnus thynnus) to Norwegian waters. Fish Res 231:105689
Phillips TB, Ballard HL, Lewenstein BV, Bonney R (2019) Engagement in science through citizen science: moving beyond data collection. Sci Educ 103:665–690
Pinder AC, Raghavan R (2013) Conserving the endangered Mahseers (Tor spp.) of India: the positive role of recreational fisheries. Curr Sci 104:1472–1475
Potts WM, Saayman M, Saayman A, Mann BQ, Van der Merwe P, Britz P, Bova CS (2021) Understanding the economic activity generated by recreational fishing in South Africa provides insights on the role of recreational fisheries for social development. Fish Manage Ecol 29:29–43
Robichaud D, English KK, Nelson TC (2017) Annual movements of acoustic-tagged White Sturgeon in the lower reaches of the Fraser River and its tributaries. Trans Am Fish Soc 146:611–625
Rypel AL et al (2021) Goodbye to "rough fish": paradigm shift in the conservation of native fishes. Fisheries 46:605–616
Schratwieser J (2015) A rejoinder to Shiffman et al., trophy fishing for species threatened with extinction: a way forward building on a history of conservation. Marine Policy 53:5–6
Sepulveda CA, Aalbers SA, Wang M, Kneebone J, Bernal D (2020) Post-release survivorship of Pacific bluefin tuna (Thunnus orientalis) captured in the California recreational fishery. Fish Res 223:105413
Shiffman DS, Gallagher AJ, Wester J, Macdonald CC, Thaler AD, Cooke SJ, Hammerschlag N (2014) Trophy fishing for species threatened with extinction: a way forward building on a history of conservation. Mar Policy 50:318–322
Shiffman DS, Gallagher AJ, Wester J, Macdonald CC, Thaler AD, Cooke SJ, Hammerschlag N (2015) A letter of clarification from the authors of "trophy fishing for species threatened with extinction." Mar Policy 53:213–214
Sneddon LU, Elwood RW, Adamo SA, Leach MC (2014) Defining and assessing animal pain. Anim Behav 97:201–212
Sportfiskarna (2025) Storfiskregistret in Storfiskregistrering S, ed. Visby, Sweden: The National Anglers Association of Sweden and the Swedish University of Agricultural Sciences
Stern PC, Dietz T, Kalof L, Guagnano GA (1995) Values, beliefs, and proenvironmental action: attitude formation toward emergent attitude objects. J Appl Soc Psychol 25:1611–1636
Stokesbury MJW, Neilson JD, Susko E, Cooke SJ (2011) Estimating mortality of Atlantic bluefin tuna (Thunnus thynnus) in an experimental recreational catch-and-release fishery. Biol Conserv 144:2684–2691
Sutter DAH, Suski CD, Philipp DP, Klefoth T, Wahl DH, Kersten P, Cooke SJ, Arlinghaus R (2012) Recreational fishing selectively captures individuals with the highest fitness potential. Proc Natl Acad Sci 109:20960–20965

Teh LCL, Ota Y, Cisneros-Montemayor AM, Harrington L, Swartz W (2020) Are fishers poor? getting to the bottom of marine fisheries income statistics. Fish Fish 21:471–482

Thiel M, Penna-Díaz MA, Luna-Jorquera G, Salas S, Sellanes J, Stotz W (2014) Citizen scientists and marine research: volunteer participants, their contributions, and projection for the future. In: Hughes RN, Hughes DJ, Smith IP (eds) Oceanography and marine biology: an annual review, vol 52. CRC Press, Boca Raton, pp 257–314

Tracey SR, Pepperell JG, Wolfe B (2023) Post release survival of swordfish (Xiphias gladius) caught by a recreational fishery in temperate waters. Fish Res 265:106742

Tuda PM, Wolff M (2015) Evolving trends in the Kenyan artisanal reef fishery and its implications for fisheries management. Ocean Coast Manag 104:36–44

Tuna Champions (2025) It's about what we do with what we catch, June 3. https://tunachampions.com.au/

van den Heuvel L, Blicharska M, Blyth S, Rönnbäck P (2020) Catch reporting in recreational fishing: Swedish anglers' attitudes and preferences, and the effect of social factors. Fish Res 223:105444

van den Heuvel L, Emma B, Malgorzata B, Rönnbäck P (2025) Effects of recreational anglers' sense of place on their stewardship intentions in private and social contexts on Gotland, Sweden. Soc Nat Res, 1–22

Venturelli PA, Hyder K, Skov C (2017) Angler apps as a source of recreational fisheries data: opportunities, challenges and proposed standards. Fish Fish 18:578–595

Vermont (2023) Master angler program in Department VFW, ed. Montpelier. Agency of Natural Resources, Vermont

Viana S, Farthing MW, Bova C, Marcone O, Sauer WHH (2025) Exploratory characterisation of recreational fishing for skipjack tuna Katsuwonus pelamis and eastern little tuna Euthynnus affinis in South Africa. African J Marine Sci 47:1–11

White JW, McLaren BD (2024) Gilgamesh to Gierach: four thousand years of fishing, fish, and water stories. Wipf and Stock Publishers

White Marlin Open (2025) Archives—2024 tournament, May 23. https://whitemarlinopen.com/archives

Wilde GR, Pope KL (2004) Anglers' probabilities of catching record-size fish. North Am J Fish Manag 24:1046–1049

Winter TJ (2024) Minnesota's native fish bill: a case study in shifting the "rough fish paradigm". Environmental Biology of Fishes

ZGWS (2025) The writings—fishing, April 6. https://zgws.org/writing-type/fishing/

Zwirn M, Malin P, Rahr G (2005) Angling ecotourism: issues, guidelines and experience from Kamchatka. J Ecotour 4:16–31

Chapter 10
Animals for Trophy Hunting

Adam G. Hart

"Can you love something and still want to kill it?"
—*Hunter*, in Trophy (2017)

Abstract Trophy hunting occupies a contentious space at the intersection of conservation, economics, and ethics. This chapter critically examines the conditions under which trophy hunting can contribute to biodiversity protection and rural livelihoods, while also highlighting the risks of ecological degradation, elite capture, and ethical backlash when governance fails. Drawing on interdisciplinary evidence, the chapter explores the economic significance of trophy hunting in biodiversity-rich but financially constrained regions, particularly in sub-Saharan Africa. It evaluates the limitations of current models and the growing pressure from international regulatory and public opinion shifts. In response, the chapter proposes a suite of pragmatic economic and regulatory reforms aimed at aligning trophy hunting with conservation goals and ethical standards. These include science-based quota systems, transparent revenue-sharing, ethical certification, hybrid land-use incentives, and integration with ecosystem service markets. Emphasizing adaptation over abandonment, the chapter argues for context-specific, community-empowered, and ecologically grounded approaches that can evolve with changing values and conservation paradigms. Ultimately, it calls for a reimagining of trophy hunting as part of a broader, more inclusive conservation finance strategy.

(Trophy (2017) is a documentary by Shaul Schwarz and Christina Clusiau that explores the ethical and economic complexities of trophy hunting and wildlife conservation)

A. G. Hart (✉)
School of Education and Science, University of Gloucestershire, Cheltenham, UK
e-mail: ahart@glos.ac.uk

N. Batini (ed.), *The Economics of Non-Human Animals*, Natural Resource Management and Policy 63, https://doi.org/10.1007/978-3-032-17580-9_10

Valuing the Hunted: Trophy Economies in a Multispecies World

While animals have historically been used by humans for food, clothing, tools, and ornamentation, these uses represent just one aspect of the long and varied relationships between species. Materials such as skins, bones, feathers, and tusks have been incorporated into human economies and cultural practices, often reflecting both practical needs and symbolic meanings. Antlers and horns, for example, have been used in tool-making and decoration, while also serving important biological functions for the animals themselves, such as defense or display. These dual roles highlight the complex ways in which human and non-human lives have intersected over time.

Birds have similarly played diverse roles in human societies. Their feathers, talons, and beaks have been used in ceremonial dress and ornamentation across many cultures, often carrying spiritual or aesthetic significance. These practices reflect deep cultural traditions, but they also raise questions about how animals are perceived and valued, whether as symbolic figures, material sources, or living beings with their own ecological and social lives.

In some societies, the display of animal parts has been associated with rites of passage, social status, or expressions of identity. Among the Maasai of Kenya and Tanzania, for instance, lion hunting has historically been linked to concepts of bravery and personal achievement, with specific animal parts worn as markers of these milestones (Goldman et al. 2013). Such practices are embedded in cultural systems that attribute meaning to human-animal encounters, though they may also reflect broader dynamics of power, tradition, and change.

Today, the display of animal trophies continues in various forms, from private collections to tourist lodges. Mounted heads, horns, and other animal parts are often presented as symbols of adventure, heritage, or prestige. These displays can be interpreted in multiple ways—celebratory, commemorative, or controversial—depending on cultural context and individual perspective. They also raise ongoing discussions about the place of animals in human economies and the values that shape our interactions with the natural world.

A visit to a tourist lodge in South Africa for example will usually involve walking under the horns of a buffalo, a kudu (a spiral-horned antelope) or even, as is the case in the restaurant at Hwange Safari Lodge in Zimbabwe, the entire head and shoulders of an elephant. Most stately homes in the UK will have deer heads mounted on the wall, often with a small brass plaque stating who shot the animal, where and when. It is not uncommon to see antique mounts of exotic species on display in such locations, including big cats, bears, and antelopes. Considerable resources were required to hunt such species in the wild and so these hunting trophies are, arguably, both mementoes and status symbols. What is not always widely appreciated is that such "trophy hunting" continues in the modern world.

Before considering the economic role and implications of trophy hunting, it is first necessary to define the term. The description of trophy hunting used by the International Union for Conservation of Nature (IUCN) is a useful starting point:

> "Trophy hunting generally involves the payment of a fee by a foreign or local hunter for a hunting experience, usually guided, for one or more individuals of a particular species with specific desired characteristics (such as large size or antlers). The trophy is usually retained by the hunter and taken home. Meat of hunted animals is usually used for food by local communities or the hunter. It may be a distinct activity or overlap with recreational or meat hunting. Many deer hunters, for example, may desire a trophy but also hunt for food or for the experience." (IUCN 2016)

The motivation behind the hunt, and involvement of money, are central to this description. So, a salaried deer manager shooting deer for population control is not a trophy hunter. However, were that manager to shoot a stag and keep the antlers for display (as many undoubtedly do), then the antlers themselves are clearly a hunting trophy, even if the hunter in this case was not motivated by obtaining the trophy. Furthermore, rather than paying for the experience, the hunter (who in this case would likely describe themselves as a deer manager) has been paid. Even if the deer were killed by a recreational deer stalker who had paid for the rights to manage deer on a parcel of land, it would be hard to call them a trophy hunter if their primary goal was to reduce deer numbers or stock their freezer, even if antlers are retained for display (Bichel and Hart 2023).

For the purposes of this chapter, trophy hunting will be defined as the selective hunting of specific animals with desired characteristics (large size, antlers, horns, tusks, etc.) with the intention of retaining parts of the animal for use as a trophy. Furthermore, for this chapter, trophy hunting will also involve payment for the hunting experience and the trophy. As we will see, in some cases such hunting involves considerable fees and often involves travel to overseas destinations.

The selective killing of wild animals for sport remains one of the most controversial practices in conservation (e.g., Evans et al. 2023). There are many active campaigns in Europe, the UK, and the US to ban trophy hunting, a morality-driven intention that usually crystallizes into calls for bans on the import of hunting trophies to hunters' home nations. In addition, and in many ways related to these campaigns, trophy hunting regularly attracts considerable negative attention in the media and in politics (Yeomans et al. 2022). Trophy hunting coverage usually focuses on charismatic and well-known species such as lions or elephants, where trophy hunting is often (incorrectly) portrayed as being a conservation threat. The reality is that these species represent only a tiny fraction of animals hunted for trophies globally, and the trade in hunting trophies of species of conservation concern is usually tightly regulated by the Convention on International Trade of Endangered Species of Flora and Fauna (CITES) (Challender et al. 2024).

At its core, trophy hunting is an economic activity; a market-based approach to wildlife utilization that generates revenue from charismatic megafauna. Its defenders argue that, when well-managed, trophy hunting provides financial incentives for wildlife conservation, supports local livelihoods, and contributes to government budgets. Meat from hunts can provide additional benefit to local communities. Some species, such as elephants and lions, can threaten livelihoods and human safety, and the value they provide through hunting can provide some incentive to maintain such species despite the risks they pose (Bichel and Hart 2023). A common phrase used in discussions of the South African hunting model, outlined below, is "it pays, it stays." Proponents of hunting argue that without the revenue hunting provides, land will be converted from habitat to agriculture or other wildlife-unfriendly uses, with subsequent loss of wildlife species and ecological function. Overall, the argument goes, commercializing wildlife provides an incentive to maintain it, and the wider habitat (to, in principle at least, the benefit of all species) (Lindsey et al. 2007).

Trophy hunting critics counter that conservation and economic claims of benefit are overstated or poorly evidenced, and that moral and ethical concerns, corruption, and perverse incentives undermine any purported benefits (e.g., Ghasemi 2021). It is often the case that those opposed to hunting do so from a personal ethical or moral position, founded on animals' rights (Bichel and Hart 2023). Any form of consumptive, exploitative wildlife use is likely to be opposed by those who embrace animal rights, but the killing of animal for a trophy is a particularly emotive topic, exemplified by the appearance of words like "evil" and "senseless" in public discourse (see discussions in Bichel and Hart 2023).

This chapter explores the economics of trophy hunting in both theory and practice. It examines the trophy hunting market, the revenue flows generated, and the incentives created for conservation or exploitation. Special attention is paid to sub-Saharan Africa where trophy hunting is often an integral part of conservation management. The chapter concludes by evaluating the strengths and limitations of trophy hunting as a conservation funding mechanism in the context of evolving ecological, social, and political pressures.

The Economics of Trophy Hunting

Defining the Market

Trophy hunting operates as a specialized niche within the wider wildlife tourism industry. Photographic wildlife tourism, where tourists travel for the experience, to see wildlife and to take photographs, is non-consumptive. While it is the case that poorly regulated or poorly managed photo-tourism can have a harmful environmental impact, and can directly harm wildlife, it is not the intention or goal of such tourism to kill animals (Higginbottom 2004; Green and Giese 2004). Hunting tourism, on the other hand, is consumptive, explicitly involving the killing of animals (Leader-Williams et al. 2005). Hunting tourism can include hunters motivated by the experience of hunting rather than the trophy itself, and such hunting is unlikely to include the killing of high-value trophy animals. It is possible, for example, in South Africa, to hunt female antelope or non-trophy (i.e., small or otherwise unremarkable) males, for management purposes or for meat (Van der Merwe et al. 2010). Trophy hunters on the other hand, often international clients, pay significant fees for the right to hunt certain animals and to take trophies home with them.

Demand for trophy hunting is shaped by several factors. One is the rarity or prestige associated with certain species, particularly the so-called "Big Five" in Africa: lion (*Panthera leo*), elephant (*Loxodonta africana*), rhinoceros (black rhino *Diceros bicornis* and white rhino *Ceratotherium simum*), leopard (*Panthera pardus*), and Cape buffalo (*Syncerus caffer*). Hunting these species carries cultural capital within trophy hunting communities and can command fees more than USD 50,000 for a single specimen, depending on size, location, and regulatory burden (Bichel and Hart 2023). Outside of Africa, species including bears, various sheep and goat species, and deer can also command high prices. The total payment typically includes permit fees, including local and central government taxes, outfitter costs, guiding services, accommodation, transport, and trophy export preparation.

Trophy hunting, wherever it takes place, is often subject to tightly regulated quotas and other regulations including the use of guides, fees, hunting method (mostly rifle, bow, or handgun), minimum calibers or ballistic performance (for rifle and handgun), duration, and so on. Navigating these regulations, and the bureaucracy involved with hunting and exporting trophies, is usually part of the service offered by hunting outfitters (discussed in Bichel and Hart 2023).

Trophy hunting markets are unusual in that the "product" is a wild animal, but what is being sold is not a product with utility value (like meat), but rather the experience of the hunt and the physical trophy (e.g., horns, skulls, or hides). The higher end of the market relies heavily on symbolic capital and, sometimes, scarcity with rarer or more dangerous species costing more. From an economic standpoint, these species function in some ways as Veblen goods: their desirability is increased by exclusivity and cost, not diminished by it. The rarer or more restricted the opportunity, the greater the perceived value. This presents a paradox for conservation: economic value may rise even as species populations decline, incentivizing exploitation unless strong safeguards are in place. Nonetheless, many trophy hunts are for relatively common species such as impala, kudu, or springbok, that cost far less (Damm 2005).

Although much focus is placed on African nations, trophy hunting of the type discussed here takes place across the world. Book Your Hunt (bookyourhunt.com) is a well-known website selling hunts, most of which would likely include trophy hunting as per the definition above. At the time of writing, it is offering 4002 hunting trips via 833 hunting outfitters (companies that organize a hunting trip) in 57 countries or regions including Argentina, Italy, Mexico, New Zealand, and the United Kingdom. To give an idea of prices, a 10-day package to hunt bighorn sheep in Mexico is selling for 7500USD, while a 28-day "classic safari" across two destinations in Tanzania is 165,000USD (not including fees per animal shot, which add to the price). However, a 7-day hunting package including full-board accommodation and four species (wildebeest, impala, blesbok, and springbok) is 2400USD.

At the real high-end of the hunting market, some bighorn sheep hunting tags (permits to hunt) can sell for more than a million USD, with one recent example setting a record of 1.3 million at an auction in Reno, Nevada in January 2025 (Collins 2025). Sheep and goats, especially species like the Markhor (Mazhar 2023), are among the most expensive hunting trophies to obtain hunting permits for. However, the previous most expensive auctioned tag was for mule deer in Arizona, selling for

725,000USD, beating the previous record, set earlier in the same auction, where a different buyer paid 500,000USD for tag to hunt a single mule deer on Antelope Island, Utah (McKean 2023).

Supply Constraints and Regulation

The supply of huntable animals is fundamentally constrained by biological limits; there are only so many trophy individuals available to hunt at any given time on any given piece of land. The number of animals will be limited by the carrying capacity of the trophy species within the hunting area and by the demographics of that species. For many trophy species, it is only the male that has the characteristics desired by hunters, and it is only older males, typically those that have passed breeding age, that will have sufficiently developed antlers, horns, or other features that make them a desirable trophy. For example, there may be hundreds or even thousands of cape buffalo roaming around a hunting area, but only a small handful of old males with sufficiently developed horns (especially the rounded bases on the top of the head known as "bosses") to make them an attractive trophy, worth the 10–2000 USD (or more) trophy fee that hunters pay. In principle, such individuals can, for most species, be removed from the population without concern for future population numbers or growth. However, the role of older males in some species can be complex, and their removal can have negative effects. This is most often discussed with respect to African elephants, where complex herd dynamics can mean that older males are involved in important roles, such as "tutoring" younger males (Allen et al. 2020). Furthermore, older males have been shown to invest more effort into finding females and are preferred by female over younger males. Consequently, their removal can have negative effects on population dynamics (Taylor et al. 2020a).

Optimal harvest theory potentially provides another lens for understanding how much hunting can occur without compromising wildlife populations. This theory is grounded in the principle of Maximum Sustainable Yield (MSY), which identifies the highest harvest level that allows populations to regenerate. While useful in theory, applying MSY in practice is fraught with uncertainty due to imperfect data and ecological variability (Goodenough and Hart 2017). In addition, MSY is a model for general exploitation whereas, by definition, trophy hunting is targeting individual animals with very specific features whose population growth and sustainable harvest may not be in line with the general population growth parameters used to calculate MSY.

The supply of huntable animals is also constrained by national and international regulations. It may be illegal for example to hunt some species, or there may be regulations that mean some hunters may not consider there to be a "supply." It is, for example, illegal to hunt any animal with a bow in the UK, but bowhunting (especially of deer) is popular in the USA (Bichel and Hart 2023). A USA-based hunter wanting to hunt a red deer stag in Scotland with a bow would be unable to do so, although the same animal could be legally hunted with a rifle. Additionally, countries typically allocate quotas for trophy species based on population estimates and conservation priorities. International frameworks such as CITES regulate cross-border movement of trophies, adding another layer of economic and bureaucratic cost, and potential obstacle (Bichel and Hart 2023). These regulatory frameworks introduce transaction costs and uncertainty but also function to shape market access and reputation. For instance, countries perceived to have transparent and science-based systems (e.g., Namibia) may be more successful at attracting high-paying clients than those with histories of corruption or poor enforcement.

The situation is further complicated by landownership and the rights of individuals to make use of wildlife on land they control. In some countries, state wildlife agencies retain ownership and control. In others, notably South Africa and Namibia, wildlife on private land is commodified, giving rise to distinct market structures and pricing mechanisms. In Namibia, some trophy hunting is conducted on private land, but some takes place within communal land, where communities may have adopted a "conservancy" model, where they oversee the use of that land and the hunting that takes place on it, as well as any photographic tourism (Naidoo et al. 2016). Professional hunters and outfitters can bring clients on to this land in exchange for a fee, but the wildlife they hunt is controlled by the conservancy and, depending on species, by centrally imposed quotas in line with wider conservation goals. In other countries, such as Tanzania, the government auctions the leases of hunting blocks, large parcels of land, on which hunting operators can set up a hunting business (Kadigi et al. 2023). Such blocks will likely have communities living alongside wildlife, and there is usually an expectation of community benefit from the hunting activity, through meat and shared revenue, as well as the upkeep of access and airstrips. Concession owners may also be expected to run anti-poaching patrols in the area, although in practice many would invest in such activities anyway to protect their livelihood. Outside of Africa, hunting often operates on privately owned land or, in the case of the USA particularly, on public land provided hunting is allowed. Land ownership, quota setting, management strategy, and national or international conservation measures can all influence the supply of huntable animals. In short, the situation is complex with multiple models in operation, sometimes even within the same region or nation.

The security of property rights and the duration of land tenure are crucial features of the trophy hunting economic landscape. In settings where property rights are clearly defined, such as privately owned land, conservancies, or well-regulated communal lands, landowners, lessees, and resource managers have strong incentives to manage wildlife sustainably. There are also strong incentives to invest in infrastructure such as fixed camps, roads and airstrips, and to foster durable and effective relationships with local communities, that can greatly reduce unregulated offtake (poaching) of wildlife and other activities that harm conservation. In contrast, areas with weak or ambiguous rights may experience something akin to the tragedy of the commons, where wildlife is overexploited due to lack of accountability or stability (e.g., Lindsey et al. 2013).

Who Gains? Revenue and Redistribution in Trophy Hunting

Gross Economic Contributions

Estimates of the economic value of trophy hunting vary significantly due to differences in methodology and a general lack of transparency across regions and sectors. A widely cited study by Lindsey et al. (2007) estimated that trophy hunting in sub-Saharan Africa generates approximately USD 200 million annually and covers over 1.4 million km^2 of land, but is clearly out of date. Currently, no single, authoritative statistic exists, at any useful level, largely because of inconsistent metrics and varied approaches used in different contexts. In some locations, and for certain species, the income generated can be substantial; in others, it may be minimal, but still locally important, a point discussed further below.

Trophy hunting contributes directly to GDP through payments for licenses, guiding services, accommodation, and logistical support. It also brings indirect benefits such as employment for trackers, cooks, and camp staff, along with multiplier effects in remote areas where economic alternatives are limited. Nonetheless, critics argue that headline figures often obscure the extent of financial leakage. A large portion of revenues may be captured by international operators or urban elites, and without strong local benefit-sharing arrangements the economic impact for rural communities can be limited (e.g., Leader-Williams et al. 2009; Peyman and Styles 2024).

Local Communities and Benefit Sharing

One of the most frequently cited benefits of trophy hunting is its potential to support rural livelihoods, particularly through community-based natural resource management (CBNRM) initiatives (Huntley 2023). In these models, communities receive a share of hunting revenues in exchange for managing wildlife and bearing the costs of living alongside potentially dangerous animals. Programs such as Namibia's communal conservancies and Zimbabwe's CAMPFIRE initiative are often highlighted as examples of how regulated trophy hunting can create tangible social and economic benefits.

In Namibia, over 80 registered conservancies benefit directly from revenues generated through both trophy hunting or photographic tourism, or both. Income is used to fund infrastructure, employment, and community development projects, including schools and clinics. According to the Namibian Association of Community-Based Natural Resource Management Support Organisations (NACSO), these programs channel several million dollars annually into rural areas and have created jobs for game guards, trackers, and administrative staff (Huntley 2023).

However, the distribution of benefits within communities may be far from uniform. Power dynamics, particularly those related to gender, class, and leadership structures, can determine who gains access to these resources. Women and marginalized groups may be excluded from decision-making processes or disproportionately underrepresented in benefit-sharing mechanisms. Moreover, some community members might be able to derive more consistent and culturally relevant benefits from livestock or agriculture, especially in areas with high rates of human–wildlife conflict (Dickman et al. 2011).

The design of lease agreements and revenue-sharing arrangements between governments, outfitters, and communities varies widely across contexts. In some models, communities receive a fixed percentage of fees; in others, they have joint management roles or limited consultation rights. The success of these systems often hinges on legal clarity, transparency, and local institutional capacity. Without strong governance, there is a risk of elite capture, whereby a small group monopolizes control over revenues or decision-making processes.

The CAMPFIRE program in Zimbabwe serves as a useful case study. Initially praised for its innovative structure and emphasis on community empowerment, it experienced a significant decline due to political interference and poor financial oversight (Mundeya 2023). To some extent, this has changed, and CAMPFIRE has improved (Koro 2022). Despite challenges, it remains an influential example of how trophy hunting revenues can be harnessed for rural development, and what happens when governance breaks down.

To improve outcomes, monitoring and evaluation systems are essential. Programs that incorporate participatory governance and independent audits tend to achieve more equitable and sustainable results. Ensuring that local people not only receive material benefits but also have meaningful agency in managing wildlife resources is a prerequisite for long-term legitimacy and conservation success.

State Revenues and Conservation Finance

In many hunting nations, hunting revenues support wildlife departments and protected area management (Bichel and Hart 2023). User fees, concession payments, and penalties from the hunting sector may be used to fund anti-poaching patrols, ecological monitoring, and infrastructure maintenance. In low-income countries with limited conservation budgets, trophy hunting can be a critical source of funding. Even though hunting revenues may represent a small percentage of national GDP (a point often raised by those opposing hunting (Gaworecki 2017)), their impact at the local level can be substantial. In many rural communities, hunting-related income provides essential financial support for conservation programs and communities that might otherwise struggle to secure funding. This localized economic contribution is particularly valuable in low-income countries, where alternative revenue streams for conservation and communities are limited. Moreover, many industries contribute small percentages to overall GDP yet remain critical to specific sectors. For example, ecotourism, artisanal fishing, and heritage conservation often account for a small fraction of GDP but play vital roles in sustaining local economies and preserving natural resources. Similarly, hunting revenues, though not a dominant force in national economic figures, can be one of the few reliable sources of funding for wildlife management in remote areas.

Nevertheless, reliance on trophy hunting creates fiscal vulnerabilities. Revenues are often unpredictable and dependent on international demand, political stability, and currency fluctuations. Furthermore, controversial hunts (such as Cecil the Lion in 2015 (Macdonald et al. 2016)) have led to international backlash and import bans that reduce market viability. The global pandemic virtually eliminated international travel, thereby hitting tourism particularly hard. However, hunting tourism was perhaps quicker to recover, largely because smaller numbers of hunters can bring in revenue that would require a far larger number of other types of tourists. Timbavati Private Nature Reserve provides a compelling case for the financial efficiency of hunting tourism compared to photographic tourism. In 2016, an analysis of the reserve's financial model revealed that the conservation levies paid by approximately 24,000 photographic tourists amounted to less than one-third of the revenue generated by just 46 hunters visiting in the same period (Timbavati Nature Reserve 2016). This stark contrast highlights how trophy hunting yields significantly more revenue per capita, allowing reserves to sustain conservation efforts with fewer visitors. In addition, hunting tourists are likely to be more accepting of travel and transport difficulties.

Economic Incentives and Conservation Trade-Offs

Incentives for Landowners and Managers

Trophy hunting can create a use-value for wildlife, transforming animals from potential liabilities into economic assets. Under the right institutional conditions, wild species can become a source of revenue for landholders, particularly through regulated hunting and tourism. These policy shifts have produced measurable changes on the ground. In South Africa and parts of Namibia, large tracts of private land have been converted from cattle production to mixed wildlife-based land use, resulting in the proliferation of private game reserves (Carruthers 2008). In some regions, this transition has contributed to increasing populations of huntable species, including several that had previously experienced declines due to overhunting, habitat loss, or human-wildlife conflict.

Wildlife ranching in South Africa exemplifies how private landowners can integrate conservation with economic sustainability. Since the 1991 legal reforms granting conditional private ownership of wildlife, many livestock farmers transitioned to wildlife-based land use, fostering a thriving industry that spans over 20 million hectares (Taylor et al. 2020b).

South Africa's wildlife ranching sector operates across three primary areas:

- Wildlife breeding and live sales: Landowners breed and sell game species, contributing to genetic diversity and conservation.
- Trophy hunting and ecotourism: Regulated hunting generates high per capita revenue, while photographic safaris attract broader tourism markets.
- Game meat production and trade: Sustainable harvesting supports local food markets and international exports.

The industry has experienced rapid growth, with an annual expansion rate of 5.6% up to the mid-2000s, accelerating to 6.75% per year due to intensive breeding practices (but see below for issues related to these practices). Wildlife ranching is now one of South Africa's fastest-growing agricultural sectors, providing employment, habitat restoration, and biodiversity conservation (Cloete et al. 2015).

Despite concerns about land use shifts, inequality, social injustice, and intensive wildlife breeding practices (discussed below), proponents argue that wildlife ranching adds significant economic value, creating skilled jobs and alternative food production systems. The model demonstrates how wild species can be transformed from liabilities into assets within a highly controlled (yet still predominantly natural) environment.

Risks of Perverse Incentives

Not all incentive structures are positive. Where oversight is weak, trophy hunting can incentivize overharvesting, artificial or accidental selection for rare traits (e.g., large horns or manes), and the commodification of genetically manipulated or captive-bred animals. In the United States, artificial deer breeding has become a lucrative industry, particularly for whitetail deer, where selective breeding is used to produce bucks with exaggerated antler growth. These deer are often raised in high-fenced enclosures, fed specialized diets, and subjected to genetic manipulation to enhance trophy appeal. While this practice increases financial returns for breeders and hunting operations, it raises concerns about genetic bottlenecks, disease susceptibility, and more general ethical considerations on the commercialization of wildlife (Bichel and Hart 2023).

Similarly, in South Africa, the selective breeding of color variant antelope has surged in popularity, although it is still a minority practice within wildlife ranching. Species such as black impala, golden wildebeest, and white springbok are bred for their unusual coat colors, which occur naturally as mutations and can be selected for in artificial breeding programs. This practice, driven by financial incentives, has led to intensive farming conditions, reduced genetic diversity, and concerns about long-term ecological impacts. Conservationists argue that breeding for novelty rather than natural selection undermines the genetic integrity of wild populations and prioritizes profit over sustainability (Hart 2017).

Also, in South Africa, the captive-bred lion industry has been a subject of intense debate, with concerns over ethical practices, conservation value, and commercial exploitation. Historically, captive lion breeding has been linked to so-called "canned hunting," where lions raised in enclosures are released into small-fenced areas for hunters to shoot, often with minimal effort required. Hunting regulations and laws legislate against these activities, but many still oppose the captive lion breeding, which is sometimes referred to as "bred for bullet" hunting, or "Blood Lions." Despite international criticism, however, the industry thrived due to high financial returns, with captive-bred lions fetching lower prices than wild lions but still generating significant revenue. Beyond hunting, captive-bred lions are also exploited for the lion bone trade, supplying markets in Asia for traditional medicine. South Africa has become the largest legal exporter of lion bones, raising concerns about wild lion poaching, as illegal traders may launder wild lion bones through the captive industry (Welz 2018).

In response to growing pressure, South Africa's government announced plans to phase out the captive lion breeding industry, citing its lack of conservation value and damage to the country's international reputation (D'Cruze et al. 2024). However, the fate of thousands of captive lions remains uncertain, as rewilding is not viable. At the time of writing, it is still possible to travel to South Africa and to shoot a captive-bred lion, released into 1000-hectares or more of African bush, for around 8000USD or less.

Ecological Outcomes

Evidence on the ecological benefits of trophy hunting remains mixed and highly context-dependent. In some well-managed areas, hunting blocks undoubtedly support higher wildlife densities than adjacent unprotected lands, especially those with extensive human encroachment or activity. Regulated hunting can, and does, contribute meaningfully to habitat conservation and species protection, which is particularly the case where revenues from hunting are reinvested in anti-poaching patrols, land management, and infrastructure (Di Minin et al. 2016). However, trophy hunting quotas may be based on outdated or incomplete data. Without rigorous ecological monitoring, there is a risk that quotas exceed sustainable yields, particularly in the face of poaching, habitat loss, and climate stressors. In these cases, the economic rationale underpinning trophy hunting breaks down, and it becomes an extractive practice rather than a tool for regenerative land management. Furthermore, studies directly comparing hunting and non-hunting areas are few and far between. Overall, we need far more data to assess the precise role that hunting plays in many parts of the world.

There are notable examples of success. In Zimbabwe, the Bubye Valley Conservancy maintains over 3700 km^2 of protected land funded largely through hunting revenues (Hart 2015). This model has supported healthy populations of lions, rhinos, and other large mammals. In northern Pakistan, a community-based trophy hunting program for the endangered markhor has led to significant population recovery, demonstrating how local revenue-sharing and tight quota controls can align community interests with conservation outcomes (Jameel et al. 2019).

Yet these successes coexist with failures. Poor regulation can result in genetic bottlenecks, skewed sex ratios, a form of artificial evolutionary selection especially when high-value males are preferentially removed, and of course population declines. Corruption, lax oversight, and opaque quota-setting processes can further erode sustainability. In some cases, trophy hunting competes directly with other land uses, such as photographic tourism or subsistence agriculture, which may offer broader economic and social benefits, particularly when managed inclusively (Dickman et al. 2011). There are also trade-offs, at least potentially, in species focus. Because trophy hunting targets a limited number of high-value species, it can skew conservation priorities and divert attention from broader ecosystem needs. If not integrated into a comprehensive conservation strategy, this narrow focus could risk undermining biodiversity at the landscape level.

Comparisons between trophy hunting and non-consumptive alternatives such as photo-tourism reveal further complexity. While non-consumptive tourism is more publicly palatable, it requires substantial investment in infrastructure, political stability, and continuous tourist traffic. In remote, arid, or politically unstable regions, or regions that lack spectacular landscapes or high densities of animals, trophy hunting often remains the most viable conservation funding tool.

Shifting Markets, Evolving Policies

International Demand and Changing Preferences

The majority of trophy hunters are from high-income countries, notably the United States, but also parts of Europe including Spain and Germany (Bichel and Hart 2023). Demand is sensitive to economic cycles, public opinion, and regulatory restrictions, as well as the recruitment of people to hunting in general, and trophy hunting in particular. High-profile controversies have led to calls for bans on the import of trophies, particularly for species listed as threatened or endangered (Challender et al. 2024). Such bans, while popular with the public, have complex economic consequences (Dickman et al. 2019). They may reduce foreign exchange income, discourage private conservation investment, and push operators toward less sustainable alternatives. Critics argue that bans often lack input from range states and may harm the very communities and habitats they intend to protect (Challender et al. 2024).

Emerging Alternatives and Hybrid Models

In response to ethical and economic critiques, many countries and operators have begun to explore alternative or complementary models to trophy hunting. These include non-consumptive wildlife tourism, conservation ranching, and payment for ecosystem services (PES) (Naidoo et al. 2011). In Kenya, where hunting has been banned since the late 1970s, photographic tourism has expanded significantly, offering a more publicly acceptable form of wildlife-based income (e.g., Nowak et al. 2019). However, its success depends on factors such as infrastructure, political stability, accessibility, and scenic appeal which are features not available in all areas. Furthermore, despite a thriving tourism industry, Kenya has seen steep declines in wildlife numbers, a fact often contrasted to the increases or stability seen in hunting countries (Hart 2020).

To address these limitations, some regions have adopted hybrid models that combine hunting and tourism. In Namibia and parts of Zambia, such integrated approaches diversify income streams while reducing reliance on any single market. These models offer resilience and flexibility, but they also require sophisticated governance structures, stakeholder coordination, and careful market segmentation. It can also be very difficult in practice to have photo-tourists staying alongside trophy hunters.

Further innovations in conservation finance are emerging. Biodiversity offsets, carbon credit schemes, conservation easements, and trust funds are gaining attention as mechanisms to monetize ecosystem services (e.g., rhino bonds (Okolo 2022)). While promising, many of these tools are unproven over time and unevenly implemented. Importantly, they often lack the immediate, direct cash flow and landholder incentives that trophy hunting, despite its controversies, can provide.

Equity, Ethics, and Global Debates

While this chapter focuses on the economic dimensions of trophy hunting, it is essential to recognize that the debate is as much ethical and political as it is material. Trophy hunting raises questions that cut across moral philosophy, postcolonial politics, and environmental justice, making it one of the most contentious topics in modern conservation.

A central ethical concern is the belief that placing a monetary value on killing wildlife, especially rare or charismatic species, is fundamentally wrong. Critics argue that such practices commodify life, reducing assumed sentient beings to tradeable assets, and reinforcing problematic dynamics where wealthy foreigners extract value from the Global South, often with limited benefits for local communities. This critique resonates particularly in deontological ethics, which holds that killing animals for sport is inherently indefensible, regardless of conservation outcomes (discussed in Bichel and Hart 2023).

In contrast, consequentialist or utilitarian arguments defend trophy hunting if it demonstrably contributes to wildlife protection and rural livelihoods. If regulated hunting generates revenue that helps conserve habitat, protect species, and support local people, some argue, then its benefits may outweigh the moral discomfort it can cause. This fundamental tension between rights-based and outcome-based ethics complicates both policy decisions and public discourse.

From an economic justice perspective, several key concerns emerge:

- Distribution of benefits: Who actually gains from trophy hunting—the local community, national government, private outfitters, or international clients?
- Opportunity costs: Are there alternative land uses, such as ecotourism or carbon finance, that could offer more inclusive and sustainable returns?
- Intergenerational equity: Does the current model prioritize short-term income over long-term biodiversity and ecosystem health?

These questions go beyond simple cost–benefit analysis. They demand an interdisciplinary approach that integrates ecology, ethics, political economy, and local cultural values. An ethically coherent conservation framework must be inclusive, context-sensitive, and responsive to both scientific evidence and community voice.

A more balanced approach would recognize the rights and interests of local people, alongside legitimate concerns for animal welfare. Ethical conservation cannot be built solely on sentiment or ideology; it must also account for the lived realities of those managing and coexisting with wildlife on the ground.

Harnessing Hunting for Habitat: Eight Reforms to Align Conservation and Policy

Given the evidence presented in this chapter, and the complex interplay of ecological, economic, ethical, and governance dimensions, there is a clear need for thoughtful reform. Trophy hunting, when poorly regulated, can undermine conservation goals and public trust. Yet under the right conditions, it has the potential to support biodiversity, fund habitat protection, and empower local communities. The following economic and regulatory proposals are offered as possible pathways to align trophy hunting more closely with conservation outcomes and ethical imperatives.

- *Ecologically Grounded Quotas with Independent Oversight*

Anchor all hunting quotas in rigorous, science-based assessments conducted by independent experts. This ensures that only surplus individuals are removed, preserving population health and ecological balance.

- *Transparent and Equitable Revenue Sharing*

Guarantee that a meaningful share of hunting revenues directly supports local communities and conservation programs. Transparent financial systems can help ensure that wildlife protection translates into real benefits for people and nature.

- *Ethical Certification and Wildlife-Friendly Labeling*

Establish international certification standards that recognize operations meeting high ethical and ecological benchmarks. Labels can help consumers and regulators support practices that respect animal welfare and habitat integrity.

- *Market Access Tied to Conservation Performance*

Condition access to international trophy markets on verified adherence to conservation and ethical standards. This creates powerful incentives for countries and operators to prioritize wildlife protection.

- *Incentives for Mixed-Use Conservation Landscapes*

Support landowners who combine sustainable hunting with photo-tourism, rewilding, or conservation ranching. These hybrid models reduce pressure on wildlife while enhancing biodiversity and economic resilience.

- *Community Stewardship and Co-Governance*

Empower local communities to co-manage hunting areas and retain a majority of the benefits. When communities are true stewards of wildlife, conservation becomes a shared and sustainable goal.

- *Linking Wildlife Protection to Ecosystem Service Payments*

Enable landholders to access payments for ecosystem services (PES) and carbon credits alongside hunting revenues. This rewards those who maintain healthy habitats and helps shift incentives toward long-term ecological care.

- *Digital Tools for Wildlife Monitoring and Accountability*

Deploy real-time digital systems to track hunts, monitor wildlife populations, and ensure compliance. These tools enhance transparency, reduce illegal practices, and build trust in conservation outcomes.

Conclusions

Trophy hunting sits at the intersection of conservation, economics, and global ethics. As a revenue-generating mechanism, it has clear potential under the right conditions, where quotas are science-based, institutions are accountable, and benefits are equitably shared. In these contexts, it can support habitat protection, fund anti-poaching, and incentivize the conservation of otherwise economically marginal landscapes. However, in the absence of these conditions, trophy hunting can become exploitative, encourage elite capture, and provoke ethical and ecological backlash.

Its economic significance is undeniable in many biodiversity-rich but underfunded regions, particularly in sub-Saharan Africa. Trophy hunting provides direct financial flows that help sustain protected areas, create employment, and, in some models, support community-led conservation. Yet these flows are often unevenly distributed and vulnerable to governance failures. At its best, trophy hunting aligns market incentives with conservation outcomes; at its worst, it reinforces inequality, depletes wildlife populations, and fuels international outrage.

As public opposition intensifies, and regulatory constraints tighten, especially in key importing countries, the future of trophy hunting as a conservation tool is increasingly uncertain. Calls for bans, eco-labeling, and reform reflect broader shifts in public values and conservation paradigms. Despite this, in many regions, no clear economic alternative has emerged that can match the scale and immediacy of funding generated by well-regulated hunting. Replacing or supplementing this revenue will require creativity, investment, and institutional innovation.

Adaptation, rather than abandonment, is likely to define the path forward. Emerging models seek to integrate trophy hunting with ethical safeguards and diversified income streams. Hybrid approaches, combining photo-tourism, conservation ranching, and sustainable hunting, are being explored to optimize land use and reduce dependence on any one model. Other alternatives, such as payment for ecosystem services (PES) and carbon credit schemes, present promising mechanisms for compensating communities and landowners for maintaining natural habitats. While these models are still maturing, they may in time provide more inclusive and durable conservation finance. In some landscapes, PES may complement or gradually replace hunting revenues altogether.

Moving forward, successful conservation strategies will need to balance economic viability with ethical legitimacy and ecological integrity. Innovations in digital monitoring, value chain transparency, certification schemes and community engagement will be essential to build trust and effectiveness. Importantly, solutions must be context-specific, recognizing that what works in Namibia for example may not apply in Cameroon or Pakistan. There is no universal blueprint, only a shared imperative to secure biodiversity while respecting social and moral complexity.

Ultimately, the role of trophy hunting in twenty-first-century conservation will depend on its capacity to evolve. Whether it remains part of the conservation toolkit or fades from relevance will be determined not just by biology or economics, but by political will, ethical discourse, and the ability of institutions to deliver just and sustainable outcomes.

References

Allen CR, Brent LJ, Motsentwa T, Weiss MN, Croft DP (2020) Importance of old bulls: leaders and followers in collective movements of all-male groups in African savannah elephants (*Loxodonta africana*). Sci Rep 10(1):13996

Bichel N, Hart A (2023) Trophy hunting. Springer Nature

Carruthers J (2008) Wilding the farm or farming the wild"? the evolution of scientific game ranching in South Africa from the 1960s to the present. Transactions of the Royal Society of South Africa 63(2):160–181

Challender DW, Sas Rolfes M, Dickman A, Hare D, Hart AG, Hoffmann M, Mallon D, Mandisodza-Chikerema RL, Roe D (2024) Evaluating key evidence and formulating regulatory alternatives regarding the UK's hunting trophies (import prohibition) Bill. Conserv Sci Pract 6(10):e13220

Cloete PC, Van der Merwe P, Saayman M (2015) Profitability of the game ranching industry in South Africa

Collins D (2025) $1.3 million Bighorn Sheep tag sets record for most expensive auction tag ever. Outdoor Life via Yahoo News. https://www.yahoo.com/news/1-3-million-bighorn-sheep-195249600.html

D'Cruze N, Elwin A, Green J (2024) South Africa is to shut down captive lion farms—experts warn the plan needs a deadline. The Conversation. https://theconversation.com/south-africa-is-to-shut-down-captive-lion-farms-experts-warn-the-plan-needs-a-deadline-227258

Damm G (2005) Hunting in South Africa: facts, risks and opportunities. African Indaba 3(4):1–23

Di Minin E, Leader-Williams N, Bradshaw CJ (2016) Banning trophy hunting will exacerbate biodiversity loss. Trends Ecol Evol 31(2):99–102

Dickman AJ, Macdonald EA, Macdonald DW (2011) A review of financial instruments to pay for predator conservation and encourage human–carnivore coexistence. Proc Natl Acad Sci 108(34):13937–13944

Dickman AJ, Cooney R, Johnson PJ, Louis MP, Macdonald DW (2019) Trophy hunting bans imperil biodiversity. Sci 365(6456):874

Evans LC, Greenwell MP, Boult VL, Johnson TF (2023) Characterizing the trophy hunting debate on Twitter. Conserv Biol 37(4):e14070

Gaworecki M. (2017) Trophy hunters overstate contribution of big game hunting to African economies: Report. Mongabay, February 10. https://news.mongabay.com/2017/02/trophy-hunters-overstate-contribution-of-big-game-hunting-to-african-economies-report/

Ghasemi B (2021) Trophy hunting and conservation: Do the major ethical theories converge in opposition to trophy hunting? People Nat 3(1):77–87

Goldman MJ, De Pinho JR, Perry J (2013) Beyond ritual and economics: Maasai lion hunting and conservation politics. Oryx 47(4):490–500

Goodenough A, Hart AG (2017) Applied ecology: monitoring, managing, and conserving. Oxford University Press

Green R, Giese M (2004) Negative effects of wildlife tourism on wildlife. In: Higginbottom R (ed) Wildlife tourism: impacts, management and planning. Common Ground Publishing, Altona, VIC, pp 81–97

Hart A (2015) Viewpoint: uncomfortable realities of big game hunting. BBC News, September 1. https://www.bbc.co.uk/news/science-environment-34116488

Hart A (2017) Conservation versus profit: South Africa's 'unique' game offer a sobering lesson. The Conversation. https://theconversation.com/conservation-versus-profit-south-africas-unique-game-offer-a-sobering-lesson-82029

Hart A (2020) The true value of trophy hunting. The Critic, January. https://thecritic.co.uk/issues/january-2020/the-true-value-of-trophy-hunting/

Higginbottom K (2004) Wildlife tourism: impacts, management and planning. Common Ground Publishing, Altona, Vic

Huntley BJ (2023) Bridging the gap: community conservancies in Namibia and Zimbabwe. In: Strategic opportunism: what works in Africa: twelve fundamentals for conservation success. Springer Nature Switzerland, Cham, pp 93–120

International Union for the Conservation of Nature (2016) Informing decisions on trophy hunting. Briefing Paper. https://cites.org/sites/default/files/eng/cop/17/InfDocs/E-CoP17-Inf-60.pdf

Jameel MA, Tabassum S, Mehmood S, Shah T, Khan MF, Kabir M, Awan MN (2019) Does trophy hunting of Kashmir Markhor really contributing in its conservation? Int J Conserv Sci 10(3):525–532

Kadigi RM, Nkuwi IR, Ligate FA, Kija H, Musamba EB (2023) Economic valuation of auctioned tourist hunting blocks in Tanzania. Open J Ecol 13(4):199–228

Koro E (2022) Zim to pay 100% of international hunting revenue to communities. Zimbabwe Independent, June 10. https://www.newsday.co.zw/theindependent/environment/article/2131/zim-to-pay-100-of-international-hunting-revenue-to-communities
Leader-Williams N, Baldus RD, Smith RJ (2005) The influence of trophy hunting on conservation. In: Baldus R, Damm G, Wollscheid K (eds) CIC technical series: best practices in sustainable hunting. CIC, Budapest, pp 37–56
Leader-Williams N, Baldus RD, Smith RJ (2009) The influence of corruption on the conduct of recreational hunting. In: Recreational hunting, conservation and rural livelihoods: science and practice, pp 296–316
Lindsey PA, Roulet PA, Romanach SS (2007) Economic and conservation significance of the trophy hunting industry in sub-Saharan Africa. Biol Cons 134(4):455–469
Lindsey PA, Balme GA, Funston P, Henschel P, Hunter L, Madzikanda H, Midlane N, Nyirenda V (2013) The trophy hunting of African lions: scale, current management practices and factors undermining sustainability. Plos One 8(9):e73808
Macdonald DW, Jacobsen KS, Burnham D, Johnson PJ, Loveridge AJ (2016) Cecil: a moment or a movement? Biol Cons 200:96–98
Mazhar U (2023) Managing common resources in Gilgit-Baltistan: a case of Markhor trophy hunt. Emerald Emerg Markets Case Stud 13(1):1–19
McKean A (2023) The $725K Mule Deer tag: auction tags set all-time record at Western Hunt expo. Outdoor Life. https://www.outdoorlife.com/hunting/auction-mule-deer-tag-western-hunt-expo/
Mundeya M (2023) Zimbabwe's CAMPFIRE conservation initiative not benefiting intended communities. The Independent, August 30. https://www.independent.co.uk/voices/campaigns/giantsclub/zimbabwe-s-campfire-conservation-b2155881.html
Naidoo R, Weaver LC, De Longcamp M, Du Plessis P (2011) Namibia's community-based natural resource management programme: an unrecognized payments for ecosystem services scheme. Environ Conserv 38(4):445–453
Naidoo R, Weaver LC, Diggle RW, Matongo G, Stuart-Hill G, Thouless C (2016) Complementary benefits of tourism and hunting to communal conservancies in Namibia. Conserv Biol 30(3):628–638
Nowak K, Lee PC, Marino J, Mkono M, Mumby H, Dobson A, Harvey R, Lindsay K, Lusseau D, Sillero-Zubiri C, 71 Signatories (2019) Trophy hunting: Bans create opening for change. Science 366(6464):434–435
Okolo N (2022) The wildlife conservation bond: exploring new market mechanisms for protecting endangered species. In: Extinction governance, finance and accounting. Routledge, pp 361–371
Peyman AJ, Styles MA (2024) Examining the influence of corruption on the practice of trophy hunting in South Africa. Conservation 4(4):577–593
Taylor LA, Vollrath F, Lambert B, Lunn D, Douglas-Hamilton I, Wittemyer G (2020a) Movement reveals reproductive tactics in male elephants. J Anim Ecol 89(1):57–67
Taylor WA, Lindsey PA, Nicholson SK, Relton C, Davies-Mostert HT (2020b) Jobs, game meat and profits: the benefits of wildlife ranching on marginal lands in South Africa. Biol Cons 245:108561
Timbavati Nature Reserve (2016) Sustainability and the funding of the Timbavati private nature reserve. https://timbavati.co.za/sustainability-and-the-funding-of-the-timbavati-private-nature-reserve/
Van der Merwe P, Saayman M, Krugell W (2010) The determinants of spending by biltong hunters. South African J Econ Management Sci 13(2):194–206
Welz A (2018) The ongoing disgrace of South Africa's captive-bred lion trade. Yale Environment360 Yale School of Environment, September 18. https://e360.yale.edu/features/the-ongoing-disgrace-of-south-africas-captive-bred-lion-trade
Yeomans N, Hare D, Dröge E, Hart AG (2022) Ten years of coverage of trophy hunting in UK newspapers. Front Conserv Sci 3:1061295

Chapter 11
Animals as Fashion

Joshua Katcher and Tracey Windsor

> "Technological progress made over the years allows us to have valid alternatives at our disposition that render the use of cruel practices unnecessary as regards animals."
> —*Giorgio Armani*

Abstract This chapter examines the fashion industry's systemic reliance on animals and the economic and ecological externalities it generates, including land degradation, pollution, exploitative labor, and opaque supply chains. It introduces "circumfauna," a macroeconomic framework for understanding the global shift away from animal-derived inputs. Fashion, which is often dismissed as frivolous despite its $1.8 trillion scale, provides a revealing lens into how unregulated, animal-based production continues to shape material economies. Circumfaunal fashion, by contrast, aligns with emerging policy, investment, and supply chain shifts that prioritize circularity, biodiversity, and resilience. Drawing on economic case studies and current regulatory trends, the chapter outlines specific policy interventions such as subsidy reform, procurement incentives, and investment in circular infrastructure. Ultimately, circumfauna is positioned as both a framework and a market signal—a means to reimagine fashion's global role while enabling more just and sustainable economies.

J. Katcher (✉)
North America Hub Strategist, Canopy, Culver City, CA, USA
e-mail: joshuakatcher@gmail.com
URL: https://www.canopyplanet.org

T. Windsor
Windsor Edge, Culver City, CA, USA
URL: https://www.windsor-edge.com

N. Batini (ed.), *The Economics of Non-Human Animals*, Natural Resource Management and Policy 63, https://doi.org/10.1007/978-3-032-17580-9_11

Introduction

There is a persistent tendency to dismiss fashion, a $1.8 trillion industry[1] (Statista 2025) projected to produce 198.4bn garments globally in 2029,[2] as mere frivolity. Even fashion's own Karl Lagerfeld once quipped, "…don't get carried away, it's only dresses" (Tschorn 2013, para. 8). What the late Lagerfeld conveyed perhaps imperfectly is that fashion, while a serious business, should not be taken *too* seriously because it's only an applied aesthetic and, therefore, inconsequential. Just as fashion itself has historically been dismissed as a trivial or decorative domain, the impacts of "faunal fashion" (defined here as fashion reliant on the bodies and byproducts of animals), and valued at approximately $201.54 billion (see Appendix for methodology), have likewise gone largely unaddressed until recently. As a result, fashion has historically operated with far greater regulatory freedom than other extractive industries like energy or food. Lawmakers have largely failed to understand fashion as both a serious vector of planetary impact as well as a nexus of strategic opportunity. This oversight has left its extractive and exploitative practices under-examined and under-regulated, while its potential to fortify, diversify, and de-risk global supply chains remains largely untapped.

The fashion industry is a global force that dominates the lives of workers, reshapes ecosystems, has driven many animal species to extinction, and transforms nonhuman animals into industrial inputs and symbols of luxury and power. More than an accessory to global capitalism, fashion is often an engine of its expansion, fueling consumerism, manufacturing human identity *en masse*, and enforcing demands that extract a toll from consumers, workers, animals, and the natural world. Fashion is also a barometer of global economic systems: a visible and material expression of substantial production and extraction systems, labor and capital flows, trade routes, and regulatory structures, concentrated in an industry of immense volume, value, and influence. These *unintended consequences* are largely hidden from public consciousness, obscured by geographically dispersed production sites and polished, heavily funded, marketing machines.

A faunal fashion value chain for merino wool, for example, could include everything from clearing native Australian land and wildlife for grazing a non-native species, to a knitted wool-blend sweater hanging on a rack in New York City, to its subsequent disposal or entry into (or rejection from) the circular economy. The first, hugely impactful step of processing one billion sheep for wool, 7.7 million tons of skins and hides, is having to dedicate fragile and dwindling resources like land, water, and fuel. Wool scouring, a process that cleans and softens greasy wool,

[1] Fashion accounts for 2% of the global gross domestic product (GDP). As of 2024, Nike holds the highest brand valuation among mass apparel companies, estimated at approximately $72 billion. Meanwhile, LVMH, whose portfolio spans multiple luxury fashion houses led the sector in market capitalization, reaching an estimated $370.5 billion by January 2025. These figures underscore the consolidation of economic power within a narrow tier of fashion industry actors.

[2] Statista Market Insights. (n.d.). Apparel market worldwide. Retrieved April 6, 2025, from https://www.statista.com/outlook/cmo/apparel/worldwide.

heavily pollutes the Australian environment with alkylphenol ethoxylates that are toxic, particularly to aquatic wildlife (Sun and Baird 1998). Each step of the supply chain introduces more risks and muddies traceability.

Several industries have recognized the competitive advantage of completely eliminating these first, most risky, harmful, and costly steps. Circumfauna, defined as the bypassing of animal inputs entirely from the production process of a given commodity, is a growing global trend, attracting increasing investment. Circumfauna is the framework needed to interrogate how animals, though largely ignored as a macroeconomic category, remain central to systems of value extraction and environmental impact. It also offers a lens to assess how shifting supply chains toward circumfaunal inputs can open new economic pathways, diversify material sources, reduce systemic risk, relieve pressure on animals, ecosystems, and indigenous and frontline communities, as well as drive innovation. More broadly, circumfauna captures a growing industrial tendency, particularly in fashion, to replace faunal materials with alternatives that bypass animal use entirely.

The drivers of this shift away from faunal materials in industrial production are diverse: ecological concerns, regulatory compliance, evolving consumer preferences, reputational risk, and strategic efforts to align with emerging sustainability trends and investment mandates. Participation in this shift does not require an ethical commitment to animal welfare; it is often motivated by considerations of cost-efficiency, risk mitigation, and market opportunity. Early circumfaunal innovations were often marginalized as niche marketing rather than recognized as systemic economic alternatives. The term Circumfauna offers a systems-level framework for understanding this phenomenon; one that moves beyond terms perceived as ideological or consumer-facing. It also is more specific than "next gen".[3] Instead, it is a targeted macroeconomic framework focused specifically on the systemic bypassing of animals in supply chains, offering greater analytical precision across sectors where animal inputs are being displaced.

Economic Impacts of Animal-Based Fashion

A circumfaunal lens considers the entire value chain, aiming to both recognize animal inputs (faunal) as a distinct and measurable category, and provide a data-driven framework for making informed decisions (circumfaunal) that can render those inputs superfluous. The absence of animals as a recognized macroeconomic category has led to a fragmented view of their role in industrial production. Unlike categories such as carbon or water, which are tracked and regulated across sectors, animal inputs are not treated as a category. This means that there is a lack of analysis, which results in

[3] While the term "next gen" is widely used to describe emerging, often technology-driven alternatives to conventional materials and practices across industries, it lacks specificity regarding faunal inputs. Circumfauna describes a specific macroeconomic shift away from the use of animals in supply chains.

a failure to measure the impact using animals has on our society and inversely, how industry impacts animals. Without a unifying concept like circumfauna, policymakers and markets have missed the opportunity to identify cross-sector patterns, reduce risk exposure, and unlock innovation and profitability through the transition to a circumfaunal economy.

The perilous outcomes of faunal fashion have been absent from accounts of mainstream economics because the lives of animals, the condition of ecosystems, and the human health implications of fashion's wage-based system are seen as external to economic activity, and as previously noted, hidden from plain sight. Fashion's reliance on faunal materials has been possible greatly due to the externalizing of societal impacts caused by the industry. When animals are used in fashion supply chains, market prices do not account for biodiversity loss, ecosystem damage, and other global harms. The terms *externalities* and *unintended consequences* are used to theoretically capture these negative societal outcomes and artificially separate them from the cause, thus allowing firms to deny culpability (Katof 2022, p. 550). Even when policy tools are intended to mitigate societal costs, industries have and will continue to resist new and existing policies, in order to protect their profits at all costs.

A top driver of forest clearing is for leather industry-linked cattle grazing and cattle feed (Mammadova et al. 2020). Luxury leather manufacturing in Paraguay is linked to environmental racism with limited access to Indigenous land and water (Correia 2022). Aquatic ecosystems can become hypoxic dead zones from fur factory farm runoff (Jones et al. 2022). While the aesthetic appearance of grazeland, pasture, and ranching may sometimes *seem* natural, these are often violent interventions with wild spaces, native biomes, and Indigenous land (Poore 2017). *When* prices start to become internalized, through stronger regulations and market interventions, the destructive faunal supply chains are likely to become less and less viable. As externalities and unintended consequences that predominantly left firms in the fashion industry unscathed have escalated, the twenty-first century policy arena will have significant long-term implications for the ability to sustain profits in industrialized animal exploitation.

In recent decades, the support for policies in human rights, environmental preservation, and animal protection is gaining momentum. Compliance with regulatory standards such as voluntary frameworks like Science Based Targets for Nature (SBTN)[4] is increasingly challenging for the animal industrial complex as societal welfare is now at the least a consideration for economic decisions. A global wave of legislation banning the sales of new fur, outlawing fur farming, or heavily regulating the fur industry to make it too risky to do business has increased significantly (Linzey and Linzey 2022). Cities in Massachusetts, Michigan, and Florida, states like California, and entire countries like Israel have passed such laws (Fur Free Alliance

---

[4] Voluntary frameworks like Science Based Targets for Nature (SBTN), a corporate framework that guides companies in setting measurable goals to reduce their impacts on nature across biodiversity, land, water, and oceans, do not recognize faunal inputs as a distinct impact category.

2025). This is having an impact, according to the fashion analytics and data site, Edited:

> "Over the past two years, real fur stocked on designers' own sites has declined. The data for 2021 revealed a 23% drop YoY, down 29% since 2019 of items containing fox, rabbit, mink and other furs. During the same period, there was an 82% YoY lift in items described as "faux-fur"." (Marci 2022, para. 5)

Geopolitical conflict and resource diversifications are leading to changing global trade conditions. Faunal materials are more likely to face sudden bans or trade barriers compared to circumfaunal products, which are subject to stricter controls and traceability requirements. Changes in tariffs can significantly affect the cost structure, market access, and competitiveness of these products. Global trade of faunal inputs and products will be growingly restricted by disease outbreaks, animal welfare regulations, and biosecurity concerns, making them subject to major disruptions.

Several economic and regulatory pressures currently threaten the stability and profitability of the animal-based fashion industry. Rising production costs, continued inflation, and expected economic downturns are major concerns for faunal fashion. Inflationary pressures and competition for resources directly impact feed, land and labor intensive animal care, raising challenges in cost management and pricing stability. Demand shocks are particularly worrisome for animal industries due to the length and vulnerability of production cycles and supply chains.

The structure of the global production network for faunal inputs will prove to be inflexible. Due to the destructive nature of industrial animal production, animals in globalized supply chains must be processed in a series of locations. Sites must be far enough out of sight to obscure worker and animal exploitation as well as environmental damage and community health risks. Maintaining a minimum distance between sites also reduces the spread of diseases that are rampant in industrial animal agriculture such as foot and mouth disease, tuberculosis, and avian influenza. In order to obscure notice, these sites are often geographically dictated to avoid affluent areas, and inversely are set near low-income communities, who will suffer direct health and safety risks from the industry.

The environmental destruction and human rights transgressions of trans-national companies are often offshored to the global periphery, leading to increased structural inequality as profits flow to the global center. As a result, the global periphery continues to be disproportionately impacted by these issues and excluded from strategies to address them. Preparedness for global events is far less possible in lower-income countries, where animal supply chains are most vulnerable.

Many other industries are considering regionalism and reshoring to improve cash flows, move closer to demand, create more agile and flexible supply chains, prepare for stricter trade and environmental policy, and lessen timing risks (Mckinsey 2021). The integration of circumfauna inputs could provide more choices for fashion and textile supply chains, while the growing and unpredictable impacts of large-scale threats on established global production networks will continue to weigh on firms. Further, as industries increasingly prioritize nearshoring and regionalized supply chains to improve agility and resilience, the vast resource extraction and environmental degradation required for animal agriculture will suddenly be center stage in developed countries.

This begs the question, *who in the developed countries will be willing to dedicate the required land and resources to meet demands of faunal fashion*? Even if we only look at one resource, land, the challenges to the industry are insurmountable. Whether production is focused offshore or onshore, arable land is essential to the faunal fashion industry. Over 70% of agricultural land is correlated with the profits of animal products (Ritchie 2017, para. 1). However, land degradation from decades of industrial use, the majority of which is related to animal commodity chains, and the related environmental impacts, are reducing the availability and profitability of arable land (Weis 2013). The significant investment required to reverse land degradation may be beyond the financial mandate of firms. Further, it is estimated that the majority of growth in farmed-animal production, which directly relies on grazing land and crop production, has already happened and the future of this industry will likely bring diminishing returns (FAO 2006). In other words, the cost of increasing production on land becomes greater as land becomes less productive and therefore less profitable. This is weighing heavily on the industries' investors. Further, competition for land use is climbing between animal agriculture, food crop, aquaculture, forestry, and energy sectors. Biofuels, often promoted as a green alternative, are increasingly taking over arable land as the push for "green energy" continues to expand (Smith et al. 2010, pp. 2941–2957). In this context, faunal materials like wool and leather, with their vast land-use requirements and long complex supply chains are ripe for circumfaunal overhaul.

Circumfaunal Clothing: Redefining Ethical Materiality

Market Growth and Adoption

By the end of 2023, investment in circumfaunal materials surpassed $500 million, increasing from $457 million the previous year, according to the pioneering Material Innovation Initiative, which shut down in 2024. Their 2023 State of the Industry Report also indicated there were 144 innovators in the space, up from 102 in the previous year. The trajectory of circumfaunal fashion appears to be toward growth, however, the challenges of commercialization and significant infrastructure investments needed to reach economies of scale are creating bottlenecks, and must be overcome to bring down premiums and reach price parity with faunal counterparts.

In June of 2022, the Danish luxury fashion label Ganni launched a wallet made from Mylo (Bolt Threads' circumfaunal leather made using mycelium, which is the root structure of mushrooms). A Vogue Business interview from November of 2022 featured Ganni founder Nicolaj Reffstrup stating that products like Mylo are designed to exceed traditional products. "Phasing out virgin animal leather by 2023 is a no-brainer if we want to reach our 50% absolute carbon reduction target by 2027 [...] brands need to place bets and take risks" (Cernansky 2022, para. 9).

And they are. From early experimentation to commercial expansion, circumfaunal materials are gaining traction as viable alternatives to faunal textiles in the fashion sector. These materials that range from mycelium-based leather to plant-derived wool, are increasingly being adopted not only for their ecological and ethical advantages but also for their potential to de-risk supply chains, reduce compliance costs, and meet evolving regulatory and consumer expectations. Ganni has since integrated innovations to replace animal skins such as Celium (made of bacterial cellulose), Vegea (made from grape waste), Ohoskin (derived from orange and cactus), and Reishi, a mycelium-based luxury leather developed by MycoWorks. Stella McCartney has similarly advanced the commercial profile of circumfaunal materials, showcasing Mirum, a plastic-free, biodegradable leather alternative made from agricultural residues, and debuting Savian, BioFluff's plant-based fur. Her SS25 Hydefy handbag, made from mycelium and sugarcane waste, is now commercially available. AnotherTomorrow recently became the first brand to launch ready-to-wear garments using Mirum, including motorcycle jackets and skirts.

Efforts to scale production capacity are accelerating. Biomaterials' company Gozen has opened a 40,000-square-foot facility in Istanbul to manufacture Lunaform, a bacterial-grown-cellulose alternative to leather that debuted in Balenciaga's Maxi Bathrobe Coat. The company aims to expand to one million square feet by 2026, with annual production capacity of up to 40,000 garments. Meanwhile, textile recycling innovator Circ, in partnership with Canopy and Fashion for Good, launched Fiber Club to consolidate demand and facilitate access to recycled feedstocks for their silky, but silk-free materials. Participating brands such as Everlane, Bestseller, and Eileen Fisher are leveraging the initiative to accelerate circular material adoption. Circ is also advancing toward commercial scale, with its first industrial facility under development and backed by five-year offtake agreements for recycled pulp and polyester. These commitments are critical for securing the long-term capital and infrastructure needed to scale high-volume material innovation. The recycled pulp will be converted into lyocell, a fiber increasingly used as a silk alternative in linings and lightweight fabrics. This model exemplifies how early offtake agreements create the runway for de-risking production, anchoring supply chains, and integrating circumfaunal materials into the global textile economy at scale. Circ's recycled fibers have been featured on major runways, including in collections by Christian Siriano and Feben. Other notable examples include Modern Meadow's Innovera™, von Holzhausen's Banbū, Ponda's BioPuff, GAIA's FLWRDWN™, a botanical replacement for feather down.

Sustainability

Global fashion firms are increasingly required to comply with stringent conservation regulations. In effect, companies face expanding requirements to address their impacts on ecosystems, not just emissions. For instance, the European Union's

Corporate Sustainability Reporting Directive (CSRD) mandates that large companies disclose their impact on biodiversity, including measures to prevent deforestation and protect endangered species, starting with fiscal year 2024 reports. Similarly, in the United States, The Securities and Exchange Commission (SEC) is considering regulations that would require companies to report on their biodiversity conservation efforts, such as habitat restoration projects and initiatives to reduce the impact on local wildlife, when these factors are significant to stakeholders or tied to company targets. These developments reflect a broader recognition that pollution and ecological harm can result from all forms of production, including those not reliant on animal-based materials, and that robust biodiversity safeguards are essential regardless of production method.

These evolving regulations were established with the advertised intent to increase transparency, pushing fashion brands to comprehensively address their environmental impact across supply chains. Perhaps the most consequential, recent global regulation relevant to circumfauna is the European Union Deforestation Regulation (EUDR).[5] This policy requires companies placing certain commodities like cattle-derived leather on the EU market to prove, via geolocation data, that those goods are not linked to deforestation after December 31, 2020.

As global policy frameworks like these evolve, circumfauna becomes an increasingly strategic tool to conceptualize and measure a fashion category with some of the highest impacts[6] and then capitalize on the opportunities to bypass and outperform that category. "Given that at least two-thirds of a brand's environmental footprint can be attributed to its choice in raw materials, more and more brands are taking an active role in promoting R&D for adaptation of next-gen materials as a necessary step towards attaining their sustainability targets" (Material Innovation 2021, p. 3).

Boosting Jobs and Strengthening Communities

While animal agriculture has often been portrayed as essential to the vitality of rural economies, this perception increasingly conflicts with reality. As Collective Fashion Justice (2023) highlights in their *Under Their Skin: A Just Transition beyond Leather* report, the profit-driven leather industry is not a harmless byproduct of the meat industry. Rather, leather is a major driver of environmental degradation, public health risks, and structural economic vulnerabilities. In the United States, employment in the leather tanning and finishing sector fell by 53% between 2003 and 2022, driven by

[5] EUDR requires companies placing commodities like cattle, soy, palm oil, timber, cocoa, coffee, and rubber on the EU market to demonstrate, using geolocation and traceability data, that products are not linked to deforestation or forest degradation after December 31, 2020. It applies to operators of all sizes and larger traders, with penalties for non-compliance including fines, confiscation of goods, and market exclusion.

[6] Fashion Global Agenda's "Pulse of the Fashion Industry" report ranks cow leather and silk as the first and second worst materials in terms of global warming, eutrophication, water scarcity, and abiotic resource depletion.

automation, declining demand, and the rise of circumfaunal materials. This reflects a broader global trend: the leather industry is already contracting, and communities dependent on animal-based economies are facing diminishing returns (Collective Fashion Justice 2023).

Transitioning away from faunal production systems offers significant opportunities for higher-value, more resilient employment. Real-world examples underscore this shift: in Radcliffe, Iowa, the Faaborg family successfully converted a pig farming operation into a specialty mushroom business (Business Record 2024). Former livestock farmers such as Craig Watts in the U.S. and operations like Halley Farms in Iowa have also transitioned to mushroom or hemp production, reporting improved working conditions, greater economic stability, and a more sustainable relationship with land use (The Guardian 2024; Rancher Advocacy Program 2024). Initiatives like the Rancher Advocacy Program and the Transformation Project provide structured support for farmers leaving industrial animal agriculture behind, helping them reorient toward circumfaunal economies.

These patterns parallel opportunities emerging within fashion supply chains. A just transition away from animal-based textiles toward circular material economies, such as textile-to-textile recycling and agricultural waste valorization (e.g., wheat straw, bagasse, pineapple leaf, fruit skins), can deliver revitalization and quality employment in rural, farming, and industrial regions, transforming what would otherwise be an expense into a new revenue stream.

Investment in processing textile waste and agricultural byproducts into fiber feedstocks for next-generation Man-Made Cellulosic Fibers (Next Gen MMCF) offers a circumfaunal model for revitalizing regional economies and displacing high-impact materials like silk. Companies like Circulose and Circ are proving that this transition can be achieved at industrial scale. Silk production is highly energy- and resource-intensive; life cycle assessments show that producing silk fabric emits approximately 19% more carbon per kilogram than polyester, largely due to the boiling of silkworm cocoons (Astudillo et al. 2014). It also requires significant water for mulberry cultivation and relies heavily on chemical processing, contributing to water pollution and ecosystem degradation (Treehugger 2022). In contrast, NextGen MMCFs made from recycled textiles and agricultural residues, rather than wood pulp or faunal materials, offer a low-carbon, circular alternative with silk-like softness, breathability, and drape (Canopy 2022), reducing reliance on deforestation-linked sourcing and Nature-negative production systems (Springer 2024).

High-technology innovations are also advancing circumfaunal transitions. AMSilk, a biotechnology company specializing in lab-grown spider silk proteins, has partnered with 21st.BIO to scale sustainable silk production through precision fermentation (AMSilk 2024; World BioMarket Insights 2024). AMSilk's biofabricated fibers are biodegradable, and derived from renewable plant-based feedstocks, achieving a 90% reduction in air pollution and over 90% less land and water use compared to traditional animal-based protein fibers (Biotech Sphere 2024). AMSilk has partnered with Adidas to integrate these materials into performance footwear and with automotive brands to develop sustainable interior components, demonstrating the wide applicability and commercial viability of circumfaunal silk alternatives.

Brewed Protein™ materials, developed by the Japanese biotechnology company Spiber Inc., are produced through a microbial fermentation process that utilizes plant-derived sugars, eliminating reliance on petrochemical or animal-based raw materials (Spiber Inc., n.d.). These protein fibers are engineered to replicate the properties of silk, wool, and cashmere, offering a robust alternative across sectors including fashion and automotive (The Worldfolio, n.d.). To support commercial scale-up, Spiber has secured over ¥10 billion (approximately $65 million) in funding (Green Queen 2024) and has established partnerships with brands such as The North Face and Goldwin, demonstrating the materials' viability in global markets.

Moreover, models like Shiringa bioleather demonstrate how rural and Indigenous communities can build circumfaunal economies by producing materials that sustain forests rather than clearing them. Harvesting latex from Amazonian trees for bioleather provides steady income, strengthens land rights, and maintains biodiversity and carbon sequestration, benefits unavailable under traditional cattle ranching systems (Shiringa 2024).

Technological Innovation

In efforts to beat out competition, firms seek to lead megatrends, drive innovation in production, and introduce new products. Scalable material technologies that supersede high-risk activities with narrow profit margins (like trapping or rearing animals for their body parts) present significant prospects. The global phenomenon of circumfauna innovation has created new markets in a number of industries. The global precision fermentation market (a form of synthetic biology in which microbes are engineered to produce proteins and other functional ingredients) includes circumfaunal collagen, silk protein (Collet 2021, pp. 207–226), mycelial and other innovations aimed at bypassing animal skins, hairs, and protein fibers (Tubb and Seba 2021; Solca 2022). It has become a key technology for creating complex organic compounds without incorporating animals in the fashion, pharmaceutical, cosmetic, food and beverage, and pet food industries. Forbes reported that, "rather than resist the inevitable, smart animal agriculture businesses are getting in on the plant-based revolution by buying or investing in plant-based brands" (Fox, 20, forbes.com).

One might think it is only in the realm of science fiction that biologists, engineers, and designers collaborate in fabricating, growing, and brewing fibers, skins, hairs, and other circumfaunal materials that once required the rearing, trapping, or confining, and exploitation or slaughtering of living beings. We are on the brink of what is being referred to as "the fourth industrial revolution" (Hassoun 2022, pp. 1–31). From cellular agriculture, biofabrication, and biosynthetics to developments in harnessing materials like algae and mycelium and the increased accessibility of production via AI, 3D, and bioprinting, everything we know about materials and fashion production is changing. Lab-Grown Leather (LGL), a UK biotech startup, successfully scaled up its cultivated animal skin tissue in late 2024, with Dr Che Connon, managing director of parent company BSF Enterprise stating, "Our tissue engineering technology has the potential to solve some of the fashion industry's greatest ethical and environmental challenges (Rock 2024)."

Circumfaunal materials are produced through industrial processes that are more compatible with digital integration, automation, AI, IoT, and advanced manufacturing technologies. This enables real-time monitoring, rapid scaling, and process optimization, which is much harder with the biological variability of unpredictable biological processes and longer cycles of animal-based supply chains. Blockchain technology is a potential solution for improving traceability and efficiency. Circumfaunal materials, such as plant-based, synthetic, or lab-grown products, typically have more linear and standardized supply chains compared to the complex, fragmented, and biologically variable nature of faunal supply chains. Blockchain's ability to streamline data, automate processes, and reduce redundancies is more effective in these straightforward, scalable networks, leading to greater efficiency gains.

Circumfaunal supply chains avoid the additional layers of regulatory scrutiny, animal welfare documentation, and biosecurity protocols required for faunal materials. Blockchain can thus be deployed more rapidly and with fewer integration challenges, accelerating improvements in transparency and operational speed. Blockchain's use-cases of enhancing data quality, verifying and authenticating sustainability claims, and providing a new avenue for collaboration between supply chain stakeholders, will all be easier to realize in circumfaunal supply chains than the more opaque and multi-layered faunal supply chains.

These developments mark a turning point. As circumfaunal innovations move beyond proof-of-concept and into scaled production with lower capital investment, they offer a compelling value proposition: reduced reliance on volatile animal supply chains; compatibility with emerging regulations like extended producer responsibility (EPR); improved material circularity; and, in some cases, significantly lower emissions and waste profiles. The growing ecosystem of startups, suppliers, and brand partnerships demonstrates that circumfaunal materials are not simply niche ethical alternatives but increasingly credible competitors in a global industry seeking to meet both compliance targets and market demand. This convergence of performance and commercial scalability underscores the need for the macroeconomic lens of circumfauna to assess the transition away from faunal inputs across industries.

Seizing the Competitive Advantage

Faunal fashion value chains, based in animal-derived materials like leather, wool, and silk, are structurally extractive, resource-intensive, and increasingly exposed to systemic risks such as regulatory tightening and increasingly volatile supply chains. In contrast, circumfaunal fashion innovation that is centered in plant-based, recycled, and biofabricated materials offers substantial environmental savings through lower water use, and minimized land impacts, while enabling higher economic efficiency through scalable, circular supply chains. Circumfaunal innovation is not merely a substitution of raw materials; it represents a structural shift toward circular, innovation-driven economies that offer higher-value employment, diversified rural development, lower supply chain risks, and better alignment with emerging biodiversity and sustainability compliance.

With faunal fashion's advantages including established trade networks, long-standing consumer trust, brand recognition, and lobbying power, it is essential for circumfaunal brands to prioritize agility and adaptability of changing market conditions through dominance in business intelligence and marketing strategies. Cirumfaunal industry should take advantage of the weaknesses of faunal fashion. With shorter lead times and more predictable production cycles, circumfaunal brands can respond relatively quickly to changes in demand. Circumfaunal can also take advantage of fewer regulatory, ethical, and global constraints by stepping in to serve demand when related issues compromise animal supply chains due to scarcity, pricing, and timing changes. In the food sector, for example, the circumfaunal Just Egg can be cheaper than chicken eggs during periods of price spikes caused by zoonotic diseases and other faunal supply chain risks.

The first industries and businesses to successfully implement ML/AI, blockchain, and other digital advancements into business operations can attract capital by improving the bottom line–generating more consistent revenue, reducing costs, optimizing spending, and saving time (Panda and Pandey 2024). Opportunities to optimize marketing spend, influence consumer taste, and overhaul supply chains have expanded dramatically in the fashion sector. Avenues for a competitive advantage include inventory management, brand discoverability, in-person experiences, and shifts in consumer segments.

Inventory management has been one of the major business intelligence challenges of the fashion sector. Overproduction of inventory not only eats into profit margins, but sabotages efforts to reduce pollution and waste amidst growing government pressure. New inventory management technologies, including AI and machine learning, enable better demand forecasting and lower inventory levels, which can help companies align circumfaunal material sourcing with real-time market needs and waste reduction.

Consumers have reported growing frustrations with product discovery and ineffective online searches. AI-powered curation, content, and search can help customers discover brands and products more effectively, making them more inclined to make a purchase. This has caught the attention of the industry as "50% of fashion executives see consumer product discovery as the key use case for generative AI in 2025" (Mckinsey 2025).

Consumers are demanding innovative and engaging in-person experiences (Liu and Zhang 2024). The re-ignition in the experiential benefits of malls and storefronts is making a comeback. Now fully emerged in a digital world, where quality and brand identity can be faked more easily, consumers are craving tactile proof of the quality of fashion and opportunities to interact with the identity of brands through the in-store experience, re-invented.

Another opportunity for marketing lies in the growing over-50 fashion consumer segment. Since the fashion industry has historically prioritized younger shoppers, an advantage can be gained in speaking to the sentiments of the "silver generation." The

2024 UBS Wealth Report on U.S. generational wealth distribution finds that 72% of total US population wealth is accounted for by those aged over 55 (2024 UBS Wealth Report).

Innovators working to commercialize and scale circumfaunal materials must adopt a systems-thinking approach rooted in deep collaboration and data-driven strategy and forecasting across the value chain. Establishing pre competitive partnerships between brands, material developers, manufacturers, and regulators is essential to building the infrastructure and market conditions necessary for success. This work requires access to patient, impact-aligned capital, as the path to replacing entrenched, subsidized animal-based systems is inherently long-term and complex. Navigating this transformation demands adaptability to shifting regulatory landscapes, supply chain fragmentation, and inconsistent demand signals. Just as importantly, embracing failure as a critical part of innovation enables these efforts to evolve and remain resilient. Together, these principles form a strategic blueprint for advancing circumfaunal innovation, not as a niche disruption, but as a viable, scalable pathway for de-risking supply chains, reducing environmental impact, and aligning material systems with the realities of a post-animal economy.

Economic Policies to Foster Circumfaunal Fashion

The dominance of faunal fashion is deeply entrenched in global economic structures. Faunal materials like leather, wool, silk, fur, and feathers are embedded in high-volume trade flows, protected by subsidies, supported by interlinked industries such as meat and dairy, and upheld by luxury markets where animal products signal status, quality, and value. Their use is not merely incidental; it is structurally reinforced across supply chains, financial systems, and cultural capital.

While the fashion industry acknowledges the diminishing timeline for sustainability goals, there are no strong coordinated industry wide solutions for circumfauna in action. Things like EPR laws, fur sale and manufacture bans, and biodiversity disclosures are promising, but have been slow to evolve and address regulatory gaps. Greater governmental intervention is necessary to create more predictable demand for circumfaunal alternatives, helping to drive economies of scale and lower costs. The regulatory landscape has long established unfair market advantages for faunal products. Even when policies are being created, they have been blocked or diluted when economic growth is prioritized over sustainability, or when just transition measures for affected workers are absent. Direct measures to counter market concentration and anti-competitive practices are essential. Structural subsidies for farmed-animal production and the absence of mandatory animal welfare disclosures have resulted in significant market distortions. These hidden costs artificially lower the price of faunal fashion materials, while emerging circumfaunal alternatives face higher barriers to entry, limited access to infrastructure, and minimal policy incentives that undermine fair competition and slow down innovation.

We need a government policy roadmap for accelerating the transition from industrial faunal material production to cirumfaunal materials. Regulatory reforms, financial incentives, and market interventions will help breach major market barriers like high costs, limited capital, accessibility hurdles, and scaling challenges for new materials. Investments in Supply Chains and Infrastructure will strengthen the effectiveness of policies, ease supply chain bottlenecks, address underdeveloped waste management, and support the transition to a workforce that is safer and benefits from upskilling in the digital age.

Finally, national campaigns, curriculum integration, and standardized labeling can foster informed demand from the public for circumfauna, increasing pressure for regulatory change while supporting early market adoption and long-term competitiveness. As we have seen, this can play out as the public makes demands for market-based transparency tools like animal welfare disclosures, certification schemes, as well as hard legal prohibitions like the global trend in fur sales and farming bans and phase-outs (Fur Free Alliance 2025). A coordination of major economic policies and regulatory interventions, many of them listed below, is essential to secure a circumfaunal fashion industry transformation.

Regulatory Reforms

- Stricter laws which phase in bans or heavy restrictions on the use of faunal materials with high environmental or animal-welfare-based ethical costs.
- Strengthened and expanded Extended Producer Responsibility (EPR), requiring brands to internalize biodiversity and/or other environmental costs.
- Waste and chemical regulation that enforces strict limits on the use and disposal of hazardous chemicals and waste in textile production.
- Proposed disclosures for the biodiversity (e.g., deforestation) impact for all fashion brands, with third-party verification.
- Equitable stakeholder engagement that includes people, workers, and communities;
- Strong and enforceable antitrust and competition policy to counter the economic growth narratives and inhibit corporate lobbying of animal agriculture megafirms.

Financial Incentives

- Correcting distorted prices that do not reflect true scarcities (land, water, energy, nutrients). Agricultural subsidies should be redirected from faunal textiles toward next-gen materials.

- Subsidies for R&D and commercialization, including significant government grants and subsidies to organizations developing and scaling circumfaunal materials.
- Dedicated finance products, such as low-interest loans, loan guarantees, and green bonds, for companies investing in circumfaunal material production and infrastructure.
- Tax credits and deductions for companies that use or produce circumfaunal materials, invest in sustainable manufacturing, or retrofit existing facilities to accommodate new materials.

Market Interventions

- Universalize government procurement mandates, for example, the NYC Environmentally Preferable Purchasing Act. Require all public agencies to source uniforms and textiles from circumfaunal materials, creating guaranteed demand and economies of scale.
- Consumer purchase incentives implemented point-of-sale rebates, tax deductions, targeted subsidies, and vouchers for the purchase of certified circumfaunal products.
- Retail pilots and small business support that exclusively features circumfaunal materials, especially in high-visibility urban markets.
- Blockchain systems that provide comprehensive supply chain transparency will encourage businesses to leave animals out of the fashion equation—as it is nearly impossible for faunal fashion brands.

Supply Chain, Infrastructure, and Workforce Support and Investment

- Investment in bio-based and circular economy infrastructure, in particular to fund the development of recycling, upcycling, and composting facilities specifically for next-gen and circumfaunal materials. Logistics hubs and digital platforms to connect small producers and brands, improving access to sustainable input.
- Public–private collaboration programs, which have successfully been used to accomplish major societal shifts and speed up technological and innovation (Katof 2022).
- Just Transition labor policies, in particular to support rural and developing communities where animal agriculture is most predominant. As subsidies shift to faunal supply chains, governmental programs can address retraining, green jobs, and income support for workers displaced from faunal supply chains.

Education and Public Engagement

- Visibility and public engagement including sustained media coverage, high-profile advocacy, and creative visibility initiatives to strengthen public acceptance.
- Education and awareness campaigns launched nationally to highlight the environmental, ethical, and performance benefits of circumfaunal materials, targeting both consumers and industry professionals.
- Standardized "Eco" and transparency labeling, including material origins and environmental impact.

Conclusions

Circumfauna offers a powerful framework for rethinking the socio-natural impacts of fashion and other global industries. It brings into focus the economic, political, cultural, and ecological forces that compel a reassessment of animals as raw materials and commodities. But its transformative potential will not be realized without sustained political and economic efforts, such as rewilding pasturelands, strengthening antitrust protections, democratizing intellectual property, and embedding bioregional principles in industrial strategy.

The motivations for bypassing animals are diverse, evolving, and often overlapping. As this field grows, it will continue to generate new productive forces, knowledge systems, and unintended consequences, many of which remain beyond our current horizon. To realize its promise, circumfaunal innovation must align with profitability and policy readiness where possible. As outlined in this chapter, the road to systemic adoption is shaped by both catalysts like the rising risk profile of faunal materials and entrenched obstacles, from industrial bottlenecks to cultural and economic support for the status quo.

Public understanding and education remain a critical battleground. Certification schemes such as Textile Exchange's Materials Matter Standard Pilot which aims to improve traceability and animal welfare in fashion supply chains for sheep wool, mohair, alpaca, and down blur consumer awareness by labeling faunal materials as "responsible" or "humane," even when they involve standard harms like castration and tail docking. This creates false equivalency with animal-free innovation, excludes circumfaunal alternatives from visibility, and undermines momentum for structural change. Similarly, lobbying groups like the Natural Fibers Alliance and the Leather Working Group actively shape narratives that portray faunal materials as inherently sustainable, often using selective metrics and industry-defined criteria. These efforts reinforce outdated norms and make reform more difficult in the absence of broader cultural consensus around biodiversity, welfare, and justice.

The path forward must be collective. Structural shifts are sustained not only through regulation or investment, but through informed public engagement. As recent research confirms (Jangde and Ahmad 2025), education is foundational, shaping policy literacy, ethical awareness, and consumer agency. Only through widely accepted knowledge can communities and institutions call with clarity and urgency for the systemic transition that circumfauna represents.

Appendix

Genuine Leather market: \$242.85 billion

Wool market: \$38.64 billion

Feather and down market: \$7.57 billion

Animal Fur Industry: \$21 billion

Estimated Total Value of Faunal Materials Across All Sectors: ≈ \$310.06 billion USD

Estimated Value Attributable to Fashion (65%): ≈ \$201.54 billion USD[7]

The global market value for genuine leather was estimated to represent 53.6% of the total leather goods market in 2022, placing the value of the genuine leather segment at approximately \$130.1 billion (Grand View Research 2023). The global wool textile market was valued at \$38.64 billion in 2023, encompassing Merino, Coarse, Mohair, Angora, Alpaca, Cashmere, and other wools (Congruence Market Insights 2025). The global down and feather market was valued at \$7.57 billion in 2023, with continued growth projected (Future Market Insights 2023). Although real fur exports fell dramatically from \$14.7 billion in 2013 to \$3.4 billion in 2023, the total fur market, including domestic and export sales, has been measured at approximately \$21 billion, primarily based on fur coat valuations. This includes rabbit, mink, fox, civet, and otter (Business of Fashion 2024; Business Research Insights 2025). This estimate aligns with prior industry reports, which placed the fur market value between \$20.1 billion and \$25.1 billion in 2021, depending on the accounting of COVID-19 impacts (We Are Fur 2021).

References

[7] Considering the leather industry's significant contribution to the category and dominance in fashion-related segments, we adopt a conservative estimate that approximately 65% of the global value of faunal materials can be attributed to the fashion sector. While market segmentation may vary across industries, this assumption reflects the widespread application of these materials within fashion and is intended to offer a reasoned approximation rather than a definitive valuation. It should be understood as an indicator of a generalized trend based on currently available data.

AMSilk (2024) AMSilk and 21st.BIO announce partnership to accelerate the production of advanced materials made from spider silk-based proteins. Retrieved from https://www.amsilk.com/amsilk-and-21st-bio-announce-partnership-to-accelerate-the-production-of-advanced-materials-made-from-spider-silk-based-proteins/
Astudillo MF, Thalwitz G, Vollrath F (2014) Life cycle assessment of Indian silk. J Clean Prod 101:203–211. https://doi.org/10.1016/j.jclepro.2015.03.093
Biotech Sphere (2024) AMSilk and 21st.BIO partnership for spider silk-based protein production. Retrieved from https://biotechsphere.com/amsilk-and-21st-bio-partnership-for-spider-silk-based-protein-production/
Business of Fashion (2024) Fur, LVMH sales, and animal welfare, November 15. Retrieved April 6, 2025, from https://www.businessoffashion.com/articles/sustainability/fur-lvmh-sales-animal-welfare/
Business Record (2024) Faaborg family in Radcliffe transitions pig operation to mushroom business at 1100 Farm, March 4
Business Record. Retrieved from https://www.businessrecord.com/faaborg-family-in-radcliffe-transitions-pig-operation-to-mushroom-business-at-1100-farm/
Business Research Insights (2025) Fur coat market size, share, trends, analysis report, 2023–2030, March 17. Retrieved April 6, 2025, from https://www.businessresearchinsights.com/market-reports/fur-coat-market-119633
Canopy (2022). Next generation solutions. Canopy. Retrieved February 1, 2022, from https://canopyplanet.org/next-generation-solutions
Cernansky R (2022, November 4). Materials startup asks brands to eliminate virgin leather if they want alternative. Vogue Business. https://www.voguebusiness.com/sustainability/materials-startup-asks-brands-toeliminate-virgin-leather-if-they-want-alternative
Collective Fashion Justice (2023) Under their skin: a just transition beyond leather. Collective Fashion Justice. Retrieved from https://www.collectivefashionjustice.org/a-just-transition-beyond-leather
Collet C (2021) Biotextiles: making textiles in a context of climate and biodiversity emergency. In: Materials experience 2. Butterworth-Heinemann, pp 207–226
Congruence Market Insights (2025) Wool market size, trends, share, growth, and opportunity forecast, 2024–2031, January. Retrieved April 6, 2025, from https://www.congruencemarketinsights.com/report/wool-market
Correia JE (2022) Between flood and drought: environmental racism, settler waterscapes, and indigenous water justice in South America's Chaco. Ann Am Assoc Geogr 1–21
FAO (2006) Livestock's long shadow: environmental issues and options. Retrieved from http://www.fao.org/docrep/010/a0701e/a0701e.pdf
Fur Free Alliance (2025) Fur bans. Fur Free Alliance, April 29. Retrieved April 29, 2025, from https://www.furfreealliance.com/fur-bans/
Future Market Insights (2023) Down and feather market size, demand & growth 2023–2033, February. Retrieved April 6, 2025, from https://www.futuremarketinsights.com/reports/down-and-feather-market
Grand View Research (2023) Leather goods market size, share & trends analysis report by product (footwear, bags, accessories, others), by distribution channel, by region, and segment forecasts, 2023–2030, February. Retrieved April 6, 2025, from https://www.grandviewresearch.com/industry-analysis/leather-goods-market
Green Queen (2024) Japan's Spiber raises $65M to scale up production of eco materials made from fermented 'brewed protein', April 16. Retrieved from https://www.greenqueen.com.hk/japan-spiber-fiber-materials-microbial-fermentation-brewed-protein/
Hassoun A, Bekhit AED, Jambrak AR, Regenstein JM, Chemat F, Morton JD, et al (2022) The fourth industrial revolution in the food industry—part II: emerging food trends. Crit Rev Food Sci Nutr 1–31

Harvey F (2024) Former livestock farmers in the US are switching to mushrooms and vegetables. The Guardian, March 3. Retrieved from https://www.theguardian.com/environment/2024/mar/03/factory-farming-transition-mushrooms-vegetables
Jangde S, Ahmad MA (2025) Integrating sustainability into equal education opportunities. In: Environmental landscape and sustainable biodiversity for healthy green growth. Springer Nature Switzerland, Cham, pp 97–103
Jones A, Labaj A, Campbell J, Libera N, Kurek J (2022) Zooplankton assemblage and body size responses to severe lake eutrophication from agricultural activities near mink farms in Nova Scotia, Canada. J Plankton Res 44(3):464–474
Katof T (2022) Review of Mariana Mazzucato's mission economy. Rev Political Econ
Linzey A, Linzey C (2022) Legislation on fur factory farming. In: An ethical critique of fur factory farming. Palgrave Macmillan, Cham, pp 11–17
Liu S, Zhang J (2024) Bibliometric analysis of omnichannel retailing: mapping research trends and future directions. Heliyon 10(6):e27118. https://doi.org/10.1016/j.heliyon.2024.e27118
Mammadova A, Masiero M, Pettenella D (2020) Embedded deforestation: the case study of the Brazilian—Italian bovine leather trade. Forest 11(4):472
Material Innovation Initiative (2021) State of the industry report: next-gen materials
Marci K (2022 November 10) Why retailers' future lies in faux fur. EDITED. Retrieved November 27, 2022, from https://edited.com/blog/why-retailers-future-lies-in-faux-fur/
Panda DK, Pandey SC (2024) A literature review on the impact of SOR theory on the retail industry and its applicability in studying blockchain technology's influence on consumer loyalty. J Retail Consum Serv 77:103523. https://doi.org/10.1016/j.jretconser.2024.103523
Poore J (2017) Back to the wild. New Sci 235(3138):26–29
Rancher Advocacy Program (2024) Transition stories. Rancher Advocacy Program. Retrieved from https://rancheradvocacy.org/transition-stories/
Ritchie H (2017, October 3) How much of the world's land would we need in order to feed the global population with the average diet of a given country? Our World in Data. https://ourworldindata.org/agricultural-land-byglobal-diets
Rock T (2024) Lab-grown leather company increases skin sample size. Leather Magazine, September 30. Retrieved from https://www.leathermag.com/news/lab-grown-leather-company-increases-skin-sample-size/?cf-view
Shiringa (2024) Bioleather and community conservation model. Shiringa. Retrieved from https://www.shiringa.bio/
Smith P et al (2010) Review. Competition for land. Roy Soc 365:2941–2957
Solca L (2022) Luxury leather goods and alternative leather: risk and growth opportunities. Luxury Stud: pursuit Luxury J 1(2):117–149
Spiber Inc (n.d.) Protein fiber. Retrieved from https://spiber.inc/en/protein
Springer (2024) Innovations in sustainable textiles. Retrieved from https://doi.org/10.1007/978-3-031-80193-8_2
Statista (2025) Apparel market worldwide—statistics & facts, February 3. Retrieved April 6, 2025, from https://www.statista.com/topics/5091/apparel-market-worldwide/
Sun C, Baird M (1998). The determination of alkyl phenol ethoxylates in wool-scouring effluent. J Text Inst 89(4):677–685. https://doi.org/10.1080/00405000.1998.11090906
The Business of Fashion & McKinsey & Company (2025) The state of fashion 2025. Retrieved from https://www.mckinsey.com/industries/retail/our-insights/state-of-fashion/
The Worldfolio (n.d.) Brewed protein: expanding the range of sustainable materials. Retrieved from https://www.theworldfolio.com/interviews/brewed-protein-expan/4955/
Treehugger (2022) Is silk sustainable? Retrieved from https://www.treehugger.com/silk-sustainable-impact-5094158
Tschorn A (2013, November 3) Diana Vreeland vs. Karl Lagerfeld: who's the wittiest of them all? Los Angeles Times

Tubb C, Seba T (2021) Rethinking food and agriculture 2020–2030: the second domestication of plants and animals, the disruption of the cow, and the collapse of industrial livestock farming. Ind Biotechnol 17(2):57–72

We Are Fur (2021) Global fur retail value, May 27. Retrieved April 6, 2025, from https://www.wearefur.com/wp-content/uploads/2021/06/Global-fur-retail-value-May-2021-Henning-study.pdf

Weis T (2013) The ecological hoofprint: the global burden of industrial livestock. Zed Books

World BioMarket Insights (2024) Biotech partners AMSilk and 21st.BIO spin a sustainable future with spider silk. Retrieved from https://worldbiomarketinsights.com/biotech-partners-amsilk-and-21st-bio-spin-a-sustainable-future-with-spider-silk/

Chapter 12
Animals in Biomedical Testing

Thomas Hartung

"The difficulty lies not so much in developing new ideas as in escaping from old ones."
— *John Maynard Keynes*

Abstract This chapter examines the economic dimensions of the transition from traditional animal testing to New Approach Methodologies (NAMs) in safety sciences. Drawing on data from regulatory agencies, industry trends, and technological innovations, it articulates how ethical motivations have been joined—if not eclipsed—by compelling economic, scientific, and policy rationales for replacing animal-based testing. It evaluates the comparative cost structures of *in vivo* versus *in vitro*/*in silico* methods, market mechanisms relevant to this field, and other socioeconomic analyses of the (lack of) progress in this field. Special attention is paid to the implications of REACH regulation in Europe, the accelerating regulatory shift in the United States (particularly under the FDA's new roadmap), and the disruptive role of artificial intelligence (AI) in reshaping toxicology as a data-driven science. The chapter concludes by framing alternatives to animal testing not as regulatory burdens but as economic opportunities, essential for global competitiveness, scientific integrity, and ethical responsibility.

From Ethics to Economics: The Changing Landscape of Animal Testing

The longstanding reliance on animal experimentation in safety sciences is now facing a disruptive shift—not from a singular ethical outcry, but from a confluence of economic, technological, and regulatory currents. Once considered indispensable for ensuring human safety, animal testing has been increasingly criticized for its

T. Hartung (✉)
Environmental Health and Engineering, Molecular Microbiology and Immunology, Whiting School of Engineering, John Hopkins Bloomberg School of Public Health, Baltimore, MD, United States
e-mail: thartun1@jhu.edu

N. Batini (ed.), *The Economics of Non-Human Animals*, Natural Resource Management and Policy 63, https://doi.org/10.1007/978-3-032-17580-9_12

costs, timelines, and limited translational relevance. In parallel, the maturation of New Approach Methodologies (NAMs), spanning *in vitro*, *in silico*, ~omics-based, and microphysiological systems (MPS), is altering the economic calculus of safety assessment.

Where once ethics dominated the discourse, today, economics has emerged as a pivotal force—what might be termed "the most important omics" (Meigs et al. 2018). From multinational pharmaceutical companies to startup biotech firms and regulatory agencies, stakeholders are realigning priorities around cost-effectiveness, scalability, and predictive reliability. This chapter dissects the economic dimensions underpinning this paradigm shift, using a foundation built on a series of publications authored by the present author and collaborators, enriched by updated data on test pricing, contract research organizations (CROs), regulatory trends, and market forecasts.

With global safety assessment expenditures now running into the tens of billions of dollars, the financial case for alternatives has never been more compelling. The transition, however, is not automatic. Structural inertia, vested interests, and regulatory conservatism still tether many decisions to outdated approaches. Understanding the economic forces—both drivers and barriers—offers a roadmap to accelerate the uptake of NAMs in global regulatory frameworks.

Animal Testing as an Economic Sector

Animal testing is not simply a scientific method; it is an entrenched economic activity with significant market implications. Each year, over 115 million animals are used globally for research and testing purposes, with regulatory testing constituting a sizable fraction of this figure. In the European Union alone, regulatory testing accounted for approximately 20% of all animal use, representing an estimated €620 million in direct testing expenditures. When extrapolated globally and updated for inflation and expanded regulatory scope (e.g., under REACH and TSCA reform), this suggests a market of $4 billion dedicated solely to animal-based toxicology.

The sector also supports a wide labor market. In Europe, estimates suggest around 60,000 experimenters and 15,000 professionals are directly employed in animal experimentation, with global figures reaching 300,000. Indirect employment through CROs, equipment providers, feed and housing suppliers, and veterinary oversight significantly expands this footprint. Contract research organizations now conduct the majority of preclinical studies, with the CRO industry valued at $79 billion in 2018—$11.2 billion of which is dedicated to preclinical services. Giants such as Charles River and Covance (LabCorp) report annual revenues in the billions, highlighting the extent to which animal-based testing has been industrialized.

However, this industrial entrenchment is increasingly offset by economic inefficiencies: slow turnaround times, high maintenance costs for animal colonies, low throughput, and most critically, limited predictive validity for human biology. False positives and negatives arising from species differences introduce risks that propagate downstream in product development, recalls, and litigation.

Comparative Cost Structures: Animal vs. Alternative Methods

The financial asymmetry between animal-based and alternative methods is stark and increasingly well documented. Sometimes, these new methods are themselves animal studies, which reduce animal numbers to achieve the same goal. For instance, a traditional two-generation reproductive toxicity study (OECD TG 416) can cost upward of €700,000 and use over 3,200 animals. In contrast, the Extended One-Generation Reproductive Toxicity Study (TG 443) reduces animal use by more than half and costs significantly less (if not expanding with new study arms to address developmental neuro- and immunotoxicity). Even more dramatically, validated *in vitro* methods such as skin corrosion (OECD TG 431, EpiDerm™, EPISKIN™) can replace animal-based Draize tests at a fraction of the cost and with greater reproducibility.

Detailed comparisons from Humane Society International and ECVAM studies have illustrated these differences. For example:

- The Draize rabbit eye irritation test costs approximately $1,800, whereas the *in vitro* Bovine Corneal Opacity and Permeability (BCOP) test costs about $1,400.
- The local lymph node assay (LLNA), also a reduction animal method, costs ~$3,000, while the full guinea pig maximization test is ~$6,000.
- Pyrogen testing using rabbits costs $475–990 per batch, while the Limulus Amebocyte Lysate (LAL) assay is as low as $85 and similar for a Monocyte Activation Test (MAT).

These figures do not capture indirect costs: time delays, regulatory burdens, or ethical compliance. The high-throughput nature of many *in vitro* systems means that hundreds or thousands of compounds can be screened rapidly with dramatically reduced per-sample costs, enabling early-stage prioritization and reducing downstream failures. *In silico* models, especially those using AI and machine learning, further reduce the need for physical testing altogether, offering predictive insights with marginal costs.

Market Expansion and Innovation: The NAM Economy

Market data from research firms such as MarketsandMarkets and Frost & Sullivan reveal that the sector of NAMs is experiencing double-digit growth, far exceeding that of traditional toxicology. *In vitro* toxicology was estimated at $6.3 billion in 2017 and projected to exceed $8.7 billion by 2022. Organs-on-Chips, although still nascent, boast a CAGR of over 36%, reflecting strong investor interest and technological promise. The global 3D cell culture market was projected to grow at over 20% annually, with applications in toxicity, efficacy, and disease modeling.

This explosion is mirrored in the biotech ecosystem. Startups and spinouts specializing in human-on-a-chip systems, AI-based predictive toxicology, and advanced ~omics platforms are attracting venture capital and forging partnerships with major pharmaceutical companies. Conferences, journal publications, and regulatory dialogues now regularly feature NAMs as central topics, indicating normalization within the scientific community.

NAMs are not simply substitutes; they are enablers. They offer mechanistic insights (e.g., transcriptomic or metabolomic perturbations), support systems-level modeling (e.g., Adverse Outcome Pathway (AOP) frameworks), and integrate human-relevant biology from the start. As such, their economic contribution transcends testing and enters the domain of innovation enablement.

Structural Barriers and Opportunity Costs

Despite clear advantages, NAMs face entrenched resistance rooted in regulatory conservatism, infrastructure inertia, and economic vested interests. The post-validation process, i.e., the time for implementation after a method was found valid, for alternatives can take years. For instance, it took six years for the OECD to accept validated alternatives to skin corrosion tests and then it often still takes decades until the animal test is actually phased out. The author led the successful validation of alternatives for the rabbit pyrogen test completed in 2003, declared validated in 2006, accepted by regulators in 2010 but finally replacing all the around 170,000 rabbits per year in Europe only in 2026. An ECVAM Workshop in 2008 identified major impediments: fragmented communication, inconsistent data sharing rules, variable implementation across sectors, and lack of global mutual recognition.

The opportunity costs are not hypothetical. Delays in accepting alternatives perpetuate the use of outdated methods, delaying market entry, increasing development costs, and failing to prevent adverse outcomes. One striking example is the pharmaceutical sector: with R&D costs per drug now surpassing €2 billion and success rates as low as 5%, in the clinical trial phase, the misdirection caused by poorly predictive animal models is economically unsustainable.

Moreover, the continued reliance on animal data has knock-on effects in product liability litigation, regulatory approval delays, and consumer trust—each carrying tangible economic repercussions. These hidden costs underscore the urgency for regulatory reform and incentivization mechanisms.

Toward a Future-Ready Bioeconomy

Alternatives to animal testing align with the principles of the emerging bioeconomy: sustainability, human relevance, precision, and digitization. They dovetail with key policy initiatives such as the EU Green Deal, and the U.S. FDA Modernization Act 2.0. Furthermore, they contribute to ESG (Environmental, Social, and Governance) metrics that are increasingly scrutinized by investors and boards.

The path forward requires coordinated investment in validation pipelines, education of regulators, and transparent public-private partnerships. Programs like Complement-ARIE, PARC, ToxCast, and Tox21 illustrate how collaboration can de-risk transitions and generate scalable platforms. Incentivization through grant mechanisms, tax relief, and expedited review pathways can further catalyze uptake.

Ultimately, embracing alternatives is not just a scientific imperative but an economic strategy. The convergence of AI, biotechnology, and regulatory modernization offers a rare moment of opportunity. Capturing it will require bold leadership, smart policy, and sustained commitment.

The True Cost of REACH: Animals and Economics

The Registration, Evaluation, Authorisation and Restriction of Chemicals (REACH) regulation of the European Union was designed to ensure a high level of protection for human health and the environment. However, it has come with a significant economic and ethical toll.

According to recent data, 4.2 million animals have been used as of December 2022 for just three systemic toxicity endpoints under REACH: reproductive toxicity (1.48 million), developmental toxicity (1.29 million), and repeated dose toxicity (132,000). An additional 1.27 million animals are currently involved in pending tests. Beyond these, another estimated 0.6 to 3.2 million animals were likely used for other endpoints, such as genotoxicity, sensitization, and ecotoxicology.

The planned amendment to REACH (Regulation EU 2022/477) could further add 3.6–7 million animals based on anticipated testing requirements. Planned extensions of Chemical Safety Assessment (CSA) to Annex VII substances (those at 1–10 t/y) may require 1.2–2.6 million more animals. The looming registration of polymers, estimated to bring tens of thousands of additional dossiers, is projected to consume several million animals as well.

The economic cost is also staggering. A single Extended One-Generation Reproductive Toxicity Study (EOGRTS, OECD TG 443) costs approximately €566,000. With at least 1,024 of such studies projected, this implies €579–€880 million in direct costs for this endpoint alone. Factoring in broader costs across systemic and ecotoxicological studies, including fees, personnel, and CRO services, the total cost of REACH animal testing could well exceed several billion euros.

Beyond financial costs, REACH's failure to fully implement NAMs despite its stated preference for alternatives (Article 1) represents a significant regulatory inertia. Read-across approaches are rejected in ~75% of compliance checks. Despite increasing acceptance of in vitro methods for endpoints like skin irritation or sensitization, *in vivo* testing remains dominant, and often required, especially in recent revisions.

Petrochemicals and complex mixtures (UVCBs) exemplify the scale of REACH's unresolved challenges. These categories alone could necessitate up to 24 million animal tests depending on how regulatory grouping is handled. The upcoming REACH revision, aligned with the EU Green Deal and Chemicals Strategy for Sustainability, presents both a risk and an opportunity: either exacerbate the testing burden or pivot toward human-relevant, cost-efficient alternatives.

Without a major shift to Next Generation Risk Assessment (NGRA), the expansion of REACH will continue to strain resources and lives—both animal and economic—undermining the European Union's vision for sustainable innovation.

U.S. Regulatory Acceleration: The FDA as a Global Catalyst

In April 2025, a coordinated wave of regulatory decisions across the U.S. marked a historic pivot away from animal testing. On April 10, the U.S. Food and Drug Administration (FDA) unveiled its new roadmap for reducing animal testing in preclinical drug safety evaluations. On the same day, the Environmental Protection Agency (EPA) recommitted(asofficiallyconfirmedinNovember2025) to phasing out vertebrate animal testing by 2035. Only weeks later, the National Institutes of Health (NIH) launched the Office of Research Innovation, Validation and announced to refocus research funding from animal tests to human-relevant models.

Central to this transformation is the FDA's centralized and coordinated authority, allowing it to rapidly adapt science-based policy—a stark contrast to the fragmented EU landscape involving ECHA, EMA, and EFSA. The FDA's roadmap explicitly acknowledges the high failure rate (>90%) of drugs successful in animal models when translated into human clinical trials. This inefficiency has severe ethical, clinical, and financial implications for the pharmaceutical industry.

The FDA is now positioning New Approach Methodologies (NAMs), including microphysiological systems (MPS), human-based *in vitro* assays, and computational toxicology, at the heart of regulatory science. These technologies offer not only enhanced predictivity and reduced reliance on ethically fraught animal models, but also promise cost and time savings and better patient outcomes. AI-based platforms and transcriptomics-enabled grouping of chemicals are being integrated into regulatory decisions.

The FDA's pivotal role in global drug regulation amplifies this transformation. Although the U.S. represents only ~4% of the global population, it dominates over 53% of the pharmaceutical market and 67% of the market for patented drugs. Consequently, NAM-based regulatory decisions from the FDA have global ramifications, effectively creating new benchmarks for drug safety that other regions—including Europe—must eventually align with.

In contrast to the EU's tentative and consultative roadmap development (slated for 2026), the FDA's measures include immediate reductions in monoclonal antibody animal testing, interagency collaborations with the US validation body ICCVAM and NIH, and NAM validation programs with clear milestones. These efforts are further supported by NIH's funding realignment to prioritize human-relevant models and training programs to counteract systemic biases favoring animal studies.

Moreover, the U.S. is investing in global harmonization: facilitating technology transfer, co-development of NAMs with Global South nations, and promoting open-access protocols and regional validation hubs. This proactive and inclusive governance strategy stands in stark contrast to the EU's decade-long discussion toward a roadmap to reduce animal testing.

As the FDA, EPA, and NIH act in concert, the U.S. emerges as the *de facto* global standard-setter in non-animal methodologies. Pharmaceutical companies—already adapting to FDA expectations—serve as early adopters and NAM accelerators. In doing so, they lower barriers for other sectors and jurisdictions.

This tectonic shift underscores the importance of agile regulation aligned with modern science. The EU, long considered a pioneer, risks being outpaced unless it rapidly aligns its internal structures, legislative mandates, and funding priorities with this global NAM momentum.

Artificial Intelligence: The Disruptive Force Redefining Toxicology

The integration of artificial intelligence (AI) into toxicology marks not an incremental improvement but a systemic rethinking of chemical safety assessment. Once the domain of rule-based expert systems and QSARs of limited applicability, toxicology has entered an era characterized by deep learning, large language models, generative modeling, and causal inference. The shift is more than technical: it represents a philosophical and methodological transformation—what some now call ToxAIcology.

AI's capacity to process, integrate, and learn from vast, heterogeneous datasets has proven particularly suited to the complex, high-dimensional nature of modern toxicology. AI-read-across tools like RASAR have demonstrated predictive accuracy (87% balanced accuracy across nine OECD endpoints) surpassing even the internal reproducibility of many animal tests (~81%). Deep neural networks now routinely outperform conventional models in tasks such as mutagenicity prediction, developmental toxicity, and even low-dose extrapolation.

Crucially, the promise of AI lies not just in performance but in scalability, adaptability, and interpretability. Novel frameworks like e-validation and the TREAT criteria (Trustworthiness, Reproducibility, Explainability, Applicability,

Transparency) reimagine how AI-based NAMs can be validated, monitored, and updated over time. Instead of freezing methods, companion AI agents allow continuous post-deployment monitoring—a necessary adaptation to models that evolve with accumulating.

AI is enabling:

- Instantretrievalofexisting(openaccess)data,
- Data prediction to overcome legacy data gaps,
- Federated learning and edge AI to protect proprietary or sensitive data,
- Causal AI to move from correlations to mechanisms,
- Explainable AI (xAI) to ensure regulatory transparency, and
- Agentic AI to automate entire toxicology workflows—from literature mining to risk modeling.

Perhaps most transformative is the co-pilot paradigm. Here, AI augments, rather than replaces, human decision-making. This hybrid approach balances empirical accuracy with ethical and legal accountability, a principle gaining traction in both regulatory guidance and public trust initiatives.

Yet AI's adoption in toxicology is not without caveats. Data quality, model interpretability, cross-disciplinary literacy, and infrastructure disparities remain obstacles—particularly for global harmonization. Initiatives like ONTOX, and the NIH's ICE platform, are helping bridge these gaps, but more work is needed to embed fairness, accessibility, and explainability into the AI infrastructure of regulatory science.

Ultimately, AI is not merely a tool for improving toxicology—it is the foundation upon which the future of safety science will be built. The challenge for the next decade is to ensure that this foundation is human-relevant, ethically grounded, globally inclusive, and scientifically robust.

The toxicology community must now confront a defining question: Will AI be harnessed to reinforce the inertia of existing systems, or will it be used to reimagine toxicology from the ground up?

Conclusions

The landscape of safety science is undergoing a once-in-a-century transformation. What began as an ethical aspiration—the reduction and replacement of animal testing—has matured into an economic, technological, and scientific imperative. This chapter has traced the trajectory of this transformation across multiple dimensions: the entrenched costs and inefficiencies of animal-based toxicology, the accelerating growth of NAMs, the mounting regulatory and political momentum on both sides of the Atlantic, and the arrival of artificial intelligence as a game-changing force in the predictive sciences. Together, these developments are not merely reforming toxicology—they are redefining it.

At the heart of this transformation lies a profound economic realignment. Animal testing is no longer just ethically problematic—it is economically irrational. The inefficiencies, delays, and low translational value of animal models impose hidden costs on industries and societies alike. NAMs, by contrast, offer scalable, mechanistically grounded, and often faster and cheaper solutions. They also align with customer demands increasingly objecting to animal testing. Their expanding market size, diverse applications, and superior human relevance make them not only viable but increasingly essential. From a business perspective, the shift is no longer about regulatory compliance—it is about competitive survival in a global market driven by innovation, precision, and public trust.

Yet economics alone cannot drive the transformation. Regulatory inertia, structural silos, and a conservative validation culture continue to slow progress. These barriers must be actively dismantled through policy reform, international harmonization, and investment in validation infrastructure. The success of the U.S. FDA and NIH in aligning policy, funding, and regulatory expectations around NAMs offers a roadmap. Europe, long a leader in alternative methods, must now reassert its role with bolder actions and streamlined governance. The future does not belong to those who merely plan—it belongs to those who execute.

Perhaps the most profound shift is epistemological: the rise of artificial intelligence and the emergence of "ToxAIcology" are redefining not only how we do toxicology, but what toxicology is. From probabilistic risk assessment to e-validation and agentic AI, these technologies offer not just better predictions, but new ways of reasoning about safety and uncertainty. Toxicology is evolving from a craft rooted in observation to a digital science rooted in mechanistic modeling and continuous learning. AI is not simply accelerating processes—it is altering the questions we ask and the evidence we consider meaningful. The future of safety science will not be written in spreadsheets and animal models, but in code, computation, and causal inference.

The path forward is clear. Policymakers must recognize that investing in alternatives is not a trade-off between ethics and efficacy—it is a strategic investment in better science, faster innovation, and greater societal resilience. Industries must recognize that adopting NAMs is not regulatory charity but business intelligence. And scientists must embrace the tools of AI and NAMs not as threats to expertise but as partners in a new scientific paradigm. Success will require courage: to shift funding priorities, to modernize legacy infrastructure, and to challenge entrenched norms. But the reward is a toxicology that is faster, fairer, and far more fit for purpose.

The era of economic indifference to animal testing is over. The economics of alternatives now make the case more compelling than any ethical argument alone ever could. It is time to act not out of moral obligation alone, but out of informed self-interest. The opportunity to create a safer, smarter, and more humane safety science is here. Whether we seize it is no longer a question of technology or principle. It is a question of will. And that will determine whether toxicology enters its renaissance—or remains a relic.

Further Reading

Bottini AA, Hartung T (2010) The economics of animal testing. Altex Special Issue 27:67–77
Hartung T (2024) The (misleading) role of animal models in drug development. Front Drug Discov 4:1355044. https://doi.org/10.3389/fddsv.2024.1355044
Hartung T, Whelan, Tong W, Califf RM (2025) Is regulatory science ready for artificial intelligence? NPJ Digital Med 8:200. https://doi.org/10.1038/s41746-025-01596-0
Kleinstreuer N, Hartung T (2024) Artificial Intelligence (AI) – it's the end of the tox as we know it (and I feel fine) - AI for predictive toxicology. Arch Toxicol 98:735–754. https://doi.org/10.1007/s00204-023-03666-2
Knight J, Hartung T, Rovida C (2023) 4.2 million and counting…the animal toll for REACH systemic toxicity studies. Altex 40:389–407. https://doi.org/10.14573/altex.2303201
Meigs L, Smirnova L, Rovida C, Leist M, Hartung T (2018) Animal testing and its alternatives – the most important omics is economics. Altex 35:275–305. https://doi.org/10.14573/altex.1807041

Chapter 13
Animals as Vehicles of Gene Drives

Nicoletta Batini

> "Do not use a cannon to kill a mosquito."
> – *Confucius*

Abstract Developed since the mid-1980s, gene drives are a technique that changes genes using genetic engineering so they spread more quickly through a population than they normally would. They are used to either exterminate entire animal populations, decrease population numbers, or change a population's genotypes. Examples include mosquito, rat, and rabbit gene drives, where millions of transgenic insects or mammals are released into ecosystems. While most engineered traits in these animals are unlikely to be favored by natural selection, gene drives can spread through an entire population. This gives gene drives the potential to unintentionally affect extraneous ecosystems and trigger the emergence of undesired and unpredicted genetic evolutions in a cascade of animal species including humans. After briefly reviewing the ecological, social, and ethical dimensions of gene drives, this chapter explores their economic impact. It demonstrates, using simple calculations and realistic example scenarios, that their potential economic costs may easily outweigh promised benefits. The chapter proposes economic and regulatory policies to govern gene drives, including a moratorium until risks are minimized, aiming to maximize socio-economic welfare.

Evolutionary Theory and Natural Adaptation

The natural world is a complex web of interactions, where every species plays a role in maintaining the balance of ecosystems. Central to this balance are the laws of natural adaptation and evolutionary theory, which describe how species evolve over

Work on this volume/chapter was conducted when the author was at the Sveriges Riksbank.

N. Batini (✉)
Independent Evaluation Office, International Monetary Fund, Washington D.C., USA
e-mail: nbatini@imf.org

N. Batini (ed.), *The Economics of Non-Human Animals*, Natural Resource Management and Policy 63, https://doi.org/10.1007/978-3-032-17580-9_13

long periods, allowing ecosystems to adapt together. This slow and gradual process of genetic mutation and natural selection ensures that changes in one species do not disrupt the intricate relationships within an ecosystem.

The theory of evolution by natural selection, first articulated by Charles Darwin and Alfred Russel Wallace in the mid-nineteenth century, is foundational to our understanding of how species adapt and evolve. Darwin's observations of finches on the Galápagos Islands, for example, demonstrated how beak shapes evolved to exploit different food sources, a process driven by environmental pressures and competition (Enciclopedia Britannica 2025). This concept of natural selection explains how advantageous traits become more common in a population over generations, leading to the gradual evolution of species.

One of the key aspects of natural evolution is its timescale (Hansen et al. 2024). Genetic mutations occur randomly, and only those that offer a survival advantage are likely to be passed on. This slow process allows ecosystems to adapt gradually. For instance, the long necks of giraffes evolved over millions of years, enabling them to reach high leaves in the savannahs of Africa (Poore 2024). This adaptation did not happen in isolation; it coincided with changes in the vegetation and the evolution of other species within the same ecosystem. Similarly, the evolution of the peppered moth during the Industrial Revolution is a classic example of rapid adaptation to environmental changes. The moths' coloration shifted from light to dark as pollution darkened the trees they rested on, providing better camouflage from predators (Smith 2024). This rapid change, however, was still part of a broader, long-term evolutionary process.

The Role of Gene Drives in Modern Science

In contrast to the slow, natural process of evolution, synthetic "gene drives"—man-engineered selfish genetic elements—represent a revolutionary tool in genetic engineering that can rapidly alter the genetic makeup of animal populations (Roberts et al. 2020). Developed since the mid-1980s, with significant advancements following the arrival of the RNA-guided CRISPR-Cas gene-editing tool without the need of complex protein engineering, gene drives can spread specific genetic traits through populations much faster than natural selection (Roberts et al. 2020).

Gene drives can be engineered into various organisms or infectious agents. The focus has been on sexually reproducing organisms, but future developments may include other types of drives. The first gene drive in a multicellular organism was demonstrated in 2011 in mosquitoes. Since the introduction of CRISPR-based techniques in 2014, developments have accelerated, with demonstrations in yeast, flies, mice, and various mosquito species (Gene Drive Network 2025). CRISPR-Cas has become the preferred tool due to its ease and flexibility, but other systems are also being developed (*ibidem*).

Most gene drive organisms (GDOs) are designed for unlimited spread, known as "global" or "self-sustaining" drives, intended for applications like disease vector eradication. Some drives are being designed to be "local" or "self-limiting," with limited spread, but these are less developed and largely speculative at this stage (Kuzma 2022).

Gene drives are categorized by their intended applications: "population suppression" to eradicate populations and "population modification" to spread desired traits. However, these distinctions can be theoretical, with unanticipated outcomes. For example, a population modification drive in mosquitoes caused extinction in a laboratory setting due to knowledge gaps (Kyrou et al. 2018). Insects are the main targets for gene drive applications, but other species, including mammals, fish, birds, nematodes, and snails, are also being considered, as well as plants (Hay and Guo 2022).

Ethical and Ecological Implications of Gene Drives in Wild Populations

Proponents of gene drives argue that the potential benefits of using GDOs to modify or reduce wild populations are substantial. GDOs, they claim, could help prevent diseases in humans and animals, boost agricultural productivity and food security, protect endangered species, control invasive and pest species, reduce pollutants and toxins, manage ecosystems, and mitigate climate change (Forbes 2016).

On the other hand, there is wide recognition that GDOs pose significant and potentially incalculable risks to human health, agriculture, the environment, biosafety, biodiversity, and biosecurity because of the complexity and contentious nature of gene drive technology; and that these risks may vastly dominate potential benefits (see, among many others, Oye et al. 2014; Albert 2020; Sirinathsinghji 2020; Kormos and Lanzaro 2022; TWN 2023; and Pilz et al. 2024). This is because, unlike traditional genetically modified organisms (GMOs), which are designed to avoid spreading, GDOs are engineered to spread genetic modifications through entire populations. In fact GDOs work by inserting transgenes into organisms than then carry and transmit the genetic engineering machinery to other organisms or future generations. This means that genetic engineering continues in each generation, making the process persistent and irreversible. Crucially, the use of GDOs to modify wild populations, rather than bred animals (or cultivated crops), introduces more complexity and unpredictability. Unintended effects cannot be fully assessed before release, making any deployment an open and irreversible experiment. The irreversibility of gene drives once released, posing a substantial risk if unforeseen negative effects occur. This is particularly concerning when modifying disease vectors, as it adds complexity to human health implications. Additionally, they note, gene drives raise the possibility of cross-species transfer, harming non-target species, which could lead to broader ecological impacts.

Besides posing unpredictable and irreversible ecological risks, gene drives raise significant ethical concerns. One major issue is the "slippery slope problem," which suggests that once we begin using gene drives for certain purposes, it may become difficult to draw the line on what is acceptable. This could lead to increasingly risky or morally questionable applications (Gene Convene Vi 2021). For example, while gene drives might initially be used to control disease vectors like mosquitoes, the technology could eventually be applied to other species, potentially leading to unforeseen ecological consequences (Resnik et al. 2024). The ethical debate is further complicated by the potential for unintended consequences, such as the spread of gene drives beyond the target population, which could disrupt ecosystems and harm non-target species (Simberloff 2012).

A real-world example of the "slippery slope problem" relates to the controversy surrounding the use of gene drives in lab mice. In 2019, researchers successfully demonstrated a gene drive in mammals, using CRISPR-Cas9 to alter the inheritance patterns in mice (ScienceAlert 2019). This experiment sparked a heated debate in the international scientific community because it showed that gene drives could be applied to more complex organisms, raising concerns about the potential for misuse and the ethical implications of altering mammalian genetics on a large scale (Quanta Magazine 2019). Additionally, the idea of exterminating entire populations, such as invasive species, is ethically problematic. Beyond the immediate ecological dangers, such as disrupting food chains and causing unintended harm to other species (Hokkanen et al. 2007), there is a moral argument against the deliberate eradication of any species. This approach can be seen as playing God, making irreversible decisions about the natural world that could have far-reaching and unpredictable consequences (Lundholm and Stackerud 1980). Historically, similar ideologies have been seen in the eugenics movement, where certain human traits were deemed superior, leading to horrific acts of racism and discrimination, including genocide. This mindset parallels speciesism, where humans prioritize certain species over others, often justifying harmful interventions (see Chapter 2). Crucially, viewing animals solely as instruments for human benefit neglects their inherent worth and the right to exist. And humans have a moral responsibility to protect and respect all forms of life, and utilizing gene drives to eradicate species for convenience fails to honor this duty (Sandler 2020).

The ethical considerations and concerns surrounding gene drives do raise the bar for advocates to demonstrate that gene drives can achieve their intended goals more efficiently and safely than other methods, such as traditional pest control or habitat management (Gene Convene Vi 2021). In other words, gene drive advocates need to show that the benefits of using gene drives, such as controlling disease vectors or invasive species, outweigh the potential ecological risks and ethical concerns. Moreover, the ethical superiority of gene drives must be established through transparent and inclusive decision-making processes that involve all stakeholders, including local communities and environmental groups (Hefferon and Herring 2020). This helps ensure that the deployment of gene drives aligns with broader societal values and ethical principles, thereby gaining public trust and acceptance.

Economic Considerations: Insights from GE Mosquito Trials

Another major hurdle for gene drives technology to be considered a legitimate tool of public policy is addressing the economic implications, namely ensuring that the deployment of gene drives is cost-effective relative to traditional alternatives and does not lead to unintended financial burdens on communities or ecosystems (ENSSER-CSS-VDW 2020). For gene drives, the WHO's Guidance Framework for Testing Genetically Modified Mosquitoes, for example, emphasizes considering socio-economic, as well as environmental and health impacts during assessments, though it does not specify a particular methodology. In parallel, the Convention on Biological Diversity (CBD) has developed broad guidelines for assessing socio-economic considerations under Article 26 of the Cartagena Protocol, focusing on the socio-economic aspects of assessments with the aim to integrate socio economic dimensions into Environmental Risk Assessments (ERA). These guidelines, however, are voluntary and yet untested in practice. Consequently, the assessment of the economic impact of gene drives remains a critical oversight in public policy regulation. This gap is particularly concerning given the potential for significant economic repercussions, both positive and negative, associated with the deployment of gene drive technologies.

For a long time, the evaluation of the effects of gene drives was not pressing because these technologies remained confined to laboratory experiments and model simulations.[1] More recently, however, the approval, testing, and release of GDOs have seen significant developments both in Brazil, Burkina Faso, and in the United States, and gene drives plans in Mali and Uganda have reached an advanced stage.[2] It has thus become both urgent and possible to evaluate first hand both some of the positive and some of the negative effects of this technology.

The first GDO mass deployment experiment was conducted in Jacobina, Brazil, by British-founded Oxitec, now a subsidiary of American biotechnology company Intrexon. Oxitec released each week, 1.2–1.8 million transgenic male mosquitoes over a period of 27 months between June 2013 and September 2015, following approval by the Brazilian National Biosafety Technical Commission (CTNBio). The authorization was based on initial tests in towns across Bahia and São Paulo to assess their effectiveness in reducing mosquito populations and disease transmission (Revista Pesquisa Fapesp. 2024). The goal of the deployment was to reduce the population of disease-carrying mosquitoes by introducing a "lethal gene" that would cause the offspring of these GM mosquitoes to die before reaching maturity (Live

---

[1] Even in laboratories, impact evaluations of simulated gene drives were at best considered probabilistic because of outstanding knowledge gaps from the potential manifestation of unintended molecular effects that can impact model parameters (NASEM 2016a, b).

[2] The Bill & Melinda Gates Foundation is the major financial sponsor of these gene drives, and of gene drive research and development globally, followed by the U.S. National Institutes of Health (NIH), and the U.S. Department of Defence Advanced Research Projects Agency (DARPA). In Africa, the Gates Foundation partnered with Open Philanthropy—a foundation founded by Cari Tuna and Dustin Moskovitz, who is one of the co-founders of Facebook and Asana to support financially Target Malaria, a consortium conducting gene drives.

Science 2019). The GE mosquitoes were released near sources of infestation, gradually surpassing the natural male population, mating with females, and transmitting the lethal gene to the eggs.

Although, according to an article published in 2015 in the journal *Scientific Reports*, the population of *A. aegypti* fell by around 95% during the period studied, the experiment did not go entirely as planned. Researchers found that some of the genes from the GE mosquitoes were passed on to the native mosquito population, which was not anticipated, creating hybrid mosquitoes. These hybrids were able to survive and reproduce, raising concerns that they might be more robust and potentially more difficult to control than the original population—a phenomenon called "hybrid vigour" (Evans et al. 2019; LiveScience 2019).

A second interesting case relates to gene drive experiments being conducted in the United States. Although there is still no evidence of these dangerous diseases spreading in the country, the presence of invasive insects including *A. ageypti* is believed by officials to pose a growing risk.[3] Reflecting this, in 2020, the Environmental Protection Agency (EPA) granted Oxitec Ltd. an experimental use permit (EUP) to also field test their transgenic mosquitoes. These trials aimed to control mosquito populations and reduce the *future* risk of the spread of diseases such as dengue fever, Zika, chikungunya, and yellow fever through local transmission. As a result, field trials began in Monroe County, Florida, in 2020 under an experimental use permit (EUP) (later extended to April 30, 2024), and expanded to Harris County, Texas, in 2021, pending state and local approvals. In March 2022 the EPA cleared Oxitec to release a maximum of roughly 2.4 billion of its transgenic mosquitoes through 2024, expanding the existing trial in Florida and start a new pilot project in the Stanislaus, Fresno, Tulare, and San Bernardino counties of California's Central Valley (EPA 2022). This last project, however, was halted in 2023 due to concerns about potential public health and environmental impacts, and the mosquitoes were never released as a result (Friends of the Earth 2023).[4]

What are the economic implications of experiments like these going awry? According to a recent policy brief the Outreach for Gene Drives (ISAAA Inc. 2022), preliminary answers to this question could be investigated through Environmental, Socio-economic, and Health Impact Assessment (ESHIA) assessments that, in addition to the impact of a treatment on the environment—as done by Environmental Risk Assessments (ERA)—consider its impacts on local and national economies as well as employment.[5] In practice, however, no assessment of such kind has yet been

[3] So far, acquisition of these diseases has been extremely low relative to population, and nearly all cases reported in these states have been associated with exposure through travel to an area affected by these diseases outside of Florida or California (CDPH 2025; CDC 2024).

[4] The California Department of Pesticide Regulation (DPR) announced the withdrawal of Oxitec's permit request, which had initially been applied for in April 2022 (Friends of the Earth 2023). Before an unregistered pesticide can be tested in the field within the state, the U.S. EPA must first approve an experimental use permit, and the DPR must approve a research authorization application. Since the Oxitec application has been withdrawn, there are currently no pending research authorization requests for studying genetically engineered mosquitoes in California.

[5] ISAAA (2022).

carried out, including for ongoing field trials, and gene drive evaluation remains confined to environmental and direct health impact assessments.

Certainly, even without an in-depth analysis, the broader economic impacts of gene drive scenarios, both locally and nationally, can be assessed through simple calculations. If these calculations yield substantial results, it's improbable that adding more details would significantly alter the overall understanding. Here are two example scenarios to illustrate this point.

Example Scenario 1: Mosquito gene drive leads to unanticipated hybridization of native species in Brazil.

Let us assume a fictitious city in the state of Bahia, Brazil, with a population of approximately 80,000 people—the size of Jacobina—called Nova Esperança. Dengue is a significant public health issue in the region, causing substantial economic and social impacts. In 2025, a biotech company releases genetically modified *A. aegypti* mosquitoes in Nova Esperança to combat diseases like dengue and Zika. These mosquitoes carry a lethal gene designed to reduce the native mosquito population.

Initially, the project is successful, reducing the mosquito population by 95%. However, after two years, researchers discover that some mosquitoes have developed resistance to the lethal gene, leading to a hybrid species that is more robust and harder to control. To compare benefits and costs of the experiment, it is necessary to compute these based on existing data.

I. Benefits

Assume that the main benefit of this gene drive is to reduce or eliminate the incidence of dengue in Nova Esperança population. If this aim was achieved, a number of economic benefits would ensue. In particular:

(1) *Health service sector savings.* Direct medical costs of treating dengue patients include hospitalization, outpatient visits, medication, and laboratory tests. The average cost of treating a dengue patient in Brazil is estimated to be around $500.[6] If the city experiences 1,700 dengue cases annually,[7] eradicating dengue could save approximately $850,000 per year in direct medical costs. Moreover, some dengue patients suffer from long-term health issues, leading to ongoing medical costs and reduced quality of life. If 10% of dengue cases result in long-term health issues, eradicating dengue could save an additional $85,000 per year in long-term healthcare costs.
(2) *Productivity gains.* Dengue leads to lost workdays and reduced productivity. On average, a dengue patient may miss about 10 days of work.[8] If 1,700 workers are affected annually, with an average daily wage of $20, the productivity gain from eradicating dengue would be over $0.3 million per year.

---

[6] Economic Impact of Dengue: Multicenter Study across Four Brazilian Regions (2015).

[7] This is calibrated on actual cases in Jacobina, Bahia, in 2012, which is prior to the release of the GDOs by Oxitec.

[8] Brazilian (2024).

(3) *Boost to tourism.* Fear of dengue can deter tourists. Eradicating dengue could make the city a more attractive destination, potentially increasing tourism revenue. If tourism revenue increases by 10% as the city becomes dengue-free, and the current annual tourism revenue is $1 million, the economic benefit would be $0.1 million per year.

Combining these factors, the total estimated economic benefit of eradicating dengue in Nova Esperança could be around $1.4 million per year.

II. Costs

Costs of the GDO-based eradication campaign in Nova Esperanca, including the cost of the unanticipated hybridization of the native mosquito population, can also be estimated making some rough assumptions.

(1) *Public spending on the GDO program.* In the real world, the cost of a typical transgenic mosquito gene drive is around $7.5–$10 per citizen in the human population.[9] Assuming the mid-range price of $8.75, for a city with 80,000 people this implies a program cost of $0.7 million.
(2) *Health service sector incremental spending.* With the resurgence of a more robust mosquito population, there could be an increase in dengue and Zika cases relative to the years pre-treatment. The cost of treating these diseases includes hospitalization, medication, and long-term care for severe cases. If the city has a population of 80,000 and 3% are affected (a slightly higher rate than pre-treatment due to hybrid vigor in the hybrid mosquitoes), with an average treatment cost of $500 per person, the total healthcare cost could be around $1.2 million per year.
(3) *Incremental spending on disease control measures.* The city would need to invest in more aggressive mosquito control measures, such as increased pesticide use, community education, and additional research into new control methods. If the annual budget for mosquito control is $1 million, and it needs to be doubled to address the resistant population, the additional cost would be $1 million per year.
(4) *Productivity losses.* Increased illness among the working population could lead to reduced productivity and economic output. If 3% of the workforce is affected, with an average loss of $20 per day per 10 days of sick leave per worker in productivity, the total cost would be $0.5 million.
(5) *Tourism losses.* Fear of mosquito-borne diseases could lead to a decline in tourism, affecting local businesses and the economy. If tourism revenue drops by 20% in a city that earns $1 million annually from tourism, the economic loss would be $0.2 million.

Combining these factors, the total estimated economic cost of dealing with resistant mosquitoes in this scenario could be around $3.6 million—*more than double the total presumptive benefits* from the GDO-based eradication campaign in the first year alone. This example highlights the potential economic burden of managing a

[9] MIT Technology Review (2016).

situation where genetically modified mosquitoes develop resistance, emphasizing the importance of careful monitoring and adaptive strategies in vector control programs.

Example Scenario 2: Mosquito gene drive causes unanticipated ecosystem services loss in California.

Let us assume a gene drive in Fresno County, the top county in California Central Valley for agricultural production.[10] Real data show that in 2023, Fresno County's agricultural production reached a record $8.6 billion.[11] This impressive figure includes a wide variety of crops, with significant contributions from fruits and vegetables. For example, grapes alone accounted for over $1.3 billion, while other top crops included almonds, pistachios, tomatoes, peaches, garlic, and nectarines.[12]

In this scenario, the eradication of mosquitoes through the hypothetical gene drive succeeds in eliminating future risks of dengue by eliminating the entire mosquito population in the county, but leads to a drop in mosquitoes own ecosystem services as well as a reduction in the population of certain bird and bat species that also provide essential ecosystem services to Fresno's agricultural sector, such as pest control.[13] Without birds to control pest populations, Fresno county farmers from the treated area experience a significant increase in crop damage.

What are the net benefits (or net costs) of this hypothetical gene drive?

I. Benefits

In line with actual evidence, the scenario assumes that the initial incidence of locally acquired dengue in Fresno is zero, and that transmission from travel-related cases in Fresno County is very rare. Given this it is challenging to quantify potential benefits of a GDO eradication campaign. While probabilistically unlikely, for the sake of argument this scenario however also assumes that, at some point, dengue nonetheless spreads locally in Fresno County through local transmission. In this unlikely event, a safe assumption for relative incidence rates would be to consider California's incidence rate significantly lower than that of Latin America, like 10–30% of that rate, given the differences in climate, infrastructure, and public health measures.[14] In that case:

---

[10] AgNet West (2024).

[11] County of Fresno (2024a).

[12] County of Fresno (2024b).

[13] Mosquitoes are crucial for ecosystems, providing food for fish, birds, bats, and dragonflies. They also help pollinate certain plants. Additionally, mosquitoes play a key role in controlling insect populations by preying on pests like aphids, mites, and beetles, which helps protect crops from potential infestations (Dove 2024).

[14] The average incidence of dengue fever in Latin America is quite high. In 2023, the region reported over 6.5 million cases and 7,300 deaths, i.e. 1000 cases per 100,000 population (Statista 2024). The average incidence rate for the Americas (which includes North, Central, and South America, as well as the Caribbean) in 2023 was approximately 305 cases per 100,000 population (WHO 2023). Considering this, it makes sense to assume that dengue would have a lower incidence rate in California compared to Latin America also due to several factors: (i) Climate and environment: Dengue is primarily spread by the *Aedes aegypti* mosquito, which thrives in warm, humid climates. Latin America has many regions with these ideal conditions, whereas California generally has a more

(1) *Health service sector savings.* Assuming dengue spreads locally in Fresno County at 20% of the incidence rate observed in Latin America, it would result in approximately 610 cases based on the size of Fresno County population. Given that the average cost of treating a dengue patient in the U.S. ranges from $1,000–$5,000, the total healthcare saving of preventing dengue could amount to around $1.8 million.
(2) *Productivity savings.* Additionally, productivity losses due to illness and recovery time could further strain the local economy. Assuming that 70% of the 610 cases are working adults, and each loses an average of 10 workdays, the productivity loss could be significant. With an average daily wage of $200, this translates to a potential productivity saving of around $0.9 million.[15]
(3) *Tourism revenue savings.* Furthermore, tourism, a vital part of Fresno County's economy, could also be adversely affected. In 2023, Fresno County generated $1.74 billion in direct travel spending (The Business Journal 2024). Assuming a 10% loss in tourism revenue due to a dengue outbreak, the averted economic loss from preventing a dengue outbreak could be around $174 million.

In total, the economic benefit of preventing a dengue outbreak in Fresno County from averting outbreak-related healthcare costs, productivity losses, and reduced tourism revenue could amount to approximately $177 million. Preventing the spread of dengue in Fresno County could therefore save the community significant financial burdens, highlighting the importance of proactive public health measures.

II. Costs

Costs of the GDO-based eradication campaign in Fresno County, including the cost of the unanticipated extinction of some bird species, can similarly also be arrived at making some broad assumptions.

A. Local economy

(1) *Public spending on the GDO program.* In the real world, the cost of a typical transgenic mosquito gene drive is around $7.5–$10 per citizen in the human population.[16] Assuming the mid-range price of $8.75, for a county like Fresno with around 1 million people this implies a program cost of $8.8 million to the local government.

---

temperate climate, which is less conducive to mosquito breeding; (ii) Sanitation and infrastructure: California has better sanitation and infrastructure compared to many parts of Latin America. Effective waste management and water systems reduce the breeding grounds for mosquitoes; (iii) Public health measures: California has robust public health systems and vector control programs that can quickly respond to and manage outbreaks, reducing the spread of the disease; (iv) Travel-associated cases: Most dengue cases in California have been travel-associated, meaning they were contracted outside the state. Local transmission is rare. Given these differences assuming for California an incidence rate of 10–30% of the rate observed in Latin America could be reasonable.

[15] In 2024Q2 the average weekly wage across all industries for Fresno County was $1075 which gives an average daily wage of $215. See BLS QWEC (2025).

[16] MIT Technology Review (2016).

(2) *Loss of agricultural revenue.* Let us assume that the annual crop loss due to pests in the treated area increases by 20%. If the agricultural sector in the affected region is worth $8.5 billion annually, similarly to in Fresno County, this results in an additional $1.7 billion in losses each year from when the loss first occurs, including the first year.

(3) *Cost of additional pest control measures.* To combat the surge in pests, farmers invest more in pesticides and other pest control measures. If the average cost of pest control increases by 15%, and the current expenditure is $300 million annually, this adds another $45 million in costs.[17]

(4) *Food price inflation and loss of purchasing power.* The combined effect of increased crop losses and higher pest control costs leads to a rise in food prices. Let's assume that farmers pass part of the increase in costs to consumers and food prices in Fresno County thus increase by 10% due to these factors. If the average household spends $5,000 annually on food, this results in an additional $500 per household per year. Fresno County had on average approximately 322,160 households between 2019 and 2023.[18] If each household were to lose $500 in a year, the total extra expenditure (and resulting purchasing power loss) would be approximately $161 million.

(5) *Second-round effects costs of food price shock.* Higher food prices can lead to increased costs for restaurants and food-related services, which may pass these costs onto consumers, further driving up prices in the "food away from home" (FAFH) category (GAO 2023). Using realistic estimates of FAFH price elasticities, a 10% increase in food prices could lead to a reduction of approximately $67 million in FAFH spending in Fresno County.,[19,20]

B. National economy

(6) *National headline inflation rate and loss of purchasing power.* Using realistic assumptions, an ecological shock in Fresno County like the one assumed here would result in an approximate 0.1% increase in the overall

---

[17] The annual cost of pesticide application in Fresno County farmland ranges from approximately $188 million to $376 million. This estimate is based on the average pesticide use of about 2.0 applications per acre, with costs ranging from $50 to $100 per acre.

[18] See Census Bureau (2024).

[19] To estimate the second-round effects of a 10% increase in food prices on food- away-from-home (FAFH) spending in Fresno County, we assume a price elasticity of demand of −0.7, which is a typical estimate for such goods, meaning a 1% price increase leads to a 0.7% decrease in quantity demanded. With 322,160 households spending $3,000 annually on FAFH, a 10% price increase would reduce total spending by approximately $67 million.

[20] This reduction could have broader economic impacts, such as decreased revenue for local restaurants and food service businesses, potentially leading to job losses and reduced economic activity in the area. Additionally, rising food prices can affect other sectors, such as transportation and packaging, due to higher costs for agricultural products (Benzinga 2024). We do not account for these effects here.

U.S. CPI level.[21] Based on the lower range of recent estimates of the relationship between inflation and consumer spending this may imply a drop in consumer spending of $7.5 billion in the year of the shock (Kikuchi et al. 2024).

(7) *Higher interest rates economic impact.* Higher CPI can lead to higher interest rates and reduced consumer spending, further slowing economic growth. Using a standard Taylor rule, the increase in interest rates necessary to curb the inflationary pressure from higher food prices would lead to a U.S. GDP loss, just in the first year, of around $27 million.[22]

Of course, the extinction of birds in Fresno can disrupt the food chain, reduce pollination and seed dispersal, and increase pest populations, leading to broader ecological instability. And since birds often migrate and interact with ecosystems far beyond their local habitats, the extinction of bird species in Fresno can disrupt these migratory patterns and affect ecosystems and species in other regions, both nationally and internationally, causing significant environmental and economic consequences. Since for simplicity we do not account here for these additional and potentially big adverse economic effects, the above hypothetical costs of the gene drive unanticipated effect on bird population are probably largely underestimating probable costs.

In summary, the eradication of mosquitoes through a gene drive leading to an unintended loss of bird species *just in the targeted area* and ignoring cascading ecosystems and human health effects could lead to an estimated total cost ranging approximately between $2 billion, just in the first year. So, the total cost of running the GDO campaign is approximately over *11 times larger* than the estimated potential benefit, using conservative estimation assumptions. When national macro effects are included, the economic costs of the GDO campaign may actually outweigh the potential benefits *more than fifty-fold.*

---

[21] To summarize the calculation: A 20% crop loss and a 15% increase in production costs would lead to a combined 27.5% price increase for Fresno County's produce. The county's significant contribution to California's fruit (at circa 50%) and vegetable production means that this translates to over 14% price increase for California's fruits and vegetables. Given California's substantial share in U.S. production of these goods (at around 35%, see CDFA 2024), and assuming that the prices of fruits and vegetables produced outside California stay the same, this results in a 6.2% increase in U.S. fruits and vegetable prices in the year of the shock. When this price increase is weighted by its respective contribution to the Consumer Price Index (CPI), which is around 1.6%, the total impact on the U.S. CPI in the year of the shock—absent other shocks—is about one tenth of a percentage point. This is a simplified estimate and actual impacts could vary based on other factors such as substitution effects, changes in consumer behaviour, and broader economic conditions.

[22] To determine the necessary interest rate increase in response to an inflation deviation, we use a standard Taylor rule. Given an equilibrium real interest rate of 2%, a target inflation rate of 2%, a zero output gap, and a previous nominal interest rate of 4%, the Taylor rule formula yields a new nominal interest rate of approximately 4.05%, indicating a 0.05 percentage point increase. Using impulse response functions (IRFs) from a standard U.S. estimated model like the FRB/US model, we can estimate the GDP impact of a 5 basis point (0.05 percentage points) increase in the federal funds rate. This increase is estimated to reduce U.S. GDP growth by approximately 0.1% in the first year, translating to a reduction of U.S. output of about $27 million.

Three-Pillar Framework for Controlling Gene Drives

Regulators, civil society, and researchers have been working together for several years to develop responsible approaches for the testing and control of gene drives (e.g., Benedict et al. 2018; Delborne 2018). However, the formulation of policies and regulations to govern gene drives is particularly challenging because gene drives are a prime example of "post-normal science" where technical knowledge alone is inadequate to address the multifaceted nature of the issue, which encompasses social, ethical, and legal dimensions (Brossard et al. 2019).

And while the 2018 Conference of the Parties to the Convention on Biological Diversity (CBD) has placed strict conditions on the environmental release of GDOs, including the need for risk assessment, the precautionary approach, and full, prior, and informed consent from affected communities (Conference of the Parties to the Convention on Biological Diversity 2018), lab and field research on gene drives continues unabated, amidst a lack of specific, binding regulations at both national and international levels driven by venture philanthropy.[23] At the same time, risk assessment methodologies for GDOs have yet to be developed, and few countries have established specific safety standards for gene drive research in laboratories. Crucially, there is no international oversight of gene drive research, nor is there an internationally agreed process for detecting and monitoring released GDOs. Furthermore, there are no mechanisms to control, recall, or reverse the effects of GDOs in nature, and no legally enforceable agreements on liability and redress for biological and economic damage caused by this technology.[24]

Although we may eventually achieve the goal of genetically modifying species to enhance public and environmental health without posing risks to people, animals, and the planet, available evidence shows that we are still very far from reaching that point (SOS, 2021). Therefore, it is crucial to implement regulatory changes at the international level to prevent gene drives from posing irreversible global risks, as advocated by several civil rights organizations (ETC Group 2023; SOS 2021). Against this background, a sensible and effective three-pillar legal framework in line with existing proposals involves:

1. *International Registry System*
    - Establish a central registry for all existing gene drives and field trials to ensure safety and facilitate discussions.
    - Mandate stringent information disclosure, including detailed descriptions of organisms, gene drive constructs, and research objectives.
    - Require researchers to develop successful and well-tested reversal drive technologies in parallel.

[23] See, for example, the program Target Malaria sponsored by the Gates Foundation. More details in Target Malaria (2022) and Bill & Melinda Gates Foundation (2022).

[24] See Gene Convene Vi (2021); and Elves (2019).

2. *Global Moratorium on Gene Drive Organisms (GDOs)*

   - Develop and implement an international moratorium—governed by the United Nations Convention on Biological Diversity (CBD)—on the research and release of GDOs until the risks associated with gene drives are reduced to levels deemed negligible or acceptable. Base decisions on comprehensive, transparent, internationally led analyses. Given the theoretical challenges in achieving such low risk, this moratorium could effectively result in a permanent global ban on the technology.

3. *Mandatory Assessments*

   - Conduct rigorous, standardized assessments of environmental, socio-economic, and health impacts for each past and proposed gene drive experiment.
   - Ensure assessments are thorough and span several years to observe long-term impacts.
   - Protect low-income countries from being used as testing grounds. The regulatory environments in these countries are often weak, and agencies may be vulnerable to political influence and corruption, which could compromise the health and economic interests of local populations.
   - Regulate sponsorship and financing of gene drive projects by private entities including by large venture philanthropists with potential conflicts of interest.[25]

This framework aims to ensure the safe and ethical development and deployment of gene drive technologies, prioritizing global safety and equity.

To ensure the safe and ethical use of gene drives, several additional safeguards must be implemented. First, gene drives should only be considered as a last resort, after all traditional methods have been exhausted and proven inadequate, ensuring that their risks are significantly smaller than the risks of no treatment. Any gene drives that exhibit unexpected developments during field trials should be suspended and thoroughly investigated to uncover predictive errors, assess costs, identify remedial actions, and extract valuable lessons. Updating biotechnology laws and regulations is crucial to close existing loopholes and address unregulated issues, while revising biotechnology treaties can enhance international collaboration. Meaningful participation of local communities and stakeholders in decisions regarding GMOs is essential, along with facilitating public discussions about the appropriate uses of GDOs in wild populations. To prevent misuse for terrorism or warfare, professional guidelines and enhanced biosecurity surveillance should be developed, and

[25] Philanthropic foundations frequently have dual economic and philanthropic interests. This duality can lead to conflicts of interest, potentially prioritizing economic gains over the well-being of local communities, especially when stakeholders in these foundations have direct or mediated investments in companies involved in the research, development, production, and deployment of biotech products.

biosafety protocols must be strengthened to prevent accidental releases. Additionally, establishing and maintaining biodiversity repositories like seed and gene banks, and designating "GMO/GDO-free" wilderness areas where people can experience life forms that have not been genetically engineered, are vital steps in managing biodiversity and ecological health. These areas must be wide enough to provide a buffer against potential genetic contamination from transgenic organisms, ensuring that native species can exist and evolve without the risk of altered genes infiltrating their populations. While the introduction and spread of transgenic fauna could pose a challenge to maintaining these GMO/GDO-free zones, proper management and monitoring can help mitigate these risks. This proactive approach ensures the preservation of natural genetic diversity, which is crucial for the adaptability and resilience of ecosystems in the face of environmental changes.

Economic policy can significantly support the implementation of the three-pillared strategy for gene drive safety and the additional safeguards. By allocating public funds for research and development, governments can ensure that safety and ethical considerations are prioritized. Economic incentives, such as tax breaks and grants, can encourage the study of issues related to the irreversibility/reversibility of gene drive technologies. Regulatory frameworks can be strengthened through economic sanctions and penalties for non-compliance, while financial support for low-income countries can help build robust regulatory systems and protect local communities. International collaboration can be enhanced by funding international bodies like the United Nations Convention on Biological Diversity (CBD) and incorporating gene drive safety standards into trade agreements. Public engagement and education can be promoted through funding for awareness campaigns and stakeholder involvement initiatives. Additionally, investment in biosecurity infrastructure and biodiversity repositories can prevent misuse and preserve genetic diversity.

By leveraging economic policy, governments and international bodies can create the conditions necessary to properly assess, monitor, and regulate gene drive technologies. This ensures that any research and decisions made are in the true interest of people and the planet, and adhere to ethical considerations rather than being driven by private interests or academic inertia. Given the significant risks associated with gene drives, including potential ecological disruptions, unintended consequences, and ethical concerns, it is crucial to apply the proper amount of caution at each stage of consideration. Economic policy can support strategic public funding, economic incentives, and robust regulatory frameworks to establish a regulatory environment with the means and institutional capability to govern gene drive technologies effectively. This approach promotes transparency, accountability, and public trust, ensuring that gene drive research and deployment are conducted responsibly and ethically. Importantly, this framework must also allow for the possibility of decisions like a permanent ban if the risks are deemed too great, ensuring that the precautionary principle is upheld to protect both human and environmental health.

Conclusions

Gene drives, enabled by advancements in genetic engineering technology, represent a novel and exciting approach to solving significant problems in innovative ways. However, unlike typical innovations, gene drives involve altering animal populations at their core, posing risks of cascading, unpredictable, uncontrollable, and irreversible effects on the entire natural world, including humans.

Currently, the ethical, public health, and economic benefits promised by gene drives appear to be vastly outweighed by the potential and emergent risks they pose. The ideation, study, exploration, and deployment of gene drives should not be driven by the economic interests of companies or individuals that fail to internalize the negative externalities. Given the magnitude and multiplicity of risks associated with gene drives, it is unlikely that any industry can assume or insure against the associated liabilities. This makes it challenging to formulate fair and efficient public policy measures to ensure that those profiting from the sale of gene drive technologies are held accountable if things go wrong.

Even if well-intentioned, proponents of gene drives must be able to prove, with high likelihood scenarios, that the benefits of gene drives, on a case-by-case basis, vastly outweigh the risks and associated costs. This assessment must consider not only environmental risks but also human and animal health risks, as well as economic, social, and livelihood impacts. The burden of proof lies with the industry, and until such proof is provided, a moratorium is appropriate, as requested by various stakeholders.

Absent comprehensive assessments on existing field trials, simple calculations for two realistic cases of gene drives conducted here indicate that the economic costs of gene drives are significantly higher than the benefits of achieving the target outcomes. This underscores the need for rigorous and comprehensive evaluations before proceeding with the deployment of gene drive technologies.

Moreover, these considerations do not account for the significant ethical issues associated with gene drives. Gene drives have the potential to permanently alter nature by modifying genomes that have evolved slowly over millions of years. This rapid and artificial alteration of genetic material can disrupt ecosystems indefinitely, as the natural evolutionary processes that have shaped these genomes are bypassed (SOS 2021; Thomasy 2024). The long-term consequences of such disruptions are difficult to predict and could have far-reaching impacts on biodiversity and ecological balance (Jablonka 2025). This raises profound ethical concerns, as such interventions can lead to unintended consequences that may be irreversible. The ethical dilemma is further compounded by the "slippery slope problem," where initial acceptance of gene drives could lead to increasingly invasive and potentially harmful genetic modifications. The permanent nature of gene drives means that any mistakes or unforeseen effects could have lasting impacts on biodiversity and ecological balance, making it imperative to approach this technology with extreme caution and robust ethical scrutiny.

Reflecting this, a three-pillar legal framework is urgently needed to regulate gene drives. This involves: (1) an international registry system for gene drives researchers and research institutions; (2) a global moratorium on gene drive organisms (GDOs) until risks are virtually eliminated or completely minimized; and (3) mandatory long-term assessments of impacts. Economic policy can support strategic public funding, economic incentives, and robust regulatory frameworks to establish a regulatory environment with the means and institutional capability to govern—and if necessary ban—gene drive technologies effectively. Additional safeguards should include suspending and investigating gene drives with unexpected developments, considering them only as a last resort, and updating biotechnology laws and regulations. Involving local communities in decisions, preventing misuse through professional guidelines, and strengthening biosafety protocols are also essential measures.

References

AgNet West (2024). Nine California Counties Among Top 10 in U.S. Ag Sales. https://agnetwest.com/nine-california-counties-among-top-10-u-s-ag-sales/

Albert H (2020) Gene drives: a controversial tool to fight malaria. Labiotech.eu. https://www.labiotech.eu/in-depth/gene-drives-controversy/

Benedict MQ, Charlwood JD, Harrington LC, Lounibos LP, Reisen WK, Tabachnick WJ (2018) Guidance for evaluating the safety of experimental releases of mosquitoes, emphasizing mark-release-recapture techniques. Vector-Borne and Zoonotic Dis 18(1):39–48. https://doi.org/10.1089/vbz.2017.2152

Benzinga (2024) The true cost of food: key factors driving food prices and why they will keep rising. https://www.benzinga.com/partner/general/24/11/41755095/the-true-cost-of-food-key-factors-driving-food-prices-and-why-they-will-keep-rising

Bill & Melinda Gates Foundation (2022) Gates foundation commits to eradicate malaria & NTDs in Africa. https://www.gatesfoundation.org/ideas/media-center/press-releases/2022/06/gates-foundation-commits-support-to-end-malaria-and-ntds-in-africa

Brazilian NR (2024) Dengue's economic and labor impact in Brazil. https://braziliannr.com/2024/03/25/dengues-economic-and-labor-impact-in-brazil/

Brossard D, Belluck P, Gould F, Wirz CD (2019) Promises and perils of gene drives: navigating the communication of complex, post-normal science. Proc Natl Acad Sci 116(26):7692–7697. https://doi.org/10.1073/pnas.1805874115

California Department of Food and Agriculture (n.d.) California agricultural production statistics. https://www.cdfa.ca.gov/statistics/

California Department of Food and Agriculture (CDFA) (2025) California agricultural production statistics, 2024 crop year. https://www.cdfa.ca.gov/statistics/

California Department of Public Health (CDPH) (2025) Dengue virus cases in California, 2016–2025. Updated January 1, 2026. Available at: https://www.cdph.ca.gov/Programs/CID/DCDC/Pages/DengueInfectionsUpdate.aspx

Census Bureau (2024).QuickFacts: Fresno county, California. https://www.census.gov/quickfacts/fact/table/fresnocountycalifornia/INC910222

Centers for Disease Control and Prevention (CDC) (2024) Zika cases in the United States. https://www.cdc.gov/zika/zika-cases-us/index.html

Cobb M (2023) Gene drives could fight malaria and other global killers but might have unintended consequences. Sci Am. Available at: https://www.scientificamerican.com

Conference of the Parties to the Convention on Biological Diversity (2018) Decision on the regulation of genetic engineering (CBD/COP/DEC/14/34). https://www.cbd.int/doc/decisions/cop-14/cop-14-dec-34-en.pdf

County of Fresno (2024a) Annual crop & livestock report. https://www.fresnocountyca.gov/Departments/Agricultural-Commissioner/Annual-Crop-Livestock-Report

County of Fresno (2024b) Fresno county's annual crop and livestock report places the county among the top of the agricultural producers in the state and nation. https://www.fresnocountyca.gov/files/sharedassets/county/v/1/resources/press-release-documents/2024-press-releases/2024-08-20-fresno-county-releases-crop-report.pdf

Delborne J et al (2018) Mapping research and governance needs for gene drives. J Responsible Innov 5(1):1–9. https://doi.org/10.1080/23299460.2017.1419413

Dove LL (2024) What would happen if mosquitoes went extinct? https://science.howstuffworks.com/science-vs-myth/what-if/what-if-mosquitoes-went-extinct.htm?

Elves C (2019) The legal regulation of gene drive technologies [PhD thesis]. University of Oxford. https://ora.ox.ac.uk/objects/uuid:8e7d4f84-cbd7-4425-a582-88b7dd5a9954

Encyclopaedia Britannica (n.d.) *Evolution: the science of evolution*. In: Encyclopaedia Britannica. https://www.britannica.com/science/evolution-scientific-theory/The-science-of-evolution. Accessed 6 Feb 2025

ETC Group (2016) The case for a global moratorium on genetically-engineered gene drives. https://www.etcgroup.org/sites/www.etcgroup.org/files/files/cbd_cop_13_gene_drive_moratorium_briefing.pdf

ETC Group (2023) Call for a global moratorium on gene drive releases. https://biosafety-info.net/articles/biosafety-science/emerging-trends-techniques/call-for-a-global-moratorium-on-gene-drive-releases/

European Network of Scientists for Social and Environmental Responsibility (ENSSER)- Critical Scientists Switzerland (CSS)- Vereinigung Deutsche Wissentschaftler (VDW)- (2020) Gene drives: what are the problems and what are the risks? https://genedrives.ch/webinar-genedrives/problems-alternatives-genedrives/

Evans BR, Kotsakiozi P, Costa-da-Silva AL et al (2019) Transgenic Aedes aegypti mosquitoes transfer genes into a natural population. Sci Rep 9:13047. https://doi.org/10.1038/s41598-019-49660-6

Forbes (2016) Bill Gates: some people think eradicating mosquitoes with genetics is scary, but I don't think it will be. https://www.forbes.com/sites/matthewherper/2016/06/10/bill-gates-says-gene-drives-to-eradicate-some-mosquito-species-could-be-ready-for-in-two-years/

Foundation for the National Institutes of Health (FNIH) (2023) Gene drive research forum: unsettled ethical issues in gene drive research. https://fnih.org/wp-content/uploads/2023/12/GDRF-Ethics-Panel.pdf

Friends of the Earth (2023) Genetically engineered mosquito experiment in California's central valley halted. https://foe.org/news/ge-mosquito-experiment-halted/

Gene Convene Vi (2021) United States: gene drives - global gene editing regulation tracker. https://www.geneconvenevi.org/articles/legal-regulation-of-gene-drive-technologies/

Gene Drive Network (2025) 2024 in review: Highlights in the field of gene drive research. Gene Drive Network. https://genedrivenetwork.org/blog/2024-in-review-highlights-in-the-field-of-gene-drive-research/

Hansen TF (2024) Three modes of evolution? Remarks on rates of evolution and time scaling. J Evol Biol 37(12):1523–1537. https://doi.org/10.1093/jeb/voae071

Hay BA, Guo M (2022) Gene drive-mediated population elimination for biodiversity conservation. When you come to a fork in the road, take it. Proc Natl Acad Sci 119(51):123–130. https://doi.org/10.1073/pnas.2218020119

Hefferon K, Herring R (2020) Engineered gene drives and their value in the control of vector-borne diseases, weeds, pests, and invasive species. In: Chaurasia A, Hawksworth DL, Pessoa de Miranda M (eds) GMOs. Topics in biodiversity and conservation, vol 19. Springer, Cham. https://doi.org/10.1007/978-3-030-53183-6_18

Hokkanen HMT, van Lenteren JC, Menzler-Hokkanen I (2007) Ecological risks of biological control agents: impacts on IPM. In: Perspectives in ecological theory and integrated pest management. Cambridge University Press, pp 246–268. https://doi.org/10.1017/CBO9780511752353.009

ISAAA (2022) Risk assessment for gene drive organisms. https://www.isaaa.org/resources/publications/policybriefs/gdn2022/default.asp
Jablonka E (2025) A new vision for how evolution works is long overdue. [Review of the book Evolution evolving: the developmental origins of adaptation and biodiversity, by K. Lala et al.]. Nature. https://www.nature.com/articles/d41586-025-00054-x
Kikuchi J, Nakazono Y, Tango K (2024) Inflation expectations and consumer spending: micro-data evidence. SSRN. https://doi.org/10.2139/ssrn.5018789
Kormos A, Lanzaro GC, Bier E et al (2022) Ethical considerations for gene drive: challenges of balancing inclusion, power and perspectives. Front Bioeng Biotechnol 10, Article 826727. https://doi.org/10.3389/fbioe.2022.826727
Kuzma J (2022) Gene drives: environmental impacts, sustainability, and governance. In Florin M-V (ed) Ensuring the environmental sustainability of emerging technologies, 2023. EPFL. International Risk Governance Center, Lausanne, pp 15–16. https://doi.org/10.5075/epfl-irgc-298445
Kyrou K, Hammond A, Galizi R et al (2018) A CRISPR–Cas9 gene drive targeting doublesex causes complete population suppression in caged Anopheles gambiae mosquitoes. Nat Biotechnol 36:1062–1066. https://doi.org/10.1038/nbt.4245
Lieb L, Schuffels J (2022) Inflation expectations and consumer spending: the role of household balance sheets. Empirical Econ 63:2479–2512. https://doi.org/10.1007/s00181-022-02222-8
Live Science (2019) Scientists can't agree on whether genetically modified-mosquito experiment went horribly wrong. https://www.livescience.com/genetically-modified-mosquitoes-create-hybrids.html
Lundholm B, Stackerud M (1980) Environmental risks associated with biological controls. In: Environmental protection and biological forms of control of pest organisms. Ecol Bull (Stockholm), pp 11–24. https://www.jstor.org/stable/20112784
MIT Technology Review (2016) Inside the mosquito factory that could stop Dengue and Zika. https://www.technologyreview.com/2016/02/17/162230/inside-the-mosquito-factory-that-could-stop-dengue-and-zika/
MVCAC (2021) If mosquitoes were eradicated, what would be the consequences? Retrieved from NewScientist. https://www.newscientist.com/lastword/mg25233643-900-if-mosquitoes-were-eradicated-what-would-be-the-consequences/
National Academics of Sciences, Engineering, and Medicine (2016a) Gene drives on the horizon: advancing science, navigating uncertainty, and aligning research with public values. The National Academies Press, Washington, DC
National Academies of Sciences, Engineering, and Medicine (NASEM) (2016b) Gene drives on the horizon: advancing science, navigating uncertainty, and aligning research with public values
Oye KA et al (2014) Regulating gene drives. Science 345:626–628. https://doi.org/10.1126/science.1254287
Pilz BC, Kosmehl N, Härlin B (2024) Gambling with nature: why gene drives are not a viable route to nature conservation. GAIA – Ecol Perspect Sci Soc 33(1):158–164. https://doi.org/10.14512/gaia.33.1.8
Poore E (2024) How 10 animals evolved their iconic features. Live Science. https://www.livescience.com/animals/how-10-animals-evolved-their-iconic-features
Quanta Magazine (2019) Gene drives work in mice (if they're female) https://www.quantamagazine.org/gene-drives-work-in-mice-if-theyre-female-20190123/
Resnik DB, Medina RF, Gould F, Church G, Kuzma J (2024) Genes drive organisms and slippery slopes. Pathogens and Global Health 118(4):348–357. https://doi.org/10.1080/20477724.2022.2160895
Revista Pesquisa Fapesp (2024) Transgenic Aedes aegypti mosquitoes hit the market. https://revistapesquisa.fapesp.br/en/transgenic-aedes-aegypti-mosquitoes-hit-the-market/
Roberts R, Marshall JM, Akbari OS (2020) Progress towards engineering gene drives for population control. The J Exp Biol 223(Suppl_1):jeb208181. https://doi.org/10.1242/jeb.208181

Sandler R (2020) Genetic engineering and moral responsibility. Conserv Biol 34(2):378–385. https://cssh.northeastern.edu/philosophy/wp-content/uploads/sites/11/2021/01/Sandler_Genetic-Engineering.pdf
ScienceAlert (2019) Scientists have successfully done a controversial 'Gene Drive' experiment on mammals. https://www.sciencealert.com/scientists-succeed-in-first-controversial-gene-drive-experiment-on-mammals
Simberloff D (2012) Risks of biological control for conservation purposes. BioControl 57:263–276. https://doi.org/10.1007/s10526-011-9392-4
Sirinathsinghji E (2020) Risk assessment challenges of synthetic gene drive organisms (TWN Biosafety Briefing). Third World Network. https://biosafety-info.net/articles/assessment-impacts/ecological/gene-drives-not-a-viable-route-to-conservation/
Smith S (2024) 10 examples of animal evolution in nature. Wildlife Informer. https://wildlifeinformer.com/examples-of-animal-evolution/
SOS (Save Our Seeds / Foundation for Future Farming) (2021) Gene drive organisms: a new dimension of genetic engineering. https://www.stop-genedrives.eu/wp-content/uploads/2021/06/GeneDriveOrganisms_-A-New-Dimension-of-Genetic-Engineering_210615.pdf
Statista (2024) Dengue in Latin America - statistics & facts. https://www.statista.com/topics/12283/dengue-in-latin-america/
Target Malaria (2022) International policy framework for genetically modified mosquitoes. https://targetmalaria.org/wp-content/uploads/2022/08/Reg_FS_EN_InternationalPolicy-_Aug22.pdf
The Business Journal (2024) Valley tourism spending soars; airport expansion 'tremendous'. https://thebusinessjournal.com/valley-tourism-spending-soars-airport-expansion-tremendous/
Third World Network (TWN) (2023) Safety briefing on gene drives. https://www.twn.my
Thomasy C (2024) CRISPR, gene drives, and the future of evolution. The Scientist. https://www.the-scientist.com/crispr-gene-drives-and-the-future-of-evolution-71699
Turchi Martelli CM et al (2015) Economic impact of dengue: multicenter study across four Brazilian regions. PLOS Neglected Trop Dis.https://doi.org/10.1371/journal.pntd.0004042
U.S. Bureau of Labor Statistics (2024) QCEW state and county map application: Fresno County, CA: 12 month percent change in employment, Total, All Industries Total Covered Jun 2023-Jun 2024 (p). https://www.bls.gov/cew/data.htm
U.S. Bureau of Labor Statistics (BLS) (2025) Quarterly Census of Employment and Wages (QCEW), full database updated through Q3 2024. https://www.bls.gov/cew/
U.S. Environmental Protection Agency (EPA) (2022) Following review of available data and public comments, EPA expands and extends testing of genetically engineered mosquitoes to reduce mosquito populations. https://www.epa.gov/pesticides/following-review-available-data-and-public-comments-epa-expands-and-extends-testing
U.S. Government Accountability Office (GAO) (2023) Food prices: information on trends, factors, and federal roles. U.S. GAO. https://www.gao.gov/products/gao-23-105846
World Health Organization (WHO) (2023) Dengue – the Region of the Americas. https://www.who.int/emergencies/disease-outbreak-news/item/2023-DON475

Part III
Parasitic Interactions

Chapter 14
Animals in Sports

Nicoletta Batini and Bruno Ćurko

> "Bullfighting is not a sport. It was never supposed to be. It is a tragedy, not a competition."
> — *Ernest Hemingway*

Abstract From ancient arenas to modern stadiums, animals have played a central role in human sports and entertainment, captivating audiences and driving significant economic activity. Yet beneath the spectacle lies a web of ethical, economic, and cultural tensions. This chapter explores the economics of animal sports, analyzing the industry's scale, the roles animals play, and the trade-offs between financial gain and animal welfare. It asks whether a future is possible where these practices are not exploitative but mutually beneficial. The chapter concludes with policy proposals aimed at reforming the sector: strengthening welfare regulations through global standards and enforcement; realigning economic incentives to reward ethical practices and penalize harmful ones; mandating transparency and data reporting to support accountability; supporting transitions in developing economies through education and alternative livelihoods; fostering innovation in ethical and virtual alternatives; and promoting public engagement to shift cultural norms. Together, these reforms aim to create a more humane, sustainable, and economically viable future for animals in sports.

Author 1: Work on this volume/chapter was conducted when the author was at the Sveriges Riksbank.

N. Batini (✉)
Independent Evaluation Office, International Monetary Fund, Washington DC, USA
e-mail: nbatini@imf.org

B. Ćurko
Humanities and Social Sciences, University of Split, Split, Croatia
e-mail: bcurko@ffst.hr

N. Batini (ed.), *The Economics of Non-Human Animals*, Natural Resource Management and Policy 63, https://doi.org/10.1007/978-3-032-17580-9_14

Global Stakes: The Scale of Animal Sports

The use of animals in sports is not just a cultural phenomenon—it is a powerful economic engine. Across continents and species, animal-based sports generate billions in revenue, support vast employment networks, and influence tourism, media, and betting industries. Yet, the true scale of this sector is often underestimated, partly due to its fragmentation across different sports, regions, and regulatory frameworks.

Horseracing: The Thoroughbred of the Industry

Horseracing remains the most economically dominant animal sport, blending centuries-old tradition with a modern, globalized enterprise. According to the International Federation of Horseracing Authorities (IFHA), the sport spans over 60 countries and plays a central role in the international regulation and coordination of thoroughbred racing. Recent estimates place the industry's global value at over $125 billion annually, with approximately 600,000 racehorses in training and more than 1 million people employed worldwide (Lindner 2025).

However, broader market analyses suggest the total economic footprint may be even larger. A 2023 report by Zion Market Research projected the global horse racing market to reach $793.9 billion by 2030, citing a compound annual growth rate (CAGR) of 8.89% from a 2022 valuation of $402.3 billion (Zion Market Research 2023). In contrast, a 2025 study by Research and Markets offered a more conservative estimate, valuing the industry at $127.3 billion in 2025, with projected growth to $182.4 billion by 2030 (Research and Markets 2025). These discrepancies reflect differing scopes of analysis—some encompassing the full ecosystem of betting, tourism, breeding, and media rights, while others focus more narrowly on core racing operations.

Major markets include the United States, United Kingdom, Japan, Australia, and Hong Kong, which host iconic races such as the Kentucky Derby, Royal Ascot, and the Japan Cup. These regions also serve as global centers for thoroughbred breeding, wagering platforms, and equine services, reinforcing horseracing's role as both a cultural institution and a powerful economic engine. Emerging markets are also reshaping the global landscape. In China, the equestrian economy is estimated at $1.58 billion, supported by over 2,000 riding clubs and nearly 700,000 active riders. Since the 2008 Beijing Olympics, equestrianism has grown rapidly, with horseback riding increasingly marketed as a symbol of cosmopolitan lifestyle and a desirable extracurricular activity for youth. India, too, is seeing a rise in civilian interest, alongside a robust saddlery export sector and expanding networks of riding centers. In the Middle East, state-backed investments in the UAE and Saudi Arabia have elevated equestrian sport as both a cultural heritage initiative and a tourism magnet, with programs supporting youth access and elite competition (EQuerry/Co 2025).

In addition to thoroughbred racing, trotting—also known as harness racing—plays a significant role in the equine sports economy, particularly in countries like Sweden, France, and the United States. Trotting involves horses pulling a two-wheeled cart (sulky) and is governed by distinct rules and breeding programs. In Sweden, for example, harness racing is a major betting sport, with events like Elitloppet drawing international attention and contributing substantially to the national racing economy.

In the United States alone, the American Horse Council estimates that horseracing contributes approximately $36 billion to the economy and employs over 450,000 people. In the United Kingdom, the sport adds around £4.1 billion to the economy and supports approximately 85,000 individuals, both directly and indirectly (Lindner 2025).

Racehorses typically have careers that span 3–4 years, though their total lifespan can reach 20–25 years. After retirement, many transition into breeding, show jumping, or recreational riding, provided they remain healthy (Lindner, 2025).

The cost of acquiring a racehorse varies widely. While some can be purchased for a few thousand dollars, elite thoroughbreds with prestigious bloodlines can fetch hundreds of thousands or even millions. The most expensive racehorse ever sold, Fusaichi Pegasus, was purchased for $70 million in 2000 after winning that year's Kentucky Derby (Lindner 2025). Annual training and maintenance costs typically range from $30,000 to $50,000 per horse, covering stabling, feed, veterinary care, and staff. Despite these expenses, a successful racehorse can generate significant returns through prize money, sponsorships, and breeding fees. Top-tier stallions may command stud fees of up to $500,000, and over a breeding career, a single horse can earn tens of millions of dollars if demand remains high (Lindner 2025).

In sum, horseracing is not only a sport but also a vast economic ecosystem—one where the value of a single horse can rival that of a luxury yacht, and where the thunder of hooves reverberates through employment, agriculture, tourism, and global finance.

Show Jumping: The Jewel of Equestrian Sport

Show jumping is among the most prestigious and economically intensive disciplines in the equestrian world, known for its elite displays of athleticism by horse and rider. Globally, it captures a substantial share of the equestrian market, which spans horse sales, training, equipment, travel, event management, and veterinary services. While precise global figures for show jumping alone are challenging to isolate, its impact is unmistakable—particularly through internationally renowned circuits such as the Winter Equestrian Festival (WEF) in the United States, World Cup qualifiers across Europe, and high-level national competitions.

In the United States, the broader equine industry—including show jumping, racing (distinct from horseracing), and recreational riding—contributed $177 billion to the economy in 2023 and supported 2.2 million jobs (AHC 2024). Events like WEF reflect the sport's powerful local economic influence, adding $352 million to Palm

Beach County's GDP and supporting over 3,300 jobs in the same year. Worldwide, the economic footprint of equestrian sport is projected to exceed $150 billion by 2025, driven by increased investment in sponsorship, tourism, and media rights.

Yet, the sport is not without its challenges. Rising operational costs—up 20–30% due to inflation, enhanced biosecurity measures, and infrastructure requirements—are reshaping access to elite competition and prompting a growing conversation about long-term financial sustainability.

Moreover, despite its commercial and cultural success, show jumping remains under scrutiny for its treatment of equine athletes. Concerns persist around improper use of whips, substandard shoeing, ill-fitting saddles, and distressing training methods such as soring. In response, governing bodies like the FEI have implemented comprehensive welfare protocols, including whip-use limits and mandatory vet checks. To maintain its social license to operate, the industry continues to pursue greater transparency in training, reduction of harmful practices, and stronger accountability through welfare-led initiatives.

Dressage and Paso Horses: Precision, Prestige, and Controversy

Competitive dressage is one of the most technically demanding and culturally prestigious disciplines in equestrian sport. Often likened to ballet on horseback, it showcases the highest levels of communication between horse and rider through a series of choreographed movements judged on precision, rhythm, and harmony. Dressage features prominently in international competitions such as the Olympic Games and FEI World Cup, and is supported by a global network of breeders, trainers, and elite riders (FEI 2023).

At the heart of classical dressage is the Spanish Riding School of Vienna, a centuries-old institution renowned for its performances with Lipizzaner stallions. These horses, trained in the art of haute école, perform advanced movements such as the levade and capriole—symbolizing the deep historical roots and artistic dimension of the sport (Spanish Riding School 2024). Similarly, Andalusian horses (Pura Raza Española) are prized for their expressive movement and temperament, making them a staple in both competitive and exhibition dressage across Europe and Latin America. The School is estimated to generate approximately €4–€5 million annually from ticket sales alone, based on average pricing and attendance figures (Vienna Tourist Board 2023). This revenue is further supplemented by guided tours, merchandise, private events, and cultural subsidies, reflecting the institution's dual role as both a tourist attraction and a national cultural treasure.

In Latin America and the Caribbean, the Caballo de Paso—notably the Peruvian Paso and Paso Fino—occupies a parallel space of cultural and competitive importance. These horses are celebrated for their naturally smooth, four-beat lateral gait, which allows for an exceptionally comfortable ride. Paso competitions are major attractions in countries like Peru, Colombia, and Puerto Rico, often tied to national identity and rural heritage (Rodriguez O'Donnell 2008).

However, both disciplines face increasing scrutiny over animal welfare, particularly regarding the use of bits and whips. In Paso competitions, horses are often subjected to severe biting systems designed to force exaggerated head positions and gait mechanics. These devices can cause intense oral pain, tongue and jaw injuries, and long-term behavioral distress (McLean and McGreevy 2010). Similarly, in both dressage and Paso events, the use of whips—though regulated—is a persistent concern. When misused, whips can inflict physical pain, provoke fear responses, and undermine the trust between horse and rider (*ibidem*). While proponents argue that these tools are essential for communication and tradition, critics highlight the ethical cost of prioritizing aesthetic performance over the horse's physical and psychological well-being. Veterinary experts and animal welfare organizations continue to call for stricter oversight, improved training standards, and a shift toward more humane practices.

As these sports evolve, the challenge remains: how to honor their cultural and competitive legacy while ensuring that equine athletes are treated with the dignity and care they deserve, not as instruments of spectacle, but as sentient partners in sport.

Greyhound Racing: A Declining but Persistent Sector

Greyhound racing, once a staple of working-class entertainment in countries such as the United Kingdom, Ireland, and the United States, has experienced a marked decline in recent decades. This shift is largely attributed to growing concerns over animal welfare and evolving public values (Pittman 2020; Holland 2025). The origins of greyhound racing lie in coursing, a traditional practice where dogs chased live prey. The sport underwent a significant transformation in the 1920s with the invention of the mechanical lure, which allowed for a more controlled and humane form of racing. This innovation led to the rapid formalization and popularization of greyhound racing, particularly among working-class communities. Its accessibility and integration with betting systems helped establish it as a widely followed spectator sport.

Despite its decline in some regions, greyhound racing continues to hold economic significance in others. In Australia, the industry remains robust, valued at approximately $2.6 billion AUD. It supports nearly 15,800 full-time equivalent jobs and involves over 30,000 registered greyhounds (IER 2024). The sport is especially prominent in New South Wales and Victoria, where it benefits from government support and generates substantial betting revenue (The Conversation 2022).

In the United Kingdom, the sport is regulated by the Greyhound Board of Great Britain (GBGB). While it still attracts millions in betting turnover, the number of active tracks has dwindled from over 70 in the 1980s to fewer than 20 today (Online Betting 2023).

In contrast, the United States has seen a near-total disappearance of the sport. Following Florida's 2020 ban on greyhound racing, only a few tracks remain, primarily in West Virginia (Pittman 2020).

The economic contributions of greyhound racing are increasingly overshadowed by ethical concerns. Critics highlight issues such as overbreeding, high injury rates, and the abandonment of dogs after their racing careers end. These concerns have fueled public opposition and legislative action, contributing to the sport's decline in many parts of the world.

Rodeo: The Rough Ride of Sport and Spectacle

Rodeo is not only a cultural tradition but also a full-fledged sport, deeply rooted in the working practices of cattle herding in the American West and northern Mexico. Evolving from cowboy skills such as bronc riding, calf roping, and steer wrestling, rodeo has transformed into a highly commercialized and regulated competitive arena. Today, it draws millions of spectators worldwide, particularly in the United States, Canada, Brazil, and Australia.

In the United States, the Professional Rodeo Cowboys Association (PRCA) governs over 600 events annually, generating more than $100 million USD in direct revenue—a figure that excludes substantial additional gains through tourism, broadcasting, and merchandise (PRCA 2023). Flagship competitions like the National Finals Rodeo in Las Vegas receive significant media coverage and corporate sponsorship, reinforcing the sport's stature in both rural heritage and mainstream entertainment.

Yet, rodeo's profile as a sport is accompanied by mounting ethical scrutiny. Animal welfare organizations challenge the physical demands placed on animals in events like bull riding and calf roping, citing evidence of stress, injury, and trauma. Although many rodeo associations have adopted veterinary monitoring and stricter welfare protocols, debates continue around whether these measures suffice. Supporters argue that rodeo represents a living heritage, combining cultural expression with athletic prowess, and maintain that participant expertise and modern standards help protect animal well-being.

As the rodeo circuit adjusts to shifting public values, it stands at a crossroads between nostalgia and reform, facing the challenge of maintaining its identity as both a sport and a symbol while adapting to the ethical imperatives of contemporary audiences.

Bullfighting: Culture, Controversy, and Commerce

Bullfighting occupies a unique space in the animal sports economy. While not a sport in the conventional sense—lacking competition or mutual consent—it is often categorized as such due to its ritualized structure and public spectacle. Economically, it remains significant in Spain, Mexico, Colombia, and parts of France and Portugal.

In Spain, the bullfighting industry is estimated to generate around €1.6 billion annually, supporting approximately 200,000 jobs, including matadors, breeders, event organizers, and hospitality workers (Fundación Toro de Lidia n.d.). The Spanish Ministry of Culture has historically recognized bullfighting as part of the country's cultural heritage, which has helped sustain public funding and tourism interest. However, the industry faces mounting challenges (The Olive Print 2025). A 2022 survey by Spain's Ministry of Culture found that only 8% of Spaniards attended a bullfight in the previous year, a sharp decline from 25% in the early 2000s (Ministerio de Cultura y Deporte 2022). Public opinion is increasingly polarized, with younger generations and urban populations expressing strong opposition to the practice. Several Spanish regions, including Catalonia and the Canary Islands, have enacted bans or restrictions, reflecting a broader societal shift. Despite this, bullfighting festivals still attract millions of tourists annually, particularly during events like Pamplona's San Fermín.

In Latin America, bullfighting continues to hold economic and cultural weight, particularly in Mexico and Colombia. In Mexico, which hosts more bullfights annually than any other country, the industry is estimated to generate over $400 million USD per year. The Plaza México in Mexico City, the largest bullring in the world, can seat over 40,000 spectators and regularly draws large crowds during the bullfighting season. The sector supports thousands of jobs, from matadors and breeders to event staff and vendors, and is closely tied to regional festivals and religious celebrations. In Colombia, cities like Bogotá, Cali, and Manizales maintain active bullfighting calendars, with events often integrated into major cultural festivals.

Bullfighting's economic contributions are undeniable in certain regions, particularly through tourism, employment, and cultural branding. However, these benefits are increasingly weighed against ethical concerns and shifting societal values. The industry's future may depend on its ability to adapt—through reforms, alternative spectacles, or cultural reinterpretation. Some proposals include non-lethal bullfighting, virtual simulations, or cultural festivals that preserve tradition without animal harm. These alternatives could allow communities to retain cultural identity while aligning with modern ethical standards. For example, unlike the lethal Spanish corrida, bullfighting in Bosnia and parts of the Balkans—locally known as *korida*—involves non-lethal contests between bulls, where the fight ends when one animal retreats. The most famous event, the Grmeč Corrida, has been held annually for over 200 years and continues to draw thousands of spectators each summer (Dnevni Avaz 2023). These events are often framed as cultural celebrations, blending tradition, music, and food, and fostering cross-community gatherings in post-conflict regions (Surk 2017). Unfortunately, despite the lack of bloodshed, animal welfare concerns persist, though organizers emphasize regulated weight classes, veterinary oversight, and the absence of weapons or human combatants (Radio Free Europe 2019). This form of bullfighting illustrates how traditional animal spectacles can persist in modified, culturally significant, yet ethically debated forms.

Other Animal Sports: Regional Economies and Niche Markets

Beyond globally recognized animal sports like horseracing or greyhound racing, a diverse array of regionally rooted animal competitions plays a significant role in sustaining local economies and cultural identities. These niche sports often operate at the intersection of tradition, tourism, and informal economies, creating complex ecosystems that are both economically impactful and socially embedded.

Camel racing in the Middle East—particularly in the UAE, Qatar, and Saudi Arabia—has evolved from a tribal pastime into a multimillion-dollar industry. The introduction of robotic jockeys in the early 2000s, prompted by international concerns over child jockeys, marked a turning point in the sport's modernization (Robot Jockey 2024). Today, camel racing is supported by state-of-the-art training facilities, breeding programs, and high-stakes prize money, with major races drawing international spectators and media attention (Maker Faire Rome 2021).

Cockfighting remains a deeply controversial yet economically and culturally significant activity in various parts of the world, particularly in Southeast Asia (notably Thailand and Indonesia), Latin America, and the Philippines. While the practice is banned or heavily restricted in many jurisdictions due to concerns over animal cruelty, it continues to thrive, often in underground circuits linked to gambling networks and local festivals.

In some countries, however, cockfighting enjoys institutional support, blurring the line between cultural tradition and animal exploitation. A prominent example is the Philippines, where cockfighting is not only legal but also televised, with licensed arenas, regulated events, and a dedicated fan base. The industry is estimated to be worth billions of dollars, driven largely by betting revenues and breeding operations (PhilLife 2018). This level of formalization highlights the sport's economic and social entrenchment, even as global pressure mounts to address the ethical implications of such practices.

Pigeon racing, particularly popular in Belgium, China, and parts of South Asia, is another niche sport with a surprisingly robust economic footprint. In China, elite racing pigeons have sold for up to $1.9 million, and the sport has attracted wealthy enthusiasts who invest heavily in breeding and training (Business Insider 2020). The industry supports specialized feed producers, GPS tracking technology, and even pigeon transport logistics. In rural areas, it can also serve as a source of supplemental income and community prestige (VOA Learning English 2020).

Elephant polo and racing, once a novelty attraction in countries like Nepal, Thailand, and Sri Lanka, have seen a sharp decline in recent years. Mounting international pressure from animal welfare organizations and changing tourist preferences have led to the cancellation of many events. In Nepal, for instance, elephant polo has been removed from festivals like the Chitwan Elephant Festival, and venues are transitioning toward observation-only sanctuaries and conservation-focused experiences (World Animal Protection 2025; Inside Himalayas 2025).

Together, these regional animal sports illustrate how deeply intertwined cultural heritage, economic opportunity, and ethical scrutiny can be. While some are adapting to modern sensibilities and regulations, others remain in legal or moral gray zones, highlighting the need for nuanced policy and public discourse.

Economic Intersections: Betting, Tourism, and Media

Animal sports are not merely isolated spectacles of entertainment: they are deeply embedded in transnational economic ecosystems that commodify both human engagement and animal labor. Their influence extends far beyond the racetrack or arena, intersecting with industries such as gambling, tourism, media, and even national branding. These connections amplify both their financial impact and the ethical complexities they entail.

Betting: The Lifeblood of the Industry

Betting is arguably the most significant economic driver behind animal sports. In many countries, wagering on horse and greyhound races is not only legal but also heavily regulated, forming a substantial part of the sports economy. The betting industry provides liquidity, sustains interest, and generates tax revenue that often feeds back into the sport itself.

In the United Kingdom, the Horserace Betting Levy Board collects a statutory levy from bookmakers, which amounted to £100 million in 2023. These funds are reinvested into the sport, supporting racecourse improvements, veterinary research, and welfare initiatives. While betting sustains the industry, it also creates incentives for overbreeding, doping, and premature retirement or euthanasia of animals deemed unprofitable. Similarly, in Australia, betting turnover on horseracing exceeded AUD $25 billion in 2022, with a portion allocated to state racing bodies for reinvestment. In Japan, horseracing is a public enterprise, and the Japan Racing Association (JRA) operates under government oversight. Betting turnover regularly exceeds ¥2.8 trillion (approx. $20 billion) annually, with profits supporting public infrastructure and social programs (JRA 2022). The Hong Kong Jockey Club, one of the world's largest betting operators, contributes billions in tax revenue and charitable donations each year.

Greyhound racing, though smaller in scale, also relies heavily on betting. In Ireland, the Greyhound Racing Ireland body reported over €100 million in annual betting turnover, which supports track operations and breeding programs. However, declining public interest and welfare concerns have led to reduced revenues and increased scrutiny.

Illegal betting also plays a role, particularly in sports like cockfighting and pigeon racing, which are popular in parts of Southeast Asia and Latin America. These underground economies are difficult to quantify but are known to involve significant sums and pose challenges for regulation and animal welfare enforcement.

Tourism: Spectacle as a Destination

Animal sports are often major tourist attractions, drawing visitors from around the world and stimulating local economies. Events like the Kentucky Derby in the United States, Royal Ascot in the United Kingdom, and the Melbourne Cup in Australia are not just races, they are cultural phenomena. These events generate millions in revenue through ticket sales, hospitality, merchandise, and associated travel.

The Kentucky Derby, for example, attracts over 150,000 attendees annually and contributes more than $400 million to the local economy. Hotels, restaurants, and transportation services all benefit from the influx of visitors. Similarly, Royal Ascot is a highlight of the British social calendar, drawing international tourists and generating £250 million in economic activity.

In Spain, bullfighting festivals such as San Fermín in Pamplona attract hundreds of thousands of tourists each year. Despite growing ethical opposition, these events remain deeply tied to regional identity and tourism marketing. In many cases, the very cultural appeal that draws tourists—heritage, tradition, spectacle—rests on practices increasingly viewed as exploitative or obsolete. The economic impact includes not only ticket sales but also spending on accommodation, food, and cultural experiences.

In Middle Eastern countries, camel racing has become a luxury tourism draw, especially in the UAE and Qatar. Events are often held in conjunction with cultural festivals and attract high-net-worth individuals, contributing to the hospitality and entertainment sectors.

However, tourism linked to animal sports is increasingly under ethical scrutiny. Many travelers now consider animal welfare when choosing destinations, and negative publicity—such as reports of abuse or poor conditions—can damage a region's reputation and economic prospects.

Media and Sponsorship: Broadcasting the Spectacle

Media rights and sponsorships have transformed animal sports into global entertainment products. Horse racing events are broadcast across continents, with dedicated channels and streaming platforms offering live coverage, analysis, and betting integration. This media presence expands the audience and monetizes viewership through advertising and subscription models. Broadcasting reinforces the normalization of animal sports, turning ethically contested practices into mainstream entertainment, often without critical framing.

In Hong Kong, the Jockey Club's races are broadcast to millions across Asia, with sophisticated digital platforms enabling real-time betting and engagement. In Japan, televised races are a staple of weekend programming, supported by mobile apps and online betting portals.

Sponsorships also play a crucial role. Major brands align themselves with prestigious events like the Dubai World Cup, Breeders' Cup, and Cheltenham Festival, gaining visibility and prestige. These partnerships bring in millions in revenue and help fund prize money, infrastructure, and promotional campaigns.

Digital transformation has further expanded the reach of animal sports. Online betting platforms, social media engagement, and virtual race simulations are reshaping how audiences interact with these events. In some cases, augmented reality and AI-driven analytics are being used to enhance viewer experience and betting strategies. Together, betting, tourism, and media form a powerful triad that not only sustains animal sports but also shields them from critique by embedding them in everyday economic and cultural life.

National Identity and Branding

In many regions, animal sports serve as living monuments to collective identity, but they also reflect the ways in which tradition can obscure ethical concerns. Events like Spain's bullfighting, officially designated as part of the country's intangible cultural heritage, or Japan's government-backed horse racing, illustrate how traditions are deeply woven into national narratives. In the Middle East, state-sponsored camel racing reinforces Bedouin heritage while attracting global media attention.

Italy's Il Palio di Siena epitomizes this convergence of history, pageantry, and risk. Held twice a year in Siena's medieval Piazza del Campo, the bareback horse race dates back to the seventeenth century and remains a central expression of Sienese identity. Yet, the event regularly draws scrutiny from animal welfare groups due to frequent injuries and fatalities. Despite veterinary inspections and safety improvements, the tight, cobbled course has resulted in fractured limbs and even deaths, like in the August 2023 Palio, where two horses were injured (Unione Sarda 2023; Wikipedia 2024). Its preservation under the guise of cultural heritage often clashes with calls for reform, illustrating the protective shield tradition can provide against scrutiny. These events also contribute to national economies through tourism, merchandising, and cultural diplomacy, further complicating efforts to reform them.

Further afield, similar dynamics play out in Mongolia, where the annual Naadam Festival features long-distance horse races across rugged terrain, sometimes 10–30 km. Jockeys are often children as young as five years old, riding semi-wild horses at full gallop without protective gear (Dobbin 2019). Although regulations now require veterinary oversight and age restrictions, enforcement is inconsistent, and injuries and fatalities remain common. Despite vast geographical differences, these events share common features: high symbolic value, popular support, and weak enforcement of animal welfare norms.

In rural Argentina and Uruguay, *carreras cuadreras*—short-distance sprint races on straight dirt tracks—are a popular tradition among gaucho communities. Similarly, in Mexico, *carreras parejeras* involve match races between two horses, often organized informally during local festivals. These events foster community cohesion but often fall entirely outside institutional oversight, leaving animals vulnerable to neglect or harm. Animal welfare concerns are widespread. Horses are often raced without adequate conditioning, veterinary care, or rest periods. The lack of oversight increases the risk of musculoskeletal injuries, dehydration, and in severe cases, collapse or death (La Voz 2023). Informal betting and the pressure to win can also encourage the use of harmful training methods or performance-enhancing substances to communal identity, such events operate outside formal animal welfare frameworks.

In the Sahara and Sahel regions, traditional camel races and donkey games take place during seasonal festivals. While camels are well adapted to desert environments, prolonged exertion in extreme heat, lack of water, and rough handling can result in visible distress. Donkeys are sometimes subjected to tug-of-war contests that push them beyond their limits, all without veterinary oversight.

While these traditions embody regional identity and provide economic and social cohesion, they also expose a persistent blind spot in global animal protection efforts. Cultural heritage has often been used—intentionally or otherwise—to shield practices that would not withstand modern welfare scrutiny. The tension between preserving cultural authenticity and safeguarding animal well-being is no longer tenable. Increasingly, the global public is calling for a future in which culture evolves alongside compassion.

Another high-profile example is the Iditarod Trail Sled Dog Race in Alaska, often dubbed "The Last Great Race." Held annually since 1973, the Iditarod covers over 1,000 miles of extreme terrain, from Anchorage to Nome, and is deeply embedded in Alaskan identity and frontier mythology. While celebrated for its endurance and historical roots—tracing back to mail routes and the 1925 serum run—the race has faced mounting criticism over animal welfare concerns. According to Humane Mushing, more than 150 dogs have died during the race since its inception, including three fatalities in 2024 and one in 2025, often from exhaustion, aspiration pneumonia, or cardiac failure (Forrester 2025; Humane Mushing 2025). In 2025, only 214 of the 528 dogs that started the race were able to finish (*ibidem*). Critics argue that the extreme distances, sub-zero temperatures, and grueling pace place dogs under immense physical stress. While organizers have implemented veterinary checks and rest requirements, advocacy groups like PETA and Humane Mushing continue to call for reform, or abolition of the event (PETA n.d.; Humane Mushing 2025). The Iditarod exemplifies the tension between cultural tradition and evolving standards of animal ethics, raising difficult questions about the cost of endurance in the name of heritage.

Disposable Athletes

While animal sports generate substantial economic benefits, these gains often come at a significant ethical cost. Across disciplines, from horse racing to bullfighting, animals are frequently subjected to conditions that compromise their welfare, health, and dignity. The very structure of many animal sports prioritizes performance and profit over the well-being of the animals involved, raising serious moral questions that are increasingly difficult to ignore in a world that is becoming more attuned to animal rights.

Horseracing is perhaps the most economically powerful animal sport, but it is also one of the most ethically fraught. Thoroughbred horses are bred for speed, often at the expense of skeletal strength and long-term health. According to the Jockey Club's Equine Injury Database, in the United States alone, approximately 1.25 horses die per 1,000 starts—a figure that translates to hundreds of fatalities annually (Jockey Club 2023). Injuries such as fractures, tendon ruptures, and internal bleeding are common, particularly on hard or synthetic tracks. Horses are often raced at a young age, before their bones are fully developed, increasing the risk of catastrophic breakdowns. The use of performance-enhancing drugs and pain-masking medications further exacerbates the problem, allowing injured horses to compete when they should be resting or recovering. Retirement is another major concern. Many racehorses are discarded once they are no longer profitable. While some are rehomed or retrained for other disciplines, a significant number are sent to slaughterhouses, often in countries with minimal welfare oversight.

Greyhound racing presents a similar pattern of exploitation. Dogs are bred in large numbers, with only a fraction making it to the track. Those who do often live in cramped kennels, receive minimal socialization, and are subjected to intensive training regimens. Injuries such as broken legs, spinal damage, and head trauma are common, particularly on poorly maintained tracks. In jurisdictions where the sport is still legal, such as parts of Australia, Ireland, and West Virginia (United States), oversight varies widely. Investigations have revealed cases of live baiting, where small animals are used to train dogs—a practice that is both illegal and deeply inhumane (Animals Australia 2025).

Perhaps most troubling is the fate of racing dogs, both greyhounds and sled dogs, after their competitive careers end. Many greyhounds are euthanized, abandoned, or sold into illegal racing circuits, particularly in regions where oversight is weak. While adoption programs exist, they are often underfunded and overwhelmed, unable to accommodate the large number of retired dogs. Even those who are adopted may carry long-term physical and psychological scars from their time on the track, including injuries, anxiety, and socialization challenges.

Sled dogs, too, face harsh and often inhumane conditions once they are no longer fast or strong enough to compete. According to PETA (2025), dogs who are no longer competitive are frequently neglected, abandoned, or killed. Some are shot, bludgeoned, or otherwise euthanized by mushers who view them as no longer economically viable. During races, the treatment of dogs can be brutal: they are not allowed to slow down even to defecate or drink, and are forced to continue running regardless of exhaustion, pain, or severe injury. As one musher reportedly stated, "better a dead dog than a slow dog" (PETA 2025). Those who survive the races may be left chained outdoors in freezing temperatures, exposed to the elements without adequate shelter. The lack of consistent veterinary care further compounds their suffering, especially as many develop arthritis and other chronic conditions from years of intense physical strain. Without proper medical support, these aging dogs often endure prolonged pain and isolation, underscoring the urgent need for reform, retirement planning, and stronger welfare protections across all forms of canine racing.

Among all sports in which animals are involved, bullfighting is unique in that it involves the deliberate killing of the animal as part of the spectacle. The bull is subjected to a prolonged and painful ordeal, often lasting 15–20 min, during which it is weakened with lances, barbed sticks (banderillas), and eventually a sword. The goal is not competition but performance, with the matador's skill measured by how gracefully he dispatches the animal. Defenders argue that the bull lives a better life than animals raised for meat, often spending years on open pastures. However, this does not negate the suffering endured in the ring. Numerous veterinary associations have condemned bullfighting as inherently cruel and incompatible with modern animal welfare standards (AVATMA 2016). At the same time, public opinion is also shifting. In Spain, a 2022 survey found that over 60% of respondents under 35 oppose bullfighting, and attendance has declined sharply over the past two decades (Ministerio de Cultura 2022). Similar trends are evident in Mexico and Colombia, where legal challenges and municipal bans reflect growing discomfort with the practice.

Other animal sports, such as camel racing, cockfighting, and pigeon racing, also raise serious ethical concerns. In camel racing, particularly in the Middle East, young camels are sometimes subjected to harsh training conditions and robotic jockeys that can cause injury. In cockfighting, birds are equipped with razor-sharp spurs and forced to fight to the death, often in unregulated and illegal settings. Pigeon racing, while seemingly benign, has been criticized for high mortality rates. Birds are often released hundreds of kilometers from home, and many die from exhaustion, predation, or disorientation. Breeding practices can also be exploitative, with birds kept in confined spaces and culled if they underperform. As global norms around animal ethics evolve, the invocation of tradition may no longer suffice to justify practices that cause suffering. The future of such events will depend on whether cultural identity can be reimagined to coexist with compassion.

Companion Sports: A Humane and Expanding Economy

As awareness of animal welfare continues to grow, so does interest in companion-based animal sports—activities grounded in cooperation, enrichment, and mutual enjoyment between humans and animals. Unlike traditional sports that often rely on animals for speed, strength, or spectacle, these emerging disciplines prioritize ethical training, voluntary participation, and positive reinforcement. From dog agility competitions and canine freestyle to therapeutic riding programs that foster healing relationships between horses and people with disabilities, these sports cultivate symbiotic bonds rather than exploitation. At the intersection of ethics and innovation, even technology is offering humane alternatives, such as virtual horseracing and robotic rodeos, that preserve cultural traditions without compromising animal welfare. Economically, this sector represents a dynamic and rapidly growing component of the broader pet and recreation industries, positioning itself as a sustainable and compassionate alternative within the landscape of animal-related sport. The increasing popularity of companion sports is indicative of a broader cultural shift in human–animal relationships, from utilitarianism and dominance to partnership and mutual respect.

Canine Agility and Performance Sports

One of the most popular and economically significant companion sports is canine agility. In these events, dogs navigate timed obstacle courses under the direction of their handlers, showcasing speed, precision, and teamwork. The sport is governed by organizations such as the American Kennel Club (AKC), UK Agility, and the Fédération Cynologique Internationale (FCI), which collectively oversee thousands of competitions annually across the globe.

The agility economy is multifaceted. It includes entry fees and prize money for competitors, a growing market for training services and professional coaching, and a thriving industry for specialized equipment such as tunnels, jumps, and weave poles. Additionally, pet nutrition and health products tailored for active dogs are in high demand, and media platforms now stream major events, attracting sponsorships and advertising revenue. In the United States alone, the pet services industry, of which agility is a growing part, is valued at over $11 billion annually (American Pet Products Association 2024). Major agility events like the AKC National Agility Championship contribute to local economies through tourism, hospitality, and event management.

Other Dog Sports: Flyball, Disc, Rally, and Outdoor Running

Beyond agility, a variety of other dog sports are gaining popularity. Flyball is a fast-paced relay race involving teams of dogs that jump hurdles and trigger spring-loaded boxes to release tennis balls. Disc dog competitions, also known as canine frisbee, combine athleticism and showmanship, with dogs performing acrobatic catches in choreographed routines. Rally obedience blends traditional obedience with agility-style movement, emphasizing communication and precision between dog and handler.

Outdoor endurance sports are also on the rise. Canicross, where dogs run alongside their owners in trail races, and skijoring, where dogs pull skiers across snowy terrain, are especially popular in Europe and North America (International Canicross Federation 2023). These sports promote fitness and bonding, often take place in natural settings, and support local tourism and outdoor gear industries. Their accessibility and low barrier to entry make them attractive to a wide range of participants, from casual enthusiasts to competitive athletes.

Ethical Equestrianism

In the equestrian world, disciplines such as trail riding, working equitation, and classical dressage offer more ethical alternatives to racing or rodeo, when practiced with animal welfare as a priority. These sports emphasize partnership, balance, and communication over speed or dominance. However, it is important to distinguish between recreational or welfare-focused equestrianism and competitive dressage, which has been criticized for harsh training methods, including hyperflexion (Rollkur), tight nosebands, and psychological stress. A 2024 international meta-analysis confirmed that hyperflexion negatively impacts equine welfare, regardless of duration or intensity (Samuelsson Radell 2024). While classical dressage, rooted in historical horsemanship, can be humane when based on positive reinforcement and biomechanical understanding, elite competitive dressage often prioritizes aesthetics and scoring over the horse's comfort (Cuckson 2024).

The economic footprint of ethical equestrian sports includes training and boarding facilities that emphasize welfare, a tack and apparel industry tailored to humane riding practices, and a network of competitions and clinics that attract tourism and sponsorship. In the United Kingdom, for example, British Dressage oversees over 17,000 members and 2,000 competitions annually, contributing significantly to the rural economy (British Dressage 2023). Ethical equestrianism also supports sustainable land use, as many riders and clubs maintain pastures and trails that double as conservation areas.

What sets companion sports apart is their mutualistic foundation: animals participate willingly, often enthusiastically, and derive physical and mental stimulation from the activity. This ethical model resonates with a growing demographic of consumers who prioritize animal welfare, sustainability, and community engagement. These sports also foster local economic development. Clubs and competitions often take place in small towns or rural areas, bringing in visitors who spend on lodging, food, and services. The cottage industry around custom gear, handmade leashes, and breed-specific equipment supports artisans and small businesses. Moreover, companion sports are inclusive and scalable. They can be practiced recreationally in backyards or parks, or professionally at national and international levels. This flexibility makes them accessible to a broad socioeconomic range, further expanding their economic footprint.

A New Playbook for Animal Sports

As the global conversation around animal welfare intensifies, the economic and regulatory frameworks that govern animal sports are increasingly under scrutiny. While these industries generate significant revenue and employment, they often do so at the expense of animal well-being. To align economic incentives with ethical imperatives, a new policy paradigm is needed, one that promotes transparency, accountability, and innovation while phasing out exploitative practices. This is particularly urgent in sectors where legacy practices continue despite mounting public and scientific concern; for instance, greyhound racing in parts of Australia or dressage techniques condemned by veterinarians. This section outlines key policy and regulatory reforms with global relevance, aimed at transforming the animal sports sector into a more humane and sustainable domain.

1. Strengthening welfare standards through regulation

The foundation of any reform must be the establishment and enforcement of robust animal welfare standards. Many countries have fragmented or outdated regulations that fail to address the realities of modern animal sports. A global framework—perhaps modeled on the World Organisation for Animal Health (WOAH) standards—could serve as a baseline for national legislation. Key regulatory reforms should include:

- Mandatory welfare audits for all licensed animal sports facilities.
- Ban on harmful training practices, such as hyperflexion in dressage or live baiting in greyhound racing.
- Minimum standards for housing, nutrition, and veterinary care, enforced through regular inspections.
- Transparent injury and fatality reporting, with public access to data.
- International cooperation is essential. Just as doping regulations in human sports are coordinated through bodies like the World Anti-Doping Agency (WADA), a similar global entity could oversee compliance in animal sports, ensuring consistency and accountability across borders.
- Realigning economic incentives.

One of the most powerful tools for reform is economic policy. Governments can use subsidies, taxes, and grants to shift the financial landscape in favor of ethical practices. For example, the Dutch government restructured agricultural subsidies in 2020 to favor animal-friendly practices, offering a useful precedent for sports contexts. Subsidies and tax incentives should be offered to:

- Organizations that adopt welfare-first training methods.
- Facilities that provide retirement and rehoming programs for animals.
- Events that promote non-exploitative companion sports, such as agility or canicross.

Conversely, tax penalties or levies could be imposed on industries that continue to rely on harmful practices. For example, a "welfare impact tax" could be applied to betting revenues from horse or greyhound racing, with proceeds redirected to animal welfare funds.

Public funding should also be reallocated. In many countries, traditional animal sports receive state support under the guise of cultural heritage. Redirecting these funds toward ethical alternatives—such as community-based agility clubs or educational programs—would signal a shift in societal values and create new economic opportunities.

3. Transparency, data, and public accountability

A major barrier to reform is the lack of reliable data. Injury rates, mortality statistics, and post-career outcomes for animals are often hidden or inconsistently reported. Governments and industry bodies must mandate comprehensive data collection and public disclosure. This transparency would:

- Enable evidence-based policymaking.
- Empower consumers to make informed ethical choices.
- Allow researchers to assess the true costs and benefits of various animal sports.

Digital platforms could play a key role. A centralized global database, accessible to regulators, researchers, and the public, could track welfare metrics across disciplines and countries. Blockchain technology might even be used to ensure data integrity and traceability in breeding and training records. Pilot initiatives such as the "EquiData" platform in Switzerland already explore the use of blockchain for veterinary record tracking.

4. Supporting transition in developing economies

In many parts of the world, animal sports are deeply embedded in local economies and traditions. Abrupt bans or restrictions could cause economic hardship and cultural backlash. Therefore, reform must be context sensitive and inclusive. International development agencies and NGOs can support this transition by:

- Funding alternative livelihoods for those dependent on exploitative animal sports.
- Supporting community-led tourism and ethical animal experiences.
- Providing training and certification in humane animal handling and sport.

For example, in regions where bullfighting or cockfighting is prevalent, governments could incentivize the development of cultural festivals that preserve tradition without animal harm—such as dance, music, or virtual simulations.

5. Innovation and ethical alternatives

Policy should also encourage innovation in the animal sports sector. This includes:

- Virtual and augmented reality experiences that simulate traditional sports without involving live animals. In 2023, a VR version of Spanish bullfighting was piloted at the Festival de Innovación in Seville, drawing thousands of visitors and sparking debate on humane preservation of tradition.
- Robotic or AI-driven competitions that preserve the excitement of racing or performance without ethical concerns.
- Investment in mutualistic sports, such as agility, skijoring, or liberty work, which emphasize cooperation and enrichment.
- Public and private research funding can accelerate the development of these alternatives, creating new markets and reducing reliance on exploitative models.
- Public engagement and cultural change.

Finally, policy reform must be accompanied by public education and cultural engagement. Laws alone are not enough; societal values must evolve alongside them. Governments, schools, and media can play a role in:

- Incorporating animal ethics into national education curricula.
- Funding community-based storytelling projects that celebrate animal-friendly traditions.
- Promoting animal welfare literacy.
- Highlighting positive examples of ethical sports.
- Encouraging youth participation in humane animal activities.
- Public campaigns, similar to those used in anti-smoking or environmental movements, can shift perceptions and build support for reform. Over time, this cultural shift can create a self-reinforcing cycle, where ethical practices become not only the norm but also the most economically viable.

While animal sports have long been embedded in human cultures, their future depends on our willingness to reimagine them through the lens of compassion, innovation, and evidence-based policy. A new regulatory playbook can safeguard both heritage and humane values without compromise.

Conclusions

The global economy of animal sports is substantial, employing hundreds of thousands and generating billions in revenue. Yet, as this chapter has shown, that success too often comes at the cost of animal welfare. Exploitation is not incidental, it is systemic, sustained by weak regulation, opaque practices, and misaligned incentives.

But this system is neither inevitable nor immutable. Change is already underway, and it can be accelerated through targeted, evidence-based policy reform.

Robust animal welfare regulation must be the cornerstone. Countries like New Zealand and the Netherlands have already implemented bans on high-risk sports like greyhound racing and bullfighting, respectively, setting a precedent. A global framework—modeled after the World Organisation for Animal Health (WOAH)—could require all licensed facilities to undergo mandatory welfare audits, enforce minimum standards for housing and veterinary care, and mandate public reporting of injuries and fatalities.

Economic incentives must be recalibrated to encourage ethical practices. For example, governments could provide tax incentives to racecourses that invest in post-retirement care for horses, as well as grants for agility clubs or therapeutic riding programs. Conversely, industries still reliant on outdated practices—like live baiting in greyhound training—could face targeted levies, with funds redirected to welfare initiatives. Germany, for instance, has begun tying racing subsidies to compliance with animal care regulations.

Transparency and data sharing are also essential. A centralized, public database tracking injury rates and post-career outcomes—similar to Australia's Greyhound

Racing Integrity Unit—could empower consumers and policymakers alike. Integrating blockchain technology into breeding records is already being piloted in Japan to ensure traceability and combat overbreeding.

Reform must be context sensitive, especially in the Global South, where animal sports like cockfighting or buffalo racing are woven into local economies. International development agencies should support transitional employment, community tourism, and cultural festivals that celebrate heritage without harming animals. In Thailand, for instance, elephant camps are gradually shifting toward no-ride, observation-only models, funded through eco-tourism.

Finally, innovation must be cultivated. Virtual alternatives, like simulated camel races already trialed in the Gulf, can help retain cultural practices while protecting animals. Investment in robotic rodeos, AI-driven equine simulators, or digital sport platforms can help build a new entertainment economy rooted in compassion and creativity.

These are not abstract ideals: they are workable, real-world solutions. If pursued collectively by governments, industry leaders, and civil society, they can transform animal sports from engines of harm into models of ethical engagement. The tools exist. The precedent is set. What remains is the political will to act.

References

American Horse Council (2024) Economic impact of the U.S. horse industry. https://horsecouncil.org/economics/

American Pet Products Association (2024) 2023–2024 APPA national pet owners survey: Industry statistics & trends. https://www.americanpetproducts.org

Animals Australia. Greyhound Racing (2025) www.animalsaustralia.org

AVATMA (2016) Informe técnico veterinario sobre el sufrimiento de toros y novillos en las lidias incruentas. Asociación de Veterinarios Abolicionistas de la Tauromaquia y del Maltrato Animal. https://avatma.org/2016/11/21/informe-tecnico-veterinario-sobre-el-sufrimiento-de-toros-y-novillos-en-las-lidias-incruentas/

British Dressage (2023) Annual report and consolidated financial statements for the year ended 31 December 2022. https://files.britishdressage.co.uk/british-dressage-annual-report-2023-1.pdf

Business Insider (2020) Why a racing pigeon just sold for $1.9 million in China. https://www.businessinsider.com/racing-pigeons-most-expensive-china-belgium-races-2019-8

Cuckson P (2024) The history of hyperflexion in dressage – and how to move away from it. Horse & Hound. https://www.horseandhound.co.uk/features/hyperflexion-in-dressage-training-879487

Dnevni Avaz (2023) Grmečka korida okupila hiljade posjetilaca: Tradicija jača od vremena. https://avaz.ba

Dobbin M (2019) Mongolia's child jockeys risk injury and death to race in Naadam festival. ABC News. https://www.abc.net.au/news/2019-10-12/mongolia-child-jockeys-risk-injury-deaths-race-naadam-festival/11537892

EQuerry/Co (2025). Market analysis: how Asia and the Middle East are redefining the equine industry. LinkedIn. https://www.linkedin.com/pulse/market-analysis-how-asia-middle-east-redefining-equine-dxfme/

FEI (2023) FEI Dressage World Cup™ Series. Fédération Equestre Internationale. https://www.fei.org

Forrester M (2025) Alaska sled dog race raises allegations of animal abuse: the 53rd annual Iditarod race kicks off on March 1. ABC News. https://abcnews.go.com/US/alaska-sled-dog-race-raises-allegations-animal-abuse/story?id=119223075
Fundación Toro de Lidia (n.d.) La tauromaquia en cifras: Impacto económico y social. https://fundaciontorodelidia.org
Holland K (2025) The Towcester greyhound race with a £175k winning prize. BBC News. https://www.bbc.com/news/articles/cy75rxg57k0o
Humane Mushing (n.d.) Ethical standards for sled dog care and racing. https://humanemushing.org/
IER (2024) Size and scope of greyhound racing in Australasia: an economic and social impact assessment. https://galtd.org.au/wp-content/uploads/2024/11/IER-Size-and-Scope-of-Greyhound-Racing-in-Australasia-2022-23-01112024.pdf
Inside Himalayas (2025) The complicated ethics of elephant-based tourism in Nepal. https://www.insidehimalayas.com/the-complicated-ethics-of-elephant-based-tourism-in-nepal/
International Canicross Federation (ICF) (2023) About Canicross, Bike-Joëring and Scootering. https://canicross.international/
Japan Racing Association (JRA) (2022) Annual Report. https://japanracing.jp/_statistics-2022/overview.html
Jockey Club. Equine Injury Database Annual Report (2023). www.jockeyclub.com.
La Voz (2023) Murió un caballo durante plena carrera cuadrera en Traslasierra [Video]. La Voz del Interior. https://www.lavoz.com.ar/sucesos/video-murio-un-caballo-durante-plena-carrera-cuadrera-en-traslasierra/
Lindner J (2025) Racehorse statistics: Market data report 2025. WorldMetrics. https://worldmetrics.org/racehorse-statistics/
Maker Faire Rome (2021) Camels are being raced by robot jockeys in Dubai. https://makerfairerome.eu/en/camels-are-being-raced-by-robot-jockeys-in-dubai/
McGreevy PD, McLean AN (2010) Equitation science. Wiley-Blackwell
Ministerio de Cultura (2022) Encuesta de Hábitos y Prácticas Culturales en España. https://www.cultura.gob.es/servicios-al-ciudadano/estadisticas/cultura/mc/ehpc.html
Online Betting (2023) The demise of greyhound racing in the UK. https://www.onlinebetting.org.uk/betting-guides/demise-of-greyhound-racing-in-the-uk.html
People for the Ethical Treatment of Animals (PETA) (2025) Tell the Iditarod to stop dogs from dying. PETA. https://support.peta.org/page/9813/action/1?locale=en-US
PhilLife (2018) Cockfighting in the Philippines: the billion dollar industry and national obsession. https://www.phillife.co/cockfighting-philippines/
Pittman C (2020) The era of greyhound racing in the U.S. is coming to an end. National Geographic. https://www.nationalgeographic.com/animals/article/greyhound-racing-decline-united-states
Professional Rodeo Cowboys Association (2023) PRCA media guide and annual report. https://www.prorodeo.com
Radio Free Europe/Radio Liberty (2019) Bosnia's bullfights: no matador, no blood, but still controversial. https://rferl.org
Research and Markets (2025) Growth trends in the $127 billion horse racing industry, 2025–2030: Featuring strategic analysis of key players. GlobeNewswire (2025). https://www.globenewswire.com/news-release/2025/01/13/3008255/0/en/Growth-Trends-in-the-127-Billion-Horse-Racing-Industry-2025-2030-Featuring-Strategic-Analysis-of-Key-Players-Churchill-Downs-The-Stronach-Group-Keeneland-Association-More.html
Robot Jockey (2024) Robot jockey. Wikipedia. https://en.wikipedia.org/wiki/Robot_jockey
Rodríguez O'Donnell A (2008) Caballo peruano de paso: Elegancia, nobleza, resistencia, tradición y embajador silencioso [Peruvian Paso horse: Elegance, nobility, resistance, tradition and silent ambassador]. Revista Peruana de Pediatría 61(3):200–201.
Samuelsson Radell E (2024) Ny studie slår fast: Hyperflexion är alltid skadligt [New study confirms: Hyperflexion is always harmful]. Tidningen Ridsport. https://www.tidningenridsport.se/ny-studie-slar-fast-hyperflexion-ar-alltid-skadligt/

Spanish Riding School (2024) About us. https://www.srs.at/en/
Surk B (2017) Bloodless bullfight gives Bosnians excuse to party. Balkan Insight. https://balkaninsight.com/2017/07/31/bloodless-bullfight-gives-bosnians-excuses-to-party-07-31-2017/
The Conversation (2022) Greyhound racing: despite waning public support, governments are spending big to keep the industry running. https://theconversation.com/greyhound-racing-despite-waning-public-support-governments-are-spending-big-to-keep-the-industry-running-184849
The Olive Press (2025) Bullfighting's protected status in Spain 'to be reviewed by Congress' after protestors gather 700,000 signatures. The Olive Press. https://www.theolivepress.es/spain-news/2025/02/17/bullfightings-protected-status-in-spain-to-be-reviewed-by-congress-after-protestors-gather-700000-signatures/
Unione Sarda (2023) Palio di Siena, two horses suffer fractures: animal rights activists protest. https://www.unionesarda.it/en/italy/palio-di-siena-two-horses-suffer-fractures-animal-rights-activists-protest-itj7m6mq
Vienna Tourist Board (2023) Visitor statistics and cultural institutions report. https://b2b.wien.info
VOA Learning English (2020) In China, pigeon racers spend big money to get winning birds. https://learningenglish.voanews.com/a/in-china-pigeon-racers-spend-big-money-to-get-winning-birds/5696324.html
Wikipedia (2024) Palio di Siena. https://en.wikipedia.org/wiki/Palio_di_Siena
World Animal Protection (2025) Chitwan Elephant Festival: Undermining Nepal's tourism goals. https://www.worldanimalprotection.org/latest/news/chitwan-elephant-festival/
Zion Market Research (2023) Global horse racing market size to surpass $793.9 Bn by 2030, exhibit a CAGR of 8.89%. On GlobeNewswire (2023). https://www.globenewswire.com/news-release/2023/04/04/2640319/0/en/Global-Horse-Racing-Market-Size-to-Surpass-793-9-Bn-Growth-by-2030-Exhibit-a-CAGR-of-8-89-Equestrian-Industry-Analysis-Comprehensive-Study.html

Chapter 15
Animals in Entertainment

Izabela Kapera and Artur Kapera

A zoo is a prison
—*Nadine Gordimer*

Abstract The entertainment sector is a lucrative industry that provides employment to millions of people worldwide and generates significant economic impact. The industry encompasses a wide range of animal applications, including zoos, dolphinariums, circuses, and the use of animals in film productions. This often raises serious concerns regarding the welfare of individual animals and species conservation. This chapter explores examples of animal use in entertainment, examining the economic aspects of the industry and addressing the ethical controversies involved. To improve the welfare of animals in entertainment, several policy proposals are suggested, including financial incentives for transitioning to sanctuary models, taxation and regulation of animal use, and the promotion of innovative technologies as alternatives. These policy proposals aim to ensure the humane treatment of animals while maintaining the economic viability of the entertainment sector.

Economic and Cultural Impact of Animals in Entertainment

The entertainment sector is not only one of the most visible areas of the cultural and creative industries but also one of significant economic importance.[1] Despite this, the topic of entertainment is often underestimated in academic literature and frequently dismissed with surprising ease as unworthy of serious analysis.[2] While research on

[1] McKee et al. (2014).

I. Kapera (✉)
Andrzej Frycz Modrzewski Krakow University, Krakow, Poland
e-mail: ikapera@uafm.edu.pl

A. Kapera
AGH University of Science and Technology, Krakow, Poland
e-mail: artur.kapera@proton.me

[2] Collis (2017).

N. Batini (ed.), *The Economics of Non-Human Animals*, Natural Resource Management and Policy 63, https://doi.org/10.1007/978-3-032-17580-9_15

entertainment remains largely scattered,[3] it is not entirely neglected. The literature contains various attempts to define entertainment, with perspectives ranging from product-oriented explanations to interpretations based on cultural experience and communication.[4] Entertainment can also be characterized by its audience-oriented, commercial nature.[5] From a business model perspective, entertainment is a form of culture that is commercially driven, does not primarily rely on government subsidies or patronage, and exists to the extent that an audience is willing to pay for it. A key aspect of entertainment is its experiential component, which is transient, time-limited, and intangible.[6] In other words, at the core of why audiences consume entertainment lies the satisfaction or "pleasure" they derive from it.[7] The modern entertainment industry—including film production, radio, television, the Internet, video games, and sports—is a multi-billion-dollar business. The total global revenue of the entertainment and media (E&M) industry increased by 5% in 2023, reaching $2.8 trillion.[8] It is important to emphasize that art and entertainment share common characteristics that are crucial for a country's economic development: they involve the creation, production, and distribution of products and services that rely on creativity and human capital as fundamental inputs.[9] However, animals are also used to provide entertainment. In fact, the entertainment industry encompasses a wide range of animal applications, from zoos and dolphinariums to circuses and the use of animals in film productions. Unfortunately, this often raises serious concerns regarding both the welfare of individual animals and species conservation. While some academic publications have addressed the issue of animals in entertainment, the topic still requires more interdisciplinary research.[10]

Animals in Zoos and Dolphinariums

Zoos

Zoos are among the most frequently visited tourist attractions worldwide and can be found in almost every country. The United States and Germany are among the nations with the highest number of such facilities (Table 15.1).

Over the years, zoos have evolved from private menageries and game reserves, accessible only to individuals of high social status, into institutions open to the general

---

[3] Vogel (2020).

[4] Cavalcanti et al. (2022).

[5] Collis (2017).

[6] Sayre and King (2010).

[7] McKee et al. (2014).

[8] PwC (2024).

[9] International Labour Office (2023a).

[10] Finn (n.d.).

Table 15.1 Number of zoos by country (Top 10 countries)

United States	350
Germany	316
United Kingdom	118
Australia	104
Japan	96
Brazil	80
India	66
Canada	40
China	34
Czech Republic	34

Based on: World Population Review, *Zoos By Country 2026,* https://worldpopulationreview.com/country-rankings/zoos-by-country[11]

public. Today, these facilities strive to be recognized not merely as entertainment venues but as institutions dedicated to wildlife conservation, public education, and scientific research.[12] Increasingly, there is a call to enhance the sustainability of their operations, with animal welfare becoming a key objective of modern zoos—both from the perspective of the animals themselves and that of human visitors.[13] In recent years, the issue of animal welfare in zoos has gained prominence, leading to the introduction of stricter legal regulations and calls for improved standards.[14]

The existence of zoos has sparked extensive debates between supporters and opponents of this form of recreation, with some animal rights activists advocating for zoo boycotts. These differing perspectives are also reflected in academic literature, where opinions on the popularity of zoos vary. Research in this area is somewhat limited, partly due to the lack of an international approach, including comprehensive studies on zoo attendance worldwide.[15] Attendance rates vary across countries and regions, influenced by factors such as population size, economic conditions, education, and cultural attitudes.[16] For instance, in 2023, Zoo, Tierpark, and Aquarium Berlin collectively welcomed 5.6 million visitors, who observed over 25,000 animals representing approximately 1,500 species. These facilities also employed around 630 staff members.[17] Some zoos and aquariums set attendance records and rank among the most visited attractions globally. According to data published by the Themed Entertainment Association, Disney's Animal Kingdom in Lake Buena Vista, Florida, United States, attracted around 14 million visitors in 2019, while the most frequently

[11] World Population Review (2004).

[12] Fa et al. (2014), Hutchins et al. (2018), Traylor-Holzer et al. (2019), Escribano et al. (2021).

[13] Rose and Riley (2022).

[14] Whitham and Wielebnowski (2013).

[15] Davey (2007).

[16] Davey (2007).

[17] Zoo Berlin (n.d.).

visited aquarium that year was Chimelong Ocean Kingdom in Hengqin, China, with an annual attendance of about 12 million visitors.[18] Collaboration and knowledge exchange play a crucial role in helping zoos fulfill their conservation objectives, particularly in programs focused on the restoration of endangered species populations. One international organization dedicated to collecting and sharing data on plants and animals in botanical gardens, zoos, aquariums, and related conservation institutions is Species360, which has been operating for 50 years. Another key organization in the development of zoos and aquariums in the fields of conservation, education, science, and recreation is the Association of Zoos and Aquariums (AZA). Based on the activities of such organizations, examples of the economic impact of zoos have been analyzed (Table 15.2).

The presence of zoological gardens influences the region in which they are located, partly because they provide employment opportunities for individuals, primarily from the local community, and attract visitors who contribute financially to the area. This has been confirmed, for example, by analyses conducted in Nigeria, which demonstrated that the local community derives social and economic benefits from the existence of a zoo.[19] Some zoological gardens see this as an additional justification for their existence. One such institution, which attracts 1.7 million visitors annually, reports that for every dollar received from tax funds, the zoo generated an average of 10 USD in economic benefits for the county in which it operates, thanks to expenditures by visitors from outside the county.[20] Over a four-year period, these visitors contributed a total revenue of $275 million, averaging $69 million USD annually, with approximately 58,115 of them staying in hotels during their trip to the zoo.[21] However, not everyone agrees with this perspective on zoological gardens. Although zoos strive to be perceived as more than just providers of entertainment, some studies confirm that people visit zoos primarily for leisure.[22] The authors' previous research on opinions about zoological gardens revealed that visitors generally view these places positively, focusing primarily on expenditures, pricing, and organizational aspects, while paying little attention to animal welfare or the conservation and educational functions that zoos seek to emphasize.[23] Meanwhile, the role of providing entertainment to visitors is not sufficient to justify removing animals from their natural habitats and placing them in enclosures.[24]

[18] Themed Entertainment Association (2022).

[19] Muhammad et al. (2022).

[20] Cincinnati Zoo (2023).

[21] Cincinnati Zoo (2023).

[22] Linke and Winterin (2011).

[23] Kapera and Kapera (2021).

[24] Catibog-Sinha (2011).

Table 15.2 AZA—Zoo and aquarium characteristic and statistic

Accreditation	253 accredited zoos, aquariums, and related facilities in 13 countries
Animals in AZA-accredited facilities	• Over 780,000 animals in the care of AZA-accredited zoo and aquarium professionals • Over 8,600 species • Over 800 Vulnerable, Endangered, Critically Endangered, and Extinct In The Wild species as categorized by the IUCN Red List
Conservation	• \$252.2 million was spent on field conservation in 119 countries in 2022 • 232 species and subspecies that benefited are listed as Endangered or Threatened under the U.S. Endangered Species Act • \$29 million was spent on AZA SAFE: Saving Animals From Extinction species programs in 2022
Economy	• Contributed more than \$22.5 billion to U.S. economy • Supported more than 198,000 full-time jobs in the U.S • Served more than 200 million annual visitors worldwide (183 million in the U.S.)

Based on: Association of Zoos and Aquariums, *Zoo and Aquarium Statistics*, https://www.aza.org/zoo-and-aquarium-statistics[25]

[25] Association of Zoos and Aquariums (n.d.).

Dolphinariums

The issue of ensuring animal welfare is particularly evident in dolphinariums. Around the world, dolphins are still being captured from wild populations for use in these facilities. More than 60% of all captive dolphins globally are held in just five countries: China (23%), Japan (16%), the USA (13%), Mexico (8%), and Russia (5%).[26] Within the EU, cetaceans are kept in 32 dolphinariums across 15 member states, with a total of 309 whales and dolphins in captivity.[27] According to trade data, between 1979 and 2008, a total of 285 live whales and dolphins were imported into the EU, despite EU Regulation CITES No. 338/97, which prohibits the import of cetaceans primarily for commercial purposes.[28] Dolphinariums attract visitors and generate revenue. Visitors can watch dolphin shows, and some facilities also offer "swimming with dolphins." Additionally, dolphin-assisted therapy or paid souvenir photos with the animals are available. Research indicates that 93% of dolphin facilities worldwide offer dolphin performances, 66% provide swimming experiences, 75% allow selfies, and 23% offer therapy sessions involving dolphins.[29] A single dolphin can generate between 400,000 and $2 million annually for a facility, meaning that all captive dolphins in the tourism industry collectively generate between $1.1 and $5.5 billion per year.[30] However, keeping these animals in captivity remains highly controversial. Within the EU, studies have been conducted, and data from dolphinariums have been gathered to assess compliance with legal requirements, including the Zoo Directive 1999/22, EU Regulation CITES 338/97, and other relevant regulations. The main findings from these analyses are presented below[31]:

- Of the 34 dolphinariums in the EU included in this report, only 14 indicated on their websites that they conducted research on cetaceans.
- Of the 13 dolphinariums visited, only four had informational boards describing the exhibited animal species.
- Among the 18 shows analyzed, 17 did not inform guests about the natural distribution of the species, eight did not discuss dolphins as mammals, and none of the 18 programs mentioned the conservation status of the species.

Dolphinariums in the EU do not meet the biological needs of captive cetaceans and fail to comply with the requirements of Directive 1999/22. Society is becoming increasingly aware of animal welfare issues and the problems associated with keeping dolphins in captivity. Despite the current high level of acceptance of dolphin entertainment, concerns about welfare are emerging: 52% of respondents believe that dolphins suffer physically and emotionally in captivity, while 47% think that no dolphin would perform tricks, kiss people, or allow them to ride on its back of its

---

[26] WAP (n.d.).

[27] Whale and Dolphin Conservation (n.d.).

[28] Whale and Dolphin Conservation (n.d.)

[29] WAP (n.d.).

[30] WAP (n.d.).

[31] Whale and Dolphin Conservation (n.d.).

own free will.[32] The same report indicates that 80% of respondents would prefer to see dolphins in the wild if given the opportunity, and one in four visitors stated that watching these animals in a dolphinarium feels wrong and that all such facilities should be closed.[33] In relation to this issue, analyses by the China Cetacean Alliance should also be considered. This is a coalition of international animal protection organizations, including the Animal Welfare Institute, Endangered Species Fund, Environment & Animal Society Taiwan, Hong Kong Dolphin Conservation Society, Kuroshio Ocean Education Foundation, Marine Connection, Nature University, and Whale and Dolphin Conservation. Their research highlights numerous problems associated with the use of animals in such facilities. The authors raise concerns regarding, for example, the structural parameters of the enclosures, including their depth, arguing that they fail to meet the complex behavioral needs of the species they exhibit. Many animals are kept in tanks that require maintenance work, and display tanks often lack shelters for the animals. Exhibit aquariums tend to be structurally simplistic, with little to no topographical variation, which can lead to boredom among the animals.[34] Additionally, the high number of visitors generates excessive noise around the tanks, especially since they are often located near loudspeakers playing music during performances. In some cases, staff behavior has also been observed to directly cause stress and discomfort to the animals. The living conditions of dolphins vary depending on the country, its regulations, and the standards in place. However, in such facilities, the needs of captive dolphins are often secondary to those of the audience, which watches and interacts with them. Some of these establishments attempt to distance themselves from the perception that their shows are purely for entertainment and emphasize their educational efforts. However, keeping dolphins in captivity for entertainment does not provide significant educational benefits. The authors of the aforementioned report stress that these facilities fail to fully utilize their potential in education.[35]

Animals in Circuses

For many years, the circus has been a significant form of international popular entertainment while remaining a rarely studied subject in academic research.[36] This is partly because the circus is considered a minor performing art and partly due to the difficulty of collecting reliable quantitative data on the industry.[37] The modern

[32] WAP (n.d.).

[33] WAP (n.d.).

[34] China Cetacean Alliance (n.d.).

[35] China Cetacean Alliance (n.d.).

[36] Malamud and Stoddart (2000).

[37] Zanola (2007).

circus, in its current form, has existed for approximately 250 years and has undergone significant development over time.[38] It is estimated that between 1,600 and 2,100 circus companies are currently registered in the EU, with most operating in France, Germany, Spain, Italy, and Belgium.[39] The circus sector in the EU employs between 11,000 and 15,000 people, a relatively small fraction of the 8.7 million individuals working in the cultural sector within the EU.[40] In 2018, about one-fifth of circus troupes had revenues exceeding 500,000 euros, three-quarters generated over 1 million euros, and one in three troupes attracted more than 30,000 spectators. Meanwhile, one in ten reported having fewer than 1,000 viewers.[41] Although contemporary circuses are moving away from the use of animals in performances, this practice is still maintained in some countries, and the biological needs of animals are not always treated as a priority.[42] Issues include inadequate diets, limited living space, poor transport conditions, insufficient social interactions, and concerns regarding training methods and the attitudes of handlers.[43] In recent years, the use of animals in circuses has become the subject of global debate, leading to the implementation of regulations in various countries regarding the use and exhibition of animals in circus performances. Measures banning or restricting the use of animals in circuses have already been adopted in approximately one-quarter of the world's countries. Most EU member states have introduced either a total or partial ban on the use of wild animals in circuses, though the scope of these regulations varies by country.[44] Representatives of the circus entertainment sector hold different views on the use of animals in performances. The European Circus Association (ECA), which represents over 130 circuses, festivals, animal trainers, and performers across 29 countries—including nearly all renowned European circuses and affiliated members worldwide[45]—asserts that "circus animals are educated and stimulated in their physical, mental, and intellectual development".[46] However, research indicates that circus animals are routinely exposed to nutritional deficiencies, diseases, pathological conditions, and stress, raising concerns about their welfare (Table 15.3).[47]

Further analyses indicate the economic benefits of reducing the use of wild animals in travelling circuses. It is emphasized that such a reduction is a more cost-effective option than the expenses associated with meeting regulatory requirements

[38] European Commission, Directorate-General for Education, Youth, Sport and Culture; Vroonhof et al. (2020).

[39] European Commission, Directorate-General for Education, Youth, Sport and Culture; Vroonhof et al. (2020).

[40] European Commission, Directorate-General for Education, Youth, Sport and Culture; Vroonhof et al. (2020).

[41] European Commission, Directorate-General for Education, Youth, Sport and Culture; Vroonhof et al. (2020).

[42] Mota-Rojas et al. (2022).

[43] Mota-Rojas et al. (2022).

[44] Kapera and Kapera (2022).

[45] European Circus Association (n.d.).

[46] European Circus Association (n.d.).

[47] Mota-Rojas et al. (2022).

Table 15.3 Regulations on the ban or restrictions on the use of animals in circuses (as of February 2025)

Country	Scope of restrictions
North and South America	
Argentina	Local bans on the use of wild animals in circuses in over 20 cities including a ban in the city of Buenos Aires
Bolivia	Nationwide ban on the use of wild and domestic animals in circuses
Brazil:	Local bans on the use of animals in circuses in 11 states and over 20 cities
Canada	Local bans on the use of animals in circuses in 33 municipal jurisdictions including Vancouver
Colombia	Nationwide ban on the use of wild animals in circuses; Local ban on the use of animals in circuses in the capital, Bogota
Costa Rica	Nationwide ban on the use of wild animals in circuses
Ecuador	Nationwide ban on the use of native wild animals; restrictions on the use of exotic animals; ban on the import of both native and exotic wild animals with circuses
El Salvador	Nationwide ban on the "Income, use or abuse of wildlife species in all kinds of entertainment"
Guatemala	Nationwide ban on the use of animals in circuses
Mexico	Nationwide ban on the use of wild animals in circuses
Panama	Nationwide ban prohibiting "entry of wild animals for use in static and travelling circuses and similar shows"
Paraguay	Nationwide ban on the use of wild animals in circuses
Peru	Nationwide ban on the use of wild animals in circuses as well as a local ban on all animals in Magdalena del Mar
USA	112 partial or full bans on performing animals in jurisdictions in the US, in 34 states
Europe	
Armenia	Nationwide ban on the use of wild animals in circuses
Austria	Nationwide ban on the use of wild animals in circuses
Belgium	Nationwide ban on the use of most wild animals in circuses (Parrots and camel are classed as domestic)
Bosnia and Herzegovina	Nationwide ban on all animals in circuses
Bulgaria	Nationwide ban on certain wild animal species in circuses, variety shows and other entertainment facilities
Croatia	Nationwide ban on the use of wild animals in circuses
Czech Republic	Nationwide ban on the use of certain species in circuses; from January 2022 circuses prohibited from obtaining and breeding wild animals and using those born after this date
Cyprus	Nationwide ban on all animals in circuses
Denmark	Nationwide ban on the use of wild animals in circuses
Estonia	Nationwide ban on the use of wild animals in circuses

(continued)

Table 15.3 (continued)

Country	Scope of restrictions
Finland	Nationwide ban on the use of wild animals in circuses and travelling animal shows
France	Nationwide ban on use of wild animals for public display/travelling circuses; prohibits keeping, acquisition, breeding and transport of animals for such use
Germany	Local in bans in more 90 towns and cities
Greece	Nationwide ban on all animals in circuses
Hungary	Nationwide ban on the use of wild-caught animals in circuses, the purchase and training of elephants and primates for circus performances and the purchase, training and use of CITES (Appendix 1) listed species in circuses
Ireland	Ban on wild animals in circuses
Latvia	Nationwide restrictions effectively banning the use of wild-caught animals
Lithuania	Nationwide ban on the use of wild mammals, birds, reptiles and amphibians in circuses
Luxembourg	Nationwide ban on wild animals in circuses
Macedonia	Nationwide ban on the use of wild animals in circuses
Malta	Nationwide ban on all animals for performances, exhibitions, shows or training for the circus
The Netherlands	Nationwide ban on the use and transport of animals in circuses, with exemptions for certain, mostly domestic, species
Norway	Use of wild species effectively banned nationwide – positive list of permitted animals only includes domestic animals (apart from camels)
Poland	Nationwide ban on the use of wild-born animals in circuses
Portugal	Nationwide ban restricting the use of wild animals in circuses
Romania	Nationwide ban on the use of wild animals in circuses (apart from certain exotic bird species and cetaceans)
Scotland	Nationwide ban on the use of wild animals in circuses
Serbia	Nationwide ban on the use of wild animals in circuses
Slovakia	Nationwide ban on the use of wild animals in circuses
Slovenia	Nationwide ban on the use of wild animals in circuses
Spain	Nationwide ban on the use of wild animals in circuses
Sweden	Nationwide ban on the use of certain species in circuses
UK	Scotland, England, and Wales have passed nationwide bans on the use of wild animals in circuses; no such legislation is currently in place in Northern Ireland. Over 200 local authorities have bans on animal circuses (more than two–thirds of these ban all performing animals, the remainder ban just wild animals)
Ukraine	Nationwide ban on "mobile menageries" and the transportation of wild animals for use in circus performances
Australia	

(continued)

Table 15.3 (continued)

Country	Scope of restrictions
Australia	Local bans on the use of animals in circuses in several towns including Hobsons Bay, Surf Coast Shire, Parramata, and Lismore
Asia	
India	Nationwide ban on the use of certain species in circuses
Iran	Use of wild animals in circuses effectively banned nationwide (no permits issued)
Israel	Nationwide ban on the use of wild animals in circuses
Lebanon	Nationwide ban on the use of certain species in circuses
Singapore	Nationwide ban on the use of wild animals in circuses
Taiwan	Nationwide prohibition on the import or export of protected wildlife for circuses
Uzbekistan	Nationwide prohibition of private ownership of wild animals in semi-wild conditions, artificial habitats or captivity, and keeping in public and travelling circuses

Source Federal Circus Bill, *Worldwide Summary*, https://www.federalcircusbill.org/briefings/worldwide-summary[48]

and conducting inspections. Attention is also drawn to taxpayer savings and the fact that circuses featuring human performers can create more jobs.[49] The reduction in animal use in circuses, along with public opinion considerations, has led circuses in recent years to seek new ways to attract audiences. One approach has been to replace live animals with life-sized holographic projections.

Animals in Films

Animals have played a fundamental role in the development and expansion of various cinematographic and audiovisual activities.[50] Their use in films has been common since the inception of cinema and has now become an extremely profitable industry.[51] However, the involvement of animals in the film industry raises concerns due to its negative impact on individual animal welfare, the potential increase in animal trade, and its effects on environmental conservation. Moreover, the portrayal of animals in films and literature often reinforces human superiority and speciesist ideology by disregarding animal autonomy, emotional experiences, and desires.[52] The issue also has a moral dimension, particularly regarding the impact of real or simulated

[48] Federal Circus Bill (n.d.).

[49] Animal Defenders International (n.d.).

[50] De Damborenea Martín et al. (2023).

[51] Martinez et al. (2022).

[52] Zavitz and Kielbiski (2021).

animal suffering on audiences.[53] The use of animals in filmmaking requires careful planning and has legal implications. Some countries attempt to regulate these issues through appropriate legislation or with the involvement of various organizations. As early as 1937, the British Parliament passed the Cinematograph Films (Animals) Act, which prohibited the exhibition and distribution of films in which animals may have suffered. This law, which bans the screening or distribution of cinematographic films produced in circumstances where animals may have been subjected to suffering, stipulates that no person may publicly exhibit or supply any cinematographic film (produced in the United Kingdom or elsewhere) for public exhibition if, in connection with its production, any scene depicted in the film was staged or directed in such a way as to involve the cruel infliction of pain or terror on any animal or the cruel provocation of any animal into a state of fury.[54] In the European Union, many of the principles outlined in various relevant directives could potentially be extrapolated or adapted to regulate this industry. However, certain areas concerning the use of animals in film and television productions remain unregulated by law.[55] In addition to legal regulations, it is also important to mention the role of organizations dedicated to ensuring the safety and well-being of animals used in film productions. One such organization is American Humane, which helps guarantee the safety and humane treatment of animal actors. American Humane's oversight extends to film, television, commercials, music videos, and computer-generated imagery (CGI). The organization is involved from the pre-production planning stage, monitors animals on set during production, and enforces guidelines. It also conducts investigations into allegations of mistreatment and cruelty, imposing sanctions on productions that fail to meet humane treatment standards. American Humane holds the exclusive right to award the "No Animals Were Harmed" certification to productions that comply with strict animal welfare standards. This phrase was first used in 1989 and has since become a registered trademark.[56] The organization has also developed the Guidelines for the Safe Use of Animals in Filmed Media, which aim to ensure the safety and well-being of all animal actors. Through its program, American Humane works to protect approximately 100,000 animals in over 1,000 productions annually, ensuring their safety and humane treatment with the help of Certified Animal Safety Representatives. Many celebrities collaborate with American Humane, advocating for animal rights. This is not the only organization working in this field. Animal Protection New Mexico (APNM) also takes a rigorous approach to the use of animals in film. It advocates for alternatives such as CGI, stock footage, animation, or other methods that do not involve live animals.[57] Film and television production companies have also introduced their own guidelines for animal use. For example, Disney requires that any proposed use of live animals be reviewed for compliance with its policies by the Disney Animals, Science, and Environment department and

---

[53] Wilkins (1981).

[54] *Cinematograph Films (Animals) Act 1937, 1937 CHAPTER 59, 1 Edw 8 and 1 Geo 6.*

[55] De Damborenea Martín et al. (2023).

[56] Malamud (2012).

[57] Animal Protection New Mexico (n.d.).

recommends adherence to American Humane Association guidelines.[58] Whenever possible, productions featuring animals should include educational elements related to animal welfare or conservation. Furthermore, the Royal Society for the Prevention of Cruelty to Animals (RSPCA) has outlined best practices for the use of animals in performances, events, and productions. According to these guidelines, filmmakers should consider at the planning stage whether live animals are truly necessary for a production and assess the risks posed to individual animals involved.[59]

Other Examples of Animal Use in Entertainment

Beyond the previously mentioned examples, animals are also used in entertainment in various other ways. This final section discusses some of these cases, highlighting potential directions for further research and the need for in-depth analysis. One such issue requiring examination is the killing of animals for entertainment. Given that a ban on commercial hunting is unlikely in the near future, this phenomenon should first be analyzed in terms of existing legal regulations in many countries. Studies on hunting tourism conducted by the authors emphasize the complexity of this issue.[60] Focusing solely on legal provisions, the following discussion presents current topics that have been subject to varying degrees of regulatory attempts in Poland. Implementing such regulations is challenging, as evidenced by two recent examples. A proposed regulation requiring periodic medical and psychological examinations for individuals licensed to own firearms for hunting purposes met with strong opposition from hunters in Poland. Similarly, hunters reacted negatively to an attempt to regulate hunting stands due to a legal loophole concerning the lack of provisions specifying procedures and rules for constructing such structures. Meanwhile, the scale of these installations raises concerns. According to information from the Polish Hunting Association (Polski Związek Łowiecki), Poland, with an area of approximately 312,000 km^2, has 116,000 hunting stands, with an additional 17,000 belonging to State Forests (Lasy Państwowe) and Game Breeding Centers (Ośrodki Hodowli Zwierzyny)[61]—resulting in an average of one hunting stand per 2.3 km^2.

The current legal framework and a certain degree of regulatory ineffectiveness are reflected in an official response received by the authors following an inquiry to government authorities:

"The Ministry of Climate and Environment, within the framework of interministerial consultations on the draft amendment to the Construction Law and certain other laws, raised concerns regarding the regulation of the construction of hunting structures. However, this concern was deemed beyond the scope of the proposed

[58] Disney (n.d.).

[59] RSPCA (n.d.)

[60] Kapera and Kapera (2020).

[61] PZŁ (n.d.).

legislative changes, which were of a derogatory nature, and was therefore not considered." Legal challenges related to hunting are addressed differently across countries. In Europe, hunters make up 1.4% of the total population, with the highest number residing in France.[62] Analyses conducted in the United States in 2022 indicate that 14.4 million people over the age of 16 participated in hunting, with hunters spending $45.2 billion on hunting-related activities.[63] However, hunting, including recreational hunting, does not encompass the entirety of the issue. Other controversial forms of animal use in entertainment include dog and cockfighting, where animals are forced into brutal fights to the death. Another widely debated practice is bullfighting, which exemplifies a human-animal relationship based on agonistic struggles initiated by humans. During a corrida, the matador kills the bull in the arena before a live audience. Literature on the subject examines the economic impact of such events, including employment opportunities on cattle ranches, rural labor, and the roles of entrepreneurs, toreros, and other workers.[64] Estimates for a single event, Feria del Toro, indicate a total economic impact of €5.3 million.[65] However, whether such financial benefits justify the killing of animals for entertainment is a question the authors deliberately leave unanswered.

Revamping Animal Entertainment: Humane Economic and Regulatory Policies

The use of animals in entertainment will not vanish rapidly. Unfortunately, options for animals already in captivity are limited. However, their welfare can and should be better ensured. Keeping wild animals in captivity requires meeting certain biological needs related to housing, nutrition, health, and mental well-being. To this end, broader legal regulations are needed in areas where such measures have not yet been implemented. In zoos, welfare standards should be strengthened wherever possible, particularly regarding enclosure sizes, diet, socialization, and the prevention of captive breeding. In some industries, more decisive actions aimed at the complete cessation of such practices would be advisable.

In the arts and entertainment industry, there is currently a growing demand for entertainment services based on modern technology, which provide instant access to content and enhance experiences through artificial intelligence and virtual reality effects.[66] The increasing application of technology in the entertainment sector has driven demand for animation, visual effects (VFX), and gaming, which is directly

[62] Benko et al. (2020).

[63] U.S. Department of the Interior, U.S. Fish and Wildlife Service (2022).

[64] Sánchez-Rivero et al. (2020).

[65] Sánchez-Rivero et al. (2020).

[66] International Labour Office (2023b).

linked to broader technological advancements, including the availability of affordable internet access. At the same time, the industry is also paying attention to environmental issues. Through their work, professionals—including artists, writers, and performers—as well as businesses and organizations can engage audiences in sustainability movements. With a commitment to environmental issues, the sector can influence consumer choices beyond the realm of art, advocating for stronger interactions between cultural work, economic contributions, and environmental responsibility.

Film, in its various forms, is one way to convey this kind of message. For example, remote camera feeds or webcams can be used by conservation organizations to raise awareness about specific species.[67] Further scientific research is also necessary to determine the number of animals used in entertainment, describe the type and duration of work performed by these animals, investigate the frequency of animal welfare-related incidents, and explore alternative methods to using live animals in film and television.[68]

A set of dedicated economic policies and regulatory reforms can be postulated to improve the well-being of animals used in entertainment and gradually make progress in their substitution with animal free entertainment activities that represent animals nonetheless. Starting with economic proposals, four key ones include:

- *Taxation and financial incentives.* Implementing taxes on businesses that use animals for entertainment can discourage their use by increasing operational costs. Conversely, providing tax breaks and grants for organizations that develop and use alternative technologies, such as virtual reality or animatronics, can incentivize innovation and reduce reliance on live animals. In the United Kingdom, for example, the government offers tax relief for film and television productions that use computer-generated imagery (CGI) instead of live animals, encouraging the industry to adopt more humane practices.
- *Research and development financing.* Allocate public funds for research and development of humane alternatives to animal-based entertainment.
- *Funding for Animal Welfare.* Establishing government-funded programs to support the rescue, rehabilitation, and care of animals previously used in entertainment can ensure their well-being. Additionally, creating financial incentives for zoos and aquariums to transition to sanctuary models that prioritize animal welfare and conservation can promote ethical treatment. The United States, for example, has several grant programs, such as the Animal Welfare Act Grant Program, which provide funding for the care and rehabilitation of animals used in entertainment.
- *Funding a Transition to Sanctuaries.* Create financial incentives for zoos and aquariums to transition to sanctuary models that prioritize animal welfare and conservation.

Regulatory proposals, alongside economic incentives, can ensure a more rapid and certain achievement of animal welfare goals. These span from outright

[67] Silk et al. (2021).

[68] Hitchens et al. (2021).

bans to measures to promote substitutive animal representation technologies in entertainment. Specifically,

- *Bans and restrictions*. Enforcing bans on the use of certain species in entertainment, particularly those that are highly intelligent or endangered, can protect vulnerable animals. Prohibiting the use of animals in specific types of performances, such as circuses and dolphin shows, can further safeguard their welfare. Implementing strict regulations on the conditions under which animals can be kept and used in entertainment, including minimum space requirements and enrichment standards, can ensure humane treatment. For example, in 2017, Italy banned the use of animals in circuses and travelling shows, joining a growing list of countries that have implemented similar bans to protect animal welfare.
- *Mandatory assessments and oversight*. Requiring regular welfare assessments and inspections of facilities that use animals for entertainment can ensure compliance with animal welfare standards. Mandating transparency and public reporting on the health and well-being of animals in entertainment can hold organizations accountable. Establishing independent oversight bodies to monitor and enforce animal welfare standards can provide an additional layer of protection. The American Humane Association's "No Animals Were Harmed" program, for example, monitors the use of animals in film and television productions, ensuring their welfare and providing certification for productions that meet their standards.
- *Reporting and transparency*. Mandate transparency and public reporting on the health and well-being of animals in entertainment.
- *Substitution with innovative technologies*. Promoting the use of virtual reality, augmented reality, and animatronics as alternatives to live animals in entertainment can reduce the need for live animals and enhance audience experiences. Encouraging the development of realistic and humane digital representations of animals for use in films, theme parks, and educational programs can further support this transition. Supporting public education campaigns to raise awareness about the benefits of using technology over live animals in entertainment can foster public support. An example of this is Disney's "The Lion King" (2019), which used advanced CGI technology to create lifelike animal characters, demonstrating the potential of innovative technologies to replace live animals in entertainment.
- *Educational campaigns*. Support public education campaigns to raise awareness about the benefits of using technology over live animals in entertainment.

In addition to the above proposals, it is key that governments work with international organizations to develop and implement global standards for the treatment of animals in entertainment. This includes revising existing treaties and agreements to include provisions for the protection of animals used in entertainment, and facilitating international cooperation to share best practices and technologies for humane alternatives to animal-based entertainment. For example, the Convention on International Trade in Endangered Species of Wild Fauna and Flora (CITES) regulates the trade of endangered species, including those used in entertainment, to ensure their protection and conservation.

Conclusions

Today, consumers have more choices than ever before regarding the type of entertainment they prefer, enabling them to make informed decisions. Every ticket purchased for venues where animals suffer provides an economic incentive for their breeding and extraction from the wild. This chapter highlighted the urgent need for standardized regulations, improved monitoring, and stricter oversight in this area, especially given the growing public opposition to certain uses of animals and the ethical concerns they raise.

For entertainment venues that also serve educational or conservation purposes, and where the discontinuation of such activities is unlikely, greater attention must be given to animal welfare. This includes enhancing standards for housing, nutrition, health care, and mental well being, as well as implementing educational and scientific initiatives and participating in wildlife conservation programs, including those conducted in natural habitats.

The entertainment sector is also witnessing a clear demand for services based on modern technology. The example of a circus discussed here demonstrates that technological advancements, such as virtual reality and animatronics, can effectively replace the exploitation of animals in performances. These innovations not only offer ethical alternatives but also enhance the entertainment experience for audiences. Furthermore, the arts and entertainment industry is experiencing increased interest and debate surrounding environmental sustainability. This sector is uniquely positioned to play a key role in raising awareness of environmental issues, promoting conservation efforts, and fostering a more compassionate and responsible approach to entertainment. By leveraging technology and adopting humane practices, the industry can contribute to the well-being of both animals and the planet.

To improve the welfare of animals in entertainment, several policy proposals were suggested, including financial incentives for transitioning to sanctuary models, taxation and regulation of animal use, and the promotion of innovative technologies as alternatives. These policy proposals aim to ensure the humane treatment of animals while maintaining the economic viability of the entertainment sector.

References

Animal Defenders International (n.d.) Restricting the use of wild animals in circuses: the economics. Congress is urged to protect wild animals. Los Angeles, Animal Defenders International. https://www.federalcircusbill.org/wp-content/uploads/2013/12/6-Congress-Brief-Economic_April-2014.pdf. Accessed 21 Feb 2025

Animal Protection New Mexico (n.d.) APNM position statement: Animals in film. https://apnm.org/wp-content/uploads/2023/03/APNM-Position-Statement-Animals-In-Film.pdf. Accessed 21 Feb 2025

Association of Zoos and Aquariums (n.d.) Zoo and aquarium statistics. Available at: https://www.aza.org/zoo-and-aquarium-statistics. Accessed 21 Feb 2025

Benko M, Náhlik A, Tomljanović K (2020) Hunters in Europe: What does it mean “the hunters population” in Europe?, Sustainable Forestry: Collection 2020, issues 81–82:159–174. https://doi.org/10.5937/SustFor2081159B

Catibog-Sinha C (2011) Zoo tourism and the conservation of threatened species: A collaborative programme in the Philippines. In: Frost W (ed) Zoos and tourism: conservation, education, entertainment? Channel View Publications, Bristol, Buffalo, Toronto, pp 9–12

Cavalcanti R, Mohandas L, Oliveira H (2022) What is entertainment? Propositions of definitions based on product, experience, culture and communication perspectives. Desenvolve Revista De Gestão Do Unilasalle 11(1):1–18. https://doi.org/10.18316/desenv.v11i1.9465

China Cetacean Alliance (n.d.) Ocean theme parks: A look inside China’s growing captive cetacean industry. Beijing.

Cincinnati Zoo (2023) #1-ranked Cincinnati Zoo boosts local economy and generates millions in tax revenue, 5 June. https://cincinnatizoo.org/1-ranked-cincinnati-zoo-boosts-local-economy-and-generates-millions-in-tax-revenue/. Accessed 21st Feb 2025

Cinematograph Films (Animals) Act 1937, 1937 CHAPTER 59, 1 Edw 8 and 1 Geo 6. https://www.legislation.gov.uk/ukpga/Edw8and1Geo6/1/59. Accessed 21st Feb 2025

Collis C (2017) What is entertainment? The value of industry definitions. In: Harrington S (ed) Entertainment values. Palgrave Macmillan, London. https://doi.org/10.1057/978-1-137-47290-8_2

Davey G (2007) An analysis of country, socio-economic and time factors on worldwide zoo attendance during a 40 year period. International Zoo Yearbook 41:217–225. https://doi.org/10.1111/j.1748-1090.2007.00007.x

De Damborenea Martín P, Bermejo-Poza R, De la Fuente Vázquez J (2023) Animal protection in filming in the context of Spain. Animals 13:1144. https://doi.org/10.3390/ani13071144

Disney (n.d.) Disney’s use of live animals in entertainment policy. https://impact.disney.com/app/uploads/2022/01/Disneys-Use-of-Live-Animals-in-Entertainment-Policy.pdf. Accessed 21 Feb 2025

Escribano N et al (2021) Global trends in research output by zoos and aquariums. Conserv Biol 35:1894–1902. https://doi.org/10.1111/cobi.13757

European Circus Association (n.d.) About ECA. https://www.europeancircus.eu/history/. Accessed 21 Feb 2025

European Commission, Directorate-General for Education, Youth, Sport and Culture; Vroonhof P, Clarke M, Goes M, Snijders J (2020) The situation of circus in the EU Member States – Study report. Luxembourg: Publications Office. https://data.europa.eu/doi/https://doi.org/10.2766/540507. Accessed 21 Feb 2025

Fa JE, Gusset M, Flesness N, Conde DA (2014) Zoos have yet to unveil their full conservation potential. Anim Conserv 17:97–100

Federal Circus Bill (n.d.) Worldwide summary. https://www.federalcircusbill.org/briefings/worldwide-summary/. Accessed 21 Feb 2025

Finn SM (n.d.) Farmed animals on film: a manifesto for a new ethic. The Palgrave Macmillan Animal Ethics Series [eBook]. https://doi.org/10.1007/978-3-031-23832-1

Hitchens PL et al (2021) The welfare of animals in Australian filmed media. Animals 11(7). https://doi.org/10.3390/ani11071986

Hutchins M, Marra PP, Diebold ED, Kreger MD, Sheppard C, Hallager S, Lynch C (2018) The evolving role of zoological parks and aquariums in migratory bird conservation. Zoo Biol 37:360–368

International Labour Office (2023a) The future of work in the arts and entertainment sector—report for the technical meeting on the future of work in the arts and entertainment sector (Geneva, 13–17 February 2023). International Labour Office, Sectoral Policies Department, Geneva, p 9

International Labour Office (2023b) The future of work in the arts and entertainment sector—report for the technical meeting on the future of work in the arts and entertainment sector (Geneva, 13–17 February 2023). International Labour Office, Sectoral Policies Department, Geneva, p 12

Kapera I, Kapera A (2020) Hunting tourism in Poland—an outline of the problem. Geography and Tourism 2(8):7–14

Kapera I, Kapera A (2021) Tourism, leisure and zoos—an outline of the problem on the example of Poland. Geography and Tourism 2(9):7–16

Kapera I, Kapera A (2022) Use of animals in entertainment—an outline of the problem. Geography and Tourism 10(1):17–24. https://doi.org/10.34767/GAT.2022.10.02

Linke S, Winterin C (2011) Conservation, education or entertainment: what really matters to zoo visitors? In: Frost W (ed) Zoos and tourism: conservation, education, entertainment? Channel View Publications, Bristol, Buffalo, Toronto, pp 69–81

Malamud R (2012) 'Film animals'. In: An introduction to animals and visual culture. The Palgrave Macmillan Animal Ethics Series. Palgrave Macmillan, London. https://doi.org/10.1057/9781137009845_4

Malamud R, Stoddart H (2000) Rings of desire: Circus history and representation. Manchester University Press, Manchester

Martinez A, Campera M, Nekaris K (2022) The use of live action, animation, and computer-generated imagery in the depiction of non-human primates in film. Animals 12:1576. https://doi.org/10.3390/ani12121576

McKee A, Collis C, Nitins T, Ryan M, Harrington S, Duncan B, Carter J et al (2014) Defining entertainment: an approach. Creat Ind J 7(2):108–120. https://doi.org/10.1080/17510694.2014.962932

Mota-Rojas D, Ghezzi MD, Domínguez-Oliva A, de la Vega LT, Boscato-Funes L, Torres-Bernal F, Mora-Medina P (2022) Circus animal welfare: analysis through a five-domain approach. Anim Behav Biometeorol 10(3):2221. https://doi.org/10.31893/jabb.22021J

Muhammad AS, Lawan I, Ibrahim S (2022) Local community perception on the impact of a zoological garden in Kano State, Nigeria. Gombe J Gen Stud 6(1):145–156

PwC (2024) Perspectives from the Global Entertainment & Media Outlook 2024–2028: Seizing growth opportunities in a dynamic ecosystem. https://www.pwc.com/gx/en/issues/business-model-reinvention/outlook/insights-and-perspectives.html. Accessed 21 Feb 2025

PZŁ (n.d.) PZŁ's position on the proposal of the ministry of climate and environment to regulate the construction of hunting towers in the provisions of the construction law act. [in Polish]. https://www.pzlow.pl/stanowisko-pzl-dotyczace-propozycji-ministerstwa-klimatu-i-srodowiska-uregulowania-budowy-ambon-mysliwskich-w-przepisach-ustawy-prawo-budowlane/. Accessed 21 Feb 2025

Rose PE, Riley LM (2022) Expanding the role of the future zoo: Wellbeing should become the fifth aim for modern zoos. Front Psychol 13. https://doi.org/10.3389/fpsyg.2022.1018722

RSPCA (n.d.) Guidelines for the welfare of performing animals. https://www.rspca.org.uk/webContent/staticImages/Performing/GuidelinesForWelfare.pdf. Accessed 21 Feb 2025

Sánchez-Rivero M, Royuela V, Franco Solís A (2020) Residents' perception and economic impact of bullfighting: the case of Feria del Toro (Olivenza, Spain). Curr Issue Tour 24(21):3057–3071. https://doi.org/10.1080/13683500.2020.1860917

Sayre S, King C (2010) Entertainment and society: influences, impacts, and innovations, 2nd edn. Routledge, New York and London

Silk M, Correia R, Veríssimo D, Verma A, Crowley SL (2021) The implications of digital visual media for human–nature relationships. People and Nature 3:1130–1137. https://doi.org/10.1002/pan3.10284

Themed Entertainment Association (2022) Theme index and museum index: the global attractions attendance report. https://aecom.com/wp-content/uploads/documents/reports/AECOM-Theme-Index-2022.pdf. Accessed 21 Feb 2025

Traylor-Holzer K, Leus K, Bauman K (2019) Integrated Collection Assessment and Planning (ICAP) workshop: helping zoos move toward the one plan approach. Zoo Biol 38:95–105

U.S. Department of the Interior, U.S. Fish and Wildlife Service (2022) National survey of fishing, hunting, and wildlife-associated recreation. https://www.fws.gov/sites/default/files/documents/Final_2022-National-Survey_101223-accessible-single-page.pdf. Accessed 21 Feb 2025

Vogel HL (2020) Entertainment industry economics: a guide for financial analysis. Cambridge University Press, Cambridge

WAP (n.d.) Behind the smile: The multi-billion dollar dolphin entertainment industry. https://www.worldanimalprotection.org.cn/contentassets/a3354bd4d557414a81970d4db1dd51c8/behind_the_smile-dolphins_in_entertainment_report-a4.pdf. Accessed 21 Feb 2025

Whale and Dolphin Conservation (n.d.) EU Zoo Inquiry Delfinaria: Ein Bericht über die Gefangenschaftshaltung von Walen und Delfinen in der Europäischen Union mit besonderer Berücksichtigung der EU-Richtlinie 1999/22/EG des Rates über die Haltung von Wildtieren in Zoos. In Zusammenarbeit mit Born Free Foundation, ENDCAP and Dolphinaria-Free Europe

Whale and Dolphin Conservation (n.d.) EU Zoo Inquiry Delfinaria: Ein Bericht über die Gefangenschaftshaltung von Walen und Delfinen in der Europäischen Union mit besonderer Berücksichtigung der EU-Richtlinie 1999/22/EG des Rates über die Haltung von Wildtieren in Zoos.

Whitham JC, Wielebnowski N (2013) New directions for zoo animal welfare science. Appl Anim Behav Sci 147(3–4):247–260. https://doi.org/10.1016/j.applanim.2013.02.004

Wilkins DB (1981) Animals in film and television. Int J Study Anim Prob 2(6):284–287

World Population Review (2026) Zoos by country 2026. https://worldpopulationreview.com/country-rankings/zoos-by-country. Accessed 14 Feb 2026

Zanola R (2007) Major influences on circus attendance. POLIS Working Papers, 89, Institute of Public Policy and Public Choice – POLIS

Zavitz T, Kielbiski C (2021) Animal oppression and solidarity: Examining representations of animals and their allies in twenty-first century media. Netw Knowl: J MeCCSA Postgrad Netw 14(2):95–109. https://doi.org/10.31165/nk.2021.142.643

Zoo Berlin (n.d.) The big headcount: Berlin's zoological facilities record a total of 26,684 animals and 5.6 million visitors. https://www.zoo-berlin.de/en/news/zoo-news/detail/the-big-headcount.Accessed 21 Feb 2025

Chapter 16
Animals for Assistance to Humans

Anna-Mari Rimppi, Henna Syrjälä, Nancy V. Wünderlich, and Julia Rötzmeier-Keuper

> "Service animals are the unsung heroes who make the impossible possible, turning disabilities into abilities."
> – *Sarah Johnson*

Abstract Animals are integral to service ecosystems, aiding in health care, accessibility, social engagement, and leisure. Despite their significant roles, the specific value outcomes of animal-based services—economic, psychological, societal, and environmental—are under-examined. This chapter investigates therapeutic, personal assistance, social engagement, and recreational services, categorizing them by purpose (health care vs. entertainment) and caretaking arrangements (service provider vs. individual consumer). It highlights the need for stronger policies and self-regulatory business practices to ensure fair treatment of service animals, as current protections are limited. Given their economic contributions, animals should be safeguarded through regulations on training, certification, and welfare, including humane handling and stress monitoring. Legal inconsistencies complicate protections for working animals, who, unlike human workers, do not receive direct compensation, raising welfare concerns. Policymakers could mandate financial provisions for animals' health care and retirement. Ethical reflection on animal agency and consent is crucial, as service roles may involve non-voluntary participation. Promoting humane training and transparent welfare protocols can enhance trust in animal-based services and encourage responsible practices.

A.-M. Rimppi (✉) · H. Syrjälä
School of Marketing and Communication, Marketing, University of Vaasa, Vaasa, Finland
e-mail: anna-mari.rimppi@uwasa.fi

H. Syrjälä
e-mail: henna.syrjala@uwasa.fi

N. V. Wünderlich · J. Rötzmeier-Keuper
Digital Markets Research Group, Faculty of Economics and Management, Technische Universität Berlin, Berlin, Germany
e-mail: wuenderlich@tu-berlin.de

J. Rötzmeier-Keuper
e-mail: roetzmeier-keuper@tu-berlin.de

N. Batini (ed.), *The Economics of Non-Human Animals*, Natural Resource Management and Policy 63, https://doi.org/10.1007/978-3-032-17580-9_16

From Assistance to Industry: The Growing Impact of Animal-Based Services

Whether comforting a patient, guiding a person through a crowd, or drawing tourists into snowy landscapes, animals are at work in today's service economy often without recognition, rights, or rest. The role of animals in assisting humans in different services has received attention in various disciplines, ranging from organizational studies (e.g., Huopalainen 2022; Mitchell 2024) and sociology (e.g., Bell 2015) to business (Tallberg et al. 2022), tourism (e.g., Fennell 2024; Mkono and Hughes 2024), and marketing research (Wünderlich et al. 2021). In this chapter, we use the term animal-based services for structured activities where animals are intentionally integrated into service processes to support or enhance customer experiences.[1] These services typically involve human–animal interactions aimed at promoting outcomes such as well-being (Lin et al. 2024), accessibility (Duncan 2000), and leisure (Lee et al. 2024).

Previous studies have highlighted the emotional and relational roles that animals play in shaping consumer service experiences and enhancing perceived value (Rötzmeier-Keuper et al. 2018). The value that animals generate in assisting humans spans many categories, ranging from economic value (i.e., cost-effectiveness, time savings, or service efficiency), psychological value (i.e., the strengthening of psychological and emotional well-being), societal value (i.e., impacts on inclusion, or collective benefit), and environmental value (i.e., ecological sustainability or naturalness of the human–animal encounters). Although a variety of value outcomes for humans are recognized in extant animal-based service research, a systematic analysis and categorization of values is lacking. This study addresses this gap by focusing on the value created in animal-based services for health care (e.g., assistance dogs, therapy animals) and entertainment (e.g., petfluencers, zoos) to capture the diversity of animal-based services. Health and entertainment purposes also represent two domains with high commercial impact. Moreover, the distinct categories of value created through human–animal interactions in these contexts can be further differentiated based on the caretaking arrangements, whether the animal's primary caretaker is the service provider or the individual consumer.

Drawing on a structured literature review, this study examines the specific value categories that emerge through human–animal interactions in four distinct animal-based service contexts—therapeutic services, personal assistance services, social engagement services, and recreational services:

[1] We utilize the term animal-based services to capture a broader range of activities compared to those defined by Animal Assisted Services International (AASI), where services are facilitated by a human service provider working with a specially qualified animal to deliver therapeutic, educational, or supportive interventions (Johnson Binder et al. 2024). The term animal based is established in fields such as tourism (Fennell 2024) and animal welfare assessments (Stygar et al. 2022), supporting its broader applicability beyond therapeutic or clinical settings.

(a) How can animal-based service types be classified based on the intended purpose (health care vs. entertainment) and the animal's caretaking arrangements (service provider vs. individual consumer)?
(b) How do value categories manifest across the identified animal-based service types?

Since existing literature has primarily focused on the value animals provide to humans—while largely overlooking the value, or lack thereof, experienced by the animals themselves—this study adopts a post-anthropocentric perspective (Askegaard et al. 2024) to critically examine the managerial and policy implications of the proposed classification, with particular attention to animal ethics and well-being. This includes acknowledging animals as more than passive tools, recognizing their potential role in shaping service experiences and raising ethical questions about their agency, consent, and welfare (Irvine 2008; Wünderlich et al. 2021).

By focusing on the value outcomes of human–animal interactions in service contexts, this chapter contributes to ongoing debates about the role of non-human actors in animal-based services, ethical consumerism, and the boundaries of value creation in multispecies settings. Understanding these dynamics is relevant for policymakers, service providers, and researchers interested in ethical service design, animal welfare, and consumer experience. Our analysis highlights how different service contexts shape human–animal relationships and calls for continued reflection on the ethical and practical implications of including animals in service ecosystems.

Categorizing Human–Animal Service Interactions

We propose a classification of animal-based services (Fig. 16.1), structured along two dimensions. The vertical axis shows the intended purpose of the service, being either health-related service, where animals support physical or mental well-being, or entertainment-related service, where animals primarily enhance leisure experiences. The horizontal axis reflects the caretaking arrangement; when the service provider is responsible for the animal's welfare, human–animal interactions are typically structured and intermittent, whereas when the consumer is the main caretaker the relationship is more continuous and intimate, as it is not mediated by a third party.

In the upper-left quadrant, we place *therapeutic services*, for example therapy animals assisting in psychological and physical rehabilitation (Quan et al. 2024). In the lower-left quadrant, we place *recreational services,* such as animal cafés, elephant rides, swimming with dolphins, and professional animal performances in tourism or leisure industries (Curtin and Wilkes 2007). In the upper-right quadrant, we place *personal assistance service*s, for example emotional support animals and privately owned assistance dogs. In the lower-right quadrant, we place *social engagement services* such as social media influencer pets, and animals used for personal branding or digital content creation (Wei et al. 2025). In the following, we elaborate on these

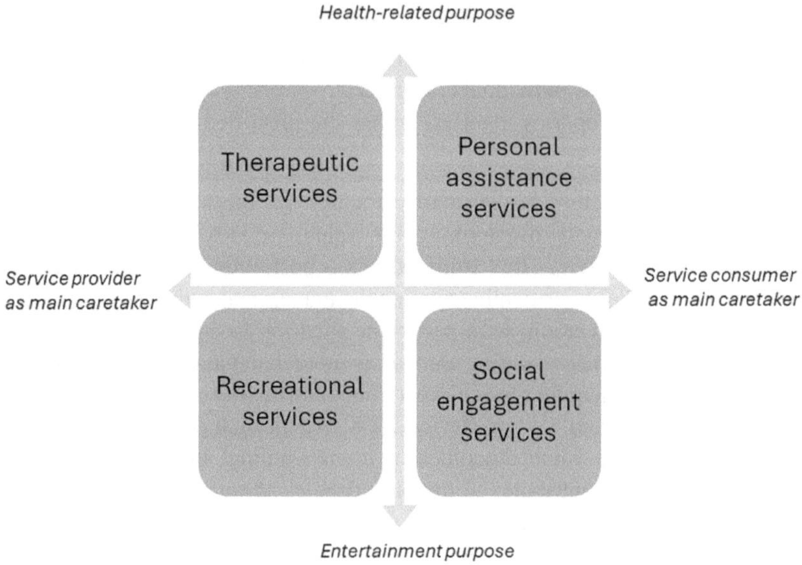

Fig. 16.1 Classification of animal-based services

different types of animal-based services and examine the value categories that animals generate within each type.

1. Therapeutic services

Therapeutic services are positioned in the matrix with the health-related purpose of having the service provider as the main caretaker of the animal. This service type emphasizes emotional and physical support, provider delivering service through structured therapy or informal well-being practices for example in mental health care (Quan et al. 2024), tourism (Lin and Li 2024), and yoga (Berbel and Praetorius 2024). Therapeutic services are primarily associated with psychological and societal value, though they also generate economic and environmental value.

Therapeutic services produce significant *economic value* by improving care efficiency and reducing treatment costs by increasing service engagement, trust, and satisfaction (Quan et al. 2024). Animal-based wellness tourism has been described as more cost-effective than traditional therapy, especially with regard to client satisfaction and accessibility (Lin and Li 2024). These economic benefits emerge alongside improvements in service quality, as animals often help therapists assess client responses more accurately and adapt interventions accordingly (Policay and Falconier 2019).

Animals create strong *psychological value* (Berbel and Praetorius 2024; Lin and Li 2024; Quan et al. 2024), as, for example, they help alleviate distress, reduce anxiety, and improve emotional regulation in individuals with depression or PTSD, adolescents in therapy, and elderly people (Berbel and Praetorius 2024; Mitchell 2024). These improvements have been linked to both physiological responses, such as reduced cortisol and increased oxytocin (Polheber and Matchock 2014), and more subjective experiences of comfort, safety, and joy (Lin and Li 2024). The mere presence of animals can foster a sense of calm and strengthen emotional resilience (Lin et al. 2024). Animals strengthen therapeutic human–human interactions and help individuals feel seen and connected (Quan et al. 2024; Lin et al. 2024). These effects are meaningful in group-based settings, such as goat yoga or equine-assisted therapy, where animals serve as bridges between people and enhance participants' willingness to engage (Berbel and Praetorius 2024). For individuals who feel alienated by traditional wellness environments or who struggle with communication and social skills, animals provide a non-judgmental presence that opens space for connection. Therapy animals have been shown to increase engagement and retention in mental health programs, especially for those who might otherwise drop out or resist care (Berbel and Praetorius 2024).

Therapeutic services also promote *societal value* by expanding access and inclusion to wellness and mental health support for individuals who may feel excluded or intimidated by conventional care environments (Berbel and Praetorius 2024). For example, for people who may not respond well to pharmacological treatments or who are excluded from traditional healthcare settings due to disability, trauma, or social stigma (Quan et al. 2024; Lin and Li 2024). In tourism, animal-based wellness offerings can be more affordable and less stigmatizing than formal psychiatric care, broadening access to emotional support (Lin and Li 2024).

Although less emphasized in the literature, *environmental value* is emerging in therapeutic services through increasing attention to animal welfare, ethical responsibility, and ecological sustainability. Increasingly, animals are framed not just as tools or passive resources, but as sentient partners whose welfare and agency matter (Quan et al. 2024). This recognition fosters a shift in how services are designed supporting more sustainable and ethically grounded care systems where animals are understood as sentient participants whose emotional and physical well-being is integral to the care process (Danby and Grajfoner 2022).

2. Personal assistance services

Personal assistance services are positioned in the matrix as services with a health-related purpose where the service consumer is also the caretaker. From crossing busy streets to easing anxiety in crowded spaces, animals working in personal assistance services are more than helpers; they are enablers of everyday freedom for the person they serve. These animals, mainly dogs, aid people with physical impairments (e.g., mobility or vision loss), psychiatric disorders (e.g., PTSD), and neurological conditions (e.g., epilepsy or autism) (Duncan 2000; Appleby et al. 2022; Singleton 2023). The dominant value outcomes associated with this service type are economic, psychological, and societal, whereas environmental value is notably absent in existing research.

Personal assistance services generate significant *economic value* by reducing long-term care needs and costs by enabling greater independence and workforce participation for individuals with disabilities (Quan et al. 2024). Lundqvist et al. (2019) demonstrated that for someone with a functional impairment, having a trained service dog can save thousands of dollars compared to having an ordinary pet dog. Beyond general cost-effectiveness there are additional ways service animals reduce expenses; handlers can cut down on medication and personal caregiver hours after getting a service animal (Singleton 2023).

While an animal might perform a task like a piece of medical equipment would, its mere presence also provides comfort and companionship in a way no gadget can (Nieforth et al. 2023), creating *psychological value*. They enhance emotional well-being, foster autonomy, enhance mobility, and boost confidence across daily life for both adults and children (Duncan 2000; Appleby et al. 2022; Lin et al. 2024). Their presence is linked to greater quality of life, reduced stress, and increased participation in social spaces. For example, guide dogs and autism assistance dogs have been shown to increase safety, ease family mobility, and improve emotional regulation, helping users feel more secure and empowered in unfamiliar environments (Lin et al. 2024; Appleby et al. 2022). The presence of animals fosters companionship and emotional resilience, reinforcing users' sense of belonging and reducing isolation (Duncan 2000), for example, strangers might initiate friendly conversation about the animal, thereby increasing the handler's social interactions and sense of acceptance in public (Nieforth et al. 2023).

Service animals offer *societal value* by increasing how assistance animals enable inclusion, dignity, and participation in community life (Duncan 2000; Quan et al. 2024). Policies such as Title III of the Americans with Disabilities Act (ADA) mandate that individuals with disabilities must be allowed to bring their service animals into public spaces, including restaurants, transportation, schools, and health-care facilities. This legal protection reflects how animals contribute to building more equitable and accessible societies (Duncan 2000). Alongside facilitating inclusiveness, assistance animals help normalize disability in workplaces and public settings by promoting independence and fostering positive interactions with others (Quan et al. 2024). In this context, animals are not only service providers but also participants in advancing social justice and community engagement.

3. Social engagement services

Social engagement services are positioned in the matrix as services with entertainment-oriented purposes where the service consumer is responsible for the animal's well-being. The rise of pet influencers—"petfluencers"—on social media illustrates how animals serve as social engagement service workers by generating mainly economic, psychological, and societal value, while environmental value is largely missing.

For their human caretakers, animal influencers generate substantial *economic value*, having been successfully commercialized as key players in the digital economy (Ngai 2023; Wei et al. 2025). These petfluencers, such as Grumpy Cat, Nala Cat, or Jiffpom pomeranian, often outperform human influencers in visibility, engagement, and audience trust, making them highly sought-after partners for brand collaborations (Ngai 2023; Wei et al. 2025; Di Cioccio et al. 2024; Lavertu et al. 2025). Petfluencers generate more consumer engagement and lead to higher purchase intentions than their human counterparts, largely because they are perceived as more authentic and credible (Di Cioccio et al. 2024). Petfluencers often charge lower fees, pose less reputational risk, and deliver equal or greater marketing value (Lavertu et al. 2025), and owners may treat this as a business venture, with some even quitting traditional jobs to focus full-time on managing their pet's brand (Lavertu et al. 2025). In tourism sector, petfluencers are increasingly used in marketing campaigns to enhance brand image, attract emotionally engaged consumers, and drive purchase behavior (Wei et al. 2025), for example, a single post by a petfluencer can significantly sway booking intentions and destination preferences (Zhang et al. 2023).

Beyond dollars and cents, animal influencers provide significant *psychological value* as people around the world follow pet accounts for wholesome entertainment, emotional connection, and a sense of shared community. For many owners, creating content with and for their animal influencer improves their own emotional well-being through creative expression, routine, and connection. Especially during emotionally taxing periods (e.g., lockdowns), posting about their pets helped owners cope with stress and gave them a feeling of productivity (Yoo et al. 2024).

Animals in social engagement services also contribute to *societal value* by shaping cultural narratives, public understanding, and ethical debates regarding animals. Animals act as cultural intermediaries, promoting empathy, knowledge sharing, and interspecies identity construction (Ngai 2023; Wei et al. 2025). For example, pet accounts serve as platforms for spreading awareness about animal-related products and care practices (Wei et al. 2025). These animals often appeal across cultural and demographic boundaries, making them widely relatable and appreciated in diverse online communities (Lavertu et al. 2025). At the same time, these representations are embedded in gendered, aesthetic, and commercial discourses that shape public attitudes toward animals (Linné 2016). Visual portrayals of farm animals as cheerful, feminine, or nostalgic reinforce idealized narratives that may obscure real welfare concerns highlighting how societal value also emerges through critique and ethical reflection (Linné 2016).

Environmental value is largely absent in social engagement services. While animals such as companion dogs in political or symbolic settings can enhance public empathy (Mitchell 2024), these emotionally resonant roles also raise questions about the sustainability and ethics of involving animals in human-centered services (Linné 2016). The commercialization of animal personas for entertainment purposes may even contribute to unsustainable consumer practices, further distancing social engagement services from broader environmental goals.

4. Recreational services

Recreational services are positioned in the matrix as services with an entertainment-oriented purpose where the service provider is the main caretaker of the animal. These services include a wide variety of activities, from wildlife shows to animal cafés and sled dog tours, where animals play a central role in shaping consumer experiences (Fennell 2024; Lee et al. 2024; Tallberg et al. 2022). All types of value are present in this type of services, while economic and psychological are dominant.

The growing demand for animal-based recreational services has significantly contributed to the *economic value* of tourism and leisure industries, where animals are utilized to maximize financial gains, justify cultural practices, and support profitable business models (Fennell 2024; Lee et al. 2024; Tallberg et al. 2022). As highlighted in Chapter 14 Animals in entertainment and 17 Animals and Tourism of this volume, these services are part of a broader entertainment economy that relies on emotional engagement and experiential value, while also raising concerns about the commodification of animals and the normalization of exploitative practices. These services often operate within an economic logic where animals are positioned as revenue-generating assets whose care, appearance, and performance are optimized for profitability (Tallberg et al. 2022). In husky tourism, the entire lifecycle of the animal from puppyhood to labor is managed to maximize economic returns, with puppies used as tourist attractions and emotional laborers in photo moments (Tallberg et al. 2022). Similarly, animal welfare practices are frequently articulated through economic benefits, where care is justified for enhancing animal performance, ensuring customer satisfaction, and securing long-term business viability, rather than for the intrinsic rights of animals (Tallberg et al. 2022). Sled dogs, pandas, and zoo animals are framed as flagship attractions that sustain revenue streams and institutional legitimacy (Fennell 2022; Guo and Fennell 2024). For example, the celebrity status of pandas transforms their affective appeal into economic value through branding, ticket sales, and public engagement (Guo and Fennell 2024).

Recreational services also generate significant *psychological value* by offering emotional support, human–animal bonding, moments of joy, companionship, and inclusion, particularly for those experiencing urban stress or social isolation (Wünderlich et al. 2021). Animal cafés and zoos have been described as spaces that promote psychological healing, relaxation, offering emotional comfort and helping people feel valued and connected (Lin and Li 2024). These interactions can offer a sense of unconditional acceptance, reduce feelings of loneliness, and reinforce a person's sense of self-worth and belonging (Lin and Li 2024). Participatory activities, such as sled dog tours or elephant-based travel, may also foster self-growth, learning, and accomplishment (Lin and Li 2024).

Recreational services also contribute to *societal value* by shaping cultural attitudes, supporting local communities, and influencing public discourse around animals. Animal-based attractions often serve as economic anchors for rural or culturally significant communities, generating employment and preserving cultural practices (Lee et al. 2024; Guo and Fennell 2024). In this way, animal-based recreational services act as sites of cultural negotiation, ethical reflection, and community development.

Although less emphasized than other value types, recreational services claim to deliver *environmental value* through conservation education, species protection, and habitat awareness. Immersive nature-based activities, such as sled dog tours or elephant encounters, can foster emotional connections to animals and landscapes, enhancing ecological appreciation (Lee et al. 2024). Yet, these experiences also risk normalizing exploitative practices when animals are treated as interactive tools rather than autonomous beings (Meng et al. 2024). Similarly, zoos and aquariums present animals as ambassadors for their species in enclosures that mimic natural settings to promote awareness and empathy (Mkono and Hughes 2024). However, these strategies may obscure the ethical complexities of captivity and offer only limited environmental value (Bell 2015). Despite these tensions, some recreational services do contribute to environmental goals. Charismatic animals such as pandas attract conservation funds and help conserve larger ecosystems (Guo and Fennell 2024), and public pressure has pushed festivals and wildlife attractions to adopt more ethical and sustainable methods (Joo et al. 2023). Thus, while some recreational services make meaningful contributions to biodiversity and ecological awareness, others risk reducing environmental value to a symbolic gesture serving entertainment or branding needs (Bell 2015).

Value Creation in Animal-Based Services: Key Considerations

The literature review of animal-based services shows that animals contribute to value creation across all service types as economic, psychological, and societal value are at least indirectly created, with different categories of value often created simultaneously. However, there are notable differences in the relative emphasis placed on different values across the service types.

While social engagement services, such as petfluencers' social media channels, primarily generate economic value, therapeutic services, by contrast, contribute more substantially to psychological value. Economic values range from cost savings to increased efficiency, typically benefitting the service provider or professional caretaker of the animal, while psychological value varies depending on the individual experiencing it. In therapeutic and recreational services, animals are integrated in the service process to benefit service customers, who experience a range of psychological values, including the alleviation of distress, reduced anxiety, and improved emotional regulation, human–animal bonding, and joy. Interestingly, observing petfluencer channels can also evoke similar psychological responses in their followers. Personal assistance services don't involve external individuals as the human caretaker, often a person with a disability, is the beneficiary of the animal's support. The psychological value generated through the animal's companionship and assistance, once trained by professional handlers, is highly individualized and context specific.

Across all service types we can observe that the strong psychological value also contributes—mostly indirectly—to broader societal value by promoting inclusion, dignity, and participation in community life. Additionally, these services may generate broader economic value by supporting a healthier population and reducing the burden on healthcare systems. Interestingly, the connection between animal-based services and *environmental value* is largely absent in existing research. Only therapeutic and recreational services are associated with the creation of environmental value. Within therapeutic services, human caretakers of animals are increasingly engaging with the welfare and agency of their "co-workers." Recreational services are related to environmental value, particularly through their efforts to promote conservation education, species protection, and habitat awareness. This growing attention to the living conditions of animals may also contribute to broader goals of ecological sustainability, as service providers may be more inclined to adopt inclusive and responsible practices that align with ecological well-being (Quan et al. 2024). It is noteworthy that social engagement services, through social media, have the potential to generate multiplier effects in raising awareness of environmental and societal issues related to animals. However, this potential remains largely under-utilized as petfluencers are often instrumentalized primarily for the economic benefit of their human caretakers.

Our analysis shows vividly that previous research has extensively documented how animal-based services create value for humans—benefiting service providers, customers, and society at large, but has overlooked the question of what value, if any, is generated for the animals themselves. This stands in sharp contrast to the reality that so many people extract considerable value from the unpaid labor of animals, often under conditions that fail to meet species-appropriate working conditions. It appears that many practices had an anthropomorphic bias that overlooked animals' interests, although animal-based services would require strong ethical standards to protect animal partners. Aligned with post-anthropocentric lenses (Askegaard et al. 2024), we argue that it is necessary to recognize animals as sentient beings rather than mere service tools. This recognition entails acknowledging their critical role in creating service value and shaping service experiences, while also raising important ethical questions regarding their agency, consent, and welfare (Irvine 2008; Wünderlich et al. 2021). Protecting animal welfare is not only an ethical responsibility but also a prerequisite for maintaining reliable and effective service quality.

Shaping Public Policy for Responsible Animal-Based Services

Our literature review on animal-based services demonstrates the significant role of animals in value creation not only on individual levels, but on the societal level, too. Therefore, we derive a reverse responsibility on the part of policymakers for the responsible treatment of animals in service ecosystems. While there is a broad societal consensus on ensuring fair working conditions for human laborers, comparable ethical considerations for animals remain underdeveloped. Precisely because animals constitute a valuable resource in generating economic value for service providers, they should be protected against exploitation. Thus, we call on public policymakers to establish robust regulations that balance human benefits with animal welfare.

Policymakers should establish clear standards for training, certification, and oversight of animal-based services. Several commercial contexts (e.g., petting zoos, animal cafés) continue to involve constrained spaces and compelled interactions that may conflict with species-specific behaviors and compromise animal welfare (Mkono and Hughes 2024). Therefore, animals' daily needs and dignity ought to be prioritized by watching regularly for signs of stress or fatigue and removing animals from situations that compromise their welfare. To make this happen, welfare safeguards should be required to be installed into operations (limit working hours, provide rest and enrichment, and use humane handling and training methods). These guidelines could be based on widely accepted welfare principles, such as the Five Freedoms (Wünderlich et al. 2021). In this way, regulations would enact comprehensive animal-based service standards to uphold animal welfare (e.g., minimum care standards, therapy animal program accreditation) while enabling responsible service delivery. As an example, some industry guidelines (e.g., veterinary associations) currently recommend assigning a "Responsible Person" to each program and involving veterinarians to monitor animal health and behavior. Such measures help institutionalize the best practices across animal-based service contexts.

Furthermore, greater coordination between human and animal-based service policies, such as therapy, tourism, entertainment, and assistance animals, may be beneficial, given the diversity of legal standards that exist across countries, service types, and species. For example, while guide dogs undergo extensive training and legal protections, emotional support animals in many countries lack standardized training (Hoy-Gerlach et al. 2019). Unlike human workers, animals do not receive monetary compensation that directly benefits their own welfare. While some human caretakers may convert the economic value into improved living conditions for the animals, there is no legal obligation to do so outside specific regulatory frameworks (Blattner 2019). Since animals are treated as goods or natural resources (Blattner 2019), animals cannot hold bank accounts or enter into contracts, policymakers could nonetheless require human caretakers to take greater responsibility for animals' welfare. For instance, they could mandate the establishment of designated accounts, contributions to a retirement fund, or enrollment in healthcare plans to ensure long-term care for working animals.

Advancing Research in Animal-Based Services

Our literature review highlights several promising directions for future research into the value of animal-based services. Firstly, our analysis reveals that only a few studies address the environmental value of animal-based services. Future research could focus on dimensions such as animal welfare, ecological impact, and sustainability across four service types. Services with an entertainment purpose, like petfluencers, deserve closer investigation for their potential educational value, such as increasing conservation awareness and audience engagement. The established role of celebrity animals (e.g., pandas) (Guo and Fennell 2024) opens avenues to investigate their symbolic function in shaping public concern for endangered species.

Secondly, given the psychological benefits across all animal-based service types, future studies could explore the potential of these services in addressing mental healthcare shortages. Animal-based tourism, found to promote mental well-being (Lin and Li 2024), might serve as an alternative mental health intervention such as their contribution to psychological resilience, emotional regulation, and stress reduction. While the positive psychological impact of animal-based services is well documented, future research should also explore the boundaries between therapeutic and personal assistance roles.

Thirdly, further exploration at the intersection of economic value and ethics is needed—especially in recreational services, where customer enjoyment may coexist with disregard for animal welfare (Meng et al. 2024). Future studies could examine how expectations, marketing narratives, and cultural backgrounds shape customers' ethical evaluations of animal-based services. Integrating social contract theory (Fennell 2022) and ethical frameworks could provide deeper insight into how consumers assess the moral acceptability of these services. The commodification of animals, particularly in recreational and social engagement services, raises concerns about the exploitation of animal labor (Guo and Fennell 2024). Research should investigate how customers perceive animals as co-creators of economic value, and whether recognizing animal agency and autonomy influences service satisfaction. For instance, in petfluencer marketing, critical analysis is needed regarding acceptable treatment of animals, sponsorship transparency, and perceived authenticity (Wei et al. 2025).

Fourth, societal value is rarely addressed directly in existing research. Future studies could investigate how individual-level values diffuse to collective societal outcomes, particularly in social engagement services. Research should examine how such representations shape or challenge public attitudes toward animal welfare (Linné 2016). Additionally, research could explore how ethical reflection on animal welfare contributes to broader societal value, especially in emerging lifestyle trends like veganism or the "One Health" movement, which promote integrated well-being for humans, animals, and ecosystems (Wünderlich et al. 2021).

Fifth, future research should explore the interactions and tensions between different types of value and between various stakeholders (e.g., providers, customers, animals). Current research remains anthropocentric, and thus, a more balanced understanding of value co-creation requires methodological advancements to better incorporate the animal's perspective (Meng et al. 2024). Furthermore, organizational scholars should investigate how animals' function in the workplaces as co-workers and how human-animal relationships shape organizational structures, leadership, and culture (Huopalainen 2022). This includes exploring employee experiences and identifying the benefits and challenges of integrating animals into services (Kelemen et al. 2020).

Finally, while some literature recognizes the caregiving role of customers, more work is needed to understand how customers function as value co-creators (Hendricks and Schmitz 2021)—especially in settings such as therapy, or tourism. Future research could conceptualize how caregiving behaviors contribute to service effectiveness, customer satisfaction, and animal well-being. It is also important to investigate how customers perceive and respond to service providers' animal welfare practices. A deeper understanding of consumer sensitivity to animal welfare could inform the ethical design and delivery of services.

Conclusions

This chapter has demonstrated that animals play a crucial and multidimensional role across a range of service contexts. Despite their importance, the specific values of animal-based services—whether economic, psychological, societal, or environmental—are not systematically explored.

Drawing on this analysis, delved into the roles of animals in therapeutic, personal assistance, social engagement, and recreational services, categorizing them based on their purpose (health care vs. entertainment) and the nature of their caretaking (service provider vs. individual consumer). It demonstrated the significant role of assistance animals in value creation not only on individual levels but on the societal level, too. Precisely because animals constitute a valuable resource in generating economic value for service providers, they should be protected against exploitation. Thus, the chapter calls on public policymakers to establish robust regulations that balance human benefits with animal welfare. These cover training, certification, and welfare, including humane handling and stress management. However, the inconsistency in legal protections across different service types and regions complicates the safeguarding of working animals, who, unlike human workers, do not receive direct compensation, raising concerns about their long-term welfare. Key recommendations from this analysis involve the provision of funds for the health care and retirement of these animals. Ethical considerations regarding animal agency and consent are crucial, as these roles often involve non-voluntary participation. Promoting humane training methods and transparent welfare protocols could build trust in animal-based services and encourage ethical practices.

Future research on this topic should address several promising directions to further understand the value of animal-based services. More studies are needed to examine the environmental value of animal-based services in terms of sustainability and welfare, investigate their potential to support mental health care, explore ethical tensions between profit and animal well-being in recreational contexts, and analyze how individual experiences shape broader societal attitudes toward animals. Finally, future research should explore the interactions and tensions between different types of value and stakeholders, incorporating the animal's perspective and understanding the role of animals as co-workers in organizational settings. By addressing these research gaps and policy suggestions, we can enhance our understanding of animal-based services and promote responsible practices that ensure the well-being of both animals and humans.

References

Appleby R, Wright S, Williams L, Stanley M (2022) Australian parents' experiences of owning an autism assistance dog. Health Social Care Commun 30(6). https://doi.org/10.1111/hsc.13805

Askegaard S, Bajde D, Arnould E (2024) Post-anthropocentric transformations of consumption in the anthropocene: beyond the nature-culture divide. In: The handbook of organizing economic, ecological and societal transformation, pp 49–67. https://doi.org/10.1515/9783110986945-003

Bell J (2015) There is no wild. Soc Anim 23(5):462–483. https://doi.org/10.1163/15685306-12341377

Berbel T, Praetorius RT (2024) Phenomenological qualitative program evaluation of Goat Yoga: "The best belly laugh." Soc Work Ment Health 22(3):335–355. https://doi.org/10.1080/15332985.2023.2299882

Blattner CE (2019) Beyond the goods/resources dichotomy: animal labor and trade law. J Int Wildlife Law Policy 22(2):63–89. https://doi.org/10.1080/13880292.2019.1658379

Curtin S, Wilkes K (2007) Swimming with captive dolphins: current debates and post-experience dissonance. Int J Tour Res 9(2):131–146. https://doi.org/10.1002/jtr.599

Danby P, Grajfoner D (2022) Human-equine tourism and nature-based solutions: exploring psychological well-being through transformational experiences. J Hosp Tour Res 46(3):607–629. https://doi.org/10.1177/1096348020978555

Di Cioccio M, Pozharliev R, De Angelis M (2024) Pawsitively powerful: why and when pet influencers boost social media effectiveness. Psychol Mark 41(7):1614–1628. https://doi.org/10.1002/mar.22000

Duncan SL (2000) APIC state-of-the-art report: the implications of service animals in health care settings. Am J Infect Control 28(2):170–180. https://doi.org/10.1067/mic.2000.106056

Fennell DA (2022) An animal welfare literacy framework for tourism. Ann Tour Res 96. Scopus. https://doi.org/10.1016/j.annals.2022.103461

Fennell DA (2024) Empathy in animal-based tourism contrasting constructed care and care ethics at a captive wildlife venue. Tour Recreat Res 49(6):1222–1237. https://doi.org/10.1080/02508281.2023.2226038

Guo Y, Fennell D (2024) What makes the giant panda a celebrity? Celebrity Studies 15(4):474–489. https://doi.org/10.1080/19392397.2023.2223731

Hendricks J, Schmitz G (2021) Value co-creation in services for animal companions. J Serv Mark 36(6):831–845. https://doi.org/10.1108/JSM-12-2020-0530

Hoy-Gerlach J, Vincent A, Lory Hector B (2019) Emotional support animals in the united states: emergent guidelines for mental health clinicians. J Psychosoc Rehabil Ment Health 6(2):199–208. https://doi.org/10.1007/s40737-019-00146-8

Huopalainen A (2022) Writing with the bitches. Organization 29(6):959–978. https://doi.org/10.1177/1350508420961533

Irvine L (2008) If you tame me: understanding our connection with animals. Temple University Press.

Johnson Binder A, Parish-Plass N, Kirby M, Winkle M, Skwerer D, Ackerman L, Brosig C, Coombe W, Delisle E, Enders-Slegers M, Fowler J, Hey L, Howell T, Kaufmann M, Kienast M, Kinoshita M, Ngai D, Wijnen B (2024) Recommendations for uniform terminology in animal-assisted services (AAS). Human-Animal Interact 12(s1). https://doi.org/10.1079/hai.2024.0003

Joo S, Bae J, Jung Y, Chun M-S, Park H (2023) Entertaining commodities or living beings? Public perception of animal welfare at local festivals in South Korea. J Agric Environ Ethics 36(1):2. https://doi.org/10.1007/s10806-022-09897-0

Kelemen TK, Matthews SH, Wan M (Maggie), Zhang Y (2020) The secret life of pets: the intersection of animals and organizational life. J Organ Behav 41(7), 694–697. https://doi.org/10.1002/job.2465

Lavertu L, Kulow K, Cowan K, Marder B (2025) Petfluencers, the Fur-Mula for sincere endorsements: examining how and when pets exhibit greater persuasion as influencers. J Advertising Res 1–16. https://doi.org/10.1080/00218499.2025.2463707

Lee S, Hong S, Kim J, Meng ZM (2024) Exploring the role of ethical experiences and psychological well-being in travel satisfaction: an animal welfare perspective in elephant-based tourism. Tour Manage Perspect 51:101248. https://doi.org/10.1016/j.tmp.2024.101248

Lin G, Li M (2024) Animal psychotherapist: the potential impacts of animal-based tourism on mental health. Tour Manage 105:104959. https://doi.org/10.1016/j.tourman.2024.104959

Lin G, Li M, Li B, Meng Y (2024) A healing journey with animals. J Hosp Tour Manage 60:252–263. https://doi.org/10.1016/j.jhtm.2024.07.006

Linné T (2016) Cows on Facebook and Instagram: interspecies intimacy in the social media spaces of the Swedish dairy industry. Telev New Media 17(8):719–733. https://doi.org/10.1177/1527476416653811

Lundqvist M, Alwin J, Levin L-Å (2019) Certified service dogs – a cost-effectiveness analysis appraisal. PLoS ONE 14(9):e0219911. https://doi.org/10.1371/journal.pone.0219911

Meng B, Chi X, Kim JJ, Untaru E-N, Han H (2024) Norm activation and self-interested process in ethical behaviours for animal tourism: exploring the function of animal co-creation and Asian cultural values. Curr Issue Tour 27(13):2066–2082. https://doi.org/10.1080/13683500.2023.2220955

Mitchell J (2024) Animals in public service: a narrative inquiry. Adm Theory Praxis 46(3):259–279. https://doi.org/10.1080/10841806.2023.2282902

Mkono M, Hughes K (2024) A state-of-the-art-review of animals in tourism: key debates and future directions. Tour Geogr 1–13. https://doi.org/10.1080/14616688.2024.2342462

Ngai N (2023) Homemade pet celebrities: the everyday experience of micro-celebrity in promoting the self and others. Celebrity Stud 14(4):437–454. https://doi.org/10.1080/19392397.2022.2070714

Nieforth L, Craig E, Behmer V, Wadsworth S, O'Haire M (2023) PTSD service dogs foster resilience among veterans and military families. Curr Psychol 42(16):13207–13219. https://doi.org/10.1007/s12144-021-01990-3

Polheber JP, Matchock RL (2014) The presence of a dog attenuates cortisol and heart rate in the Trier Social Stress Test compared to human friends. J Behav Med 37(5):860–867. https://doi.org/10.1007/s10865-013-9546-1

Policay R, Falconier M (2019) Therapy dogs in couple and family therapy: a therapist's perspective. Contemp Family Therapy.

Quan SX, Lam C, Schabram K, Yam KC (2024) All Creatures great and small: a review and typology of employee-animal interactions. J Manage 50(1):380–411. https://doi.org/10.1177/01492063231191090

Rötzmeier-Keuper J, Hendricks J, Wünderlich NV, Schmitz G (2018) Triadic relationships in the context of services for animal companions. J Bus Res 85:295–303. https://doi.org/10.1016/j.jbusres.2018.01.003

Singleton JK (2023) Benefits of being teamed with a service dog for individuals living with visible and invisible disabilities. Healthcare 11(22):2987. https://doi.org/10.3390/healthcare11222987

Stygar AH, Krampe C, Llonch P, Niemi JK (2022) How far are we from data-driven and animal-based welfare assessment? A critical analysis of European quality schemes. Front Animal Sci 3:874260. https://doi.org/10.3389/fanim.2022.874260

Tallberg L, García-Rosell J-C, Haanpää M (2022) Human-animal relations in business and society: advancing the feminist interpretation of stakeholder theory. J Bus Ethics 180(1):1–16. https://doi.org/10.1007/s10551-021-04840-1

Wei W, Zhang L, Ying T, Zheng Y (2025) Pet influencer marketing appeal in hotel booking: exploring the power of message appeal and boundary conditions. Int J Hosp Manage 126:104094. https://doi.org/10.1016/j.ijhm.2025.104094

Wünderlich NV, Mosteller J, Beverland MB, Downey H, Kraus K, Lin M-H (Jenny), Syrjälä H (2021) Animals in our lives: an interactive well-being perspective. J Macromarketing 41(4):646–662. https://doi.org/10.1177/0276146720984815

Yoo S, Pu K, Truong KN (2024) Behind the pup-ularity curtain: understanding the motivations, challenges, and work performed in creating and managing pet influencer accounts. In: Proceedings of the CHI conference on human factors in computing systems, pp 1–17. https://doi.org/10.1145/3613904.3642367

Zhang L, Wei W, Rathjens B, Zheng Y (2023) Pet influencers on social media: the joint effect of message appeal and narrator. Int J Hosp Manage 110:103453. https://doi.org/10.1016/j.ijhm.2023.103453

Chapter 17
Animals for Traction and Transport

Nicoletta Batini

Abstract Draft and pack animals have not only supported agriculture and livelihoods, facilitated human migration, and revolutionized warfare—they have profoundly shaped the course of history. Even with the advent of mechanized transport, animals remain indispensable in many parts of the world, especially in regions with limited infrastructure. Their economic value is estimated to surpass even that of the modern transportation industry. Despite their invaluable contributions, working animals often endure harsh conditions, physical strain, and inadequate care. When they become too weak to work, they are frequently killed, highlighting the aberration of a use-and-discard culture towards these precious working partners. Recognizing and enhancing the economic value of draft and pack animals is essential for sustainable development and ethical treatment. Structural and economic reforms are urgently needed to implement proper social protection measures for working animals, like retirement, universal care, and the right to proper food, water, rest, and shelter. Both public and private finance can support these efforts and provide the necessary incentives for alternative transportation methods.

"Aut viam inveniam aut faciam"[1]

—Hannibal

[1] The phrase "Aut viam inveniam aut faciam", which translates to "I shall either find a way or make one", is attributed to Hannibal, the Carthaginian general. He is said to have uttered it when his generals told him it was impossible to cross the Alps with elephants, reflecting his determination and resolve to overcome obstacles but also, implicitly, the faith Hannibal put in the brawn and adaptability of elephants (Bradford 2004).

Work on this volume/chapter was conducted when the author was at the Sveriges Riksbank.

N. Batini (✉)
Independent Evaluation Office, International Monetary Fund, Washington D. C., USA
e-mail: nbatini@imf.org

N. Batini (ed.), *The Economics of Non-Human Animals*, Natural Resource Management and Policy 63, https://doi.org/10.1007/978-3-032-17580-9_17

Unparalleled Abilities

Non-human animals are remarkable at transporting themselves, objects for their survival, and their young, each in their own and unique way. Birds fly, fish swim, and mammals run or climb, and in all these activities they vastly outperform unaided human animals in locomotion due to their specialized adaptations and their incredible strength.

Each mode of non-human animal self-transport is highly specialized (Vogel 2003). Birds like eagles and falcons can fly at high speeds and altitudes, covering vast distances that humans cannot achieve without the aid of technology like airplanes; while insects such as bees and dragonflies are incredibly agile in flight, capable of ultra-rapid manoeuvres and hovering. Looking at locomotion through water, fish are highly efficient swimmers, with species like the sailfish reaching speeds of up to 68 mph (110 km/h) (Block and Finnerty 1994); while among marine mammals dolphins, orcas and whales are powerful swimmers, capable of long-distance travel and deep dives that humans cannot match without equipment (Schreiber and Burger 2002). In running, cheetahs are notoriously the fastest land animals thanks to their body structure, spine flexibility, and muscle composition, capable of reaching speeds up to 60–70 mph (97–120 km/h) in short bursts (Hudson et al. 2011)—with a top speed is about 7.6 times faster than current world champion Noah Lyles' average speed during his 100 m sprint (World Athletics 2021); while other animals, like pronghorn antelopes, far exceed human capabilities in endurance, being able to sustain high speeds over long distances (Byers 1997). At the same time, many primates, such as monkeys and apes, are exceptional climbers, using their strong limbs and tails to navigate trees with ease; while mountain goats like ibex can scale steep, rocky terrains with extraordinary agility and balance.

Thanks to these natural abilities and instincts, non-human animals achieve unfathomable feats in how far, high and deep they can move. For example, the Arctic tern, a bird the size of a crow, travels from its breeding grounds in the Arctic to the Antarctic and back again each year to experience two summers every year. During this trip covers over 44,000 miles round-trip, the longest migration of any animal (Otte 2025). Likewise, monarch butterflies travel up to 3,000 miles from North America to central Mexico to escape the cold winter. They use the sun's position and possibly the Earth's magnetic field to navigate this incredible journey (Otte 2025). Born in freshwater rivers, salmon migrate to the ocean to mature and then return to their birthplace to spawn. This journey involves navigating through various obstacles, including predators and strong currents (Otte 2025). And humpback whales migrate up to 16,000 miles annually between their feeding grounds in polar waters and their breeding grounds in tropical waters. Their migration is one of the longest among mammals (Otte 2025). When travelling vertically, animals are unparalleled by unaided human. The Cuvier's beaked whale for example holds the record for the deepest dive by a mammal, reaching depths of nearly 9,842 feet (3,000 m) (Otte 2025). Moving upwards and downwards, one famous example is the Cingino Dam in Italy, where ibex climb the nearly vertical walls to lick salt and minerals from the stones thanks to their specialized hooves, which have a hard outer rim and a soft, grippy centre (Atlas Obscura 2016).

At the same time, animals have developed various strategies to carry and protect their young. Kangaroos have pouches for their joeys, while many bird species carry their chicks on their backs or in their beaks (Drickamer et al. 2001). Some fish, like cichlids, carry their fry in their mouths for protection. Many animals transport objects for survival. Ants, for instance, can carry objects many times their body weight to build nests or store food (Hölldobler and Wilson 1990). Beavers transport branches and mud to construct intricate dams that alter waterways and create new habitats (Müller-Schwarze and Sun 2003). Crucially, animals' movements are primarily driven by survival instincts and environmental cues. In this sense, their self-transport is both energy efficient and energy-conservative since non-human animals—contrary to human animals—do travel primarily for essential reasons like finding food, seeking shelter, or migrating to breeding grounds rather than by reasons beyond necessity, like those persuaded by human animals such as exploration, leisure, business, and cultural experiences.

Harnessed for Human Gain

Humans have utilized the strength and abilities of animals for transport and traction for thousands of years. From the earliest agricultural societies to modern times, this practice has played a crucial role in shaping economies, cultures, and even the outcomes of wars. This required tweaking the animal's behavioural instincts or biology, initially by selecting animals with desirable traits like tameness and adaptability and using selective breeding, training, and providing food and shelter, and also limiting these to induce dependency and obedience. Modern domestication continues with advanced breeding techniques and animals' genetic modification to improve traits for companionship, work, and food production (Clutton-Brock 1999).

The global number of animals currently in use for transport and traction is large. Just looking at the most used animal categories, there are approximately 58 million horses, 24 million camels, 44 million donkeys, and 9 million mules worldwide (Food and Agriculture Organization of the United Nations 2021). While exact numbers of domesticated yaks can vary, it is estimated that there are around 13 million yaks in Tibet alone and over 0.6 million in mainland China (Chinese Academy of Sciences 2006; Norlha 2018).

A Brief History

The domestication of animals for work began around 6,000 years ago. The first animals to be domesticated for traction were likely oxen, which were used to pull ploughs and carts. In ancient Mesopotamia, evidence of oxen-drawn ploughs dates back to around 4,000 BCE (Smith 1995). These early tools allowed for more efficient farming, leading to surplus food production and the growth of early cities. As civilizations expanded, so did the variety of animals used for work. Horses, donkeys, and mules became essential for transportation and agricultural tasks. Horses, in particular, were prized for their speed and strength. By 2,500 BCE, horses were being used to pull chariots in Sumer (Postgate 1992). The invention of the chariot revolutionized warfare and transportation, allowing for faster movement of troops and goods.

In Egypt, oxen were used to pull ploughs as early as the III Dynasty (around 2,700 BCE). The Egyptians also utilized donkeys for transport and camels for long-distance trade routes across the desert (Brewer and Teeter 1999). The introduction of the camel around 0 AD significantly enhanced trade across the Sahara and other arid regions (Bulliet 1975).

The Romans also utilized a variety of animals to meet their agricultural needs. Overall, the use of animals for traction and transport was integral to the functioning and expansion of ancient Rome (Harris 2011). Oxen were commonly used to pull ploughs, turning the soil for planting crops. This increased agricultural productivity and supported the growing population of the Roman Empire. Donkeys and mules were also employed to carry goods to market, navigating the rugged terrain of the countryside. For transportation, animals were essential in moving people and goods across the vast expanse of empire. Horses pulled chariots and carriages, facilitating travel and communication over long distances. Horses' ability to carry more weight and move faster than humans meant that they also helped develop and expand trade networks and allowed people to come into contact with diverse cultures. The Roman road network, renowned for its engineering, was designed to accommodate these animal-drawn vehicles, enhancing trade and military mobility.

During the medieval period, the use of animals for traction and transport became even more widespread. In Europe, horses were used extensively for ploughing fields, pulling carts, and as mounts for knights in battle. The medieval knight on horseback became a symbol of the era (Bennett 1998). In Asia, water buffaloes were commonly used in rice paddies, while elephants were employed for heavy lifting and transportation in India and Southeast Asia. The versatility of these animals made them invaluable for both agricultural and military purposes (Sukumar 2003).

In military contexts, animals have long been vital for both logistics and combat. Horses forever changed human conflict when, by the 1000s BC, they had become common features of the battlefield. They were the primary animals used in combat, serving as mounts for cavalry and for pulling chariots and artillery. The effectiveness of cavalry units was evident in battles from ancient times through the Napoleonic Wars (1803–1815) and the American Civil War (1861–1865) (Keegan 1993). Horses, for example, were the backbone of the Roman cavalry, providing speed and manoeuvrability on the battlefield. They allowed for rapid troop movements and effective reconnaissance. Elephants, though used less frequently, were employed in certain military campaigns to intimidate and trample enemy forces. In 218 BC, Hannibal led his Carthaginian army, including 37 elephants, across the Alps to invade Italy during the Second Punic War (Roman Empire Times 2024). This daring feat remains one of the most celebrated military achievements in ancient history. Likewise, camels were used in desert regions for their ability to carry heavy loads over long distances without water, supporting military logistics in arid environments, like during the Battle of Ullais in 633 AD, during the early Islamic conquests, which showcased the strategic use of camels in warfare (Bulliet 1975; Donner 1981).

During World War I, horses were used extensively for cavalry charges, transportation of troops, and hauling supplies.[2] However, the advent of machine guns and trench warfare reduced their effectiveness in direct combat (Gilbert 1994). Despite this, horses remained crucial for logistical support, especially in difficult terrains where motorized vehicles could not operate.

World War II saw a continued, albeit reduced, use of horses. They were employed for transportation in challenging landscapes and by some armies for cavalry charges (Budiansky 1997). Additionally, other animals played vital roles during the war. Mules were used for transporting ammunition and supplies through rugged landscapes, while dogs served as messengers, sentries, and search and rescue animals (Storey 2022). Carrier pigeons were also used extensively during both world wars to carry messages across enemy lines. Their ability to navigate back to their home lofts made them reliable messengers in situations where other forms of communication were compromised (Storey 2022).

Modern Uses

With the advent of mechanized vehicles in the twentieth century, the use of animals for traction and transport began to decline. Tractors and trucks replaced oxen and horses in agriculture and transportation. However, in many parts of the world, tens of millions of animals are still used for these purposes due to economic and environmental reasons, especially in regions where modern infrastructure is limited. In rural and remote areas of many developing countries, animals remain the most reliable and cost-effective means of transportation. They are used to carry goods, water, and other necessities, which supports local economies and livelihoods. In those countries, animals are essential for transporting agricultural products from farms to markets. This helps farmers access broader markets and increases their income. In some regions, like Africa and Asia, the economic impact of animal transportation is significant. In Ethiopia, for example, donkeys contribute to the transportation of 12 million tons of goods annually (Tegegn 2021). Similarly, rough estimates suggest that Tibetan yaks transport around 420 million tons of goods every year (author's calculation).

In addition to transport, animals continue to be used in large parts of the world in agriculture for tilling soil, harrowing, planting, ridging, weeding, mowing,

---

[2] Both the novel *War Horse* by Michael Morpurgo and its film adaptation directed by Steven Spielberg highlight the significant contributions and hardships faced by horses on the battlefield during this war. They poignantly depict the bond between soldiers and their horses, emphasizing the emotional and physical toll of war on these animals.

harvesting, and operating mills; in forestry for logging by the ability of some animals of uprooting trees; and in construction to cargo-lift and operate pulleys (Matheny and Leahy 2007). Beyond the iconic sentinel canary used to detect the presence of carbon monoxide, animals, notably dogs, ponies, mules, and donkeys have also been used for centuries in mining to pull wagons full of mined material (Chadwick et al. 2013). Although this was common mostly prior to the introduction of electric haulage, this practice still stands today in several countries especially in regions with difficult terrain where modern vehicles cannot easily operate and in small-scale or artisanal mining operations, where pack animals like mules and donkeys might still be used to transport supplies and equipment to and from mining sites (Farid 2014). Animals' strength and endurance make them ideal for these labour-intensive activities.

Finally, animals are also employed for transport in tourism, for activities such as horse-drawn carriages, elephant treks, and camel and mule rides, contributing to local economies by attracting tourists and generating income for local communities (García-Rosell 2022; and Chap. 18 in this book).

Transporting Animals

Beyond enhancing human mobility for millennia, animals have themselves been transported by humans throughout history for diverse purposes. In ancient Rome, for example, animals like lions, bears, and elephants were brought from distant lands to entertain the masses in Roman circuses (Jennison 2005). In 1493, on his second voyage to the New World, Christopher Columbus brought two dozen horses to the islands of Hispaniola and Cuba, revolutionizing transportation and agriculture in the Americas (Phillips and Phillips 1992).[3] In 1515, a rhinoceros was transported from India to Lisbon and later depicted in a famous woodcut by Albrecht Dürer. Another notable example is the transportation of giraffes, such as the one gifted to Charles X of France from Egypt in the early nineteenth century, involving a long and arduous journey from Africa to Europe (Blancou and Parsonson 2008).

Technological advancements were designed to facilitate the transport of animals. The introduction of specialized ships, trains, and vehicles ensured the safe and efficient movement of these animals across vast distances. For example, circus trains in the nineteenth century were designed to transport elephants and other large animals across the country. In modern times, with the globalization of the food and textile industries, animals are often transported live to reach import destinations, where they are slaughtered upon arrival for cost, tax and "freshness" reasons.

[3] Prior to this reintroduction, horses had gone extinct in the North American continent around 10,000 years ago.

Economic Impact of Draft and Pack Animals

In allowing humans to move heavy loads, cultivate large areas of land, and travel long distances more efficiently than they could on their own, animals have played a key role in human migration, in food production and agricultural sustainability, in connecting civilizations, in promoting demographic growth, and in the making of empires like those of the Incas, the Mongols, the Persians, the Ottomans, and the Romans. While some advancements might have been possible without animals, it is clear that animals have been indispensable for, and played a central role in the growth of human economies and the accumulation of resources, ultimately leading to today's level of economic progress and global wealth. Their contributions not just accelerated human development. Draft and pack animals shaped the course of history.

Although it is practically impossible to quantify the monetary value of these contributions due to the vast historical and economic contexts involved, and estimating the value of animals' current economic contributions via transport and traction, we can try to get a sense of their scale based on some simple math and using valuations from machine-operated sectors in comparison.

Let us take, for example, the transportation sector. In a year, the existing world stock of pack and draft animals—horses, camels, donkeys, mules, and yaks—together transport a massive amount of weight. This can be estimated to be between 5 and 27 billion tons of weight annually depending on whether we assume that the load is packed on or pulled by the animal.[4] To put this into perspective, the total weight transported in 2023 by *all* types of maritime shipping in the world—not just container ships—was 11 billion tons (corresponding to 80% of global goods) (Statista Research Department 2024a). Cumulatively, in an average year, the animals also travel much longer than the global fleet, at 1.1 trillion km, about ten times the total distance

[4] These estimates are conservative because they exclude oxen, since the exact number of draft oxen in the world today is difficult to pinpoint due to the variability in data collection across different regions. Assuming horses transport an average load carrying capacity of 100 kg, which is 20% of their average body weight of 500 kg, results in horses transporting an estimated 1.45 billion tons annually. Camels, with an assumed carrying capacity of 300 kg, can be estimated to transport around 1.8 billion tons. Donkeys, assumed to carry 50 kg (20% of their average body weight of 200 kg), are estimated to move 550 million tons. Mules, with an assumed capacity of 125 kg (25% of their average body weight of 500 kg), are estimated to handle 281.25 million tons. Yaks, assumed to carry 130 kg, are estimated to transport 455 million tons. The sum of these estimates gives a total carrying capacity of the existing stock of horse, camels, donkeys, mules, and yaks of about 5 billion tons. These numbers have to be multiplied by 6–7 if we assumed that the same animals are used to pull carts with loads since most animals can pull about 150% of their own weight while only carry around 20–25% of their own weight. So the carrying capacity of the stock of existing draft and pack animals excluding oxen can be put conservatively between 5 and 27 billion tons per year, given each type of animal's average distance travelled per day and average days worked in a year, once rest and non-working days are accounted for.

travelled by all marine freights in the world in a year (Statista Research Department 2024b).[5]

Even though animals transport more weight and cover greater distances annually compared to all the ships in the world combined, the value of the transport services carried out by animals is considerably lower in pure economic terms due to the nature of goods typically transported by animals (e.g. agricultural products, basic goods) despite the fact that transport by draft or pack animals is considerably less efficient than transport by sea. So while in 2023, the total value of marine freight globally was estimated to be around $650 billion (UNCTAD 2023; Statista Research Department 2024b), the value of transport services by animals globally—assuming an average price per ton transported between $2 and 6 dollars[6]—could easily be in the range of $10 billion to $157 billion, which is between 1 and 16% of the GDP in 2023 of all low-income countries combined.

In practice, the true value of transportation by animals developing countries is likely much higher than what simple economic metrics can capture. Animals are often the only viable means of transportation in remote or rugged areas, making them essential for connecting communities to markets, health care, and education. While the direct economic value of goods transported by animals might seem lower, the indirect benefits are substantial, as animals enable trade and commerce in otherwise isolated regions, supporting local economies and livelihoods. Additionally, animals play a crucial role in the daily lives of many communities, not just for transportation but also for agricultural work, food production, and cultural practices. This multi-faceted role adds to their overall value. Furthermore, animal transport is often more sustainable and environmentally friendly compared to mechanized transport, especially in areas where fuel and maintenance for vehicles are not readily available. Therefore, the existential role of animals in supporting the livelihoods, economies, and cultures of low-income countries significantly enhances their true value.

Another interesting sector to focus on in gauging the economic value of draft and pack animals contribution is agriculture. As mentioned above, animals "of burden" are crucial for farming worldwide, powering nearly half of all cultivated land and hauling a quarter of all carts (Endalew and Ayalew 2016). In Ethiopia, for example, where agriculture accounts for a significant portion of GDP and employs a large part of the population; 85% of small-scale farmers rely on animals for farming tasks like ploughing, weeding, and transporting products and inputs.[7] Around six million oxen

[5] This cumulative distance is estimated multiplying the total of animals by type by the average daily distance that is usually travelled by each animal type in a day, and in turn, multiplying this result by the number of days in a year in which animals are likely to be working allowing for rest and non-working day (a number that is equalled to 200 days).

[6] The value of the transportation services provided by animals is approximately ten times lower than that of maritime transport. This estimate was obtained by equating marginal cost and marginal benefit, and measuring marginal cost based on the surveyed price of renting out a donkey in Ghana for a week ($2.26–3.67) in relation to the amount (in tons) that a donkey can carry in a week (0.28–0.63 tons)) (Mercier 2018; Maggs et al. 2021).

[7] In Ethiopia, small-scale farmers are incredibly important to the agricultural sector. They are responsible for producing about 94% of the country's food crops and 98% of its coffee, which is

help with crop cultivation with traditional ploughs called "maresha", which has been integral to Ethiopian agriculture for centuries, aiding in seedbed preparation and other cultivation tasks (Tefera 2011). Oxen are affordable, can access areas tractors cannot, and do not need fuel or repairs (although operating them is not cost-free. See the section below). In fact, tractors are rarely used in the highlands due to cost, rough terrain, and small, scattered fields. Instead, draft animals' power about all of the cultivated land there. Additionally, animals such as donkeys, horses, and mules are commonly used for transporting goods to markets and people back and forth, especially in rural areas where modern transportation infrastructure is limited.

As of 2022, the GDP from agriculture in Ethiopia generated thanks to the use of pack and draft animals was roughly $14.5 billion. Within this, Ethiopia's total agricultural exports, mostly coffee, fresh-cut flowers, fresh vegetables, sesame seeds, and pulses, were valued at $3.3 billion (International Trade Administration 2024). Assuming that agricultural production follows a standard (Cobb–Douglas) production function specification, and that animals contribute to output with a share similar to that commonly assumed for capital (agricultural machines) in agricultural production functions,[8] these figures imply that Ethiopian oxen generate between $2.9 and 7.5 billion in income yearly, that is about 2–4.5% of Ethiopia's GDP, and up to *over half* of the country's total agricultural income. Each oxen then generates about *half* of the per capita income of a typical small-scale farmer.

In a similar vein, tourism activities involving transport by animals, such as trekking, horse safaris, and cultural tours, significantly contribute to local economies worldwide. In regions like the Himalayas, yaks, mules, and horses are essential for trekking and mountaineering expeditions, providing vital services and income for local communities. Horseback riding tours in Africa, North and South America, and Central Asia attract tourists seeking unique experiences, while camel and elephant rides in the Sahara, Rajasthan, and Southeast Asia are major attractions, offering unique ways to explore natural landscapes and connecting with local cultures (see also Chap. 18 in this book).

Quantifying the exact global value of tourism using animals for transport is challenging due to the diverse range of activities and regions involved. However, examples can give a handle of the economic impact involved. In Argentina, the cost of a horse safari can vary depending on the duration and the level of luxury. For example, a 7-night horse safari in Patagonia can cost around $900 per person *per night*. Another option, an 8-day safari through the Andes, is priced at approximately $7,175 (Black Saddle n.d.). Mule rides at the Grand Canyon, an activity attended by thousands of visitors and offered year round with different options available depending on the season and the rim of the canyon, typically starts at around $155 per person (Grand Canyon Trust 2024). The cost of a camel trek safari in the Sahara ranges from around $9 to $13 USD for a short ride (30 min to an hour) in places like Marrakech (Moroccan Journeys, n.d.). For longer treks, however, during overnight stays in luxury desert

Ethiopia's leading export. These farmers cultivate around 95% of the total agricultural land (IGAD 2018).

[8] That is 0.2–0.6.

camps, prices can start from approximately \$68 to \$105 USD per person (Vagabonds of the World, n.d.).

Neglect Versus Care Costs

The widespread reliance on animals for traction and transport in developing countries presents several challenges, in terms of both animal welfare and economically. From a welfare perspective, working animals often face harsh conditions. Animals used for transportation frequently face physical strain and injuries. For example, donkeys and horses can suffer from back injuries, lameness, and sores due to heavy loads and poorly fitted harnesses. Severe mistreatment has been documented in many parts of the developing and developed world, including starvation, beatings, and being forced to work while injured (Animal Ethics, n.d.). Such conditions lead to significant physical and psychological suffering for the animals. In some regions, working animals are hosted in poor living conditions and do not receive proper veterinary care, leading to untreated illnesses and infections, which lead to significant pain and suffering (Starkey 2004). Animals also may experience health issues due to inadequate nutrition, water, and rest. The lack of access to clean water and appropriate shelter further exacerbates their plight. In addition, long hours of work and harsh environmental conditions can cause unbearable stress and fatigue in animals. This is particularly evident in regions with extreme temperatures, where animals may not have sufficient protection from the elements or rest breaks. Moreover, the use of animals for transport in urban areas can expose them to additional hazards, such as traffic accidents and pollution (Eurogroup for Animals 2022).

Ensuring draft and pack animals' well-being is essential for ethical and sustainable use. However, challenges such as feed inadequacy, limited use of animals outside of cultivation periods, and the need for improved animal health and management practices persist. Economically, the costs associated with maintaining working animals in healthy and pain-free conditions can be significant. These costs include veterinary care, feed, and equipment. Veterinary expenses are particularly high, as working animals are prone to injuries and diseases due to the strenuous nature of their tasks (Bangura n.d.). Additionally, the cost of proper nutrition and shelter can be burdensome for owners, especially in low-income regions (Starkey 1999). The economic viability of using animals for traction and transport is often influenced by factors such as farm size, cropping patterns, and the availability of institutional support (Bangura n.d.).

Similarly, transporting animals can involve significant animal welfare and economic costs. Despite advances in means of animal transportation and increasingly strict regulation, the transportation of animals continues to raise significant concerns about their welfare. Animals often endure transport lasting several days or even weeks, during which they face risks such as exhaustion, dehydration, injuries, illnesses, and even death (Eurogroup for Animals 2024a).

From an economic standpoint, although transporting animals can be cost-effective for farmers and meat producers, it also comes with economic losses from indirect costs related to animal welfare, such as stress, injuries, and high mortality. For instance, in Australia, one of the world's largest live exporters, cattle from the Northern Territory in Australia face some of the longest journeys, travelling up to 2,500 km to reach east coast abattoirs, resulting in increased stress, injuries, and mortality, impacting the industry's economic viability (Meat and Livestock Australia 2021). Similarly, road accidents in the United States, such as the 2024 truck crash that killed 22 cows, highlight the need for improved transport conditions and safety measures (Investigate Midwest 2024). In Brazil, the live export of cattle has faced criticism for poor transport conditions, leading to economic losses due to high mortality rates (World Federation for Animals 2023). Additionally, live export vessels often subject animals to crowded and inadequate conditions, resulting in high mortality rates, as seen in Australia in 2021, where over 1.37 million animals were exported, and many did not survive the journey (Department of Agriculture, Water and the Environment 2021). Direct costs associated with freight charges, special handling requirements, and long-distance travel, along with indirect costs such as stress, injuries, and mortality, contribute to the overall economic burden of transporting live animals over long distances.

Revolutionizing Animal Welfare in Traction and Transport

As argued earlier in this chapter, animals used for transport and traction are vital to developing economies, generating major income that is crucial for these countries. These animals help in various agricultural activities, transportation of goods, and even tourism, thereby supporting the livelihoods of many people. However, these animals often suffer due to overwork, inadequate nutrition, and a neglected environment. This suffering raises serious ethical concerns, but also impacts the efficiency and sustainability of their use. Ensuring the welfare of these animals is essential for maintaining their health, physical and emotional well-being, and, ultimately productivity, which in turn supports the economic stability of the communities that rely on them. Therefore, it is imperative to adopt more sustainable and humane practices to improve the life of these animals while also enhancing economic efficiency.

If implemented, these six top economic policy and regulatory proposals could make a significant difference in addressing these challenges:

- *Standards for animal care.* One key recommendation is the establishment of minimum standards for draft and pack animal care [5] (https://wfa.org/shaping-a-sustainable-future-new-recommendations-for-global-biodiversity-and-animal-welfare/). This implies that animal owners provide proper veterinary services, proper nutrition, and adequate shelter to their working animals at all times. Governments can play a crucial role in providing training and resources to animal owners, helping them to improve the welfare of their animals (Humane Action Pennsylvania 2022).

- *Public schemes in support of animal care standards.* Since caring for and allowing proper rest and nutrition for draft and pack animals is costly to the owners, it is critical, however, that governments also help fund these efforts especially when it comes to poorer owners. This can be done through a combination of direct funding, subsidies, and collaboration with veterinary services and animal welfare organizations. Governments can also help set up dedicated animal owners-centred cooperatives in rural and peri-urban areas, as well as medical insurance schemes and/or health savings accounts for rural communities and poorer owners to ensure that the standards can be met affordably by all animal owners (The Social Work Graduate, n.d.).
- *Social protection for animals that work in transport/traction.* A step forward from these first two proposals combined involves setting up a system of social protection for animals that work in transport and traction. Drawing parallels between animal labour and human labour, it becomes evident that both require adequate rest, nutrition, and health care to maintain productivity and well-being. Just as human workers benefit from social protection measures such as health insurance and labour rights, animals used for labour should also be afforded similar protections (Israeli 2024). This includes access to veterinary care, proper nutrition, and humane working conditions (Emory University 2014). By ensuring that animals are well cared for, their productivity and longevity can be enhanced, ultimately benefiting the owners and the broader economy (Israeli 2024). The funding of these social protection schemes could be similar to that suggested in funding simple standard compliance schemes. For success, both require the funding of proper enforcement tools including a registry of working animals.
- *Retirement plans.* Furthermore, the concept of social protection for animal workers can be extended to include retirement plans for older animals. Just as human workers are entitled to retire after years of service, animals should also be allowed to retire and live out their old age without working. This can be facilitated through government-supported retirement funds or government-sponsored sanctuaries where retired animals can receive the care they need.
- *Urban regulations.* Another proposal is the implementation of stricter regulations on the use of animals for transport, particularly in urban areas, to reduce the risks associated with traffic and pollution. Bans to the use of animals for draught of heavy loads (including touristic carriages) should be introduced to prohibit animals to carry or pull heavy loads during the hottest or coldest seasons of the year as these have too often proven deadly for the animals themselves (Wanted in Rome 2020).
- *Incentives for alternative transportation methods.* Additionally, promoting alternative, sustainable methods of transport and traction can help alleviate the burden on working animals. For example, the introduction of affordable, motorized equipment can reduce the reliance on animal power. Encouraging the use of renewable energy sources for transport can also contribute to this goal (World Federation for Animals 2024).

There are several examples of public–private collaborations that have successfully raised the standards of animal welfare in transportation. The World Association for Transport Animal Welfare and Studies (TAWS) has been involved in various programs across Africa to promote the use of animal power for transportation (Sims et al. 2003). These programs focus on training farmers and providing them with the necessary equipment, such as ox carts and harnesses. In countries like Ethiopia and Madagascar, these initiatives have significantly improved the efficiency of transporting agricultural products to markets.

In the mountainous regions of Nepal, pack animals like yaks and mules are essential for transporting goods. Various non-governmental organizations (NGOs) have implemented programs to improve the welfare and efficiency of these animals (Animal Nepal 2025). These programs include veterinary care, training for handlers, and the provision of better equipment. As a result, the transportation of goods in these remote areas has become more reliable and efficient.

In Rajasthan, India, camels are traditionally used for transporting goods across the desert. Programs supported by local governments and NGOs have focused on improving the health and working conditions of these camels (Help in Suffering 2022). Initiatives include veterinary camps, training for camel handlers, and the introduction of more efficient harnesses and carts. These efforts have helped sustain the livelihoods of many families who depend on camel transport.

In Kenya, donkeys are widely used for transporting water, firewood, and agricultural products. Organizations like the Donkey Sanctuary Kenya have implemented programs to improve the welfare of working donkeys (The Donkey Sanctuary 2025. See also AU-IBAR 2018). These programs provide veterinary care, training for donkey owners, and community education on proper animal care.

These programs demonstrate the ongoing importance of animals in transportation and the positive impact that targeted initiatives can have on both animal welfare and local economies. By adopting these measures, governments can help create a more sustainable and ethical system for using animals in labour. This not only improves the welfare of the animals but also supports the livelihoods of the people who depend on them, ensuring a more equitable and humane approach to animal labour.

Transforming Animal Transportation Practices

It is now widely recognized that improving transport conditions and implementing stricter live animal transport regulations can help enhance animal welfare globally and also mitigate correlative economic losses. Some experts argue that reducing the number and length of journeys, and, at the same time, establishing universal safe transport conditions can go a long way in achieving these goals, benefiting both animals and their handlers. Reports of animals enduring extreme temperatures, overcrowded conditions, insufficient headroom and bedding, and inadequate food, water, and rest have sparked debates about the need for stricter regulations (Brussel

Times 2023, 2024a, 2024b; Eurogroup for Animals 2024a, 2024b; Compassion in World Farming 2024a, 2024b; Robin de Bois and Animal Welfare Foundation 2024).

To foster progress in this area, organizations like Compassion in World Farming, the Eurogroup for Animals, FOUR PAWS, and the Federation of Veterinarians of Europe (FVE) have called for reforms to improve animal welfare during transport, including shorter journey times, better conditions, and mandatory veterinary oversight (FOUR PAWS 2023; Compassion in World Farming 2024b; Eurogroup for Animals 2024c; Federation of Veterinarians of Europe 2024). FOUR PAWS, for example, has been vocal about the need for stricter regulations, such as limiting transport times to eight hours and banning live exports to third countries due to the inhumane conditions animals often face during these journeys (FOUR PAWS 2023). Similarly, the FVE has advocated for updated transport rules based on scientific expertise, including increased space allowances, veterinary supervision during loading and unloading, as well as the designation of independent animal welfare officers on transport vessels, and stringent temperature controls to ensure animals' well-being during transport (Federation of Veterinarians of Europe 2024).

Transforming animal transportation practices requires comprehensive policies that prioritize animal welfare and sustainability. The European Commission's Animal Transport Guides project, funded between 2015 and 2017, developed practical guidelines for the transport of livestock such as cattle, pigs, poultry, sheep, and horses within Europe and to third countries. These guidelines emphasize the need for humane treatment, proper handling, and adequate rest periods during transport (European Commission 2023). Additionally, the Eurogroup for Animals advocates for a strategy to reduce and replace live animal transport, promoting a shift towards meat and carcass trade to minimize the stress and suffering associated with long-distance transport (Eurogroup for Animals 2020).

An international treaty on animal transportation could further strengthen these efforts by establishing uniform standards and enforcement mechanisms across countries. The Council of Europe's European Convention for the Protection of Animals during International Transport (ETS No. 193) is an example of such an initiative, aiming to protect animals during cross-border transport. This treaty, revised in 2003, sets out specific requirements for the transport of animals, including space allowances, feeding, watering, and rest periods (Council of Europe 2003). Implementing similar international agreements could ensure that animals are transported under humane conditions, regardless of their destination.

Conclusions

The historical and ongoing use of animals for traction and transport underscores the deep-rooted partnership between humans and animals. This relationship has been pivotal in the development of human societies, with animals playing crucial roles in agriculture, warfare, and transportation. In various regions, animals continue to play a critical economic role in agriculture, generating substantial income. Despite this, the economic value of animal transport services is lower compared to other modes of transport due to the nature of goods typically transported by animals.

At the same time, the welfare of draft and pack animals remains a significant concern worldwide. Ensuring the well-being of these animals and their equitable contribution to human economies comes with substantial costs, including veterinary care, feed, and equipment. Thus, maintaining their well-being requires considerable investment. As a result, challenges such as inadequate nutrition, limited use outside cultivation periods, and the need for better animal health and management practices persist.

Governments must step up to honour the invaluable contributions of working animals by playing a central role in transforming animal welfare standards. This includes establishing minimum care requirements for draft and pack animals, providing training, and offering funding support. Ensuring proper veterinary services, nutrition, and shelter is crucial. Public schemes, including subsidies and collaborations with veterinary services, can help make these standards affordable, especially for poorer owners. Implementing universal social protection measures for working animals, akin to human labour rights, can enhance their well-being and productivity at the same time.

Additionally, governments can coordinate and support retirement plans for older working animals, ensuring they live out their later years in comfort and dignity. Enforcing stricter urban regulations to protect animals from harsh conditions and promoting alternative transportation methods with economic incentives can alleviate the burden on working animals. Overall, addressing the abuse and neglect of these animals requires a multifaceted approach, including the enforcement of animal welfare standards, education of animal owners, and the general promotion of sustainable alternatives to animal labour. By adopting these measures, we not only significantly enhance the well-being of working animals but also set a precedent for a more compassionate and ethical approach to our shared environment. Moreover, improving animal welfare contributes to the economic stability of animal owners, creating a win–win situation that underscores our commitment to sustainable and humane practices.

References

African Union Inter-African Bureau for Animal Resources (AU-IBAR) (2018) Animal welfare strategy for Africa: executive summary. https://www.au-ibar.org/resources/animal-welfare-strategy-africa-awsa-executive-summary

Animal Ethics (n.d.) Animals used as workers. https://www.animal-ethics.org/animals-used-workers/

Animal Nepal (2025) A voice for the voiceless. https://www.animalnepal.org.np/

Atlas Obscura (2016) Watch these amazing alpine goats scale a near-vertical dam. Atlas Obscura. https://www.atlasobscura.com/articles/watch-these-amazing-alpine-goats-scale-a-nearvertical-dam

Bangura JV (n.d.) Appropriate animal drawn equipment for Sierra Leone. https://openknowledge.fao.org/server/api/core/bitstreams/1cdb7847-fa47-4575-9774-9fa4715836e8/content/x5483b1f.htm
Bennett M (1998) The Cambridge illustrated atlas of warfare: the middle ages, 768–1487. Cambridge University Press
Black Saddle (n.d.) Jakotango riding safaris in Argentina, Patagonia. https://black-saddle.com/jakotango
Blancou J, Parsonson I (2008) Historical perspectives on long distance transport of animals. Vet Ital 44(1):19–30. https://www.academia.edu/14605914/Historical_perspectives_on_long_distance_transport_of_animals
Block BA, Finnerty JR (1994) Endothermy in fishes: a phylogenetic analysis of constraints, predispositions, and selection pressures. Environ Biol Fishes 40(3):283–302
Bradford E (2004) Hannibal. Pen and Sword Books Ltd.
Brewer DJ, Teeter E (1999) Egypt and the Egyptians. Cambridge University Press
Brussels Times (2024a) EU continues to allow dangerous vessels to transport live animals. https://www.brusselstimes.com/eu-affairs/994345/eu-continues-to-allow-dangerous-vessels-to-transport-live-animals
Brussels Times (2023) EU auditors: 'Live animal transport at the expense of animal welfare'. Brussels Times
Brussels Times (2024b) Record number of animals seized for protection against abuse. Brussels Times
Budiansky S (1997) The nature of horses: exploring equine evolution, intelligence, and behavior. Free Press
Bulliet RW (1975) The camel and the wheel. Harvard University Press
Byers JA (1997) American pronghorn: social adaptations and the ghosts of predators past. University of Chicago Press
Chadwick MJ, Highton NH, Lindman N (2013) Environmental impacts of coal mining & utilization: a complete revision of environmental implications of expanded coal utilization. Elsevier.
Chinese Academy of Sciences (2006) Domestication of yaks. https://english.cas.cn/newsroom/archive/china_archive/cn2006/200909/t20090923_41966.shtml
Clutton-Brock J (1999) A natural history of domesticated mammals. Cambridge University Press
Compassion in World Farming (2024a) Farm animal welfare research papers. https://www.ciwf.org.uk/research/animal-welfare/
Compassion in World Farming (2024b) Animal transport research briefs. https://www.ciwf.org.uk/research/live-transport/
Council of Europe (2003) European convention for the protection of animals during international transport (ETS No. 193). https://www.coe.int/en/web/conventions/full-list?module=treaty-detail&treatynum=193
Department of Agriculture, Water and the Environment (2021) Live animal export statistics. https://www.agriculture.gov.au/biosecurity-trade/export/controlled-goods/live-animals/live-animal-export-statistics
Donner FM (1981) The early Islamic conquests. Princeton University Press
Drickamer LC, Vessey SH, Jakob EM (2001) Animal behavior: mechanisms, ecology, evolution, 5th ed. McGraw-Hill
Emory University (2014, August 14) Understanding parallels of human and animal parenting can benefit generations to come. https://news.emory.edu/stories/2014/08/young_rilling_parenting_science/index.html
Endalew B, Ayalew Z (2016) Assessment of the role of livestock in Ethiopia: a review. Am-Eurasian J Sci Res 11(5):405–410. https://doi.org/10.5829/idosi.aejsr.2016.11.5.22464
Eurogroup for Animals (2020) A strategy to reduce and replace live animal transport: towards a meat and carcasses-only trade. Eurogroup for Animals, Brussels. https://www.eurogroupforanimals.org/files/eurogroupforanimals/2020-12/Eurogroup-for-Animals_A-strategy-to-reduce-and-replace-live-animal-transport.pdf

Eurogroup for Animals (2022) Animal welfare during transport. https://www.eurogroupforanimals.org/library/animal-welfare-during-transport
Eurogroup for Animals (2024a) Live animal transport. https://www.eurogroupforanimals.org/what-we-do/areas-of-concern/live-animal-transport
Eurogroup for Animals (2024b) Live animal transport: due time to change the rules. https://www.eurogroupforanimals.org/library/live-animal-transport-due-time-change-rules
Eurogroup for Animals (2024c) White Paper on the revision of Council Regulation (EC) 1/2005. Eurogroup for Animals
European Commission (2023) Animal welfare during transport. https://food.ec.europa.eu/animals/animal-welfare/eu-animal-welfare-legislation/animal-welfare-during-transport/animal-transport-guides_en
Farid S (2014, May 5) Beasts of burden. Reuters: the wider image. https://widerimage.reuters.com/story/beasts-of-burden
Federation of Veterinarians of Europe (2024) FVE's positions on animal transport: overview and recent developments. https://fve.org/publications/fves-positions-on-animal-transport-overview-and-recent-developments/
Food and Agriculture Organization of the United Nations (2021) FAOSTAT: live animals. https://www.fao.org/faostat/en/#data/QA
FOUR PAWS (2023) Statements on EU animal welfare proposals. https://www.four-paws.org/our-stories/press-releases/december-2023/statements-on-eu-animal-welfare-proposals
García-Rosell J-C (2022) Animals in tourism: theoretical and practical insights. https://www.jcgarciarosell.com/post/animals-in-tourism-theoretical-and-practical-insights
Gilbert M (1994) The first world war: a complete history. Henry Holt and Company
Grand Canyon Trust (2024) Grand Canyon tourism fuels Arizona's economy. https://www.grandcanyontrust.org/blog/grand-canyon-tourism-fuels-arizona-economy
Harris WV (2011) Rome's imperial economy: the grandeur and the failure of an idea. Oxford University Press
Help in Suffering (2022) Camel welfare program Jaipur and camel rescue Center Bassi. https://helpinsuffering.org/camel-shelter/
Hölldobler B, Wilson EO (1990) The ants. Harvard University Press
Hudson PE, Corr SA, Payne RC, Wilson AM (2011) Functional anatomy of the cheetah (Acinonyx jubatus) forelimb. J Anat 218(4):375–385. https://doi.org/10.1111/j.1469-7580.2011.01344.x
Humane Action Pennsylvania (2022) The intersection of social work and animal welfare. https://humaneactionpittsburgh.org/the-intersection-of-social-work-and-animal-welfare/
IGAD (2018) A review of Ethiopian agriculture: Roles, policy and small-scale farming systems. https://land.igad.int/index.php/documents-1/countries/ethiopia/rural-development-1/275-a-review-of-ethiopian-agriculture-roles-policy-and-small-scale-farming-systems/file
International Trade Administration (2024) Ethiopia—agricultural sectors. https://www.trade.gov/country-commercial-guides/ethiopia-agricultural-sectors
Investigate Midwest (2024) Millions of livestock die each year while being transported. https://goodmenproject.com/featured-content/millions-of-livestock-die-each-year-while-being-transported-those-cases-are-rarely-investigated-by-the-usda/
Israeli A (2024) Human labor and natural labor in Henry David Thoreau's works. Mod Intellect Hist. https://doi.org/10.1017/S1479244324000131
Jennison G (2005) Animals for show and pleasure in ancient Rome. University of Pennsylvania Press
Keegan J (1993) A history of warfare. Knopf, Alfred A
Maggs HC, Ainslie A, Bennett RM (2021) Donkey ownership provides a range of income benefits to the livelihoods of rural households in northern Ghana. Animals 11:3154. https://doi.org/10.3390/ani11113154
Matheny G, Leahy C (2007) Farm animal welfare, legislation, and trade. Law Contemp Probs 70(1):325–358. https://scholarship.law.duke.edu/lcp/vol70/iss1/10

Meat & Livestock Australia (2021) W.LIV.2024—the live export industry annual transport mortality report 2020. https://www.mla.com.au/research-and-development/reports/2021/w.liv.2024---the-live-export-industry-annual-transport-mortality-report-2020/
Mercier S (2018) The cost of transporting cereals in West Africa. IFPRI Discussion Paper 01759
Moroccan Journeys (n.d.) Camels in the Sahara Desert, Morocco. https://moroccanjourneys.com/camels-in-the-sahara-desert-morocco/
Müller-Schwarze D, Sun L (2003) The Beaver: natural history of a wetlands engineer. Cornell University Press
Norlha (2018) Yaks and transport on the Tibetan Plateau. https://www.norlha.com/blogs/life-at-norlha-blog/yaks-and-transport
Otte J (2025) 8 incredible animal migrations that will blow your mind. Discov Wild Sci. https://discoverwildscience.com/8-incredible-animal-migrations-that-will-blow-your-mind-1-263823/
Phillips WD, Phillips CR (1992) The worlds of Christopher Columbus. Cambridge University Press
Postgate JN (1992) Early Mesopotamia: society and economy at the dawn of history. Routledge
Replace live animal transport. https://www.eurogroupforanimals.org/files/eurogroupforanimals/2020-12/Eurogroup-for-Animals_A-strategy-to-reduce-and-replace-live-animal-transport.pdf
Robin de Bois and Animal Welfare Foundation (2024) 64 EU-approved livestock carriers. https://www.animal-welfare-foundation.org/files/downloads/Report_64-livestock_AWF_RobindesBois_FINAL_March24-BD.pdf
Roman Empire Times (2024) Hannibal ad Portas: how 37 African elephants crossed the Alps. Roman Empire Times. https://romanempiretimes.com/hannibal-ad-portas-how-37-african-elephants-crossed-the-alps/
Schreiber RW, Burger J (2002) Biology of marine birds. CRC Press
Sims BG, Inns F, O'Neill D (2003) Equipment for working animals, with emphasis on equids in developing countries. World Association for Transport Animal Welfare and Studies (TAWS). https://www.taws.org/TAWS2003-Equipment-Sims-Inns-Oneill-Paper.pdf
Smith BD (1995) The emergence of agriculture. Scientific American Library.
Starkey P (2004) Moving forward with animal power for transport: How people, governments, and welfare organizations can make an impact: examples from Africa and Madagascar. World Association for Transport Animal Welfare and Studies (TAWS). http://www.taws.org/TAWS04-Starkey-Transport-8april04-16.pdf
Starkey PH (1999) Empowering animal traction development: practical methods for small multidisciplinary survey teams. Animal Traction Network for Eastern and Southern Africa (ATNESA). http://www.atnesa.org/Empowering99/Empowering99-Starkey-www.pdf
Statista Research Department (2024a) Container shipping—statistics & facts. https://www.statista.com/topics/1367/container-shipping/
Statista Research Department (2024b) Ocean shipping—statistics & facts. https://www.statista.com/topics/1728/ocean-shipping/
Storey N (2022) 10 animals that played an important role in the second world war. History Hit. https://www.historyhit.com/animals-in-the-second-world-war/
Sukumar R (2003) The living elephants: evolutionary ecology, behavior, and conservation. Oxford University Press
Tefera M (2011) Oxenization versus Tractorization: options and constraints for Ethiopian framing system. J Sustain Dev Afr 13
Tegegn E (2021, February 6) Ethiopia's donkey population at risk. The Reporter Ethiopia. https://www.thereporterethiopia.com/10847/
The Donkey Sanctuary. (2025). About Us. https://thedonkeysanctuarykenya.org/
The Social Work Graduate (n.d.) Veterinary social work. https://www.thesocialworkgraduate.com/post/veterinary-social-work
United Nations Conference on Trade and Development (UNCTAD) (2023) Review of maritime transport 2023: towards a green and just transition. Geneva, UNCTAD
Vagabonds of the World (n.d.) Sahara desert tour. https://vagrantsoftheworld.com/sahara-desert-tour/

Vogel S (2003) Comparative biomechanics: life's physical world. Princeton University Press
Wanted in Rome (2020, August 18) Italy: royal palace of Caserta bans horse-drawn carriages after horse's death. https://www.wantedinrome.com/news/italy-royal-palace-of-caserta-bans-horse-drawn-carriages-after-horses-death.html
World Athletics (2021) World records. https://www.worldathletics.org/world-records
World Federation for Animals (2023) Brazil's court order to shut down live export: a significant but not yet final win for animal welfare. https://wfa.org/brazils-court-order-to-shut-down-live-export-a-significant-but-not-yet-final-win-for-animal-welfare/
World Federation for Animals (2024) Shaping a sustainable future: new recommendations for global biodiversity and animal welfare. https://wfa.org/shaping-a-sustainable-future-new-recommendations-for-global-biodiversity-and-animal-welfare/

Part IV
Commensalistic and Mutualistic Interactions

Chapter 18
Animals and Tourism

Siobhan I. M. Speiran

> Wilderness without wildlife is just scenery.
> —*Lois Crisler*

Abstract Tourism has long been entangled with colonial infrastructures, shaping travel networks that historically benefited imperial powers while often exploiting local populations and landscapes. This chapter examines the lasting impacts of these global systems as manifested in contemporary wildlife tourism context, in which more-than-human animals (henceforth, 'animals') are frequently commodified as attractions, labourers, and souvenirs. Despite the central role of animals in the industry, ethical concerns surrounding their welfare have largely been overlooked. Through an interdisciplinary lens—including postcolonial and posthuman critiques—this chapter interrogates the economic structures that sustain exploitative wildlife tourism practices. It evaluates the industry's global reach, examines its ecological consequences, and introduces the concept of animal-positive practices. A number of successful case studies from around the world are examined. The chapter concludes by proposing economic policy and regulatory interventions aimed at reducing harmful tourist–animal interactions, and fostering conditions that support animal agency, well-being, and resilient multispecies communities.

Selling the Wild: Ethics, Economics, and the Future of Wildlife Tourism

International tourism is a phenomenon and driver of globalization, developed alongside imperial systems of trade, leisure, and transportation. Historically, colonial empires played a major role in shaping early tourism—establishing hospitality infrastructures and transportation networks to facilitate travel for elite and wealthy visitors from imperial nations. In this way, tourism has long intertwined with colonial exploitation; as local populations and landscapes were commodified for visitors'

S. I. M. Speiran (✉)
Faculty of Environmental & Urban Change, York University, Toronto, ON, Canada
e-mail: speiras@yorku.ca

N. Batini (ed.), *The Economics of Non-Human Animals*, Natural Resource Management and Policy 63, https://doi.org/10.1007/978-3-032-17580-9_18

enjoyment, economic benefits flowed primarily to colonial powers rather than to the host communities (Greiner and Toivanen 2024, pp. 223–233).

Animals—referred to as 'more-than-human' beings in some discussions—have been deeply embedded in tourism since its beginnings, and often subjected to the same unequal power dynamics. Millions of animals have been used as attractions, reinforcing their roles as spectacles for tourists (Barua 2017) or as commodified "souvenirs," leaving them with little control over their own existence (Fennell et al. 2024, p. 3824; Hooper 2022). Despite their central presence across many facets of the tourism industry, ethical considerations surrounding their treatment have been significantly overlooked in both academic research and tourism practices. Tourism scholars describe this issue as "virtually terra incognita"—an unexplored territory in ethical discussions (Fennell 2014, p. 983; Fennell et al. 2024).

Today, the concept of animal-based tourism evokes a wide variety of human–animal interactions, including elephant rides, swimming with dolphins, safari expeditions, sloth selfies, dog sledding, birdwatching, cat cafés, and visits to local zoos. Across this ever-growing list of attractions, both wild and domesticated species serve as the main draw. While acknowledging that domesticated animals may serve as attractions, labourers, or consumables in tourism contexts, this chapter focuses specifically on the wildlife tourism sector.

Wildlife tourism, defined broadly, is a niche of nature-based tourism centred on encounters with non-domesticated animals, either free-ranging or in captivity, typically in or near protected areas (Higginbottom 2004; Speiran and Hovorka 2024). Wildlife management for tourism exists along a continuum: from minimal human interference, where animals roam freely, to increasing levels of intervention (e.g., food provisioning) and, ultimately, to full captivity in restrictive and impoverished enclosures (ibid.).

Following Fennell, "what we see in tourism and what we know about the nature of tourism operations can be vastly different" (Fennell 2022a). Captive wildlife tourism includes millions of individual animals living in at least 10,000 zoos and aquaria worldwide (Fennell 2013; Speiran and Hovorka 2024). Determining exact numbers is a challenge, however, given the multitude of wild animals used in unregulated, non-accredited, or illegal tourism settings. For example, it is estimated that more than half a million animals are part of non-accredited, non-zoo wildlife attractions worldwide that harm their welfare or conservation (Moorhouse et al. 2015). Furthermore, investigations by journalists (Daly 2019), academics (Baker et al. 2013), NGOs (WFA 2023), and conservation authorities (IUCN 2016) reveal the prevalence of unethical wildlife attractions, as well as, the intertwined nature of the wildlife trade and tourism industry (D'Cruze et al. 2017; Moorhouse et al. 2017a).

In June 2019, *National Geographic* published a special issue exposing the hidden cruelty behind wildlife tourism (Daly 2019). The investigative piece followed a journalist and photographer through six countries, uncovering troubling practices at popular wildlife attractions—particularly those believed to harm the animals involved. The resulting article and visuals documented a range of exploitative scenarios across the growing wildlife tourism industry, including elephant rides in Thailand, performing bears in Russia, and photo opportunities with baby sloths in the Amazon. The report concluded that many of these operations "maximise profits by exploiting animals from birth to death" and that "people who love animals can unknowingly fuel their suffering" (ibid.). It would thus appear that to investigate the lives of animals entangled in this phenomenon is to reveal the capitalist contours of an industry that commodifies and consumes wild animals' lives and bodies for profit and pleasure (Barua 2019).

This chapter considers how animals are engaged in the global wildlife tourism economy to reassess their true economic value to the industry and propose ways to better reflect this value in economic decision-making. This work is rooted in interdisciplinary scholarship across animal-based tourism, wildlife conservation, and animal welfare, and draws on insights from feminist care theory (Donovan 2006), animal labour studies (Blattner et al. 2019; Coulter 2016), and ecofeminist thought (Yudina and Grimwood 2016). It also engages postcolonial (Akama et al. 2011) and posthuman (Thomsen et al. 2021) critiques of wildlife tourism and animal studies, weaving these perspectives together to address this timely subject.

The chapter begins by examining the exclusionary capital–colonial logics that underpin wildlife tourism, before evaluating the global scale of the industry and its contemporary economic and ecological impacts. It subsequently develops the concept of animal-positive practices, aligning them with existing regulatory frameworks and economic incentives designed to protect socio-ecological systems. Finally, it recommends future public policy interventions aimed at reducing consumptive (and illegal) tourist–animal interactions, while fostering conditions that promote animal agency and support good lives for the animals involved in tourism.

The Origins of Wildlife Tourism

Contemporary forms of animal-based tourism can be traced back to early written records describing the use of animals for entertainment (e.g., Roman Colosseum *venationes* and the walled menageries of ancient Assyria, Egypt, and Babylonia) and subsistence (e.g., hunting and fishing) (Nóbrega Alves and Duarte Barboza 2018). Imperial menageries symbolized the dominion of the wealthy classes, whose collections of displaced animals, and often Indigenous peoples, laid the foundation for zoological gardens that reinforced colonial identities (Deckha 2012; Nóbrega Alves and Duarte Barboza 2018). Class relations and global capitalism cemented the abject status of animals, with zoos becoming "part of the repertoire marking cities as places of high culture and their inhabitants as paradigmatic humans, compared to the natural realm of the colonies and hinterlands and their inhabitants" (Deckha 2012, p. 528). Moreover, the historical animalization of racialized and gendered "subaltern" human groups is central to colonial logics (Hovorka 2015; Mbaiwa and Hambira 2023).

This "colonial baggage" remains diffuse throughout the tourism industry today, embedded in its research, development, and practice (Greiner and Toivanen 2024, p. 234). Some scholars argue that tourism operates as a modern form of colonialism (i.e., neocolonialism), through which the Global North continues to exert political, economic, and socio-cultural dominance over the Global South (Akama et al. 2011). Tourism development, for example, is often framed as a pathway to economic advancement for marginalized communities. This financial vulnerability, however, is frequently manipulated by powerful actors who impose unequal and exploitative economic arrangements (Akama et al. 2011). In Kenya, for instance, wildlife tourism and conservation programmes were developed jointly to protect wildlife parks for foreign tourists—often at the expense of pastoral, nomadic Maasai communities, who were displaced and denied access to their ancestral lands (ibid.).

Rather than viewing the relationship between tourism and empire as fixed, we might instead consider the liminal zones created by tourism as spaces in which to "listen carefully for subaltern voices"—including those of animals (Zuelow 2024, p. 351). From the past to the present, tourism has also offered colonial subjects opportunities to express agency (e.g., protest) otherwise restricted under colonial regimes (Akama et al. 2011; Zuelow 2024). Similarly, this chapter encourages attentiveness to how animals assert forms of agency within tourism landscapes—for example, by resisting or leveraging tourism encounters through acts such as injuring tourists, refusing participation in attractions, or stealing valued items to trade back for food (Fennell 2022c).

The Economic Impact of Wildlife Tourism

The economic impact of the global wildlife tourism market is difficult to quantify due to its integration with adjacent industries that also rely on animals—such as agriculture, entertainment, and the pet trade. Complicating matters further, wildlife tourism may be just one component of multi-activity travel, or even incidental to the primary purpose of a trip. Barbara Noske introduced the term *animal–industrial complex* to describe the web of economic activities and sectors interconnected through their use of animals (1989). Richard Twine later expanded on this concept, describing it as the "partly opaque and multiple sets of networks and relationships between the corporate (agricultural) sector, governments, and public and private science" (Sorenson 2014; Twine 2012, p. 23). Animal-based tourism intersects with both legal and illegal industries involving animal products, labour, entertainment, and companion animals.

Wildlife tourism is a developing and diversifying sector within the broader category of nature-based tourism. The *World Bank* reported in 2016 that the tourism industry, writ large, generates 10.4% of global Gross Domestic Product (GDP) and supports 292 million jobs worldwide (Twining-Ward et al. 2018; WTTC 2019). With more than half the world's population now residing in urban areas—a figure projected to rise—demand for wildlife tourism is expected to grow in parallel (Higginbottom 2004; Twining-Ward et al. 2018). Currently, wildlife tourism comprises over 20% of global tourism, with millions of trips taken each year and an annual growth rate of 10% (Moorhouse et al. 2015; Twining-Ward et al. 2018). A 2019 report by the

World Travel & Tourism Council estimated that wildlife tourism generates over $120 billion annually and supports more than 21 million jobs worldwide (WTTC 2019). While this growth offers opportunities to support host economies and ecosystems through tourism revenue, it will undoubtedly be challenged by intensifying climate change (Mkono and Hughes 2024).

The *World Travel & Tourism Council*—defining wildlife tourism as the non-consumptive viewing and experiencing of non-captive wildlife in their natural habitat—reports that wildlife tourism accounts for over a third of all travel and tourism in Africa, 1.6% in Europe, 2% in North America, 5.8% in the Asia–Pacific region, and 8.6% in Latin America (2019). A few examples from countries renowned for wildlife tourism illustrate this variation: in India, tourism is a leading net foreign exchange earner and the largest service industry (ibid.); in Tanzania, it is the main driver of growth and employment, and was the top contributor of foreign exchange receipts in 2018 (CABI 2019; World Bank 2024); in Mexico, foreign exchange income from tourism in 2023 set a new historical record (Duran 2024).

Yet, the prevalence of foreign-owned tourism companies (e.g., hotels, airlines, and tour operators) often leads to revenue leakage, limiting the potential benefits to local communities and providing minimal job mobility for tourism workers. Wildlife tourism, however, can support less-developed, biodiverse regions through direct employment (e.g., rangers, guides, hospitality) and indirect employment (e.g., transportation, suppliers, vendors), thereby bolstering developing economies (Higginbottom 2004). This is especially true in the case of community-based wildlife tourism in which profits are retained and reinvested into the host community's healthcare, education, and infrastructure (Alam and Nayak 2024).

At its core, wildlife tourism relies on the commodification of nature, yet it can also serve as a powerful conservation tool—for instance, through the establishment of protected areas and the provision of *ecosystem services*. Protected areas (including national parks, reserves, and private conservation zones) often depend on tourism revenue, permits, and concessions for their sustainability. The global cost of developing and maintaining protected areas is estimated at approximately $10 billion, and the revenue generated by wildlife tourism significantly exceeds these costs (Balmford et al. 2015). Nonetheless, comprehensive economic evaluations of park tourism's impact remain limited in many developing countries (Chidakel et al. 2021). Addressing this gap, a study of South Luangwa National Park in Zambia found that tourism contributes approximately 40% of local household income and accounts for at least half of business growth in the surrounding gateway community—despite high levels of revenue leakage (ibid.).

Given that wildlife tourism is estimated to be worth five times more than the illegal wildlife trade, it can offer a viable alternative to poaching and trafficking of protected species by contributing to sustainable livelihoods through ecosystem services, environmental education, and the employment of former poachers as anti-poaching rangers—all of which supports the *United Nations' Sustainable Development Goals* (WTTC 2019). In China, for example, over 60% of anti-poaching rangers were formerly poachers who were incentivized to transition into conservation work (Lotter et al. 2016).

Wildlife tourism can generate multiplicative effects that benefit other sectors, including agriculture, hospitality, transportation, and artisanal goods. This diversification is vital, as overdependence on tourism revenue (especially in regions vulnerable to pandemics, climate change, or political instability) poses risks to economic stability, and conversely, conservation in the case of overtourism (Stone 2024). Travel restrictions during COVID-19 led to the collapse of several wildlife tourism-dependent economies and a corresponding increase in habitat loss and poaching (Mearns et al. 2023). The impact of travel restrictions, as well as the seasonal nature of tourism, can also create job insecurity, especially for demographics with limited social protection (e.g., women) (Tran and Walter 2014).

Although wildlife tourism holds potential for supporting local livelihoods, education, and conservation, these benefits are often undermined by asymmetrical power relations among stakeholders—least of all the animals themselves, who are typically treated as commodities rather than recognized as stakeholders in the tourism industry (Speiran and Hovorka 2024). Even organizations mandated with improving the sustainability and ethics of tourism have customarily not "held animals in any regard (e.g., [United Nations World Tourism Organization])" and continue to conceptualize them as resource-components of broader categories of nature (Fennell 2014). Tourism revenue often fails to meet the expectations set to fund comprehensive conservation efforts (Tumusiime and Vedeld 2012), and can incentivize unethical wildlife attractions that harm the welfare of involved species and endanger their conservation (Moorhouse et al. 2017a).

These realities underscore the need for continued research and advocacy in support of what wildlife tourism ultimately depends on—the animals themselves—and how their true economic value can be recognized such that they are afforded a "life worth living" (Mellor 2016). Following Fennell, tourism and conservation are fundamentally human enterprises in which animals owe us nothing (2014). Fennell critiques wildlife tourism models that frame animals as "earning their keep" as a rationale for their care or conservation, arguing that such logic assumes animals have a stake in tourism, when in reality they are treated as pawns (2014). Ultimately, we must confront the dominant theoretical foundations of tourism literature, which consistently marginalize animal interests, reducing their bodies, lives, and labour to economic abstractions rather than acknowledging their intrinsic worth and agency. The following sections explore these challenges in depth, along with their far-reaching consequences for animal welfare and conservation.

The Ecological Impact of Wildlife Tourism

Wildlife tourism has served as a crucial catalyst in prompting governmental support of biodiversity conservation, although the extent and effectiveness of such measures can vary widely (Higginbottom 2004). Tourism activities and development can significantly impact the behaviour of wildlife and ecological dynamics (Cohen 1978). As a result of this anthropogenic pressure on the environment from tourism, animals

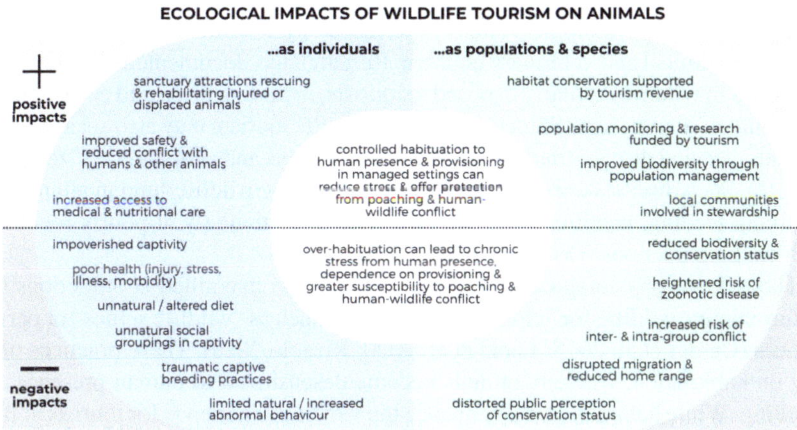

Fig. 18.1 Positive & negative ecological impacts of wildlife tourism on wild animals at individual (e.g., rescue, stress, abnormal behaviour) and population/species levels (e.g., habitat conservation, biodiversity loss, disrupted migration). *Source* Author's own work

may undergo changes in foraging, migration, reproduction, and predator avoidance behaviours. This section outlines the positive and negative contributions to ecology by focusing on both the individual and species-level impact of wildlife tourism (summarized in Fig. 18.1).

The ecological impacts associated with tourism-related development are substantial. Infrastructure expansion (including trails, roads, lodges, and enclosures) can fragment habitats and disrupt ecological processes (Ascensão et al. 2022; Sánchez Porras 2024). Increased tourist access often contributes to deforestation and habitat loss (Newsome 2021), while sensitive ecological corridors and breeding or nesting sites may be disturbed by human presence and activity (Shannon et al. 2017). Some tourism developments, such as high-end hotels and lodges, are situated in ecologically fragile areas (i.e., near critical breeding, feeding sites, and watering holes) (Akama et al. 2011). The movement of tourists across ecosystems can also facilitate the introduction of non-native species who pose a risk to native species, and in turn threaten ecological stability (Anderson et al. 2015).

Pollution and waste are also consequences of wildlife tourism development and pose risks to the health of individuals within the ecosystem. Littering, light, noise, and water pollution degrade habitats and disrupt the natural behaviours of wildlife (Roe et al. 1997). Littering and human food waste can lead certain species, especially scavengers, to become dependent on human provisioning, increasing the likelihood of illness or human-wildlife conflict (Cui et al. 2021; Santos et al. 2019). Light pollution from tourist establishments can disrupt migratory and nocturnal activities (Wolf and Croft 2012). Noise pollution can cause distress and disorientation in wildlife (Belsoy and Korir 2012). Finally, water pollution from litter and chemicals (e.g., sunscreen) can endanger both freshwater and marine life (Downs et al. 2022).

Crucially, the physiological stress experienced by wildlife as a result of tourism is a serious ethical and veterinary concern. Research has documented elevated stress responses in wildlife regularly exposed to tourists, including increased cortisol levels and immune suppression (Shutt et al. 2014). Wildlife tourism may also act as a vector for pathogen and disease transmission between humans and animals (i.e., "zoonotic" disease). Such diseases are more likely to spread during wildlife-human interactions involving feeding, handling, or close observation, particularly at poorly regulated, high-traffic attractions (Odeniran et al. 2018).

The risks of physiological stress and zoonoses are magnified at attractions that feature captive wildlife for "close-up" encounters such as "wildlife selfies" or performances (Carder et al. 2018; Lenzi et al. 2020; Rizzolo 2020). These practices often rely on habituation, wherein animals become desensitized to human presence and handling. While habituation may enhance the viewing experience for tourists at free-living, non-captive wildlife attractions (Knight 2009), it can compromise individual welfare by increasing vulnerability to poaching and disease. Habituation can also destabilize ecological communities by disrupting inter- and intra-species (including predator–prey) dynamics (Bach and Burton 2017; Green and Gabriel 2020). For example, animals may avoid or be displaced from habitats due to overcrowding or consistent human activity. Species with complex social structures, such as elephants and primates, are especially vulnerable to disturbances in group cohesion and social hierarchies (Costa et al. 2023; Szott et al. 2019).

Accreditation systems exist for some forms of wildlife tourism—such as those offered by the World Association of Zoos and Aquariums (WAZA), the Global Federation of Animal Sanctuaries (GFAS), and various certification programmes (e.g., sustainabletourism.net; gstcouncil.org). However, less than 1% of tourism businesses are formally certified. A report by World Animal Protection (WAP) on wildlife tourism revealed that just one-third of the 62 travel trade associations examined had sustainability initiatives visible on their websites (WAP 2023). Furthermore, only three had animal welfare guidelines, and only one actively tracked their enforcement. Of the estimated 7000–10,000 zoological parks and sanctuaries worldwide that are open to the public, only 1300 are accredited by WAZA and just 150 by GFAS (ibid.). This disparity has led researchers to argue that most wildlife attractions operate without adherence to recognized ethical standards or oversight mechanisms (Blackett et al. 2017).

Wildlife tourism attractions that are harmful to animals and ecosystems may be subject to "greenwashing"—a marketing tactic used to appear ethical and/or sustainable. Terms like ecotourism and sustainable tourism remain profitable but unregulated. Attractions often conceal the aversive conditioning and drug-induced sedation used to ensure wild animals (especially predator species) tolerate constant proximity and handling from changing crowds of tourists (Carder et al. 2018; Cohen 2013). These attractions are popularized by tourists who share stories and images on social media platforms such as *Facebook, Instagram, TikTok, Twitter, YouTube,* and *TripAdvisor* (Lenzi et al. 2020; von Essen et al. 2020).

Social media can intensify these dynamics by encouraging and normalizing close-contact interactions with wild animals serving as photo-props. These "wildlife selfies" shape public perceptions of what is acceptable and desirable when engaging with wild animals, reinforcing demand for proximate—and often exploitative—experiences. Viral images and videos not only reflect these trends but actively drive them (Lenzi et al. 2020; Tomassini et al. 2024). Unfortunately, most tourists remain unable to recognize the signs of poor animal welfare or conservation practices, evidenced by positive online reviews of problematic attractions on forums such as *TripAdvisor* (Moorhouse et al. 2015, 2017a, b).

Conversely, there is plenty of evidence that—when managed responsibly—wildlife tourism can have a positive ecological impact, supporting conservation through several key mechanisms (Higginbottom 2004). The economic and social benefits of tourism can serve as strong incentives for operators and local communities to protect the ecosystems that sustain their livelihoods (Campbell 2007). Revenue generated from tourism can be reinvested into conservation projects, either through the operator's own initiatives or by supporting external organizations. For example, tourism can provide essential funding to enable habitat restoration, biodiversity monitoring, and anti-poaching measures through the creation and maintenance of national parks and wildlife reserves (Higginbottom 2004). Tourism can thus offer a sustainable alternative to extractive land uses, encouraging governments and communities to preserve ecosystems (Broadbent et al. 2012). Finally, wildlife tourism can also serve an educational role, fostering environmental awareness among tourists which may cultivate broader support for conservation (Larm et al. 2018).

Tourism has consequently been described as holding an "ambivalent position in relation to biodiversity" (van der Duim and Caalders 2002, p. 744), and as a "double-edged sword for the socio-environmental movement" (Mowforth and Munt 1998, p. 156). Like sustainable development, biodiversity is a triadic, "compound concept" composed of genetic, species, and ecosystem diversity (van der Duim and Caalders 2002, p. 746). As van der Duim and Caalders observe, the "simultaneous maximization or optimization of all these is not possible" (ibid.). Thus, hard choices and trade-offs are often necessary to determine which aspect of biodiversity conservation to prioritize (McShane et al. 2011). Ultimately, if tourism contributes net negative impacts to biodiversity, this not only threatens ecological stability, but also increases the vulnerability of both ecosystems and individual species to anthropogenic disturbances and disease—which may ultimately lead to extinction (Benson et al. 2019). The collective impact of these anthropogenic pressures, whether direct or indirect, determines the long-term viability of wildlife populations and the overall sustainability of wildlife tourism development.

Although tourism revenue can contribute to conservation, such as by funding protected areas (Steven et al. 2013; Tumusiime and Vedeld 2012) and supporting zoo and aquarium operations (Higginbottom 2004), it also raises tensions between maintaining ecological integrity and pursuing economic gain (Khater et al. 2024). Having considered the broader ecological impacts of wildlife tourism, the following section develops a theory of animal-positive practices and explores integrative approaches to valuing animals as both individuals and populations within wildlife tourism contexts.

Animal-Positive Practices in Wildlife Tourism

This section advances interdisciplinary and innovative approaches to promote animal-positive practices in wildlife tourism. It grounds these approaches in case studies that highlight the challenges and opportunities faced in safeguarding the socio-ecological environments where tourism occurs. Each case study concludes with targeted recommendations for public policy interventions aimed at reducing consumptive (and illegal) wildlife tourism. Animal-positive practices in wildlife tourism are explored across three registers, guided by the following conceptual frameworks: the conservation-welfare nexus, animal labour and interspecies solidarity, and Fennell's (2022a) seven hypernorms for wildlife tourism. Animal-positive practices are defined as:

1. *Beneficence.* Practices that prioritize beneficence toward animals, advancing both individual (i.e., welfare) and population-level (i.e., conservation) outcomes, rather than focusing solely on harm mitigation;
2. *Recognition.* Practices that value animals beyond their passive utility as tourism attractions or labourers, recognizing them as relational beings who benefit from interspecies solidarity and who are supported in their right to inhabit tourism landscapes on their own terms;
3. *Agency.* Practices that acknowledge wild animals as stakeholders in tourism, with legitimate interests in the protection of their ecological communities and the freedom to express agency and consent.

Effective policy frameworks that support animal-positive practices should be designed to integrate these principles in the design and regulation of wildlife tourism. In this way, tourism models can be fostered that are ethically responsible and sustainable for multispecies tourism communities.

The Conservation-Welfare Nexus

Animal welfare is commonly defined as the state of an animal as it attempts to cope with its environment (Fraser and Broom 1990). It is holistically assessed based on multiple elements, including biological functioning (i.e., health), feelings (i.e., affective state), and the naturalness of living conditions (Mellor et al. 2020). An animal's welfare is not an entirely objective state; it is influenced by the animal's own perception of its welfare and that of other group members (Ohl and Putman 2014).

The multidisciplinary field of animal welfare science examines the lives of animals and their individual experiences within human-ordered and governed systems. To shift the focus toward providing positive welfare, the *UK Farm Animal Welfare Council* introduced the concepts of a "life worth living," a "life not worth living," and a "good life," later adapted into the "Quality of Life Scale" by Green and Mellor

(2011; Mellor 2016). It is unrealistic, however, to expect the total elimination of negative affective experiences, or the continuous provision of positive experiences, throughout an animal's lifetime. Thus, a "life worth living" for animals in wildlife tourism ideally "achieves a net balance over time that favours positive experiences" (Mellor 2016, p. 12).

Progressive zoos worldwide have developed creative strategies to advance animal welfare, such as environmental enrichment (Mellor 2016). This involves identifying and providing species-appropriate stimuli that promote good welfare. Enrichment is a crucial management strategy for captive animals, requiring continual refinement and consistent application (Bachetti et al. 2024). There is also compelling evidence that human–animal relationships impact welfare and, in some cases, can be enriching (Claxton 2011). Such relationships may benefit animals by fostering the acceptance of human constraints, facilitating learning, reducing injury risk, and promoting positive welfare states both in the short term (e.g., reassurance, relaxation, enrichment, exploration, playfulness) and the long term (e.g., improved health, reduced stress, increased resilience) (ibid.).

The 2020 update to the widely used *Five Domains* model of animal welfare included human–animal interactions, along with an emphasis on "various forms of comfort, pleasure, interest, attachment, confidence, and a sense of being in control"—all of which can enhance welfare (Mellor et al. 2020, p. 7; see also Fig. 18.2 for a visual summary). These additions recognize the influence of subjective states on animal welfare and are attuned to expressions of agency, choice, and consent in wildlife attractions (Mellor et al. 2020).

Animal welfare and conservation must be viewed as interconnected priorities rather than competing objectives. As Paquet and Darimont (2010, p. 14) argue, they are "two sides of the same coin." While welfare initiatives focus on individuals

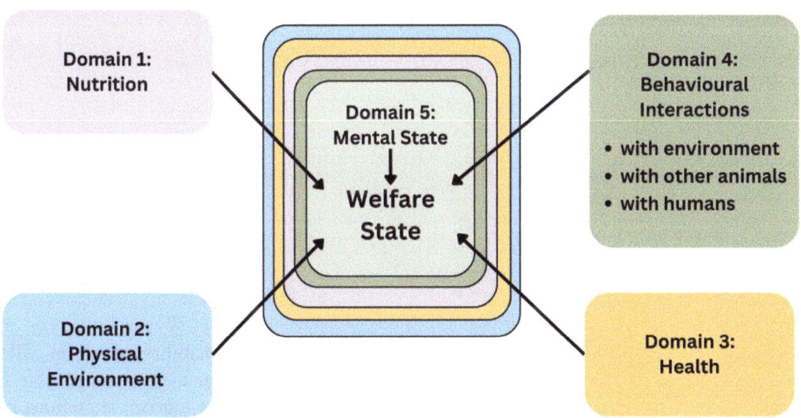

Fig. 18.2 The 2020 five domains model for animal welfare assessment and monitoring. Adapted from Wilkins et al. (2024), who adapted from Mellor et al. (2020)

and conservation typically targets populations and ecosystems, ecosystems are ultimately assemblages of individuals. Achieving sustainable wildlife tourism outcomes requires integrating welfare and conservation goals through coordinated policy action. This concept, sometimes called the conservation-welfare nexus (Fig. 18.3), is the subject of several sub-disciplines and animal ethics approaches, including zoo and wildlife reintroduction studies (Swaisgood 2010), compassionate conservation (Ramp and Bekoff 2015), conservation welfare (Beausoleil et al. 2018), and increasingly animal tourism research (Fennell et al. 2023; Speiran and Hovorka 2024).

Complementary to this concept are the *One Health* and *One Welfare* approaches, which highlight how compromised animal welfare can, in turn, harm human well-being and environmental health (Tarazona et al. 2019). Moreover—from an economic perspective—poor animal health can cause stress and increased energy expenditure which threatens productivity and renders animal industries unsustainable (ibid.). To be truly equitable, a One Health, One Welfare model must "[rethink] social justice through a multispecies lens" (Ruckert et al. 2020, p. 643, citing Celermajer et al. 2020). This includes recognizing that animals can serve as "indicators of human health and welfare" in multispecies communities and partnerships (e.g., wildlife attractions) (Jordan and Lem 2014).

In 2022, the *United Nations Environment Assembly* recognized the critical interdependence of sustainable development, environmental protection, and animal welfare

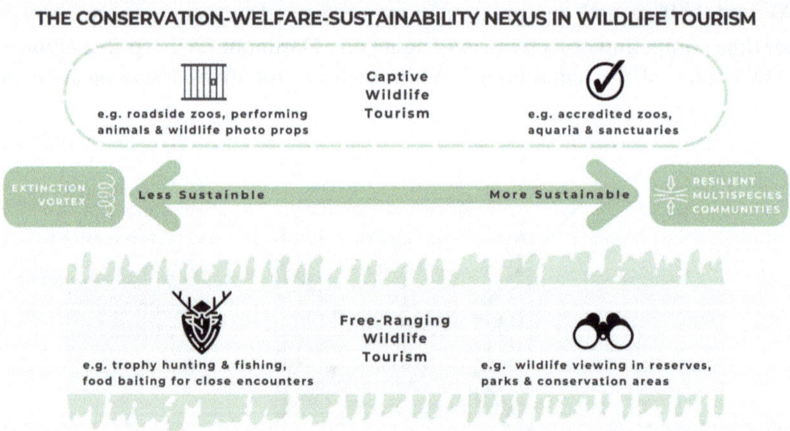

Fig. 18.3 This figure demonstrates the conservation-welfare-sustainability nexus in wildlife tourism. The centre of the image depicts a spectrum from *less sustainable* to *more sustainable.* Less sustainable, explicitly "consumptive" captive and free-ranging wildlife tourism attractions negatively impact animal welfare and conservation outcomes for involved species. If biodiversity loss and animal use are too intensive, they can lead to an extinction vortex. Captive and free-ranging wildlife tourism attractions which are non-consumptive, and improve animal welfare and conservation outcomes for involved species, are more sustainable. Such attractions can foster resilient multispecies communities. *Source* Author's own work

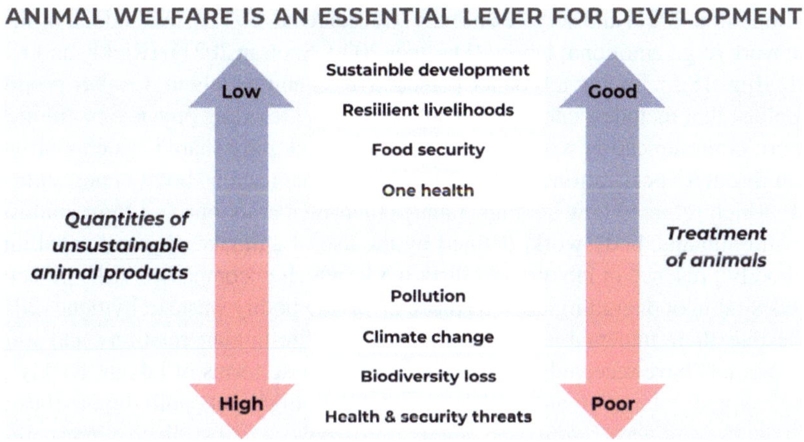

Fig. 18.4 Adapted from the world federation for animals report entitled: "Unveiling the Nexus: The Interdependence of Animal Welfare, Environment & Sustainable Development"

(WFA 2023). In response, the *World Federation for Animals* published a report which affirms that "animal welfare is an instrumental lever for development" (see Fig. 18.4), such that high welfare is integral to addressing environmental challenges and the UN's Sustainable Development Goals (SDGs) (WFA 2023, p. 3). Despite the sweeping scope of the SDGs, there is little mention of the role of domesticated or wild animals and no mention of animal welfare, which, as Kline et al. note, contrasts with One Health objectives (Keeling et al. 2019, 2022). To align wildlife tourism with global objectives, tourism operators must prioritize positive mental experiences for animals by providing choice, control, agency, and opportunities to express natural behaviours, access to stimulating, species-appropriate environments and social groups.

Empowering tourists with the tools to identify and assess ethical standards in wildlife tourism is essential to driving industry-wide improvements in animal welfare and conservation (Fennell et al. 2023; Moorhouse et al. 2017a). Fennell et al. (2023) developed an evaluative rubric that enables tourists to assess and report on animal welfare, governance, and conservation practices at captive wildlife tourism sites. These efforts are further supported by Fennell's animal welfare literacy framework (2022b) and educational syllabus (2022) both of which can guide policy and education initiatives aimed at fostering more ethical tourism practices.

Animal Labour and Interspecies Solidarity

Animals have been entwined in the tourism industry for centuries as labourers, performing various types of work, including performative work (e.g., bull fighting (López-López and Quintero Venegas 2021), value-added work (e.g., transportation

(Vasilopoulou 2021) and service animals (Hansen et al. 2021)), and hidden or intangible work (e.g., emotional labour (Dashper 2020; Speiran 2021)) (Rickly and Kline 2021) (Fig. 18.5). Taking a broader perspective on animal labour, Coulter proposes a typology that includes: care work, which involves providing physical or emotional support; communication work, which includes developing shared systems of interaction through vocalizations, gestures, and even unconscious bodily cues; emotion work, which refers to how animals manage their own emotions and form emotional ties with humans; body work, defined by the use of animals' physical capabilities and bodily presence in labour; and dirty work, which encompasses tasks perceived as undesirable or degrading, such as those involving bodily waste or hygiene (2016).

Despite their undeniable contribution to wildlife-human relations and industries, animals have received little recognition for these forms of labour. Rickly and Kline's edited volume on animal labour in tourism highlights both the obvious and often overlooked ways animals engage in tourism work across diverse international contexts (2021). The volume also explores the theoretical implications of recognizing animals as (co-)workers within the industry (ibid.). Considering what "good work" for animals entails, Blattner et al. consider the political and philosophical questions surrounding how labour rights, consent, legal and political status, and allied advocacy movements interface with animal labour (2019).

Like human labour, animals can experience oppressive and harmful forms of work, but work may also provide animals with a source of meaning, self-development, and social membership (Blattner et al. 2019). Unregulated and unethical wildlife tourism attractions represent a form of institutionalized harm inflicted by humans on animals. Addressing this harm requires replacing exploitative attractions with humane alternatives that benefit both human and animal workers (Blattner et al. 2019; Coulter 2016). In cases where eliminating such attractions is not feasible, meaningful improvements must be made to enhance the working conditions of both human and non-human participants (ibid.).

The growing body of scholarship that seeks to improve the lived realities and status of animals through an animal labour perspective often centres interspecies

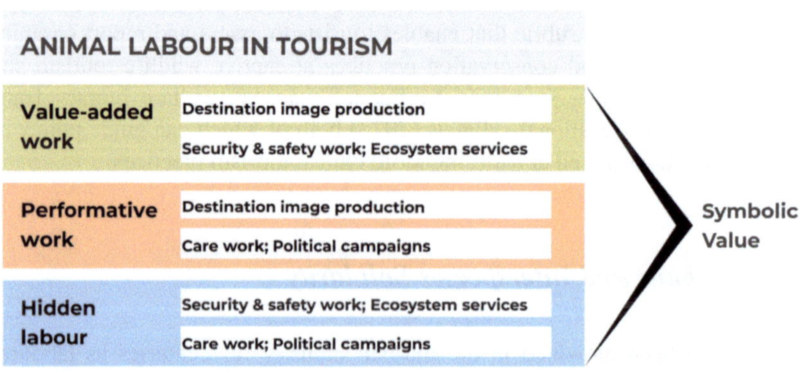

Fig. 18.5 "Approaches to animal work in tourism" adapted from Rickly and Kline (2021)

justice and solidarity (Blattner et al. 2019; Coulter 2016). Interspecies solidarity offers a lens through which to reimagine the meaning and experience of labour, both in routine interactions and within broader political contexts (Coulter 2016, 2017). Fundamentally rooted in empathy, it acknowledges the intertwined emotional and rational dimensions of wildlife-human relationships (ibid.). Two allied conceptual frameworks that support the lives of animals in tourism through a posthuman, interspecies justice approach include Thomsen et al.'s *multispecies livelihoods* (2021) and Kline et al.'s *wildlife equity theory* (2022). These approaches challenge reductionist, anthropocentric tourism practices in which animals are viewed as "underprivileged and oppressed counterparts," emphasizing that "the multilateral recognition of intrinsic value and ethical rights of all biodiversity is fundamentally linked to progress for all" (Kline et al. 2022, p. 2). The multispecies livelihoods framework positions tourism as a tool to address ecological crises and improve animal welfare, ultimately promoting wildlife-human coexistence (2021). Underscoring a moral obligation to recognize animals as active participants in shaping tourism experiences, there is a need for interdisciplinary inquiry to develop ethical guidelines for the use of wild animals in tourism, elevate their role as stakeholders in tourism governance, challenge exploitative practices, and foster locally managed economic development (Fennell 2014; Fennell and Sheppard 2021; Kline et al. 2022; Thomsen et al. 2021).

Scholars and advocates considering the lives of animal labourers in wildlife tourism can also benefit from the application of Coulter's humane jobs concept, which is grounded in interspecies solidarity (Blattner et al. 2019; Coulter 2017). The humane jobs concept also prompts us to consider the potential for animals to engage in work that is meaningful to them and from which they derive value. To reconceptualize a wildlife tourism attraction as a "multispecies workplace" and community, humane jobs would be "characterised by respect and reciprocity," with animals "afforded protections and positive entitlements underscored by interspecies solidarity" (Coulter 2017, p. 73). Potential humane jobs within and adjacent to wildlife tourism include conservation canines (D'Souza et al. 2019), travelling with guide dogs (Hansen et al. 2021), and conspecific care work in zoos and sanctuaries (Speiran 2021).

While the specifics of implementing labour rights for animals in policy are beyond the scope of this chapter (these are dealt extensively in Chapter 16 of this book), Cochrane (2016) recommends five plausible and essential rights—already established in international treaties and national laws—that can be extended across species lines. These include: "the right to representation by a labour union, the right to a decent standard of remuneration, the right to healthy and safe working conditions, the right to rest and leisure, and the right to a decent retirement" (2016, p. 27). Policies supporting these rights would provide animals with a political voice and stakeholdership, remuneration (e.g., food, health care, retirement funding), and opportunities for rest and recreation that are valued by the animals, rather than by their employers. Valuing animals as "members of" and "workers within" the tourism community can inform more caring, innovative, and inclusive wildlife-human relations (Cochrane 2016, p. 31).

Seven Hypernorms for Wildlife Tourism

Speiran and Hovorka identify three major challenges in addressing the use of animals in wildlife tourism in ways that improve sustainability (2024). First, unethical and unsustainable practices across the industry frequently endanger animal welfare and wildlife conservation, thereby undermining broader sustainable development goals. Second, significant knowledge gaps persist in the study of wild animal welfare, compounded by limited welfare literacy among tourists and tourism practitioners. Third, wild animals are rarely afforded agency or considered stakeholders in tourism, despite being co-creators and co-participants in tourism research and practice. In short, animals remain the "unseen majority" of tourism (2024).

Sustainable tourism has been the subject of academic attention for nearly four decades, yet there seems to have been relatively little change in tourism operations (Moscardo and Murphy 2014). In both theory and practice, the interests of global players involved in nature-based tourism, ecotourism, and wildlife tourism contradict those of the local communities where tourism occurs, creating a "climate of uncertainty and disruption in the lives of people and the animals upon which they depend" (Fennell 2022a).

To address these tensions within wildlife tourism, policy innovations might include context-specific welfare assessments (Bansiddhi et al. 2020; Carder et al. 2016; Speiran 2025), mandatory education for tourism operators on recognizing animal agency, and regulatory mechanisms that ensure animals have the right to avoid or exit human encounters (Fennell 2022a, c; Guo and Fennell 2024). A key policy question regarding the regulation of captive wildlife attractions is how to ensure these attractions go beyond the provision of basic care to ensure a "life worth living" for the wild animals involved. Insights from animal welfare science underscore the importance of promoting positive affective states—such as play, comfort, and pleasure—by enriching captive conditions to support emotional and social well-being (Mellor 2016; Mellor et al. 2020; Webb et al. 2019). As Melfi recommends, wild animals in captivity should be provided with a "luxurious life [...] conditions in which [they] thrive rather than just survive" (Melfi 2009, p. 579).

Policy frameworks guiding animal-based tourism have traditionally overlooked animals' agentive capacity to express their desires, fears, and interests. Fennell addresses this gap by proposing the concept of *animal-informed consent*—a framework which suggests animals can express assent, consent, or dissent through their exhibited behaviour, emotions, and physiological states (2022c). Integrating such a concept into tourism policy could transform industry standards by formally recognizing animal agency in wildlife-human encounters. To that end, Fennell (2022a, b) proposes seven normative principles called "hypernorms" to serve as ethical benchmarks for global wildlife tourism governance. These hypernorms include: *(1) the pinnacle of practice, (2) recognition of beneficence, (3) non-maleficence, (4) enhancing literacy and education, (5) justice, (6) recognition of agency and self-determination,* and *(7) animal-informed consent.* Together, these principles can serve as the foundation for policy instruments and certification schemes aimed at improving animal welfare outcomes across wildlife tourism operations (Fennell 2022a, p. 3).

The development and enforcement of such ethical guidelines present challenges, however, especially when navigating the tension between global policy norms and diverse local practices. In many tourism contexts, such as in the Global South, cultural, economic, and ecological realities shape how wild animals are used, valued, and protected in tourism. Any policy approach must therefore be sensitive to the situated knowledge, multispecies relationships, and local culture of the host community, while remaining committed to the overarching goals of justice, sustainability, and animal welfare (Fennell 2022a). As Mbaiwa observes, local community involvement in wildlife tourism planning and implementation is crucial to encourage a positive, supportive experience and enhances the potential for profit from active rather than passive involvement (2023).

Case Studies: Examples of Successful Animal-Positive Wildlife Tourism Policy Frameworks

Elephant Tourism in Southeast Asia

Backdrop. Asian elephants, endangered across their native Southeast Asia, number 30,000–50,000 in the wild and 10,000–15,000 in captivity (Baker and Winkler 2020). Countries relying on elephant-based tourism employ mahouts (human keepers) to manage captive populations, but traditional training methods often subject elephants to physical and psychological stress (Rizzolo and Bradshaw 2018).

In Nepal, elephant-back safaris require elephants to carry heavy loads for several hours, sometimes up to nine trips daily during peak season (Szydlowski 2022). The COVID-19 'anthropause' temporarily halted tourism, easing demand but causing welfare challenges; elephants faced isolation, food shortages, and inadequate care due to staffing cuts (Szydlowski 2022). Within months, a quarter of captive elephants near Chitwan National Park were illegally sold to India, likely becoming "begging elephants" or temple elephants, enduring harsh conditions (Szydlowski 2022; Vanitha et al. 2010).

Declining tourism revenue motivated collaborations between NGOs and elephant owners to establish chain-free facilities and retirement sanctuaries. However, high acquisition costs—around $90,000 USD per elephant—pose financial barriers to reform (Szydlowski 2022). In India, mahouts face low literacy rates and unstable incomes, prompting calls for targeted support programs in education, healthcare, and housing to improve career stability (Hs et al. 2025). Cross-sector collaboration among social services, governments, and NGOs is thus essential for sustainable livelihoods and welfare-driven tourism (Hs et al. 2025).

In Thailand, captive elephants outnumber wild ones, primarily engaged in rides, performances, and interactive experiences (Baker and Winkler 2020). Thai sanctuaries rescue elephants from exploitative venues, but must buy the elephant outright to secure their freedom. Some sanctuaries rely on donor funding for rehabilitation, while others offer less-invasive interactions like viewing, feeding, and bathing elephants to attract tourists.

Alternative livelihoods for elephants can be scarce, especially for those in tourism-driven economies (Bansiddhi et al. 2020). Thailand's wildlife tourism context offers few humane economic options, leading some to contend that elephants would fare worse without the financial stability provided by tourism (Baker and Winkler 2020). Research shows educating tourists before their visits can shift demand toward venues with better welfare standards, allowing ethical tourism to become more viable (Flower et al. 2021; Moorhouse et al. 2017b).

Pathways forward and policy roadmap. Policy recommendations to promote animal-positive practices for elephant tourism in Southeast Asia include:

- Phasing out exploitative practices (e.g., rides, performances) and transitioning to observation-only, or more ethical, harm-reductive interactions (e.g., walking with, feeding).
- Educating tourists to influence consumer choices and redirect revenue to ethical venues.
- Strengthening CITES enforcement to curb illegal trade and ensure transparent ownership records.
- Providing financial incentives (e.g., subsidies/tax benefits) for attractions adopting chain-free, ride-free sanctuary models (e.g., Elephant Nature Park (elephantnaturepark.org) in Chiang Mai).
- Supporting mahouts through career stability programmes, literacy initiatives, and social protections.
- Implementing licensing for mahouts, ensuring certified humane handling practices.
- Encouraging NGO-government collaboration to improve elephant tourism management and develop ethical industry standards.

Wildlife Tourism in Costa Rica

Backdrop. Costa Rica is a global leader in conservation, with one of the highest proportions of protected land and robust legal protection for wildlife designated as a public asset under law (Hernández-Ulate and Cruz 2015). The country's wildlife legislation prohibits owning, feeding, or interacting with wild animals outside veterinary or husbandry contexts (Speiran 2025). Enforcement relies primarily on fines, however, which may not be a strong enough deterrent.

Wildlife tourism in Costa Rica is non-consumptive, focusing on wildlife viewing in national parks and licensed sanctuaries. Sanctuaries, though legally designated as zoos, operate with a rehabilitative, sustainable, and care-focused mandate. Sanctuaries which rescue, rehabilitate, and reintroduce wildlife are entirely, or partly, non-profit and do not breed animals in captivity for reintroduction (with some exceptions) (Speiran 2021, 2025). Tourists visiting sanctuary attractions in Costa Rica thus encounter wild animals that were rescued and ultimately cannot be released due to injury, illness, or overhabituation to human presence (e.g., former 'wild pets').

Despite strong regulations, illegal wildlife tourism persists through clandestine activities and attractions which may involve food-baiting and hotels, restaurants, and unlicensed sanctuaries that keep captive wildlife. In response to ethical concerns surrounding such human-wildlife interactions, the #StopWildlifeSelfies campaign was launched by Costa Rica's *Institute of Tourism* in 2019, following a study that ranked the country 7th globally for Instagram images depicting direct human contact with wild animals (WAP 2017). This responsive initiative further reinforces Costa Rica's leadership in ethical tourism and environmental education.

Rapid urban expansion without adequate safeguarding infrastructure has led to injuries among arboreal species—particularly primates and sloths—who are frequently rescued from electrocutions on telecommunication lines and road collisions (Sánchez Porras 2024). To alleviate wildlife suffering, the burden of safeguarding interventions, wildlife rescue and rehabilitation has shifted onto legitimate, non-profit sanctuaries (e.g., Las Pumas Rescue Centre and Sanctuary (laspumascr.org)) (Speiran 2021). Fortunately, the establishment of wildlife corridors (e.g., hanging bridges) and increased public awareness around risks to wildlife — driven by sanctuaries, non-profits, and Costa Rica's electrical companies—represent meaningful progress in mitigating these risks.

Pathways forward and policy roadmap. Policy recommendations to promote animal-positive practices for wildlife tourism in Costa Rica include:

- Legal protections alone cannot address "wildlife selfie" culture and illegal tourism activities.
- Stronger enforcement strategies—including higher penalties and investigations into illegal operations—are needed.
- Tourist education should be mandated, with awareness campaigns and pledges against harmful interactions.
- Government support for community-based conservation must be strengthened, including mandatory contributions from tourism developers to fund sanctuaries and infrastructure protections, such as insulated electrical wiring and wildlife corridors.
- A conservation tax on incoming tourists could fund these projects, while an alliance between Costa Rica's electrical companies (*Institute of Electricity* and *Coopelesca*), the *Institute of Tourism*, and the *Ministry of Environment and Energy* could ensure coordinated efforts to protect habitats and wildlife.

Wildlife Tourism in Botswana

Backdrop. Botswana's *Community-Based Natural Resource Management Program* (CBNRM) was introduced in 2007 to promote economic development, attract investment, and involve local communities in wildlife tourism (Mbaiwa 2023). The policy aimed to generate socio-economic benefits while fostering conservation efforts. Currently, 39% of Botswana's land is designated for wildlife utilization, meaning much of it is commodified for tourism (ibid.).

The CBNRM programme includes national parks, game reserves, and controlled hunting areas. In 2014, Botswana banned trophy hunting due to concerns over declining wildlife populations, but the decision was perceived to be influenced by animal rights groups rather than local needs. While photographic tourism expanded following the ban, the government reinstated hunting in 2019. This was a response to rising human-wildlife conflicts—particularly crop damage and injuries associated with elephants—leading to community frustration and an increase in poaching incidents (Mbaiwa 2023; Mbaiwa and Hambira 2023).

Critics argue that opposition to trophy hunting, especially from Global North stakeholders, often dismisses Botswana's sustainable wildlife harvesting practices. Locals view restrictive conservation approaches as impractical, instead recommending a dual tourism model, where photographic safaris operate in key areas and trophy hunting is confined to marginal zones (Mbaiwa and Hambira 2023). An overemphasis on charismatic megafauna (e.g., elephants, lions, rhinos), however, can risk overlooking other species. This includes species involved in human-wildlife conflict, as observed between farmers and endangered African wild dogs (Fraser-Celin et al. 2018). Wildlife tourism may help mitigate these conflicts, especially when combined with community-led conservation efforts. A notable example is Kenya's Sera Rhino Sanctuary (sarunibasecamp.com/sera-conservancy/), where tourists can track endangered rhinos while supporting local employment. Revenue generated supports education, healthcare, habitat restoration, and anti-poaching initiatives. Promoting community ownership of wildlife tourism is vital for both socio-economic development and ecological sustainability (Fraser-Celin et al. 2018; Mbaiwa and Hambira 2023).

Pathways forward and policy roadmap. Policy recommendations to promote animal-positive practices for wildlife tourism in Botswana include:

- Encourage community ownership and stakeholdership in wildlife tourism governance to promote socio-economic development and ecological sustainability.
- Diversify tourism attractions beyond charismatic species (e.g., megafauna).
- Reframe "human-wildlife conflict" as human disputes over wildlife to address underlying social inequalities.
- Develop integrated management plans that foster collaboration across industry sectors and government agencies.
- Promote less-consumptive alternatives, such as photographic tourism, while supporting community-led and managed economic options for regions unsuitable for this model.

Conclusions

Animals have long been implicated in tourism practice since its outset as "colonial subjects" and "lively commodities" (Barua 2017; Belcourt 2014). The industry relies on their bodies, labour, and charismatic appeal, while generally failing to seriously consider their interests, welfare, and long-term survival (Speiran and Hovorka 2024).

While the role of animals in unregulated wildlife tourism has received increasing recognition from academics, in practice animals figure little more than passive participants, at best, and as expendable resources, at worst. A major challenge in providing good lives and working conditions for animals in tourism is the discrepancies that emerge when establishing universal norms for animal use—norms that can challenge the cultural legacies of how those species are encountered in local tourism contexts (Fennell 2022a). There is no universal solution to the diversity of challenges facing the unethical and unsustainable use of wildlife for tourism purposes.

Current conservation efforts often lack ethical, care-based approaches that centre the well-being of individual animals. Although tourism revenue can contribute to conservation, such as by funding protected areas (Steven et al. 2013; Tumusiime and Vedeld 2012) and supporting zoo and aquarium operations (Higginbottom 2004), it also raises tensions between maintaining ecological integrity and pursuing economic gain (Khater et al. 2024). The commodification of wildlife within the capitalist framework of tourism has been historically ingrained since the industry's inception. A "market environmentalist" mindset, paired with a lack of regulation and transparency, further complicates efforts to improve sustainability in the wildlife tourism industry (Belicia and Islam 2018). Ultimately, a "green capitalism" approach values animals and their ecological communities based on their profitability, which poses risks to species that may not generate income, potentially driving them to extinction (Mbaiwa 2023).

These are the stakes for animals in an industry where revenue becomes the ultimate arbiter of what constitutes their permissible use. Bearing witness to the lives and experiences of animals in tourism requires grappling with an entrenched, dominionistic relationship to wild beings—and with the ethics of (re)producing false versions of nature and wildness for profit.

To enhance the treatment of animals in wildlife tourism, a relational operating ethic should be implemented—one that applies a precautionary principle acknowledging wild animals' interest in remaining undisturbed and occupying suitable habitats on their own terms. This approach necessitates a fundamental shift in the industry's economic and regulatory frameworks, prioritizing non-exploitative tourism models that phase out harmful practices such as performances and rides, replacing them with ethical, observation-based interactions. Diversifying wildlife tourism beyond attractions focused on charismatic species (e.g., megafauna) and intensive encounters (e.g., wildlife selfies) toward sustainable economic alternatives (e.g., wildlife-viewing attractions) would help regions dependent on traditionally intensive tourism transition to more ethical, less-exploitative models while minimizing economic loss.

Strengthening enforcement mechanisms, particularly through more rigorous implementation of international agreements like CITES (cites.org), is essential to curbing the illegal wildlife trade and ensuring transparent ownership records. Additionally, financial incentives must be introduced to encourage the transition to sanctuary-based models that eliminate restrictive wildlife encounter conditions utilizing sedatives and/or restraints to force interactions. Beyond structural reforms, empowering those directly involved in animal tourism (e.g., mahouts) through career stability programmes, literacy initiatives, and humane handling certifications can promote ethical stewardship. Education remains a key pillar in this transformation; tourists must be made aware of the ethical implications of their choices through awareness campaigns and pledges that actively redirect consumer spending toward responsible venues.

Legal protections alone, however, are insufficient to address deeply ingrained tourism habits like wildlife selfies and exploitative encounters at unregulated attractions. Stronger enforcement measures, including higher penalties and more frequent investigations into exploitative operations, must be coupled with community-based conservation efforts that integrate local voices from the host community into wildlife tourism governance. Governments should mandate contributions from tourism developers to fund preventative measures, establishing wildlife corridors, subsidizing sanctuaries, and safeguarding infrastructures, and contributing to a conservation tax which supports habitat protections. Industry-wide collaboration—especially between governmental agencies, conservation organizations, and local communities—is crucial to developing ethical tourism standards that move beyond mere regulation to promote holistic, non-consumptive alternatives.

Animals and humans are equally relevant to tourism geographies, as they "both occupy and compete in space and place" (Mkono and Hughes 2024, p. 2). Healthy animal populations and biodiverse habitats attract tourists and generate ethical and fiscal support through mechanisms such as entrance fees to protected areas and investment in habitat preservation. Ultimately, a future where animal welfare is fully integrated into tourism requires an industry-wide reorientation—one that recognizes wild animals not as commodities, but as autonomous beings deserving of ethical consideration and respectful coexistence.

References

Akama JS, Maingi S, Camargo BA (2011) Wildlife conservation, safari tourism and the role of tourism certification in Kenya: a postcolonial critique. Tour Recreat Res 36(3):281–291. https://doi.org/10.1080/02508281.2011.11081673

Alam R, Nayak D (2024) Developing local support for wildlife conservation through community-based ecotourism: a study of Jim Corbett Tiger Reserve, India. Tour Plan Dev 22:182–206

Anderson LG, Rocliffe S, Haddaway NR, Dunn AM (2015) The role of tourism and recreation in the spread of non-native species: a systematic review and meta-analysis. PLoS ONE 10(10):e0140833. https://doi.org/10.1371/journal.pone.0140833

Ascensão F, D'Amico M, Barrientos R (2022) No planet for apes? Assessing global priority areas and species affected by linear infrastructures. Int J Primatol 43(1):57–73. https://doi.org/10.1007/s10764-021-00207-5

Bach L, Burton M (2017) Proximity and animal welfare in the context of tourist interactions with habituated dolphins. J Sustain Tour 25(2):181–197. https://doi.org/10.1080/09669582.2016.1195835

Bachetti ÉDS, Viol LY, Viana-Junior AB, Young RJ, De Azevedo CS (2024) Global overview of environmental enrichment studies: what has been done and future directions. Animals 14(11):1613. https://doi.org/10.3390/ani14111613

Baker L, Winkler R (2020) Asian elephant rescue, rehabilitation and rewilding. Anim Sentience 5(28). https://doi.org/10.51291/2377-7478.1506

Baker SE, Van Kesteren F, Zommers ZA, D'Cruze N, Macdonald DW, Cain R (2013) Rough trade: animal welfare in the global wildlife trade. Bioscience 63(12):928–938. https://doi.org/10.1525/bio.2013.63.12.6

Balmford A, Green JM, Anderson M, Beresford J, Huang C, Naidoo R, Walpole M, Manica A (2015) Walk on the wild side: estimating the global magnitude of visits to protected areas. PLoS Biol 13(2):e1002074

Bansiddhi P, Brown JL, Thitaram C, Punyapornwithaya V, Nganvongpanit K (2020) Elephant tourism in Thailand: a review of animal welfare practices and needs. J Appl Anim Welfare Sci 23(2):164–177. https://doi.org/10.1080/10888705.2019.1569522

Barua M (2017) Nonhuman labour, encounter value, spectacular accumulation: the geographies of a lively commodity. Trans Inst Br Geogr 42(2):274–288. https://doi.org/10.1111/tran.12170

Barua M (2019) Animating capital: work, commodities, circulation. Prog Hum Geogr 43(4):650–669. https://doi.org/10.1177/0309132518819057

Beausoleil NJ, Mellor DJ, Baker L, Baker SE, Bellio M, Clarke AS, Dale A, Garlick S, Jones B, Harvey A, Pitcher BJ, Sherwen, S, Stockin KA, Zito S (2018) "Feelings and fitness" not "feelings or fitness"—the Raison d'être of conservation welfare, which aligns conservation and animal welfare objectives. Front Vet Sci 5. https://doi.org/10.3389/fvets.2018.00296

Belcourt B-R (2014) Animal bodies, colonial subjects: (re)locating animality in decolonial thought. Societies 5(1):1–11. https://doi.org/10.3390/soc5010001

Belicia T, Islam M (2018) Towards a decommodified wildlife tourism: why market environmentalism is not enough for conservation. Societies 8(3):59. https://doi.org/10.3390/soc8030059

Belsoy J, Korir J (2012) Environmental impacts of tourism in protected areas. J Environ Earth Sci 2:64–73

Benson JF, Mahoney PJ, Vickers TW, Sikich JA, Beier P, Riley SPD, Ernest HB, Boyce WM (2019) Extinction vortex dynamics of top predators isolated by urbanization. Ecol Appl 29(3). https://doi.org/10.1002/eap.1868

Blackett TA, McKenna C, Kavanagh L, Morgan DR (2017) The welfare of wild animals in zoological institutions: Are we meeting our duty of care? Int Zoo Yearb 51(1):187–202. https://doi.org/10.1111/izy.12143

Blattner CE, Coulter K, Kymlicka W (eds) (2019) Animal labour: a new frontier of interspecies justice? Oxford University Press, Oxford. https://doi.org/10.1093/oso/9780198846192.001.0001

Broadbent EN, Zambrano AMA, Dirzo R, Durham WH, Driscoll L, Gallagher P, Salters R, Schultz J, Colmenares A, Randolph SG (2012) The effect of land use change and ecotourism on biodiversity: a case study of Manuel Antonio, Costa Rica, from 1985 to 2008. Landscape Ecol 27(5):731–744. https://doi.org/10.1007/s10980-012-9722-7

CABI (2019, February 25) Tourism the main source of foreign exchange for Tanzania. CABI Digital Library. https://www.cabidigitallibrary.org/do/10.5555/collection-news-66066/full/

Campbell LM (2007) Local conservation practice and global discourse: a political ecology of sea turtle conservation. Ann Assoc Am Geogr 97(2):313–334. https://doi.org/10.1111/j.1467-8306.2007.00538.x

Carder G, Proctor H, Schmidt-Burbach J, D'Cruze N (2016) The animal welfare implications of civet coffee tourism in Bali. Anim Welf 25(2):199–205. https://doi.org/10.7120/09627286.25.2.199
Carder G, Plese T, Machado F, Paterson S, Matthews N, McAnea L, D'Cruze N (2018) The impact of 'selfie' tourism on the behaviour and welfare of brown-throated three-toed sloths. Animals 8(11):216. https://doi.org/10.3390/ani8110216
Celermajer D, Chatterjee S, Cochrane A, Fishel S, Neimanis A, O'brien A, Reid S, Srinivasan K, Schlosberg D, Waldow A (2020) Justice through a multispecies lens. Contemp Polit Theory 19:475–512
Chidakel A, Child B, Muyengwa S (2021) Evaluating the economics of park-tourism from the ground-up: leakage, multiplier effects, and the enabling environment at South Luangwa National Park, Zambia. Ecol Econ 182:106960. https://doi.org/10.1016/j.ecolecon.2021.106960
Claxton AM (2011) The potential of the human–animal relationship as an environmental enrichment for the welfare of zoo-housed animals. Appl Anim Behav Sci 133(1–2):1–10. https://doi.org/10.1016/j.applanim.2011.03.002
Cochrane A (2016) Labour rights for animals. In: The political turn in animal ethics. Bloomsbury Academic, London, pp 15–32
Cohen E (1978) The impact of tourism on the physical environment. Ann Tour Res 5(2):215–237. https://doi.org/10.1016/0160-7383(78)90221-9
Cohen E (2013) "Buddhist compassion" and "animal abuse" in Thailand's Tiger Temple. Soc Anim 21(3):266–283. https://doi.org/10.1163/15685306-12341282
Costa RFP, Romano V, Pereira AS, Hart JDA, MacIntosh A, Hayashi M (2023) Mountain gorillas benefit from social distancing too: close proximity from tourists affects gorillas' sociality. Conserv Sci Pract 5(1):e12859. https://doi.org/10.1111/csp2.12859
Coulter K (2016) Animals, work, and the promise of interspecies solidarity, vol 26. Springer, New York
Coulter K (2017) Humane jobs: a political economic vision for interspecies solidarity and human-animal wellbeing. Polit Anim 2(1):67–77
Cui Q, Ren Y, Xu H (2021) The escalating effects of wildlife tourism on human–wildlife conflict. Animals 11(5):1378
Daly N (2019) Suffering unseen: The dark truth behind wildlife tourism. National Geographic
Dashper K (2020) More-than-human emotions: multispecies emotional labour in the tourism industry. Gend Work Organ 27(1):24–40. https://doi.org/10.1111/gwao.12344
D'Cruze N, Machado FC, Matthews N, Balaskas M, Carder G, Richardson V, Vieto R (2017) A review of wildlife ecotourism in Manaus, Brazil. Nat Conserv 22:1–16. https://doi.org/10.3897/natureconservation.22.17369
Deckha M (2012) Toward a postcolonial, posthumanist feminist theory: centralizing race and culture in feminist work on nonhuman animals. Hypatia 27(3):527–545
Donovan J (2006) Feminism and the treatment of animals: from care to dialogue. Signs: J Women Cult Soc 31(2):305–329. https://doi.org/10.1086/491750
Downs CA, Cruz OT, Remengesau TE Jr (2022) Sunscreen pollution and tourism governance: science and innovation are necessary for biodiversity conservation and sustainable tourism. Aquat Conserv Mar Freshwat Ecosyst 32(5):896–906
D'Souza R, Hovorka A, Niel L (2019) Conservation canines: exploring dog roles, circumstances, and welfare status. In: Animal labour: a new frontier of interspecies justice? Oxford University Press, Oxford
Duran P (2024, February 15) Mexico breaks foreign exchange income record thanks to tourists. Mexico Business News. https://mexicobusiness.news/policyandeconomy/news/mexico-breaks-foreign-exchange-income-record-thanks-tourists
Fennell DA (2013) Contesting the zoo as a setting for ecotourism, and the design of a first principle. J Ecotour 12(1):1–14. https://doi.org/10.1080/14724049.2012.737796

Fennell DA (2014) Exploring the boundaries of a new moral order for tourism's global code of ethics: an opinion piece on the position of animals in the tourism industry. J Sustain Tour 22(7):983–996. https://doi.org/10.1080/09669582.2014.918137

Fennell DA (2022a) Bridging the global-local animal-based tourism divide. Ann Tour Res 96:103459. https://doi.org/10.1016/j.annals.2022.103459

Fennell DA (2022b) An animal welfare literacy framework for tourism. Ann Tour Res 96:103461. https://doi.org/10.1016/j.annals.2022.103461

Fennell DA (2022c) Animal-informed consent: sled dog tours as asymmetric agential events. Tour Manage 93:104584. https://doi.org/10.1016/j.tourman.2022.104584

Fennell DA, Sheppard V (2021) Tourism, animals and the scales of justice. J Sustain Tour 29(2–3):314–335. https://doi.org/10.1080/09669582.2020.1768263

Fennell DA, Coose S, Moorhouse TP (2022) An animal welfare syllabus for wildlife tourism. J Sustain Tour 31:1071–1089. https://doi.org/10.1080/09669582.2022.2142597

Fennell DA, Moorhouse TP, Macdonald DW (2023) Towards a model for the assessment of conservation, welfare, and governance in wildlife tourism attractions. J Ecotourism 23:166–193. https://doi.org/10.1080/14724049.2022.2156523

Fennell DA, Kline C, Mkono M, Grimwood BS, Sheppard VA, Dashper K, Rickly J, Burns GL, Bertella G, von Essen E (2024) Tourism, animals & the vacant niche: a scoping review and pedagogical agenda. Curr Issues Tour 27:3820–3848

Flower EK, Burns GL, Jones DN (2021) How tourist preference and satisfaction can contribute to improved welfare standards at elephant tourism venues in Thailand. Animals 11(4):1094. https://doi.org/10.3390/ani11041094

Fraser A, Broom D (1990) Farm animal behaviour and welfare. CAB International, Wallingford

Fraser-Celin V-L, Hovorka AJ, Silver JJ (2018) Human conflict over wildlife: exploring social constructions of African wild dogs (*Lycaon pictus*) in Botswana. Hum Dimens Wildl 23:341–358. https://doi.org/10.1080/10871209.2018.1443528

Green VM, Gabriel KI (2020) Researchers' ethical concerns regarding habituating wild-nonhuman primates and perceived ethical duties to their subjects: results of an online survey. Am J Primatol 82(9). https://doi.org/10.1002/ajp.23178

Green T, Mellor DJ (2011) Extending ideas about animal welfare assessment to include 'quality of life' and related concepts. N Z Vet J 59(6):263–271

Greiner A, Toivanen M (2024) Colonial baggage: an introduction. Itinerario 48(3):223–234. https://doi.org/10.1017/S0165115324000263

Guo Y, Fennell D (2024) To touch or not to touch: navigating the ethical and monetary dilemma in giant panda tourism. Tour Hosp 5(4):1309–1326. https://doi.org/10.3390/tourhosp5040073

Hansen M, Rickly JM, Halpern N, McCabe S (2021) A working holiday: from home to destination with a guide dog. In: Kline C, Rickly JM (eds) Exploring non-human work in tourism: from beasts of burden to animal ambassadors. De Gruyter Oldenbourg, München, pp 143–158. https://doi.org/10.1515/9783110664058-009

Hernández-Ulate A, Cruz J (2015) Protected wild areas and eco-tourism in Costa Rica. In: Panosso Netto A, Trigo L (eds) Tourism in Latin America. Springer, Cham, pp 127–141. https://doi.org/10.1007/978-3-319-05735-4_7

Higginbottom K (2004) Wildlife tourism: impacts, management and planning. https://www.semanticscholar.org/paper/9f07c59cd23689d39244f9aef80fe6b4012d2896

Hooper J (2022) Cat-poo-chino and captive wildlife: tourist perceptions of balinese kopi luwak agrotourism. Soc Anim 1(aop):1–21

Hovorka AJ (2015) The gender, place and culture jan monk distinguished annual lecture: feminism and animals: exploring interspecies relations through intersectionality, performativity and standpoint. Gend Place Cult 22(1):1–19. https://doi.org/10.1080/0966369X.2014.993546

Hs KK, Kumar CS, Bhukya A (2025) Assessing the living conditions of mahouths and their awareness towards welfare program: a socioeconomic study. Asian Res J Arts Soc Sci 23(5):70–76. https://doi.org/10.9734/arjass/2025/v23i5682

International Union for Conservation of Nature (2016) Engaging communities to combat illegal wildlife trade: a theory of change [Policy brief]. https://iucn.org/sites/default/files/2022-10/01-policy-brief-engaging-communities-to-combat-illegal-wildlife-trade-a-theory-of-change.pdf
Jordan T, Lem M (2014) One health, one welfare: education in practice veterinary students' experiences with community veterinary outreach. Can Vet J 55(12):1203
Keeling L, Tunón H, Olmos Antillón G, Berg C, Jones M, Stuardo L, Swanson J, Wallenbeck A, Winckler C, Blokhuis H (2019) Animal welfare and the United Nations Sustainable Development Goals. Front Vet Sci 6:336. https://doi.org/10.3389/fvets.2019.00336
Khater M, Ibrahim O, Sayed MN E, Faik M (2024) Legal frameworks for sustainable tourism: balancing environmental conservation and economic development. Curr Issues Tour 28:3693–3714
Kline CS, Hoarau-Heemstra H (Hin), Cavaliere CT (2022) Wildlife equity theory for multispecies tourism justice. J Travel Res. https://doi.org/10.1177/00472875221129254
Knight J (2009) Making wildlife viewable: habituation and attraction. Soc Anim 17(2):167–184
Larm M, Elmhagen B, Granquist SM, Brundin E, Angerbjörn A (2018) The role of wildlife tourism in conservation of endangered species: implications of safari tourism for conservation of the Arctic fox in Sweden. Hum Dimens Wildl 23(3):257–272
Lenzi C, Speiran S, Grasso C (2020) "Let me take a selfie": implications of social media for public perceptions of wild animals. Soc Anim 31:64–83. https://doi.org/10.1163/15685306-BJA10023
López-López Á, Quintero Venegas GJ (2021) Animal dark tourism in Mexico: bulls performing their own slaughter. In: Kline C, Rickly JM (eds) Exploring non-human work in tourism: from beasts of burden to animal ambassadors. De Gruyter Oldenbourg, München, pp 69–82. https://doi.org/10.1515/9783110664058-005
Lotter WD, Roberts KA, Singh R, Clark K, Mander D, Khadka M, Guerrero J (2016) Anti-poaching in and around protected areas: training guidelines for field rangers. International Ranger Federation. https://www.internationalrangers.org/wp-content/uploads/Anti-poaching-Training-Guidelines.pdf#page=9.10
Mbaiwa JE (2023) Commodification of wildlife resources in the Okavango Delta, Botswana. In: Conservation, markets & the environment in Southern and Eastern Africa: commodifying the 'wild'. Boydell & Brewer, Woodbridge
Mbaiwa JE, Hambira WL (2023) Can the subaltern speak? Contradictions in trophy hunting and wildlife conservation trajectory in Botswana. J Sustain Tour 31(5):1107–1125. https://doi.org/10.1080/09669582.2021.1973483
McShane TO, Hirsch PD, Trung TC, Songorwa AN, Kinzig A, Monteferri B, Mutekanga D, Thang HV, Dammert JL, Pulgar-Vidal M, Welch-Devine M, Peter Brosius J, Coppolillo P, O'Connor S (2011) Hard choices: making trade-offs between biodiversity conservation and human well-being. Biol Cons 144(3):966–972. https://doi.org/10.1016/j.biocon.2010.04.038
Mearns K, Dube K, Donkor FK (2023) Locking in lessons from the COVID-19 pandemic for tourism destinations: a case study of wildlife destinations. In: COVID-19, tourist destinations and prospects for recovery: volume three: a South African and Zimbabwean perspective. Springer, Cham, pp. 153–165
Melfi VA (2009) There are big gaps in our knowledge, and thus approach, to zoo animal welfare: a case for evidence-based zoo animal management. Zoo Biol. https://doi.org/10.1002/zoo.20288
Mellor DJ (2016) Updating animal welfare thinking: moving beyond the "Five Freedoms" towards "a Life Worth Living." Animals 6(3):21
Mellor DJ, Beausoleil NJ, Littlewood KE, McLean AN, McGreevy PD, Jones B, Wilkins C (2020) The 2020 five domains model: including human-animal interactions in assessments of animal welfare. Animals 10(10):1870. https://doi.org/10.3390/ani10101870
Mkono M, Hughes K (2024) A state-of-the-art-review of animals in tourism: key debates and future directions. Tour Geogr 27:653–665. https://doi.org/10.1080/14616688.2024.2342462
Moorhouse TP, Dahlsjö CAL, Baker SE, D'Cruze NC, Macdonald DW (2015) The customer isn't always right—conservation and animal welfare implications of the increasing demand for wildlife tourism. PLoS ONE 10(10):e0138939. https://doi.org/10.1371/journal.pone.0138939

Moorhouse TP, D'Cruze NC, Macdonald DW (2017a) Unethical use of wildlife in tourism: what's the problem, who is responsible, and what can be done? J Sustain Tour 25(4):505–516. https://doi.org/10.1080/09669582.2016.1223087

Moorhouse TP, D'Cruze NC, Macdonald DW (2017b) The effect of priming, nationality and greenwashing on preferences for wildlife tourist attractions. Glob Ecol Conserv 12:188–203. https://doi.org/10.1016/j.gecco.2017.11.007

Moscardo G, Murphy L (2014) There is no such thing as sustainable tourism: re-conceptualizing tourism as a tool for sustainability. Sustainability 6(5):2538–2561. https://doi.org/10.3390/su6052538

Mowforth M, Munt I (1998) Tourism and sustainability: new tourism in the third world. Routledge, Abingdon

Newsome D (2021) The collapse of tourism and its impact on wildlife tourism destinations. J Tour Futur 7(3):295–302. https://doi.org/10.1108/JTF-04-2020-0053

Nóbrega Alves RR, Duarte Barboza RR (2018) From roman arenas to movie screens. In: Ethnozoology. Elsevier, London, pp 363–382. https://doi.org/10.1016/B978-0-12-809913-1.00020-X

Noske, B. (1989). Humans and other animals: beyond the boundaries of anthropology. Pluto Press, London

Odeniran PO, Ademola IO, Jegede HO (2018) A review of wildlife tourism and meta-analysis of parasitism in Africa's national parks and game reserves. Parasitol Res 117(8):2359–2378. https://doi.org/10.1007/s00436-018-5958-8

Ohl F, Putman RJ (2014) Animal welfare at the group level: more than the sum of individual welfare? Acta Biotheor 62(1):35–45. https://doi.org/10.1007/s10441-013-9205-5

Paquet P, Darimont C (2010) Wildlife conservation and animal welfare: two sides of the same coin? Anim Welf: 14. https://doi.org/10.1017/S0962728600001433

Ramp D, Bekoff M (2015) Compassion as a practical and evolved ethic for conservation. Bioscience 65(3):323–327

Rickly JM, Kline C (eds) (2021) Exploring non-human work in tourism: from beasts of burden to animal ambassadors. De Gruyter, München. https://books.google.ca/books?id=WvWUwgEACAAJ

Rizzolo JB (2020) The rise of selfie safaris and the future(s) of wildlife tourism. In: Wildlife tourism futures. Channel View Publications, Bristol

Rizzolo JB, Bradshaw GA (2018) Human leisure/elephant breakdown: impacts of tourism on Asian elephants. In: Wild animals and leisure, pp 113–131. Routledge, Abingdon

Roe D, Leader-Williams N, Dalal-Clayton B (1997) Take only photographs, leave only footprints: the environmental impacts of wildlife tourism. https://www.semanticscholar.org/paper/befc9a027bfd13c529e74e3848649bd386bc69f6

Sánchez Porras R (2024) Desarrollo de puentes aéreos para el desplazamiento seguro de monos en Costa Rica. Rev Cienc Ambient 59(1):1–14. https://doi.org/10.15359/rca.59-1.1

Santos ER, Ferrari SF, Beltrão-Mendes R, Gutiérrez-Espeleta GA (2019) Anointing with commercial insect repellent by free-ranging Cebus capucinus in Manuel Antonio National Park, Quepos, Costa Rica. Primates; J Primatol. https://doi.org/10.1007/s10329-019-00748-7

Shannon G, Larson CL, Reed SE, Crooks KR, Angeloni LM (2017) Ecological consequences of ecotourism for wildlife populations and communities. In: Blumstein DT, Geffroy B, Samia DSM, Bessa E (eds) Ecotourism's promise and peril: a biological evaluation. Springer, Cham, pp 29–46. https://doi.org/10.1007/978-3-319-58331-0_3

Shutt K, Heistermann M, Kasim A, Todd A, Kalousova B, Profosouva I, Petrzelkova K, Fuh T, Dicky J-F, Bopalanzognako J-B, Setchell JM (2014) Effects of habituation, research and ecotourism on faecal glucocorticoid metabolites in wild western lowland gorillas: implications for conservation management. Biol Cons 172:72–79. https://doi.org/10.1016/j.biocon.2014.02.014

Sorenson J (2014) Critical animal studies: thinking the unthinkable. Canadian Scholars' Press, Toronto

Speiran SI (2021) 11 Monkey see, monkey do: the work of primates in Costa Rican sanctuaries. In: Kline C, Rickly JM (eds) Exploring non-human work in tourism. De Gruyter, München, pp 181–206. https://doi.org/10.1515/9783110664058-011
Speiran SIM (2025) A field-based Conservation Welfare Assessment Framework for Costa Rican primate sanctuaries. Hum-Anim Interact 13(1). https://doi.org/10.1079/hai.2025.0011
Speiran SIM, Hovorka AJ (2024) Bringing animals in-to wildlife tourism. Sustainability 16(16). https://doi.org/10.3390/su16167155
Steven R, Castley JG, Buckley R (2013) Tourism revenue as a conservation tool for threatened birds in protected areas. PLoS ONE 8(5):e62598
Stone LS (2024) Over reliance on wildlife tourism: impacts and policy implications. In: Wildlife tourism dynamics in Southern Africa: contemporary issues, challenges and prospects for sustainable development. Springer, Cham, pp 101–113
Swaisgood R (2010) The conservation-welfare nexus in reintroduction programmes: a role for sensory ecology. Anim Welf 19(2):125–137. https://doi.org/10.1017/S096272860000138X
Szott ID, Pretorius Y, Koyama NF (2019) Behavioural changes in African elephants in response to wildlife tourism. J Zool 308(3):164–174. https://doi.org/10.1111/jzo.12661
Szydlowski M (2022) Elephants in Nepal: correlating disease, tourism, and welfare. J Appl Anim Welf Sci 25:126–138. https://doi.org/10.1080/10888705.2022.2028628
Tarazona AM, Ceballos MC, Broom DM (2019) Human relationships with domestic and other animals: one health, one welfare, one biology. Animals 10(1):43. https://doi.org/10.3390/ani10010043
Thomsen B, Thomsen J, Copeland K, Coose S, Bryan H, Prokop K, Cullen K, Vaughn C, Rodriguez B, Muha R, Arnold N, Winger H, Chalich G (2021) Multispecies livelihoods: a posthumanist approach to wildlife ecotourism that promotes animal ethics. J Sustain Tour 31:1195–1213
Tomassini L, Bertella G, Grasso C, Lenzi C (2024) The space of animal justice in wildlife sanctuaries: a posthuman perspective. J Ecotour 23(1):38–55
Tran L, Walter P (2014) Ecotourism, gender and development in northern Vietnam. Ann Tour Res 44:116–130
Tumusiime D, Vedeld P (2012) False promise or false premise? Using tourism revenue sharing to promote conservation and poverty reduction in Uganda. Conserv Soc 10(1):15. https://doi.org/10.4103/0972-4923.92189
Twine R (2012) Revealing the 'animal-industrial complex'—a concept and method for critical animal studies. J Crit Anim Stud 10(1):12–39
Twining-Ward L, Li W, Bhammar H, Wright E (2018) Supporting sustainable livelihoods through wildlife tourism. World Bank, Washington, DC. https://doi.org/10.1596/29417
van der Duim R, Caalders J (2002) Biodiversity and tourism: impacts and interventions. Ann Tour Res 29(3):743–761
Vanitha V, Thiyagesan K, Baskaran N (2010) Daily routine of captive Asian elephants (Elephas maximus) in three management systems of Tamil Nadu, India and its implications for elephant welfare. J Sci Trans Environ Technov 3(3):116–122
Vasilopoulou C (2021) The donkeys of Santorini: workers or slaves? In: Kline C, Rickly JM (eds) Exploring non-human work in tourism: from beasts of burden to animal ambassadors. De Gruyter Oldenbourg, München, pp 159–180. https://doi.org/10.1515/9783110664058-010
von Essen E, Lindsjö J, Berg C (2020) Instagranimal: animal welfare and animal ethics challenges of animal-based tourism. Animals 10(10):1830. https://doi.org/10.3390/ani10101830
Webb LE, Veenhoven R, Harfeld JL, Jensen MB (2019) What is animal happiness?: What is animal happiness? Ann N Y Acad Sci 1438(1):62–76. https://doi.org/10.1111/nyas.13983
Wolf ID, Croft DB (2012) Observation techniques that minimize impacts on wildlife and maximize visitor satisfaction in night-time tours. Tour Manag Perspect 4:164–175. https://doi.org/10.1016/j.tmp.2012.08.002
World Animal Protection (2017) A close-up on cruelty: the harmful impact of wildlife tourism attractions in Latin America. https://www.worldanimalprotection.us/siteassets/reports-programmatic/a-close-up-on-cruelty-report.pdf

World Animal Protection (2023) Tracking the travel industry: how Canada's travel companies are failing wildlife. https://www.worldanimalprotection.ca/siteassets/reports-pdfs/Tracking-the-travel-industry-2023-10/?utm_medium=google_grant&utm_source=google_grant&utm_campaign=google_grant&ea.tracking.id=google_grant
World Bank (2024) Tanzania Economic Update, Issue 20: overcoming demographic challenges while embracing opportunities. https://documents1.worldbank.org/curated/en/099031124044543127/pdf/P1796101f356d10fa1b47215b969e1205b2.pdf
World Federation for Animals (2023) Unveiling the nexus: the interdependence of animal welfare, environment & sustainable development
World Travel & Tourism Council (2019) The economic impact of global wildlife tourism: travel & tourism as an economic tool for the protection of wildlife. http://wttc.org/Portals/0/Documents/Reports/2019/Sustainable%20Growth-Economic%20Impact%20of%20Global%20Wildlife%20Tourism-Aug%202019.pdf
Yudina O, Grimwood BSR (2016) Situating the wildlife spectacle: ecofeminism, representation, and polar bear tourism. J Sustain Tour 24(5):715–734. https://doi.org/10.1080/09669582.2015.1083996
Zuelow EGE (2024) Afterword: tourism and empire. Itinerario 48(3):348–354. https://doi.org/10.1017/S0165115324000305

Chapter 19
Animals and Ecosystem Services

Nicoletta Batini

"In nature nothing exists alone"
—*Rachel Carson*

Abstract Animals provide key ecosystem services like pollination, pest and disease control, and seed dispersal, which are crucial for ecosystem balance and floral health. Conserving these animal populations is essential for maintaining healthy ecosystems and thriving economies. Despite their significant economic contributions, these services often go unrecognized in traditional economic metrics. This chapter focuses on the economic value of selected ecosystem services provided by wildlife and the need to invest in conservation initiatives to promote a sustainable future for animals, humans, the planet, and our economies as well. It proposes a multi-faceted approach to achieving this, including Payment for Ecosystem Services (PES) programs, sustainable eco-tourism, conservation trust funds, incentives for sustainable agriculture, and strengthened wildlife protection laws. By internalizing the value of these ecosystem services in economic policies, we can ensure animal well-being, conservation, and thriving economies.

Pillars of Ecological and Economic Prosperity

Animals play an indispensable role in the functioning and maintenance of ecosystems, acting as key providers of essential services that sustain both natural environments and human societies. Faunal ecosystem services (FES) encompass a broad range of benefits derived from animal populations, including provisioning, cultural, and regulatory services (Gutierrez Arellano and Mulligan 2018). These services are

Work on this volume/chapter was conducted when the author was at the Sveriges Riksbank.

N. Batini (✉)
Independent Evaluation Office, International Monetary Fund, Washington D.C., USA
e-mail: nbatini@imf.org

N. Batini (ed.), *The Economics of Non-Human Animals*, Natural Resource Management and Policy 63, https://doi.org/10.1007/978-3-032-17580-9_19

not only vital for ecological balance but also contribute significantly to economic activities and human well-being (Dasgupta, 2021; Pascual et al. 2023).

One of the primary contributions of fauna to ecosystem services is in the realm of provisioning. Animals provide various resources such as food, fiber, and other raw materials that are crucial for human sustenance and industry. Beyond their tangible outputs, animals also hold immense cultural significance, shaping human traditions, practices, and values across diverse societies (Millennium Ecosystem Assessment 2005).

Regulatory services, often less visible but equally critical, are where animals truly shine as ecosystem stewards. Through functions such as pollination, pest and disease control, and seed dispersal, animals facilitate the health and stability of ecosystems. Pollinators, for instance, are essential for the reproduction of many plant species, ensuring biodiversity and agricultural productivity. Pest and disease control provided by predatory and parasitic species helps maintain the health of crops and natural vegetation, reducing the need for chemical interventions. Seed dispersal by various fauna promotes forest regeneration and the propagation of plant species, maintaining ecosystem diversity and resilience (Kremen and Miles 2012). Finally, carbon sequestration contributes significantly to climate regulation and the mitigation of global warming.

Beyond their provision and regulatory services, animals play a crucial role in ecosystems because life is intricately interconnected like a web, where nothing exists in isolation (Carson 2002). The presence of keystone species, such as wolves and elephants, significantly influences the structure and functioning of entire ecosystems, demonstrating the profound interdependence among species (Paine 1969). This interconnectedness means that the loss or decline of one species can have cascading effects on others, leading to ecosystem imbalance and degradation (Estes et al. 2011). The complex relationships among species support biodiversity, enhance ecosystem resilience, and contribute to the stability of natural environments (Pascual et al. 2023). Collectively, these functions enable a balanced and thriving ecosystem, indirectly supporting the production of other economic services. The intricate interplay between animals and their environment underscores the importance of preserving faunal populations and their habitats (IUCN 2023).

This chapter focuses solely on regulatory services, as Chapters 6–10 and 11 comprehensively address animals as food and their roles in fashion and clothing, respectively; while Chapter 18 deals with animals and tourism which is one of the main cultural values often attributed to them. As we delve deeper into the various facets of faunal ecosystem services in this chapter, we will explore the myriad ways in which animals contribute to ecological and economic systems, highlighting their contribution to human economies and the need for their conservation and sustainable management.

Nature's MVPs: Animals in Pollination, Seed Dispersal, Pest Control, and Carbon Sequestration

Regulatory services are perhaps the most critical but often underappreciated contributions of faunal populations. These include pollination, pest and disease control, and seed dispersal—functions that maintain ecosystem health and stability.

Pollination services are invaluable to ecosystems, driving biodiversity and the continuity of numerous plant communities. Insects such as bees and butterflies are essential pollinators for many plant species. Their work sustains not only ecosystems but also human economies. According to the Intergovernmental Science Policy Platform on Biodiversity and Ecosystem Services (IPBES), pollination services contribute approximately $235 billion to $577 billion annually to global agriculture (IPBES 2016). For example, bees alone are responsible for pollinating about 70 of the 100 crop species that feed 90% of the world (Klein et al. 2007).

In addition to pollination, animals play a crucial role in regulating ecosystems through natural pest and disease control. Predatory species such as birds and bats help manage pest populations, reducing the need for chemical pesticides and fostering healthier ecosystems. For instance, a single bat can consume up to 1,000 mosquitoes in an hour, providing natural pest control that benefits both ecosystems and agricultural productivity (Boyles et al. 2011).

Animals also provide essential seed dispersal services. Birds, mammals, and insects play pivotal roles in distributing seeds, promoting forest regeneration and plant diversity. Elephants, for example, can disperse seeds over large distances, contributing to the spread of tree species and the maintenance of diverse plant communities. This natural process ensures ecosystem resilience and the ability to recover from disturbances, maintaining ecological balance and health (Campos-Arceiz and Blake 2011). The following sections delve into the economic value of key regulatory services provided by animals, showcasing examples that range from the smallest to the largest species in the animal kingdom: bees, ladybugs, owls, elephants, and whales.

The Economics of Pollination Services: The Vital Role of Bees

Bees play a vital role in global agriculture through their pollination services, which are essential for the production of many crops. The economic value of bee pollination is immense, with estimates suggesting that bees contribute approximately $215 billion per year to global agriculture (Global Honey Organization 2024). This figure highlights the significant economic impact of bees on food production and security.

One of the largest examples of bee pollination's economic value is seen in the almond industry in California. Almonds are entirely dependent on bee pollination, and California produces about 80% of the world's almonds. The almond industry generates billions of dollars in revenue, with pollination services being a critical component. Beekeepers are typically paid between $165 and $240 per colony for pollination services, with the average payment being around $203 per colony for almond pollination (Bee Keeper Facts 2024). A colony, which typically consists of thousands of bees and a queen, is the basic unit of a beekeeping operation. For a beekeeper moving 2,000 colonies into almond orchards, this can gross around $300,000 (Bee Keeper Facts 2024). However, most beekeepers net only about 5–10% of this amount due to various costs involved (Bee Keeper Facts 2024). The economic insurance value of wild pollinators in almond orchards has been studied, showing that wild pollinators can enhance the stability and productivity of almond crops (Henselek et al. 2016).

Another significant example is the global honey market, which was valued at $8.94 billion in 2023 and is projected to grow to $15.59 billion by 2032 (Fortune Business Insights 2023). Honey production relies heavily on bee pollination, and beekeeping provides a primary source of income for millions of people worldwide. This not only strengthens the resilience of farmers' livelihoods but also supplements their incomes, contributing to economic stability in many regions (Global Honey Organization 2024).

The Economics of Pest and Disease Control Services: Owls and Ladybugs

Both owls and ladybugs exemplify the benefits of using natural predators for pest and disease control, offering eco-friendly solutions that support sustainable agriculture and ecosystem health. By leveraging the natural behaviors of these animals, farmers and gardeners can create more resilient and balanced ecosystems. This approach aligns with the principles of integrated pest management (IPM), which emphasizes the use of natural predators, crop rotation, and other sustainable practices to manage pests effectively.

Owls play a crucial role in pest and disease control by preying on rodents and other small mammals. Their presence in agricultural areas helps reduce rodent populations, which can cause significant crop damage and spread diseases. Barn owls (*Tyto alba*), among other owl species, are particularly effective at controlling rodent populations, offering a sustainable alternative to chemical rodenticides. For example, a single barn owl family can consume several thousand rodents in a year, significantly impacting local rodent populations (Bontzorlos et al. 2024). Encouraging natural predators like owls in gardens and farms promotes biodiversity and ecological balance. Furthermore, by controlling rodent populations, owls indirectly reduce the risk of diseases such as hantavirus, leptospirosis, and plague, which rodents can transmit to humans. The economic benefits of using owls for pest control are substantial, as they help reduce crop losses and the need for expensive chemical pesticides (Bontzorlos et al. 2024).

Ladybugs, on the other hand, are well known for their ability to control aphid populations and other garden pests. These insects are voracious predators, consuming large quantities of aphids, mites, and other harmful insects. A single ladybug can eat up to 5,000 aphids in its lifetime (Indogulf BioAg 2023). Ladybugs are often used as biological pest control agents due to their effectiveness and minimal environmental impact. By establishing a permanent population of ladybugs, farmers and gardeners can maintain pest control throughout the growing season, reducing the need for chemical pesticides (Indogulf BioAg 2023). Additionally, ladybugs contribute to the overall health of plants by preventing infestations that can weaken and damage crops, thus supporting higher yields and better-quality produce. The economic impact of using ladybugs for natural pest control is significant, with studies showing that predatory insects like ladybugs could save soybean farmers in northern United States an estimated $4.6 billion annually on insecticides (Landis and Isaacs 2012). The study found that by increasing predator-friendly habitats, such as planting buckwheat strips and maintaining natural grasslands and forests within 1.5 miles of the soybean fields, the abundance of ladybugs could be significantly increased. This, in turn, helped control soybean aphids, the most destructive pest in the region.

The Economics of Seed Dispersal: Monkeys and Birds

Large frugivores, animals that primarily consume fruits, like apes and monkeys, play a critical role in seed dispersal, contributing significantly to forest regeneration and ecosystem health (Chaves et al. 2018). These animals ingest seeds along with the fruits they eat and later excrete them in different locations. This natural process helps maintain plant diversity, supports forest growth, and enhances ecosystem resilience. In a similar way, frugivore birds play a vital role in seed dispersal, as they transport seeds to new locations through various methods, such as passing seeds through their digestive tract, carrying them on their feathers and beaks, and through hoarding behaviors (Sorensen et al. 2022).

Large frugivores are essential for the dispersal of large-seeded trees, which are vital for carbon storage and other ecosystem services. Bello et al. (2021) examined the economic impacts of seed dispersal loss by three key large frugivores: woolly spider monkeys (*Brachyteles arachnoides*), black howler monkeys (*Alouatta guariba*), and guans (*Pipile jacutinga*) all of which are essential for the dispersal of large-seeded trees in tropical forests, which store high amounts of carbon. The study finds that the seed dispersal services provided by these animals can contribute to carbon sequestration valued at $3.94 to $15.42 per hectare per year (Bello et al. 2021). Taking Ivindo National Park in Gabon as an example, the seed dispersal services provided by large frugivores like woolly spider monkeys, black howler monkeys, and guans are essential for forest regeneration and carbon sequestration. Given the park's area of 300,000 hectares, a rough estimate based on results in Bello et al. (2021) suggests that this can generate significant revenue through carbon offsets, ranging from $1.18

million to $4.63 million per year.[1] This economic valuation stresses the importance of conserving seed-dispersing animal populations to maintain forest ecosystems and their associated ecosystem services.

The Economics of Carbon Sequestration: Whales and Elephants

A key additional ecosystem service that animals provide is carbon sequestration. This refers to the capture and storage of carbon dioxide (CO_2) from the atmosphere, which helps regulate the climate and mitigate global warming. While plants and forests are well known for their carbon sequestering abilities, animals also play crucial roles in this process. Various faunal populations contribute to this process through their interactions with the environment.

Marine animals, both small and large, play a significant role in carbon sequestration. Through a process called the "biological pump," marine organisms facilitate the transfer of carbon from the surface waters to the deep ocean. Phytoplankton, for instance, absorb CO_2 during photosynthesis. When these microscopic plants are consumed by zooplankton and other marine animals, the carbon is transferred through the food web.[2] As marine organisms die, they sink to the ocean floor, effectively sequestering carbon in the deep ocean (Henson et al. 2016). The economic value of marine carbon sequestration services has been estimated to be significant. According to a study by Nellemann et al. (2009), coastal and marine ecosystems provide an estimated $25 billion per year in carbon sequestration benefits.

Whales play a crucial role in marine ecosystems, providing a range of ecosystem services that contribute to the health and productivity of the oceans. One of the most significant services is their contribution to carbon sequestration through the "whale pump" and "whale fall" processes (Roman and McCarthy 2010; NOAA 2024). Whales facilitate the transfer of nutrients from the deep ocean to the surface waters, promoting the growth of phytoplankton, which are the foundation of marine food webs. Phytoplankton not only provide food for a variety of marine organisms but also play a vital role in carbon sequestration by absorbing CO_2 during photosynthesis. Specifically, the "whale pump" involves whales feeding at depth and releasing nutrient rich feces at the surface, which fertilizes the water and stimulates phytoplankton growth (Roman and McCarthy 2010). This process enhances the biological carbon pump, where carbon is transferred from the surface to the deep ocean, effectively sequestering carbon and mitigating climate change (Henson et al.

[1] The calculation is based on the economic value of seed dispersal services, with the lower estimate being $3.94 per hectare per year and the upper estimate being $15.42 per hectare per year, applied to the park's 300,000 hectares.

[2] Zooplankton include various species, such as tiny crustaceans (like copepods), jellyfish, larvae of larger animals (like fish and crabs), and other microscopic animals. They typically feed on phytoplankton and other small particles in the water.

2016). According to Fabio Berzaghi and his colleagues, a thriving whale population could boost phytoplankton productivity by as much as 1% globally (Berzaghi et al. 2022). This increase in phytoplankton is significant because phytoplankton play a crucial role in carbon sequestration by absorbing CO_2 during photosynthesis. More phytoplankton means more CO_2 is removed from the atmosphere, which can help mitigate the effects of climate change. It is estimated that increasing whale populations could boost phytoplankton productivity by 1% globally, which would help absorb 37 billion metric tons of CO_2 annually—equivalent to offsetting all human global CO_2 emissions in a year (Chami et al. 2019).[3]

Whales also support the food web by providing a food source for other marine animals. Their carcasses, known as "whale falls," create complex ecosystems on the ocean floor, sustaining a variety of scavengers and deep-sea organisms. This process further contributes to nutrient cycling and carbon sequestration in the deep ocean (Nellemann et al. 2009; Roman and McCarthy 2010; NOAA 2024). In addition to their role in carbon sequestration, whales contribute to the overall health and resilience of marine ecosystems. Their movements and behaviors help to distribute nutrients across vast oceanic regions, supporting the growth of marine life and maintaining biodiversity. Before the era of commercial whaling, which led to a dramatic decline in whale populations by over 80% worldwide, whales enhanced the ocean's ability to sequester carbon and carry out other ecosystem functions. The preservation and protection of whale populations are therefore essential for maintaining the balance and productivity of marine ecosystems, as well as for their contributions to climate regulation and carbon sequestration (Berzaghi et al. 2019).

Large terrestrial herbivores also contribute to carbon sequestration. Megafauna such as elephants and bison play a role in maintaining grasslands and savannahs, which are important carbon sinks. By grazing and trampling, these animals promote the growth of grasses that have deep root systems, capable of storing substantial amounts of carbon in the soil (Doughty et al. 2016). Forest elephants play a crucial role in tropical forest ecosystems, offering a range of services that enhance the health and productivity of these environments. One of their most significant contributions is to carbon sequestration by maintaining forest structure and dynamics. Through their browsing and trampling activities, forest elephants create gaps in the canopy, allowing sunlight to reach the forest floor and fostering the growth of new vegetation. They also promote the growth of diverse plant species, which are essential for tropical forest food webs and play a vital role in carbon sequestration by absorbing CO_2 during photosynthesis. Additionally, forest elephants help maintain forest health by consuming a variety of plant species and dispersing seeds over large distances, thereby increasing plant diversity and density. Lastly, their movements and behaviors distribute nutrients across vast forested areas, supporting diverse plant and animal life and maintaining biodiversity (Berzaghi et al. 2019, 2023; Campos-Arceiz and Blake 2011). Based on the ecosystem services that whales and forest animals provide,

---

[3] Global carbon dioxide emissions from fossil fuels and industry totalled 37.01 billion metric tons ($GtCO_2$) in 2023. Emissions are projected to have risen by about 1% in 2024 to reach a record high of 37.41 $GtCO_2$. See Statista (2024).

particularly their contributions to carbon sequestration and nutrient cycling, Ralph Chami and his colleagues estimated the value of a live forest elephant to be $1.75 million, while they estimate value of a live whale to be around $2 million (Chami et al. 2022). These are not just theoretical estimates: the carbon sequestration services provided by these animals can be monetized through carbon credit markets. Organizations and countries can invest in conservation projects to offset their carbon emissions and meet climate goals, creating a financial incentive to protect these species. A concrete example of this possibility is Gabon's initiative to fund forest conservation through the Central African Forest Initiative (CAFI). The presence of live, healthy forest elephants in Gabon is a key indicator of effective conservation and sustainable management practices. By preserving its rainforests and protecting these majestic creatures, Gabon aims to improve the living standards of its people through job creation and sustainable resource harvesting. This effort not only maintains Gabon's natural treasures and biodiverse ecosystems but also highlights the critical role of forest elephants in promoting ecological health and carbon sequestration (Berzaghi et al. 2023). Based on this scheme, Gabon became the first African country to receive payments for preserving its rainforests. In a historic agreement with Norway, Gabon received $150 million over 10 years for reducing greenhouse gas emissions from deforestation and degradation, as well as for the absorption of carbon dioxide by natural forests. This agreement, which includes a carbon price floor of $10 per certified ton, provides a significant financial incentive for Gabon to continue its conservation efforts (CAFI 2019).

Empowering Ecosystem Champions: Policy Proposals to Protect and Boost Key Animal Populations

The regulatory services provided by animals, such as pollination, seed dispersal, pest control, and carbon sequestration, are vital for the health of our planet, human populations, and economies. As previously discussed, these ecosystem services support biodiversity, enhance food production, and ensure that ecosystems remain resilient in the face of various changes brought about by human encroachment of nature. Therefore, efforts to conserve and restore these animals are both crucial and welcome, as they bolster economic and planetary prosperity beyond merely ensuring animal well-being. Investing in these conservation initiatives promotes a sustainable future for all living beings.

The Convention on Biological Diversity (CBD) has been instrumental in fostering global efforts to preserve faunal ecosystem services and animal welfare. Under the CITES (Convention on International Trade in Endangered Species of Wild Fauna and Flora) and the Montreal Protocol, the CBD has set ambitious goals to protect biodiversity and ensure the sustainable use of natural resources. The Kunming-Montreal Global Biodiversity Framework (GBF), adopted during the COP15 in December 2022, outlines four long-term goals and 23 action targets to be achieved by 2030.

These goals include conserving at least 30% of the world's land and sea areas, restoring degraded ecosystems, and reducing threats to biodiversity. The framework emphasizes the importance of ecologically representative, well-connected, and equitably governed systems of protected areas, recognizing the rights of indigenous peoples and local communities. By promoting sustainable use and fair distribution of profits derived from genetic resources, the CBD aims to turn the negative trend in biodiversity loss and ensure a world living in harmony with nature by 2050.

There are numerous ways in which economic policy and regulatory reform can support CBD goals in the implementation phase of these biodiversity targets with aim to bolster animal well-being, conservation, and faunal ecosystem services. Implementing such measures creates a win–win-win–win scenario, benefiting animals, people, economies, and the planet. Here are six top ideas:

1. *Payment for Ecosystem Services (PES) Programs*

Payment for Ecosystem Services (PES) programs are a powerful economic policy tool to incentivize the conservation of faunal ecosystem services. Under such programs, landowners, local communities, or countries receive financial compensation for managing their land or resources in ways that maintain or enhance ecosystem services provided by wildlife. For instance, creating PES schemes to reward the conservation of pollinators like bees, which are vital for agricultural productivity, could promote biodiversity and support local economies.

One successful example of a PES program is the Costa Rican Payments for Environmental Services (PES) program, which pays landowners to preserve forests that provide critical habitat for wildlife, including various fauna that contribute to ecosystem services such as water regulation and carbon sequestration (Pagiola 2008). The program, initiated in 1997, is funded through Costa Rica's fuel tax and water charge, as well as through the sale of carbon credits and Certificates of Conservation of Biodiversity. Landowners receive direct payments for the environmental services their lands provide when they adopt sustainable land-use and forest-management techniques. The program has been highly effective in reducing deforestation and promoting forest conservation, with more than 18,000 families benefiting from the program and over 1.3 million hectares under PES contracts. The PES program bundles together the provision of four main environmental services: carbon sequestration, biodiversity protection, water regulation, and landscape beauty (UNFCCC n.d.). By incentivizing sustainable practices, the program helps protect primary forests, allows secondary forests to flourish, and promotes forest plantations to meet industrial demands for lumber and other wood products. Other countries that have implemented similar PES programs include Mexico, China, and Brazil (Global Land Use Change 2017). These programs provide financial incentives to landowners for adopting sustainable land-use practices, thereby promoting biodiversity conservation and ecosystem services. By expanding these programs globally and tailoring them to specific faunal ecosystem services, governments and organizations can ensure that conservation efforts are financially sustainable.

2. *Wildlife Tourism and Eco-Tourism Development*

Wildlife tourism and eco-tourism offer significant economic opportunities while promoting the conservation of faunal ecosystem services. By developing tourism infrastructure that highlights wildlife and their habitats, countries can create jobs, generate revenue, and fund conservation projects (see Chap. 18). For example, the gorilla trekking industry in Rwanda and Uganda has been highly successful, attracting tourists from around the world and generating substantial income for local communities and conservation efforts (Lepp 2007).

Policies that promote sustainable eco-tourism should ensure that tourism activities do not disrupt wildlife behavior or habitat. Establishing guidelines, carrying capacity limits, and eco-certifications can help minimize negative impacts on wildlife. Revenue from eco-tourism can be reinvested in habitat restoration, anti-poaching efforts, and community development projects that benefit both humans and wildlife. Several successful examples of these policies already exist. For example, Bhutan's tourism policy, known as High Value, Low Impact Tourism, is designed to promote sustainable tourism while ensuring the protection of wildlife and their habitats. The policy includes a minimum daily package rate (MDPR) and a sustainable development fee (SDF), which contribute to conservation efforts that safeguard the well-being of local wildlife. These funds are used for habitat preservation and minimizing human-wildlife conflicts (Tourism Council of Bhutan 2021). The Galapagos Islands, a UNESCO World Heritage Site, have implemented stringent tourism regulations to protect the health and well-being of their unique wildlife species. Visitors must be accompanied by a naturalist guide and adhere to rules enforced by the Galapagos National Park Directorate (GNPD), such as maintaining a safe distance from wildlife, not feeding animals, and following designated trails. These measures help preserve the islands' biodiversity and ensure that tourism activities do not harm the animals or their habitats (Galapagos Conservancy n.d.). Likewise, South Africa has embraced community-based tourism initiatives that prioritize wildlife conservation and the well-being of local species (van Megen and Anthony 2025). These initiatives involve local communities in tourism planning and management, ensuring that they benefit from tourism while also protecting wildlife. Examples include the Wild Coast Sun and the Amakhala Game Reserve, which support anti-poaching efforts and provide sustainable livelihoods for local people (see, for example, Amakhala Game Reserve n.d.).

3. *Conservation Trust Funds and Green or Blue Bonds*

Conservation trust funds and green bonds are innovative financial instruments that can provide long-term funding for conservation projects focused on maintaining faunal ecosystem services. Conservation trust funds are independent, legally established funds that manage financial resources dedicated to biodiversity conservation. Green bonds are debt securities issued to raise capital for environmentally beneficial projects, including wildlife conservation and habitat restoration. For example, the Seychelles Conservation and Climate Adaptation Trust (SeyCCAT) uses proceeds from a debt-for-nature swap to fund marine and coastal conservation projects, including efforts to protect marine fauna and their ecosystem services (Srivastava 2024). With respect to bonds, a notable example is the Wildlife Conservation Bond, also known as the Rhino Bond, issued by the World Bank in partnership with the Global Environment Facility (GEF), which raised $150 million to support the protection of black rhinos in South Africa (World Bank 2021a). By creating similar financial instruments focused on faunal ecosystem services, governments and private sector partners can secure sustainable funding for conservation initiatives.

4. *Incentives for Sustainable Agriculture and Forestry*

Promoting sustainable agriculture and forestry practices that protect and enhance faunal ecosystem services is crucial for biodiversity conservation (Batini 2021). Economic policies can provide incentives for farmers and foresters to adopt practices that support wildlife, such as agroforestry, organic farming, and reduced chemical use. These practices can benefit pollinators, pest control species, and seed dispersers, contributing to healthier ecosystems and increased agricultural productivity.

For instance, the European Union's Common Agricultural Policy (CAP) includes agri-environmental schemes that provide payments to farmers who implement environmentally friendly practices (Pe'er et al. 2014). By expanding such schemes and incorporating specific measures to protect faunal ecosystem services, countries can promote sustainable land use while supporting rural economies. Another important example is the REDD + (Reducing Emissions from Deforestation and Forest Degradation) program, which provides financial incentives to countries to reduce deforestation and forest degradation. By protecting forests and enhancing sustainable land management, REDD + helps preserve the habitats of many wildlife species and supports the ecosystem services they provide, including carbon sequestration and biodiversity conservation (Angelsen et al. 2012).

5. *Strengthening Wildlife Protection Laws and Enforcement*

Effective wildlife protection laws and robust enforcement are essential for safeguarding faunal ecosystem services and preserving animal welfare. Strengthening legal frameworks to combat wildlife trafficking, habitat destruction, and illegal hunting can help protect endangered species and their ecosystems (Brockett et al. 2023). Implementing stricter penalties for wildlife crimes and increasing funding for enforcement agencies can enhance the effectiveness of these laws. For example, in 2018, Botswana implemented a ban on trophy hunting to protect its wildlife, including iconic species like elephants and lions. This ban was part of a broader effort to strengthen wildlife protection laws and enforcement, aiming to safeguard the country's rich biodiversity and promote sustainable tourism. The ban has been credited with helping to stabilize and even increase wildlife populations in the region, demonstrating the positive impact of robust wildlife protection measures. Similarly, the "Ending the Captivity of Whales and Dolphins Act" in Canada bans the capture and keeping in captivity of cetaceans, except for specific research purposes (Parliament of Canada 2019). This act is a significant step toward ensuring the welfare of these marine animals and preserving their role in the wild. Likewise, the Lacey Act in the United States bans interstate or foreign commerce involving any fish, wildlife, or plants taken, possessed, or sold in violation of state or foreign law, providing a strong legal tool against wildlife trafficking (North Carolina Wildlife Federation 2013). Establishing best practice standards for various biomes and encouraging countries to adopt these standards under the Convention on Biological Diversity would further enhance global wildlife protection efforts and promote sustainable biodiversity conservation.

International cooperation is also critical for addressing transboundary wildlife conservation challenges. For example, the African Elephant Coalition, comprising 32 African countries, works to protect elephants through coordinated efforts to combat poaching and illegal trade in ivory (CITES 2021). By fostering similar regional and international alliances, countries can strengthen their capacity to protect wildlife and the ecosystem services they provide.

6. *Embedding Ecosystem Services in National Income Statistics*

Ecosystem services provided by wildlife are vital for maintaining ecosystem balance and supporting economies. However, these services are not embedded in GDP or national income metrics, which means their significant contributions often go unrecognized in traditional economic evaluations (Dasgupta, 2021). To address this gap, it is crucial to integrate the value of ecosystem services into national income statistics. By embedding ecosystem services in national income statistics, we can ensure that conservation efforts are valued as essential contributors to economic prosperity and growth. This approach aligns with the United Nations System of Environmental-Economic Accounting (SEEA), which provides a framework for incorporating the value of natural resources and ecosystem services into national accounts. Recognizing the economic value of these services can lead to more informed policy-making and resource allocation, ensuring that conservation initiatives are adequately funded and prioritized (UN 2024).

National accounting systems, like the System of Environmental-Economic Accounting (SEEA), aim to integrate environmental and economic data by quantifying the supply and use of ecosystem services in both physical and monetary terms. These systems monitor changes in ecosystem assets and conditions over time, providing valuable data for policy-making, cost–benefit analysis, and raising awareness about the importance of ecosystems. Incorporating ecosystem services into national accounts ensures that the economic contributions of wildlife services are recognized and valued, promoting more informed and sustainable decision-making.

CGE Models (Computable General Equilibrium Models), such as the General Equilibrium Model of Ecosystem Services (GEMES), play a complementary role by integrating ecosystem services and natural capital into economic analyses (see, for example, World Bank 2021a, b; Johnson et al. 2023; von Jeetze et al. 2023). These models simulate interactions between households, producing sectors, and governments, linked through commodity and factor markets. By doing so, they help quantify the economic impacts of changes in ecosystem services, supporting the development of policies that balance economic growth with environmental sustainability. Together, national accounting systems and CGE models provide a comprehensive framework for recognizing and internalizing within national account statistics the value of ecosystem services in the way we value wildlife services.

Conclusions

Ecosystem services provided by animals, such as pollination, seed dispersal, pest control, and carbon sequestration, are essential for the health of our planet, human populations, and economies. These services support biodiversity, enhance food production, and ensure ecosystem resilience in the face of various changes brought about by human encroachment on nature. The economic contribution of these services, although substantial, often goes unrecognized in traditional economic metrics. Investing in conservation initiatives not only preserves these crucial services but also promotes economic and environmental sustainability. The Convention on Biological Diversity (CBD) and the Kunming-Montreal Global Biodiversity Framework (GBF) play pivotal roles in setting ambitious conservation goals and ensuring the sustainable use of natural resources.

To achieve these biodiversity targets and bolster animal well-being, conservation, and faunal ecosystem services, a multi-faceted approach is necessary. Developing Payment for Ecosystem Services (PES) programs can financially incentivize landowners and communities to maintain ecosystem services. Promoting wildlife tourism and eco-tourism can generate revenue while protecting wildlife habitats through established guidelines and eco-certifications. Conservation trust funds and green bonds can provide long-term funding for biodiversity conservation projects. Additionally, economic policies that incentivize sustainable agriculture and forestry practices can enhance ecosystem services. Strengthening wildlife protection laws and enforcement is essential for safeguarding faunal ecosystem services and preserving animal welfare.

While there is no direct market for these services, their contribution to the global economy and environmental health is enormous and needs to be internalized. Recognizing and integrating the value of these services into economic policies and decision-making processes is crucial for achieving a sustainable future where animal well-being, conservation, and ecosystem services thrive.

References

Amakhala Game Reserve (n.d.) Conservation on Amakhala. https://www.amakhala.co.za/conservation/conservation-on-amakhala

Angelsen A, Brockhaus M, Sunderlin WD, Verchot LV (eds) (2012) Analysing REDD+: Challenges and choices. CIFOR

Batini N (2021) The economics of sustainable food: smart policies for health and the planet. Island Press and International Monetary Fund

Bee Keeper Facts (2024) The economics of beekeeping: pollination service payments. [Bee Keeper Facts]. https://beekeeperfacts.com/economics-of-beekeeping/
Bello C, Culot L, Ruiz Agudelo C, Galetti M (2021) Valuing the economic impacts of seed dispersal loss on voluntary carbon markets. Ecosyst Serv 52:101362
Berzaghi F et al (2023) Mega herbivores modify forest structure and increase carbon stocks through multiple pathways. Proc Natl Acad Sci 120(5):e2201832120
Berzaghi F, Chami R, Fullenkamp C et al (2022) Value wild animals' carbon services to fill the biodiversity financing gap. Nat Clim Chang 12(7):598601
Berzaghi F, Longo M, Ciais P, et al (2019) Carbon stocks in central African forests enhanced by elephant disturbance. Nat Geosci 12(9):725–729
Bontzorlos V, Cain S, Leshem Y et al (2024) Barn owls as a nature-based solution for pest control: a multinational initiative around the mediterranean and other regions. Conservation 4(4):627–656
Boyles JG, Cryan PM, McCracken GF et al (2011) Economic importance of bats in agriculture. Science 332(6025):4142
Brockett C, Woolaston K, Deane F, et al (2023) Best practice mechanisms for biodiversity conservation law and policy. Camb Prism Extinction 1:e16. https://doi.org/10.1017/ext.2023
Campos-Arceiz A, Blake S (2011) Mega gardeners of the forest—the role of elephants in seed dispersal. Acta Oecologica 37(6):542–553
Central African Forest Initiative (CAFI) (2019) Gabon signs landmark deal to preserve rainforest and cut emissions. https://www.cafi.org/news/gabon-signs-landmark-deal-to-preserve-rainforest-and-cut-emissions
Chami R et al (2022) The value of nature to our health and economic well-being: a framework with application to elephants and whales. In: Paganetto L (eds) Economic challenges for Europe after the pandemic. Springer Proceedings in Business and Economics. Springer, Cham. https://doi.org/10.1007/978-3-031-10302-5_7
Chami R, Cosimano TF, Fullenkamp C et al (2019) Nature's solution to climate change. Finance Dev 56(4). https://www.imf.org/en/Publications/fandd/issues/2019/12/natures-solution-to-climate-change-chami
Chaves ÓM, Bicca-Marques JC, Chapman CA (2018) Quantity and quality of seed dispersal by a large arboreal frugivore in small and large Atlantic forest fragments. PLoS ONE 13(3):e0193660. https://doi.org/10.1371/journal.pone.0193660
CITES (1973) Convention on international trade in endangered species of wild fauna and flora
CITES (2021) The African elephant coalition's position on elephants and ivory trade. Convention on International Trade in Endangered Species of Wild Fauna and Flora Conservation. University of Antwerp for CLIMATEFIT
Convention on Biological Diversity (CBD) (1993) Text of the convention. https://www.cbd.int/
Convention on Biological Diversity (CBD) (2022) Kunming-Montreal global biodiversity framework. https://www.cbd.int/
Dasgupta P (2021) The economics of biodiversity: the Dasgupta review. HM Treasury
Doughty CE, Wolf A, MoruetaHolme N, Jetz W, Malhi Y, Svenning JC (2016) Megafauna extinction, tree species range reduction, and carbon storage in Amazonian forests. Ecol Lett 19(8):936945
Estes JA, Terborgh J, Brashares JS et al (2011) Trophic downgrading of planet Earth. Science 333(6040):301–306. https://doi.org/10.1126/science.1205106
Fortune Business Insights (2023) Honey market size, share, analysis, industry trends, 2032. https://www.fortunebusinessinsights.com/industry-reports/honey-market-100551
Galapagos Conservancy (n.d.) Galápagos national park rules. https://www.galapagos.org/travel/park-rules
Global Honey Organization (2024) Honey, biodiversity and economy in low- and middle-income countries. https://www.globalhoney.org/news-gho/honey-biodiversity-and-economy-in-low-and-middle-income-countries/
Global Land Use Change (2017) PES as an instrument to foster a 'green economy'. https://globallandusechange.org/wp-content/uploads/2017/10/WWF_Information_PES-2015_final.pdf

Gutierrez-Arellano C, Mulligan M (2018) A review of regulation ecosystem services and disservices from faunal populations and potential impacts of agriculturalisation on their provision, globally. Nat Conserv 30:1–39. https://doi.org/10.3897/natureconservation.30.26989
Henselek T et al (2016) The economic insurance value of wild pollinators in almond orchards. J Econ Entomol 109(3):1234–1242
Henson SA, Sanders R, Madsen E, Painter SC (2016) A reduced estimate of the strength of the ocean's biological carbon pump. Geophys Res Lett 43(17):87308739
Indogulf BioAg (2023) Biological pest control agent profiles: Ladybugs (Coccinellidae)
IPBES (2016) Assessment report on pollinators, pollination and food production. Intergovernmental Science Policy Platform on Biodiversity and Ecosystem Services
IUCN (2023) Recognizing and valuing ecosystem services in protected & conserved areas. International Union for Conservation of Nature. https://iucn.org/resources/informationbrief/recognizingandvaluingecosystemservicesprotectedconservedareas
Johnson JA, Baldos ULC, Corong E, Hertel T, Polasky S, Cervigni R, Roxburgh T, Ruta G, Salemi C, Thakrar S (2023) Investing in nature can improve equity and economic returns. Proceedings of the National Academy of Sciences 120(27): e2220401120. https://doi.org/10.1073/pnas.2220401120
Klein AM, Vaissière BE, Cane JH et al (2007) Importance of pollinators in changing landscapes for world crops. Proc Roy Soc Lond B Biol Sci 274(1608):303313
Kremen C, Miles A (2012) Ecosystem services in biologically diversified versus conventional farming systems: benefits, externalities, and tradeoffs. Ecol Soc 17(4):40. https://doi.org/10.5751/ES05035170440
Landis DA, Isaacs R (2012) Increasing predator-friendly land can help farmers reduce costs. AgBioResearch. https://www.canr.msu.edu/news/increasing_predator_friendly_land_can_help_farmers_reduce_costs
Lepp A (2007) Residents' attitudes towards tourism in Bigodi village, Uganda. Tour Manag 28(3):876 885
Millennium Ecosystem Assessment (2005) Ecosystems and human wellbeing: biodiversity synthesis. World Resources Institute. https://www.millenniumassessment.org/documents/document.356.aspx.pdf
Nellemann C, Corcoran E, Duarte CM, et al (2009) Blue carbon: the role of healthy oceans in binding carbon. United Nations Environment Programme
NOAA Fisheries (2024) Whales and carbon sequestration: can whales store carbon? https://www.fisheries.noaa.gov/feature-story/whales-and-carbon-sequestration-can-whales-store-carbon
North Carolina Wildlife Federation (2013) America's Top 10 federal conservation laws for the protection, preservation and enhancement of wildlife and wild places. https://ncwf.org/blog/americas-top-10-federal-conservation-laws/
Pagiola S (2008) Payments for environmental services in Costa Rica. Ecol Econ 65(4):712–724
Paine RT (1969) A note on trophic complexity and community stability. Am Nat 103(929):91–93
Parliament of Canada (2019) Ending the captivity of whales and dolphins act. https://laws-lois.justice.gc.ca/eng/annualstatutes/2019_11/page-1.html
Pascual U, Balvanera P, Anderson CB, Chaplin-Kramer R, Christie M, et al. (2023) Diverse values of nature for sustainability. Nature 620:813–823. https://doi.org/10.1038/s41586-023-06462-4
Pe'er G, Dicks LV, Visconti P, et al (2014) EU agricultural reform fails on biodiversity. Science 344(6188):1090–1092
Rachel Carson (2002) Silent spring. Houghton Mifflin Harcourt, p 51
Roman J, McCarthy JJ (2010) The whale pump: marine mammals enhance primary productivity in a coastal basin. PLoS ONE 5(10):e13255. https://doi.org/10.1371/journal.pone.0013255
Sorensen MC, Mueller T, Donoso I, et al (2022) Scatter-hoarding birds disperse seeds to sites unfavorable for plant regeneration. Mov Ecol 10:38. https://doi.org/10.1186/s40462-022-00338-1

Srivastava V (2024) Seychelles debt for nature swap: Debt restructuring for marine conservation." CLIMATEFIT International Best Practice Factsheet, Case ID: 15. University of Antwerp. Available at: https://climatefit-heu.eu/wp-content/uploads/2024/07/15_Seychelles-DNS.pdf
Statista (2024) Global CO_2 emissions by year 1940–2024. https://www.statista.com/statistics/276629/global-co2-emissions/
Tourism Council of Bhutan (2021) Tourism policy of the Kingdom of Bhutan. https://bhutan.eregulations.org/media/Tourism%20Policy.pdf
United Nations Framework Convention on Climate Change (n.d.) Payments for environmental services program|Costa Rica. https://unfccc.int/climate-action/momentum-for-change/financing-for-climate-friendly-investment/payments-for-environmental-services-program
United Nations Statistics Division (2024) System of Environmental-Economic Accounting: Ecosystem Accounting (SEEA EA). Statistical Papers, Series F, No. 124. United Nations, New York. https://digitallibrary.un.org/record/4069081
van Megen L, Anthony BP (2025) Exploring community-based wildlife tourism from an environmental justice perspective: a case study of the wild olive tree camp in South Africa. Hum Ecol. https://doi.org/10.1007/s10745-025-00575-z
von Jeetze et al (2023) Projected landscape-scale repercussions of global action for climate and biodiversity protection. Nat Commun https://www.nature.com/articles/s41467-023-38043-1
World Bank (2021a) Wildlife conservation bond (Rhino Bond). https://www.worldbank.org/en/news/press-release/2021/03/23/world-bank-launches-wildlife-conservation-bond-to-protect-black-rhinos-in-south-africa
World Bank (2021b) The economic case for nature: a global earth-economy model to assess development policy pathways. Washington, DC, World Bank. https://www.worldbank.org/en/topic/environment/publication/the-economic-case-for-nature

Chapter 20
Animals as Pets

Philip Howell

> "Not Carnegie, Vanderbilt, and Astor together could have raised money enough to buy a quarter share in my little dog."
> —*Ernest Thompson Seton*

Abstract This chapter explores the complex and rapidly expanding pet economy, beginning with an overview of its global scale and structure. Even allowing for the speculative nature of industry-sourced data, the pet sector is undeniably vast: in the United States alone, it probably exceeds $150 billion annually, with comparable growth trends emerging in China, Europe, and beyond. This chapter examines the commodification of companion animals, the shifting boundaries between property and personhood, and the challenges of pricing beings that are both emotionally invaluable and economically significant. Drawing on interdisciplinary perspectives, it considers the positive and negative externalities of pet keeping—from emotional and health-related benefits to regulatory gaps, abandonment, and illicit trade. The chapter concludes by arguing for a more nuanced economic and policy framework that reflects the moral, emotional, and social roles pets play in human lives. Proposed reforms include subsidised veterinary care, stricter regulation of breeding and the exotic pet trade, improved adoption infrastructure, and the internalisation of pets' public health contributions. Ultimately, the pet economy demands an approach that transcends market logic, integrating ethical stewardship with economic insight.

Beyond Property: The Economics of Pets

Pets have long been overlooked by economists—perhaps because of the discipline's pragmatic as well as anthropocentric logic (see McMullen 2016), and perhaps just because it is inherently difficult for any of us to conceive of consumer goods who are also our companions. This does not mean companion animals (the term preferred in academic writing) are beyond the reach of economic analysis. But even some recent,

P. Howell (✉)
University of Cambridge, Cambridge, UK
e-mail: philip.howell@geog.cam.ac.uk

N. Batini (ed.), *The Economics of Non-Human Animals*, Natural Resource Management and Policy 63, https://doi.org/10.1007/978-3-032-17580-9_20

pioneering studies in pet economics (Hall et al. 2017; Weimer and Vining 2024) tend to sidestep the more complex questions surrounding relationships between humans and companion animals, and here the property value of pets is as much problem as opportunity. To begin unpacking this field, we can start with a broad overview of the pet economy, then explore the various markets for pets, and assess the costs and benefits of what has been called the "pet revolution" (Hamlett and Strange 2023).

Along the way, we must consider the ongoing expenses of pet ownership and efforts to quantify the value of companion animals' lives. It quickly becomes apparent that conventional economic frameworks, while yielding surprising and insightful conclusions, often struggle with the deeper questions of what pets are and what they mean to us. Most notably, we must acknowledge that pets are not merely "the ultimate consumer good" (Grier 2003, 64), but also what Bernays (2018) calls "sentient property"—entities that defy treatment as ordinary goods. The emerging field of pet economics offers valuable insights into our relationships with these "lively commodities" (Barua 2016), but public policy pathways serving the interests of humans and animals will ultimately depend on perspectives that challenge and expand the boundaries of traditional economic thought.

Consumers as Well as Consumer Goods: The Pet Economy

Let me start with the obvious, however: pets are very big business. Even allowing for the fact that global statistics are speculative, and often sourced from the pet sector itself, the pet industry is huge. In the United States, the American Pet Products Association (APPA) suggests that the current pet market is worth more than $150bn, made up of pet food sales ($65.8bn) and veterinary care ($39.8bn), with the remaining $46.3bn coming variously from pet supplies, sales of live animals, over-the-counter medicines, and a host of other services. This spending primarily caters (using the APPA's high estimate) to the 90 million dogs resident in nearly two-thirds of households, and 95 million cats living in nearly half of American homes.[1] These figures are, in fact, fuzzy, and dubious at worst (see Kavin 2016, xiv); but even if we take these figures with justified caution, the United States (at least) looks like a mature market for pet goods and services.

Global information is patchy—or perhaps patchier—but it gives us rough points of comparison. The 2025 *World Population Review* counts 69.9 m dogs and 74.1 m cats in the United States, for instance, which is probably more accurate than APPA's figures. China is said to be home to 27.4 m dogs and 53.1 m cats, with Russia at 17.6 m dogs and 23.3 m cats, followed by the United Kingdom (12.7 m dogs, 11.9 m cats) and Japan (12 m dogs, 7.3 m cats).[2] We should be wary about taking contemporary

[1] Data from American Pet Association, summary of State of the Industry Report, 2025, n.d.: https://americanpetproducts.org/industry-trends-and-stats, last accessed 27 May 2025.

[2] World Population Review, Pet Ownership Statistics by Country, n.d.: https://worldpopulationreview.com/country-rankings/pet-ownership-statistics-by-country#title, last accessed 27 May 2025.

Western practices and preferences as the norm (Gray and Young 2011) but there is a strong argument for the rapid recent spread of Western styles of pet keeping to much of the rest of the world. In China, for example, Lu et al (2022) speak of the "late start" of the country's pet economy compared to developed countries, but with astonishing recent increases in spending, from 72.5bn yuan in 2015 to 252bn yuan in 2019. The short- and long-term trends indicate significant growth across the world. The global pet goods market is forecast to have a compound annual growth rate of 6.8% by 2032, for instance, with pet care products and veterinary services being the main drivers.[3]

Given the role of U.S. corporations, it is no surprise that the United States accounts for half of the estimated global pet market. The United States remains a significant net exporter in the "vast world trade in tins of cat and dog food" (Vale and Vale 2009, 225). The top U.S. players (with some of their more familiar brands) are Colgate Palmolive (Hill's Pet Nutrition/Science Diet), Mars Petcare (Whiskas, Cesar, Pedigree, and Royal Canin) and PetSmart (Simply Nourish). Together with the Swiss-based giant Nestlé (Purina Petcare), these businesses claim a quarter of the global market share for pet supplies. Corporate consolidation is notable. By contrast, as I will go on to emphasise, the breeding, sourcing, and retailing of pets remains relatively small-scale (Nestlé Purina's investment in the pet adoption website Petfinder notwithstanding).

Historically, the cost of keeping a companion animal has been modest and arguably more than offset by the various services they have performed, including companionship. But can we say that pets today are still "low-cost investments" (Gray and Young 2011, 27)? If we consider pet services as well as pet food, the answer is surely no. Mark Cushing (2021, 52) estimates that American families spend an average of $1225 each year looking after their pets, and this figure looks something of an underestimate. In the United Kingdom, the RSPCA suggests that for a medium-sized dog like a cocker spaniel, the annual costs are between £1000 and £3000 per year. The lifetime cost is then estimated as between £11,000 and £43,000, not taking into account insurance, emergency medical bills, and end-of-life care.[4] Across the Atlantic, these figures look on the high side. The American Kennel Club (AKC), citing an article in *Money*, suggests that a small dog with an average life expectancy of 15 years costs $15,051, a medium dog living 13 years costs $15,782, and a large dog living 10 years costs $14,480; but then again, the AKC goes on to note that *Forbes* estimates lifetime costs ranging from $17,650 to a massive $93,520.[5]

Medical expenses are particularly substantial (perhaps $9000 to $13,000 over a pet's lifetime, according to the Animal Health Institute in 2019: Bisco and Fier

---

[3] Global Market Insights, Pet Care Market – By Type, By Animal, By Distribution Channel, Global Forecast 2024–2032, June 2024: https://www.gminsights.com/industry-analysis/pet-care-market, last accessed 27 May 2025.

[4] RSPCA, Pet Cost Calculator, n.d: https://www.rspca.org.uk/adviceandwelfare/costofliving/petcalculator?species=dog&size=medium&breed=Cocker+Spaniel, last accessed 27 May 2025.

[5] American Kennel Club, Average Costs by Dog's Size, n.d.: https://www.akc.org/expert-advice/lifestyle/how-much-spend-on-dog-in-lifetime/#:~:text=Average%20Costs%20by%20Dog's%20Size&text=According%20to%20an%20article%20in,life%20expectancy%20of%2010%20years, last accessed 27 May 2025.

2020, 2). Pet insurance is an evolving market with clear growth potential. In the United Kingdom, it is said that around a third or even half of pets are insured, but as recently as 2017 only 2% of American households with pets were insured, meaning that perhaps only one dog in a hundred was covered. Albeit from this extremely low baseline, the take-up of insurance in the United States is impressive, growing by an average of 20% each year since 2020, reaching a premium volume of $4bn. With modern insurance bundles covering wellness and preventative care as well as emergency interventions, it is no surprise that premiums have risen substantially. This is indicative of pet owners' willingness to pay, but it also suggests how difficult it is for pet owners of modest means to calculate accurately and prepare accordingly. The pet insurance business (at least in the United States) is poorly regulated and lacks the transparency that consumers need to make informed decisions (Bisco and Fier 2020).

All the same, there is little difficulty in justifying an economic focus on companion animals and the pet economy. Pets (as secondary consumers) are part of a vast consumer industry, and the willingness of pet owners to care for their animals shows little sign of slowing down.

From Poodles to Pythons: Inside the Pet Trade

When we turn to the sale of pets, a natural set of questions arises: *What kind of market is this? How does it function? Does it function well?* Rather than diving straight into familiar territory, it may be more revealing to begin with what appears to be a niche market: the trade in so-called "exotic" pets. This specialised market has a long and complex history, yet it often escapes scrutiny, overshadowed as it is by the more conventional companion animals. Exotic birds (apparently the third most numerous pet in the United States) are a prime example. Pet birds have long ranged from cheap finches and canaries—the latter very easy to mass produce, as with the Harz or Hartz roller canaries in Germany, subsequently bred in the United States for the domestic market—but exotics number wildly expensive parrots and birds of prey. Exotic fish are also significant, though similarly neglected. Fish require more in the way of equipment, obviously, but they also retail at different price points, from batch produced goldfish to koi carp and other "ornamentals," sometimes even kept as investment opportunities. Pet shops, which date from the later nineteenth century in Europe and the United States (Grier 2006), were helpful in supplying fish tanks and birdcages for fancy pets like these. Canaries and goldfish were the stock in trade of the five-and-dime stores, but specialist pet stores were ideally suited to the exotic pet trade (see Fig. 20.1), and they were later supplemented by department stores. In the Western world, high street brick-and-mortar pet shops have virtually disappeared, often in response to animal welfare concerns, but for a century or so pet shops were an important part of the exotic pet market, and a waystation on the journey from the wild to our houses and gardens.

Fig. 20.1 Former pet store, Camden Parkway, London, 2025. Photograph by author

The trade in wild animals kept as pets has survived the demise of pet stores. The exotic pet trade is flourishing, and worth at least $5bn today in official estimates, though perhaps as much again, or possibly up to four times as much, when we include the shadowy illegal trade (Collard 2020, 10). This "parallel universe of exotic animals" (Cushing 2021, 251) is only a tiny fraction of the global pet market, clearly, but it serves to remind us that pets are not born but *made*, and not through the magical sleight of hand that Marx called "commodity fetishism," a dead object taking on a life of its own. In this case, the trade is dependent on animals' capacities for reproduction (as all animal breeding is), but it relies on capture (80% of exotic pets are not captive bred), a system of global trafficking and wholesale warehousing, all "links in the chain of dislocated animal lives" (Biehler 2024, 218). Exotics are shuttled through networks of dealers and distributors, ending up on the auction block on their journey to point of sale. Since demand outstrips supply for many species, the costs of this process, the negative externalities, can be measured in the depleted wild populations living in compromised habitats.

There are vast differences when we turn to more traditional pets, though all pet animals are similarly fetishised and commodified. We should note the informal and small-scale nature of the market for pet animals of this sort. Reflecting on the history of the pet revolution in modern Britain, for instance, Jane Hamlett and Julie-Marie Strange (2023, 70) note in passing that "The dog market remained hard to crack." The Victorians could buy pet dogs from street sellers, market traders, and from dealers, in a largely open market characterised by local suppliers, with few restrictions or effective regulations. Purchasers could also be matched with suppliers through neighbourhood contacts or newspaper advertisements, and only perhaps with pedigree dogs do we see the efflorescence of a specialist and integrated market.

In many ways, surprisingly little has changed, though we can substitute the internet for newspaper ads and street hawkers. Pets like dogs enter our lives in a number of ways, often quite informally. They can come for free, perhaps from friends or relatives, or at relatively low cost from shelters, though there are usually prices of sorts, in the form of adoption fees for neutering, microchipping, and vaccination. As far as supply goes, we have nothing to compare with the corporate consolidation in the pet food, supplies, and services sector. Dog breeders remain relatively small-scale and independent: as the journalist and writer Kim Kavin (2016, 234) argues, with pardonable exaggeration, "almost everyone dealing in dogs is a mom-and-pop business, or slightly larger at best." Breeders do come in very different forms, from pedigree dog enthusiasts to hobby and backyard breeders, all the way to the so-called "puppy mills." There are "inadvertent" and black market breeders too, though all these terms are contentious; we should be careful not to assume that small-scale hobby breeders are welfare-conscious, and large-scale commercial operations are not. In the United Kingdom, perhaps half of all pet dogs come from unlicensed breeders (Yeates and Bowles 2017, 22) and in the United States, there are said to be 7000 unlicensed "puppy mills" in operation. Regulation is uneven at best and inadequate at worst.

If we follow the likes of Mark Cushing (2021, 163–167), large-scale commercial breeders, despite their public reputation, serve the pet market well. Cushing argues that in the last couple of decades in the United States, the market for pets is characterised not by oversupply but undersupply. If this is right (the argument is not universally accepted), then we need to look at the market as a whole—including the role of shelters that we usually think of as dealing with the dismal consequences of reckless overproduction. Shelters, in this view of the market, are nothing more than second-hand pet retailers, an *additional* source of supply rather than the antithesis of rampant commodification. Shelter animals, since they come at the price of an adoption fee, are still consumer goods of a sort. Prospective pets still need to perform their appeal to potential buyers, and shelters need to market them accordingly. Shelters are well versed in shifting these animals, but shelter activists have been accused of engaging in "retail rescue" by commercial breeders tired of being tagged as running "puppy mills." Some rescue dogs may even have been purchased from "puppy mills" or from auctions, making some shelters the equivalent of the pet stores that have fallen out of public favour. Likewise, the "canine freedom trains" or "underhound railways" taking shelter dogs from places like the rural American South (or from much further abroad) to forever homes in the metropolitan North are arguably just a different form of animal wholesaling.

The distinction between "saving" and "selling" is uncomfortably unclear. There is a persuasive argument to be made that pet breeding is an integrated market, however loosely organised. If we again take dogs as exemplary, there is, in the United States, a highly organised wholesale distribution system connecting the relatively small-scale breeders with individual pet buyers, via a handful of mega-distributors (Kavin 2016).

Some, even prominent pet enthusiasts, lean into the benefits of such a system. The writer Mark Cushing (2021), in advocating a pet in every American home, challenges the animal welfare argument that the market for dogs is imperfect because of the numbers of dogs that end up in dog shelters. If it *is* imperfect, Cushing argues, the problem is that there are simply not enough dogs to go around. Striking a note that followers of Hayek or Friedman might endorse, Cushing suggests that well-intentioned interventions, such as spay-and-neuter programmes and campaigns against "puppy mills" as well as pet stores, have merely backed up a demand which the shelters simply cannot meet on their own. Large-scale commercial breeding, albeit tamed by effective regulation, is in this view the only way of meeting the "Great American dog shortage."[6]

There does not seem to be the same dog "shortage" in the United Kingdom, where overpopulation still seems to be the norm, along with high levels of abandonment, though more basic research is necessary. The global pet dog market does seem to be tighter now than in previous decades, and shortfalls in supply are reported in other countries, such as Japan, but there too animal abandonment is significant (Mattes 2021). But part of the problem has been recognised as one of information asymmetry. As Weimer and Vining (2024, 63) point out, the pet dog market puts the consumer at a distinct disadvantage, one of the consequences being the abandonment of dogs that have not lived up to owners' expectations. The problem in the "used dog market" (Weimer and Vining 2024, 83) is less acute, since shelters have time to understand resident dogs, and adoptive owners have more time to figure out what they are getting. But even in the United States, even healthy and happy dogs are still abandoned and euthanised—because consumers, even in the teeth of a putative dog shortage, just don't want *these* animals. Consumer preference puts a premium on puppyhood, naturally, or on specific breeds or superficial characteristics (think of the "black dog problem" hindering the chances of adoption for some animals). Hedonic pricing models, discounting less valuable animals or less valuable traits, are one way of reducing adoption times and avoiding the worst consequences of failure to be adopted (Reese et al. 2017). But as defective products, unwanted dogs have lost their premium. They are at best "low-priced options" (Kavin 2016, 144), a status that low shelter prices or adoption fees sadly encourage. Increasing commercial breeding (together with discouraging spay-and-neuter) will not stop an inherent "negativity bias" (we are led by many circumstances to believe that dogs in shelters are there because they have problems), and actions like this might well make things worse. Liberalisation will likely not solve the market's problems. There are good reasons for speaking not just of imperfect markets but also of market *failure*.

At what we can think of as the luxury end of the market, by contrast, we might consider pedigree dogs and cats as easier to model. We might think of "purebreds" as Veblen goods—status goods where the more expensive the price the greater the demand. Pedigree prices mean that puppy breeding can be a lucrative business,

---

[6] Jennifer Kingson, 'The Great American Dog Shortage', *Axios* 13 August, 2021: https://www.axios.com/2021/08/13/the-great-american-dog-shortage, last accessed 27 May 2025.

whether practised more, or less, ethically.[7] On the one hand, this is just a market driven by consumer demand, and questions of intrinsic value are irrelevant from the point of economics. But on the other, this is a system that pushes the most marketable characteristics, often to the detriment of the animals themselves. Breeds can after all be thought of as brands (Worboys et al. 2018; Kavin 2016), and the adjective "pure" is no more than a piece of canny marketing. The fad or fashion aspects of the market for purebreds are a notable downside of the pet dog market (Herzog 2006). Consumers may plump for breed stereotypes and superficial features, adding to the general information asymmetry associated with pet buying. The obvious problem for dogs is once again the failure of the "canine supply chain" compromising animals' interests and leading to abandonment and worse.[8] Consumers certainly need education, but the supply side of the market is the other face of the problem. Consumer credulity goes hand in hand with breeder cupidity (Yeates and Bowles 2017, 23, 24).

Above all, we cannot separate the pet market from the paradoxes of what the historian Katherine Grier (2003) has called "shopping for friends." Purchasing pets is "an awkward process, with the animal caught somewhere between consumer good and emotional subject" (Hamlett and Strange 2023, 49). What is distinctive about companion animals is that they are "living property," sharing both the characteristics of objects and those of persons. That the market for pets is predominantly profit-driven may seem a redundant observation, but it is still worth emphasising given that we shy away from this admixture of the sentimental and the hard-nosed. This is a world away from the neutral model of the market, in which sellers are placed in touch with buyers, where the latter can rely on the former, with built-in regard for both the consumers' rights and the welfare needs of animals. Instead, it looks like the modern market is driven by the worst aspects of consumer culture and the suppliers who enable it.

The Pet Effect: Gains, Costs, and Consequences

If we turn to the wider economic significance of owning a pet, we might consider the costs and benefits of pet keeping, and here we might start with demand: why we want pets in our lives. For most of us, pets provide a profound sense of emotional grounding, companionship, and purpose. They offer comfort in grief, joy in routine, and a sense of connection that is essential or even existential. In households with children, pets very often play a formative role—teaching empathy, responsibility, and emotional expression. Caring for a pet can instil a sense of routine and accountability, offering children early lessons in nurturing, patience, and the necessity as well as

[7] Cynthia A. Measom, 'Power of Pedigree: Investing in Purebred Dog Breeds for Financial Gain', *Yahoo! Finance*, 26 May 2023: https://finance.yahoo.com/news/power-pedigree-investing-purebred-dog-213305361.html, last accessed 27 May 2025.

[8] 'Rising Puppy Prices', *The Economist* 28 May 2020: https://www.economist.com/britain/2020/05/28/rising-puppy-prices, last accessed 27 May 2025.

the consequences of care. Pets can also serve as educational companions, sparking curiosity about biology, behaviour, the natural world, and our responsibilities. More broadly, pets can help reduce tensions within families, acting as buffers in moments of stress or conflict, and fostering a sense of shared care and affection. For some, pets are even vital for living in the world—making journeys possible, for instance, that might otherwise be too lonely, too daunting, or too emotionally difficult to undertake without support. In this way, pets become part of the moral and emotional fabric of a household, shaping daily rhythms and long-term decisions alike. These intangible benefits—difficult to quantify but impossible to ignore—are a crucial part of the pet economy's hidden ledger. This is what animal advocates call the "pet effect."

Building on this emotional foundation, we can say that pets contribute to more measurable forms of well-being. The benefits to individuals and to society of companion animals (this version of the "pet effect" has been termed "zooeyia": Hodgson and Darling 2011) are readily extolled by pet lovers and allies, enthusiastically abetted by the pet industry. In the language of positive externalities, pets have been lauded "as builders of social capital, as agents of harm reduction, as motivators for healthy behavior change, and as potential participants in treatment plans" (Hodgson et al. 2015, 526). Thinking just of health benefits, early exposure to pets—particularly in infancy—has been linked to reduced risks of allergies and asthma. Studies have consistently shown that children raised in homes with dogs or cats tend to develop stronger immune systems and are less likely to become sensitised to common allergens (Ownby et al. 2002; Gern et al. 2004), which suggests that pets may play a subtle but significant role in shaping long-term physical health.

Putting these benefits into the discipline of the balance sheet, companion animals are supposed to save Americans $23bn in annual health care costs, according to a recent survey by HABRI, the Human Animal Bond Research Institute (Clower and Thornton 2023). Some of the claims made for the health benefits of keeping pets are inevitably *parti pris*, and the results of other non-aligned meta studies range from the cautiously positive (Hussein et al. 2021) to the frustratingly inconclusive (Scoresby et al. 2021). Nevertheless, it is possible to begin to quantify the economic value that pets bring, not just to their owners but also to the societies of which they are a part. In a sustained attempt to measure "zooeyia," for instance, David Weimer and Aiden Vining's (2024) recent analysis of pet dogs stands out. Weiner & Vining's consideration of the economic impact of dogs on our health is a subsidiary of an attempt to calculate the economic value of a dog's life—the canine equivalent of the Value of a Statistical Life (VSL), which in cost-benefit analyses is the monetary value individuals and institutions put on the cost of reducing the risk of mortality. Based on research on American dog owners' willingness to pay for medical treatment for their pets, Weimer & Vining's estimated *Value of a Statistical Dog's Life* (VSDL) comes in at between $7000 and $13,000. This calculation of the value of the dog to human owners leads into an estimate of the presumed benefit of each year of a dog's life. In these calculations, a rough estimate of the Value of a Dog Life Year (VDLY), the yearly benefit to the dog owner, is $1500.

It is important to be clear about this last figure, which is generated from survey respondents' willingness to pay for a hypothetical treatment that might reduce the risk of mortality and associated suffering to their pet. So, it is only a rough and somewhat sideways measure of the benefits that pet dogs may bring to their owners, and rather indirectly to society. It is only based on dogs and their American owners, so that the economic value of companion animals remains debatable. All the same, Weimer and Vining suggest one framework by which the value of a pet dog's contribution to human wellbeing might be established, and because of the reference to the reduction of suffering to the pet (not just the damage to the owner's wallet), there is at least a partial nod to the animal's intrinsic value. Weimer and Vining make the point that law courts and insurance companies already use calculations like this for human lives, and they suggest entirely reasonably that the lives of pet dogs should be valued far beyond their market "replacement cost." Weimer and Vining do not mention the fact that any movement in this direction is likely to trigger defensiveness on the part of veterinarians and insurers and end up increasing pet premiums and making responsible petkeeping even less accessible (Cushing 2021, 180–185)—but this is at least a start when it comes to the measurement of the positive externalities of petkeeping.

There are, however, compound "negative externalities" which must also be borne in mind. As a counter to "zooeyia," we could venture to call this "zoozimia"—should we want a word to capture the general harm, injury, damage for which pets and other animals are variously responsible. Pets have long been recognised as a vector for disease, for instance, so we obviously should not represent pets as always and everywhere therapeutic. Attacks by pets, particularly dog attacks, are another clear downside: in the United States, dog attacks cost perhaps $1bn a year (Dziura 2013a, b), though such attacks are dismissed as statistically insignificant by advocates such as Cushing (2021, 138). In the United Kingdom, a single police force has been reported as spending £215,000 in an eight-month period kennelling dogs seized as dangerous or given up by their owners under recent dangerous dogs legislation.[9] The costs of keeping even well-behaved or more welcome pets are a significant economic burden, one that reflects their value to us but can also lead to pet abandonment. Where abandoned dogs join the ranks of strays, the costs and benefits of dog management policies must be carefully assessed before joining in with the chorus of approval for pets' contribution to the economy.

It is important to stress that these negative outcomes are rarely the fault of the animals themselves. Rather, they are typically the consequence of reckless breeding practices, inadequate training, poor socialisation, as well as neglectful ownership. These are issues that involve complex social and human–animal negotiations, extending well beyond the responsibility of either individual pets or individual owners (Westgarth et al. 2019). Studies such as Patronek et al. (1996) have shown that many cases of pet relinquishment stem from mismatches between owner expectations and animal behaviour—issues that could often be mitigated through better education and support. But McMillan et al. (2011) further emphasise that dogs from commercial

[9] BBC News, 25 March 2025: https://www.bbc.co.uk/news/articles/c0rzk2q7vrko#:~:text=A%20police%20force%20spent%20more,Cambridgeshire%2C%20which%20spent%20£159%2C041, last accessed 28 May 2025.

breeding operations are more likely to exhibit behavioural problems, underscoring the long-term social costs of unethical breeding. So: rather than focusing on defective goods, we need once more to emphasise the institutional framework of contemporary pet keeping.

Finally, there are some questions for environmental economists. We have already noted the negative externalities of the growing enthusiasm for exotic pets. But environmental externalities characterise every form of pet keeping. In their provocatively titled *Time to Eat the Dog*, for instance, Brenda and Robert Vale (2009) estimated the environmental cost of keeping various pets. Not surprisingly, horses are rated as one of the most environmentally expensive companion animals. Cats, ignoring their predations of wildlife, have a much lower carbon footprint. But dogs are significant actors: calculating for the top ten dog-owning nations, the Vales come up with a footprint of between 465,909 km^2 on a dried dog food diet (not suitable for humans), and 828,283 km^2 for an appropriate human diet (Vale and Vale 2009, 237), which is to say, "we need another New Zealand just to feed the dogs of the top 10 dog-owning nations" (Vale and Vale 2009, 238).[10] We might quibble with these calculations, and the Vales somewhat comically provide estimates for goldfish and canaries, as well as calculating the energy lost through catflaps (minimal), but the point is taken: pets have an environmental cost to be set against the economic benefits of "zooeyia." Do the positive externalities outweigh the negatives? Should pet owners be given tax credits, on the basis of the money they save the health care system, as Cushing (2021, 141) suggests? The answers (for the nonpartisan) are not clear: the "magic effect" of owning a pet (Hussein et al. 2021) remains resistant to economic analysis.

Between Property and Personhood: Criminal Markets

Pets are, if we turn away from human enslavement, unique in occupying a contested middle ground between property and persons. Historically, pets have always been property, and little or nothing more. But, particularly in the Western world, and particularly in more recent times, pets have been assigned an "emotional" or sentimental value (see Fletcher 2009), a recognition of an intrinsic worth that transcends the market. Pragmatically, we recognise that nonhuman animals become quasi-persons when it comes to questions of damages and custody and criminal abuse, and the legal case for treating animals at least as "sentient property" (Bernays 2018) is growing. The default position of both law and economics, treating pets as personal property, looks increasingly inadequate, as we will see with discussions of pet theft (Allen and Wyatt 2024; Harris 2018).

Law is changing, but what about economics? Here, Weimer and Vining's (2024) argument for calculating the value of companion dogs is rather less convincing. The case against valuing a pet dog only by its fair-market replacement cost is well made, and putting a dollar value on the services provided to human owners is appealing

[10] Note that the Vales do not seem to include street dogs in their calculations.

too. But as policy economists, Weimer and Vining skirt around the emotional value of pets to their owners, or at best fold this in with a calculation of instrumental value, or perhaps the actual value of intrinsic properties, based on willingness to pay arguments. Sentimental or emotional value is harder to calculate. Sentimental value is complex because it is dynamically dependent on situation and context, and if we readily accept that (say) a wedding ring's emotional value changes with a divorce, the same can be said of who keeps the pet dog after a breakup, assuming that there is joint custody. Pitting intrinsic value against instrumental value arguably misses the fluidity of such sentimental logic.

Tellingly, if I can end with another niche market, consider in more detail the phenomenon of pet theft, where sentimental valuation is brought into contact with what only seems to be the antithesis of market value. Willingness to pay here takes on a much darker shade. As I have argued elsewhere in relation to "dognapping" (kidnapping of pet dogs for ransom), this cruel practice forces owners to put a price on their sentimental attachment to their pet animals (Howell 2015, 61–82). The replacement cost consideration is obviously inadmissible: the specific individual animal is irreplaceable. But this does not mean that economic considerations are irrelevant—quite the opposite. The *irreplaceability* of the pet is at the heart of the criminal business model.

The straightforward comparison is with human kidnapping for ransom. As we know from the economics of kidnapping—"economic kidnapping" or the "hostage trade"—this is "a rational problem with rational causes" (Briggs 2001, 9). Crucially, kidnapping is a self-governing kind of market (Shortland 2019) with "self-enforcing contracts" that make it in the interest of both parties to find a resolution. As Richard Freeman noted in his classic discussion of the economics of crime, such criminal activity is subject to "strategic gaming" (Freeman 1999, 3532), not just on the part of criminals but also for the police and the public. But it is not just the relation between the rewards involved, the chance of being caught, and the extent of punishment. With both human and pet kidnapping, we can extend the economic analysis of black markets to the crucial phenomenon of emotional attachment. The threat of violence should not obscure the fact that social norms and expectations regulate both the criminal and the victim's loved ones. "Reputation" here cuts two ways—instilling fear, but only up to a point, after which it becomes counterproductive. The other element is the informal market regulation. Early on, the use of "go-betweens," agents, middlemen, and intercessors was practised (if not as elaborate as in the kidnap for ransom trade today: see Shortland 2019); along with the apparently strong emphasis on information and surveillance. We see this with dognapping, and the role of criminal middlemen is a particularly prominent element. Ransoms can easily be disguised as rewards. But there are other features. The first is the fact that society and its institutions naturally place much less emphasis on pets as opposed to people. The reward for the criminal is lower, but so too are the risks. Secondly, this is a low-cost enterprise, needing little in the way of organisational capacity. Thirdly, the opportunities for criminals are enhanced. Pet dogs are liable to stray and need to be exercised. Dogs can be lifted from front or back gardens or from the streets. And fourthly, returning to the social valuation of companion animals, the law has offered very little protection, either to the animals or owners who suffer from predatory criminals. In Britain, many pet dogs were not even legally recognised as property of any value at all until 1845 (before that time, most were not considered as having any useful purpose), and only with the Pet Abduction Act of 2024 has the emotional bond between animals and owners been fully recognised in U.K. law.

Criminal markets—whether decisively black or more ambiguously grey—have only belatedly been recognised in the economics of pet keeping, with Weimer and Vining discussing dog breeding in the most unscrupulous "puppy mills" or backyard breeding, the grey tipping into black where dogs are bred for illegal practices such as dogfighting (Weimer and Vining 2024, 77). But Weimer and Vining treat these practices only as situations where information asymmetries are prominent and where negative externalities are obvious. Dognapping (Stickle et al. 2024) is a phenomenon where the economic analysis of crime could readily be extended. We could even say that criminal markets everywhere haunt the culture of petkeeping, and they are surely likely to follow its expansion. More abstractly, we can argue that the meaning of "pet" shifts as the animal transitions from the breeder to the marketplace to the home—from product to commodity to family member—and back again to commodity when it is held to ransom. The market (whether white, grey, or black) always enfolds companion animals, even in spaces like the home where refuge from market rationales is most prized. The lesson is perhaps that exchange value can never be separated from qualitative or use value. The relations that have been cultivated between the consumer and this living consumer good (sponsored and encouraged by producers and retailers and the entire pet industry) are precisely what make pets and pet owners vulnerable.

Pets and Public Policy

What can be done? What should be done? Many animal rights theorists take the "abolitionist" view that nothing short of phasing out pet keeping is the answer, though often allowing for exceptions in the short run for rescued animals. Most take the view that treating pets and other animals as property is at the heart of the problem, and that acknowledging the intrinsic value of nonhuman animals is the first and necessary and even sufficient step. These are long-term ambitions that foresee a wholesale social transformation and smack of the utopian. But it has also been argued that there are policy interventions, including reform of property law, by which the intrinsic value of animals can be at least partially recognised (McMullen 2016). The stakes are obviously high, from public health and consumer protection to animal welfare and environmental impact. The pet economy is growing in scale and complexity, and it demands thoughtful economic and regulatory policy reform. Assuming that we do not take what seem like reformist wins as merely different forms of defeat, what economic policies relating to pets might we promote?

One pressing issue is the rising cost of keeping a pet, particularly bearing in mind veterinary care. Rising costs can deter responsible pet ownership and lead to abandonment or neglect. If pets do provide benefits, and if those benefits outweigh the negatives, then some forms of state support may be justified. For veterinary care, for instance, governments could consider: subsidising basic veterinary services, particularly for low-income households; introducing price ceilings on essential procedures or medications, similar to models used in human healthcare; expanding pet insurance schemes with public–private partnerships to reduce out-of-pocket costs. For pet services in general, the market will continue to dominate, but quality control in pet food and products must be strengthened with mandatory labelling, regular inspections, and enforcement of nutritional standards—all ensuring that affordability does not come at the cost of safety. In too much of "pet nation" (Cushing 2021), regulations are absent, inconsistent, or unenforced.

When it comes to supply, more effective oversight of both private and commercial breeding is urgently needed. Those operations that do really deserve the despised name of "puppy mills" continue to produce animals with serious health and behavioural issues, as do many smaller breeders. But governments will need a legal definition of what is and what is not unacceptable, and of course the power and desire to make those standards stick. Societies should welcome stricter licensing and inspection regimes for breeders and a system of registration backed up with real teeth. Some markets might not be acceptable at all. The trade in exotic pets poses ecological, ethical, and public health risks, and there is a strong case for enforcing a ban, however unpopular this will be. Governments should at the very least tightly restrict the private ownership of species captured from the wild. Countries must coordinate collectively to more effectively dismantle trafficking networks.

We cannot continue to avoid our collective responsibilities by blaming consumer demand, but states need to promote responsible ownership, rather than make the default our right to own animals for our pleasure. Running public awareness campaigns to shift consumer demand towards adoption and ethical sourcing, and away from reliance on commercial breeders, looks like a sensible first option. Authorities might explore maintaining adoption platforms that connect shelters with potential adopters and perhaps offer tax incentives or subsidies for adopting rather than purchasing pets. Microchipping and registration are necessary to improve traceability and accountability.

We also need to research the role of pets as economic assets for society. We ought, without reducing human–animal relationships to an accounting exercise, particularly one that is calibrated only to what pets can do for us, to disseminate the awareness of the positive benefits of pets to public health and social cohesion, aiming to internalise the externalities. Governments might explicitly incorporate pets into public health strategies, for instance, especially for questions of mental health, ageing, and rehabilitation. As pets become more integrated into daily life, for instance, we should expect travel and housing policies to adapt accordingly. We should welcome standardised pet travel regulations across transport providers and borders. Pet-friendly housing policies, particularly in public or subsidised housing, can also be encouraged. And we ought to support pet-inclusive urban planning, such as in the provision of parks, or transit access, and emergency shelters. Politicians should recognise the role of companion animals in disaster planning, healthcare settings, and social services, particularly for the most marginalised communities.

In sum, the pet economy can no longer be considered a niche or sentimental domain—it is a dynamic and consequential sector that intersects with public health, environmental policy, and social welfare. It is of central relevance to a host of public policy debates with vital economic significance. Effective regulation should balance economic efficiency with ethical responsibility, acknowledging that pets are not merely a special kind of consumer good, but living beings embedded in critical ways in individual and collective lives. Reforming this economic and political culture is a matter of protecting animals, but also of building a more humane and resilient society.

Conclusions

Pet keeping is a strange and fascinating phenomenon. It is, as Grier (2003, 62) puts it, "the choice by a human being to recognize a particular animal as an individual, bring it into close physical proximity, and establish a relation of stewardship." This is not based only on commodification—the pet as just another consumer good—but more accurately on *possession*: a personal, affective relationship with a sentient being from another species. We cannot reduce other animals to things: as Erica Fudge (2008, 50) observes, "We need pets to have minds in order for them to be pets." This recognition of animal subjectivity complicates the economic picture—but it does not invalidate it. On the contrary, the emerging field of pet economics reveals how market considerations are ever-present, even in our most intimate relationships with animals.

Treating pets as property can yield surprising insights, for instance—such as viewing rescue shelters as "used dog showrooms." But it also risks unhelpfully flattening the moral and emotional dimensions of pet keeping. The market, as Jeff Nunokawa (1994, 4) warns, casts its shadow even over the "fur babies" of the family. Dognappers and traffickers are quick to assign a price to a pet's life, even if we are reluctant to do so ourselves. Pets must be seen as more than property, and conventional economic analyses, even when they attempt to elevate the value of pets, cannot rest solely on replacement costs or willingness-to-pay metrics. As we have seen in the case of exotic pets, animals must be reconfigured—socially, biologically, and symbolically—before domesticity can become destiny. This process, which Collard (2020) calls "animal fetishism," detaches animals from their autonomous existence, and reassigns them instead a human-centred use-value. Something similar occurs with pets, though often with more benign consequences: a "good life" can be suggested as part of the trade-off in which animals are supposed to accept becoming companions of pets.

Pet keeping nevertheless offers the possibility of something more mutual, less instrumental—a relationship motivated by compassion rather than mere utility

(Haraway 2007; Markovits and Crosby 2014). If this is accepted, then the economics of pets must be expanded to include non-market values, drawing on insights from fields such as ethics, law, sociology, and animal studies, among many others. Thinking more generally, if economists are to overcome their profound silence on the place of animals and their interests (McMullen 2016), then a sustained engagement with these fields is non-negotiable.

At the same time, the practical implications of this expanded view are increasingly clear. Public policy is an inevitable concomitant of an interest in the economics of pets. Regulatory reforms are desperately needed to reflect the real and symbolic importance of pets in society. If we are to take seriously the idea that pets are more than property, then our policies must reflect that complexity—not just in theory, but in practice.

References

Allen D, Wyatt T (2024) Non-human animals as property: what this means when companion animals are stolen. In: Hunnicutt G, Twine R, Mentor K (eds) Violence and harm in the animal industrial complex. Routledge, Abingdon, pp 180–193

Barua M (2016) Lively commodities and encounter value. Environment and Planning d: Society and Space 34(4):725–744. https://doi.org/10.1177/0263775815626420

Bernays KA (2018) We've still got feelings: re-presenting pets as sentient property. Ariz Law Rev 60(2):485–508. Retrieved from https://heinonline.org/HOL/LandingPage?handle=hein.journals/arz60&div=18&id=&page=

Biehler DD (2024) Animating central park: a multispecies history. University of Washington Press, Seattle

Bisco JM, Fier SG (2020) Licensing and reporting in the U.S. pet insurance market. J Insur Regul 39(2):1–19. https://content.naic.org/sites/default/files/jir-za-39-02-el-licensing-pet-market.pdf

Briggs R (2001) The kidnapping business. The Foreign Policy Centre, London

Clower TL, Thornton TE (2023) The health care cost savings of pet ownership. Human Animal Bond Research Institute, Washington

Collard R-C (2020) Animal traffic: lively capital in the global exotic pet trade. Duke University Press, Durham, NC

Cushing M (2021) Pet nation: the inside story of how companion animals are transforming our homes, culture, and economy. Penguin, New York

Dziura M (2013a) Should we beware of dog or beware of breed?. J Law Econ Policy 10:463–487. https://heinonline.org/HOL/LandingPage?handle=hein.journals/jecoplcy10&div=19&id=&page=

Dziura JD (2013b) Dog bites: a modern epidemic. J Am Vet Med Assoc 242(1):36–40

Fletcher G (2009) Sentimental value. Journal of Value Inquiry 43(1):55–65. https://doi.org/10.1007/s10790-009-9152-1

Freeman RB (1999) The economics of crime. In: Ashenfelter OC, Card D (eds) Handbook of labor economics, vol 3C. North-Holland, Amsterdam, pp 3529–3571. https://doi.org/10.1016/S1573-4463(99)30043-2

Fudge E (2008) Pets. Acumen, Stocksfield

Gern JE et al (2004) Effect of dog ownership on immune development and atopic diseases in infants. Journal of Allergy and Clinical Immunology 113(2):307–314. https://doi.org/10.1016/j.jaci.2003.11.017

Gray PB, Young SM (2011) Human–pet dynamics in cross-cultural perspective. Anthrozoös 24(1):17–30. https://doi.org/10.2752/175303711X12923300467285
Grier KC (2003) Buying your friends: the pet business and American consumer culture. In: Strasser S (ed) Commodifying everything: relationships of the market. Routledge, Abingdon, pp 43–70
Grier KC (2006) Pets in America: a history. University of North Carolina Press, Chapel Hill
Hall S, Dolling L, Bristow K, Fuller T, Mills D (2017) Companion animal economics: the economic impact of companion animals in the U.K. CABI, Wallingford
Hamlett J, Strange J-M (2023) Pet revolution: animals and the making of modern British life. Reaktion, London
Haraway D (2007) When species meet. University of Minnesota Press, Minneapolis
Harris L (2018) Dog theft: a case for tougher sentencing legislation. Animals 8:78. https://doi.org/10.3390/ani8050078
Herzog H (2006) Forty-two thousand and one dalmatians: fads, social contagion, and dog breed popularity. Soc Anim 14(4):383–397. https://brill.com/view/journals/soan/14/4/article-p383_3.xml
Hodgson K, Darling M (2011) Zooeyia: an essential component of One Health. Can Vety J 52:189–191. https://pmc.ncbi.nlm.nih.gov/articles/PMC3022463/
Hodgson K, Barton L, Darling M, Antao V, Kim FA, Monavvari A (2015) Pets' impact on your patients' health: leveraging benefits and mitigating risk. J Am Board Fam Med 28(4):526–534. https://doi.org/10.3122/jabfm.2015.04.140254
Howell P (2015) At home and astray: the domestic dog in Victorian Britain. University of Virginia Press, Charlottesville
Hussein SM, Soliman WS, Khalifa AA (2021) Benefits of pets' ownership, a review based on health perspectives. J Intern Med Emerg Res 2(1):1–9. https://doi.org/10.37191/Mapsci-2582-7367-2(1)-020
Kavin K (2016) The dog merchants: inside the big business of breeders, pet stores, and rescuers. Pegasus, New York
Lu X, Jiang Y, Li Y, Wang M, Wu J (2022) Current situation of pet economy development under post-epidemic period. Acad J Bus Manag 4(9):117–123. https://doi.org/10.25236/AJBM.2022.040917
McMillan FD, Duffy DL, Serpell J (2011) Mental health of dogs formerly used as breeding stock in commercial breeding establishments. Appl Anim Behav Sci 135(1–2):86–94. https://doi.org/10.1016/j.applanim.2011.09.006
McMullen S (2016) Animals and the economy. Palgrave Macmillan, London
Markovits AS, Crosby KN (2014) From property to family: American dog rescue and the discourse of compassion. University of Michigan Press, Ann Arbor
Mattes S (2021) Kawaii pets and animal abandonment in Japan. In: Reese LA (ed) Animals in the City. Routledge, Abingdon, pp 95–126
Nunokawa J (1994) The afterlife of property: domestic security and the Victorian novel. Princeton University Press, Princeton
Ownby DR, Johnson CC, Peterson EL (2002) Exposure to dogs and cats in the first year of life and risk of allergic sensitization at 6 to 7 Years of Age. JAMA 288(8):963–972. https://doi.org/10.1001/jama.288.8.963
Patronek GJ et al (1996) Risk factors for relinquishment of dogs to an animal shelter. J Am Vet Med Assoc 209(3):572–581. https://doi.org/10.2460/javma.1996.209.03.572
Reese LA, Skidmore M, Dyar W, Rosebrook E (2017) No dog left behind: a hedonic pricing model for animal shelters. J Appl Anim Welfare Sci 20(1):52–64. https://doi.org/10.1080/10888705.2016.1236693
Scoresby KJ, Strand EB, Ng Z, Brown KC, Stilz CR, Strobel K, Barroso CS, Souza M (2021) Pet ownership and quality of life: a systematic review of the literature. Vety Sci 8(12):332. https://doi.org/10.3390/vetsci8120332

Shortland A (2019) The economics of kidnapping in developing countries. Vision of Humanity, September 2019. Retrieved from https://www.visionofhumanity.org/the-economics-of-not-being-kidnapped/

Stickle B, Vose B, Miller JM (2024) A video data analysis of pet theft incidents: an examination of offense form, situational dynamics, & offender characteristics. Deviant Behavior, published online 8 July 2024. https://doi.org/10.1080/01639625.2024.2378111

Vale R, Vale B (2009) Time to eat the dog: the real cost of sustainable living. Thames and Hudson, London

Weimer DL, Vining AR (2024) Dog economics: perspectives on our Canine relationships. Cambridge University Press, Cambridge

Westgarth C, Christley RM, Marvin G, Perkins E (2019) The responsible dog owner: the construction of responsibility. Anthrozoös 32(5):631–646. https://doi.org/10.1080/08927936.2019.1645506

Worboys M, Pemberton N, Strange J-M (2018) The invention of the modern dog: breed and blood in Victorian Britain. Johns Hopkins University Press, Baltimore

Yeates J, Bowles D (2017) Breeding and selling of companion animals. In: Maher J, Pierpoint H, Beirne P (eds) The Palgrave international handbook of animal abuse studies. Palgrave Macmillan, London, pp 15–38

Chapter 21
Reimagining Economics with Non-human Animals at the Center

Nicoletta Batini

Abstract This concluding chapter synthesizes the key insights of *The Economics of Non-Human Animals*, a volume exploring how non-human animals are commodified within global economic systems. Drawing on contributions from diverse authors, the book reveals how animal exploitation is structurally embedded in modern economies and closely linked to broader market failures such as environmental degradation, inequality, and displacement. Common threads include the invisibility of animals in economic theory despite their foundational role in human prosperity, the normalization of their suffering, and the shared extractive logic that harms both animals and marginalized human communities. These conclusions were deepened through a post-production virtual workshop, where authors reflected on overlapping themes and future directions. The chapter outlines proposals for integrating animal welfare into policy and for developing economic models that reflect multispecies well-being. It calls for a shift toward coexistence and shared prosperity—an economy grounded in compassion, interdependence, and justice for all sentient beings.

> "Are not two sparrows sold for a penny? Yet not one of them will fall to the ground outside your Father's care."
>
> —*Matthew 10:29*

A World Inseparable from Animals

From the dawn of human civilization, non-human animals have been indispensable to our survival, prosperity, and identity. They have served as sources of energy, labor, companionship, and inspiration. They have shaped our landscapes, our cultures, and

Work on this volume/chapter was conducted when the author was at the Sveriges Riksbank.

N. Batini (✉)
Independent Evaluation Office, International Monetary Fund, Washington D.C., USA
e-mail: nbatini@imf.org

N. Batini (ed.), *The Economics of Non-Human Animals*, Natural Resource Management and Policy 63, https://doi.org/10.1007/978-3-032-17580-9_21

our economies. Yet, despite this deep interdependence, economics has largely failed to account for their presence, let alone their contributions. Animals are often treated as if they were inert resources—like fossil fuels or timber—valued solely for their extractable utility, without recognition of their sentience, agency, or ecological roles.

This book has argued that this oversight is not only ethically troubling but also economically flawed. A world without animals is unimaginable, not only from an emotional or ecological standpoint but also from an economic one. The chapters in this volume have explored the many ways in which animals underpin human economies, and how their exclusion from economic models represents a profound blind spot. This concluding chapter draws together those insights to propose a new economic vision—one that recognizes animals as co-creators of value, not just resources to be exploited.

Interdependent Economies: Humans and Non-human Species

Chapters 1 through 5 have revealed the profound interdependence between human and non-human animals. Far from being peripheral, animals are foundational to economic systems. The domestication of animals catalyzed the agricultural revolution, enabling settled societies, trade, and technological innovation. Animals provided not only sustenance and materials but also labor, mobility, and protection.

Today, their economic relevance endures. Farm animals and fisheries are not just contributors to the global economy: they are its nutritional foundation. Pollinators like bees are indispensable to global food production. Working animals sustain livelihoods across continents. Companion animals, often dismissed as luxuries, underpin a multibillion-dollar industry encompassing veterinary care, nutrition, insurance, and entertainment. Sport and service animals similarly contribute to sectors ranging from therapy to law enforcement.

Beyond measurable outputs, animals enrich human life in ways that defy quantification: emotional bonds, cultural traditions, and social cohesion. These contributions, though rarely captured in economic models, are deeply valued. An economy without animals is not merely diminished—it is unthinkable. It would mean the collapse of food systems, the unraveling of ecosystems, and a profound erosion of human well-being.

It follows that a world that fails to recognize the value of animals is not only ecologically and ethically compromised: it is economically incoherent. As demonstrated through novel metrics in this book, thriving animal populations correlate with stronger economic performance. Biodiversity, particularly faunal diversity, is not a luxury but a fundamental pillar of economic infrastructure. True economic resilience is inseparable from ecological integrity.

And yet, despite their indispensable contributions to economies past and present, animals remain largely invisible in mainstream economic thought. When acknowledged, they are typically reduced to commodities—measured by market price, not by sentience or social complexity. Their suffering, extinction, and welfare are externalities, not core concerns. Their role is often obscured further. Rather than being recognized as distinct agents within ecological systems, animals are frequently categorized under the broad label of "natural capital." While this classification acknowledges their ecological importance, it often fails to account for their individuality and agency, reinforcing an economic framework that overlooks the intrinsic value of living beings.

This reductionist view reflects a deeper ideology—what this volume has termed "economic speciesism"—which frames animals as inferior and exploitable. By casting them as inputs—free, replaceable, and voiceless—economic systems have extracted immense value from animals without reckoning with the cost. Domesticated animals have powered agriculture, industry, and transport, only to be rendered invisible in national accounts.

Of course, this logic is far from new. History is filled with examples of marginalized groups—enslaved people, Indigenous communities, women, children, and people with disabilities—systematically excluded from economic recognition while their labor, knowledge, or bodies were exploited. In some parts of the world, other marginalized groups—such as migrant workers, prisoners, and caste-oppressed individuals—have likewise been denied full economic personhood, even as their labor and contributions remain essential to the systems that exclude them. The same rationale that once justified human subjugation now underpins the economic erasure of animals. Exclusion has always been a tool of control.

Just as with many human hierarchies, this one is not rooted in strength but in constructed superiority. We are not faster than cheetahs, stronger than elephants, smarter than octopuses, or more resilient than insects. Our dominance stems not from physical prowess or universal intelligence or moral authority, but from our capacity to manipulate through tools, machines, and stories. It is through cunning, abstraction, and the ability to reshape meaning that we have imposed hierarchies and restructured ecosystems. From hunting apex predators to domesticating laborers, from factory farming to genetic engineering, our control has been systemic and strategic, not natural or inevitable. Meanwhile, animals—innocent, often trusting, and unable to anticipate the scale of our interventions—have borne the cost. It was not weakness, but grace, that made them vulnerable.

Even if we accept that this exploitation is ethically indefensible and economically shortsighted, we face a deeper challenge: how do we value non-human life? Economics thrives on quantification, yet many of the benefits animals provide, like companionship, ecological balance, cultural meaning, resist pricing. Traditional models equate value with utility or market price, a logic that has justified deforestation, overfishing, and extinction without accounting for ecological roles or intrinsic worth. To this end, this book has explored alternative frameworks that begin to close this gap. Intrinsic valuation recognizes animals as beings with interests and rights. Instrumental valuation accounts for their contributions to human welfare.

Non-market valuation methods, such as contingent valuation and deliberative democratic approaches, offer tools to capture these broader values. These are not just technical adjustments; they are moral and political acts. What we choose to value shapes what we protect.

Industrial Predation

Chapters 6 through 13 explore the many ways animals are used—often violently and systematically—for food, fashion, recreation, experimentation, and genetic manipulation. These uses are not only ethically fraught but also frequently economically irrational, driven by outdated assumptions, market failures, and unaccounted externalities.

To begin with, animal-based food systems (Chapter 6) dominate global agriculture and trade, generating trillions in revenue. Yet the prevailing methods—especially factory farming, aquaculture, and commercial fishing—carry immense hidden costs: environmental degradation, public health risks, and the suffering of trillions of sentient beings. These systems persist not because they are efficient, but because they are subsidized, normalized, and deeply embedded in global supply chains. One of the mechanisms that sustains them is abstraction: meat, dairy, and fish are marketed in ways that obscure their origins, using sanitized packaging, euphemistic language, and appealing imagery that disconnects consumers from the living beings behind the products. Factory farms and industrial fisheries are deliberately kept out of sight, both geographically and culturally, so that the violence and suffering remain invisible, and ethical discomfort is minimized. In this way, the system not only exploits animals but also manipulates perception, allowing cruelty to continue behind a veil of convenience and denial. Compounding this, the animal food industry actively promotes the idea that animal-based products are essential for health, despite growing scientific consensus that excessive consumption is linked to chronic illnesses such as heart disease, diabetes, and certain cancers. This manipulation of public perception has contributed to a global epidemic of preventable diseases, shifting the burden of cost onto public health systems and individuals while shielding the industry from accountability.

Building on this, recreational hunting and fishing (Chapters 7 and 8) are often framed as cultural traditions or conservation tools. However, the reality is more complex. Wildlife is treated as *res nullius*—unowned until killed—ignoring the many forms of value animals hold while alive: ecological, aesthetic, relational, and economic. While in principle there is demonstrable economic and cultural value in hunting and fishing—from food sovereignty to ecosystem management—these practices are often poorly regulated, poorly enforced, or both, especially in remote areas where oversight is minimal and "what the eye doesn't see" becomes a license for excess. On the other side of the coin is the animal's loss of life, which is frequently unnecessary and ethically troubling, particularly when non-lethal alternatives exist. Trophy angling (Chapter 9), in particular, often targets the largest and most fecund marine species, which can undermine biodiversity and ecosystem services. While some regions are shifting toward catch-and-release practices and species protection, enforcement remains uneven, and ecological impacts—such as sublethal stress, injury, and mortality—continue to raise concerns. The chapter highlights that, when well-managed, trophy fisheries can contribute to conservation through ethical catch-and-release, citizen science, and incentive-based regulation. It also emphasizes the importance of reducing fish suffering and mortality, expanding the definition of a "trophy" to include species diversity and local significance, and promoting stewardship that respects both ecological and animal welfare values. Similarly, trophy hunting (Chapter 10) remains deeply contested. Critics view it as ethically contradictory: wealthy hunters killing iconic species such as lions, elephants, and leopards in the name of conservation especially at a time when wildlife populations are dwindling globally. While ecological outcomes vary and are highly context-dependent, public concern persists over potential disruptions to population dynamics and the social structures of these species. The chapter notes that, when carefully regulated, trophy hunting can support conservation goals and local livelihoods as some examples show. However, realizing these benefits requires robust governance, fair revenue distribution, and meaningful community involvement. Without such reforms, and amid increasing regulatory and public scrutiny, the sector must evolve or risk being regulated out of existence.

Framing the killing or harming of animals as a means to fund conservation raises difficult ethical and practical questions. While often justified by the need to generate revenue, create local employment, or deter poaching by allowing a few to kill legally, such practices reflect a broader commodification of wildlife. This logic frequently sidelines more inclusive, non-extractive conservation models. Even wildlife breeding is increasingly marketed as a solution; yet breeding animals for sale or controlled killing undermines the very idea of wildness, turning conservation into a form of managed exploitation. In this framing, animals are preserved not for their intrinsic value, but for their utility, often in ways that contradict the ecological goals they are meant to serve.

This pattern of extractive use continues in the fashion industry (Chapter 11), which still relies heavily on animal-derived materials like fur, leather, and wool. Despite the availability of viable, technologically advanced, more profitable, and often more sustainable alternatives, the production of these materials remains resource-intensive, polluting, and ethically troubling. Externalities, such as chemical runoff, greenhouse gas emissions, and animal suffering, are rarely priced into the final product, distorting market signals and perpetuating harm.

Meanwhile, in the realm of biomedical and psychological research (Chapter 12), animals continue to be used extensively, even as new technologies, notably New Approach Methodologies (NAMs) and Non-Animal Technologies (NATs), prove more accurate, cost-effective, and humane. The continued reliance on animal models not only raises ethical concerns but also introduces scientific and economic inefficiencies, including costly errors in predictive biology. Transitioning to non-animal methods is not just a moral imperative, it is a matter of scientific progress and economic prudence.

At the frontier of technological intervention, gene drives and genetic manipulation (Chapter 13) present perhaps the most profound risks. These technologies, often justified in the name of disease control or agricultural efficiency, can irreversibly alter ecosystems. The cascading effects of such interventions are impossible to fully predict, and the economic consequences of ecological collapse could be catastrophic. Here, more than anywhere, a precautionary, ethics-driven regulatory framework is urgently needed.

Taken together, these chapters reveal a common thread: animals are typically used not because it is absolutely necessary or efficient, but because dominant economic models fail to challenge the fact that a small subset of actors has monopolized the way we see and use animals, whether for profit, or through recreational and cultural practices that involve unnecessary harm or killing. These practices reflect a deeper ideology of instrumentalism: a belief by some that animals exist solely for human use, regardless of the broader consequences. This persists despite widespread public opposition to animal cruelty and exploitative practices. Surveys across multiple countries consistently show that between 70% and 90% of people support stronger animal welfare protections and oppose activities such as trophy hunting, animal testing, and industrial farming (Ipsos; Eurobarometer; YouGov; Humane Society International). Ultimately, the chapters show that the line between use and abuse is not just ethical, it is economic. When animals are reduced to inputs, their true value is lost. And when that value is lost, so too is the stability of the systems that depend on them.

Domesticated Toil

Chapters 14 through 17 examine parasitic interactions—those in which animals are used for human entertainment, assistance, and labor, often without recognition, reciprocity, or protection. These relationships raise urgent ethical and economic questions: If animals are workers, what rights do they have? What protections should be in place to ensure their dignity and well-being?

Across sports, entertainment, service, and transport, animals contribute immense value—economically, socially, and emotionally. In recreational and sporting contexts (Chapter 14), animals such as horses, bulls, camels, and dogs generate significant revenue and cultural capital. Yet the line between tradition and exploitation is often blurred. While some practices are rooted in heritage, others are driven purely by profit, with little regard for animal welfare. Public policy must distinguish between these uses and incentivize animal-positive practices that respect both cultural identity and ethical responsibility.

Similarly, the entertainment industry (Chapter 15), from circuses and zoos to film and marine parks, relies heavily on animal performers. Though lucrative, this sector often subjects animals to confinement, stress, and unnatural behaviors. The chapter proposes a shift toward sanctuary-based models, financial incentives for humane alternatives, and stronger regulation to ensure that economic viability does not come at the cost of animal suffering.

In service roles (Chapter 16), animals assist humans in healthcare, accessibility, and social engagement. Their contributions are profound, yet their welfare is often overlooked. Unlike human workers, service animals receive no compensation, no retirement, and limited legal protection. The chapter calls for comprehensive policies that include certification standards, stress monitoring, and financial provisions for healthcare and retirement. It also raises deeper questions about agency and consent: can animals truly choose to serve, and if not, what ethical obligations do we bear?

The same questions apply to working animals in transport and agriculture (Chapter 17). Draft and pack animals have shaped human history, enabling migration, trade, and even warfare. Today, they remain vital in many regions, especially where infrastructure is limited. Their labor, often undervalued, may in fact rival the economic output of entire sectors of the modern transportation industry. Yet they endure harsh conditions, physical strain, and inadequate care. Addressing this requires enforceable welfare standards, public–private funding mechanisms, and long-term social protections that recognize animals not as tools, but as laboring beings.

Taken together, these chapters challenge us to rethink the moral and economic frameworks that govern animal labor. If we accept that animals work—intentionally or not—then we must also accept that they deserve protections. We already extend such protections to vulnerable human populations: children, the elderly, and people with disabilities. These groups, like animals, are often dependent, voiceless in legal systems, and at risk of exploitation. The parallels are not incidental, they are instructive.

In fact, early animal protection laws helped inspire child protection laws, reflecting a shared recognition that dignity, safety, and flourishing are not privileges, but rights owed to those who cannot advocate for themselves. Recognizing these principles in the treatment of animals is not radical. It is a return to the original ethical impulse that once inspired protections for vulnerable humans. Yet while those human protections have since been expanded and enshrined in law, animals have been largely left behind. Extending justice to them now is not a leap forward, but a long-overdue act of moral consistency and economic ethics.

Entangled Lives

Chapters 18 through 20 highlight mutualistic interactions, where animals and humans benefit from shared relationships, such as in tourism, ecosystem services, and companionship. Although this mutualism is often uneven, aspirational, or conditional, and structured by power imbalances, economic incentives, and cultural narratives that favor human interests, analysis in these chapters offer a glimpse of what a symbiotic economy might look like—one that values animals not for their utility alone, but for their presence, their agency, and their contributions to a shared world.

In the realm of wildlife tourism, animals have long been cast as attractions, laborers, or commodities—shaped by colonial legacies and global market demands (Chapter 18). Yet, new models are emerging that challenge this extractive logic. Animal-positive tourism initiatives, grounded in ecological respect and community benefit, show that it is possible to design economic systems where animals are not merely used, but respected as co-inhabitants of shared spaces. These models offer examples of a more reciprocal relationship, one that values animal agency and well-being alongside human livelihoods.

Animals also sustain human economies in less visible but no less vital ways (Chapter 19). Through pollination, pest control, seed dispersal, and other ecosystem services, they uphold the very systems that make agriculture, forestry, and climate regulation possible. These contributions are rarely accounted for in traditional economic metrics, yet they are foundational to planetary health. Recognizing and compensating these services—through conservation incentives, ecosystem service payments, and biodiversity protections—can help rebalance the scales, acknowledging animals not as tools but as ecological partners.

Even in the intimate sphere of pet companionship (Chapter 20), the dynamics of mutualism are complex. Pets offer emotional support, health benefits, and social connection, while also driving significant economic activity. But they are also subject to commodification, breeding practices, and legal frameworks that often fail to reflect their sentience. The emerging field of pet economics challenges us to rethink value, not just in terms of market exchange, but in terms of care, reciprocity, and interdependence.

Together, these chapters suggest that a more just and sustainable economic relationship with animals is not only possible: it is already taking shape in scattered but promising ways. True mutualism may remain an ideal, but it is one worth striving for: a vision of shared flourishing that redefines prosperity across species lines.

Three Pillars for an Economy of Coexistence

As we confront the ecological, ethical, and economic consequences of our treatment of non-human animals, a new framework is urgently needed—one that moves beyond exploitation and toward coexistence. This path forward rests on three interdependent pillars: Recognition, Remuneration, and Non-Use. Together, they offer a foundation for reimagining our economic systems in ways that honor the agency, value, and dignity of animals.

Pillar 1—Recognition: Valuing the Invaluable

The first step is to recognize animals not merely as passive resources or background actors in human economies but as active participants in economic systems and as moral subjects. While animals may not engage in economic reasoning in the human sense, many of their actions—from guiding individuals with disabilities, to competing in horse races, to performing in entertainment all the way to locating survivors in disaster zones—are the result of cognitive decisions made in response to training, environmental cues, and social relationships. These decisions are purposeful, adaptive, and often collaborative, directly contributing to economic value and human well-being.

In this broader and more inclusive understanding, animals can be seen as non-human economic agents: beings whose intentional actions shape economic outcomes and sustain both ecological and social systems. And even when they are not making cognitive decisions, animals remain vital to economies—often through their suffering or death—as humans exploit them for food, labor, or materials, frequently ignoring their capacity to feel pain. Yet, their contributions remain largely invisible in GDP calculations, overlooked in trade policy, and excluded from legal protections. Recognizing animals as cognitive and economic participants challenges us to rethink the boundaries of economic agency and to embed their value into the structures of economic thought, law, and policy.

One of the central challenges in integrating animals into economic thinking is the question of value. While traditional economics does distinguish between value and price, it often relies on monetary valuation—using a single numeraire, money—to compare and prioritize different kinds of value. As a result, what cannot be priced or marketed—such as animal well-being, companionship, ecosystem stability, or cultural meaning—is often excluded from policy consideration, despite being deeply valued by society. This narrow focus on marketable value hides the real costs of animal suffering, confinement, and loss of autonomy behind the illusion of cheap products and efficient systems.

This book has shown that more inclusive valuation frameworks are possible. These include intrinsic valuation, which recognizes animals as beings with their own interests and rights, and instrumental valuation, which accounts for their contributions to human welfare. These two forms of value are not mutually exclusive; for instance, a companion animal may hold deep intrinsic value for a family while also providing measurable psychological and social benefits—just as a pollinator species may be valued both for its ecological role and its inherent right to exist. Non-market valuation methods, like contingent valuation and deliberative democratic approaches, offer promising tools for capturing these broader values.

Just as environmental economists have pushed for the inclusion of natural capital in national accounting systems, we must now advocate for the recognition of animal capital—not as property, but as sentient participants in our shared economies. This includes integrating animal well-being into cost–benefit analyses, impact assessments, and sustainability metrics. It means developing animal-inclusive indicators of economic performance, such as animal welfare-adjusted GDP or multispecies well-being indices. Practical examples of this kind of integration are beginning to emerge. For instance, the United Kingdom has explored incorporating animal welfare into agricultural cost–benefit analyses (Farm Animal Welfare Committee), the One Welfare framework links animal, human, and environmental well-being in policy

(García Pinillos et al. 2016), and organizations like World Animal Protection have advocated for including animal welfare in the UN Sustainable Development Goals (World Animal Protection).

Crucially, recognition must go beyond utility. Unlike ecosystems or infrastructure, animals are sentient beings capable of suffering, joy, and social connection. This moral dimension makes their recognition not only an economic necessity but an ethical imperative. Sentience should be a threshold criterion for inclusion in economic and legal frameworks, just as vulnerability and dependency are for human populations.

To make this ethical and economic recognition meaningful, we must confront the systemic concealment of animal suffering embedded in current legal and economic structures. Today's laws often enable, rather than prevent, the obfuscation and sanitization of violence against animals. For instance, "ag-gag" laws in parts of the United States not only criminalize undercover investigations in factory farms but also prohibit photographing or filming concentrated animal feeding operations (CAFOs)—even from public spaces—thereby suppressing journalistic and public scrutiny. This legal shielding not only allows animals to suffer in silence but also permits unsanitary and unsafe practices to persist, posing significant risks to human health through the spread of zoonotic diseases, antibiotic resistance, and environmental contamination which, in turn, can lead to unfathomable public and private economic costs. Similarly, misleading food labels—like "free-range" or "humane certified"—often lack rigorous standards, fabricating a narrative of ethical treatment while concealing harsh realities.

The legal classification of animals as property further entrenches this invisibility, reducing sentient beings to economic units with no intrinsic rights. In contrast, some jurisdictions show examples of a more transparent future: the United Kingdom's mandatory CCTV in slaughterhouses allows regulators to monitor animal treatment, and the EU's animal welfare laws include bans on extreme confinement and support for welfare impact assessments. Building on such measures, mandatory labeling requirements could be introduced, grounded in evidence from continuous monitoring systems, to ensure that consumers are informed about the actual conditions under which animals are raised, transported, and slaughtered. Switzerland, for example, has recently introduced mandatory animal-welfare labeling for certain painful practices, offering a partial model of consumer-oriented transparency. These examples show that legal frameworks can either obscure or illuminate the suffering behind consumption. If people were fully aware of the suffering embodied in what they consume—whether food, fashion, or pharmaceuticals—they would be empowered to make more ethical and sustainable choices. Legal reform must therefore aim not only to protect animals but to dismantle the mechanisms that normalize and conceal their exploitation.

Encouragingly, some progress has been made. Countries like Germany and Switzerland have amended their constitutions to recognize animal dignity and welfare. Since 1992 Switzerland recognized in its Constitution the dignity of animals as living beings with inherent worth, while in 2002, Germany became the first EU country to include animal protection in its Basic Law (Grundgesetz), stating that "the state shall protect the natural foundations of life and animals" (Basic Law for the Federal Republic of Germany, Art. 20a). Similarly, Italy's 2022 constitutional reform established animal protection as a fundamental state objective, binding legislation and economic activity to its pursuit. And Ecuador's 2008 Constitution went further, granting rights to nature, including animals, recognizing their right to exist and regenerate (Constitución de la República del Ecuador 2008).

Ultimately, recognition is about re-centering our economic vision. It is about acknowledging that animals are not marginal to our prosperity: they are foundational to it. And it is about building systems that reflect this truth, not only in theory but in practice.

Pillar 2—Remuneration: Toward Social Policy for Animals

If we are to take animals seriously as participants in our economies, we must also take seriously their right to fair treatment. This includes retribution for harm and remuneration for labor. Animals who work—whether in agriculture, entertainment, therapy, companionship, service, or sport—deserve protections akin to those we afford vulnerable human workers. This means ensuring access to basic needs: food, shelter, medical care, and rest. It means recognizing the right to retirement after a life of labor and the right to express instinctual behaviors, maintain social bonds, and live free from chronic stress or confinement. These are not radical demands: they are extensions of principles already applied to children, the elderly, and other dependent populations.

A comprehensive social policy for animals would build on these precedents, establishing workplacc standards, welfare guarantees, and public investment in animal well-being. It would also require reparative justice for past and ongoing harms, including habitat destruction, forced labor, and systemic neglect. One foundational step is the establishment of minimum care standards for working animals, particularly those used in transport, agriculture, and tourism. These standards should include access to veterinary care, proper nutrition, and adequate shelter. Governments can play a critical role by funding training programs for animal owners, especially in rural and low-income areas, and by supporting compliance through subsidies, cooperatives, and animal health savings accounts.

Beyond basic care, animals used for labor should be included in social protection systems. Drawing parallels with human labor rights, this includes healthcare, rest periods, and humane working conditions. For example, retirement plans for older animals, like government-supported sanctuaries or retirement funds, would allow animals to live out their final years in dignity, rather than being discarded or overworked until death. In urban areas, stricter regulations on animal labor are essential to prevent suffering from traffic, pollution, and extreme weather. Bans on the use of animals for heavy loads during peak heat or cold seasons, as seen from New York to Rome, Santorini, Jaipur, or Petra are a necessary step. At the same time, governments should incentivize alternative transportation methods, such as affordable electric carts or renewable-powered vehicles, to reduce reliance on animal labor.

Animals also serve in highly specialized roles—as guide dogs, police and military animals, emotional support companions, and athletes in sports like racing or equestrian events. They also play critical roles in search and rescue operations, helping to locate people trapped in avalanches, earthquakes, and other disasters, often succeeding where machines or humans cannot. Additionally, some animals are trained to detect diseases such as cancer, diabetes, or infections, using their acute senses to identify subtle biological changes, making them invaluable in both emergency response and medical diagnostics. These animals often undergo intense training and face demanding conditions. A just economic framework must recognize their labor and ensure legal protections against overwork, injury, and abuse, access to medical care and psychological well-being (especially for service animals exposed to trauma), retirement and rehoming programs after their service ends, and ethical oversight of breeding, training, and competition standards.

In sports, where animals generate significant revenue, there is a strong case for profit-sharing mechanisms that fund lifelong care for the animals involved. Regulatory bodies should enforce strict welfare standards, and public funding should support independent monitoring to prevent exploitation.

Of course, one might ask: why advocate for such comprehensive protections for animals when so many humans around the world still lack access to basic rights and services? This is a valid and urgent concern. However, the two causes are not mutually exclusive. In fact, they are deeply interconnected. A society that expands its circle of care to include non-human beings is often one that is also more attentive to the needs of its most vulnerable human members. Justice is not a finite resource; extending it to animals does not diminish our capacity to fight for human dignity: it enhances it. By recognizing the labor and suffering of animals, we reinforce a broader ethic of compassion, responsibility, and interdependence that can strengthen all social justice movements.

Ultimately, a social policy for animals is not only a matter of compassion, it is a matter of justice and economic foresight. Animals contribute to our economies in visible and invisible ways. Ensuring their well-being enhances their productivity, reduces public health risks, and reflects the values of a society that recognizes interdependence across species.

Pillar 3—Non-use: Beyond Commodification

Perhaps the most transformative pillar in rethinking human–animal relationships is the principle of non-use—a rejection of the idea that animals exist solely for human benefit. This does not mean severing all human–animal relationships, but rather reconfiguring them to prioritize existence over extraction. Non-use challenges the commodification of animals in tourism, agriculture, entertainment, food production, and even conservation. It asks us to imagine economies where animals are not valued for what they produce, but for who they are.

Realizing this vision requires a profound cultural shift—one that touches food systems, legal frameworks, education, economic models, and everyday habits. It calls for reimagining our place in multispecies communities, where respect and restraint replace dominance and utility. However, this vision is not utopian; it is already taking shape in diverse and grounded ways. In food systems, for example, some emerging models are experimenting with ethical coexistence, allowing for the consumption of animal-derived goods like eggs and milk without compromising animal autonomy or life. Sanctuary-based dairies let cows live out their full natural lives without forced impregnation or separation from their calves, offering milk only when it is truly surplus. Similarly, some small-scale farms collect eggs from free-roaming hens who are not selectively bred for overproduction and are never culled when their laying slows. These approaches prioritize the animals' well-being, freedom, and natural rhythms, reframing food production as a relationship of care rather than extraction. While still rare, such models point toward a future where interspecies coexistence can include ethical forms of nourishment that do not depend on killing or exploitation. In this context, non-use does not require the complete elimination of animal-derived products, but rather a transformation in how they are sourced—emphasizing consent, care, and coexistence, and redefining food not as a product of domination, but as a potential expression of interspecies reciprocity.

A similar reimagining is taking place in the realm of hunting. Can the essence of hunting—the skill, the connection to nature, the ritual of the chase—be preserved without taking life? In some Indigenous and traditional cultures, hunting has long been more than a means of obtaining food. It is a spiritual and relational practice, where tracking and observing animals is a form of respect and learning. The hunt may end without a kill and still be considered meaningful, even successful. Modern interpretations of non-lethal hunting are emerging in recreational and conservation contexts. One of the most prominent examples is camera hunting or photo safaris, where animals are tracked and "shot" with cameras instead of guns. These experiences require many of the same skills as traditional hunting—patience, stealth, deep knowledge of animal behavior—while allowing animals to live undisturbed. In some regions, former trophy hunting reserves have been transformed into photographic tourism destinations, generating sustainable income while protecting wildlife. There are also virtual hunting simulations and augmented reality experiences that replicate the thrill of the chase without any real-world harm. These can serve as educational tools or recreational outlets, satisfying the human drive for pursuit while fostering empathy and ecological awareness.

Reimagining hunting in this way opens up new possibilities for ethical engagement with wildlife. It challenges the assumption that the value of the hunt lies in the kill and instead centers the experience, the relationship, and the reverence for life. In a world increasingly shaped by ecological limits and moral reconsideration, non-lethal hunting offers a path forward, one that honors tradition while embracing a future of coexistence. Of course, suffering is a natural part of life in the wild—animals hunt, compete, and die—but this does not justify causing harm that is avoidable, disproportionate, or lacking ecological or cultural necessity, especially when alternatives exist that honor both tradition and life.

This principle of non-use is also gaining ground in the realm of scientific research, particularly in medical, psychological, and psychiatric studies. For decades, animals have been subjected to invasive experiments in the name of human health. Yet today, a growing body of evidence shows that non-animal methods—such as organ-on-a-chip technologies, advanced computer modeling, and human cell-based assays—are not only more ethical but often more predictive of human outcomes. These innovations challenge the assumption that animal suffering is a necessary cost of scientific progress. Instead, they point toward a future where knowledge is pursued without harm, and where the integrity of life is upheld even in the pursuit of healing.

Arguably, the most ambitious expression of non-use lies in the creation of vast, untouched, and unextractive spaces—places where animals are not managed, harvested, or displayed, but simply allowed to be. Some conservation models are already embracing this shift. The "Half-Earth" proposal by E.O. Wilson and the 30 × 30 biodiversity framework adopted by the UN Convention on Biological Diversity aim to protect large portions of the planet from extractive use, prioritizing ecological integrity over economic gain (Wilson 2016; CBD 2022). Examples of this vision in practice include Costa Rica, where ecotourism has been restructured to minimize human–wildlife contact and maximize habitat preservation, and Namibia, where community-based conservancies have successfully combined wildlife protection with local economic empowerment, reducing poaching and increasing biodiversity. These efforts recognize that the most effective way to support animal flourishing is often to step back—to create conditions where animals can recover in numbers, maintain social and ecological relationships, and live free from human interference. Taking inspiration from such models, policy frameworks elsewhere must begin to internalize the broader ecological value of wildlife—not only for the services they provide, such as pollination or seed dispersal, but for their role in maintaining resilient ecosystems. Mechanisms like Payment for Ecosystem Services (PES), conservation trust funds, incentives for sustainable agriculture, and strengthened wildlife protection laws can help scale these approaches. Strengthened wildlife protection laws and sustainable eco-tourism models are also essential to ensure that conservation is not only ecologically sound but also economically viable.

Avoiding commodification also demands rethinking policy frameworks. Voluntary corporate pledges are not enough; we need enforceable regulations, biodiversity taxes, and reinvestment mandates that ensure those who profit from nature also pay to protect it. This includes philanthropic and private sector involvement, which must be tightly regulated. Too often, philanthropy serves as a gateway for covert, profit-driven agendas under the guise of conservation. Strict, enforceable contracts must ensure that all contributions are genuinely in service of wildlife protection, not as a vehicle for indirect profit, but as a commitment to value life over return.

Equally vital is education: children and adults alike must learn to love and understand nature not through cages, spectacles, or extractive tourism, but through respectful, immersive experiences—like feeding a chicken, observing an insect's life without the need to crush it, or swimming quietly among fish—that cultivate empathy rather than ownership. Without this cultural foundation, policy alone cannot undo the deep-rooted logic of commodification.

Governments have a powerful role to play in this transformation, starting with early education that fosters ecological literacy and empathy, and extending to the way cities are designed, food systems are supported, and public spaces are shaped to encourage coexistence rather than control. Because ultimately, non-use is not about withdrawal: it is about responsibility. It is about building systems that honor the intrinsic value of animal life and that allow for coexistence without control. In this sense, non-use is not only the most radical idea, it is also the most necessary.

Threads in the Tapestry: Rethinking Our Place in the Economy of Life

We often speak of civilization as progress—of how far we have come in building systems of governance, trade, and technology. Yet behind this polished façade lies a hidden barbarism: the continued exploitation of the vulnerable, often out of sight and out of mind. One of the most persistent and overlooked economic injustices is the treatment of non-human animals. Their suffering is not incidental to our economic systems, it is embedded within them. Addressing this is not a distraction from human-centered economic justice; it is integral to it. As Gandhi so wisely reminded us, "The greatness of a nation and its moral progress can be judged by the way its animals are treated." A society that shows compassion toward animals reveals a deeper moral capacity, one that inevitably extends to how it treats its most vulnerable people as well.

Of course, not all humans are complicit, and not all animals are exploited; there are countless individuals, communities, and ecosystems that embody care, reciprocity, and resistance to extractive norms. But these examples exist in tension with, and often in defiance of, dominant systems that continue to externalize harm and normalize exploitation.

In fact, the same extractive logic that treats animals as disposable commodities also harms the world's poorest people. Industrial food systems, built on animal exploitation, contribute to health crises through poor nutrition, environmental degradation, and antibiotic resistance. These systems disproportionately affect low-income communities, who face limited access to healthy food and bear the brunt of pollution and ecological collapse. Meanwhile, Indigenous peoples are displaced from ancestral lands, losing access to ecosystems that once sustained them—ecosystems now repurposed for livestock, monoculture, and resource extraction, including the depletion of wildlife populations. These are not separate crises; they are symptoms of the same economic paradigm—one that prioritizes profit over life, and extraction over reciprocity.

In the vast tapestry of life on Earth, humans are but a single thread—one among millions of species, a mere fraction of the planet's staggering biological wealth. Yet, in our economic models, our industries, and our narratives, we place ourselves at the center, often blind to the intricate and indispensable economies of non-human animals. Forests hum with transactions, oceans operate on delicate exchanges, and ecosystems sustain themselves through networks more ancient and efficient than any human market. And it is largely on these networks that our own economies have developed and thrived. We are, quite literally, cutting the branch on which we sit.

It is time to rethink this relationship. And while it may seem difficult to account for animals in economic systems, we are not without tools. Decades of economic theory have given us the means to model complexity, uncertainty, and interdependence. From auction theory to behavioral economics, from game theory to environmental valuation, we have developed sophisticated frameworks for understanding value beyond price. If we can model the intricacies of carbon markets and high-frequency trading, we can also model the moral and ecological costs of animal exploitation. Not only can it be done: it is one of the most urgent and meaningful frontiers for economic thought today.

This book has shown why a new economic model is urgently needed, and begun to explore how it might be realized. Human economies are not separate from nature; they are deeply and irrevocably entangled with the lives of non-human animals. From horses that powered empires to bees that pollinate billion-dollar crops, from silkworms that clothed royalty to microbes that ferment our food, non-human life has shaped every corner of human prosperity. These contributions are not peripheral: they are foundational, visible in both the vast networks of global trade and the intimate routines of daily life.

Building on this recognition, the book calls for a model that not only acknowledges these interdependencies but also reimagines our relationship with non-human animals. This model is neither abstract nor theoretical: the book offers concrete economic policy and regulatory proposals, some inspired by real-world successes, to embed animal welfare and ecological interdependence into economic systems.

What emerges is a vision of shared prosperity, one that includes all sentient beings and is grounded not in domination, but in coexistence.

Change begins not with certainty, but with conviction; and the conviction to do better is already here. *The hope is that these pages are not only read, but reflected upon, used, and carried forward; that they offer not just critique, but inspiration for a more just and compassionate future.*

References

Animal Welfare Board of India v. A. Nagaraja & Ors. Supreme Court of India (2014)
Asociación de Funcionarios y Abogados por los Derechos de los Animales (AFADA) v. Gobierno de la Ciudad de Buenos Aires. Argentina (2015)
Basic Law for the Federal Republic of Germany. Art. 20a (2002)

Constitución de la República del Ecuador (2008)
Convention on Biological Diversity (2022) Kunming-Montreal global biodiversity framework
European Commission (2016) Attitudes of Europeans towards animal welfare. Special Eurobarometer 442, European Union, Mar 2016. https://europa.eu/eurobarometer/surveys/detail/2096
Farm Animal Welfare Committee (2020) Opinion on the welfare of farmed animals at killing. Department for Environment, Food & Rural Affairs, UK Government
García Pinillos R et al (2016) One welfare—a platform for improving human and animal welfare. Vet Rec 179(16): 412–413
Humane Society International (2020) Global public opinion on animal protection issues: summary of key findings. Humane Society International. https://www.hsi.org/wp-content/uploads/2020/06/global-opinion-survey-summary.pdf
Ipsos (2018) Global views on animal welfare. Ipsos. https://www.ipsos.com/en/global-views-animal-welfare
Wilson EO (2016) Half-Earth: our planet's fight for life. Liveright
World Animal Protection (2018) Animal protection and the United Nations sustainable development goals. https://www.worldanimalprotection.org
YouGov (2022) Most Britons support a ban on the import of hunting trophies. YouGov. https://yougov.co.uk/topics/politics/articles-reports/2022/06/15/most-britons-support-ban-import-hunting-trophies

MIX
Papier aus verantwortungsvollen Quellen
Paper from responsible sources
FSC® C105338

If you have any concerns about our products,
you can contact us on
ProductSafety@springernature.com

In case Publisher is established outside the EU,
the EU authorized representative is:
Springer Nature Customer Service Center GmbH
Europaplatz 3, 69115 Heidelberg, Germany

Printed by Libri Plureos GmbH
in Hamburg, Germany